VERMONT GUIDE

BE A TRAVELER – NOT A TOURIST!

OPEN ROAD TRAVEL GUIDES SHOW YOU
HOW TO BE A TRAVELER – NOT A TOURIST!

*Whether you're going abroad or planning a trip in the United States, take Open Road along on your journey. Our books have been praised by **Travel & Leisure, The Los Angeles Times, Newsday, Booklist, US News & World Report, Endless Vacation, American Bookseller, Coast to Coast**, and many other magazines and newspapers!*

Don't just see the world – experience it with Open Road!

ABOUT THE AUTHOR

John J. Bentley IV is also the author of Open Road's *Egypt Guide*. He makes his home in South Royalton, Vermont.

BE A TRAVELER, NOT A TOURIST - WITH OPEN ROAD TRAVEL GUIDES!

Open Road Publishing has guide books to exciting, fun destinations on four continents. As veteran travelers, our goal is to bring you the best travel guides available anywhere!

No small task, but here's what we offer:

• All Open Road travel guides are written by authors with a distinct, opinionated point of view – not some sterile committee or team of writers. Our authors are experts in the areas covered and are polished writers.

• Our guides are geared to people who want to make their own travel choices. We'll show you how to discover the real destination – not just see some place from a tour bus window.

• We're strong on the basics, but we also provide terrific choices for those looking to get off the beaten path and experience the country or city – not just see it or pass through it.

• We give you the best, but we also tell you about the worst and what to avoid. Nobody should waste their time and money on their hard-earned vacation because of bad or inadequate travel advice.

• Our guides assume nothing. We tell you everything you need to know to have the trip of a lifetime – presented in a fun, literate, no-nonsense style.

• And, above all, we welcome your input, ideas, and suggestions to help us put out the best travel guides possible.

VERMONT GUIDE

BE A TRAVELER - NOT A TOURIST!

John J. Bentley IV

OPEN ROAD PUBLISHING

OPEN ROAD PUBLISHING

We offer travel guides to American and foreign locales. Our books tell it like it is, often with an opinionated edge, and our experienced authors always give you all the information you need to have the trip of a lifetime. Write for your free catalog of all our titles.

**Catalog Department, Open Road Publishing
P.O. Box 284, Cold Spring Harbor, NY 11724**

*E-mail:
Jopenroad@aol.com*

1st Edition

Front cover photo©FPG International. Back cover photos©Kim Grant, Boston. Maps by James Ramage.

TABLE OF CONTENTS

INDEX   441

SIDEBARS

1. INTRODUCTION

Vermont. Just saying it soothes the soul. It's a universal thing, whenever anybody thinks of the Green Mountain State, those same pleasant images come to mind – covered bridges, quaint village greens with gazebos and steepled churches; a cool, crisp valley gushing with every shade of orange, yellow and red; a pastoral dairy farm with an old-fashioned barn; a fresh cooked dinner of roast rack of lamb next to a cozy fire after shushing down the slopes.

It's a cliche and a stereotype, but fortunately when it comes to Vermont, the stereotype holds. The Green Mountains are as beautiful as ever and the skiing at Killington, Stowe, Sugarbush, and a dozen other resorts is still the best east of the Mississippi. Flip through this guide and you will find that Vermont offers hundreds of lodging and dining opportunities at charming inns and bed and breakfasts, many of which are family-owned and date to the 19th century, or even the 18th century.

But before we move on, I would be remiss not to let on that there's more to Vermont than just its well-earned reputation as a four season holiday mecca for skiers and leaf-peepers. A rural state that has kept development in check, Vermont rarely conjures up images of vibrant cities and towns with museums that any major city would be glad to claim as its own. But Burlington, Montpelier, Rutland, and St. Johnsbury are all enjoying cultural and economic rebirths. Migrants from all over America and the world have moved to these towns out of respect for traditions and have maintained their essence while breathing new life into them. As a result, visitors can now enjoy both Vermont's traditional offerings like maple sugar on snow gatherings, and a ride through a covered bridge, but also respected and hip cultural events from the renowned Marlboro Chamber Music Festival to the Vermont Reggae Fest, one of the best this side of Jamaica.

In this book, I have tried to give you the best of the classic Vermont as well as the exciting aspects of the new. Accommodations listings feature healthy doses of both old-fashioned bed and breakfasts, as well as new condo developments and ski resorts, offering the latest facilities and conveniences. I laid out a basic road map for finding your way to major and minor destinations and attractions, but at the same time, I urge you to undertake random exploration. Vermont is so small that no matter how far you go, you haven't gone far enough to get lost – unless of course you find yourself in New Hampshire.

2. OVERVIEW

BENNINGTON COUNTY

Often called the "Gateway to Vermont" (Brattleboro is also known by the same title) **Bennington** is a town and region steeped in history and well-endowed with natural and historical attractions, but too often passed over by travelers on their way to ritzier destinations like Manchester and Wilmington. The first town chartered by New Hampshire west of the Connecticut River in 1749, Bennington was a bastion of political activity before and during the Revotionary War, when the state's early leaders such as Ethan Allen met at the famous Catamount Tavern on Monument Avenue to plot strategy and tactics for struggles like the Battle at Bennington which turned the tide of the Revolutionary War in the Champlain Valley against the British. Today, the 306-foot obelisk Bennington Monument that was built to commemorate that battle dominates the regional skyline and serves as a beacon to those entering the town and the state. It is also the area's most popular tourist destination, though the area boasts an impressive assortment of historical and natural attractions.

Among the attractions of Bennington itself is the **Bennington Museum**, featuring the largest collection of Grandma Moses paintings in the country, the **Old First Church and Burying Grounds** where Robert Frost and dozens of Revolutionary War soldiers and leaders are interred, and the **Hemming Motor News** headquarters where you can wax nostalgic at an old-fashioned filling station and collect antique auto-related souvenirs and memorabilia. Meanwhile, the surrounding countryside – all encompassed in the **Green Mountain National Forest** – features dozens of opportunities for outdoor recreation, whether it be hiking the **Appalachian** and **Long Trails**, canoeing the scenic **Battenkill**, or exploring covered bridges on the **Walloomsac River**.

North of Bennington are the historic villages of **Shaftsbury** and **Arlington**, both featuring hundreds of historic buildings and historic atttractions such as the **Norman Rockwell Museum & Exhibition**. Rockwell

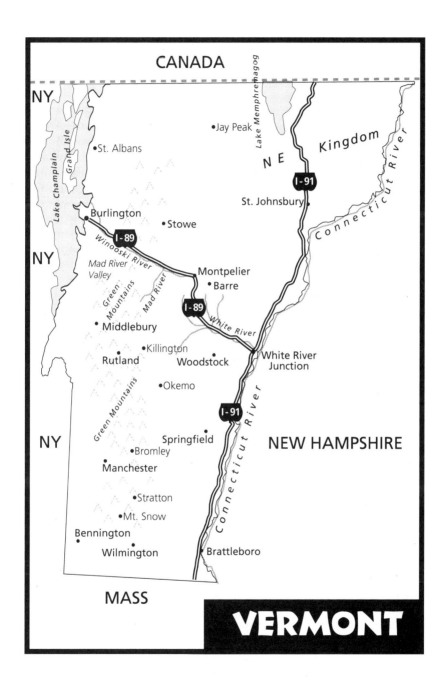

CANADA

NY

Lake Memphremagog

• Jay Peak

Lake Champlain

Grand Isle

• St. Albans

N E   Kingdom

I-91

Connecticut River

St. Johnsbury •

• Burlington

• Stowe

I-89

Winooski River

NY

Mad River
Valley

Montpelier
• Barre

Green
Mountains

Mad River

I-89

White River

• Middlebury

• Killington

Rutland   Woodstock

White River
Junction

• Okemo

Connecticut River

I-91

NY

Springfield •

• Bromley

NEW HAMPSHIRE

Manchester

Green Mountains

• Stratton

• Mt. Snow

Bennington
•

• Brattleboro

Wilmington

Connecticut River

MASS

VERMONT

used to live in Arlington, and at this exhibition you can take guided tours given by men and women who used to work for him as models. Many of these attractions take little time to enjoy, so even if you are on your way to another part of the state or on your way home, it is easy to enjoy the southwestern corner of Vermont.

MOUNT SNOW

With more than 130 runs covering 500 acres and a southern location that makes it the most convenient major ski resort for folks from Boston and New York, the **Mt. Snow** and **Haystack** ski areas are quickly turning the Deerfield Valley into one of the fastest developing tourist destinations in Vermont. And while this leads some to bypass it, fearing larger crowds and less snow, modern snowmaking techniques and the opening of hundreds of new hotel rooms and condo's annual have insured that the skiing experience at Mt. Snow is one of the highest rated in the East.

Of course skiing isn't all the area has to offer. Mt. Snow offers numerous opportunities for cyclists, hikers, and of course leaf-peepers, while the Harriman and Somerset reservoirs are fine, and often over-looked, venues for fishermen, boaters, and swimmers. The area also offers a wide choice in lodging and dining, ranging from establishments like the Hermitage and the Inn at Sawmill Farm that are among the finest inns in America, to a long list of condo's, lodges, B&B's, and motels that can accommodate all budgets.

BRATTLEBORO & WINDHAM COUNTY

One of the first areas in present-day Vermont to be settled by Europeans, the southeast corner of the state offers visitors a variety of attractions, from the month-long world renowned **Marlboro Music Festival** in July and August to the bustling town of **Brattleboro** and the charming villages of **Grafton** and **Newfane**.

Originally developed by the British army which constructed Fort Dummer just south of present-day Brattleboro to protect settlements in New Hampshire, the region thrived in the 19th century by virtue of its commercially important location on the Connecticut River, and the establishment of major commercial firms like the Estey Organ Company. Today, that importance has dominished somewhat, but its legacy has left Brattleboro and towns like **Putney** with an old-timey charm that retains its authenticity due to the fact that the region is not overrun with tourists. Indeed, the region does not feature the obvious draws like major ski areas and standout historic sites, but between the area's natural beauty and offerings ranging from some of the state's most impressive covered bridges to the very fine Brattleboro Museum and Art Center, it certainly warrants a lookin' over if not several days of your time. Besides, if you want to go skiing, Mt. Snow with its 135 runs is but 25 minutes from Brattleboro on Route 9.

MANCHESTER & THE HEART OF THE GREEN MOUNTAINS

Few towns better meet the definition of a New England resort than **Manchester**, Vermont. Attracting the vacationing elites of New York, Boston, and Washington since the post-Civil War years when families like the Lincolns, Grants, and Roosevelts made it a regular summer destination. Manchester is considered Vermont's first major tourist attraction, and it remains one today. With numerous beautiful estates from the Lincolns' former Hildene Estate, to the Equinox resort, Manchester Village is among the most picturesque villages in Vermont with numerous quality inns and restaurants, while nearby Manchester Center is the shopping capital of Vermont with dozens of outlet and retail stores ranging from Orvis to Calvin Klein.

For those more interested in sports and recreation, this chapter also covers four of Vermont's major ski resorts including **Bromley**, **Stratton**, **Okemo**, and **Magic Mountain**, as well as the towns of **Dorset**, **Londonderry**, and **Weston**, best known as the home of the famous Vermont Country Store.

THE OTTAUQUECHEE RIVER VALLEY

Just west of White River Junction along the modest **Ottauquechee River**, the 25 mile stretch of Route 4 from Route 100 to Interstate 89's Exit 1 draws perhaps more visitors and tourists than any in the state, with the possible exception of Route 100 between Warren and Stowe. The major attraction is the handsome, gentrified village of **Woodstock**. Known for its green, romantic Victorian inns, and the beautiful surrounding countryside with its rolling hills and classic farm houses, Woodstock is often described as the "quintessential New England village" and the "most photographed town in Vermont." But accolades aside, Woodstock is home to some fascinating attractions, including the **Billings Farm & Museum** where you can visit a working dairy farm that pioneered environment-friendly farming, and the **Marsh-Billings National Historic Park** on Mount Tom, featuring Laurence Rockefeller's former summer home-turned museum.

Almost as famous is the neighboring village of **Quechee**, site of "Vermont's Grand Canyon," the 165-foot deep **Quechee Gorge**, a famous balloon festival in June, and the renowned **Simon Pearce Glass and Pottery** works where you can watch master artists at work and eat in a fine restaurant in a renovated mill while gazing over waterfalls. Both Quechee and Woodstock boast among the best recreational facilities in Vermont, including fine golf courses and excellent cross-country skiing, hiking, and biking. The area is particularly popular during the foliage season in October, so be sure to make your reservations well in advance.

Situated about 12 miles west of Woodstock is the township of **Plymouth**. Not nearly as popular, gentrified, or developed as Woodstock and Quechee, Plymouth is the hometown of the 30th President of the United States, **Calvin Coolidge**. On Route 100A, Silent Cal's home village of **Plymouth Notch** – from the room where he was born to the parlor in which he took the oath of office and the cemetery in which he is buried – has been entirely maintained and is open to the public from May until October. Without subjecting you to a deluge of tacky souvenirs and meaningless exhibits, it not only teaches about Calvin Coolidge, but provides a fascinating glimpse of life in rural New England around the turn of the century. Just up the road from Plymouth Notch is the **Calvin Coolidge State Park**. Part of the Coolidge State Forest (everything in these parts is named "Coolidge"), the park includes camping sites and trails for hiking and biking.

KILLINGTON & RUTLAND

According to Vermont legend, a certain 18th century traveler, Rev. Samuel Peters, was traveling the Green Mountains. After ascending what we now know as Mt. Killington (then called Mt. Pisgah after the mountain in Jordan from which Moses first saw the Promised Land), and beholding the beautiful green expanse of moutains and valleys, he christened the area "Verd Mont." Later the area's English-speaking settlers shortened the name out of linguistic convenience to "Vermont" and the name – meaning "Green Mountains" – has remained ever since.

Should Rev. Peters ascend Killington today (probably in a gondola) he would hardly recognize the area, for today **Killington**, with its sister peak and resort **Pico**, is the largest ski area east of the Mississippi with more than 200 trails. The surrounding area is covered with condos, lodges, shops, and other facilities to accommodate the tens of thousands of visitors who come to ski, bike, and hike the mountain slopes. Unfortunately, the developments are almost exclusively modern and the area lacks the old New England charm that characterizes most of Vermont, though many find it a worthy tradeoff for Killington's excellent recreational opportunities and facilities.

Just 15 miles east of Killington on Route 4, Vermont's traditional second city, **Rutland**, was the capital of the country's marble industry in the 19th century, and while it has not been a major tourist destination, the city's recent renaissance makes it worthy of a visit. Its downtown has been revitalized and the town makes an excellent base not only for accessing Killington, but for visiting nearby attractions such as the **Marble Museum** in Proctor and **Lake Bomoseen** near Vermont's border with New York.

STOWE & MT. MANSFIELD

To many, **Stowe** is synonymous with Vermont. For skiers, between **Stowe Mountain Resort** and **Smugglers' Notch**, the area offers more than 100 runs and 500 acres of world class skiing on Vermont's highest peak, **Mt. Mansfield**, as well as unlimited opportunities for cyclists, hikers, showshoers, cross-country skiers, or virtually anybody else who enjoys sport and recreation in a beautiful natural setting. Combine that with a picturesque village, complete with steepled churches and a classic village green; classic inns and resorts like the **Trapp Family Lodge**; and the **Ben & Jerry's** headquarters in nearby Waterbury, and you could argue – though certainly against the objections of a few locals – that few destinations in Vermont offer a more complete version of the "Vermont Experience."

But one of the beauties of Vermont, and Stowe is certainly no exception, is that even when you're in a major tourist hub, you only have to jump in your car or even on your bike and within minutes you can sample the "true Vermont" of working dairy farms and country stores.

THE MAD RIVER VALLEY

In addition to featuring two of Vermont's most established and esteemed ski areas, and the only one managed by a cooperative in Mad River Glen, the **Mad River Valley** south of I-89 and Stowe between Montpelier and Burlington, is also one of the oldest ski regions in the state. Visitors have more opportunities to sample vintage old school accommodations and eateries than in other ski areas in the state. The two towns, **Waitsfield** and **Warren**, that serve as the commercial and social anchors for the region, have weathered the development that big time tourism entails better than most and have by and large maintained their historic character.

In addition to skiing, the two resorts, **Mad River Glen** and **Sugarbush**, offer unlimited opportunities for hikers, cyclists, and shoppers. If the local offerings are not enough, the Mad River Valley is within easy driving distance of attractions ranging from the art galleries and cultural happenings of Burlington to the most famous hike in Vermont (the **Camel's Hump** near Huntington and Bolton).

BURLINGTON & THE CHAMPLAIN VALLEY

The **Lake Champlain Valley** in northeastern Vermont is unlike any other region in the state. While most of Vermont is characterized by sloping mountains and quaint villages, the northern Champlain Valley is defined by the lake and at times almost has a maritime feel to it. **Burlington**, the region's centerpiece, is a bustling city of 30,000 with an ever-increasing cultural vibrancy. Restaurants, music, and sights from **Shelburne Farms** to the Ethan Allen Homestead make Burlington a worthy attraction, particularly for culture and history afficianados.

The Lake itself of course, is the obvious attraction, especially for those who enjoy boating and fishing. You can easily combine water recreation with Burlington, but to truly sample Champlain's beauty, you should head to the Lake Champlain islands to the north, where civilized distractions are few and the lake truly defines one's lifestyle.

THE NORTHEAST KINGDOM

Often described by it inhabitants as the "Vermonters' Vermont," the **Northeast Kingdom** (a term coined in the 1940's by then-U.S. Senator George Aiken) is the most remote, and many claim the most beautiful, part of the state. In large part because of its isolation, the Kingdom has not seen the massive development linked to tourism like some other parts of the state, and while this certainly means that those who make the extra effort to reach it are rewarded with the most pristine wilderness in Vermont, it also translates into fewer economic opportunities for its residents.

In any case, its offerings are many and diverse. The region's main town, **St. Johnsbury**, is home to the famous **Fairbanks Museum and Planetarium**, as well as numerous beautiful buildings including the **St. Johnsbury Athenaeum**, one of the oldest unadulterated art galleries in America, and a gem of Victorian building. For skiers, **Jay Peak** and **Burke Mountain** are smaller than the Killingtons and Stowes of the world, but their nothern locations mean the best snow in the state and smaller crowds. For cyclists, hikers, and cross-country skiers, the same rule applies and the scenery is consistently beautiful. Finally, the Kingdom's many small villages, the best known of which is **Craftsbury Common**, are among the most charming in the state, and again, without being overrun by tourists, they have retained their original character.

MONTPELIER & CENTRAL VERMONT

Finally, there is plenty to explore along the White River that flows from the Montpelier region (there are actually four branches) to the Connecticut River at White River Junction. From Woodstock and Quechee, you can take Route 4 to White River Junction and then take Route 14 along the White River as far as you like; it's quite a pretty drive.

At **Sharon**, 13 miles from White River Junction, you can take a scenic detour on **Route 132** to the beautiful village of **Strafford**, known for its Meeting House and the **Justin Smith Morrill Homestead**, a historic Victorian mansion that was once the home of the man who drafted the Morrill Homestead Acts that provided land grants for colleges across the United States. You can also reach Sharon by taking the scenic Pomfret Road from Woodstock. Five miles beyond Sharon, just before South Royalton, with its classic village green and church steeple, is Dairy Hill Road and **Joseph Smith Monument**, built to commemorate the Mormon prophet's birthplace. Yet another scenic rural road, Dairy Hill Road will eventually lead you to Turnbridge and Route 110. You can also get on Route 110 at South Royalton itself. It is a scneic 27-mile drive lined with farms; you'll pass the villages of Tunbridge and Chelsea from South Royalton to the eastern edge of **Barre** which borders Montpelier.

You can also continue along Route 14 through Bethel, East Randolph, North Randolph, and the town of **Brookfield**, home of the famous **Floating Bridge** (take a detour on Route 65 west) before the final 11 miles to Barre – itself home to the **Rock of Ages Granite Quarries** (the largest in the world), which you can visit along with the manufacturing division. You can watch as dozens of craftsmen carve and engrave headstone, statues, and other granite products.

Just northwest of Barre is **Montpelier**, the charming and handsome state capital distinguished by the elegant capital building and several fine restaurants, including two operated by the **New Engand Culinary Institute**.

3. A SHORT HISTORY

BEFORE THE ARRIVAL OF EUROPEANS

Though it's difficult to say based on archaeological evidence, scholars believe that the area that now comprises Vermont apart from the Champlain Valley was not heavily populared by Native Americans. It is believed that the Iroquois and Algonguin tribes frequented the area for hunting purposes and were in the process of vying for dominance over the region when European settlers who arrived in the 18th century pre-empted both tribes.

CHAMPLAIN & THE FIRST EUROPEANS

The first European to set foot in the territory that now comprises the State of Vermont was the French explorer **Samuel Champlain**. Escorted by Algonguin Indians, Champlain arrived from Canada to explore the region around the lake which now bears his name. Though he established no permanent settlement, Champlain and his Algonguin allies were in Vermont long enough to engage in a battle with the Iroquois that forever would sour relations between the French and the Iroquois (who would later play an instrumental role in Britain's victory in the French and Indian Wars that led to Canada's becoming part of the British Empire).

In 1666, construction of a fort and shrine to St. Anne on Isle La Motte by Captain La Mothe marked the first European settlement in Vermont, though essentially the area remained completely undeveloped and un-settled by Europeans until the British constructed Fort Dummer south of what is now Brattleboro in the southeast corner of the state.

THE CONFLICT BETWEEN NEW YORK & NEW HAMPSHIRE

After the its defeat at the hands of the British in the French and Indian Wars in 1763, France relinquished all claims to what is now Vermont as settlement of the region by Englishmen began in earnest, and in chaos. The Province of New York claimed that its charter given by King Charles II in 1664 granted it control over all territory west of the Connecticut River, while New Hampshire's 1741 charter stated that its territorial control was to extend west "until it meets with our other governments." These vague definitions of colonial sovereignty, drawn up by British royal officials in London and approved by King George III, are a classic example of colonial misrule and led to an unnecessary conflict between the two colonies.

After the French defeat in 1763, the matter was further complicated when King George issued a proclamation reinforcing New York's claims to all land west of the Connecticut, but New Hampshire, which had granted charters for settlements in Vermont to its own citizens since 1741 and had invested considerable resources in those settlements, refused to recognize New York's sovereignty.

ETHAN ALLEN & THE REVOLUTIONARY WAR ERA

In 1770, a native-born Vermonter named **Ethan Allen** emerged with some of his companions who called themselves the **Green Mountain Boys** and began to resist the authority of New York, while at the same time buying up New Hamshire granted lands in the Champlain Valley. By 1775, however, the conflict between the colonists and Britain began to supercede that between the Green Mountain Boys and the neighboring provinces that laid claim to Vermont. In what became a legendary act of heroism, Ethan Allen led the Green Mountain boys on May 10, 1775, across Lake Champlain to New York where they captured the critically strategic **Fort Ticonderoga**, which set the stage for a two year tug-of-war over the important Lake Champlain Valley. In July 1777, British forces recaptured Ticonderoga only to lose it again within two months after suffering heavy losses at the **Battle of Bennington** that August.

Meanwhile the three-way conflict between New York, New Hampshire, and Vermonters, who pleaded to the Continental Congress for independence, was far from being resolved. Impatient with the inflexibility of neighbors and a Contintental Congress they felt did not take them seriously, Vermont leaders proclaimed the independent **Republic of Vermont** in July 1777 in Windsor, Vermont. Though it would have joined the Union at any time during the Revolution, Vermont was never invited to do so and the Republic remained in existence for 14 years until 1791, when it was finally admitted as the 14th state.

THE 19TH CENTURY

As it was for all of America, the 19th century was a period of great growth and change for Vermont. The early part of the century saw a fast growth in popularion as settlers arrived from southern colonies to exploit the state's fertile soil and unclaimed lands. By the 1830's two new developments were taking the state's economy in a new direction. The first was the growth of **sheep farming**. The sheep were bred for wool which led to the second important phase, the development of textile mills and early industrialization. Towns on rivers, the water of which was used for power, saw nearly exponential growth while technological developments paved the way for economic growth after the sheep industry began to weaken by the middle of the century.

By the 1840's industrialization took a new turn in Vermont as the state found itself on the cutting edge of technology development. In the 1820's the Smith Rifle Company in Windsor began to mechanize the manufacture of rifles. This marked the beginning of the **machine tool industry** which Vermont dominated throughout the middle of the 19th century. Also during this period, towns like Middlebury and Rutland began to dominate the increasingly important marble industry, which really took off after the coming of the railroads in the 1850's.

Politically, Vermont began to assume an increasingly Republican identity which was cemented during the Civil War, in which Vermont lost more men per capita than any state in the Union. Vermont would remain firmly Republican until the post-World War II era 100 years later.

Despite economic growth fueled by the marble and machine tool industries, Vermont began to suffer a loss of popularion during the mid-1800's as people increasingly began to head west in search of opportunities. Perhaps ironically, this migration was largely facilitiated by the efforts of Vermont Congressman Junstin Smith Morrill, who played an instrumental rol in passing the great Land Grant Acts which facilitated the settlement of the western territories and the establishment of the land grant universities.

THE 20TH CENTURY

The early 20th century was not especially kind to Vermont. The state continued to lose popularion to migration while the once important machine tool and marble industries lost their economic preeminance. These trends would continue until well into the post-WW II era, when tourism spurred by the growth of the ski industry began to redefine and strengthen the state's economic base.

Also furthering the state's stronger economy in recent decades has been an increased migration to Vermont of people from other states.

Since the 1960's a growing number of people from primarily urban roots have discovered Vermont's beauty and charm and have decided to move there for quality of life reasons.

That many of these new Vermonters are well educated and relatively wealthy has certainly contributed to the state's improved economic fortunes. They have also reshaped the state's demography and political character. In 1936, Vermont was one of only two states (Maine was the other) not to vote for Franklin Roosevelt's reelection. However, by the mid-1990's, Vermont had changed to the extent that not only was it consistently reelecting Democratic governors and its Democratic U.S Senator, Patrick Leahy, but Vermont's only delegate to the House of Representatives, Bernard Sanders, was the only independent and Socialist in the Congress.

4. LAND & PEOPLE

LAND

Covering 9,564 square miles with an average elevation of 1,000 feet, Vermont is only the forty-second largest state of the fifty states. Its landscape, dominated by the Green Mountains and the Champlain Valley, is largely the creation of the same pushing on the earth's crust 500,000 years ago that created the Appalachians and most of the mountains in the eastern United States (the Green Mountain range is in fact a northwestern extension of the Appalachians), as well as the last ice age 10,000 years ago which is largely responsible for the creation of Lake Champlain and many of the valleys and riverways throughout the state.

The **Green Mountains** dominate the center of the state and include such peaks as Killington, Mansfield and Pico, and comprise the state's preeminent geological and topographical feature. Other ranges, which were created by the same pressures on the earth's crust that created the Green Mountains, include the **Taconics**, which stretch from Bennington County into Massachusetts; the **Granite Hills** in the center of the state which left Vermont endowed with some of the greatest granite deposits on earth; and the **Red Sandrock Hills**, extending from St. Albans to Addison County.

The largest and most important river in Vermont – even though it technically belongs to New Hampshire – is the **Connecticut River**, which stretches the entire length of the state before continuing south through Massachusetts, Connecticut, and on to the Atlantic Ocean. Other major rivers, all of which flow through valleys formed during the past ice age, include the **White River** and its various branches that flow from the center of the state to the Connecticut at White River Junction; the **Winooski** flowing from the Champlain Valley to the Green Mountains; and the **Battenkill** in the southwestern corners of the state.

PEOPLE

Vermont's first inhabitants were probably members of the Iroquois and Algonquin Indian tribes who lived in the Champlain Valley. Though the French were the first Europeans to set foot in Vermont in the 17th century, the first major migrations were by English colonists from the southern New England colonies of Massachusetts, Connecticut, and New Hampshire. Vermont's popularion remained primarily English until the mid- and late-19th century when the railroad, and the granite and marble industries, began to attract migrants, many of them first generation Americans of other European backgrounds. Another major group to enter the mix were French-Canadians who began arriving in substantial numbers in the early 20th century.

Today, Vermont's popularion is still more than 90% Caucasian, though in the past two decades more Asians and Latinos have found their way to urban centers like Burlington.

5. PLANNING YOUR TRIP

BEFORE YOU GO

WHEN TO VISIT

With the possible exception of late April and early May, when melting snows turn much of the state into a giant mud pit, Vermont is a fantastic destination throughout the year. Of course, Vermont's seasons are very well defined and when you travel depends on the type of experience you're looking to enjoy. If you want to ski, obviously you have to come during winter (December through late March or early April), while if you're keen to sample the colors of foliage, you must come during fall, preferably October.

Winter

Vermont is one of the most popular winter destinations in America, thanks in no small part to the excellent **skiing** offered by more than a dozen resorts including Killington, Stowe, and Sugarbush. The season, which in terms of good snow conditions (though snow is never guaranteed) usually lasts from December through late March. In addition to skiing, Vermont during winter offers excellent cross-country skiing, snowmobiling, sledding, and even hiking.

Vermont is also very beautiful in the winter, and particularly during the Christmas season, the entire state assumes a festive and almost magical feeling. Special celebrations are held throughout the state for Christmas and New Year's and inns, hotels, and restaurants pull out all the stops to make your holiday a festive one. Of course, holiday seasons, which also incude Presidents' Weekend, also mean the biggest crowds, fewer vacancies, and higher rates.

VERMONT TRAVEL INFORMATION

As you begin planning your visit to Vermont, you should call the **Vermont Department of Tourism and Marketing**, *Tel. 802/828-3237 or 800/VERMONT. They will provide you with a healthy amount of information (and some flat out propaganda) about whatever it is you want to know concerning visiting Vermont. You should also beam up their web site at* **www.travel-vermont.com**. *The web site provides good information, but even more important it features hundreds of links to virtually everything in Vermont, from hotels and ski resorts to general stores and chambers of commerce.*

Though it should go without saying, winter in Vermont is cold, with temperatures hovering around freezing or below nearly all of the time, so if you do not enjoy cold, Vermont in the winter is not the place to come. Also keep in mind that driving conditions can be difficult because of ice and snow and drivers need to take extra care to avoid accidents.

Spring & Summer

In the interests of full disclosure, it must be said that spring in Vermont is not the best time to visit the state. It's difficult to predict exactly when the snows will melt but when they do – and it's usually in early or mid-April – it leads to three weeks or a month of what locals term "mud season," which pretty much says it all. The mud generally subsides by mid-May when summer starts to kick in.

True summer lasts from June through early September when insects begin to disappear and nightime thermometer readings begin to dip into the low 30's Fahrenheit. The season is characterized by green, green, and more green, as well as numerous opportunities for outdoor recreation. Ski resorts turn their trails over to hikers and cyclists while rivers and lakes lure fishermen and boaters. Summer is also the time to visit Vermont's historic sites and museums, many which close in October.

Autumn

Vermont's fall foliage is legendary and for a month from the last week in September through October, the tourist volume is the highest of the year. What this means is that if you plan to sample the sparkling orange, reds, and yellows of the turning leaves, you really should make plans and reservations in advance, especially if you plan to visit during a weekend. Also, keep in mind that hotel rates are considerably higher during October than they are during the rest of the year.

WHAT TO PACK

Given the wide range of weather throughout the year, when you will travel will determine what you need to pack in terms of clothing. For **winter**, you defintely need to bring a heavy jacket, sweaters, hats, gloves, long underwear, and whatever else you need to stay warm. In **autumn**, tempertures can vary widely from balmy days in the 70's to freezing nights. You probably do not need to bring your full winter wardrobe, but you should, particularly if you plan to visit during late October or November, bring a jackets, some sweaters, and gloves. You should also have enough light clothing in case you're lucky enough to hit a patch of Indian Summer. **Summer** temperatures range from cool nights in the 50's to hot days in the 80's and 90's. You'll probably want to bring shorts, short sleeve shirts, and a swim suit, as well as slacks and pants and shirts heavy enough to at least keep you comfortable in an over-airconditioned dining room.

Whenever you travel, you should also bring whatever personal items you require, such as prescription medicines and toiletries. You'll also want to bring a camera, sunglasses (some of Vermont's coldest days can also be the sunniest), and of course personal documents like a driver's license, insurance cards and, if you're coming from overseas, your passport.

MAKING TRAVEL ARRANGEMENTS

Most visitors to Vermont make their own arrangements, particularly if they are driving from New York or Boston, and do not need to fly. If you feel more comfortable arranging your trip through a travel agent, by all means do so, but we'd recommend that you take time to research exactly what sort of accommodations you'd like to sample, particularly if you want to stay in one of Vermont's many fine inns and B&B's (bed and breakfasts). Travel agents are generally more accustomed to making bookings in large brand name hotels, and are unlikely to be familiar with particular establishments in Vermont.

However you prefer to make arrangements, keep in mind that if you plan to visit Vermont during a holiday or long weekend – or any time in October for that matter – you need to make reservations in advance. If you're able to visit during a time when it's not high season or some holiday, you can enjoy more flexibility – and cheaper rates – and even wing it as you go. Those compulsive planners should consider when making arrangements what it is you want to accomplish in Vermont. If there are particular historic sites you wish to visit, for example, look them up to see when they're open.

DEALS & DISCOUNTS

Though Vermont is not much of a package tour destination, there are plenty of deals and discounts to be had, particularly at the major ski resorts, both during summer and fall. Typically, hotels and resorts offer a wide assortment of weekend and multi-day packages that bundle lodging, some dining, and access to ski slopes or during the summer, golf courses and other facilities, for prices that are considerably lower than what you'd pay if you arranged each facet separately. To find out about discount packages beam up the *www.travel-vermont.com* web site and browse the sites of resorts and hotels to see what they offer. If you make arrangments at an inn or small hotel, ask them if they offer any discount packages.

BY AIR

The only major commercial airport in Vermont itself is **Burlington International Airport** serviced by:
• **Continental**, *Tel. 800/525-0289*
• **United**, *Tel. 800/241-6522*
• **USAir**, *Tel. 800/428-4322*

Two commuter airlines also fly into Burlington:
• **Business Express**, *Tel. 800/345-3400*
• **Comair**, *Tel. 800/927-0927*

However, keep in mind that flights into Burlington can be more expensive than flying into the major airports listed below.

In New Hampshire, **Lebanon Municipal Airport** in West Lebanon is about 10 minutes from White River Junction on Route 89 from Exit 1 and Route 4. However, Lebanon is only served by **USAir Express**, *Tel. 800/428-4322,* and flights are limited and expensive.

More convenient in terms of available flights and cost is **Manchester Airport** in Manchester, New Hampshire. Serviced by Southwest, *Tel. 800/435-9792*, Continental, USAir, and Delta Connection, *Tel. 800/345-3400,* Manchester is approximately two hours from White River Junction and most of eastern Vermont by car – most major rental companies operate out of Manchester. Otherwise, **Vermont Transit Lines**, *Tel. 800/552-8738, 800/451-3292,* offers direct service from the Manchester Airport to White River Junction four times daily (10:25am, 2:55pm, 5:55pm, &

10:40pm). If the departure times from the airport are inconvenient, take a taxi to the downtown depot where another half dozen buses depart daily for White River Junction.

A bit further away, Boston's **Logan Airport** is approximately 2.5 hours from the White River Junction region by car. All major car rental companies operate out of Logan, or you can take one of the hourly shuttles to South Station in downtown Boston and catch one of a half dozen daily buses to White River Junction. The advantages of flying to Boston, particularly if you are traveling some distance, include the availability of flights and lower costs than flying into one of the smaller regional airports.

Visitors to northern Vermont should consider flying into **Montreal** for similar reasons, while **Hartford** and **Albany** are within an hour's drive from most destinations in southern and western Vermont, respectively.

BY CAR

Vermont is approximately two to four hours from Boston and four to seven hours from New York City, depending on where in Vermont you're headed to. Driving to Vermont is recommended because once you arrive, having your own car is virtually essential to getting around the state. For directions to specific destinations in Vermont, look at the appropriate destination chapter.

BY BUS

Vermont Transit Lines, *Tel. 802/864-6811,* offers daily direct service from New York, Boston, Montreal, Albany, and Manchester and Keene, NH, to White River Junction, Burlington, and Rutland. From those cities you can make connections to virtually every region within Vermont. A one-way ticket between Boston and White River is approximately $30, while to New York, it's about $45.

BY TRAIN

Amtrak's **Vermonter**, *Tel. 800/USA-RAIL,* departs Washington DC at 7:40am and stops at Baltimore, Wilimington DE, Philadelphia, New York City, Newark NJ, Metro Park NJ, Trenton, NJ, Bridgport CT, Hartford CT, Meriden CT, New Haven CT, Springfield MA, Amherts MA, Northampton MA, Brattleboro VT, Keene NH, Windsor VT, White River Junction VT, Randolph VT, Montpelier VT, Waterbury-Stowe, Burlington VT, St. Albans, and Montreal, Canada. A one way ticket to Washington, DC from White River Junction costs about $85; from New York City $65; and less to destinations in Connecticut, Massachusetts, New Hampshire, and within Vermont.

A second train to Rutland, the **Ethan Allen Express**, departs Washington DC at 3am daily (#299), and at 10:40am Monday-Thursday (#291), and 1:05pm Friday-Saturday (#293), it stops at Baltimore, Wilimington DE, Philadelphia, and New York City (arriving at 6:38am. 2:15pm & 4:19pm respectively) where you must catch a connecting train with the same number. Train #299 departs Penn Station at 7:10am, #291 at 3:55pm, and #293 at 5:40pm en route to Yonkers, Croton-Harmon, Poughkeepsie, Rhinecliff-Kingston, Hudson, and Albany. Again you must transfer or board trains with the same number departing at 9:55am, 6:40pm, and 8:20pm respectively and **arriving in Rutland** at 12:30pm, 9:05pm, and 10:45pm. Trains depart Rutland in the other direction at 1:25pm and 5:25pm. A one-way fare from Rutland to New York city is approximately $55.

BY BOAT

Ferries link **Port Kent, New York** and **Burlington** at the King Street Dock off College Street. Ferries leave every 70 minutes from 9am-8:30 pm for $12.75 per vehicle and driver one-way ($23 round-trip); $3.25 every additional adult passenger. Ferries between **Plattsburgh, New York** and **Grand Isle, Vermont** depart every 20 minutes in each direction; fees for car and driver is $7, extra additional passengers $2.50 (children under 12 $.50). Finally, south of Shelburne, there is a ferry between **Essex, New York** and **Charlotte, Vermont**; ferries depart hourly in the early morning and late evening (6am-7am, 9:30pm-11pm) and every half hour from 7am-10pm during summer; ferries depart less frequently during other seasons. The fee for one car and driver is $7 one-way (round-trip $12.50); additional adult passengers cost $2.25.

For further information about ferries between northern Vermont and New York, contact the **Lake Champlain Transportation Company,** *King Street Dock, Burlington VT 05401, Tel. 802/864-9804, Web site: www.ferries.com*; or get one of their schedule pamphlets available at hotels, highway rest-stops and other sources of tourist information.

GETTING AROUND VERMONT

BY CAR

Because of its rural character, Vermont is not well-endowed with public transportation, so a car is very, very handy. Cars can be rented all airports in and around Vermont.

It is also possible to rent a car at several points within Vermont. In Burlington, **Avis** *(Tel. 800/331-1212)* , **Budget** *(Tel. 800/244-9429)* and **Hertz** *(Tel. 800/654-3131)*, and **Thrifty** *(Tel. 802/863-5500, toll free 800/ FOR-CARS)* all operate out of **Burlington International Airport. Avis** also has an office in Rutand *(Tel. 802/773-1317)*, and **Enterprise Rent-A-Car** has outlets in Rutland *(Tel. 802/773-0855)* , Barre *(Tel. 802/479-5400)*, and South Burlington *(Tel. 802/863-2111)*.

BY BUS

Vermont Transit Lines *(Tel. 802/864-6811)* does offers service between most major towns and resorts. Call for information about fares and schedules.

ACCOMMODATIONS

Vermont has always been known for its **inns** and **bed and breakfasts (B&B's)**, many of which are charming, family-run affairs situated in renovated 19th and early 20th century homes and farmhouses. Technically a "bed and breakfast" refers to a smaller establishment (usually ten rooms or less) that includes breakfast in its rates, and does not serve other meals, while the term "inn" denotes a larger establishment that very often includes a full-fledged restaurant and perhaps other facilities as well. However in this book, we have lumped them together since many establishments that call themselves inns are in fact B&B's, and vice versa.

Prices for inns and B&B's vary according to standards of luxury, amenities, and services. Often a comfortable, homey room in a small B&B can cost as little as $45 a night, while the truly exceptional inns may charge as much as $200-$300 a night or more. Prices also vary according to season with the most expensive rates charged during the foliage season (October) and major holidays like Christmas.

In recent years with the boom of the ski industry, there has been an exponential growth in the number of rooms available in larger, modern **hotel and resort establishments**. Invariably not as charming as the inns and B&B's, they usually offer the amenities and services expected of name brand hotels anywhere. Also, at major ski resorts, condominiums are readily available. Again, prices vary according to facilities and amenities, and very often they can often be rented as part of a "ski and stay" package that bundles accommodations, dining, and ski and recreation fees for considerably less than if you paid for each facet separately.

For information about hotels, condo's and resorts, contact the **Vermont Department of Tourism and Marketing**, *Tel. 800/VERMONT*, or visit their website at *www.travel-vermont.com*. You can also contact resorts and hotels directly by looking up their listings on the Vermont web site or in this book.

If you're looking for cheaper accommodations, there are many motels and motor inns through Vermont, where you can stay for as little as $45 a night. For more information, contact the Vermont Department of Marketing and Tourism at the number and web site listed above or check the listings in this book.

Finally, there are literally hundreds of **camping grounds** for recreation vehicles and tents in both state parks and at privately-operated grounds. Rates typically range from $10-$30 per night. For complete listing of campgrounds in Vermont, visit the **Vermont Campground Association** at their web site: *www.campvermont.com* and request a copy of the publication, *Vermont Campground Guide*, which features a complete listing of campgrounds in Vermont. For information about camping in state parks, contact the **Vermont Department of Forests, Parks & Recreation**, *103 South Main Street, Waterbury VT 05671-0603, Tel. 802/241-3655,* or visit their web site at *www.state.vt.us/anr/fpr/parks*.

6. BASIC INFORMATION

ADVENTURE TRAVEL

Vermont is so small that it doesn't afford the opportunities for adventure travel that some of the larger states do. However, it is possible to arrange multi-day or even multi-week hiking, biking, and boating trips. For more information, beam up *www.travel-vermont.com* and check out the links, or contact the organizations listed below:

VERMONT ADVENTURE GUIDES, *P.O. Box 3, North Ferrisburgh VT 05473. Tel. 802/425-6211, 800/425-8747, Fax 802/425-6218. E-mail: cabin@adventureguidesvt.com. Web site: adventureguidesvt.com.*

Organizes hiking, cycling, and canoeing trips.

GREEN MOUNTAIN CLUB, *4711 Waterbury/Stowe Road (Route 100), Waterbury Center VT 05677. Tel. 802/244-7037, Fax 802/244-5867. E-mail: gmc@sover.net. Web site: www.greenmountainclub.org.*

The Green Mountain Club can provide information about hiking in Vermont, including advice about how to organize multi-day hikes on such famous routes as the Long Trail.

AMERICAN EXPEDITIONS & AMERICAN PIONEER TOURS, *86 Lake St., Burlington VT 05401. Tel. 802/864-7600.*

CHILDREN

Vermont is a very child-friendly destination. It's safe, relatively cheap, and the vast recreational opportunities are usualy open to kids as well as adults. Major resorts almost always offer supervised activities such as ski lessons for children as well as day care facilities.

Camps

Vermont is famous for its summer camps to which upper, and later middle class, urban types from Boston and New York have been disposing their children for nearly a hundred summers. For information about summer camps in Vermont, contact the **Vermont Camping Association,** *278 Main Street., Burlington VT 05401, Tel. 888/882-2677.*

CREDIT CARDS

Most lodging and dining establishments as well as major retailers accept credit cards. When an establishment accepts Visa, Mastercard, and American Express, listings in this book will indicate "Major credit cards accepted." The vast majority of these establishments will also accept the Discover Card.

CRIME

In virtually every category of crime, particularly those of a violent nature, Vermont boasts among the lowest rates in America – it is indeed one of the safest states in the country in that respect. Having said that, we must remind you that there are exceptions to every trend and you should always take the same basic precautions you would take anywhere else. Always lock your car and hotel rooms securely, and never leave your valuables unattended in public. Also, whenever possible stash plane tickets and other important documents, as well as valuables in a hotel safety deposit box when circumstances do not dictate that you must carry them on your person.

FOOD & DRINK

Vermont's inns and hotels and the restaurants associated with them have long been known for the high quality American country cuisine served by their chefs. This cuisine typically includes such dishes as roast rack of lamb, roast chicken, and fresh vegetables prepared in a myriad of ways. Yankee favorites like prime rib and seafood dishes like Maine crab cakes are also common. Very fine and expensive restaurants often specialize in European cuisines, such as French and Italian, and with the spread of cuisines across America and the recent influx of folks from other parts of America and the world, it is also possible these days to find every type of cuisine from Chinese to Mexican. Such diversity is especially prevalent in the major resort areas and cities and towns such as Burlington.

By and large, eating out will take a modest bite out of your pocket book. It is difficult to find very cheap eats, but at the same time, a meal that would cost $60 or more in New York or Los Angeles will not set you back more than $40-$50 in Vermont.

HEALTH

The weather presents the greatest health risk to visitors Vermont, and wearing appropriate clothing and using common sense should mean that even the coldest winter day will not be a problem. In the winter, and on cold days in fall and spring, always be sure to wear plenty of warm clothing, drink plenty of fluids, and know your personal limits when you're outdoors. Exposure to low tempertures can lead to sickness or even death in a hurry (even a few hours), if you're not able to recover warmth in a hurry. So if you go hiking or skiing off well-traveled trails be sure to let people know where you're going and when you plan to return, and make sure you have plenty of warm clothing.

While winter cold presents the biggest threat, the summer heat and sun can also be problematic. If you're exposed to sun too long – especially when taking part in physically strenuous activity – heat stroke and heat exhaustion can set in without your knowing it. Even when it's hot, be sure to wear enough clothing to protect yourself from the sun, wear plenty of sun block, and most importantly, drink lots of fluids (and I don't mean beer). Caffeinated drinks like colas are not a very good idea because the caffeine is diuretic and actually accelerates the dehydration process.

Tap water is generally safe, and if you have any worries at all about drinking out of the tap, bottled water is readily available. You should not however, drink from lakes, streams, or rivers without first purifying it by filter or purification tablets.

Finally, in case of emergency, check in the Practical Information sections of each destination chapter in this book for telephone numbers for ambulances and health centers. In some communities, the standard "911" is the correct number but in many areas, you will need to dial a local number.

SHOPPING

By and large shopping isn't the first thing that pops into one's mind when considering Vermont, but from galleries stocked with locally produced crafts to sugar houses selling every maple product known to man, Vermont does offer shoppers unique opportunities. One factor that makes shopping in Vermont special is that unlike the rest of America, indeed the rest of the world, Vermont has not turned into one big stretch mall dominated by franchise and chain stores. And though the likes of Walmart have made some inroads, Vermont is a place where the village general store is still a focal point for many communities.

STAYING OUT OF TROUBLE

By any standard, Vermont is one of the safest states in the US and should you take basic precautions and follow state and federal rules, you should enjoy a problem free vacation. Here are some precautions and guidelines worth following:

• Copy all personal documents (passport, insurance cards, driver's license) and keep them separate from the originals. This can make life easier should you lose the originals.

• Keep important documents in hotel safes whenever you're not using them.
• Do not flaunt valuables and only keep as much money on your person as necessary.
• If traveling from Canada or any other point overseas, make sure that your passport, visa, and other documents are in order. Any document that is out of order can cause major headaches and delays at the border.
• Avoid excessive drinking, particularly in public and when you are alone with strangers. Of course, don't even consider drinking and driving.

TAXES

Taxes is the main hidden cost for both travelers and residents in Vermont. Sales taxes are 6%, and hotel and meal taxes are another 9% – they add up in a hurry. Listed prices in this book **do not include** these taxes.

TELEPHONES

All of Vermont is within the **802 area code**, and whenever dialing a Vermont number from outside the state, you must dial 1-802 first. You also need to dial 1-802 for many in-state calls when you are not dialing within the immediate community. For our foreign visitors, remember that when dialing any part of the United States, or to another country, you must dial "1" and then the appropriate area code or country code before dialing the actual number.

TIME

Vermont is on Eastern Standard Time (EST), five hours behind Greenwich Mean Time, and three hours ahead of Pacific Coast Time.

TIPPING

The 15% rule applies to most cases in Vermont unless circumstances dictate otherwise.

WHERE TO FIND OUT MORE ABOUT VERMONT

You can begin by calling *Tel. 800/VERMONT* and asking for information or getting online and going to *www.travel-vermont.com*. Both will lead to the Vermont Department of Tourism and Marketing, which will you send all sorts of glossy brochures and magazines like *Vermont Life Explorer* and *Vermont Life*. It's mostly propaganda and the sugarcoated writing can make for less than sensational reading, but the information is quite helpful and will give you not only a general idea about what Vermont and its different regions have to offer, but tons of particulars about hotels, shops, coming attractions, and everything else a visitor to Vermont might be interested in. Below is the full address:

Vermont Department of Tourism & Marketing, *6 Baldwin Street, 4th floor, Drawer 33, Montpelier VT 05633-1301. Tel. 802/828-3237, Fax 802/ 828-3233. E-mail: vttravel@dca.state.vt.us. Website: www.travel-vermont.com.*

Magazines like *Vermont Life* and *Vermont Magazine* are good sources of tourism information, including up to date listings of local cultural events like concerts and festivals. For more specific local information, regional dailies and weeklies like the *Burlington Free Press* and the *Rutland Herald* can also be helpful, as are the promotional publications put out by regional tourist boards or chambers of commerce in heavily traveled destinations like Stowe and Killington.

For more information about hotels, shops, and you may also consider getting in touch with the **Vermont Chamber of Commerce**, which publishes seasonal magazine guides, and the **Vermont Lodging and Restaurant Association**, and the specific regional tourism offices listed below. If you're looking to find out about specific types of recreation, we list contact info for statewide organizations such as the Green Mountain Club, the Department of Fish & Wildlife, and the Vermont Ski Areas Associations which can provide comprehensive infomation about opportunities in Vermont.

VERMONT CHAMBER OF COMMERCE, *P.O. Box 37, Montpelier VT 0501-0037. Tel. 802/223-3443, Fax 802/223-4257, ext. 111. E-mail: info@vtchamber.com. Website: www.vtchamber.com.*

VERMONT LODGING & RESTAURANT ASSOCIATION, *3 Main Street. Suite 100, Burlington VT 05401. Tel. 802/660-9001. Fax. 802/802) 660-8987. E-mail: vtlra@ad.com. Website: www.visitst.com.*

For regional information, contact:
- **Burlington & Environs**, *Tel. 877/686-5253. E-mail: Vermont@vermont.org. Website:www.vermont.org.*
- **Lake Champlain Islands & Northwestern Vermont**, *Tel. 800/262-5226. E-mail: ilandfun@toether.net.*
- **Stowe, Waterbury, & Smugglers' Notch**, *Tel. 877/247-8693. E-mail: lvcc@together.net or stowe@sover.net. Website: www.stoweinfo.com.*
- **Northeast Kingdom**, *Tel. 888/884-8001. Website: www.vermontnekchamber.org.*
- **Montpelier, Mad River Vally, & Waterbury,***Tel. 877/4968. E-mail: cvermontll@aol.com. Website: www.central-vt.com.*
- **Middlebury & The Lower Champlain Valley**, *Tel. 800/733-8376. E-mail: addcoc@together.net. Website: www.midvermont.com.*

- **Killington & Rutland**, *Tel. 800/756-8880. E-mail: rrccvt@aol.com. Websites: www.killington.com; www.rutlandvermont.com.*
- **Woodstock, Randolph & Orange County,** *Tel. 888/848-4199. E-mail: mail@randolph-chamber.com.*
- **Upper Connecticut Valley (White River & Queechee),** *Tel. 888/663-6656. E-mail: quechee@queechee.com.; u.v.chamber@valley.net. Website: www.queechee.com.*
- **Southern Connecticut Valley, including Ludlow**, *Tel. 802/885-2779. E-mail: spfldcoc@vermontel.com.*
- **Southeastern Vermont (Stratton, Brattleboro & Mt. Snow),** *Tel. 877/887-2378. E-mail: londcham@vermontel.com; info@visitvermont.com. Website: www.southernvermont.com.*
- **Southwestern Vermont (Bennington & Manchester),** *Tel. 877/768-3766. E-mail: benncham@sover.net. Websites: www.bennington.com; www.vtweb.com*

7. SPORTS & RECREATION

BIKING

With a combination of low traffic, well maintained roads, and beautiful scenery, Vermont is an ideal destination for road cyclists, while the Green Mountains afford limitless opprtunities for mountain bikers. To get an idea about biking opportunities in Vermont, pick up a copy of John Freidin's book, *Twenty-Five Bicycle Tours in Vermont*. We have also listed in each destination chapter, places to rent bikes and get information about regional opportunities. Listed below are several outfits that organize bike tours throughout Vermont, including inn-to-inn tours.

BIKE VERMONT, *P.O. 207, Woodstock VT 05091. Tel. 802/457-3553, 800/257-2226. E-mail: bikevt@bikevt.com. Web site: www.bikevt.com*

BICYCLE HOLIDAYS, *1394 Munger St., Middlebury VT 05753. Tel. 800/292-5388.*

MAJIC MOUNTAIN CYCLING LTD., *RR1 Box 608, Moretown VT 05660. Tel. 802/496-2641.*

CANOEING

Rivers such as the **Battenkill**, the **White River**, and the **Connecticut River**, as well as numerous lakes and ponds offer excellent canoeing opportunities in beautiful settings. For information about canoeing in specific regions, look up listings in this book's destinations chapters. For information about tours and renting equipment, contact the organizations listed below.

VERMONT ADVENTURE GUIDES, *P.O. Box 3, North Ferrisburgh VT 05473. Tel. 802/425-6211, 800/425-8747, Fax 802/425-6218. E-mail: cabin@adventureguidesvt.com. Web site: adventureguidesvt.com.*

Organizes hiking, cycling, and canoeing trips.

AMERICAN EXPEDITIONS & AMERICAN PIONEER TOURS, *86 Lake St., Burlington VT 05401. Tel. 802/864-7600.*
BATTENKILL CANOE LTD., *Tel. 802/363-2800, 800/421-5268.*
WILDERNESS TRAILS, *Tel. 802/295-7620.*

FISHING

Vermont's more than 300 lakes, rivers and streams offer numerous opportunities for fishermen. For information about everything from licenses (required) to where to catch what when, contact the **Vermont Dept. of Fish and Wildlife**, *Tel. 800/VERMONT, Web site: www.anr.State.vt.us/fw/fwhome.*

HIKING & BACKPACKING

With its rural character and extensive wilderness, Vermont features excellent and extensive hiking for all types from casual walkers looking to sample the fresh air and beautiful scenery to dedicated adventurists who come from all over the world to spend weeks exploring some of America's most famous trails such as the **Long Trail** and the **Appalachian Trail**. While hiking is most popular during summer and the fall foliage season, it is also an excellent way to enjoy the beauty of Vermonts winter, however, hiking is not recommended from the end of winter snowmelt in late-March/April until mid to late-May when the Mud Season not only renders trails virtually impassable and extremely hard on shoes, but also finds them extremely fragile and vulnerable to ecological damage.

Vermont tourist authorities wlil be more than happy to provide information about hiking throughout Vermont. We'd also recommend that if you're considering anything more than an afternoon stroll, that you contact the **Green Mountain Club** at *Route 100, Waterbury Center VT 05677, Tel. 802/244-7037,* Vermont's most important hiking association of hikers, and a major contributor to the maintenance of Vermont's trails on both public and private lands. The Green Mountain Club is also the publisher of a series of books and guides, such as the *Day Hiker's Guide to Vermont* and *Guide Book of the Long Trail*, considered by many to be indispensable for hikers and backpackers.

The **Green Mountain National Forest**, which covers more than 300,000 acres primarily in the southwestern part of the state, features hundreds of miles of scenic hiking trails as well as camping facilities and canoeing, fishing, and wildlife viewing. For information about the Forest, including suggestions, accessibility, and rules and regulations, contact the **Forest Supervisor's Office**, *231 Morth Main Street, Rutland VT 05701; Tel. 802/747-6700;* or *PO Box 519, Rutland VT 05702, Tel. 802/773-0300.*

TIPS FOR HIKERS

Though Vermont's mild terrain makes hiking a fun, safe and feasible recreational activity for people of all ages and most levels of physical fitness (those with chronic physical ailments should consult their doctor before hitting the trail), all hikers should follow some basic guidelines to protect themselves and the hiking environment.

1. Whenever hiking off major roads, always consult and carry a map.

2. Unless you are a very experienced hiker and really know what you are doing, always hike with at least one other person.

3. Always let somebody else know when and where you plan to hike.

4. Always bring plenty of water and a flashlight; you never known when you might get lost and both are critical.

5. Be aware of your own physical limits and do not hesistate to rest, stop, and/or turn around when you get tired. Fatigue can lead to serious injury or worse.

6. Consult a weather forecast before setting off; Vermont weather can change in a hurry and strong rains, winds, or a sudden change in weather can spell disaster.

HUNTING

Hunting is an integral part of life for many Vermonters and the first day of deer season has become something of a state holiday. Out of ignorance, I have not addressed hunting thoughout this book; however, if you contact the **Vermont Dept. of Fish and Wildlife**, *Tel. 800/ VERMONT, web site: www.anr.State.vt.us/fw/fwhome.*, they will send you literature telling you everything you need to know about hunting in Vermont – from the calendar of the various seasons and license require ments, to listings of hunter-friendly lodging establishments.

SKIING, CROSS-COUNTRY SKIING & SNOWBOARDING

While the Green Mountains are not big enough or high enough to compete with the Rockies or the French Alps, Vermont is the undeniable "Ski Capital of the East" and the sport is an integral part of winter life and the state's economy. Generally the season begins around mid-November; even if not much snow has fallen, it is cold enough that the resorts can crank up their snowmaking machines – snowmaking was practically invented in Vermont – to provide suitable conditions. The season generally ends in early-mid April though its always hard to predict. Sometimes the snow is virtually gone by the end of March while in some years the biggest storms of the year happen in April. In any case, the best skiing is from January through mid-March. By the end of March, icing can be a problem in the mornings while by afternoons, even if there is a lot of snow, exposure to the sun gives it a consistency resembling mashed potatoes.

When and where you ski depends on many factors. Vermont features more than a dozen major resorts, each of which has something a little different to offer. Experienced skiers undoubtedly want to head for the big mountain resorts like Sugarbush, Mad River Glen, Stowe, Mount Snow, and the biggest of them all, Killington. These areas offer the most variety, the longest runs, and more choice. They are also big enough to feature many easy runs for beginners and the most choice in terms of instruction packages. On the other hand, families may consider smaller resorts like Burke or Magic Mountain which are smaller and less crowded.

For an introduction to Vermont's skiing opportunities, visit the web site *www.skivermont.com*, or contact the **Vermont Ski Areas Association,** *26 State Street, P.O. Box 368, Montpelier VT 05601, Tel. 802/229-6917* and ask for information.

We have listed major **cross-country skiing** venues in the destination chapters. For a complete list, contact the **Vermont Chamber of Commerce,** *Tel. 802/223-3443; e-mail: vtg99@vtchamber.com; web site: www.vtchamber.com,* and request that they mail you a copy of their winter guide.

SNOWMOBILING

With its healthy snowfalls and rural landscape, Vermont is perfect for snowmobiling and it is certainly one of the most popular winter pastimes among Vermonters. Through the destination chapters, we have listed snowmobile clubs and companies that rent snowmobiles and give instruction and tours.

For comprehensive information sbout snowmobiling in Vermont, contact the **Vermont Association of Snow Travelers (V.A.S.T.),** *P.O. Box 839, Montpelier VT 05601, Tel. 802/229-0005, toll free 888/884-8001, Fax 802/223-4316, Web site: www.vtvast.org.*

8. MAJOR EVENTS

Vermont's calendar is overflowing with events and happenings, from music festivals that attract thousands to local affairs like church dinners and Old Home Days parades in the summer. Listed below are some of the highlights. For a more complete listing of Vermont happenings, visit the Vermont Department of Tourism and Marketing's web site at *www.travel-vermont.com* or call them at *Tel. 800/VERMONT* and request information.

The **Vermont Chamber of Commerce**, *Tel. 802/223-3443; e-mail: vtg99@vtchamber.com; web site: www.vtchamber.com,* which publishes seasonal guidebooks in magazine form, is also a good source.

WINTER

The Christmas and New Year holidays give Vermonters and visitors alike an excuse to whoop it up, and the holiday season is packed with events from colorful Christmas Tree lightings to large New Years and First Night celebrations.

PRELUDE TO CHRISTMAS (Manchester) – This series of events held from late November through December in Manchester includes musical performances, a Christmas tree lighting in Manchester Village, and a torchlight parade with fireworks on New Year's Eve.

STOWE WINTER CARNIVAL – Held during the last week in January, this special event features a wide assortment of winter sports competitions, parties, and exhibitions.

BROOKFIELD ICE HARVEST – Held annually during the last week in January, the Ice Harvest features amazing ice sculptures that are judged in competition.

SPRING & SUMMER

DISCOVER JAZZ FESTIVAL – Held in Burlington in the second week in June, the Discover Jazz Festival is the only Vermont jazz fest to attract the likes of Herbie Hancock and Clark Terry.

BEN & JERRY'S ONE WORLD, ONE HEART FESTIVAL – Sponsored by Vermont's best loved ice cream makers, this annual late-June festival held at Mount Ellen features dozens of vendors selling food, clothing, and other goodies, as well as music by popular rock and folk acts.

FOURTH OF JULY – America's birthday is celebrated in Vermont with colorful parades and fireworks at major resorts like Stratton. Check the local paper for event listings.

OLD HOME DAYS – Many villages celebrate themselves with Fourth of July-like parades. Dates vary according to city.

VERMONT MOZART FESTIVAL – A series of concerts given throughout Vermont during July.

MARLBORO MUSIC FESTIVAL – The most highly acclaimed chamber music event in the region, if not the country, is held annually in Marlboro from mid-July through mid-August; call for information at *Tel. 802/254-2394.*

AUTUMN

NEW WORLD FESTIVAL – This Labor Day weekend festival celebrates Celtic and French-Canadian music with lovely performances galore.

VERMONT STATE FAIR – Held over the first two weeks of September, the Vermont State Fair is the biggest and most popular in the state.

BENNINGTON ANTIQUE AUTO & MOTORCYCLE SHOW – A car lover's delight held annually in mid-September in Bennington, home to the *Motor Hemming News.* Call *Tel. 802/447-3311* for information.

TUNBRIDGE WORLD'S FAIR – This old-timey fair is a consistent favorite with Vermonts, and is held in mid-September annually.

SUGARBUSH BREWERS' FESTIVAL – The foliage season kicks off in late September with this event held in Lincoln Peak. Brewers from across Vermont and New England have booths and tents where you can taste all varieties of beer and food, watch demonstrations about the brewing process, and ride chairlifts from which you can enjoy spectacular views of the Mad River Valley.

9. VERMONT'S BEST PLACES TO STAY

TRAPP FAMILY LODGE, *700 Trapp Hill Road, Stowe, VT 05672. Tel. 802/253-8511, 800/826-7000. Fax 802/253-5740. E-mail: info@trappfamily.com. Web site: www.trappfamily.com. Rates: $100-$250. Major credit cards.com.*

"A mountain resort in the European tradition," founded and owned by the Trapp family whose story inspired the smash musical and movie *The Sound of Music.* The Trapp Family Lodge is a 2,500-acre resort with a myriad of facilities and a hillside setting overlooking the Little River Valley that is nothing less than breathtaking. Lodging options include a variety of rooms and suites, ranging in price (not inluding holiday rates or special packages) from $98 to $650 in one of two main lodge buildings. Though the original lodge burned down in the early 1980's, the new lodges have recaptured much of the Austrian mystique. Rooms combine comfort and modern amenities with old world standards of decor and comfort. There are also condos available on a time share basis.

Recreational facilities include a full service cross-country ski center with more than 100 kilometers of groomed trails, three pools indoor and out, a fitness center, sleigh riding, miles and miles of hiking and biking trails, and oodles of planned activities ranging from the Vermont Mozart Society outdoor concerts to volleyball and tennis tournaments. There are also three eateries: an Austrian tea house that serves breakfast and lunch; the main semi-formal dining room serving fine continental cuisine with a German twist; and a handsome lounge serving refreshments and upscale bar food. Various meal plans are available; call or talk to your travel agent about special packages with cheaper rates than the rack rates listed above.

Even if you do not stay at the Trapp Family Lodge, it is well worth a visit.

THE HERMITAGE INN, *Coldbrook Road, Wilmington VT 05363. Tel. 802/464-3511, Fax 802/464-2688. E-mail: hermitag@sover.net. Web site: www.hermitageinn.comm. Rates: $150-$300 per room. Major credit cards accepted.*

One of America's great country inns, the Hermitage is actually more like a resort for the rich and famous from another era. Set on an estate comprising hundreds of scenic acres at the base of Haystack Mountain that include a trout pond, 50 kilometers of cross-country ski trails, a tennis court, a swimming pool, and an on-site skeet shooting range (game birds are also hunted in season), the inn offers a superb combination of luxurious accommodations, a first-rate restaurant, and an atmosphere that is approriately informal but elegant.

For lodging there are 30 individually appointed, deluxe rooms with beautiful antique furnishings located in various buildings throughout the estate. The main inn building, known as the Main House, contains four elegant, antique-laden guestrooms in addition to the famous fireplace lounge and the restaurant. Adjoining the Main House is the Wine House, home to the Hermitage's renowned wine cellar. It features seven guest rooms, each of which contains a working fireplace. Across the meadow from the Main House, the Carriage House affords those staying in its four guestrooms a private parlor and a sauna. Finally, the Brookbound Inn, about a mile down Coldbrook Road from the main inn, is a beautiful house with 14 guestrooms and a wonderful woodpaneled living room with a stone fireplace. Whatever incovenience the distance from the Main House may lend, it is more than compensated for by the clay tennis court and swimming pool that its guests enjoy direct access to.

But the Hermitage experience is more than just staying in deluxe accommdations. The grounds include a sugar house, a gamebird farm where pheasants, ducks, and geese are raised, a skeet shooting range, and as I mentioned before, more than 50 kilometers of some of the most beautiful cross-country skiing trails in Vermont.

An integral part of staying at the Hermitage is the dining. Perfectly classy and elegant without pretension, the Hermitage embodies the ideal country resort, and the restaurant is no exception. Ideally, an evening begins with a refreshment and perhaps some hors d'oeuvres in the fireplace tavern before moving on to the dining room – where the stars of the meal are traditionally the finely prepared game bird specials and a glass or two (or three) from one or more of the Hermitage's more than 2,000 selections. Game birds such as duck, goose, and pheasant are raised on the inn's premises and the wine cellar holds more than 30,000 bottles. Dress is smart casual and full meals will set you back at least $30-$40, but it's worth every penny.

JACKSON HOUSE INN & RESTAURANT, *37 Route 4 West, Woodstock VT 05091. Located just beyond Woodstock High School west of the Woodstock Green on Route 4 on the right. Tel. 802/457-2065, 800/448-1890, Fax 802/457-9290. E-mail: innkeepers@jacksonhouse.com, or posadajh@aol.com. Web site: www.jacksonhouse.com. Rates: $175-$200 for rooms, $250-$300 suites. Credit cards: Visa, Mastercard, American Express.*

One of the finest inns in Vermont, Jackson House features about a dozen rooms and suites, all elegant, comfortable, and filled with enough quality antiques to be museum exhibits in their own right. Each room includes air-conditioning and private bath and is individually appointed with beautiful and comfortable furniture and ornamentation. The Josephine Tasher Bonaparte room (all rooms and suites have names to match), for example, features an antique mahogany bed with brass mounts, a gem of an old ceiling fan, and is decorated with bronze statuettes. Suites are even more fantastic – the Wales Johnson has a queen sleighbed made of cherry wood, a marble top bureau, a gas fireplace, and a jacuzzi in the bathroom. It also has a private entrance to the patio and gardens.

In addition to its lodging facilities, Jackson House Inn is also home to one of the finest restaurants in Woodstock, and while the prices are steep (they include breakfast, evening champagne refreshments and hors d'oeuvres), the experience is well worth the splurge. You can feast on variations of fine continental cuisine in a beautiful dining room distinguished by its cathedral style ceiling, beautiful wooden furniture, and an open hearth granite fireplace. But the food is the real star. While most dishes are from the continental old school, the chef has given them a little extra thrust without changing their essence or turning them into some fruity nouveau experiment. In 1998-1999, the menu included such items as the classic French seafood soup bouillabaisse, grilled veal chop with merlot butter and jumbo asparagus, and Atlantic grilled grouper with fiddleheads and cabbage. He is a bit more experimental with appetizers like yellowfin tartar with pickled ginger and wasabi tobikko and eggplant canneloni. For dessert you may choose from the tray of fine pastries and baked goods.

WOODSTOCK INN & RESORT, *14 Village Green, Woodstock VT 05091. Tel. 802/457-1100, 800/448-7900, Fax 802/457-6699. Web site: www.woodstockinn.com. Rates: rooms begin at about $100, and there are numerous 2,3 day and longer packages that bundle meals, skiing, golf and other activities. Call for info. Major credit cards accepted.*

Perhaps the most famous – and certainly one of the finest – of all inns in Vermont, the Woodstock Inn combines the comfort and personal service of a country inn with the facilities of a resort in a classic Vermont setting on Woodstock's legendary green. There are 144 rooms, all tastefully furnished with country furniture and decor, featuring modern amenities such as air-conditioning, cable television, and telephones; 44 rooms also include a fireplace.

The main inn building includes a gift shop, tavern, and two eateries including a very fine dining room serving gourmet continental and American country. There is also a fitness center with squash, indoor tennis, massage, and aerobics, and guests also enjoy access and special rates at the Suicide Ski Area and the Woodstock Country Club golf course designed by Robert Trent Jones. Be sure to call about special packages offered throughout the year that may enable you to enjoy all of these facilities and opportunities for less than if you paid for them separately.

Though the Inn is more famous, its restaurant consistenly receives high marks from critics and guests alike. The cuisine is mainly fine American and continental and the menu typically features more seafood than you usually find in Vermont restaurants, in addition to the usual assortment of superb steak, lamb, and poultry dishes. Appetizers are typically $7-$8 while entrees range from $20 for the maple roasted chicken for example, to $24 for double lamb chops au jus. The house specialty, char-grilled tiger shrimp and scallop, is $22. For dessert, there is an assortment of pastries and baked goods, many of which are sinfully rich and delicious, but if you're watching calories, there is also sorbet and sometimes fruit. Reservations are advised, particularly during holiday and foliage seasons, and dress is just this side of formal – men are encouraged to wear jackets; jeans and t-shirts are prohibited.

THE EQUINOX & THE CHARLES ORVIS INN, *Route 7A, Manchester Village VT 05254. Tel. 802/362-4700, 800/362-4747, Fax 802/362-1595. E-mail: reservations@equinoxresort.com. Web site: www.equinoxresort.com. Rates: $150-$500 for rooms and suites at the Equinox; $600-$1000 for luxury suites in the Charles Orvis Inn. Major credit cards accepted.*

Originally established in 1769, the Equinox and its luxury adjunct, the Charles Orvis Inn, are truly one of Vermont's signature landmarks and offer guests a unique combination of luxury accommodations and first-rate recreational opportunities. Restored to its colonial-era glory with splendid antiques and colonial and Victorian decor, the Equinox offers rooms and suites beautifully appointed with top of the line amenities. Larger suites and the superduper luxury suites in the Charles Orvis Inn feature fireplaces, extra sitting rooms and private patios.

Recreation facilities include the Gleneages golf course, two swimming pools (including one indoor), tennis, the British School of Falconry where you can learn the art of flying and hunting with falcons, and the Land Rover Driving School which provides instruction in off-road jeep driving. There is also a full-fledged gym and weight room, a library, a bar, and two restaurants.

TOPNOTCH AT STOWE RESORT & SPA, *4000 Mountain Road (Route 108), Stowe VT 05672. Tel. 802/253-8585, 800/451-8686, Fax 802/253-9263. E-mail: topnotch@sover.net. Web site: www.topnotch-resort.com. Rates: $75 per person per night & up. Major credit cards accepted.*

Situated on 120 acres overlooking Mt. Mansfield, this highly acclaimed modernist (many ceiling to floor glass walls) resort lives up to its name as it features the most impressive facilities and amenities in Stowe, if not all of Vermont. Guests have a choice between staying in one of the 92 individually and lavishly appointed rooms and suites or one of the 15 fully equipped townhouse condo's with fireplaces, kitchens, balconies, and other amenities.

The most impressive aspects of Topnotch, however, are the recreational facilities that include indoor and outdoor tennis courts, on-site cross-country skiing, an acclaimed spa and fitness center, two swimming pools, mountain bike rentals, and horseback riding. Other distractions include an all-out beauty shop (facials, masseurs et al), a gift shop, a bar, fine dining at the highly regarded restaurant Maxwell's, and presentations of movies on the big screen four times a week. Finally, if nothing else, the lobby with its freestanding stone fireplace and gothic-like ceiling is worth a visit. Call for package deals with discounts for rooms, the spa, skiing, golf, and tennis.

10. BRATTLEBORO & WINDHAM COUNTY

One of the first areas in present-day Vermont to be settled by Europeans, the southeast corner of the state offers visitors a variety of attractions – from the month-long world-renowned **Marlboro Music Festival** in July and August to the bustling town of **Brattleboro** and the charming villages of **Grafton** and **Newfane**. Originally developed by the British army which constructed **Fort Dummer** just south of present-day Brattleboro to protect settlements in New Hampshire, the region thrived in the 19th century by virtue of its commercially important location on the Connecticut River and the establishment of major commercial firms like the Estey Organ Company.

Today, that importance has diminished somewhat, but its legacy has left Brattleboro and towns like **Putney** with an old-timey charm that retains its authenticity due to the fact that the region is not overrun with tourists. Indeed, the region does not feature the obvious draws like major ski areas and standout historic sites, but between the area's natural beauty and offerings ranging from some of the state's most impressive covered bridges to the very fine **Brattleboro Museum and Art Center**, it certainly warrants a looking over, if not several days of your time. Besides, if you want to go skiing, **Mt. Snow** with its 135 runs is but 25 minutes from Brattleboro on Route 9.

ARRIVALS & DEPARTURES

By Air

Bradley International Airport in Hartford, Connecticut, is 1.5 hours from Brattleboro and probably the nearest major airport. Just over the Connecticut River from White River Junction, an hour north of Brattleboro (45 minutes from Bellows Falls), is the **Lebanon Municipal Airport** in Lebanon, New Hampshire. However, Lebanon is only served by USAir Express, *Tel. 800/428-4322,* and flights are limited and expensive. More convenient in terms of available flights and cost is **Manchester Airport** in Manchester, New Hampshire, approximately 1-1.5 hours from Brattleboro by way of Route 9 in New Hampshire. Serviced by Southwest, *Tel. 800/435-9792*, Continental, *Tel. 800/525-0289*, USAir, *Tel. 800/428-4322*, and Delta Connection, *Tel. 800/345-3400.*

Major rental companies operate out of Manchester. Otherwise, **Vermont Transit Lines,** *Tel. 800/552-8738, Tel. 800/451-3292,* offers service from the Manchester Airport to Keene, NH and from Keene to Brattleboro.

Other alternatives include Boston's **Logan Airport** (2 hours from Brattleboro), approximately 2.5 hours from the Woodstock-Quechee region by car; **La Guardia** and **JFK** airports in New York City (4-5 hours from Brattleboro), and **Montreal**.

By Car

Interstate 91 (I-91) links Brattleboro and Brattleboro County directly with Springfield MA, Hartford CT, and (after intersecting with I-95) with New York City to the south. It also joins Brattleboro to points in northern Vermont such as Windsor and White River Junction, where it intersects with I-89 which leads to central New Hampshire and major destinations within Vermont including Montpelier, Burlington; and via Route 100, resort areas such as Stowe and the Mad River Valley. The region is linked to Mount Snow (southern Vermont's permier ski area), Bennington, and the Manchester region by Route 9.

By Bus

Vermont Transit Lines, *Tel. 802/254-6066,* links Brattleboro and Bellows Falls with Keene, NH, Ascutney-Windsor, Hanover NH, and White River Junction where connections can be made for Montreal and points throughout northern, central, and western Vermont, including Montpelier, Burlington, Rutland, and St. Johnsbury. From Keene NH, connections can be made for Manchester NH, and Boston. Vermont Transit also provides service south to Springfield MA, where Greyhound connections can be made for New York, Hartford, Philadelphia, and other destinations through the region and the United States generally.

By Train

Amtrak's **Ethan Allen**, *Tel. 800/USA-RAIL,* stops in both Brattleboro and Bellows Falls, and links both with Windsor, White River Junction, Randolph, Montpelier, Waterbury-Stowe, Burlington, St. Albans, Swanton, and Montreal to the north. Trains leaving for these destinations depart from Brattleboro at 5pm and from Bellows Falls at 5:35pm.

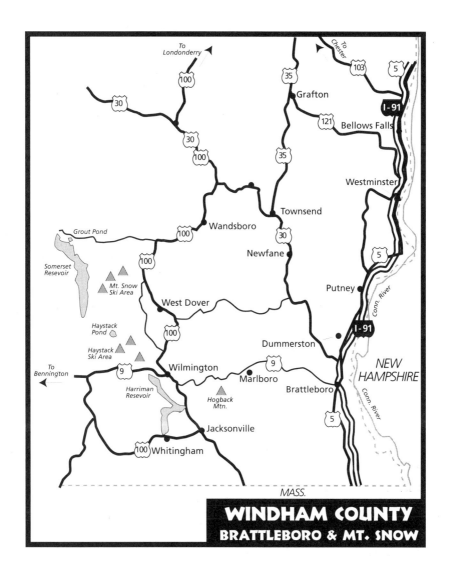

WINDHAM COUNTY
BRATTLEBORO & MT. SNOW

Trains depart south from Brattleboro at noon, and Bellows Falls at 11:26am for the following destinations: Amherst and Springfield, MA; Hartford, Berlin, Meriden, New Haven, Bridgeport, and Stamford, CT; New York, NY (Penn Station); Newark, Metropark, and Trenton, NJ; Philadelphia, PA; Wilmington, DE; Baltimore, BWI Airport and New Carrollton, MD; and Washington DC. A one-way ticket from Brattleboro to Washington costs approximately $80. Reservations are required.

ORIENTATION

A town of 12,500, **Brattleboro** is the first major town (with apologies to Guildford) on the north-south interstate **I-91** after it enters Vermont from Massachusetts. It is also the regional hub in that most of the area's major roads intersect in or near it. **Route 9** links Brattleboro with Keene, NH to the east, and Marlboro (10 miles), Wilmington-Mount Snow (20 miles), and Bennington (40 miles) to the west.

Route 30 leads northwest to Newfane, Townsend, and eventually Stratton and Manchester in the western part of the state. Finally, **Route 5** and I-91 run alongside each other and the Connecticut River to Dummerston, Putney, Westminster, and Bellows Falls before continuing on to Windsor, White River Junction, and the Northeast Kingdom.

GETTING AROUND

It's always much easier to get around Vermont if you have your own vehicle, and Windham County is no exception. If you arrive in Brattleboro, or anywhere else in the area, and you would like to rent a car, **Enterprise Rent-a-car**, *Tel. 802/257-4700*, can arrange to deliver the car to you, or you can arrange to pick it up. You can also try **Thrifty Car Rental**, *Tel. 802/254-9900*.

Within Brattleboro itself, the **Brattleboro Town Bus**, *Tel. 802/254-4541*, offers service within the town itself. Call for information or consult the folks at your hotel for more information.

WHERE TO STAY

Bellows Falls & Westminster

RIVER MIST BED & BREAKFAST, *7 Burt Street, Bellows Falls VT 05101. Tel. 802/463-9023, 888/463-9023, Fax 802/463-1571. E-mail: rmistbnb@vermontel.com. Web site: www.river-mist.com. Rates: $65-$100. Credit cards: Visa, Mastercard.*

This small family-run Victorian B&B features only three comfortable rooms and is known for its warm hospitality and good breakfasts.

BLUE HAVEN CHRISTIAN BED & BREAKFAST, *6963 Route 5, Westminster VT 05158. Tel. 802/463-9008, 800/228-9008, Fax 802/463-*

0669. E-mail: bluhaven@sover.net. Web site: www.virtualvermont.com/band/ bluehaven. Rates: $45-$110. Credit cards: Visa, Mastercard.
Situated in a restored 1830's school house with five rooms (canopy beds and private baths) including a suite with a kitchenette. Breakfast included.

Brattleboro

LATCHIS HOTEL, *50 Main Street, Brattleboro VT 05301. Tel. 802/ 254-6300, Fax 802/254-6304. Web site: www.brattleboro.com/latchis. Rates: $65-$150. Credit cards Major credit cards accepted.*
Situated right downtown, the Art Deco Latchis has recently been restored to its 1930's glory and now features 30 rooms and suites, all with modern amenities. The Latchis also contains quite a good restaurant and brewery.

CROSBY HOUSE, *45 Western Avenue, Brattleboro VT 05301. Tel. 802/ 257-4914, 800/528-1868. E-mail: tomlynn@sover.net. Web site: www.sover.net/ ~tomlynn. Rates: $90-$145. Credit cards: Visa, Mastercard, American Express.*
This elegant 19th century building with decor and antiques to match, features only three guestrooms with queen beds, private baths, and fireplaces. Breakfast is served in an equally elegant dining room.

"40 PUTNEY ROAD" BED & BREAKFAST, *40 Putney Road, Brattleboro VT 05301. Tel. 802/2546268, 800/941-2413, Fax 802/258-2673. E-mail: frtyptny#@sover.net. Web site: www.putney.net/40purneyrd. Rates: $80-$170. Major credit cards accepted.*
Situated on the West River within walking distance of downtown, "40 Putney Road" features four more-than-comfortable antique-laden rooms with private baths, cable television,fireplaces, and telephones.

QUALITY INN & SUITES, *Putney Road (Route 5 North off I-91 Exit 3), Brattleboro VT 05301. Tel. 802/254-8701, Fax 802/257-4727. Rates: $80-$120. Major credit cards accepted.*
A full-fledged modern hotel with modern rooms and amenities like cable television, in-room telephones, and air-conditioning. Premises include an indoor pool, a bar, a dining room, meeting rooms and saunas/ whilrpools. Scores low in the Vermont charm department.

DALEM'S CHALET, *16 South Street, Brattleboro VT 05301. Tel. 802/ 254-4323, 800/462-5009. E-mail: info@dalemschalet.com Web site: www.dalemschalet.com. Rates: $50-$90. Major credit cards accepted.*
An alpine style chalet on a 20 acre estate, Dalem's includes 27 rooms with cable television and other amenities, as well as a restaurant serving German and Austrian cuisine.

MOLLY STARK MOTEL, *829 Marlboro Road, Brattleboro VT 05301. Tel. 802/254-2440. Rates: $35-$60. Major credit cards accepted.*
The recently refurnished rooms are simple, but comfortable and include such amentities as telephones, private baths, and cable television.

Grafton
THE OLD TAVERN AT GRAFTON, *Main Street & Townsend Road, Grafton VT 05146. Tel. 802/843-2231, 800/8431801, Fax 802/843-2245. E-mail: tavern@sover.net. Web site: www.old-tavern.com. Rates: $125-$250. Major credit cards accepted.*
Operated by the Windham Foundation (Vermont's largest non-profit foundation), The Old Tavern is one of the oldest inns in Vermont (founded 1801) and features 66 beautifully appointed rooms and suites, a dining room serving excellent American cuisine, a bar, tennis courts, a game room and other facilities such as a laundry room. There is also cross-country skiing right out the door.
THE INN AT WOODCHUCK HILL FARM, *244 Woodchuck Hill Road, Grafton VT 05146. Tel. 802/843-2398, Fax 802/843-2872. Web site: www.woodchuckhill.com. Rates: $70-$140. Credit cards: Visa, Mastercard.*
Situated on a 200-acre estate on the top of a hill in a restored house dating to the 1780's, the Inn at Woodchuck Hill Farm has seven guestrooms and suites with kitchettes and fireplaces. The estate also features hiking trails, a pond, a sauna, and magnificent views of the Green Mountains.

Marlboro
COLONEL WILLIAMS INN, *Route 9, Marlboro VT 05344. Tel. 802/257-1093, Fax 802/257-4460. E-mail: colwinn@sover.net. Web site: www.colonelwilliamsinn.com. Rates: $100-$150. Major credit cards accepted.*
Colonel Williams Inn features a dozen rooms in a restored 1769 farmhouse. All rooms have a private bath and some also contain a fireplace. There is also a restaurant on the premises and sitting rooms with fireplaces and television. Pets can stay in the carriage house.

Newfane & Townsend
WINDHAM HILL INN, *311 Lawrence Drive (P.O. Box 44), West Townsend VT 05359. Tel. 802/874-4080, 800/944-4080, Fax 802/874-4702. E-mail: windham@sover.net. Web site: www.windhamhillinn.com. Rates: $200-$400 with full meal plan. Credit cards: Major credit cards accepted.*
Right out of your Vermont fantasy, the secluded Windham Hill Inn is a beautiful country inn set on a 160-acre estate with magnificent views, first-rate 5 course dining, and 21 luxurious and spacious suites. Recreation possibilities include hiking or snowshoeing on the Inn's beautiful

grounds, tennis, and relaxing in the pool. For a preview go their web site featuring hundreds of pictures.

FOUR COLUMNS INN, *230 West Street (P.O. Box 278), Newfane VT 05345. Tel. 802/365-7713, 800/787-6633, Fax 802/365-0022. E-mail: frcolinn@sover.net. Web site: fourcolumnsinn.com. Rates: $100-$300. Major credit cards accepted.*

Situated on a 150-acre estate on the Newfane Green, the Four Columns Inn is recognized as one of the finest inns throughout Vermont, and its restaurant is even more highly touted. A baronial building constructed in the colonial style during the 19th century, the Inn features 15 elegantly appointed rooms and suites with private baths. Some suites also contain two-person jacuzzis and fireplaces – very romantic indeed. Recreationally, there is a pool on the premises as well as gardens with a brook, a pond, and walking paths on which to stroll.

OLD NEWFANE INN, *Route 30 (off the Village Green), Newfane. Tel. 802/365-4427, 800/789-4427. Rates: $100-$200. Major credit cards accepted.*

Originally established more than 200 years ago (1787), the Old Newfane offers eight elegantly apointed rooms, but it is primarily known for its award-winning restaurant, which specializes in French and continental cuisine.

WEST RIVER LODGE, *117 Hill Road, Brookline in Newfane, VT 05345. Tel. 802/365-7745. E-mail: wrlodge@sover.net. Rates: $80-$130. Credit cards: Visa, Mastercard.*

A small lodge with eight rooms in a classic farm-style house, West River Lodge is especially convenient for those keen to ride horses as it is located next to the West River Stables. Guests can just take breakfast or opt for a full meal plan that includes dinner.

Putney

HICKORY RIDGE HOUSE, *53 Hickory Ridge Road, South Putney VT 05346. Tel. 802/387-5709, 800/380-9218, Fax 802/387-4328. E-mail: E:@hickoryridgehouse.com. Web site: www.hickoryridgehouse.com. Rates: $105-$165. Credit cards: Visa, Mastercard.*

Listed on the National Historic Register of Historic Places, Hickory Ridge House features six guestrooms with private baths and fireplaces. Two miles from the village on a dirt road, it is an eight acre estate with cross-country skiing and hiking on the premises.

RANNEY-CRAWFORD HOUSE, *1097 Westminster West Road, Putney VT 05346. Tel. 802/387-4150, 800/731-5502. Rates: $90-$110. Credit cards: Visa, Mastercard.*

An early 19th century colonial style house on beautiful grounds with gardens, the Ranney-Crawford House features homey, comfortable rooms.

The management is helpful in organizing recreational activities such as biking and hiking tours, as well as giving general advice.

PUTNEY INN, *Just off I-91 Exit 4 (P.O. Box 181), Putney VT 05346. Tel. 802/387-5517, 800/653-5517. E-mail: putneyin@sover.net. Web site: www.putney.net/inn. Rates: $60-$140. Major credit cards accepted.*

Located within walking distance of the village center, the Putney Inn includes 25 rooms with modern amenities like private baths and cable television situated in a modern adjunct to the 200-year-old farmhouse. The dining is regarded as some of the finest in the region.

Area Camping

TOWNSEND STATE PARK, *RR 1 Box 2650, Townsend VT 05353. Tel. 802/365-7500 (summer), 802/886-2434 (off-season). Base rates: $11-$15. Credit cards: Visa, Mastercard. Open mid-May through Columbus Day (mid-October).*

Situated on the West River at the base of Bald Mountain (there's a beautiful hike to the summit), Townsend State Park features 30 tent/trailer sites (4 lean-to's) and tenting platforms. There is a sanitation station, showers, and fishing and boating in the nearby Townsend Reservoir.

FORT DUMMER STATE PARK, *434 Old Guilford Road, Brattleboro VT 05301-3653. Tel. 802/254-2610 (summer), 802/886-2434 (off-season). Base rates: $11-$15. Credit cards: Visa, Mastercard. Open mid-May through Labor Day (first week in September.*

Located just south of downtown Brattleboro off I-91 it Exit 1, Fort Dummer State Park is located on and named for the first European military fort in Vermont. Today it is a modest 200 acre park with 50 campsites for tents and trailers, several hiking trails, showers, and picnic acreas.

BRATTLEBORO NORTH KOA, *RD 2 Box 560, Putney VT 05346. (Located off Route 2.8 miles south of I-91 Exit 4, 3.5 miles north of Ext 3.) Tel. 802/254-5908, 800/562-5909 (for reservations). Base rates: $16-$20. Major credit cards accepted.*

One of the best managed campgrounds around, North KOA includes 42 shaded sites with a grill and a table; sewage, electric and cable hookups, and water are also available as are sites for longer trailers. Facilities include a swimming pool, game rooms, television lounge, dump station, and a small store that can meet basic needs.

MOSS HOLLOW CAMPGROUND, *RD#4 Box 723, Brattleboro VT 05301. (Take Route 9 eight miles to Marlboro College and follow signs to the dirt road.) Tel. 802/368-2418. Base rates: $10-$15. Credit cards: Visa, Mastercard. Open May 15- October 15.*

Seemingly in the middle of nowhere, Moss Hollow features 50 sites with hookups flush toilets, hot showers, and wood. Recreationally there are oodles of dirt roads and trails for hiking and biking, and there's trout fishing nearby.

CAMPERAMA CAMPGROUND, *Depot Road (off Route 30 seventeen miles northwest of Brattleboro), Townsend VT 05353. Tel. 802/365-4315, 800/ 63-CAMPS (for reservations). Base rates: $18-$23. Credit cards: Visa, Mastercard. Open May 15-October 15.*

There are 219 sites with showers, picnic areas, ice, fire pits, swimming pool, bastball and volleyball courts – what else do you need?

WHERE TO EAT

Bellows Falls, Rockingham & Saxtons River

INN AT SAXTON'S RIVER, *27 Main Street, Saxton's River VT. Tel. 802/869-2110. Open for lunch and dinner. Credit cards: Visa, Mastercard.*

This restaurant and pub serves hearty country cuisine and lite fare in an elegant but casual environment.

MISS BELLOW'S FALLS DINER, *90 Rockingham Street downtown, Bellow's Falls. Tel. 802/463-9800. opend daily from around 7am until 9pm-10pm. Credit cards: Visa, Mastercard.*

Serving classic diner food in a vintage 1930's Worcester diner; very popular with the locals for good reason.

LESLIE'S, *Route 5, Rockingham VT. Tel. 802/463-4929.Open Wednesday-Monday 5pm-9pm. Credit cards: Visa, Mastercard.*

A very friendly, relaxed, and casual establishment, Leslie's specializes in freshly prepared ingredients and healthy dishes. Pasta is made on the premises. Expect to pay $15-$25 for a full meal.

Brattleboro

T.J.'S BUCKLEY, *132 Eilliot Street, Brattleboro VT 05301. Tel. 802/ 257-4922. Credit cards not accepted. Open nightly for dinner. Checks accepted but no credit cards.*

T.J. Buckley's is one of the most eclectic restaurants in Vermont, if not the US or the world! Situated in a vintage 1927 Worcester diner, T.J.'s is in fact very much the opposite of a diner. It seats only a handful and is recognized as serving the finest food in town made with the freshest ingredients. The menu is limited and rotates nightly; entrees typically cost $25-$30. An excellent locale for a date or intimate meal, it is very popular, so call as far in advance as possible to make reservations.

LATCHIS GRILLE & WINDHAM BREWERY, *50 Main Street, Brattleboro VT 05301. Tel. 802/254-6300, Fax 802/254-6304. Web site: www.brattleboro.com/latchis. Major credit cards accepted. Open daily except Monday for lunch and dinner.*

Located in a renovated Art Deco hotel in the heart of downtown

Brattleboro, the Latchis Grille serves high-end American and country cuisine along with ales and lagers brewed on the premises. The atmosphere is classy and a bit old-fashioned but casual.

JOLLY BUTCHER'S, *Route 9, West Brattleboro VT 05103. Tel. 802/ 254-6043. Open daily 11:30am-2:30pm, 5pm-10pm and on Sundays from noon-9pm. Major credit cards accepted.*

Specializing in steak and seafood (there is alive lobster tank) and featuring a salad bar, the Jolly Butcher's is a decent – though certainly not spectacular – eatery serving classic American fare for reasonable prices (entrees $8-$20).

MARINA ON THE WATER, *Putney Road, Brattleboro VT 05301. Tel. 802/257-7563. Open from 11:30am-11pm daily except for Mondays and Tuesdays (4pm-11pm). Closed Mondays and Tuesdays in the winter. Major credit cards accepted.*

Located on the West River which it overlooks, the Marina serves good seafood and other dishes for reasonable prices. It is especially pleasant when weather permits patio dining. A full meal costs $20-$25 including beverages.

Marlboro

SKYLINE RESTAURANT, *Route 9, Marlboro VT. Tel. 802/464-3536. Open year around for breakfast, lunch and dinner, except in April-May when it closes at 3pm. Major credit cards accepted.*

Located on Hogback Mountain, the Skyline is known as the restaurant with the "100 mile view" as it overlooks parts of Vermont, New Hampshire, and Massachusetts. In addition it serves more than decent American style food in a charming cozy atmosphere that is enhanced by the fireplace for most of the year. For dinner the menu features plenty of pasta, steak, and salads accompanied by fresh bread, while its breakfast receives high marks for its waffles and pancakes, served of course with pure Vermont Maple syrup.

Newfane

OLD NEWFANE INN, *Route 30 (off the Village Green), Newfane. Tel. 802/365-4427, 800/789-4427. Open nightly except Monday for dinner from 6pm-9:30pm. Major credit cards accepted.*

One of the most acclaimed restaurants in Vermont, the Old Newfane Inn combines vintage colonial atmospherics (the inn was originally founded in 1787) with superb French cuisine for very reasonable prices. From an extensive menu (there are more than a dozen choices for both appetizers and entrees) you may choose for starters ($6-$10; soups $3.75) one of several classic French favorites such as escargots Bourguignonne, smoked goose paté, and french onion soup or perhaps stuffed veal, smoked Nova Scotia salmon, or marinated herring.

The list of entrees is equally compelling. Freshwater and seafood delights might include king crab flambée, filet of sole amandine, shrimp scampi and the French classic, frog legs provencale. There is also a wide selection of grilled fare (rack of lamb, chateaubriand, and a variety of steaks), game dishes, and variety of dishes served with sinfully delicious sauces such as beef brochettes Bordelaise, veal scallopine marsala, and even a curry of the day. Entree prices ranged from $15-$30, and desserts include a selection of freshly prepared pastries and baked goods with sorbet and fruit also available.

FOUR COLUMNS INN, *230 West Street (P.O. Box 278), Newfane VT 05345. Tel. 802/365-7713, 800/787-6633, Fax 802/365-0022. E-mail: frcolinn@sover.net. Web site: fourcolumnsinn.com. Open for dinner 6pm-9pm nightly except for Tuesdays. Major credit cards accepted.*

Situated in an elegantly restored barn that joins the inn's Greek Revival main building, the Four Columns Inn features a more diverse if not as extensive menu as its neighbor, the Old Newfane Inn. The half dozen appetizer list typically includes a soup, a light pasta, and several seafood, meat and fowl dishes (appetizers range from about $5 for the soup to $10.) Entree choices range from American specialties as grilled Black Angus sirloin and North Atlantic salmon to Asian inspired delights like Peking Duck, and seared tuna with noodles in coconut milk with lemongrass. Vegetarians can be accommodated (call in advance for more choice), and appetizers can be converted into main courses.

Putney

PUTNEY INN, *Just off I-91 Exit 4 (P.O. Box 181), Putney VT 05346. Tel. 802/387-5517, 800/653-5517. E-mail: putneyin@sover.net. Web site: www.putney.net/inn. Major credit cards accepted.*

In an elegant but relaxed dining area befitting a classic country inn, the Putney Inn restaurant serves first-rate American and gourmet country fare made (when possible) with fresh and locally produced ingredients.

CASA DEL SOL, *Route 5 in downtown Putney. Tel. 802/387-5318. Open 11:30am-2pm, 5pm-8pm April-January (closed February & March). No credit cards accepted.*

Who would've thunk it? Genuine Mexican food right here in Putney – not Taco Bell, not Tex-Mex – but real Mexican cooked home style by first generation immigrants. Dishes include seafood, meat, and vegetables and range from $5-$15.

SEEING THE SIGHTS

Brattleboro

Built on the site of the first European settlement in what is now Vermont, Brattleboro was founded as a town in 1753 when New Hampshire granted it a charter. It was named for **Colonel William Brattle** who served in the nearby Fort Dummer (for which Dummerston is named), built to protect the seetlments from Indian raids. Initially, Brattleboro did not develop as quickly as other towns and cities like Windsor, Burlington, and Middlebury, but by the latter half of the 19th century, it had become a mid-sized manufacturing center.

However until **Jacob Estey** established the **Estey Organ Company** in the 1850's, Brattleboro, unlike most Vermont towns, was not associated with one particular industry or craft the way shipping shaped Burlington or Rutland became synonymous with marble. At its height before the turn of the century, the Estey Organ Co. employed more than 500 employees, most whom lived in a neighborhood known as Esteyville.

However, while organs were still manufactured in Brattleboro until the 1950's, the industry was not able to sustain the town, particularly with the onset of the Depression in the 1930's. Like many Vermont towns that thrived on industries in the 19th century which became obsolete in the 20th, Brattleboro suffered a flat economy and low morale for much of the 20th century. Today, however, it is enjoying a revival fueled by tourism and the establishment of successful institutions like **World Learning & the School for International Training**, and the **Brattleboro Retreat**, a drug and alcohol rehabilitation center which is the town's largest employer.

BRATTLEBORO MUSEUM AND ART CENTER, *Main And Vernon Streets, Brattleboro VT 05301. Tel. 802/257-0124. Open Tuesday-Sunday noon-6pm from mid-May through October. Admission: $2-$5.*

This small gem of a museum testifies to Brattleboro's impressive artistic and industrial heritage. Several rooms are dedicated to paintings, photographs, and sculptures reflecting the work of native sons William Mead, a famous architect, and highly esteemed sculptor brother, Larkin Mead. Another room is dedicated entirely to Estey organs, manufactured here in Brattleboro during the late 19th and early 20th century.

CREAMERY BRIDGE, *.25 mile west on Route 9 from I-91 Exit 2.*

Named for the old Brattleboro Creamery, this hansome lattice bridge is 80 feet long and was built in 1879 as a replacement for a prior bridge.

Route 5 & I-91 North of Brattleboro

Both I-91 and Route 5 lead north along the Connecticut River; 91 is faster and more efficient, while 5 is appropriate for those keen for a more leisurely drive and the opportunity to explore smaller roads and absorb some local color. North of Brattleboro there is little in the way of major attractions, but the drive is pleasant – particularly in the autumn – and the towns of Putney, Bellows Falls, and Rockingham are not without appeal.

RUDYARD KIPLING & NAULAKHA

*One of the nuggets of Brattleboro history is the short-lived residence of famed Victorian author Rudyard Kipling. With his image as the embodiment of Britsh India, it surprises many to find out that the great writer lived in Vermont, let alone that he wrote his most famous work, **The Jungle Book**, here; after all, it is hard to imagine two places more different from each other than Vermont and India, and Mr. Kipling was intensely protective (some describe him as "paranoid") of his private life.*

*Kipling moved to Brattleboro in 1892 after he married a local girl, and though he planned to live out the rest of his life here, bickering with his in-laws, an inability to adjust to Yankee society and Vermont winters led Kipling to move back across the pond after only four years. The home where he lived, known as **Naulakha** (a version of the Hindu word "jewel"), was a beautiful mansion in Dummerston off Route 5 that was only restored to its former glory recently after a British company purchased it. Unfortunately, it is not open to the public, though it can be rented for weddings and other special events.*

Putney

A handsome village nine miles north of Brattlenoro that was once home to the perfectionist (and cousin of President Rutherford B. Hayes) John Humphrey Noyes, Putney features an assortment of 19th century buildings and many Federal style houses, and today is home to some colorful little shops like the **Putney Clayschool** and **Hearthstone Books**. Putney is on Route 5 (aka "Putney Road" in Brattleboro) off I-91, Exit 4. Continuing north and east of Putney Village, Route 5 passes through beautiful farmland and is lined with signs advertising farms selling maple syrup, pumpkins or whatever happens to be in season. Roughly half-way between Exits 4 and 5 on Route 5 is **Santa's Land**, a tacky Christmas theme village featuring rides, a petting zoo, gift shops, and if you're lucky a visit with Santa himself. *(Open May through Christmas 10am-6pm daily. Tel. 802/ 387-5550) .*

PUTNEY HISTORICAL SOCIETY MUSEUM, *Town Hall, Putney VT 05346. Tel. 802/387-5862. Open during business hours and by appointment. Admission free.*

Besides artifacts, documents, and photographs, the museum features a collection of local Native American artifacts.

Westminster

About ten miles north of Putney on Route 5, the modest hamlet of Westminster was one of the earliest towns in Vermont to be granted a charter in 1735, when it was determined to be a suitable place for a station on the King's Highway which was under construction at the time. Today its claim to fame is the **Westminster MG Car Museum**, featuring thirty MG models. Unfortunately the museum and its splendid collection is only open once a year around Columbus Day. Call *802/722-3708* for information.

Bellows Falls

Roughly 25 miles north of Brattleboro on Route 5 (off I-91 Exit 5 if coming from the south, Exit 6 from the north), **Bellows Falls** was a major railroad junction and manufacturing center in the 19th century that like so many Vermont towns has struggled to redefine itself in the 20th. Built near the impressive Bellows Falls, named for a prominent citizen and landowner, **Colonel Benjamin Bellows**, the village (in the Town of Rockingham) took off economically after the construction of the first true canal in the United States, in 1802. For much of the latter half of the 20th century, as businesses folded and buildings emptied, Bellows Falls has been charcaterized by a sense of depression; however, recently the establishment of a regional internet service provider (Sovernet), and the development of a new art center as well as an increase in tourism has lifted hopes for a revival.

To get a flavor for the area's history, you might want to take in the museum, housed with the town library: **Rockingham Public Library & Museum**, *65 Westminster Street, Bellows Falls VT 05101. Tel. 802/463-4270. Library hours vary from 9am-8pm and 1pm-8pm every other day except for Wednesday when it closes. Museum open 2-4pm Wednesdays and by appointment. Admission free.*

From Bellows Falls, the 14 mile drive north on Route 5 and then northwest on **Route 103** through Rockingham and Bartonsville, past several covered bridges up to **Chester**, is one of the most scenic in the area. Chester (see the "Precision Valley" chapter) is a very picturesque little town featuring an impressive assortment of restored Victorian houses and inns. You can also take in the scenery by joining a **Green Mountain Flyer Scenic Railroad** excursion. See sidebar on the nest page for details.

THE GREEN MOUNTAIN FLYER SCENIC RAILROAD

One of the most enjoyable ways to explore the beauty of Vermont is to ride the **Green Mountain Flyer** from Chester Depot to Bellows Falls (or vice versa). A vintage 1930's diesal passanger train, the Flyer will take you on a 26-mile journey along the scenic Williams River Valley where you can enjoy viewing covered bridges, the waterfalls at Brockway Mills Gorge, and classic Vermont pastoral landscapes.

In operation from the last week of June through mid-October (the ride is especially beautiful during the foliage season), and on certain dates in December and February, the Flyer departs daily from Bellows Falls at 11am and 2pm. A roundtrip to Chester takes two hours and fares cost $12 for adults and $7 for children under 12 (children under 3 years are free). Of course, if you take the morning Flyer, you can return from Chester on the 3:10pm train and spend several hours taking in Chester's sites. During certain dates in October, the Flyer extends its route to Ludlow. For further information contact the Green Mountain Railroad, Tel. 800/707-3530 or 802/463-3069.

Route 121 & Grafton

From Bellows Falls, the underdeveloped and scenic **Route 121** leads 10 miles to the northwest and the town of **Grafton**. Initially developed as a stop on the Boston-Montreal stagecoach highway, Grafton was a hub for the local sheep industry and developed as a minor center for industry which used the Saxtons River for power. Though these industries are now long obsolete as foundations of economic growth, Grafton has successfully maintained its historic village center district and remade itself into a popular tourist destination. From Grafton, you can take Route 35 north seven miles to Chester (from which you can return to Bellows Falls by way of Route 103); or you can take Route 35 ten miles south to Townsend from whence Route 30 leads a further 18 miles south to Brattleboro.

HALL COVERED BRIDGE, *Off Route 121, 3-4 miles from Bellows Falls.*
This 120-foot bridge is a replica built in 1982 as a replacement for a prior bridge which collapsed under the weight of a passing oversized truck.

KIDDER HILL COVERED BRIDGE, *About 250 meters from the junction of Routes 35 and 121 on Kidder Hill Road.*
A slight 68 feet long, the Kidder Hill Bridge was built in 1870 and substantially restored in the mid-1990's. Like other bridges on the Saxtons River, including the Hall Bridge, it was a replacement for a prior bridge swept away after the great rains of 1869.

GRAFTON HISTORICAL SOCIETY MUSEUM, *Main Street, Grafton VT 05146. Tel. 802/843-2305. Open 1:30pm-4pm on Saturdays and Sundays from Memorial Day (late May) through Columbus Day (mid October). Admission: $1.*

Located in an 1845 house, the museum includes seven rooms of exhibits featuring the usual assortment of photographs, documents and artwork, as well as antique firefighting equipment and a collection of 18th and 19th century furnishings.

GRAFTON MUSEUM OF NATURAL HISTORY, *Main Street, Grafton VT 05146. Tel. 802/843-2347.*

Route 9 Between Brattleboro & Wilmington

The winding and steep **Route 9** between Brattleboro and Wilmington is among the most scenic in the area. It is a particularly enjoyable drive west to east, because of the extent of the visibility (on clear days anyway) across the Connecticut Valley into New Hampshire and south into Massachusetts. However, when the road is slick or icy, Route 9 can also be one of the more dangerous drives in Vermont, so take care.

Just west of the village of Marlboro (5 miles east of Wilmington and 12 miles west of Brattleboro) at Hogback Mountain is the **Southern Vermont Natural History Museum**. Featuring hundreds of exhibits with more under construction, its primary emphases are birds, particularly those native to the region. Visitors can also take walks in the nearby woods, eat a picnic, and visit the museum's gift shop. Parking is free and the museum is handicap-accessible. *The Museum is open daily from 9-5 from Memorial Day-mid/late October, and sporadically during winter (call to find out). Admission: $2 adults; $1 youth 18 and under. Tel. 802/464-0048.*

MARLBORO HISTORICAL SOCIETY MUSEUM, *Main Street, Marlboro VT 05344. Tel. 802/254-9152. Open Saturdays 2pm-5pm on Saturdays. Admission free*

Located in a restored 1813 schoolhouse and the Newton House, the Society features the usual assortment of documents, furnishing, and photographs relating to local history. It also sponsors lectures, tours, and classes.

Route 30

Another picturesque drive from Brattleboro is **Route 30**, which passes by the famous West Dummerston Covered Bridge and through the village of Newfane en route to Townsend and East Jamaica where it intersects Route 100 near the major ski resort of Stratton (see "Manchester & the Heart of the Green Mountains"). From East Jamaica, you can take Route 100 twenty-three miles south to Wilmington and then Route 9 20 miles east back to Brattleboro. You can also take Route 35 north from

Townsend to Grafton, a handsome village whose attractions include several covered bridges.

WEST DUMMERSTON BRIDGE, *Off Route 30 seven miles from dowtown Brattleboro.*

Built in 1872 and substantially restored in the early 1990's, this bridge which spans 280 feet over the West River, is the longest covered bridge in Vermont (the Cornish-Windsor Bridge over the Connecticut River is technically in New Hampshire).

Newfane

With its beautiful common and courthouse – **Newfane** became the county seat in 1787 – this is one of the most picturesque villages in Vermont.

HISTORICAL SOCIETY OF WINDHAM COUNTY, *Route 30, Newfane VT 05345. Tel. 802/365-4148. Openn from mid-May through mid-October from noon-5pm Wednesday-Sunday.*

As the museum for the whole county, the Society features more extensive exhibits than most local societies and its subject matter covers the entire region. It also sponsors lectures, discussions, and tours.

Townsend

Situated at the junction of Route 30 and Route 35 which leads north to Grafton and Route 121 (leads east to Bellows Falls), **Townsend** features several interesting shops and the impressive Scott Covered Bridge off Route 30 to the west.

SCOTT COVERED BRIDGE, *On Route 30 one and a half miles south and west of the junction with Route 35 in Townsend.*

Built in 1870, this classic lattice style bridge spans more than 270 feet overall with the lattice span reaching over 160 feet.

NIGHTLIFE & ENTERTAINMENT

Though the Brattleboro region does not attract as many tourists as many other regions in Vermont, it still features its share of culture. The most notable event is undoubtedly the **Marlboro Music Festival**, the most highly acclaimed chamber music event in the region if not the country. It is held annually from mid-July through mid-August; call for information, *Tel. 802/254-2394.*

The other major musical event of the year is the **New England Bach Festival** sponsored by the **Brattleboro Music Center** and held annually in the late summer-early autumn. For information about this festival and other music events sponsored by the Music Center, call *802/247-4523* or contact the **Brattleboro Area Chamber Of Commerce** which can provide information about other events throughout the region (*180 Main Street, Brattleboroe VT 05301. Tel. 802/254-4565, Fax 802/254-5675. E-mail: bratchmb@sover.net. Web site: sover.net/~brachmb@sover.net*).

For a simple drink or night on the town, there are several bars in downtown Brattleboro and many inns and restaurants have taverns within their confines.

SPORTS & RECREATION

Biking

It goes without saying that bikers will want to get out of Great Brattleboro, but the rest of the region is fine territory for road biking. **Routes 30, 103, 121,** and **5** (especially north of Putney) are all excellent. Also north of Putney, the **Westminster Road** off Route 5 north of town offers some steeper and more challenging riding. The area is a little short on good mountain biking, but the Mt. Snow region 25 miles west of Brattleboro via Route 9 offers numerous opportunities. See the "Mt. Snow" chapter for details.

BRATTLEBORO BICYCLE SHOP, *178 Main Street, Brattleboro. Tel. 802/254-8644, 800/BRATBIK. Open daily. Major credit cards accepted.*

Provides rentals, service, and accessories.

GRAFTON PONDS NORDIC & MOUNTAIN BIKE CENTER, *Townsend Road, Grafton VT 05146. Tel. 802/843-2400. Major credit cards accepted.*

Most of the 90 kilometers of cross-country ski trails are open to bikers in the summer.

WEST HILL SHOP, *Putney, VT. Tel. 802/387-5718. Major credit cards accepted.*

Full service, bike rentals and retail sales.

Boating/Canoeing/Kayaking

Both the West River and the Connecticut are viable venues for kayaking and canoeing, and are fairly easy paddles.

VERMONT CANOE TOURING CENTER, *by the Veterans Memorial Bridge on Putney Road (Route 5), Brattleboro VT 05301. Tel. 802/257-5008, 802/254-3908. Major credit cards accepted.*

Rents canoes and kayaks and organizes expeditions and tours.

Cross-Country Skiing

There are also many cross-country skiing opportunities in the Mount Snow area 20 miles west of Brattleboro on Route 9; see the "Deerfield Valley and Mount Snow" chapter for more information.

BRATTLEBORO OUTING CLUB, *Brattleboro VT 05301. Tel. 802/ 254-4081. Major credit cards accepted. Trail fees: $8.*
25 kilometers of trails; rentals available.
GRAFTON PONDS NORDIC & MOUNTAIN BIKE CENTER, *Townsend Road, Grafton VT 05146. Tel. 802/843-2400. Major credit cards accepted.*
Operates a substantial 90 kilometers of beautiful trails and offers full services including rentals, tours, and instruction.

Fishing

For river fishing, the **Connecticut** is an excellent source for trout (brook and rainbow), large mouth bass, and pickerel, while the **West River** and **South Pond** (just south of Marlboro) also feature several types of trout.

Golf

There are also many golfing opportunities in the **Mount Snow** area 20 miles west of Brattleboro on Route 9; see the "Deerfield Valley and Mount Snow" chapter for more information.
BRATTLEBORO COUNTRY CLUB, *Route 30, Brattleboro VT. Tel. 802/257-7380. 9 holes. Green fees: $22-$25. Major credit cards accepted. Carts available.*
BELLOWS FALLS COUNTRY CLUB, *Bellows Falls VT. Tel. 802/463-9809. 9 holes. Green fees: $16-$21. Carts available.*

Hiking

Near Brattleboro, **Fort Dummer State Park**, *Tel. 802/254-2601/ summer, Tel. 802/886-2434/off-season,* is open from May through Labor Day (first week in September) and features several very modest hikes.

Skiiing & Snowboarding

The **Maple Valley Ski Area at Sugar** in West Dummerston, *Tel. 802/ 254-6083,* is a very modest ski area with three lifts and 50 acres of ski area. For more advanced skiiers especially, the **Mount Snow** and **Haystack** ski areas 25 miles west and north from Brattleboro on Route 100 (by way of Route 9) are probably more suitable. If your base is north, say in Bellows Falls or Grafton, **Mt. Asutney** in Windsor, **Okemo** bear Ludlow, and **Magic Mountain** in Londonderry are major ski areas within an easy drive.

Sledding & Sleigh Rides

GRAFTON PONDS NORDIC & MOUNTAIN BIKE CENTER, *Townsend Road, Grafton VT 05146. Tel. 802/843-2400. Major credit cards accepted.*

Snowshoeing

There are also many snowshoeing opportunities in the Mount Snow area 20 miles west of Brattleboro on Route 9; see the "Deerfield Valley and Mount Snow" chapter for more information.

GRAFTON PONDS NORDIC & MOUNTAIN BIKE CENTER, *Townsend Road, Grafton VT 05146. Tel. 802/843-2400. Major credit cards accepted.*

SHOPPING

Brattleboro

ELF'S WORKSHOP, *Fairfield Plaza on Putney Road (Route 5), Brattleboro. Tel. 802/257-6941. Open daily. Major credit cards accepted.*

Specializes in candle making for which it offers classes, but also sells other arts and crafts.

J. GALANES & SONS, *116 Main Street, Brattleboro. Tel. 802/254-5677. Open daily. Major credit cards accepted.*

Galanes features a combination of sports equipment and accessories, along with Vermont souvenirs and specialty products including foods like maple syrup.

LE TAGGE SALE, *In the Rollerdome on Putney Road (Route 5), Brattleboro. Tel. 802/254-9224. Open daily 10am-6pm. Credit cards accepted.*

Located in an old skating rink, Le Tagge is a cheeky sort of place selling all sorts of of antiques and used goods – a fun place to look for a bargain.

THE OUTLET CENTER, *Off Exit 1, I-91, Brattleboro. Tel. 802/254-4594; toll free 800/459-4594. Open daily. Major credit cards accepted.*

The Outlet Center offers outlet and discount shopping for a dozen name brands including Van Heusen, Carters Chilldrenware, Hanes, Playtex, Factory Handbag, and others.

TOM & SALLY'S HANDMADE CHOCALATES, *55 Elliot Street, downtown Bratttleboro. Tel. 802/. Hours: 10am-6pm Monday-Saturday; noon-5pm Sunday during peak seasons. Credit cards: Visa, Mastercard.*

This family-owned operation has turned chocolate making into an art and their rich (pun intended) array of candies make wonderful gifts.

VERMONT ARTISAN DESIGNS, *106 Main Street, Brattleboro. Tel. 802/257-7044. Website: www.vtartisans.com. Open daily. Major credit cards accepted.*

Featuring the works of hundreds of local and regional artists, including pottery, paintings, blown glass, jewelry and more.

VERMONT MAPLE MUSEUM & SUGARBUSH SCOTTIES, *1991 Marlboro Road off Route 9, West Brattleboro. Tel. 802/254-2903.*

Putney

BASKETVILLE, *Main Street, Putney. Tel. 802/387-5509. Website: www.basketville.com. Open daily 9am-5pm. Major credit cards accepted.*

In addition to all types of baskets produced locally and around the world, Basketville features a wide variety of handicrafts and home accessories.

THE CHRISTMAS TREE SHOPPE AT SANTA'S LAND, *Route 5 (Exit 4, I-91), Putney. Tel. 800/726-8299. Open May through Christmas 10am-6pm daily. Major credit cards accepted.*

Townshend & West Townshend

MARY MEYER STUFFED TOYS FACTORY STORE, *Route 30, Townshend. Tel. 802/365-7793, 800/451-4387. Open daily May-December. Major credit cards accepted.*

Features all sorts of stuffed animals and teddy bears, many sold at discount rates.

EXCURSIONS & DAY TRIPS

THE PRECISION VALLEY

Just north of Windham County (30-40 minutes from Brattleboro), Southern Windsor County and the area around the towns of **Windsor** and **Springfield** is known as the **Precision Valley** because it was here that the machine-tool industry was developed in the 19th century.

The southernmost of the two, Springfield is on Route 11 off I-89 and Route 5 12 miles north of Bellow Falls. Its main attraction is the **Hartness House** mansion, the former home of a Vermont Governor and industrialist James Hartness, which has been converted into an inn with a fine restaurant and several small historical exhibits, including a fascinating antique observatory. From Springfield, you can take Route 11 ten miles west to the picturesque village of **Chester**, known for its many beautiful Victorian buildings and quaint village green. To get back to the Woodstock-Quechee region, take 103 west from Chester to Route 100 North to Plymouth Union and then Route 4 east.

Fifteen miles beyond the turnoff for Route 11 and Springfield, on Route 5 and off I-91 (Route 5 is slower but more scenic) is Windsor, "Birthplace of Vermont" and home of the **American Precision Museum**, which contains a wonderful collection of tools, machines and firearms from the 19th century. Vermont was proclaimed a republic in 1777 in a local tavern (now known by the more respectable "Constitution House") which is also open to the public as a museum. Just north of Windsor on Route 5 are **Simon Pearce Glass** (a second branch of the operation in Quechee) and the **Catamount Brewery**.

Finally, just south of Windsor, Route 44 takes you past **Mount Ascutney** where there is a resort with a skiing area, and **Mt. Ascutney State Park** where you can hike or bike to the summit with magical views of the Connecticut River Valley, the Berkshires, and the Green Mountains. (See the "Precision Valley" Chapter for more information.)

PRACTICAL INFORMATION

Chambers of Commerce
BRATTLEBORO AREA CHAMBER OF COMMERCE, *180 Main Street, Brattleboroe VT 05301. Tel. 802/254-4565, Fax 802/254-5675. E-mail: bratchmb@sover.net. Web site: sover.net/~brachmb@sover.net.*

Medical Emergencies
Ambulance – *Tel. 257-8222 or 911*
Brattleboro Memorial Hospital, *9 Belmont Avenue, Brattleboro. Tel. 802/257-0341*

Police
State Police – *Tel. 254-2382*
Brattleboro Police – *Tel. 254-2321*

11. DEERFIELD VALLEY & MT. SNOW

With more than 130 runs covering 500 acres and a southern location that makes it the most convenient major ski resort for folks from Boston and New York, the **Mt. Snow** and **Haystack** ski areas are quickly turning the **Deerfield Valley** into one of the fastest developing tourist destinations in Vermont. And while this leads some to bypass it, fearing larger crowds and less snow, modern snowmaking techniques and the opening of hundreds of new hotel rooms and condos annually have insured that the skiing experience at Mt. Snow is one of the highest rated in the East.

Of course, skiing isn't all the area has to offer. Mt. Snow offers numerous opportunities for cyclists, hikers, and of course leaf-peepers, while the **Harriman** and **Somerset reservoirs** are fine, and often overlooked, venues for fishermen, boaters, and swimmers. The area also offers a wide choice in lodging and dining, ranging from establishments like the Hermitage and the Inn at Sawmill Farm that are among the finest inns in America, to a long list of condos, lodges, B&B's, and motels that can accommodate all budgets.

See map on page 55 for destinations in this chapter.

ARRIVALS & DEPARTURES
By Air

The nearest major airport is **Bradley International Airport** in Hartford, CT, 1.5-2 hours from Wilmington. Other airports in the region within a reasonable driving distance include **Manchester** in New Hampshire (1-2 hours), **Logan Airport** in Boston (2-3 hours), **Albany**, NY and JFK and La Guardia airports in New York City (4-5 hours). Cars can be rented at all major airports.

By Car

Mount Snow, Wilmington and the Deerfield Valley is located at and around the **junction of Route 9 and Route 100**, with most establishments located on Route 100. Route 9 is an east-west thoroughfare which leads 20 miles east to Brattleboro and I-91, which comes straight from New York, Hartford, and Springfield, MA. From New York City, you can also take I-87 to Albany-Troy where you need to take Route 7 to Bennington, VT, and then Route 9 east 20 miles to Wilmington.

From the Boston area, take Route 2 west until it intersects Route 112 North which meets Route 100 in Vermont; or when Route 2 meets I-91, take it north to Brattleboro, and then Route 9 west to Wilmington. You can also take one of two routes through New Hampshire: take Route 3 to Nashua, 101A and 101 to Keene, and Route 9 through Brattleboro and on to Wilmington; or, you can take I-93 to Manchester, 101 to Keene and then get on Route 9.

From Montreal and cities in western Vermont, like Rutland and Burlington, take Route 7 south to Bennington and then Route 9 east 20 miles to Wilmington. From points in the Green Mountains, take Route 100 south, and from destinations in eastern Vermont, find your way to I-91 take it south to Brattleboro and then Route 9 west to Wilmington.

By Bus

Mount Snow and the Deerfield Valley is one region of Vermont that is not served by Vermont Transit Lines; the nearest major depots are in Bennington and Brattleboro, which offers more links to regional destinations. However, a company called **Absolute Edventures, Inc.** has stepped in and provides direct shuttle service between Mount Snow and New York, NY, and Hartford CT. Buses typically depart once or a twice a day depending on the season and a roundtrip from New York costs $65 ($50 for Hartford).

For information about schedules and bus depot locations, as well as reservations (required) contact Edventure by phone or e-mail: *Tel. 802/ 464-2810 or 212/921-9161; E-mail: absoluteedventures@sprynet.com.*

By Train

The nearest **Amtrak** stop is in **Brattleboro** which is linked to destinations across Vermont (including White River Junction, Randolph, Montpelier, and Burlington among others) as well as major Eastern Seaboard destinations like Hartford, New York, Philadelphia, Wilmington, Baltimore, and Washington, DC.

For complete schedules, fare information, and reservations, call Amtrak, *Tel. 800/USA-RAIL,* or your local travel agent. For a **taxi** at the station, call *802/254-5411.*

ORIENTATION

The **Deerfield Valley** comprises two major towns: **Wilmington**, located at the junction of east-west **Route 9** (also known as the "Molly Stark Trail) and north-south **Route 100**; and **Dover**, which consists of several villages north of Wilmington on and around Route 100. West Dover, for example, is actually on Route 100, while the village of Dover is east of Route 100 on Dover Hill Road.

The ski areas Mount Snow and Haystack as well as many condos, inns and restaurants are located on and around **Handle Road** and **Cold Brook Road**, which run roughly parallel to Route 100 and can be reached by turning west on one of several roads, the most major of which is **Tannery Road** just north of West Dover.

GETTING AROUND

The easiest way to get around is with your own car. Otherwise, the Deerfield Valley Transit Association (DVTA) operates a local **bus shuttle** known as the **Moo-ver** which links Wilmington (the terminus is the Deerfield Valley Medical Center) with Dover and the Mount Snow Base Area. There are many stops along Route 100, which are clearly marked, and there is generally one bus every hour from 7am-10pm, though during the ski season (late November through late March), and from July 2 through mid-October, there are two buses every hour. For more information call *802/464-8487*.

If you need to rent a car, both **Enterprise Rent-a-car**, *Tel. 802/257-4700*, and **Thrifty Car Rental**, *Tel. 802/254-9900*, have offices in Brattleboro.

WHERE TO STAY

There are literally dozens of condo properties and rentals. We have listed an assortment, but to receive comprehensive information call *800/245-SNOW*.

MOUNT SNOW CONDOMINIUMS, *299 Mountain Road, Mount Snow VT 05356. Tel. 802/464-7788, 800/451-4211. E-mail: msresoff@sover.not. Web site: www.mountsnow.com. Rates: $200-400 per night. Major credit cards accepted.*

The Mount Snow Resort operates four condominium properties; all are available in "ski & stay" packages that include lower rates for ski passes and other discounts. The most moderately priced **Deer Creek Condos** feature an assortment of 2-3 bedroom units within walking distance of the slopes and include private baths, kitchens, phones and television. Guests can use the saunas and jacuzzis at the Snow Lake Lodge.

Slightly more expensive, and a shuttle ride away from the slopes, are the **Snow Mountain Village Condominiums** and the **Snowtree Condominiums**. Both feature 1-3 bedroom studios and condos equipped with a full package of modern amenities, and both offer access to facilities at the Base Lodge including jacuzzis, the gym, and the pool. Finally, the **Seasons Condominiums at Mount Snow** are literally slopeside and also feature modern apartments as well as an inhouse pool, jacuzzis, and saunas.

SNOW RESORTS, *P.O. Box 757, Mount Snow VT 05356. Tel. 802/464-2177, 888/451-MTSNOW (ext. 4). E-mail: snowres@sover.net. Web site: www.mountsnow-vt.com.*

Snow Resorts is the largest rental company in the area and offers townhomes, houses, a wide variety of condos, many of which include facilities like jacuzzis, pools, and perhaps a gym.

RENTALS ONLY CONDOMINIUMS & HOMES, *P.O. Box 1450, West Dover VT 05356. Tel. 802/464-0904, 800/833-0904. E-mail: rentonly@sover.net. Web site: www.rentalsonly.com.*

Rentals Only operates several condominium properties and also rents a variety of private homes and apartments, some slopeside.

CHIMNEY HILL OWNERS ASSOCIATION, INC., *P.O. Box 415, 9 Haystack Road, Wilmington VT 05363. Tel. 802/464-2182.*

Chimney Hill is an area in Wilmington just northwest of the village center featuring a variety of homes and apartments for rent as well as an assortment of recreational facilities, including pools, tennis courts, and ice skating. Rates beging at about $500 for a weekend in the winter ($250 in summer).

NORTH REAL ESTATE, *P.O. Box 8, Route 100, West Dover VT 05356. Tel. 802/464-2196.*

Rents private multi-bedroom homes, many of which include amenities such as hot tubs beginning at $200 a night (multinight stays).

MOUNTAIN RESORT RENTALS, *P.O. Box 1804, West Dover VT 05356. Tel. 802/464-1445. E-mail: rentverm@sover.net. Web site: www.mountainresortrentals.com.*

Offers a wide variety of chalets, apartments, townhouses, and houses throughout the Mount Snow area.

GRAND SUMMIT RESORT HOTEL & CONFERENCE CENTER, *Mountain Road, Mount Snow VT 05356. Tel. 802/464-7788, 800/451-4211. E-mail: msresoff@sover.not. Web site: www.mountsnow.com. Rates: $100-$300. Major credit cards accepted.*

Mount Snow's spanking new piece de resistance boasts more than 200 rooms and suites, several restaurants, valet parking, a health club with sauna, a gym, swimming pools, and of course a slopeside location. The charm of a country inn or B&B is certainly lacking, but the facilities and the prices are hard to beat, especially with special "ski & stay" packages that include dining and ski passes.

SNOW LAKE LODGE, *199 Mountain Road (at the base of Mount Snow Lifts), Mount Snow VT 05356. Tel. 802/464-7788, 800/664-6535. E-mail: msresoff@sover.not. Web site: www.mountsnow.com. Rates: $80-$180. Major credit cards accepted.*

The main Mt. Snow lodge before the establishment of the Grand Summit, the Snow Lake Lodge has nearly 100 rooms and is located at the base of the Mount Snow ski area. Typically modern and not especially charming, its rooms all include amenities like telephones and television, while facilities include jacuzzis, hot tubs, and whirlpools. For dining and entertainment there is a decent restaurant as well as a pub and a nice lounge, both of which sometimes feature live entertainment.

BEST WESTERN – THE LODGE AT MOUNT SNOW, *Handle Road (P.O. Box 755), West Dover 05356. Tel. 802/464-5112, 800/451-4289. Rates: $75-$180. Major credit cards.*

A modern 50-room lodge situated about a quarter of a mile from the Mount Snow Lifts, the Best Western is smaller and more moderately placed than the Grand Summit Resort. The rooms are not overwhelming, but all include clean bathrooms, telehones, and cable television, and many also feature fine views. Other facilities include a heated pool, a dining room, and a nice lounge with good views and large fireplace. All in all, the Best Western offers good value and family-friendly environment with a great location and decent amenities.

KITZHOF LODGE, *Route 100 (HCR 63, Box 14), West Dover VT 05356. Tel. 802/464-8310, Tel. 800/388-8310. E-mail: kitzhof@together.net. Web site:kitzhof.com. Rates: $7-$150. Major credit cards accepted.*

Situated less than a mile from the Mount Snow lifts (the Moo-ver shuttle is convenient), the Kitzhof Lodge is a slightly rustic chalet-style affair with 25 rooms including several suites. All rooms have private baths, telephones, and cable television, and there is also a dining room, and a lounge with a fireplace (BYOB) where you can relax and mingle with other guests.

THE HERMITAGE INN, *Coldbrook Road, Wilmington VT 05363. Tel. 802/464-3511, Fax 802/464-2688. E-mail: hermitag@sover.net. Web site: www.hermitageinn.comm. Rates: $150-$300 per room. Major credit cards accepted.*

Undoubtedly the region's premier inn, the Hermitage is actually more like a resort for the rich and famous from another era. Consisting of hundreds of acres that include a trout pond, 50 kilometers of cross-country ski trails, a tennis court, a swimming pool, and an on-site skeet shooting range (game birds are also hunted in season), the inn consists of about 30 individually appointed, deluxe rooms located in various buildings throughout the estate, including at the Brookbound Inn about a mile down Coldbrook Road.

Each building consists of several rooms with private baths and elegant sitting parlors; one also includes a sauna. The main inn building itself contains four guestrooms in addition to the lounge and the Hermitage's highly acclaimed restaurant which is known for its wine selection (over 40,000 bottles) and its game bird specials featuring goose, duck, and pheasant – some birds are raised on the premises.

Selected as one of my *Best Places to Stay* – see Chapter 9 for more details.

INN AT SAWMILL FARM, *Crosstown Road, West Dover VT 05356. Tel. 802/464-8131, Fax 802/464-1130. Rates begin at $250 a night. Major credit cards accepted.*

Even fancier and more expensive than the Hermitage, the Inn at Sawmill epitomizes elegance and luxury. Built in 1770, this beautiful inn includes 20 antique-laden, immaculately decorated and furnished rooms and suites, with fireplaces, salons, cushy baths and canopy beds. The restaurant is legendary for its gourmet continental and American country cuisine, and in particular its wine cellar with more than 30,000 bottles of fine wines. Finally, the grounds include beautifully maintained gardens, a trout pond, and a swimming pool. Note: the inn is closed from April 7 to May 21 each year.

DEERHILL INN & RESTAURANT, *Valley View Road, West Dover VT 05356. (Turn east off Route 100 just north of the Dover Town Offices.) Tel. 802/464-3100, 800/99-DEER9, Fax 802/464-5474. E-mail: deerhill@sover.net. Web site: www.deerhill.com. Rates: $100-$350. Major credit cards accepted.*

This highly acclaimed inn features 15 rooms and suites, each beautifully decorated with antiques and many of which include fireplaces. The restaurant serves inspiring country cuisine by candlelight, and there is also a small art gallery and a porch/terrace with mountain views.

WHITE HOUSE OF WILMINGTON, *Route 9 East, Wilmington. Tel. 802/464-2135, 800/541-2135. E-mail: whitehse@sover.net Web site: www.whitehouseinn.com. Rates: $110-$220. Major credit cards accepted.*

Situated just east of Wimington Village from which it is within walking distance, the White House is a handsome (surprise!) white Victorian farmhouse with a dozen tastefully appointed rooms, some of which include fireplaces. Known for its duck, the in-house restaurant serves continental and American country dishes by candlelight in a cozy and elegant dining room; there is also a lounge. The White House One-Stop Outdoor Adventure Center operates a cross-country ski touring facility that rents skis and snowshoes and maintains 25 kilometers of trails. It also rents sleds and tubes which you can use on their hill. Other facilities include two pools (one indoor) and a spa with a whirlpool and sauna.

WHITINGHAM FARM B&B AND BARN, *742 Abbie Morse Road, Whitingham VT 05361. Tel. 802/368-2620, 800/310-2010. E-mail: whitingbb@aol.com. Web site: www.whitinghamfarm.com. Rates: $90-$140. Major credit cards accepted.*

Featuring only three bedrooms, the Farm offers a unique opportunity to sample the beauty and solitude of Vermont country living. Situated on a 50 acre farm, the 1860 Greek Revival home decorated with antiques and oriental rugs is elegantly old-fashioned, but comfortable and homey. The grounds are beautiful and waiting to be explored by hiking, cross-country skiing, snowshoeing, or even by sleigh depending on the seasons and your wishes.

DEERFIELD VALLEY INN, *Route 100, West Dover VT 05356. Tel. 802/464-6333, 800/639-3588, Fax 802/464-6336. E-mail: deerinn@vermontel.com. Web site: www.deerfieldvalley.com. Rates: $75-$175. Credit cards: Visa, Mastercard.*

Listed in the National Register of Historic Places, the Deerfield Valley Inn is a small bed & breakfast with nine elegant, comfortable rooms; all of which have private baths and cable television and some of which also have fireplaces.

THE INN AT QUAIL RUN, *Smith Road (turns east off Route 100 beween Wilmington and West Dover), Wilmington VT 05363. Tel. 802/464-3362, 800/34-ESCAPE. E-mail: quialrunvt@aol.com. Web site: www.bbonline.com/vt/quailrun. Rates: $80-$160. Major credit cards accepted.*

Not as fancy or luxurious as other inns, but comfortable and charming nonetheless, the Inn at Quail Run operates 15 rooms, all of which have private baths and cable television. Other facilities include an oversized jacuzzi, a sauna, and a dining room where a full breakfast is served every morning.

THE INN AT MOUNT SNOW INN & OTHER PROPERTIES, *Route 100, West Dover VT 05356. Tel. 802/464-3300. Rates: $80-$200. Major credit cards.*

The Inn at Mount Snow is a 14 room establishment in the tradition of Vermont inns. Rooms and suites are handsomely decorated with country decor and features amenities such as private baths; suites include jetted tubs and fireplaces. There is also a lounge with a fireplace and pleasant views of the Green Mountains.

The same folks who operate the Inn at Mount Snow also operate a handful of other lodges and inns. **The Inn at Mount Snow Lodge** has 30 rooms with private baths and cable television as well as a game room and a restaurant. A restored farmhouse on a 50 acre estate (with beautiful gardens in the summer) between Haystack and Mount Snow on the Handle Road, the **Handle House** is more intimate and charming with only six guestrooms, all with private bath and cable television. Finally, adjacent to the Inn at Mount Snow, the **Ironstone Lodge** includes 30 modern guestrooms with bath, television, and balconies, as well as a tavern and an inn style restaurant serving traditional Vermont country fare.

HORIZON INN, *Route 9 (P.O. Box 817), Wilmington VT 05363. Tel. 802/464-2131, 800/336-5513, Fax 802/464-8302. E-mail: horizon@sover.net. Web site: www.horizoninn.com. Rates: $60-$120. Major credit cards accepted.*

A sort of upscale motel, the Horizon Inn has 30 rooms, all equipped with private baths, cable television, and in-room phones as well as a restaurant, a heated pool, and a sauna.

VINTAGE MOTEL, *Route 9 West, Wilmington VT 05363. Tel. 802/ 464-8824, 800/899-9660. Web site: www.vintagemotel.com. Rates: $50-$100. Major credit cards accepted.*

A simple but decent motel with 18 rooms, all of which include private baths, cable television and in-room telephones.

WHERE TO EAT

TWO TANNERY ROAD, *Tannery Road (off Route 100), Mount Snow. Tel. 802/464-2707. Web site: www.sover.net/˜captsls/. Open nightly except Monday 6pm-10pm. Major credit cards accepted.*

Situated in an 18th century house that was once a Roosevelt family summer home, Two Tannery Road includes an elegant dining room serving fine American and Mediterranean cuisine, and a cozy tavern featuring a bar that was once in the famed Waldorf Astoria in New York City. The dining room serves an assortment of soups ($5) and hot and cold appetizers ($8-$10), such as smoked duck with mozzarella, baked Vermont cheddar with smoked ham, and country pate. All are excellent, but keep in mind that entrees are invariably hearty affairs like breaded veal dijon topped with Chardonnay herb butter, New York sirloin with whiskey brown sauce, and shrimp sauteed with garlic butter, portabello mushroom, and white wine sauce. For a lighter, less formal meal, the Tavern serves a variety of upscale sandwiches, soups and salads.

THE HERMITAGE INN, *Coldbrook Road, Wilmington VT 05363. Tel. 802/464-3511, Fax 802/464-2688. E-mail: hermitag@sover.net. Web site: www.hermitageinn.com. Major credit cards accepted.*

Perfectly classy and elegant without pretension, the Hermitage embodies the ideal country resort, and the restaurant is no exception. Ideally, an evening begins with a refreshment and perhaps some hors d'oeuvres in the fireplace tavern before moving on to the dining room, where the stars of the meal are traditionally the finely prepared game bird specials and a glass or two (or three) from one or more of the Hermitage's more than 2,000 selections. Game birds such as duck, goose, and pheasant are raised on the inn's premises and the wine cellar holds more than 30,000 bottles. Dress is smart casual and full meals will set you back at least $30-$40, but it's worth every penny.

INN AT SAWMILL FARM, *Crosstown Road, West Dover VT 05356. Tel. 802/464-8131, Fax 802/464-1130. Open nightly for dinner from 6pm-9:30pm. Major credit cards accepted.*

Epitomizing class and sophistication, the Inn at Sawmill Farm serves extremely fine continental cuisine in an elegant country envirnonment where everything from the restrained decor and first-rate service makes dining an experience to remember. Meals typically begin with immaculately prepared soups, salads, and/or appetizers such as lobster bisque or warmed goat cheese over a fresh assortment of greens. For entrees, the chef specializes in preparing game meats and birds such as duck, as well as rack of lamb and seafood. All meals should be accompanied by one of 30,000 selections of wine from their renowned cellar, and bread baked freshly on the premises. For desserts there is typically a variety of sinfully rich and a few somewhat lighter baked goodies and pastries, as well as sorbet and fruit. Make reservations, dress sharply though ties are not required, and be prepared to pay at least $30 per person.

DEERHILL INN & RESTAURANT, *Valley View Road, West Dover. Tel. 802/464-3100. Open for dinner 6pm-9pm Thursday through Monday. Major credit cards accepted.*

Served in a hillside fireplace dining room with colorful (some say "gaudy") decor, Deerhill's menu features a diverse selection of well prepared gourmet American cuisine. The appetizer ($7.50-$10) menu for example, might include items such as escargot (French snails), bruschetta with tomato garlic sauce, or avocado and curried crab, as well as soups and salads. Entrees are generally more familiar and range from roast ducking and grilled New York sirloin to southwestern spicy chicken and grilled pork chop with maple apple glaze. If you want to keep things interesting, try one the rare wines from South America from the extensive, award - inning wine list.

LE PETIT CHEF, *Route 100 North, Wilmington. Tel. 802/464-8437. Open nightly form 6pm except Tuesday. Major credit cards accepted.*

Located in a cozy restored farmhouse, the highly regarded Petit Chef is a chef-owned (Betty Hillman) affair specializing in traditional French cuisine. Dress is casual and reservations are requested (and advised). Ideally you should arrive a bit early to enjoy a refreshment and some hors d'oeuvres in the lounge. Meals are hearty and fine, comprised of French favorites ranging from coq au vin (chicken in rich red wine sauce) and duck confit to other meat, seafood and poultry specialties.

WHITE HOUSE OF WILMINGTON, *Route 9 East, Wilmington. Tel. 802/464-2135, 800/541-2135. E-mail: whitehse@sover.net Web site: www.whitehouseinn.com. Open for dinner 5:30-9pm nightly except Tuesday, Sunday brunch 11am-2:30pm. Major credit cards accepted.*

Situated in a classic Vermont Victorian mansion, the self-proclaimed "quintessential country inn" serves a tasty menu of continental and American country fare, such as baked brie and smoked trout for appetizers (each $6.50) and entress like roast pork loin, filet mignon, and the house specialty, boneless stuffed duck ($22.95). Perhaps even more tempting, though certainly not mutually exclusive, is the Sunday brunch buffet ($14.95) featuring a dazzling assortment of sweet and savory goodies including French toast, eggs bennedict, meats from ham and turkey to sausages, fruits, fresh breads, and much more.

PONCHO'S SHIPWRECK, *10 South Main Street (Route 100), Wilmington Village. Tel. 802/464-9320. Open nightly for dinner at 4pm and for lunch on Saturdays and Sundays. Major credit cards accepted.*

Family-owned and "shipwrecked" since 1972, Poncho's serves a staggering array of American, Mexican and seafood fare in a cozy, lantern-lit dinning room. Meals may begin with any one of more than two dozen appetizers ranging from steam mussels and littleneck clams Portuguese style to one of three different nachos and Maryland crab cakes; there are also four types of soups and chili.

The entree portion of the menu is divided into three sections, each larger than an entire menu in most restaurants. "Steaks, Chicken & Ribs" features a wide variety of grilled fare, much of it "southern style" (Texas barbeque and hickory smoked chicken, for example). For seafood, there are New England style dishes like boiled lobster and baked stuffed sole as well as Portuguese style clams or mussels (with tomatoes, garlic, herbed wine sauce and linguicia sausage). Finally Mexican favorites feature well prepared versions of the familiar fajitas, burritos, tacos, and chicken rellenos. There is also a children's menu and live entertainment is often featured as well.

ANCHOR SEAFOOD, *8 South Main Street, Wilmington. Tel. 802/464-2112. Open daily for lunch and dinner. Credit cards: Visa, Mastercard, American Express.*

Located in Wilmington village, the Anchor is a New England seafood house serving classic baked, broiled, boiled and fried, seafood including clams, shrimp, salmon, swordfish, sole, haddock, and of course lobster. Steak, chicken, and veal items are also available. Appetizers ($2-$10) range from escargot (snails) and baked stuffed clams to non-seafood favorites like potato skins with cheese and bacon, and hot buffalo wings. If you're not up for a full meal, consider an appetizer with a clam chowder or perhaps a salad, and there is also a special section on the menu titled

"Light Fare," featuring smaller portions of fried clams and scallops, as well as burgers and salads.

JULIO'S WOOD-FIRED PIZZA, *Route 100, West Dover (south of the village center). Tel. 802/464-1154. Open daily except Wednesdays from 4pm until 9pm (10pm on Fridays and Saturdays). Credit cards not accepted.*

Julio's serves some of the area's best and most popular pizza, which is the way it should be given that pizza is virtually all that they serve. Patrons may choose from 15 of the house specialties ranging from the simple three-cheese Margherita to "Julio's Favorite" topped with several cheeses, roasted vegetabes, garlic, and goat cheese; or they design their own, picking from nearly a dozen types of cheese, even more vegetables, and a half dozen meats and sausages. Pies come in three sizes: nine inches, 12 inches, and 16 inches, and prices start at $6.75 for a nine inch Margherita. You have the choice of eating at the restaurant or ordering take-out in advance; they will cook the pizza for you or simply prepare it so that you may bake it yourself and enjoy it fresh out of the oven at home.

JULIE'S CAFE, *Route 100, West Dover (south of the village center). Tel. 802/464-2078. Open 11am-9pm Sunday through Thursday (10pm on Friday and Saturday). Major credit cards accepted.*

The upscale sister of Julio's, Julie's Cafe serves a modest selection of well prepared dishes, most of which are Italian or southwestern. At the heart of the menu are the pasta and vegetarian selections headlined by "Julie's Signature Pasta" ($16.95, $18.95 with shrimp), a tasty collection of pasta topped with olives, artichoke hearts, sun-dried tomatoes, pine nuts and either chicken or shrimp (a vegetarian version is also possible). There are also several substantial meat and fish dishes (grilled ribs or fish for example), as well as lighter but satisfying dinner salads. For lunch the menu also includes several excellent sandwich selections including turkey with brie, burgers, and wraps.

ALONZO'S PASTA & GRILLE, *West Main Street (Route 9 West), Wilmington. Tel. 802/464-2355. Open daily from 4pm-10pm and from 9:30am-4pm for Sunday Brunch. Major credi cards accepted.*

Located in the Wilmington Village, Alonzo's is a casual, family-friendly eatery serving good American and Italian cuisine for very decent prices. Appetizers ($4-$6) include such American favorites as buffalo wings and nachos, while for entrees ($8-$15) there is a wide assortment of pastas, grilled fare (including steaks, ribs, pork loin, and fish), as well as Italian dishes like lasagna, ravioli, and Chicken parmigiana. For those with less than a full appetite, Alonzo's offers a selection of light fare ($7-$9) including burgers, sandwiches, and salads. Finally, there is also a children's menu, and a small bar with a television and a smoking section in the basement.

SEEING THE SIGHTS

It is the superb skiing and the natural beauty, along with the recreational opportunities, which brings visitors to the Deerfield Valley – not its historical or cultural attractions, and honestly there is little in the way of sightseeing within Mount Snow's immediate vicinity. However, there are numerous attractions within about 20 miles in any direction that can be explored in as little as a half-day.

Driving south of Wilmington on Route 100, the condos and relative urbanization of the Mount Snow Resorts quickly gives way to Vermont's more typical picturesque dairy farms. Less than 10 miles south of Wilmington is the hamlet of **Jacksonville**, home of the **North River Winery**. Located on Route 112 just south of the junction with Route 100, it is housed in an 1850's farmhouse and offers free tastings and tours (call in advance), as well as sales. *Open daily 10am-5pm. Tel. 802/368-7557.*

At Jacksonville, Route 100 turns west en route to Whitingham where the **Whitingham Farm B&B**, *Tel. 802/464-2135,* offers wonderful countryside sleigh rides in the winter. However, two miles west of Jacksonville before Whitingham is a turnoff to the south, which leads to a small memorial park built in honor of **Brigham Young**, perhaps the most important figure in the development and success of the Church of the Latter Day Saints (the Mormon Church) Born in Whitingham in 1801, Young was converted to the new faith as a teenager, and in 1844 he became leader of the Church after the murder of the Mormon Prophet Joseph Smith. Young led the Mormons away from the persecution they suffered in the east and Midwest to what is now Utah, where he founded Salt Lake City and lived until his death in 1877. Interestingly enough, the founder and Young's predecessor as leader, Joseph Smith, was also born in Vermont, in Sharon in the White River Valley.

From Whitingham, continue west on Route 100 until you reach Heartwellville. From there you can continue north on Route 8 which will lead you to Searsburg on Route 9, eight miles west of Wilmington, or you can turn south on Route 100 which turns into Route 8 in Massachusetts. It will lead to Route 2 which continues west to **Williamstown, MA** (20 miles from Heartwellville), which is the home of the prestigious **Williams College** as well as the **Sterling and Francine Clark Art Institute**, *Tel. 413/458-9545; open daily).* Though located in a very small town in an area many would think of as the "boonies," the Institute is a world class museum that includes in its collection more than 30 Renoirs, as well as works by such prominent artists as Winslow Homer and Frederick Remington.

There is other worthwhile sightseeing in **Brattleboro**, which is only 20 miles east of Wilmington on Route 9; **Marlboro** (10 miles east), which features a natural history museum and the scenic **Hogback Mountain**;

and **Bennington** and **Arlington**, 20 miles west of Wilmington, where you can visit such sights as the Bennington Monument, Robert Frost's grave in the historic Old First Church, and the Norman Rockwell Museum in Arlington where the maestro of Americana lived for more than 20 years. See the "Brattleboro & Windham County" and the "Bennington" chapters for details.

NIGHTLIFE & ENTERTAINMENT

Like Vermont's other resort areas, the Deerfield Valley hosts its fair share of musical and cultural events, particularly around Christmas-New Year's and during the summer and foliage seasons. The most notable event is undoubtedly the **Marlboro Music Festival**, the most highly acclaimed chamber music event in the region. It is held annually from mid-July through mid-August in Marlboro, which is just 10 miles east of Wilmington on Route 9. Call for information, *Tel. 802/254-2394.* Another major high culture event is the **Williamstown Theatre Festival**, held in Williamstown, MA and featuring cutting edge plays and theatre from June-August; call for further information, *Tel. 413/597-3400.*

For further information about these and other events, contact the **Mount Snow Valley Chamber Of Commerce**, *P.O. Box 3, Wilmington VT 05365, Tel. 802/464-8092, E-mail: info@visitvermont.com, Web site: visitvermont.com.*

For an old-fashioned adult refreshment after a long hard day of skiing or golfing (life's tough, isn't it?), most lodges and inns operate their own taverns. There are also several local blue collar type bars, like the **Village Pub** in Wilmington Village.

For more involved nightlife, try the establishments listed below:
THE SNOW BARN, *Base of Mount Snow . Tel. 802/464-1100 (Ext. 4693). Open nightly until late. Major credit cards.*

Features dancing, live bands (Thursday-Sunday), and all sorts of food (mostly the pizza-bar variety) and drink. Stay tuned for special attractions and events like the Reggae Weekend in April.

DEACON'S DEN, *Route 100, West Dover. Tel. 802/464-9361. Open daily from 3pm until late. Major credit cards accepted.*

Serves all sortsof beers and spirits as well as sandwiches, pasta, pizza and other barroom favorites. Live music and dancing featured on the weekends.

SPORTS & RECREATION
Biking

The recently developed **Valley Trail** from Mount Snow to Wilmington Village is designed for biking, as well as hiking and snowmobiling in the winter. For road biking, Route 100 and Route 112 south of Wilmington in the Jacksonville and Whitingham area are less developed and trafficked than between Wilmington and Dover; however, many of the roads off of Route 100 in Dover are less traveled and quite scenic.

Mount Snow features some of the best mountain biking in Vermont with a course developed for professionals on **Mount Snow** itself, open to the public – call for information about access. There is also excellent mountain biking at **Harriman Reservoir** where a course along a rail bed begins at the Mount Mills West picnic area on Woods Road 2.5 miles west of Wilmington on Route 9; and at **Woodford State** Park 12 miles west of Wilmington on Route 9.

BONKERS BOARD ROOM, *Dover Center on Route 100, West Dover. Tel. 802/464-2536. Open daily. Major credit cards accepted.*

Specializes in snowboard equipment and acessories in the winter and bikes in the summer, including rentals.

Boating

You can canoe and kayak on both **Harriman Reservoir** (two miles west of Wilmington on Route 9), and on the smaller **Somerset Reservoir** which can be accessed five miles west of Wilmington by way of Route 9 and then running north for a short bit.

Cross-Country Skiing & Snowshoeing

In addition to the operations listed below, there is also excellent nordic skiing in Woodford and Bennington – see the "Bennington" chapter for more information.

HERMITAGE SKI TOURING CENTER, *Coldbrook Road, Mount Snow Valley 05363. Tel. 802/464-3511. Web site: www.hermitageinn.com. Trail fees: $14.*

The Hermitage operates 55 kilometers of beautiful trails and offers lessons and rentals; it's also a great place to stay or at least dine.

SITZMARK SKI TOURING CENTER, *East Dover Road, Wilmington. Tel. 802/464-3384. Trail fees: $10.*

Offers 40 kilometers of trails, lessons, and rentals.

WHITE HOUSE ONE-STOP OUTDOOR ADVENTURE CENTER, *Route 9 East, Wilmington. Tel. 802/464-2135, 800/541-2135. E-mail: whitehse@sover.net Web site: www.whitehouseinn.com. Trail fees: $12.*

The White House operates 25 kilometers of trails and provides rentals, lessons, and tours; it also rents sleds and tubes.

HIGH ALTITUDE ROUTE 100, *Route 100 West Dover. Tel. 802/464-0536. Open daily 8am-7pm. Major credit cards accepted.*

A full-fledged sporting goods store specializing in winter sports equipment, accessories and apparel including ski, snowboard, and snowshoe rentals and sales.

Golf

HAYSTACK GOLF CLUB, *Mann Road, Wilmington. Tel. 802/464-8301. Web site: www.haystackgolf.com. 18 holes. Green fees: $40-$45. Major credit cards accepted. Carts available.*

MT. SNOW COUNTRY CLUB, *Route 100 Mount Snow, West Dover VT. Tel. 802/464-5642. 18 holes. Green fees: $43. Major credit cards accepted.*

SITZMARK, *East Dover Road, Wilmington. Tel. 802/464-3384. 18 holes. Green fees: $12. Credit cards accepted. Carts available.*

SOMEDAY RESORT, *Sugar Lot Road, West Dover. Tel. 802/464-5807.*

Hiking

The **Valley Trail**, which begins at Mount Snow and extends to Wilmington Village, offers good hiking; it can be accessed at the corner of Tannery Road and the Handle Road in West Dover among other places. The ski slopes of **Mount Snow** itself offer more challenging hikes with less traffic and better scenery. You can also hike around the **Harriman Reservoir** and at **Woodford State Park** 12 miles west of Wilmington on Route 9.

Skiing & Snowboarding

MOUNT SNOW & HAYSTACK, *Handle Road, Mount Snow VT 05356. Tel. 800/599-5754, 800/245-SNOW. E-mail: vacasva@sover.net. Web site: www.mountsnow.com. Lift Rates at Mount Snow (including Haystack): $35-$55 per day (less for multiday passes and for juniors, youth, and seniors); only Haystack: $27-$40. . Lifts operate from 8:30am-4pm.*

With more than 134 runs and trails covering 500 acres with nearly 30 lifts, Mount Snow and Haystack represent the second largest skiing area in Vermont and the East Coast after Killington & Pica. It's a good thing, because of with its southerly location and relative proximity to major popularion centers like New York and Hartford, it is also one of the most popular. While Mount Snow has been expanding and will be looking to further capitalize on its hosting of the **Winter Extreme Games** in February 2000, Haystack has been going through hard times, something which its new owners, the American Skiing Company (who also own Mount Snow, Killington, and a host of other major eastern ski resorts), hopes to rectify.

Equipment can be rented at Crisports at the base lodges at both Haystack and Mount Snow; full rentals (poles, skis, and boots) begin at $30 for adults with lower rates for children and for multiday rentals; or any of the many ski and sporting goods shops in the area (some listed below). Snowboards with boots can also be rented by the day ($25). There arc also numerous ski and snowboard clinics and lessons for adults and children of all ages. You can join a group lesson, which is considerably cheaper, or arrange a private or family lesson. At Haystack, you can also partake in **telemark lessons**.

EQUIPE SPORT, *Base of Mount Snow, Mount Snow. Tel. 802/464-2222. Open daily. Major credit cards accepted.*

Specializes in snowboard and skiing equipment and accessories, including rentals.

HIGH ALTITUDE ROUTE 100, *Route 100 West Dover. Tel. 802/464-0536. Open daily 8am-7pm. Major credit cards accepted.*

A full fledged sporting goods store specializing in winter sports equipment, accessories and apparel including ski, snowboard, and snow-shoe rentals and sales.

BONKERS BOARD ROOM, *Dover Center on Route 100, West Dover. Tel. 802/464-2536. Open daily. Major credit cards accepted.*

Specializes in snowboard equipment and acessories in the winter and bikes in the summer, including rentals.

Sledding

You bring your own sled to the Carintha Base Lodge at Mount Snow where slopes are lighted from 5pm-9pm.

WHITE HOUSE ONE-STOP OUTDOOR ADVENTURE CENTER, *Route 9 East, Wilmington. Tel. 802/464-2135, 800/541-2135. E-mail: whitehse@sover.net Web site: www.whitehouseinn.com.*

Rents sleds and tubes in addition to maintaining 30 kilometers of trails used primarily for cross-country skiing.

Sleigh Rides

WHITINGHAM FARM, *742 Abbie Morse Road, Whitingham VT 05361. Tel. 802/368-2620, 800/310-2010. E-mail: whitingbb@aol.com. Web site: www.whitinghamfarm.com. Rates: $90-$140. Major credit cards accepted.*

Enjoy an hour-long sleigh ride in the beautiful countryside of Whitingham south of Wilmington, secluded from Mount Snows's resort developments. Reservations required.

Snowmobiling

HIGH COUNTRY, *Route 9 West, Wilmington. Tel. 802/464-2108, 800/626-7533. E-mail: highetry@sover.net. Web site: www.southvermont.com/wilmington/highcountry. Major credit cards accepted.*

Offers lessons, tours, and rentals; tends to use very new and up-to-date equipment.

VTS, INC. SNOWMOBILE TOURS, *Route 100, West Dover. Tel. 802/464-3280, 800/686-1275. Major credit cards accepted.*

Tours, lessons, and rentals.

SHOPPING

BONKERS BOARD ROOM, *Dover Center on Route 100, West Dover. Tel. 802/464-2536. Open daily. Major credit cards accepted.*

Specializes in snowboard equipment and acessories in the winter and bikes in the summer, including rentals.

THE CHRISTMAS BARN,*Route 9 West, Wilmington VT 05363. Tel. 802/464-3138, 800/245-5252. Open daily 10am-5pm. Major credit cards accepted.*

Situated in a charming old renovated barn, the Christmas Barn sells all sorts of colorful ornaments and Christmasy gifts.

EQUIPE SPORT, *Base of Mount Snow, Mount Snow. Tel. 802/464-2222. Open daily. Major credit cards accepted.*

Specializes in snowboard and skiing equipment and accessories, including rentals.

HIGH ALTITUDE ROUTE 100, *Route 100 West Dover. Tel. 802/464-0536. Open daily 8am-7pm. Major credit cards accepted.*

A full fledged sporting goods store specializing in winter sports equipment, accessories and apparel including ski, snowboard, and snowshoe rentals and sales.

ROSEATE CREATIONS, *7 North Main Street, Wilmington. Tel. 802/464-1466.*

"A gallery of artistic excellence," Roseate sells all sorts of arts and crafts from quilts and jewelry baskets and photography.

TADDINGERS, *Route 100 at Haystack Access Road, Wilmington. Tel. 802/464-3727. Open daily from 10am-6pm. Major credit cards accepted.*

Featuring seven stores in one including Orvis sporting goods and apparel (namely fly flishing and hunting), a Christmas theme shop, gourmet foods, and antiques.

LEFT BANK ANTIQUES, *Wilmington Village. Tel. 802/464-3224.*

Your area store for all sorts of antiques.

EXCURSIONS & DAY TRIPS

BENNINGTON & ARLINGTON

Twenty miles west of Wilmington on Route 9, Bennington is one of the oldest towns in Vermont and is home to a beautiful old district where you'll find the impressive **Bennington Monument**, built to commemorate the Battle of Bennington (1777), a cemetery where **Robert Frost** is buried, and an impressive museum housing the country's largest collection of Grandma Moses paintings, as well as a diverse assortment of American art and historic artifacts.

Fifteen miles north of Bennington on scenic Route 7A, **Arlington** is a handsome and picturesque village and is home to several attractions, including several covered bridges and a museum about Norman Rockwell who lived there in the 1930's, 40's, and 50's. See the "Bennington" chapter for more details.

BRATTLEBORO & EASTERN WINDHAM COUNTY

The twenty mile stretch of **Route 9** between Wilmington and Brattleboro is a winding beautiful affair. En route you will pass through **Marlboro** (9 miles east of Wilmington), known for its world class music festival in the summer, and home to a fine natural history museum. **Brattleboro** itself is a town on the rebound and (by Vermont standards anyway) is bustling and active with commerce and people on the move. Its primary attraction is a modest but impressive art museum featuring a beautiful collection of Espey Organs, which were in fact manufactured in Brattleboro.

From Brattleboro you can continue north along **Route 5** or **I-91** to towns like **Putney** and **Bellows Falls**. Many of the local roads in this area are quite beautiful and feature classic Vermont scenes, like rolling hills dotted with the barns and livestock of dairy farms. You can also drive up **Route 30** through the handsome village of **Newfane** up to the town of Jamaice where it meets Route 100 – take that south and it's 30 miles to Wilmington.

See "Brattleboro & Windham County" chapter for more details.

THE PRECISION VALLEY

As an excursion, see Chapter 10, *Brattleboro & Windham County*. For much greater detail, go to the Precision Valley chapter.

PRACTICAL INFORMATION

Chambers of Commerce
MOUNT SNOW VALLEY CHAMBER OF COMMERCE, *P.O. Box 3, Wilmington VT 05365. Tel. 802/464-8092. E-mail: info@visitvermont.com. Web site: visitvermont.com.*

Medical Emergencies
Ambulance – *Tel. 362-2323*
Deerfield Valley Health Center, *Wilmington. Tel. 464-5311*
Brattleboro Memorial Hospital, *9 Belmont Avenue, Brattleboro. Tel. 802/257-0341*

Police
State Police – *Tel. 254-2382*
Wilmington Police – *Tel. 464-8593*
Dover Police – *Tel. 464-2020*

12. BENNINGTON & ARLINGTON

Often called the "Gateway to Vermont" (Brattleboro is also known by the same title), **Bennington** is a town and region steeped in history and well-endowed with natural and historic attractions, but too often passed over by travelers on their way to ritzier destinations like Manchester and Wilmington. The first town chartered by New Hampshire west of the Connecticut River in 1749, Bennington was a bastion of political activity before and during the Revotionary War. The state's early leaders, including Ethan Allen, met at the famous Catamount Tavern on Monument Avenue to plot strategy and tactics for struggles like the Battle at Bennington, which turned the tide of the Revolutionary War in the Champlain Valley against the British.

Today, **Bennington Monument**, a 306-foot high obelisk built to commemorate that battle, dominates the regional skyline and serves as a beacon to those entering the town and the state. It is also the area's most popular tourist destination, though the area boasts an impressive assortment of historic and natural attractions.

Among the attractions of Bennington itself is the **Bennington Museum**, featuring the largest collection of Grandma Moses paintings in the country, the **Old First Church and Burying Grounds** where Robert Frost and dozens of Revolutionary War soldiers and leaders are interred, and the **Hemming Motor News** headquarters where you can wax nostalgic at an old-fashioned filling station and collect antique auto-related souvenirs and memorabilia. Meanwhile, the surrounding countryside – all encompassed in the **Green Mountain National Forest** – features dozens of opportunities for outdoor recreation, whether it be hiking the Appalachian and Long Trails, canoeing the scenic Battenkill, or exploring covered bridges on the Walloomsac River.

North of Bennington are the historic villages of **Shaftsbury** and **Arlington**, both featuring hundreds of historic buildings and atttractions such as the **Norman Rockwell Museum & Exhibition**. Rockwell used to live in Arlington and at this exhibition you can take guided tours given by men and women who used to work for him as models. Many of these attractions take little time to enjoy, so even if you are on your way to another part of the state or on your way home, it is easy to enjoy the southwestern corner of Vermont.

ARRIVALS & DEPARTURES

By Air
The closest commercial airport to Bennington is in **Albany, New York**, which is approximately 50 miles away by Route 7. Boston's **Logan Airport** (150 miles away), is further, but often more convenient in terms of the number of flights and availability. In Vermont itself, **Burlington International Airport**, is serviced by Continental, *Tel. 800/525-0289*, United, *Tel. 800/241-6522*, USAir, *Tel. 800/428-4322*, and the commuter airlines, **Business Express**, *Tel. 800/345-3400*, and **Comair**, *Tel. 800/927-0927*. Burlington is approximately a two hour drive (mostly very scenic) from Bennington on Route 7.

Another viable option is **Manchester, NH** serviced by Southwest, *Tel. 800/435-9792*, Continental, *Tel. 800/525-0289*, USAir, *Tel. 800/428-4322*, and Delta Connection, *Tel. 800/345-3400*. It is less than a two hour drive by way of Route 110 and Route 9.

By Car
Bennington is located at the junction of Routes 9 (east-west) and Route 7 (north-south). From Rutland, Middlebury, Manchester, and Burlington (including the Lake Champlain region) you need to take Route 7 south. From Boston, take Route 2 West past Williamstown to Route 7 and then head north.

From New Hampshire and eastern Vermont, find your way to Route 91, take it to Brattleboro, and then ride Route 9, 40 miles west to Bennington. Route 100 to Route 7 by way of Route 11 is most convenient for those traveling from any point in central Vermont north of Londonderry. From points south on Route 100, such as Route 9, simply continue south on Route 100 and then go west on Route 9 at Wilmington.

From New York, I recommend taking Route 87 to Albany from whence you can take Route 7/9 east to Bennington. Arlington is on Route 7, 15 miles north of Bennington. Cars can be rented at all major airports.

By Bus
Vermont Transit Lines, *Tel. 802/442-4808*, provides direct service to Bennington and Arlington. Three buses daily depart from Albany, NY to

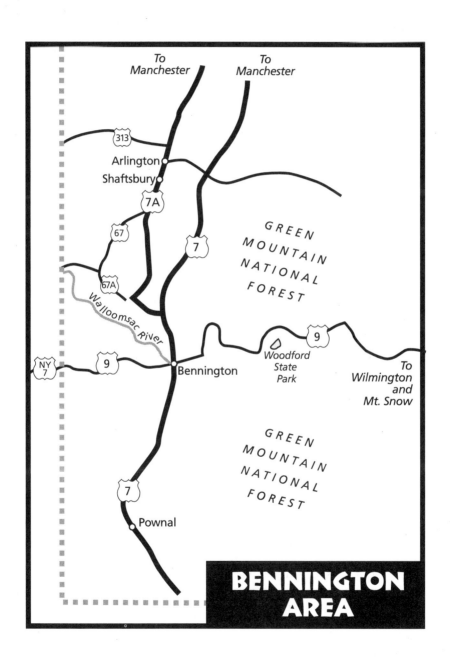

To
Manchester

To
Manchester

313

Arlington
Shaftsbury

7A

67

7

GREEN
MOUNTAIN
NATIONAL
FOREST

67A

Walloomsac River

9

Woodford
State
Park

NY
7

9

Bennington

To
Wilmington
and
Mt. Snow

GREEN
MOUNTAIN
NATIONAL
FOREST

7

Pownal

BENNINGTON AREA

Bennington (and one daily to Arlington), and continue on to Manchester (VT), Wallingford, Rutland, Brandon, Middlebury,Vergennes and Burlington. At Rutland, you can make connections for Montpelier and White River Junction where buses make daily runs to the Northeast Kingdom, Boston, New York, Maine, and points in New Hampshire. Make connections in Burlington for Montreal and Canadian destinations. Ticket prices range from $10-$40 (more if you make Greyhound connections to destinations beyond the Northeast) depending on the distance of your journey.

By Train

Amtrak's **Ethan Allen Express**, *Tel. 800/USA-RAIL,* does not stop in Bennington County, but it does stop in Albany twice a day (once from Rutland, once on the way to New York). Several trains daily depart for points through New York State, including New York City, Syracuse, and Rochester, as well as other destinations in the Northeast such as Philadelphia, Springfield MA, New Jersey, Washington D.C. and others.

Amtrak's other service to Vermont, the **Vermonter**, stops in Brattleboro VT (40 miles east on Route 9) twice daily: once on the way north (5pm) to Bellows Falls, Windsor, White River Junction, Randolph Center, Montpelier, Waterbury-Stowe, Essex-Burlington, St. Albans, and Montreal. The southbound train departs Brattleboro at noon for Amherst and Springfield, MA; Hartford, Berlin, New Haven, Bridgport, and Stamford, CT; New York City; Newark, Metropark, and Trenton, NJ; Philadelphia; Wilmington, DE; Baltimore; BWI Airport, New Carrollton, MD; and Washington D.C.

ORIENTATION/GETTING AROUND

Located in Vermont's southwest corner, Bennington County is largely dominated by the **Green Mountain National Forest** which engulfs it. With no true interstates passing through the region, the over-trafficked **Route 9** (east-west) and **Route 7** (north-south) serve as the area's main arteries. They intersect in the city of **Bennington**, the region's largest town, creating a sometimes traffic disaster known as "Malfunction Junction." From Bennington, Route 9 leads west to New York state only four miles away and on to Albany. To the east, it winds its way up through the Green Mountains to Wilmington (20 miles from Bennington), and on to Marlboro, Brattleboro and the Connecticut River Valley.

Route 7 links Bennington with Massachusetts to the south by way of the town of Pownal, best known for its auto race track, while to the north it's a 16 mile straight shot to Arlington (featured in this chapter) and on to the upscale mountain tourist mecca of Manchester (25 miles), Middlebury, and eventually Burlington and Canada.

More scenic than the interstate-like Route 7 is **Historic Route 7A**. Tracing an old stagecoach route, it begins at Route 67A, an east-west road that begins at Route 7 on the northern edge of Bennington and continues east along the scenic Wallomsac River, along which route you'll find plenty of ccovered bridges. Route 7A passes through the minor town of Shaftsbury en route to Arlington, Sunderland, and Manchester.

While the entire county is contained in the Green Mountain National Forest, the wilderness itself is primarily east of Bennington and Route 7. There are entrances to the park from Route 7 and Route 9 at Woodford State Park, roughly 10 miles east of Bennington.

As noted before, Route 9 and Route 7 are the main highways for the region, and also access Bennington itself. In town, Route 7 doubles as North Street (north of the junction with Route 9) and South Street (south of the junction) and is lined with stores, eateries, and businesses, including several gas stations. Meanwhile Route 9 morphs into East Main Street (east of the Route 7 junction) and West Main Street. East Main is home to a number of motels as well as such landmarks as the First Church, where Robert Frost is buried, and the Bennington Museum. It also leads to the Bennington Monument and passes through historic Old Bennington.

WHERE TO STAY
Arlington

ARLINGTON INN, *Route 7A, Arlington VT 05250. Tel. 802/375-6532, 800/875-2724. Rates: $80-$210. Major credit cards accepted.*

From the 19th century Greek Revivial mansion to the first class rooms equipped with fireplaces and jacuzzis, this inn – now 150 years old – lives up to its reputation as a classic Vermont country inn. Located less than 10 miles from the historic town of Manchester, it contains 19 rooms, meeting rooms, tennis facilities, business services, and a tavern and first-rate restaurant.

WEST MOUNTAIN INN, *River Road (half mile west on Route 313 from Route 7A at Arlington), Arlington VT 05250. Tel. 802/375-6516, Fax 802/375-6553. E-mail: info@westmountaininn.com. Web site: www.westmountaininn.com. Rates: $150-$250. Major credit cards accepted.*

Set on a 150 acre estate overlooking the beautiful Battenkill River Valley, this fine inn located in a huge country house offers guests magnificent views and comfortable lodging in 18 stylish rooms. On-site recreational opportunities include cross-country skiing, skating, and sledding in the winter, and hiking, biking, and hanging out with the resident llamas in the summer and fall. The elegant West Mountain Inn restaurant is renowned for its innovative fine cuisine and is open to the public on a reservation basis.

INN ON COVERED BRIDGE GREEN, *RD 1 Box 1272 (River Road), Arlington VT 05250. Tel. 802/375-9489, 800/726-9480. E-mail: cbg@sover.net. Web site: cimarron.net/usa/vt. Rates: $100-$150. Major credit cards accepted.*
Situated on the scenic Battenkill River and the Arlington Green, this inn was once the home and studio of famed Americana painter Norman Rockwell and was originally built in 1792. There are five comfortable guestrooms, all different from one another, with fireplaces – one features an in-room whirlpool.

EQUINOX MOUNTAIN INN, *Mount Equinox Skyline Drive off Route 7A north of Arlington (P.O. Box 2405), Arlington VT 05250. Tel. 800/MTN-VIEW. Rates: $85-$140. Major credit cards accepted. Open from May through October.*
Recently restored, this small inn requires something of a hair-rising drive up the toll road, Skyline Drive ($6 per vehicle) up Mount Equinox. The inn is now owned by a group of Carthusian monks, and the views are simply among the best in Vermont, particularly during foliage season. Rooms are comfortable and each has its own view. There is also a fine restaurant serving $25 dinners, an impressive oval bar, and a number of hiking trails for you to explore the surrounding wilderness.

HILL FARM INN, *RR#2 Box 2015, Arlington VT 05250. Located off Route 7A between Manchester and Arlington. Turn off at Battenkill Canoe. Tel. 802/375-2269, 800/882-2545, Fax 802/375-9918. Rates: $65-$150. Major credit cards accepted. No smoking.*
Named for the Hill family to whom King George granted this land in 1775, this classic Vermont estate has been turned into a fine inn. The Main Inn, built in 1830, contains seven unique rooms, all with king or queen beds, and five of which have private baths. Also available are five rooms and one two-room suite located in the Guest House (built 1790). Three of the rooms feature a private bath, while the suite (known as the Lilac) contains a kitchenette, woodstove, private bath, and queen bed. From the end of May through October, 24 cabins (all with porch and private shower) are available, the largest of which, "Butternut," contains two bedrooms. Rates include breakfast. Call for information about discounts – particularly in the off-season (January through April).

ROARING BRANCH LOG CABIN RESORT, *Sunderland Hill Road (off Route 7), Arlington VT 05250. Tel. 802/375-6401, Fax 802/375-6401. E-mail: rblogcab@sover.net. Web site: www.roaringbranch.com. Rates: $600-$700 per cabin per week. Credit cards: Visa, Mastercard, American Express. Open Memorial Day (mid-May) through Columbus Day (mid-October).*
Great for a family vacation (including pets), these 80-year-old cabins set in pine woods are rented for a weekly basis during the summer and early fall, and feature 103 bedrooms, kitchens, fireplaces, and hot

showers. The resort grounds contain several recreational facilities, including tennis courts, fishing, swimming, and a playground for children.

Bennington

THE FOUR CHIMNEY'S, *21 West Road, Old Bennington VT 05201. Tel. 802/447-3500. Rates: $95-$185. Credit cards: major credit cards accepted. No smoking.*

Originally constructed in 1783, and restored in 1910 after a fire, the Four Chimney's is a superb inn with 11 rooms and a dining room open to the public serving fine cuisine. Rooms are spacious, comfortable, and decorated in old-fashioned style, but feature a host of modern amenities, including television, phones, fireplaces, and jacuzzi's.

THE HENRY HOUSE, *Rural Road 1 Box 214, North Bennington VT 05401. Tel. 802/442-7045, 888/442-7045, Fax 802/442-3045. Rates: $85-$135. Credit cards: Visa, Mastercard. No smoking.*

Named for a Revolutionary War hero, William Henry, who fought in the Battle of Bennington, this historic inn is a true gem. Overlooking the Henry Covered Bridge on the Walloomsac River, it only features five rooms and a handful of comfy salons where guests can read and chat. The most impressive room is "The Ballroom" (all of the rooms have names), so named becaused it served that function during Lt. Henry's tenure here in the 18th century. Laden with antiques, it boasts 14-foot ceilings and a four poster canopy bed worthy of royalty – or at least one of General Washington's officers.

MOLLY STARK INN, *1067 East Main Street, Bennington VT 05201 Tel. 802/442-9631, 800/356-3076, Fax 802/442-5224. E-mail: mollystarkinn@vermontel.com. Web site: www.mollystarkinn.com. Rates: $70-$175. Credit cards: major credit cards accepted. No smoking.*

Located conveniently near downtown Bennington on Route 9, the Molly Stark Inn is a Victorian style inn with six comfortable rooms, including private baths complete with bearclaw bathtubs; and a superduper cottage suite complete with a jacuzzi.

ALEXANDRA B&B, *Route 7A & Orchard Road, Bennington VT 05201. Tel. 802/442-5619, 888/207-9386, Fax 802/442-5592. Rates: $85-$125. Major credit cards accepted. No smoking.*

Alexandra contains four comfortable and spacious guestrooms, endowed with cable television, privates baths, and four poster beds. Well groomed grounds, a porch, and an assortment of handsomely decorated salons enhance the country house atmosphere.

SOUTH SHIRE INN, *124 Elm Street, Bennington VT 05201. Tel. 802/ 447-3839. E-mail: sshire@sover.net. Rates: $105-$160. Credit cards: Visa, Mastercard.*

Designed by prominent Bennington area archictect, William Bull, this Victorian-era inn is a gem of a building with nine guestrooms and a mahogany-laden library. The rooms all feature private baths, air-conditioning, and telephones. Most also contain fireplaces and four have jacuzzis. Very convenient access to downtown Bennington and an excellent choice overall.

BEST WESTERN NEW ENGLANDER MOTOR INN, *Route 7A & Northside Drive, Bennington VT 05201. Tel. 802/442-6311, 800/528-1234. Rates: Major credit cards accepted.*

BW features all the charm and amenities that one might expect from a brand name motel, including a number of "deluxe" (i.e. standard) rooms, including some with jacuzzi's and/or refrigerators, as well as a restaurant, lounge, and free continental breakfast.

PARADISE MOTOR INN, *141 West Main Street, Bennington VT 05201. Tel. 802/442-8351. Credit cards: Visa, Mastercard, Discovery.*

It may not quite live up to its name, but this is definitely a cut above most motels in Vermont and is endowed with 76 rooms and suites (some with jacuzzi's), a pool, a couple of tennis courts, and a restaurant and lounge.

BENNINGTON MOTOR INN, *143 West Main Street, Bennington VT 05201. Tel. 802/442-5479, 800/359-9900. Rates: $45-$65. Major credit cards accepted.*

The rooms are a bit small, but homier than those in brand name motels and feature cable television all the same.

HARWOOD HILL MOTEL, *2 miles north of downtown on Route 7A, Bennington VT 05201. Tel. 802/442-6278, Fax 802/442-6278. Rates: $50-$70. Major credit cards accepted.*

Harwood Hill contains about 20 units (some in cabins), equipped with cable television, and air-conditioning. Other facilities include picnic tables and barbeque grills for guest use.

Shaftsbury

HILLBROOK MOTEL, *Route 7A (about 5 miles north of Bennington), Shaftsbury VT 05262. Tel. 802/447-7201. Rates: $50-$100. Credit cards: Mastercard, Visa, Disovery.*

Rooms features cable television and in-room air-conditioning, and motel grounds include a pool and picnic tables.

Area Camping

WOODFORD STATE PARK, *HCR 65 Box 928, Bennington VT -5201. Located off Route 9 about 12 miles east of Bennington. Tel. 802/447-7169 (summer), 802/483-2001 (off-season). Base rates: $13-$17. Credit cards: Visa, Mastercard. Open mid-May through Columbus Day (mid-October). Pets allowed on leash.*

Situated on the Adams Reservoir in the Green Mountain National Forest, Woodford State Part features 103 sites for trailers and tents (20 with lean-to's) as well as a beach, picnic area, and restrooms, but no hot showers. The Reservoir affords fishing and boating opportunities (row boats and canoes are available for rental), and several miles of hiking trails. Also the Long Trail and Appalachian Trail pass through the Green National Forest just a couple of miles to the west. Call for reservations in advance, particularly for holiday weekends and foliage season.

LAKE SHAFTSBURY STATE PARK, *RD#1 Box 266, Shaftsbury VT 05262. Off Route 7A two miles south of Arlington. Tel. 802/375-9978 (summer), 802/483-2001 (off-season). Base rates: $16. Credit cards: Visa, Mastercard. Open mid-May through Labor Day.*

This scenic and isolated state park offers great hiking, swimming and boating (canoes and row boats are available for rent), as well as picnic areas and a beach, but only has 15 camp sites which are generally only rented to groups. Call in advance to make reservations.

CAMPING ON THE BATTENKILL, *RD 2 Box 3310, Arlington VT 05250. On Route 7A less than a mile north of Arlington Village. Tel. 802/375-6663, 800/830-6663. Base rates: $17-$23. Credit cards: Visa, Mastercard. Open from the third week of May through October. Pets allowed with proof of rabies vaccination.*

This 100-plus site campground (with nine for tents) offers access to the beautiful Battenkill River with its covered bridges and excellent swimming and fishing. The campground itself features both open and wooded sites, a dumping station, a playground, fire pits, hot showers and restrooms, and LP gas.

GREENWOOD LODGE AND CAMPSITES, *P.O. Box 246, Bennington VT 05201. Located on Route 9, eight miles east of Bennington (just west of Woodford State Park). Tel. 802/442-2547. Rates: $14. Open May 15 through the third week in October.*

A great option for those interested in cheap lodging, Greenwood features a hostel and 30 campsites for tents and trailers on a 120 acre parcel in the midst of woods and wilderness. Amenities include restrooms and showers, a dump station, and electric hookups. On-site recreation facilities include a rec room, playing field, horseshoe pits, and a basketball court. The nearby Long Trail and Adams Reservoir at Woodford State Park offer excellent opportunities for hiking, biking, fishing and swimming.

PINE HOLLOW CAMPGROUND, *RR1 Box 343, Pownal VT 05261. Located on Barbers Pond Road 6.5 miles south of Bennington on Route 7. Tel. 802/823-5569, Fax 802/823-5569. Rates: $14-$18. Major credit cards accepted. Open mid-May through mid-October.*

Situated on Barbers Pond, Pine Hollow features 50 campsites for tents and trailers in grassy and wooded areas; showers, ice, and firewood are available at extra cost. The pond and its surrounding environs offer opportunities for trout fishing (catch and release), swimming, hiking, and biking.

WHERE TO EAT

If Bennington and Arlington are unable to satsify your desires for haute cuisine (Arlington can make a pretty good case for itself), consider paying a visit to Manchester (25 miles north of Bennington, 10 miles north of Arlington), or the Mount Snow region (25 miles east on Route 9 and Route 100) – both of which are well endowed with high-end dining establishments. They are listed in the "Manchester & the Heart of the Green Mountains" and the "Mount Snow" chapters, respectively.

Arlington

ARLINGTON INN, *Route 7A, Arlington VT 05250. Tel. 802/375-6532. Hours: opens nightly at 5:30pm, closes around 11pm. Major credit cards accepted. Reservations required.*

Set in a stately 19th century Greek Revival mansion, the Arlington Inn serves superb haute cuisine in a setting that is nothing short of elegant. You will sit at an immaculately set table, complete with white tablecloth and candles, in a classicly decorated Victorian dining room. Romantic intimacy is enhanced by a crackling fire in winter and beautiful flowers in summer.

The food itself, which may by enhanced by your choice from an extensive wine list, combines the best and freshest of local ingredients with classic and nouveau French and American recipes, such as roasted Long Island Duckling in pear and port sauce and venison tournedos in wild mushroom marsala souce. Appetizers include a classic French onion soup and a Caesar salad, as well as American and French classics such as escargot (snails) in a puff pastry and Maine crab cakes. The dessert tray is typically loaded with an assortment of sinfully rich and delicious pastries, ice cream, and sorbets. Prices range from $5.50-$9 for soups and appetizers, and from $19-$26 for entrees.

WEST MOUNTAIN INN, *River Road (off Route 313 west from Route 7A in Arlington), Arlington VT 05250. Tel. 802/375-6516. Hours: 8am-9:30am for breakfast; 6pm for hor d'oevres, dinner served 6:30-8:30; 9am-1pm for Sunday brunch. Credit cards: major credit cards accepted.*

This cozy, intimate, and elegant inn's restaurant specializes in creative and innovative country and continental cuisine. Dinners are "semi a la carte," meaning that there is a prix fixe five course meal for $35 that offers some choice for appetizers and entrees. Appetizers typically include three choices, including a soup and a daily special. This is followed by a green salad and a sorbet to refresh your pallet before taking on the entrees. Entree offerings often include a number of interesting choices, such as apple smoked pork chops in cherry sauce with candied sweet potatoes, ratatouille stuffed peppers with cous cous and leeks, veal cordon bleu and black angus filet mignon. For desserts, you may choose from an array of pastries and cakes, or take sorbet or ice cream. Reservations are required for those not staying at the inn as residents.

EAST ARLINGTON CAFE, *located on Old Mill Road East Arlington Village off Route 7, Exit 3 (head west from the exit), and east of Arlington and Route 7A off Route 313, East Arlington VT 05250. Tel. 802/375-6412. Open for lunch and dinner Tuesday-Saturday in winter, Sunday in summer and fall. Credit cards: Visa, Mastercard.*

This casual and cozy eatery serves a variety a freshly prepared and tasty foods for lunch and dinner, including soups, salads, sandwiches and burgers, pasta, steak, and poultry.

CHAUNCEY'S, *Route 7A (two miles north of Arlington Village), Arlington VT 05250. Tel. 802/375-1222. Breakfast hours: 7am-10:30am Tuesday-Saturday, 7am-12:30pm Sunday. Lunch: 11:30am-2pm Tuesday-Saturday, 12:30pm-3pm Sunday. Dinner: 5:30pm-9pm Friday & Saturday. Closed Mondays. Credit cards: Visa, Mastercard, American Express.*

This casual but classy restaurant specializes in New England-style seafood, pasta, veal, and various combinations thereof, although chicken, steak, and other foods are also available and are more than decent. The lunch menu features smaller portions of the same as well as sandwiches, soups, and salads. For breakfast, you can choose from pancakes, egg dishes, rolls, muffins and pastries.

THE SUGAR SHACK, *Route 7A, Arlington VT 05252. Tel. 802/375-6747. Hours vary, but generally open 9am-5pm. Credit cards: Visa, Mastercard.*

Situated on a working farm, the Sugar Shack is a bake shop, sugar house, and antique shop all wrapped into one. They sell a wonderful array of pies, and maple products as well as deli items like sandwiches.

Bennington
THE FOUR CHIMNEY'S, *21 West Road, Old Bennington VT 05201. Tel. 802/447-3500. Credit cards: major credit cards accepted. Open 11:30am-2pm, 5pm until about 10pm; Sunday noon-2pm and 5pm-9pm. Open only for lunch on Monday.*

The Four Chimney's offers superb continental and American cuisine in a typical country inn setting. The rotating menu is limited and usually features lamb, fish (often salmon), and fowl, but the wine list is extensive. Prices generally range from $7-$15 for lunch and from $15-$35 for dinner.

BENNINGTON STATION, *150 Depot Street, Bennington. Tel. 802/ 447-1080. Open daily from 11:30am-4pm, 4:30pm-9pm (10pm on Friday & Saturday); Sunday 11am-2:30pm (brunch) & 4pm-8pm. Major credit cards accepted.*

This wood-paneled restored railroad station features an extensive menu of steak, seafood, pasta, poultry, and sandwiches with prices ranging from $7-$25. The food is excellent and the service is friendly and professional. The create-your-own-pasta is a signature dish.

ALLDAYS AND ONIONS, *519 Main Street, Bennington VT 05201. Tel. 802/447-0043. Open daily from 8am until about 10pm. Credit cards: Visa, Mastercard.*

This popular downtown restaurant is known for its omelets, pasta, sandwiches and lunch, and slightly more hearty fare at night. Prices are reasonable with virtually everything costing under $15. Live entertainment is featured every Wednesday and when the weather permits, there is outdoor dining.

GEANNELIS' RESTAURANT, *925 East Main Street, Benninton VT 05201. Tel. 802/442-9833. Open daily 7am-8pm. Credit cards: Visa, Mastercard.*

Another popular eatery, Geannelis' food has a home-cooked taste that is particularly enjoyable at breakfast when you can feast on great french toast, egg dishes and other goodies. Breakfast and lunch also feature tasty renditions of your favorite American dishes and soups. Takeout available.

JAKES STEAK & SEAFOOD AT THE AUTUMN INN, *924 East Main Street Route 9), Bennington VT 05201. Tel. 802/447-7625. Hours: 4pm-9pm nightly, open for breakfast and lunch according to season and demand. Credit cards: Visa, Mastercard, American Express.*

Offerings include a variety of decent but not out-of-this-world steak and seafood dishes like calamari, shrimp, pasta, and grilled and fried fish. Appetizers include soups and salads. Prices range from $2-$7 for appetizers and $8-$16 for entrees. When the weather is warm, diners can sit outside on the terrace.

THE VERMONT STEAKHOUSE, *716 East Main Street (Route 9), Bennington VT 05201. Tel. 802/447-1226. Hours: 11am-midnight daily. Credit cards: Visa, Mastercard.*

Specializing in steak and other typical American poultry, seafood, and pasta dishes, the Vermont Steakhouse offers satisfying meals and good value (entrees range from $8-$18). There is also a lounge with a full bar and smoking section.

PARADISE RESTAURANT, *141 Main Street (Route 9), Bennington VT 05201. Tel. 802/442-5418. Hours: 11:30am-9pm daily. Credit cards: Visa, Mastercard, American Express.*

Situated in the motor inn of the same name, the Paradise Restaurant offers a relaxed and casual setting in which to enjoy pasta, roast chicken, or steak and other meats such as veal. The food is essentially American but with some ethnic flavors thrown in, as in the pastas. The establishment includes a bar and lounge, as well as a terrace where you might enjoy dining during the summer or on warm fall and spring nights. Prices are affordable (entrees range from $9-$15) – a good place for a family meal.

SONNY'S BLUE BENN DINER, *Route 7 (one mile of the junction of with Route 9), Bennington VT 05201 Tel. 802/442-8977. Hours: 5am-10 or 11pm. No credit cards.*

"Blue Benn," as the locals call it, is by far and away Bennington's favorite diner. Intimate (a euphimism for "cramped" in this case) and colorful, its menu features an interesting mix of diner favorites like burgers and eggs, as well as foods like tofu and vegetarian dishes that cater to college kids and granola types.

KAY'S COUNTRY BAKE SHOP & CIDER MILL, *Route 9 (west of downtown Bennington), Bennington VT 05201. Tel. 802/442-4459. Open from May 1 through the Christmas – New Year's holiday season 8am-6pm. Major credit cards accepted.*

A sort of hybrid Vermont deli-bakeshop, Kay's serves great soups and sandwiches as well as Vermont specialty foods, cider, and whatever produce is in season.

SEEING THE SIGHTS
Bennington

Situated at the junction ("Malfunction Junction") of Routes 7 and 9, **Bennington** is most famous for the Revolutionary War battle that bears its name (but was actually fought in New York) and the 306-foot obelisk monument built in honor of that early American victory. But while Bennington's greatest claim to fame is a battle that was not actually fought there, it does feature prominently in Vermont history and is home to some of the more impressive historical sites in the state. The majority of these attractions are located along West Main Street (Route 9 west of the junction with Route 7) and in the western part of Bennington to which it leads, known as **Old Bennington**. It is here that we begin the tour.

HEMMING MOTOR NEWS, *West Main Street (Route 9) just beyond the second light west of the intersection with Route 7, Bennington VT 802/447-1571. Hours: 9am-5pm Monday through Friday.*

Old car afficianados will recognize the *Hemmings Motor News* as a bible of sorts for those interested in antique automobiles. Their publishing headquarters, located here, features an auto-modfied shop full of books, posters, and other souvenirs, as well as a vintage filling station and several beautiful old cars.

ONE WAY TO SEE BENNINGTON

*One of the most fascinating and informative ways to approach sightseeing in Bennington is to join a tour and attend a lecture given by **Tordis Isselhardt**, a local historian and guide based at the **Bennington Center/Images from the Past** (her shop) at 155 West Main Street in Bennington (Tel. 802/442-3202). Her lectures consist of slide shows with historical photographs, which in combination with her engaging tours and lectures, are very effective in bringing the past back to life. The Center also features a small shop selling Bennington and Vermont-related paraphernalia. Call to arrange a tour and to learn shop hours, as they vary according to her tour schedule.*

THE BENNINGTON MUSEUM, *West Main Street (one mile west of the junction of Routes 7 and 9), Bennington VT 05201. Tel. 802/447-1571. Hours: 9am-5pm daily from March 1-December 23; 9am-5pm on Saturdays, Sundays & holidays only January 2 through the end of February. Group tours available. Admission: $5 adults, children under 12 are admitted free of charge.*

As the museum literature so accurately states, the Bennington Museum presents "Americana at its best," from the largest collection of work by folk artist **Grandma Moses** to vintage Continental Army uniforms and the Stars & Stripes flag (thought to be the oldest in existence) flown at the Battle of Bennington.

One of the oldest – founded in 1875, it moved to this site in 1928 – and best endowed museums in Vermont in terms of the variety and quality of its exhibits, the Benninton Museum features more than ten galleries, ranging from the Grandma Moses Room and her relocated schoolhouse to the Bennington Pottery Gallery. History buffs will be interested in the collection of Revolutionary War era paraphernalia, including objects in the Church Gallery – so named because it was formerly part of the St. Francis de Sales Roman Catholic Church – such as money issued by the Republic of Vermont, and one of Ethan Allen's bar tabs from the famed Catamount Tavern (see sidebar below).

Meanwhile, those interested in art will probably enjoy the pottery, painting, glass, and historic furniture and tool displays.

GRANDMA MOSES

Few artists have projected an ideal of Vermont to so many Americans as Anna Mary Roberston Moses. Born in 1860 across the state line in Eagle Bridge, New York (from whence the schoolhouse in the museum was relocated in 1972), Anna Moses lived virtually a full life as a farmer's wife before becoming a national sensation at the age of 80 (which explains the title "Grandma") – when one of her exhibits caught on with critics in New York City.

Recalling an earlier and simpler age when life revolved around the farm, the church, and the local community, both Grandma Moses and her paintings seemed to speak to a nostalgic America as it entered World War II and the fast-paced word of technology, television, and electronic communications. An immediate celebrity, Grandma Moses received audiences with President Truman and other politicians, a string of honorary degrees, and was even featured on the cover of Time magazine. She passed away in 1961 at the age of 100; the largest collection of her work is here at the Bennington Museum.

THE OLD FIRST CHURCH & THE OLD BURYING GROUND, *West Main Street (Route 9) just up the hill from the Bennington Museum, Bennington VT 05201. Open to the public during the summer.*

Atop the hill at the end of West Main Street, above the Bennington Museum and down the street from the Bennington Monument, stands the oft-neglected **Old First Church** and the **Old Burying Ground**, final resting place of poet and part-time Vermont resident **Robert Frost**. Designed by architect Lavius Fillmore and built in 1806, the white wooden church with a square tower featuring an open belfry and Palladian windows is a true beauty. But it is the cemetery, and specifically Frost's grave, that attracts most attention. You shouldn't have any problem finding the site, which is behind the church, because there are signs throughout to lead you, but nor should you rush through the rest of the cemetery either, for it contains many vintage and fascinating Colonial-era headstones – many of which mark the graves of soldiers from the Battle of Bennington, including British redcoats and Hessian mercenaries in addition to Continental Army soldiers. Also resting here are five Vermont Governors and many prominent members of the Bennington community from throughout the town's history.

Frost himself is buried with his wife and children at a site marked by two simple marble stones. Under his beloved wife Elinor's grave are the words, "Together wing to wing and oar to oar." His own name is accompanied by Frost's classic phrase, "I have a lover's quarrel with the world."

Old Bennington – Monument Avenue & The Bennington Monument

At the Old First Church, there is an intersection between Route 9 and **Monument Avenue**, a quiet street lined with trees and stately 19th century buildings that marks the beginning of **Old Bennington**. Bennington was the first town chartered by New Hampshire west of the Connecticut River (1749), and it was on this street that many of its earliest prominent citizens lived, including Ethan Allen and Isaac Tichenor who served as Governor of Vermont.

Monument Avenue was also the site of the famous **Catamount Tavern** where the Green Mountain Boys met for refreshments and to plan their political and military operations. Here also was the weapons cache which the British attempted to capture in August 1777, provoking the Battle of Bennington which marked the beginning of the turning of the tide against the British in the Champlain Valley. Most visitors make their way to the northern end of Monument Avenue and the towering **Bennington Monument**; if you make your way to the southern end, you will find yourself at **Southern Vermont College** and the 1914 mansion of Edward H. Everret. A turn of the century masterpiece, it is open to the public during regular business hours in the summer.

THE BENNINGTON MONUMENT, *located on the northern end of Monument Avenue off Route 9 (turn right) about one mile west of the intersection with Route 7, Bennington VT 05201. Tel. 802/828-3051 (Division for Historic Preservation in Montpelier). Hours: 9am-5pm daily from mid-April through October 31. Admission: $1.*

Standing 306 feet, 4.5 inches and built of Sand Hilly Dolomite from Hudson Falls, New York, the obelisk-shaped Bennington Monument is the city's signature landmark and one of the tallest battle monuments in the world. Indeed its grandeur – especially given that the battle, while significant, was by no means the most important of the war – seems out of place in Vermont where architectural beauty is typically characterized by modesty and simplicity.

Financed by monies collected from Vermont, New Hampshire, Massachusetts, and the federal government by the Bennington Historical Society, the monument's construction began in 1887 and was completed in 1891, in time to celebrate the centennial of Vermont's admission to the Union. Designed by Boston architect John Phillip Rinn, it features a 37 square foot base, more than 400 steps, and is topped by a gilt star. Other monuments on the site include a plaque dedicated to John Stark by New Hampshire in 1977, and a handsome statue of Seth Warmer erected in 1910. In 1952, the Bennington Monument Association handed owner-

THE BATTLE OF BENNINGTON

In the summer of 1777, the future of Vermont and the 13 Colonies fighting for their independence from Britain was in flux. Vermont, whose citizens had been in a constant struggle to free themselves from both New York and New Hampshire who claimed the territory as their own, had declared its independence and became the Republic of Vermont on July 7. Meanwhile, British regiments under **General John Burgoyne** *were rapidly advancing down the Champlain Valley, threatening to cut off New England from the rest of the colonies, a potentially fatal blow for the aspiring Republic. As August approached, the British forces threatened to take a substantial cache of arms located in Old Bennington. Alarmed and threatened, the infant Republic of Vermont secretly appealed to New Hampshire for assistance. It was granted and a force of 2,000 consisting mostly of untrained farmers from New Hampshire and Massachusetts was assembled under the leadership of* **John Stark**, *a veteran of the early struggles of Bunker Hill and Valley Forge.*

On August 16 after a hard rain on the 15th, this ragtag force launched a surprise attack on Burgoyne's army at Wallomsac Heights five miles north of Bennington. Inspired according to legend by Stark's battlecry, "They will be ours or Molly Stark will lie a widow," the Americans fought bravely and were initially successful as the British were caught off guard by the attack and slow to recover because of the rain and mud. However, the Red Coats mustered a counterattack and Stark's men were falling back when the Green Mountain Boys under the command of Seth Warner arrived from Manchester and sent the British and their Hessian allies into retreat back north.

The price of 800 dead, wounded and prisoners was costly for Burgoyne whose new vulnerability caught up with him later that October when he surrendered after another defeat after the Battle of Ticonderoga. This was a major turning point in the war as pro-independence forces regained control of the Champlain Valley and removed the threat of the severance of northern New Engand and New York from the rest of the colonies.

ship of the monument to the state. Today, visitors can enter the monument, but fear not, an elevator is now used to transport folks to the top where the view of surrounding landscapes, though hampered by the rock slits, is impressive. There is also a small diorama at the entrance which recreates the battle, speaking of which, you should remeber did not take place here, but five miles to the northwest in New York State.

Route 9 West of Monument Avenue

Continuing west on **Route 9**, you will soon find yourself in New York, but not before passing Bennington's finest inn, the **Four Chimney's Inn & Restaurant**; the huge **Camelot Village Craft Center**; the **Bennington Center for the Arts**; and the **Vermont Confectionary**, a candy-lover's delight.

Back Downtown

Retracing your steps on Route 9/East Main Street will take you back to the "Four Corners," another name for the Route 9-Route 7 intersection. This newer downtown replaced Old Bennington as the city center in the 1820's and 1830's when mills were developed along the Walloomsac River, and the hillsides of Old Bennington proved inadequate as sites for factories and lacked access to major highways for transporting goods. The factories have long gone dormant, but the 19th century brick buildings remain as a reminder of Bennington's industrial past. Today, most contain offices, shops, and other businesses; the marble post office is particularly impressive.

South of Downtown on Route 7

Unless you are a racing fanatic on your way to Pownal, there is little of note on the Green Mountain State's side of the border, apart from the modest Lake Potter and Barker Pond. However, just over the state line in Massachusetts is **Williamstown**, home of the prestigious **Willliams College** and the **Clark Museum of Art**, featuring an impressive collection of European and American art, including more than a dozen Renoirs.

West of Bennington on Route 9

Take Route 9 west from downtown Bennington, and before you can say "Ethan Allen" you will find yourself in the thick of the Green Mountain National Forest in one of the largest undeveloped tracts of land in the state. Twelve miles on to the right you will come to **Woodford State Park**, one of the area's premier destinations for folks seeking to enjoy the outdoors.

During the summer, campsites are available for trails and tents, and **Adams Reservoir** provides a venue for boating, fishing, swimming and hiking. It is also in this region (about 4 miles west of the park) that the **Appalachian** and **Long Trails** (by this time merged) pass through the area. In the winter, trails in the park are used by cross-country skiers and showshoers. For further information, contact the park – *Tel. 802/447-7169 (summer), 483-2001 (off-season)* – or the **Green Mountain National Forest**, *P.O. Box 519, Rutland VT 05702, Tel. 802/773-0300 or 773-0324*. Also see the "Where to Stay" section above for information about camping and the "Sports & Recreation" section below for tips about hiking, biking, skiing, and snowmobiling.

Beyond Woodford State Park, Route 9 winds its way up the Green Mountains towards **Wilimington** and the popular resort area around **Mt. Snow** 20 miles from Bennington. One of the most popular destinations for skiers and tourists in Vermont, this region is well developed and features many quality inns and restaurants in addition to excellent skiing in the winter and golf and hiking in the summer and fall. (See the "Mt. Snow" chapter for details.) From Wilimington you can take Route 100 North up through the Green Mountains to virtually every major ski area in the state including Killington, the Mad River Valley, and Stowe; or you can continue east another 20 miles to **Brattleboro** and the Connecticut River Valley (see the "Windham County" chapter). Route 100 South takes you straight to **Massachusetts** by way of **Whitingham**, significant as the birthplace of Mormon leader Brigham Young.

North of Bennington

For many visitors, Bennington is a simple landmark on the way to destinations north along Route 7 such as Manchester, Rutland, Middlebury and Burlington. However, there is much to be explored between Bennington and Manchester, not the least of which is the handsome scenery along Route 67 and 67A, and Historic Route 7A, which you should take in any case unless you're in a massive hurry.

North Bennington

Taking **North Street** (Route 7) from downtown will lead you to an intersection with Northside Drive (just beyond the well marked Chamber of Commerce offices). From this intersection, continue straight to stay on Route 7, the most direct route to Manchester and beyond; or turn west (left) on Northside drive to **North Bennington**, which begins at the fork of the road with 67A continuing west and Route 7A going north. Even if you intend to head north, I'd recommend taking **Route 67A** along the Walloomsac River and then bearing right on **Route 67** which then connects with Route 7A – it's only a five mile loop, but offers you the chance to see three covered bridges, and if you have the time, to visit the **Park-McCullough House**, a beauty of a Victorian Mansion dating to the 1860's (see below).

About a mile beyond the intersection with Route 7A on Route 67A, on the right, is **Bennington College**. The city's premier institution for higher education, Bennington College is small liberal arts college (just over 500 students), known for its liberal and feminist politics – it was originally a women's college but is now coed – and in the mid-1980's made headlines for its tuition costs ($17,000-plus) which at the time was the highest in the nation and deemed by critics to be out of proportion to the quality of education provided, which was not exactly on a par with Harvard or Princeton.

Almost immediately opposite Bennington College, on the south side of Northside Drive, is Silk Road and the **Silk Covered Bridge** over the picturesque Walloomsac River. Built in the 1840's and named for a local family, Silk Bridge is the first of three along Route 67A. To visit the second and third bridges, continue on Route 67A and turn right on **Murphy Road**. This will take you by (not through as traffic has been closed since 1986) the **Paper Mill Bridge**, dating to 1889. Continue along Murphy Road and make the clockwise loop back to Route 67A and you will pass through the **Henry Bridge**. Named for a store owner from a prominent local family named Henry, whose name is also attached to the nearby classy little inn (see "Where to Stay" above), the bridge was originally constructed in 1840 and completely renovated in 1989.

THE VERMONT VALLEY FLYER SCENIC RAILWAY

*One of the most enjoyable ways to enjoy the beauty of Vermont is to spend an afternoon riding through the countryside on one of the old-fashioned trains operated by the Green Mountain Railroad Corps. This outfit operates three main routes, including Chester-Bellow Falls, Burlington-Middlebury, and the **Vermont Valley Flyer** between **Manchester** and **Arlington**, which during the autumn (mid-September through mid-October) is extended to **North Bennington**. The Valley Flyer is a vintage 1940's train that takes a beautiful route through the Valley between the Taconic and Green Mountain ranges, along the Battenkill, and past such landmarks as Mt. Equinox and the Hildene estate.*

From July 3 until September 6 there are two departures daily from Manchester (11am & 2pm) and Arlington (11:45am & 2:45pm). A round-trip either way takes one hour and 15 minutes and costs $10 for each adult and $6 for children aged 3-12. When the route is extended to North Bennington, there are two departures daily from Manchester (10am & 2pm) to Arlington and two from N. Bennington (11:45am & 3:45om) to Arlington. Trains depart Arlington for Manchester at 12:25 pm and 4:25pm, and for North Bennington at 10:40am and 2:40pm. A round-trip between North Bennington and Manchester takes three hours and costs $14 per adult and $10 per child aged 3-12. Call 802/463-3069 for details and directions to train platforms.

Back on Route 67A continue north on Park Street and follow the signs for the Park-McCullough House. on West Street:

PARK-MCCULLOUGH HOUSE, *located at the corner of Park and West Streets, North Bennington. Tel. 802/442-5441. Open late May through October daily except Tuesday and Wednesday from 10am-3pm. Admission: $5 adult, $4 seniors, $3 children 12-17 years, children under 12 enter free.*

Built by Trenor Park during the Civil War, this knock-your socks-off 35 room mansion was the home of Vermont Governor **John McCullough** (1902-1904). It remained in the family until 1965 when it was turned over to the state and listed on the National Register of Historic Places. Visitors can take guided tours of the mansion with its classic Victorian decor and furnishings, and grounds featuring beautifully maintained gardens, a carriage house, and a gem of a children's playhouse. During the summer, **concerts** are periodically given on the grounds; contact the museum office or check out local publications for performance schedules.

Route 7A to Arlington

From the Park-McCullough House, turn right on West Street to get on Route 67 which you take north and east to get on Historic Route 7A, the major stagecoach highway in the region during the 18th and 19th centuries. Just north of the intersection is the quaint hamlet of Shaftsbury. Historic **Shaftsbury Village** features numerous buildings dating to the 18th and 19th centuries, including the home of Governor Joshua Galusha (1809-1813), the local Greek Revival-style academy, a Baptist Church, and a handsome Town House. Located in the former Baptist Meeting House is the **Shaftsbury Historical Society** featuring several modest museum exhibits concerning local history. *Entrance is free and the Society is open from 2pm-4pm Monday through Saturday from early June to mid-October.*

North of Shaftsbury village to the east (right coming from the south, lies **Lake Shaftsbury State Park,** *Tel. 802/375-9978/summer, Tel. 802/483-2001/off-season,* a popular venue for camping, hiking, picnicing, swimming, and fishing during the summer. See "Sports & Recreation" below for information about recreation at Lake Shaftsbury.

Arlington

Located roughly 15 miles north of Bennington and 10 miles south of Manchester, **Arlington** is home to a number of interesting attractions such as the Norman Rockwell Museum and several covered bridges, as well as a handful of very fine inns, restaurants, and shops. First settled in the 1760's, Arlington was known as a hotbed of Tory sympathizers during the Revolutionary Era, though many prominent American and Vermont nationalists (Vermont was an independent republic from 1777-1791) like Ethan Allen and Thomas Chittenden (the first governor of Vermont) lived here as well. Later it became a minor industrial center with a variety of mills and a railroad car factory.

Arlington's **historic district** situated along the Roaring Branch River on E. Arlington Road, Old Mill Road and Maple Street, is dotted with buildings dating to the 18th and 19th centuries, and is now home to numermous shops and eateries. On East Arlington Street you can also check out the covered **Chiselville Bridge**. More than 100 feet long, it was built in 1870. A second covered bridge, the **West Arlington Bridge**, spans the Battenkill River on the other side of Route 7A off Route 313. Particularly photogenic, it was built in 1852.

NORMAN ROCKWELL EXHIBITION AND GIFT SHOP, *Route 7A, Arlington VT 05252. Tel. 802/375-6423. Hours: 9am-5pm daily. Admission: $2.*

Located in a small reconverted church, this small exhibition contains hundreds of illustrations, paintings, ads, and other works by the master of Americana, Norman Rockwell. Best known for his work for the *Saturday Evening Post*, Rockwell lived in Arlington from 1939 to 1953 on the Covered Bridge Green in West Arlington near the West Arlington covered bridge. He often described his time in Vermont as the best in his life, but he felt the need to move back to Massachusetts after his wife fell ill. Here you can watch a 15 minute video about his life and work, and take a tour guided by local men and women, some of whom served as models for Rockwell more than 40 years ago.

North of Arlington Village

Roughly five miles north of Arlington Village is the **Skyline Drive** turnoff for **Mt. Equinox**, where during the summer and autumn you can enjoy some of the most spectacular views in Vermont. A toll road ($6 per vehicle), Skyline Drive is steep and winding, so be careful. There is an inn at the top (see "Where to Stay" above) and hiking trails around the summit. A great place for a family hike and picnic.

Manchester (including Manchester Village and Manchester Center) is approximately 10 miles north of Arlington on Route7 and Route 7A.

NIGHTLIFE & ENTERTAINMENT

Performing Arts

During the summer especially, you can expect a smattering of major acts to pass through the region, including the Vermont Symphony Orchestra, the Vermont Mozart Society, and others from out of state. Many appear in the context of **Summer Under the Tent**, a series of concerts held every Wednesday through Saturday for a month from mid-July to mid-August. Look in local publications for information or call the Bennington Area Chamber of Commerce, *Tel. 802/447-3311.* A variety of

BENNINGTON & ARLINGTON AREA EVENTS

First Night Bennington – *December 31. A family-friendly, substance-free New Year's celebration including food, music, arts, and fire works.*

Mayfest Craft Fair – *Memorial Day Weekend. A celebration of crafts with art vendors, exhibitions, and classes as well as food and entertainment. Held in downtown Bennington.*

Ethan Allen Days – *3rd weekend in June. A reenactment of a Revolutionary Battle held in Arlington.*

4th of July – *A parade is held in Bennington while Willow Park is the site of a celebration including food, live music, and of course fireworks.*

Summer Under the Tent – *Wednesday-Saturday mid-July through mid-August. A series of concerts held in downtown Bennington.*

Bennington Battle Day – *August 16. On this unique Vermont holiday, Bennington holds a parade and sponsors a variety of other activities including games, music, and firemen's competitions. Of course all sorts of food is available.*

Festival of Tree's – *Thanksgiving-early December. The Bennington Museum sponsors a display of colorfully decorated trees, wreaths and other Christmasy items, which are judged in a competition.*

Second Weekend After Labor Day – *The third weekend in September sees the* **Annual Antique Auto & Motorcycle Show** *in Bennington and* **Quiltfest,** *a celebration of quilts with vendors, demonstrations, and displays.*

For more details, contact the Brattleboro Area Chamber of Commerce, Tel. 802/447-3311, Fax 802/447-1163. E-mail: benncham@sover.net. Web site: www.bennington.com.

music and theater is also featured throughout at the year at **Bennington Center for the Arts** (see below), the **Park-McCullough House** off Route 67, *Tel. 802/442-5441;* and at educational institutions such as **Bennington College**, *Tel. 802/442-5401*, **Southern Vermont College**, *Tel. 802/442-5427*, and the **Sonatina School of Music**, *Tel. 802/442-9197, 5 Catamount Lane, Bennington, VT 05401.*

BENNINGTON CENTER FOR THE ARTS, *Gypsy Lane (west of the Bennington Monument off Route 9), Bennington VT 05201. Tel. 802/447-0564. Art exhibits and performances are featured from April through December.*

The Bennington Center for the Arts is a multiplex for the arts featuring two theaters for the performing arts in addition to four art galleries. The galleries (open Tuesday-Sunday 11am-5pm) are used for a variety of exhibits every year ranging from painting and photography to

Native American sculpture, while theaters are employed from May through October for concerts and plays. The Bennington Center for the Arts is the home of the **Old Castle Theatre Company**, a professional theater troupe since 1972 that puts on several plays and musicals annually.

Bars & Lounges

In Bennington, there are several popular drinking spots on East Main Street, such as **Carmody's** and the **Madison Brewery**. Many of the restaurants listed above also contain some sort of bar, but there's little in the way of raging nightclubs.

SHOPPING

Listed below is just a sampling of the shopping opportunities in the Bennington-Arlington area. For a complete listing, contact the **Arlington Chamber of Commerce,** *P.O. Box 245 (Route 7A), Arlington VT 05250, Tel. 802/375-2800, Fax 802/442-5494, Web site: www.arlingtonvt.com;* or the **Bennington Area Chamber of Commerce**, *Veterans's Memorial Drive (Route 7 North), Bennington VT 05401, Tel. 802/447-3311, Fax 802/447-1163, E-mail: benncham@sover.net, Web site: www.bennington.com.*

Serious shoppers (as well as serious eaters and sightseers) should consider paying a visit to **Manchester**, 25 miles north of Bennington (10 miles north of Arlington), where in Manchester Center there are dozens of high-end outlet stores, antique dealers, and crafts shops. See the "Manchester & the Heart of the Green Mountains" chapter for details.

Arlington & East Arlington

CANDLE MILL VILLAGE, *East Arlington-West Wardsboro Road aka "Old Mill Road" (turn east just off Route 7A just south of Route 313), East Arlington VT 05252. Tel. 800/772-3759. Major credit cards accepted.*

Candle Mill Village is a complex of shops including The Music Box Shop, The Happy Cook (cooking accessories), The Cookbook Corner, and The Candle Mill Shop (where you can dip your own candles). Call for details about particular shops.

EAST ARLINGTON ANTIQUES, *two outlets on Maple Street, and Old Mill Road in East Arlington VT 05252. Tel. 802/375-9607/375-6144. Open daily 9am-5pm. Credit cards: Visa, Mastercard.*

These two locales serve as outets for more than 100 local antique dealers and crafts-people. One is located in an old movie theater, the other in an old post office – both worth a visit.

THE SUGAR SHACK, *Route 7A, Arlington VT 05252. Tel. 802/375-6747. generally open during normal business hours 9am-5pm. Credit cards: Visa, Mastercard.*

Situated on a farm along the Roaring Branch River, the Sugar Shack sells an interesting array of maple products, baked goods, antiques, and country versions of deli sandwiches.

BENNINGTON POTTERY

*Just as Quechee is known for glassblowing and Johnson is famous for textiles and clothing, so Bennington is synonymous in the Vermont artistic community with pottery. The industry actually took root here in the late 19th century when **Norton Pottery** – which remained in business until 1894 – began producing high quality, functional, but beautiful earthenware distinguished by its cobalt-blue decorations. In the 19th century, the **United States Pottery Company** also earned a nationwide reputation for its granite and clay jars and containers.*

*Quality examples from both companies can be found in the Bennington Museum on Main Street, and while both have gone out of business, the pottery tradition is continued at the **Bennington Potters' Yard** at 324 County Street where the Bennington Potters have been producing high quality jars, vases and other beautiful pieces for more than 50 years. You can take a tour of the factory and purchase items for wholesale prices – just be sure to pack them well because they're undoubtedly very fragile. To find the Yard, turn east off North Street/Route 7 three blocks north of the intersection of Route 7 & Route 9. Tel. 802/447-7531. Hours: 9:30am-8pm Monday-Saturday, noon-5:30pm Sunday. Major credit cards accepted.*

Bennington

THE APPLE BARN & COUNTRY BAKE SHOP, *Route 7 (south of downtown Bennington), Benninton VT 05201. Tel. 802/447-7780, 888/APPLES. Open daily 9am-6pm (later during Christmas holiday season). Major credit cards accepted.*

A Vermont specialty food store selling maple products, chocolates and fudge, wines, baked goods, and as the name suggests all sorts of apple-related products such as cider and apple pie. Goods can be shipped.

CRAFT CENTER AT CAMELOT VILLAGE, *Route 9 – 60 West Road (west of downtown and Monument Avenue), Bennington VT 05201. Tel. 802/447-2979. Hours: 9:30am-5:30pm daily. Major credit cards accepted.*

Features a variety of shops, including a huge antique center featuring the wares of more than 100 dealers, as well as all types of gifts, souvenirs, and Vermont specialty foods like maple products and cheeses.

STONEWALL'S ANTIQUES, *136 Monument Avenue (.5 mile south of Old First Church), Bennington VT 05201. Tel. 802/447-1628. Hours: 10am-5 pm "or by chance." Credit cards: Visa, Mastercard.*

Classic New England antiques for sale including furniture, china, silver, and other household accessories.

SPORTS & RECREATION

Biking

Apart from Route 7 between Bennington and Manchester, most of the roads in the Bennington area are not only viable for cycling, but scenic as well, particularly along the **Walloomsac** and **Battenkill** rivers and in the **Green Mountain National Forest** east of Route 7 and along Route 9 east of Bennington. *Vermont Life* magazine publishes a map of Vermont (*"Vermont Life Bicycle Vermont Map & Guide"*) with directions and cycling routes through the state, including one through Bennington and Alrington. Cyclists should also consider consulting the book *25 Bicycle Tours in Vermont* (Back Country Publications) by John S. Freidin, also available throughout the state. For information and maps of trails in the Green Mountain National Forest, write or call Green Mountain National Forest, *P.O. Box 519, Rutland VT 05702, Tel. 802/773-0300 or -0324.*

Mountain bikes can be rented in Bennington at **Cutting Edge North** in Bennington, *Tel. 802/442-8664.*

Boating & Canoeing

The Battenkill River, which runs along Route 313 off Route 7A at Arlington, is considered one of the most beautiful in Vermont and is excellent for canoeing. For lake-style canoeing or boating, you can rent rowboats at Lake Shaftsbury in the **Lake Shaftsbury State Park** off Route 7A between and Bennington and Arlington, *Tel. 802/375-9978;* and rowboats and canoes at Adams Reservoir in **Woodford State Park** about 12 miles east of Bennington on Route 9, *Tel. 802/447-7169.*

BATTENKILL CANOE LTD, *Route 7A Box 2445-1, Arlington VT 05250. Tel. 802/363-2800, 800/421-5268. E-mail: bk@bettenkill.com. Web site: www.battenkill.com. Open daily 9am-4:30pm April 15 through November 1. Major credit cards accepted.* ·

The combination of the Battenkill River and the Green Mountains is a winner for folks who love the outdoors, and for those interested in spending more than just a few hours out on the trail, Battenkill Canoe Ltd. offers a variety of hiking and canoeing expeditions, ranging from day trips to hiking-canoeing adventures lasting up to two weeks. Some of the longer expeditions take travelers from inn to inn while others involve camping, and they will take you not only to Vermont, but Maine and Canada as well.

The shop is open daily from April 15 through November 1, but you can call, e-mail, or fax for information and reservations during the winter.

Cross-Country Skiing

In the immediate vicinity of Bennington, the area in and around **Woodford State Park** 12 miles east of Route 9, *Tel. 802/ 483-2001,* in the Green Mountain National Forest features about 50 miles of trails. Contact the **Prospect Mountain Cross-country Ski Center** in Woodford, *Tel. 802/ 442-2575,* for maps, ski and equipment rentals, guided tours, and instruction.

Within half an hour (or perhaps a bit more depending on conditions) are several cross-country ski centers in the Manchester region 25-30 miles north on Route 7, and the Mount Snow area about 25 miles east of Bennington on Route 9, and north on Route 100 from Wilmington. In Manchester, there are about eight miles of trails around **Hildene,** *Tel. 802/362-1788,* where you can also rent equipment.

There are more options around Mt. Snow and Willington. The **Hermitage Cross-Country Ski Center** on the Handle Road (off Route 100) north of Wilmington, *Tel. 802/464-3511,* features more than 50 kilometers of beautiful trails, and also offers instruction and rentals. Other options include **Sitzmar,** *Tel. 802/464-3384,* with 40 kilometers of trails, instruction, and rentals; **Timber Creek**, *Tel. 802/363-0999,* with 15 kilometers of trails, equipment rentals, and instruction; and the **White House Hotel**, *Tel. 802/464-6578,* with 25 kilometers of trails, rentals, guided tours, and instruction.

Fishing

The **Battenkill** and **Walloomsac** rivers are both quite good for fishing, as are **Lake Shaftsbury** in the Lake Shaftsbury State Park off Route 7A between and Bennington and Arlington, *Tel. 802/375-9978;* **Adams Reservoir** in **Woodford State Park** *about 12 miles east of Bennington on Route 9, Tel. 802/447-7169;* and **Barbers Pond** on Barbers Pond Road in Pownal about 7 miles south of Bennington on Route 7. Boats can be rented at all of these pond and lake locations.

For fishing opportunities beyond the region discussed in this chapter, turn to the "Mt. Snow," "Manchester & the Heart of the Green Mountains," and the "Middlebury & Lower Champlain Valley" chapters.

Golf

Check out the "Mt. Snow" and "Manchester and the Heart of the Green Mountains" chapters for information about other golfing opportunities accessible from the Bennington and Arlington regions.

MT. ANTHONY COUNTRY CLUB, *3 Bank Street. (P.O. Box 947), Bennington VT 05201. Tel. 802/447-7079. Semi-private; 18 holes. Rates: $25 all week. Carts available for rent. Call for tee times. Major credit cards accepted.*

Hiking

There are excellent hiking opportunities throughout the Bennington region, namely along the picturesque **Walloomsac** and **Battenkill** rivers, and in the **Green Mountain National Forest** which technically encompasses the entire region, but whose wilderness is primarily east of Route 7 and on both sides of Route 9. The two state parks, **Woodford State Park** on Route 9 12 miles east of Bennington, *Tel. 802/447-7169/summer, Tel. 802/483-2001/off-season;* and **Lake Shaftsbury State Park** (between Bennington and Arlington off Route 7A, *Tel. 802/375-9978/summer, Tel. 802/483-2001/off-season,* features modest trails around the Adams Reservoir and Lake Shaftsbury respectively. For guided tours and walks (including inn-to-inn tours), contact the **Walking Tours of Southern Vermont** in Arlington, *Tel. 802/375-1141.*

Some of the most rewarding hiking in the region in terms of natural beauty and views is on **Mount Equinox** on Skyline Drive off Route 7A just north of Arlington. To reach the mountaintop and the hiking, you must first drive up a toll road ($6 per vehicle). The mountain (owned by Carthusian monks) is open during the summer and autumn only. Free parking is available at the top.

Also passing through the Green Mountain National Forest in this region are the **Appalachian** and **Long Trails**, which merge to the north near Rutland and run roughly parallel to Route 7 about 10 miles to the east. There are numerous trailheads and possibilities when it comes to hiking these famous trails. For more details contact the **Green Mountain Club**, *Route 100, Waterbury Center VT 05677, Tel. 802/244-7037.* The Club is responsible for maintaining the Long Trail and publishes numerous books, maps and pamphlets about the Long Trail (*The Long Trail: A Footpath in the Wilderness*) and hiking in Vermont generally; many of these publications are readily available at bookstores throughout Vermont. Also, consider contacting the **Green Mountain Forest Service**, *Green Mountain National Forest, P.O. Box 519, Rutland VT 05702, Tel. 802/773-0300 or -0324.* They can provide detailed topographical maps and general information about hiking, camping, and other types of recreation in the Green Mountain National Forest.

Skiing

Two of Vermont's major ski areas, **Mount Snow & Haystack**, *Mount Snow, Tel. 802/464-8092; Haystack, Tel. 802/464-8501,* and **Stratton**, *Tel. 800/STRATTON,* are (assuming decent driving conditions) are 30 and 35 miles respectively and less than an hour's drive from downtown Bennington, and can be reached by going east 20 miles to Wilmington and north on Route 100. Also about 30 miles away, near Manchester, is the **Bromley Mountain** ski area, *Tel. 802/824-5522,* on Route 11.

Snowmobiling

For comprehensive information about snowmobiling in Bennington County and throughout Vermont, contact the **Vermont Association of Snow Travelers** at *P.O. Box 839, Montpelier VT 05601, Tel. 802/229-0005; Tel. 802/229-4202 for trail conditions.*

TWIN BROOKS GUIDED SNOWMOBILE TOURS, *Route 9 (east of Bennington), Woodford VT 05201. Tel. 802/442-4054. Major credit cards accepted.*

Offers snowmobile tours in Woodford State Park and the Green Mountain National Forest, as well as instruction, rentals, and snowmobile storage.

EXCURSIONS & DAY TRIPS

NORTH OF BENNINGTON

Rutland, 30 miles north of Manchester, is Vermont's second largest city, but is not really considered an attraction. Nearby Killington, however, is the East's largest and most popular ski area. For more details, see the "Killington & Rutland" chapter.

EAST OF BENNINGTON

Route 9 East is a beautiful highway that winds up the Green Mountains to its intersection with Route 100 at Wilmington (20 miles from Bennington). About halfway in between is **Woodford State Park** and **Adams Reservoir**. You can easily spend a day or two here (there is camping) hiking, fishing, swimming, or engaging in just about any outdoor activity. During the winter the area is popular with snowmobilers and cross-country skiers. (See the "Sports & Recreation" section above for details.)

Just north of Wilmington in the Deerfield Valley are the **Mt. Snow** and **Haystack** ski areas, which attract tens of thousands of tourists and skiers annually. The countryside is beautiful and the region is teeming with quality inns, restaurants, and recreational opportunties. See the "Mt. Snow Region" chapter for more details.

Twenty miles beyond Wilmington is **Brattleboro**, a town similar to Bennington in size and even in appearance. It is home to an impressive little museum as well as several restaurants and inns. Surrounding towns such as Newfane, Putney, and Marlboro all feature scenic drives, good restaurants, and various minor attractions. See the "Brattleboro" chapter for more information.

PRACTICAL INFORMATION

ATM's & Banks

CHITTENDEN BANK, *401 Main Street, Bennington 05201. Second branch: Kocher Drive, Bennington. Tel. 802/442-7605, 802/447-7522.*

VERMONT NATIONAL BANK (VNB), *West Main Street, Bennington VT 05201.*

Chamber of Commerce

ARLINGTON CHAMBER OF COMMERCE, *P.O. Box 245 (Route 7A), Arlington VT 05250. Tel. 802/375-2800, Fax 802/442-5494. Web site: www.arlingtonvt.com.*

BENNINGTON AREA CHAMBER OF COMMERCE, *Veterans's Memorial Drive (Route 7 North), Bennington VT 05401. Tel. 802/447-3311, Fax 802/447-1163. E-mail: benncham@sover.net. Web site: www.bennington.com.*

Medical Emergencies & Services

Emergencies– *Tel. 911*

SOUTHWESTERN VERMONT MEDICAL CENTER, *100 Hospital Drive, Bennington VT 05201. Tel. 802/442-6361.*

13. MANCHESTER & THE HEART OF THE GREEN MOUNTAINS

Few towns better meet the definition of a New England resort than **Manchester**. Attracting the vacationing elites of New York, Boston, and Washington since the post-Civil War years when families like the Lincolns, Grants, and Roosevelts made it a regular summer destination, Manchester is considered Vermont's first major tourist attraction, and it remains one today. With numerous beautiful estates from the Lincolns' former Hildene Estate to the Equinox resort, Manchester Village is among the most picturesque villages in Vermont with numerous quality inns and restaurants, while nearby **Manchester Center** is the shopping capital of Vermont, with dozens of outlet and retail stores ranging from Orvis to Calvin Klein.

For those more interested in sports and recreation, this chapter also covers four of Vermont's major ski resorts: **Bromley**, **Stratton**, **Okemo**, and **Magic Mountain**, as well as the towns of **Dorset**, **Londonderry**, and **Weston**, best known as the home of the famous Vermont Country Store.

ARRIVALS & DEPARTURES

By Air

Continental's **Colgan Air**, *Tel. 800/253-FARE,* flies two to four times daily between Rutland and Boston. **Lebanon Municipal Airport** in West Lebanon, New Hampshire, is within an hour-hour and half drive from most of the region. It is serviced by **USAir Express**, but flights are relatively expensive and infrequent *(Tel. 800/428-4322 at the airport, Tel. 800/943-5436 for general info and reservations).*

Also within a reasonable driving distance (about 110 miles from Rutland by way of I-89 and Route 4) is the upstart airport in **Manchester, N.H.**, serviced by Continental, United, USAir, and Southwest. The **Vermont Transit Line** bus company, *Tel. 802/864-6811,* operates bus routes directly from the airport to White River Junction where you can make connections to Rutland. From Rutland you can make a connection to Dorset, Manchester or Ludlow; you can also rent a car at any major stop along the way.

Boston's **Logan Airport** is another option, and is a 3-4 hour drive to Windsor. All major rental car agencies operate out of Logan, and while Vermont Transit no longer provides direct service from Logan to White River Junction, there are frequent shuttles to the main bus depot at South Station in downtown from Boston, and there are no fewer than a half dozen departures daily to White River Junction. In White River you can reach Dorset, Manchester, and Ludlow via Rutland.

Finally, Montreal and Albany are also within hours by automobile of the Manchester region. Albany in particular, is convenient, and you can catch a train or bus to Rutland where you can make a Vermont Transit bus connection to Dorset, Manchester or Ludlow.

By Car

Having your own car is certainly the easiest and most convenienct way to reach Manchester and the southern Green Mountains. From New York City and southern New York State, take Interstate 87 to Albany and then New York Route 7 to Bennington, Vermont. From Bennington it is a 25 mile drive north on Route 7 or the more scenic Route 7A.

From Massachusetts and Connecticut, you can take Interstate 91 to southeastern Vermont. From Brattleboro, Route 30 leads directly to Bondville (Stratton) where it meets Route 100 which continues north through Londonderry, Weston and Ludlow. Route 30 continues west to Bromley and Manchester. If you're coming from northeastern Vermont or New Hamshire, make your way to Route 100 by way of Route 4 from the White River Junction-Quechee-Woodstock region and then take it south to Ludlow. Or, from points south like Windsor, take Route 131 West, or Route 11 from Springfield and Chester.

Finally, from northwestern destinations like Rutland, Burlington, and Middlebury, simply take Route 7 south straight to Manchester.

By Bus

Vermont Transit Lines, *Tel. 802/864-6811,* offers direct service between Manchester *(Village Valet on Route 7; Tel. 802/362-1226)* and Albany NY, Rutland, Burlington, Middlebury and about a dozen minor Vermont destinations in between. It also links Ludlow *(Chamber of*

Commerce on Route 100; Tel. 802/228-5830) to Rutland and Brattleboro where connections can be made for New York City, Springfield MA, Hartford CT, and Boston. From Rutland, you can also make connections to those destinations as well as Montreal and major destinations throughout Vermont, including Montpelier, White River Junction, Middlebury, and St. Johnsbury.

By Train
Amtrak's **Ethan Allen Express** links Rutland and Albany, NY – the closest Amtrak stops to Manchester – with major destinations on the northeastern seaboard. It departs Washington DC at 3am daily (#299), and at 10:40am Monday-Thursday (#291), and 1:05pm Friday-Saturday (#293). It stops at Baltimore, Wilimington DE, Philadelphia, and New York City (arriving at 6:38am. 2:15pm & 4:19pm respectively) where you must catch a connecting train with the same number. Train #299 departs Penn Station at 7:10am, Train #291 at 3:55pm, and Train # 293 at 5:40pm en route to Yonkers, Croton-Harmon, Poughkeepsie, Rhinecliff-Kinston, Hudson, and Albany. Again you must transfer or board trains with the same number departing at 9:55am, 6:40pm, and 8:20pm respectively and arriving in Rutland at 12:30pm, 9:05pm, and 10:45pm. Trains depart Rutland in the other direction at 1:25pm and 5:25pm. A one-way fare from Rutland to New York City is approximately $55. In Rutland, you can rent a car or catch a Vermont Transit Lines bus to Dorset or Manchester.

The **James Jeffords Railroad Station** is located next to the transportation center behind the Walmart in downtown Rutand. There are virtually no facilities. Call *800/USA-RAIL* to make reservations and inquire about schedules and fares.

If your destination is Ludlow, Londonderry or some other point on or around Route 100, you might conside Amtrak's **Vermonter** route which departs Washington DC at 7:40am and stops at Baltimore, Wilimington DE, Philadelphia, New York City, Newark NJ, Metro Park NJ, Trenton, NJ, Bridgeport CT, Hartford CT, Meriden CT, New Haven CT, Springfield MA, Amherst MA, Northampton MA, Brattleboro VT, Keene NH, Windsor VT, and arrives at White River Junction VT at 6:30pm. You can get off at Windsor or White River Junction and take a cab, or rent a car and drive west on Route 131 or Route 4 west to Route 100.

You can also take the Vermonter north to destinations like Randolph, Montpelier, Waterbury-Stowe, Burlington, St. Albans and Montreal Canada. Going south to destinations above (except Randolph, Montpelier, Waterbury-Stowe, Burlington, St. Albans and Montreal), the Vermonter departs White River Junction at 10:35am. A one way ticket to Washington, DC costs about $85, New York City $65, and less to destinations in Connecticut, Massachusetts, New Hampshire, and Vermont.

ORIENTATION

This chapter covers a region than includes several major towns and ski areas. To the west, on Route 7 and Route 7A where it meets **Routes 11** and **30** coming from the east, is the major destination of Manchester. About 25 miles north of Bennington by both Route 7 and Route 7A (the more scenic of the two), Manchester actually consists of two villages or hubs – **Manchester Village**, address for such landmarks as the Equinox Hotel, is about a mile south on Route 7A of **Manchester Center**, home to the hundreds of shops and outlet stores which are the other main source of Manchester's fame. Five miles north of Manchester Center on Route 30 is **Dorset**, a small, picturesque village that is itself home to many fine lodging and dining establishments.

From Manchester, the joined Routes 30 and 11 lead east through Manchester Depot about seven miles before splitting. Route 11 continues north past the **Bromley ski area** (about 10 miles east of Manchester) and the hamlet of Peru before intersecting the major north-south artery, Route 100, at Londonderry. Five miles east of Londonderry on Route 11 is the Magic Mountain ski area. Meanwhile, Route 100 north leads to Weston, known for its country store and eventually the town of Ludlow (19 miles north of Londonderry) and the Okemo ski area. Continuing south about eight miles on Route 100 from Londonderry leads to the small village of Rawsonville and to its west, Bondville, which is actually on Route 30.

From Route 30 in Bondville, the Stratton Mountain Access Road winds just a few miles to the **Stratton Mountain** ski slopes and resort. Route 100 continues south to Jamaica, Vermont and eventually on to Wardsboro, Mt. Snow and Wilmington where it intersects with Route 9. Finally the Stratton area can also be accessed from Arlington (10 miles south of Manchester on Routes 7 and 7A) in the summer by the Kelly Stand Road.

GETTING AROUND

Having your own automobile is definitely the easiest way to get around, though you can get around the individual villages and resorts on foot. There is a regular public shuttle between Ludlow, Okemo, Chester and Springfield known as the **Town and Village Bus**, *Tel. 888/869-6287,* or speak with the folks at your hotel for information. A ten-ride ticket costs about $4. Many hotels, particularly those catering to skiers, offer some sort of shuttle to the slopes; they can also assist you in reaching a regional airport or bus terminal by providing or arranging transportation.

For rental cars, **Avis**, *Tel. 800/331-1212*, **Budget**, *Tel. 800/244-9429*, and **Hertz**, *Tel. 800/654-3131* all operate out of Burlington International Airport. **Avis** also has an office in Rutland, *Tel. 802/773-1317*. **Enterprise Rent-A-Car** has outlets in Rutland, *Tel. 802/773-0855*, Barre, *Tel. 802/479-5400*, and South Burlington, *Tel. 802/863-2111*.

WHERE TO STAY
Dorset
DORSET INN, *Route 30 (Church and Main streets on the Green), Dorset VT 05251. Tel. 802/867-5500, 800/835-5284, Fax 802/867-5542. Rates: $150-$250. Credit cards: Visa, Mastercard, American Express.*

"Vermont's oldest continuously operating inn," the Dorset Inn is an elegant colonial three storied affair with 30 rooms and a very fine restaurant. Appointed with antiques and colonial decor, the rooms are elegant and comfortable (but without phones); guests will also enjoy relaxing in the bar and dining in the restaurant where the specialties include crispy duck and roast rack of lamb. Adults only and no smoking.

INN AT WEST VIEW FARM, *802/867-5715, 800/769-4903, Fax 802/867-0468. E-mail: westview@vermontel.com. Web site: vtweb.com/innatwestviewfarm. Rates: $90-$160. Credit cards: Visa, Mastercard, American Express.*

Known for its charm, elegance and romantic atmosphere, the Inn at West View features 10 individually appointed rooms complete with four postered beds and private baths; some also have televisions. Guests can also enjoy golf priviliges, fine country dining in the Auberge Restaurant, lounging in the tavern, and the opportunity to relax and mingle in one of several cozy sitting rooms.

BARROWS HOUSE INN & RESTAURANT, *Route 30, Dorset. Tel. 802/867-4455. Web site: www.barrowshouse.com. Rates: $100-$250. Major credit cards accepted.*

Known for its restaurant, Barrows House consists of a restored 1804 farmhouse-turned-inn, as well as seven elegantly appointed cottages with private baths, bedrooms, and sitting areas.

Londonderry (including Peru & Bromley)
In addition to being very close to the Bromley ski area, staying in Londonderry, and especially south Londonderry, is also very convenient (especially if you have your own transportation) for those skiing Stratton Mountain and Magic Mountain.

BROMLEY VILLAGE, *Route 11, Peru VT 05152. Tel. 802/824-5458, 800/865-4786. Web site: www.bromley.com. Rates: $100-$350. Major credit cards accepted.*

Guests at Bromley Village may stay either at the Sun Lodge, offering full amenities such as private bath, cable television, and access to the recreational facilities including the pool and gym/spa facilties; or in the condos which range from 1-4 bedrooms with kitchens, fireplaces, and access to gym/sauna facilities. Both are within meters of Bromley's ski slopes.

THE WILEY INN, *Route 11 (P.O. Box 37), Peru VT 05152. Tel. 802/ 824-4195, 888/343-6600, Fax 802/824-4195. E-mail: wileyinn@sover.net. Web site: www.wileyinn.com. Rates: $80-$200. Credit cards: Visa, Mastercard.*

Located within minutes of Bromley, the Wiley Inn offers romantic atmospherics and fine amenities which make it an excellent choice for those keen to enjoy the Vermont inn experience. It includes 12 rooms and suites, two of which have fireplalces and jacuzzis, as well as an outdoor hot tub, a lounge and a library for relaxing. The dining room serves fine country cuisine.

HIGHLAND HOUSE (FROG'S LEAP INN), *Route 100, Londonderry. Tel. 802/824-3019, 877/FROGSLEAP, Fax 802/824-3657. E-mail: frog@frogsleapsinn.com. Web site: www.frogsleapinn.com. Rates: $100-$250. Major crdit cards accepted.*

Situated on a 32-acre estate, the Highland House/Frog's Leap Inn was originally constructed in 1842 and features 17 guestrooms, a beautiful and intimate dining room, on-site cross-country ski trails, a swimming pool, and a tennis court. Also noteworthy is the hospitality of innkeepers Kraig and Dorenna Hart, and the service which manifests itself in the delivery of Godiva chocolates, Pellegrino, and coffee to the rooms daily.

LONDONDERRY INN, *Route 100 (P.O. Box 301-69), South Londonderry VT 05155. Tel. 802/824-5226, Fax 802/824-3146. E-mail: londinn@sover.net. Web site: cimarron.net/usa/london.html. Rates: $40-$120. Checks accepted, no credit cards.*

A restored homestead from the 1820's, the Londonderry Inn features simple but very comfortable rooms as well as a convenient location near the Bromley, Stratton, and Magic Mountain ski areas. On-site facilities also include a cozy tavern, a game room with billiards, and several lounging areas.

SWISS INN, *Route 11 (RR 1, Box 140), Londonderry VT 05148. Tel. 802/824-3442, 800/84-SWISS. E-mail: swissinn@sover.net. Web site: www.swissinn.com. Rates:$50-$100. Major credit cards accepted.*

Though a bit plain looking from the outside, the Swiss Inn offers very good value for its comforts and amenities. There are nearly 20 rooms, all of which are equipped with private baths, telephones, and televisions. The in-house restaurant serves very good Swiss and German food, including fondue and raclette, and there are also several sitting rooms for lounging, a game room, and a lounge serving refreshments.

MAGIC VIEW MOTEL, *Route 11 (RR1 Box 22), Londonderry VT 04145. Tel. 802/824-3793, Fax 802/824-3794. Web site: members.aol.com/ magikview. Rates: $45-$90. Major credit cards accepted.*

Magic View offers 18 rooms with amenities including private bath, cable television, and in-room fridges, as well as proxitimity to (and good views) of Magic Mountain. It is also very near to Bromley (10 minutes), Okemo (20 minutes), and Stratton Mountain (15 minutes).

Ludlow, Okemo & Proctorsville

Plymouth, Londonderry, and especially Chester, with its many historic inns, are all viable and convenient alternative locations in which to stay for those skiing Okemo.

OKEMO MOUNTAIN RESORT, *77 Okemo Ridge Road, Ludlow VT 05149. Tel. 802/228-2079, 800/786-5366. E-mail: okemor@tds.net. Web site: www.okemo.com. Rates: $75-$400. Major credit cards accepted.*

Okemo Mountain Resort maintains five separate rental and condo resorts, each of which is within meters of the slopes and offers such amenities as cable television, kitchens or kitchennettes, telephones, private baths and showers, and access to a variety of recreational facilities like saunas, weight rooms, and so on.

The more moderately priced establishments include the Okemo Mountain Lodge, Ledgewood, and Kettle Brook. The **Mountain Lodge** is located near the base lodge with easy access to ski lifts, and consists of one bedroom condos with small kitchens, cable television, fireplaces, and telephones. Prices essentially range from under $100-$200 per night, depending on when you plan to stay.

Located on the slope near the Ledgewood trail for which it is named, the **Ledgewood** resort offers more spacious units with three or four bedrooms, and amenities similar to those at the Mountain Lodge, except Ledgewood has its own skating pond. Prices are also comparable ($200-$450) when divided per person.

Also slopeside, **Kettle Brook** features a variety of units ranging from one bedroom units to three bedroom condos with full kitchens and expanded sitting areas. Prices begin at about $90 per night for the one bedroom efficiencies.

The two pricier resorts, Solitude Village and Winterplace, are distinguished by their better views, fancier and more amenity-laden condos, and more and better recreational facilities. **Solitude Village** features a variety of units ranging from one to five bedrooms (some of which are in townhouses), and its own private swimming pool and gym facilities. It is also home to the Gables Restaurant. Meanwhile, **Winterplace** offers two and three bedroom units with similar amenities.

TRAILS END ACCOMMODATIONS, *P.O. Box 316, 101 Main Street, Ludlow VT 05149. Tel. 802/228-8363, 888/872-4511, Fax 802/228-2233. E-mail: trails@mail.net. Web site: www.skivt.com. Rates: nightly rates begin at $100. Major credit cards accepted.*

Situated on the Sachem ski trail, Trails End offers your choice of 1-4 bedroom condos, all of which feature fireplaces, cable television, phones, and a kitchen; many also have great views, and some even have saunas or whirlpools.

SLOPESIDE ONLY CONDOMINIUM RENTALS, *Lamere Square (Main Street), Ludlow VT 05149. Tel. 802/228-8999, Fax 802/228-8946. Web site: www.2.cyberrentals.com/vt/socrok.html. Rates begin at around $100 per night. Major credit cards accepted.*

Slopeside Only offers an assortment of 1-4 bedroom condos, all of which include private bath, cable television, access to a swimming pool, and are within walking distance of Okemo slopes.

THE GOVERNOR'S INN, *86 Main Street, Ludlow VT 05149. Tel. 802/228-8830, 800/GOVERNOR. Web site: www.innbook.com. Rates: $100-$300. Credit cards: Visa, Mastercard.*

Perhaps the finest lodgings in Ludlow, the Governor's Inn is a beautifully appointed three story Victorian House that was once the summer home of Vermont governor Wallace Stickney (hence the name) that now features eight individually decorated rooms and one suite. The restaurant offers very fine dining and complimentary refreshments are provided in the afternoon. Make reservations well in advance. Keep in mind that smoking is prohibited and children are not permitted. Bed and Breakfast and full meal plans are both offered.

THE CASTLE, *Junction of Routes 103 and 131 (Box 207), Proctorsville VT 05153. Tel. 802/228-7222, 800/697-7222. Web site: thecastle-vt.com. Rates: $130-$300. Credit cards: Visa, Mastercard.*

One of the most luxurious establishments in the region, the Castle is a restored 1904 English Country Manor-style inn with ten individually appointed rooms with antiques, private baths, extra space for lounging, and even compact disc players; six rooms also include fireplaces, and a handful boast whirpools. The elegant wood paneled dining room serves fine country and continental cuisine. Bed and breakfast as well as full meal plans are offered.

ECHO LAKE INN, *Route 100 north of Ludlow village (P.O. Box 154), Ludlow VT 05149. Tel. 802/228-8602, 800/356-6844, Fax 802/228-3075. E-mail: echolkinn@aol.com. Web site: www.vermontlodging.com.echolacke.html. Rates: $70-$200. Major credit cards accepted.*

Located near Echo and Amherst Lakes as well as the Okemo and

Killington ski areas, Plymouth Notch (Calvin Coolidge's birthplace and hometown) and Woodstock, the Echo Lake Inn is hard to beat for location. It also features an assortment of recently renovated rooms with modern facilities, but 19th century atmospherics (the inn was founded in the 1840's), and more private, modern condos with kitchens, as well as private bath and bedrooms. Other facilities include jacuzzi, a pool, a lighted tennis court, and a fine restaurant with outdoor porch seating in the summer and early fall.

COMBES FAMILY INN, *953 E. Lake Road (RFD 1 Box 275), Ludlow VT 05149. Tel. 802/228-8799, 800/822-8799, Fax 802/228-8704. E-mail: billcfi@aol.com. Web site: www.combesfamilyinn.com. Rates: $80-$120. Major credit cards accepted.*

Simple, hospitable and comfortable, the Combes Family Inn offers guests an opportunity to sample true country living. Located four miles from the Okemo slopes, it includes 11 rooms, a sitting room and a dining room where innkeepers Bill and Ruth serve homecooked breakfasts and dinners.

CAVENDISH POINTE HOTEL,*Route 103 (P.O. Box 525), Ludlow VT 05149. Tel. 802/226-7688, 800/438-7908, Fax 802/226-7689. Rates: $60-$180. Major credit cards accepted.*

A full fledged hotel bordering on being a resort, Cavendish Pointe has more than 70 comfortable rooms featuring amenities such as in-room telehones, cable television, modern, spacious baths, and refrigerators. Other facilities include hot tubs, an indoor pool, lounge and game room, conference facitilies and a decent restaurant. The Okemo slopes are two miles away and shuttle service is provided.

BEST WESTERN LUDLOW COLONIAL MOTEL, *93 Main Street, Ludlow VT 05149. Tel. 802/228-8188, Fax 802/228-7731. Web site: www.bestwesternludlow.com. Rates: $50-$175. Major credit cards accepted.*

Consisting of a renovated 1825 home and a modern adjunct, Ludlow's Best Western offers a combination of a convenient village location and comfortable rooms with amenities like phones, clean full baths, in-room telephones, and cable television.

ALL SEASONS INN MOTEL, *112 Main Street, Ludlow VT 05149. Tel. 802/228-8100, Tel. 888/228-8100, Fax 802/228-4915. E-mail: happym@tds.net. Web site: www.virtualvermont.com/allseasons. Rate:$70-$200. Major credit cards accepted.*

The All Seasons features nearly 20 rooms, all of which include private bath, cable television, telephones, and refrigerators; a few also have kitchenettes. Its Main Street location is perfect for those interested in exploring the village and who enjoy walking. It is also within minutes of Okemo by car. Less than inspiring architecturally.

TIMBER INN MOTEL, *112 Route 104 South, Ludlow VT 05149. Tel. 802/228-8666. Web sites: www.vermontlodging.com & www.okemostayandski.com. Rates:$50-$125. Major credit cards accepted.*

Located a mile and half from the Okemo ski slopes, the Timber Inn not only lives up to its name – it's a fine wooden rustic structure – it offers clean, simple rooms with private baths and television, and also features jacuzzi and sauna.

Manchester

THE EQUINOX & THE CHARLES ORVIS INN, *Route 7A, Manchester Village VT 05254. Tel. 802/362-4700, 800/362-4747, Fax 802/362-1595. E-mail: reservations@equinoxresort.com. Web site: www.equinoxresort.com. Rates: $150-$500 for rooms and suites at the Equinox; $600-$1000 for luxury suites in the Charles Orvis Inn. Major credit cards accepted.*

Originally established in 1769, the Equinox and its luxury adjunct, the Charles Orvis Inn, are truly one of Vermont's signature landmarks and offer guests a unique combination of luxury accommodations and first-rate recreational opportunities. Restored to its colonial-era glory with splendid antiques and a mix of colonial and Victorian decor, the Equinox offers a variety of rooms and suites, all of which are beautifully appointed and enjoy first-rate amenities.

Larger suites and the fantastic luxury suites in the Charles Orvis Inn feature fireplaces, extra sitting rooms and private patios. Recreational facilities include the Gleneages golf course, two swimming pools (including one indoor), tennis, the British School of Falconry where you can learn the art of flying and hunting with falcons, and the Land Rover Driving School, which provides instruction in off-road jeep driving. There is also a full fledged gym and weight room, a library, a bar, and two restaurants.

Selected as one of my *Best Places to Stay* – see Chapter 9 for more details.

THE RELUCTANT PANTHER INN AND RESTAURANT, *West Road (one block north of the Equinox), Manchester Village VT 05254. Tel. 802/362-2568, 800/822-2331, Fax 802/362-2586. E-mail: panther@sover.net. Web site: www.reluctant panther.com. Rates: $150-$450. Major credit cards accepted.*

One of the most luxurious and romantic inns in Vermont, the Reluctant Panther is located in a a beautifully restored 1850 building that includes sixteen rooms and four suites, in addition to a very fine restaurant. Rooms are individually decorated with many featuring four poster beds and antique furnishings. Those really looking for a romantic – and indulgent – getaway should consider the two fireplace suites, with one in the bedroom and one in front of the two-person jacuzzi. Inquire about golf packages and other special rates.

VILLAGE COUNTRY INN, *Route 7A (P.O. Box 408), Manchester Village VT 05254. Tel. 802/362-1792, 800/370-0300, Fax 802/362-7238. E-mail: vci@vermontel.com. Web site: www.villagecountryinn.com. Rates: $120-$350. Major credit cards accepted.*

Another fine luxury establishment, the Village Country Inn is a beautiful country estate distinguished by lovely gardens with fountains, a pool, and a gazebo outside, while inside guests can enjoy excellent dining, the tavern with mountain views, and superb accommodations. There is an assortment of elegantly appointed and antique-laden rooms and suites, some of which have fireplaces and/or in-room jacuzzis.

1811 HOUSE, *Route 7A, Manchester Village 05254. Tel. 802/362-1811, 800/432-1811, Fax 802/362-2443. Web site: www.1811.com. Rates: $100-$225. Major credit cards accepted.*

This quaint but elegant inn built in the 1770's features six beautiful guestrooms, each individually decorated with antique oriental rugs, and featuring four poster beds and fireplaces. The 1811 House also includes a pub to match serving more than 50 whiskeys (many rare single malt) and imported high end beers and ales.

WILBURTON INN, *River Road, Manchester Village 05254. Tel. 802/ 362-2500, 800/648-4944. E-mail: wilbuinn@sover.net. Web site: www.wilburton.com. Rates: $100-$250. Major credit cards accepted.*

The "Grand Victorian Estate" (which actually resembles a Tudor estate) features 20 acres of beautiful grounds and superb views. Rooms are spacious and all are indivually appointed with antiques and a fireplace. The formal fine dining restaurant serves excellent pricey continental cuisine, while a more casual establishment serves upscale American tavern fare.

THE INN AT MANCHESTER, *Route 7A (Box 41), Manchester Village VT 05254. Tel. 802/362-1793, 800/273-1793, Fax 802/362-3218. E-mail: iman@vermontel.com. Web site: www.innatmanchester.com. Rates: $100-$200. Major credit cards accepted.*

A beautiful 1880 white house on a four acre estate, the Inn at Manchester features nearly 20 elegantly appointed rooms and suites. All accommodations include beautifully appointed rooms, air-conditioning, and private baths, with some also featuring fireplaces. Other charms include the marble terrace and small pool in the beautifully maintained and peaceful gardens.

MANCHESTER VIEW, *Route 7A (P.O. Box 1268), Manchester VT 05254. Located north of Manchester Center. Tel. 802/362-2199, 800/548-4141, Fax 802/362-2199. E-mail: manview@vermontel.com. Web site: www.manchesterview.com. Rates: $80-$210. Major credit cards accepted.*

Manchester View features 35 rooms and suites, all of which include a private bath, cable television, and telephones; some also have fireplaces, private balconies, and or whirlpools. Other on-site facilities include a meeting room and basic business services, a restaurant, a pool, and a modest gym with weights.

PALMER HOUSE, *Route 7A, Manchester Center VT 05254. Tel. 802/ 362-3600. Web site: www.palmerhouse.com. Rates: $60-$120. Major credit cards accepted.*

Probably the nicest hotel in town, the Palmer House offers a combination of spacious comfortable rooms that include cable television, air conditioning, telephones, and refrigerators. Other facilities include a spa with a whirlpool and sauna, tennis, a pool, and some business centers. The views are quite nice and the atmosphere is enhanced by nice decor and antiques, including an antique doll collection.

ASPEN MOTEL, *Route 7A (P.O. Box 548), Manchester Center VT 05254. Tel. 802/362-2450, Fax 802/362-1348. Web site: www.thisisvermont.com/aspen. Rates:$50-$100. Major credit cards accepted.*

A friendly motel, the Aspen includes 22 rooms with air conditioning, coffee makers, private baths, and cables television. There is also a two bedroom cottage with a kitchen and fireplace. Other facilities include a small pool, and guests enjoy tennis and golf privileges.

Stratton Mountain

STRATTON CONDOMINIUMS, *Stratton Access Road, Stratton VT 05155. Tel. 802/297-4000, 800/STRATTON (Tel. 800/787-2886), 800/843- 6967. E-mail: infostratton@intrawest.com. Web sites: www.stratton.com & www.ridestratton.com. Rates: $150-$700. Major credit cards accepted.*

Stratton Mountain offers a variety of 1-4 bedroom condos, all of which feature amenities such as private baths, cable television, and telephones, and some of which include kitchens or kitchenettes, fireplaces, and laundry facilities. Lodgers enjoy not only easy access to the slopes and restaurants and shops at the Village Square, but also enjoy priviliges at Stratton's recreational facilities such as saunas, gym, whirlpools, etc. Call for special "ski & stay" packages combining lodging, left tickets, and dining – it can significantly cut expenses.

STRATTON MOUNTAIN INN, *Stratton Access Road, Stratton VT 05155. Tel. 802/297-4000, 800/STRATTON (Tel. 800/787-2886), 800/843- 6967. E-mail: infostratton@intrawest.com. Web sites: www.stratton.com & www.ridestratton.com. Rates: $100-$400. Major credit cards accepted.*

Stratton Mountain Inn offers a combination of great access to the slopes and Stratton's other goings on, as well as more than 100 modern rooms with full amenities. Featuring a gym, saunas, two restaurants, and a lounge with nightly live entertainment, the Stratton Mountain Inn offers the most in Stratton in the way of facilities and amenities.

STRATTON VILLAGE LODGE, *Stratton Access Road, Stratton VT 05155. Tel. 802/297-4000, 800/STRATTON (Tel. 800/787-2886), 800/843-6967. E-mail: infostratton@intrawest.com. Web sites: www.stratton.com & www.ridestratton.com. Rates: $100-$250. Major credit cards accepted.*

This modern alpine-style lodge has nearly 100 rooms equipped with all modern amenities and facilities like full private baths, cable television, telephones, in-room microwaves, coffee makers, and refrigerators. Guests also enjoy the privilege of using the gym and sauna facilities at the Stratton Mountain Inn. The Lodge offers terrific access to the slopes and other facilities, but lacks the charm of some of the region's older inns. Call for special "ski & stay" packages combining lodging, lift tickets, and dining – it can significantly cut expenses.

WHERE TO EAT

Dorset

DORSET INN, *Route 30 (Church and Main streets on the Green), Dorset VT 05251. Tel. 802/867-5500, 800/835-5284, Fax 802/867-5542. Open for dinner 7:30am-10am (breakfast; 11:30am-2pm (lunch); 5:30pm-9pm (dinner). Credit cards: Visa, Mastercard, American Express.*

Established in 1796, "Vermont's oldest continuously operating inn" includes one of the area's finest restruants. Elegantly appointed with colonial-style decor, it features such house specialties at roast rack of lamb, seafood, and crispy duck, as well as an extensive wine list and a tavern (open 4pm-midnight).

BARROWS HOUSE INN & RESTAURANT, *Route 30, Dorset. Tel. 802/867-4455. Web site: www.barrowshouse.com. Breakfast served from 8am-9:30am. Open for dinner at 6pm daily. Major credit cards accepted.*

Situated in an 1804 inn six miles north of Manchester, the Barrows House serves a moderate but well rounded selection of American, New England, and continental specialties including steaks and filets, seafood, vegetables and pastas. While many of the excellent dishes are standard fare in these parts such as Maine crabcakes, grilled black angus steak, and roasted free range chicken, there are usually some different and unique items as well, such as sauteed calves' liver with sherried bacon and onions. Entrees ranges from $10-$25, and a rotating assortment of salads, appetizers, and desserts are also featured.

SOUTH DORSET GENERAL STORE, *Route 30, South Dorset. Tel. 802/362-5153. Open daily for breakfast and lunch.*

The General Store offers a wide selection of excellent sandwiches, pastries, and other baked goods from scones to biscotti, which are especially nice for those in a bit of a rush or in need of something for the road.

SWEET CREAMS, *Route 30 across from the Green in Dorset. Tel. 802/ 867-5966. Open daily for late breakfast and dinner.*

Specializing in baked goods, coffees and desserts, Sweet Creams prepares more than decent sandwiches and salads.

Londonderry
HIGHLAND HOUSE AT FROG'S LEAP INN, *Route 100, Londonderry. Tel. 802/824-3019, 877/FROGSLEAP. Open Thursday-Monday from 6pm and Sunday brunch. Major credit cards accepted.*

Situated in the 1842 Frog's Leap Inn with beamed ceilings and antique furnishings, the Highland house is a fine setting in which to enjoy a candlelit dinner. While the menu features many selections typical of similar restaurants in Vermont such as grilled New York Sirloin, nouveau seafood, and pastas, it also always includes a series of unique, if not electectic dishes. Appetizers ($3-$8) might include venison, duck, and rabbit pie with seasonal vegetables, as well as sushi roll with mixed greens; while for an entree you could try venison medallions sauteed with chanterelle mushrooms in cognac and cream sauce. Entrees range in price from $15-$20, and for dessert there is a selection of freshly prepared cakes, tarts and other pastries.

SWISS INN, *Route 11, Londonderry (west of the village center). Tel. 802/ 824-3442, 800/84-SWISS. Open nightly for dinner from 5:30pm. Major credit cards accepted.*

Specializing in Swiss and German entrees such as fondue (chicken, beef, or cheese), raclette (melted cheese on potatoes, with picked onions and cornishons), and beef stroganoff, the Swiss Inn offers casually elegant, candlelit dinners for reasonable prices. Most entrees are priced between $10-$20. Accompaniments include your choice from a fine wine list, appetizers such as herring in sour cream, soups, and smaller versions of fondue and raclette, as well as salads, fresh French bread, and to top it off, freshly prepared desserts from the dessert tray. Reservations recommended.

LONDONDERRY INN, *Route 100, South Londonderry. Tel. 802/824-5226. Open for dinners from 5:30pm-8:30pm on holidays and weekends only. Checks accepted, no credit cards.*

Located in a converted 1826 homestead about 15 minutes from Stratton, the Londonderry Inn serves hearty, simple and tasty New England and continental cuisine. The rotating menu usually includes several soups and chowders, salads, and typical American favorites like wings and nachos for appetizers; entrees range from baked ham and steak to mushroom ravioli and baked salmon. Very often some type of game fowl or meat is also featured. All entrees come with bread, a salad, and seasonal vegetables and prices range from $10-$20. Desserts are refreshingly simple and old-fashioned: brownie sundae, apple crisp and the like.

Ludlow & Weston

THE GOVERNOR'S INN, *86 Main Street, Ludlow VT 05149. Tel. 802/ 228-8830, 800/GOVERNOR. Web site: www.innbook.com. Seating at 7pm. Credit cards: Visa, Mastercard.*

One of the most elegant and charming inns in Vermont, the Victorian era Governor's Inn was once the summer residence of Vermont governor Wallace Stickney, and even if you do not have the opportunity to stay in the wonderful establishment, at least you should splurge for an evening. Specializing in continental and gourmet fare, meals typically consist of immaculately prepared game meats and fowl as well as superb soups, salads, and sinfully rich desserts. It's expensive (expect to pay at least $40 per person), and reservations are recommended.

INN AT WESTON, *Route 100 in Weston Village. Tel. 802/824-6789. Web site: www.innweston.com. Open nightly for dinner from 5:30pm. Major credit cards accepted.*

This fine restaurant is located in a beautifully restored farmhouse-turned inn. Ranging in price from $15-$30, the choice of entrees ranges from standard country favorites like rack of lamb and game meats such as quail and venison, to more continental specialties like ravioli and scaloppini of veal.

ECHO LAKE INN, *Route 100 (north of Ludlow village), Ludlow. Tel. 802/228-8602, Fax 802/228-3075. Web site: www.vermontlodging.com.echolacke.html. Open for dinner from 6pm-9pm (tavern open from 4pm). Major credit cards accepted.*

This acclaimed restaurant and inn which dates to the 1840's specializes in groumet but hearty cuisine reflecting seasonal local produce. The menu typically consists of game meats and fowl, such as pheasant, venison, and rabbit (as well as sausages comprising of all the aforementioned or whatever else can be used), as well as Vermont favorites like goat cheese, locally caught or farmed trout, and locally produced vegetables. In summer and early autumn there is outdoor porch seating and a tavern serves lighter fare as well as adult refreshments. A full meal typically costs $20-$30,

MICHAEL'S SEAFOOD & STEAK TAVERN, *Main Street (Route 103), Ludlow. Tel. 802/228-5622. Open nightly for dinner from 5pm-9:30pm. Major credit cards accepted.*

Michael's is a very decent steak and seafood house decked out in semi-classy Americana decor, that also features pasta, a salad bar and an assortment of typical American style appetizers (wings, etc). Full meals typically cost about $20 (more with an appetizer) and there is also a salad bar and a children's menu.

Manchester

THE EQUINOX, *Route 7A, Manchester Village VT 05254. Tel. 802/ 362-4700, 800/362-4747, Fax 802/362-1595. E-mail: reservations@equinoxresort.com. Web site: www.equinoxresort.com. Major credit cards accepted.*

Manchester's most famous lodging and dining establishment includes two eateries. The less formal **Marsh Tavern** is open for breakfast, lunch and dinner. For breakfast, there is an assortment of fruit, egg, and sweet dishes while for lunch you may choose from high end sandwiches, soups, and salads. With dishes like steamed clams and mussels in a tomato lobster broth and grilled venison with Hasty pudding, supper at the Marsh would by other standards be considered fine dining. On weekends there is live entertainment; expect to pay $10-$20 per meal and more if you take multiple courses and/or alcohol.

A truly elegant eatery, the **Colonnade** specializes in fine country dining with the emphasis on roasted and grilled meats (vegetarians should call ahead to make arrangements).

THE RELUCTANT PANTHER INN AND RESTAURANT, *West Road (one block north of the Equinox), Manchester Village VT 05254. Tel. 802/ 362-2568, 800/822-2331, Fax 802/362-2586. E-mail: panther@sover.net. Web site: www.reluctant panther.com. Open for dinner on weekends and holidays. Major credit cards accepted.*

One of Manchester's most luxurious inns, the Reluctant Panther boasts a dining room to match. The dining room is cozy, elegant, and intimate while the cuisine is generally continental with Swiss-style specialties. Call for reservations and expect to pay at least $30 per person for a full meal including beverages.

VILLAGE COUNTRY INN, *Route 7A (P.O. Box 408), Manchester Village VT 05254. Tel. 802/362-1792, 800/370-0300, Fax 802/362-7238. E-mail: vci@vermontel.com. Web site: www.villagecountryinn.com. Open nightly for dinner from 6pm-9pm. Major credit cards accepted.*

Set in a handsome dining room with candles, white table cloths and fireplace, the Village Country Inn specializes in French and continental cuisine. Appetizer choices typically include items such as Les Escargot Bourguignonne, goat cheese with baked radicchio, and crab cakes, while entrees range from heavyweights like roast rack of lamb, seared salmon with herb cream and grilled venison in Port wine sauce, to "Lighter Fare" (usually vegetarian fare) like roasted vegetable napoleon with basil pesto, and stir fried tofu with gingered vegies. Most entress range from $15-$25.

WILBURTON INN, *River Road (off Route 7A), Manchester Village 05254. Tel. 802/362-2500, 800/648-4944. E-mail: wilbuinn@sover.net. Web site: www.wilburton.com. Open nightly for dinner from 6pm-9pm. Major credit cards accepted.*

Situated in a handsome Victorian era inn (though it's somewhat Tudor in Style), the Wilburton's elegant dining room serves an assortment of nouveau and traditional country fare. Grilled fish, steaks, and interesting vegetarian items like lentil stew with grilled vegetables, are generally well prepared and accompanied by bread freshly baked on the premises (as are the desserts). Appetizers cost between $4-$8 while entrees range from $15-$25. There is also a more casual eatery, the Billiard Room, which serves upscale American-style bar food.

THE BLACK SWAN, *Route 7A (next to the Jelly Mill), Manchester Village. Tel. 802/362-3807. Open nightly, except Tuesdays and Wednesdays, from 5:30pm. Major credit cards accepted.*

Situated in a restored brick house from the 1830's, the Black Swan offers very fine continental and American country dining in an elegant setting made cozy by the warmth provided by several fireplaces. The relatively extensive menu typically includes several soups and appetizers ranging from French classics like "Country Pate" and mussels in white wine and cream, to the heartier calamari and warm goat cheese wrapped in prosciutto. For entrees there are usually a half dozen pastas in addition to a dozen "Specialites" which are dominated by French classics like coq au win, frogs legs provencale, and roast pork loin sauteed in calvados with apples; several seafood and fish dishes are also regularly featured. Entrees range from $15-$25 and the Black Swan also includes a tavern and private dining rooms which can be arranged upon request.

SIRLOIN SALOON, *Route 30 & 11, Manchester Center. Tel. 802/362-2600. Open daily for dinner from 5:30pm (4:30 on weekends). Major credit cards accepted.*

A nice change both in cuisine and temperment from the upscale dining which dominates the region (and ideal for families), the Sirloin Saloon offers good grilled fare (steaks, chicken, seafood) for good value ($10-$20) in a friendly and relaxed setting. In addition to the grilled goodies, the Saloon features a fairly extensive salad bar.

LITTLE ROOSTER CAFE, *Route 7A South, Manchester Center. Tel. 802/362-3496. Open daily for breakfast and lunch.*

Specializing in breakfast and lunch, this cafe is the place if you're keen to enjoy a leisurely breakfast (say, rich Belgian waffles topped with cream and Vermont maple syrup) or a lunch designed to do more than just help you reach dinner. Gourmet coffees, high end sandwiches, and light entrees are the main features; you can expect a full breakfast or lunch for less than $15 – assuming you take it easy on the wine.

Stratton Mountain Area (including Bondville & Jamaica)
PORTOBELLO'S, *Liftline Lodge at Stratton Mountain. Tel. 802/292-1912. open for dinner at 6pm from Wednesday-Saturday (and Sundays in winter and foliage season). Major credit cards accepted.*

This elegant eatery at Stratton Mountain serves a fascinating assortment of nouveau Mediterranean and international dishes (the menu rotates daily) ranging from original versions of classics like filet mignon de boeuf beaujolais with potato leek pancake to butternut risotto with asparagus and other mixed vegetables. Offerings also typically include various game and rare meats such as venison, ostrich, and antelope prepared in a variety of cutting-edge gourmet sauces. Formal attire (jacket and tie) is expected for men and reservations are recommended. The wine list is strong and you expect to spend at least $35 per person for a full meal.

RED FOX INN, *Bondville Village (one mile off Route 30). Tel. 802/297-2488. Serving dinner from 6pm-10pm, tavern opens from 4pm until 1pm. Major credit cards accepted.*

The Red Fox features a great dining room-pub combination situated in a restored barn, the centerpiece of which is a fantasticly large fieldstone fireplace. The menu, which rotates with the seasons, typically features an assortment of about a half dozen appeitizers, many of which are seafood-based (Maine crabcakes, scallops fiorella, smoked salmon), as well as a modest variety of American and continental entrees ranging from Vermont rack of lamb to blackened swordfish. There is a separate menu for children and the pub often features live entertainment, including live Irish music on Tuesday nights.

OUTBACK AT WINDHALL RIVER, *Route 30 (.25 mile south of the Stratton Access Road) Bondville. Tel. 802/297-3663. Open for dinner at 5pm nightly, for lunch from 11:30am-3pm Friday-Sunday. Major credit cards accepted.*

Set in a very pleasant location overlooking the Windhall River in Bondville, the Outback includes a pub featuring numerous beers on tap, a pool table, and live entertainment on weekends. Its menu features upscale bar food such as wings, calamari, chowder, and variety of sandwiches which are also served at lunch. The dinner menu offers a choice of about a half dozen American and Italian dishes such as pasta, grilled sirloin, rack of lamb, and some type of seafood. Entree prices range from $10-$25.

CAFE ON THE CORNER, *Liftline Lodge on Stratton Mountain. Tel. 802/297-2600. Open daily from 7am-noon Monday-Friday, 7am-1pm weekends and holidays. Major credit cards accepted.*

An excellent choice for beginning the day or recovering from a long evening, the Cafe serves excellent gourmet, filling breakfast dishes

ranging from eggs and cornbeefed hash to belgian waffles, three egg
omelettes and Italian style frittatas.

SEEING THE SIGHTS

Manchester

Manchester is one of the few resort destinations in Vermont that was
actually founded as such, when establishments such as the **The Equinox**
in Manchester Village served as a summer haven for rich folks from
Boston, Connecticut and New York. By the late 19th century, such
prominent personalities as Mary Todd Lincoln (wife of President Abraham
Lincoln), the wife of Ulysses S. Grant, Theodore Roosevelt, and William
Howard Taft were regular visitors. It was during this time that Manchester
also established itself as a commercial hub as merchants sought to cash in
on the town's wealthy visitors and residents.

Today, with its many upscale inns and restaurants, Manchester
Village has retained its status as a premier destination for wealthy tourists,
while Manchester Center has further developed into a commercial center
with hundreds of shops and outlet stores. In terms of sightseeing, the
beautifully maintained Village with its colonial and Victorian-era buildings is itself the main attraction, but there are a number of small museums
(or in the case of the Hildene Estate, large museums) and other attractions
worth visiting.

AMERICAN MUSEUM OF FLY FISHING, *Route 7-A & Seminary
River, Manchester VT 05254. Tel. 802/362-3300. Hours: 10am-4pm daily from
May 1 through October 31; 10am-4pm Nibday through Friday November 1-May
30. Admissions: $2 (by donation).*

Fishermen and lovers of technology and gadgetry will enjoy the
thousands of rods, reels, and other memorabilia, some of which is
hundreds of years old. Also fun is the wide variety of art and creative
expressions celebrating the love of fishing, and the lectures, classes, and
auctions held throughout the year.

HILDENE ESTATE (HOME OF ROBERT TODD LINCOLN),
*Route 7-A in Mancchester Village, Manchester VT 05254. Tel. 802/362-1788.
Hours: 9:30am-4pm daily mid-May through October. Cross-country skiing begins
in mid-December.*

Built on the side of a hill around the turn of the century, this beautiful
neo-Georgian mansion was the summer home of Abraham Lincoln's
grandson, Robert Todd Lincoln, until 1975. The grounds include acres
of beautifully maintained gardens and nature trails, while the house is
decorated with original furnishings and family belongings; the estate also
hosts numerous cultural events and concerts (call for information), and
in the winter the trails are used for cross-country skiing.

SOUTHERN VERMONT ART CENTER, *West Road (off Route 7A or Route 30 west of Manchester Center), Manchester VT 05254. Tel. 802/362-1405. Open Tuesday-Saturday 10am-5pm & Sunday noon-5pm from may through October; Monday -Saturday 10am-5pm from December through mid-March. Admission: $3 donation.*

Situated on a 400 acre-plus estate listed on the National Register of Historic Places, the Southern Vermont Art Center includes galleries presenting sculpture, painting, and other art; a concert hall; a beautiful garden with nature trails; a restaurant operated by The Equinox; and a gift shop which includes a gallery of work aimed at collectors.

VERMONT WAX MUSEUM, *Routes 11 & 30, Manchester Center. Tel. 802/362-0609. Open daily 10am-5pm.*

The Vermont Wax Museum consists of three restored Victorian-era buildings, nearly 100 wax figures dressed in antique and historical clothing, and an assortment of other historical and artistic exhibits. There is also a gift shop.

MANCHESTER HISTORICAL SOCIETY, *Manchester VT. Tel. 802/362-3747. Admission by appointment only.*

Features a modest collection of local historical memorabilia.

VERMONT STATE CRAFT CENTER AT THE EQUINOX, *Route 7A Manchester Village, Manchester VT 05452. Tel. 802/362-3321. Hours: open daily except Wednesdays from 10am-5pm (winter), 10am-6pm (summer).*

Features rotating exhibits with arts and crafts produced primarily in Vermont. Classes, lectures, and demonstrations are also presented.

Dorset

Just a handful of miles north of Manchester on Routes 30 and 7, the various villages comprising the town of Dorset are quiet picturesque affairs, but offer little in the way of historic attractions

DORSET HISTORICAL SOCIETY MUSEUM, *Dorset VT 05251. Tel. 802/867-4450. Open Saturday 10am-noon and by appointment. Admission by donation.*

Features the standard assortment of artifacts and photos relating to local history, in addition to extensive geneaological histories of many local residents.

Route 11 to Londonderry

From Manchester, Route 11 (and Route 30) East will take you past the Bromley ski area (8-10 miles depending from where in Manchester you depart) and the hamlet of Peru before taking you to Londonderry (18 miles from Manchester). A one-time mill town of little historic significance, Londonderry now thrives on its convenient location from three major ski areas: Bromley, Stratton, and Magic Mountain. The more handsome village of **South Londonderry** is seven miles south of Londonderry itself.

North of Londonderry on Route 100 – Weston

Five miles north of Londonderry on Route 100, Weston is a small but thriving hamlet that in the past half century has become synonymous with the famous **Vermont Country Store**, a store and mail order business from the old school (see Weston under "Shopping" below). Other attractions include the many restored homes and other buildings which were first built during the town's first commercial boom in the mid-19th century.

FARRAR-MANSUR HOUSE AND OLD MILL MUSEUM, *off Route 100, Weston VT. Tel. 802/824-8190. Farrar-Mansur House hours: daily 1pm-5pm daily from Memorial Day (late May) through Columbus Day (mid-October). Old Mill hours: daily 10am-4pm Memorial Day. Admission by $2 donation.*

Built by Oliver Farrar in 1797 and sold to Franklin Mansur in 1857, the Farrar-Mansur House has been preserved in its 19th century condition and features numerous exhibits including fine furniture, kitchenware, a collection of tall and shelf clocks, American paintings, and metalworks including fine examples of copper, brass, and silverware.

Situated on a pond next to the Farrar-Mansur House, the Old Mill Museum was a sawmill turned grist mill that now contains a fascinating assortment of agricultural exhibits, including a granary, tinsmithing tools, and numerous examples of farming tecnology from the past 200 years.

Ludlow

Once a minor manufacturing center that specialized in the reworked wool known as "shoddy" – much in demand during the post-Civil War cloth shortage – Ludlow, 10 miles north of Weston, is today a fairly wealthy town dependent on the tourism business, much of which is centered around the nearby Okemo ski area. Not especially attractive as a village, the town of Ludlow does feature several interesting attractions apart from the stunning natural beauty of the region:

BLACK RIVER ACADEMY MUSEUM, *High Street, Ludlow VT 05149. Tel. 802/228-5050. Hours: noon-4pm Wednesday-Sunday from Memorial Day (late May) through Columbus Day (mid-October).*

Calvin Coolidge's alma mater, the Black River Academy now features a relatively extensive three story museum that includes numerous exhibits related to local history and Calvin Coolidge.

CROWLEY CHEESE FACTORY, *Healdville (just off Route 103 just past the Crowley Cheese Store), in Ludlow. Tel. 802/259-2340. Factory hours: 8am-4pm daily. Gift shop hours: 10am-5pm daily except Sunday when it opens at 11am. Admission is free.*

The oldest cheese factory still operable in the United States, the Crowley Factory – unlike the more famous Cabot establishment – still makes cheese the old-fashioned way: by hand. The process, while not riveting, is interesting and the product (samples are provided) is quite good.

NIGHTLIFE & ENTERTAINMENT

Ludlow-Okemo

Throughout the year – particularly around major holidays such as Christmas and the Fourth of July – many special events and concerts are held in Ludlow and Okemo, including performances by the **Vermont Symphony Orchestra**. For detailed information (usually published every season), pick up a copy of the locally available *Okemo Magazine* and contact the **Ludlow Area Chamber of Commerce**, *P.O. Box 333, Ludlow VT 05149, Tel. 802/228-5830, Fax 802/228-7642, Web site: www.vacationinvermont.com.*

BRICK HOUSE, *South Main Street, Ludlow. Tel. 802/228-4249. Open nightly from 5pm. Credit cards accepted.*

A fun tavern and restaurant featuring a rotating selection of local brews on tap and live entertainment on the weekends.

Manchester

To learn about concerts and special events held in Manchester and the region generally, pick up a copy of the *Manchester and the Mountains Area Guide* and contact the **Manchester and the Mountains Chamber of** Commerce, *RR2 Box 3451, Manchester Center, VT 05255, Tel. 802/362-2100, Fax 802/362-3451, E-mail: mmchamber@sover.net. Web site: www.manchesterandmtns.com.*

Summer is an especially busy time for concerts and musical events. The **Vermont Symphony** Orchestra, *Tel. 800/VSO-9293*, recently made Manchester its summer headquarters and regularly performs in such beautiful settings as Hildene and Hunter Park. The **Manchester Music Festival**, held annually and several dates in July and August, features concerts held by groups and orchestras consisting of established professionals up and coming stars from around the region. For information, make the following contacts: *Tel. 800/639-5868; web site: www.vtweb.com/mmf.*

Special events in winter are concetrated around Christmas and New Year's, when public tree lightings, the **Manchester Winter Carnival**, and concerts are held. Contact the Chamber of Commerce for details.

Stratton

Special events are held throughout the year in Stratton, ranging from fireworks and concerts on New Year's Eve, to similar celebrations on July

Fourth. For further information, contact **Stratton Mountain**, *RR 1 Box 145, Stratton Mountain VT-5155, Tel. 800/STRATTON, Fax 802/297-4300, Web site: www.stratton.com.*

MULLIGANS, *Village Square at Stratton Mountain on the Stratton Mountain Access Road. Tel. 802/297-9293. Open from 11am-2pm. Major credit cards accepted.*

Featuring live entertainment, three bars, and more than 60 beers on tap, Mulligans has staked a strong claim to title of Stratton's premier aprés-ski establishment. Food is served from 11am-10pm.

RED FOX INN, *Bondville Village (one mile off Route 30). Tel. 802/297-2488. Serving dinner from 6pm-10pm, tavern opens from 4pm until 1pm. Major credit cards accepted.*

The Red Fox includes a very pleasant if low key pub that features live Irish music every Tuesday night when Irish food is also served.

OUTBACK AT WINDHALL RIVER, *Route 30 (.25 mile south of the Stratton Access Road) Bondville. Tel. 802/297-3663. Open for dinner at 5pm nightly, for lunch from 11:30am-3pm Friday-Sunday. Major credit cards accepted.*

Featuring numerous beers on tap, a game room and a pool table, the OutBack Tavern regularly features live entertainment, particularly on weekends and holidays.

SPORTS & RECREATION
Biking

In the Manchester-Dorset region, you can devise numerous loops on roads such as Route 7A, Route 11, Route 30, and particularly Routes 315, 313, and 153 near Rupert. For mountain biking, **Stratton Mountain** with its chairlifts offers a great setup for bikers of all levels, and **Green Peak** in Dorset features several miles of trails amongst the old marble quarries. Bikes can be rented at Stratton *(Tel. 800/7872886)* where a gondola day pass costs about $20 per adult.

In the eastern portion of the area, there is plenty of good road riding on Routes such as 131, 103,155, and on many local roads.

BATTENKILL SPORTS CYCLE SHOP, *Junction of Route 7 and Routes 11 & 30 in Manchester. Tel. 802/362-2734. Open 9:30am-5:30pm daily. Major credit cards accepted.*

MOUNTAIN CYCOLOGY, *5 Lamere Square, Ludlow. Tel. 802/228-2722. Major credit cards accepted.*

EIGER SNOWBOARDS, SKATE, BIKE, HIKE, *Route 7A, Manchester Center. Tel. 802/362-0804. Major credi cards accepted.*

Rentals, services, and retail sales for all snowboarding, skating, biking, and hiking equipment and accessories.

Cross-Country Skiing

EQUINOX SKI TOURING CENTER, *Union Street, Manchester Village. Tel. 802/362-4700.*

There are 35 kilometers of trails for cross-country skiing and snowshoeing; instruction and rentals availables.

FOX RUN SKI TOURING CENTER, *Ludlow VT. Tel. 802/228-8871. Trail fees: $13.*

Fox Run features 20 kilometers of trails and can provide equipment rentals and instruction.

HILDENE, *Route 7A, Manchester. Tel. 802/362-1788. Trail fees: $10.*

With only 15 kilometers of trails, Hildene is more modest than others, but the scenery is beautiful; rentals are offered but no instruction.

STRATTON MOUNTAIN CROSS-COUNTRY CENTER, *Stratton Mountain Resort on Stratton Mountain Access Road. Tel. 802/297-1880, 297-4115. Trail fees: $12.*

Stratton offers more than 30 kilometers of trains on varied terrain as well rentals, instruction, and guided tours.

VIKING CROSS-COUNTRY SKI CENTER, *Little Pond Road (off Route 100), Londonderry. Tel. 802/824-3933, 824-6578. Trail fees: $12.50.*

There are 30 kilometers of trails as well as instruction, rentals, and tours.

WILD WINGS SKI TOURING CENTER, *North Road (off Route 11), Peru (next to Bromley). Tel. 802/824-6793. Trail fees: $10.*

Wild Wings features 25 kilometers of groomed trails as well as rentals and instruction; concentrates on families.

Fishing

The **West River** which passes north of South Londonderry (on Route 100) is known for its trout fishing.

Off Route 100 north of Ludlow, the **Amherst**, **Echo**, and **Rescue lakes** are all popular fishing locales with an assortment of trout, bass, and perch.

KEVIN LADDEN GUIDE & OUTFITTER, *64 Tucker Road, South Hill, Ludlow VT 05149. Tel. 802/228-5195..*

Kevin Ladden offers an assortment of clinics and tours, as well as equipment sales and rentals.

The **Battenkill River**, particularly south of Manchester and west of Arlington, is a very popular fishing venue and features several types of trout. The ponds off the Kelly Stand Road (see "Stratton" below), are also very accessible.

THE ORVIS STORE, *Route 7A, Manchester Center. Tel. 802/362-=3750. Open daily 9am-6pm. Major credit cards accepted.*

South of Stratton Mountain, the **Kelly Stand Road** (from Manchester take Route 7 to Arlington where it intersects the Kelly Stand Road) accesses the **Stratton**, **Bourne**, and **Branch ponds**, all of which offer decent fishing.

KIDDERBROOK OUTFITTERS, *Stratton VT. Tel. 802/297-4450.* Rents equipment and provides clinics.

Golf

GLEANEAGLES GOLF COURSE AT QUINOX, *Equinox Hotel, Manchester Village. Tel. 802/362-3223. 18 holes. Green fees: $60-$90. Major credit cards accepted.*

OKEMO VALLEY GOLF CLUB, *77 Okemo Ridge Road, Ludow VT 05149. Tel. 802/228-8871. 18 holes, driving range, practice greens, pro shop. Major credit cards accepted.*

STRATTON MOUNTAIN COUNTRY CLUB, *Stratton Mt. Access Road, Stratton. Tel. 802/297-4114. 27 holes. Green fees: $56-$66. Major credit cards accepted. Carts available.*

FOX RUN, *Fox Lane, Ludlow. Tel. 802/228-8871. 9 holes. Green fees: $22-$27.*

Hiking

In the Ludlow & Okemo region, **Mount Okemo** features numerous hiking trails on and around the ski slopes, including the Healdville Trail off Route 103 north of Ludlow. There is also good hiking around **Lowell Lake** off the Magic Mountain access road, and in **Camp Plymouth State Park** and **Calvin Coolidge State Park**, north of Route 100A.

Horseback Riding

MOUNTAIN VIEW RANCH, *Danby. Tel 802/293-5837.*

Skiing (alpine resorts, including summer activities)

BROMLEY, *Located in Peru, Vermont 10 miles east of Manchester and eight miles west of Londonderry. (Mailing address: P.O. Box 110, Manchester Center VT 05255). Tel. 802/824-5522. Web site: www.bromley.com. Lift rates: $30-$45 – less for multiday tickets, you & junionrs, and senior citizens. Hours: 8:30am-4pm.*

Bromley features more than 40 runs and trails, divided practically evenly between difficult, easy, and moderate difficulties, and serviced by 9 lifts. Lessons, day care, and rentals (usually about $25 per day for full equipment per adult) are all available.

During the summer and autumn, you can take enjoy scenic a chairlift ride ($6 per adult) – a great way to view the area, particularly during foliage season. An **alpine slide** is also in operation during the summer and early autumn.

MAGIC MOUNTAIN, *Route 11 (P.O. Box 536), Londonderry VT 05148. Tel. 802/824-5645, Fax 802/824-5199. Lift rates: $20 (weekdays) – $35 (weekends; less for multiday passes, juniors, and seniors. Hours: 8:30am-4pm.*

Newer, smaller (30 trails & four lifts), and less known, Magic Mountain is a cheaper alternative to the larger resorts which may be appropriate for beginners and families keen on good value. Lessons, equiment rentals, and snowboards are also available and Magic Mountain now features snow tubing, an easier way to enjoy speeding down steep inclines.

OKEMO MOUNTAIN, *Off Route 100 & Route 103 in Ludlow. Tel. 802/228-4041,800/78-OKEMO. Web site: www.okemo.com. Lift rates: $45 – less for multiday passes, young adults, juniors, and seniors. Hours: 8:30am-4pm.*

One of Vermont's fastest growing ski resorts, Okemo features 96 trails fed by 13 lifts, and offers a large assortment of lesson and clinic packages through its Cutting Edge Learning Center. Rentals are also available at the base lodge (as well as nearby ski shops), and snowboards are also available. The resort can also provide day care for children in both summer and winter.

STRATTON MOUNTAIN, *Stratton Mountain Access Road off Route 30 and Route 100 in Bondville (RR 1 Box 145, Stratton Mountain VT 05155. Tel. 800/STRATTON, Fax 802/297-4300. Web site: www.stratton.com.) Lift rates: $45 daily, less per day for multiday passes. Hours: 8:30am-4pm.*

One of Vermont's most famous and modern resorts, Stratton features 90 trails over 400 acres with 12 lifts. Like other resorts, it offers rentals, lessons, and care and clinics for children. During the summer, Stratton opens its slopes to bikers and hikers.

Sleigh Rides

HORSE FOR HIRE SLEIGH RIDES, *Off Route 11 in Peru (just east of Bromley). Tel. 802/824-3750.*

MERCK FOREST AND FARMLAND CENTER, *Route 315, Rupert (northwest of Dorset). Tel. 802/394-7836.*

SUN BOWL RANCH, *Stratton Mountain. Tel. 802/297-9210,*

TAYLOR FARM SLEIGH RIDES, *Route 11, Londonderry. Tel. 802/824-5690.*

SHOPPING
Dorset

AMERICAN QUILTS, MARIE MILLER, *Route 30, Dorset. Tel. 802/867-5969. Open daily 10am-5pm. Major credit cards accepted.*

Features hundreds of beautiful quilts and other textiles, many of which are heirlooms and collectors' items.

OLD COW'S TAIL ANTIQUES, *Route 30, Dorset. Tel. 802/362-3363. E-mail: cowstail@sover.net. Open daily 10am-6pm. Credit cards: Visa, Mastercard, Discover.*

PELTIER'S MARKET, *On the Green, Dorset. Tel. 802/867-4400. Open daily. Major credit cards accepted.*

A charming store featuring Vermont specialty goods and foods including maple products, cheeses, and much more – a good place for gift shopping.

Manchester

Manchester, and Manchester Center in particular, is renowned for its shopping. Not only does the area feature the usual assortment of Vermont specialty stores and antique dealers, but Manchester Center is home to dozens of **outlet stores** for such name brands as Armani, Calvin Klein, Brooks Brothers, Donna Karan and Levi's to name but a few. We have listed several; to receive a more complete list, pick up a copy of the *Manchester and the Mountains Area Guide,* widely available throughout the region and the state or contact the **Manchester and the Mountains Chamber of** Commerce, *RR2 Box 3451, Manchester Center, VT 05255, Tel. 802/362-2100, Fax 802/362-3451, E-mail: mmchamber@sover.net. Web site: www.manchesterandmtns.com.*

BATTENKILL & HIGH RIDGE OUTLETS CENTERS, *Route 7, Manchester Center VT 05255. Tel. 802/362-2958. Open daily (hours vary according to store). Major credit cards accepted at most stores.*

These neighboring outlet centers features outlet store for major name brands including **Anne Klein** *(Tel. 362-2958),* **Polo Ralph Lauren** *((Tel. 362-2340),* **Bose** *((Tel. 362-4902),* **Donna Karan** *((Tel. 362-5272),* **Gund** *((Tel. 362-9200),* **Jockey** *((Tel. 362-3555),* **Van Heusen, Home Fashions** *((Tel. 362-8111),* **Ellen Tracy** *((Tel. 362-4443)* in addition to others.

EQUINOX ANTIQUES-MARK REINFURT, *29 Main Street, Manchester Center. Tel. 802/362-3540, Fax 802/362-0806. Web site (including catalog): www.equinoxantiques.com. Open daily 10am-6pm. Major credit cards accepted.*

EQUINOX MOUNTAIN ANTIQUES CENTER, *Route 7A in Sunderland (just south of Manchester Village). Tel. 802/362-5459. Open daily 10am-5pm. Credit cards: Mastercard, Visa.*

Situated in a historic late 18th century building, the Center features the wares of more than 35 dealers.

EQUINOX SQUARE, *Routes 11 & 30, Manchester Center. Most shops open daily. Major credit cards accepted by most shops.*

Another assortment of brand name outlet stores. Resident shops include **J. Peterman**, **Burberry's**, **Easy Spirit** and the **Johnston & Murphy Factory Store**.

MAGIC SLEIGH, *Main Street (Route 7A), Manchester Center. Tel. 802/362-2197. Major credit cards accepted.*

A wonderfully colorful Christmas store featuring all sorts of beautiful ornaments and decorations from all over the world.

MANCHESTER COMMONS, *Off Route 7A on Routes 30 & 11, Manchester Center. Tel. 800/955-SHOP. Open daily (hours vary according to each outlet). Major credit cards accepted at most shops.*

Along with Manchester Square just down the block, Manchester Commons is perhaps the major outlet center in the area in terms of number of name brand stores. Those represented include **Calvin Kein** *(Tel. 362-5260)*, **TSE Factory Store** *(Tel. 362-0622)*, **Coach** *((Tel. 362-1771)*, **Cole-Haan Company Store** *(Tel. 362-1145)*, **Baccarat** *((Tel. 362-4132)*, **Dansk** *((Tel. 362-2451)*, **J. Crew**, and others.

MANCHESTER MARKETPLACE, *Routes 11 & 30, Manchester Center. Tel. 802/362-4321. Open daily (hours may vary for each shop). Major credit cards accepted.*

Outlet stores include **Carter's Childrenswear** *(Tel. 362-0254)*, **Linen Barn**, **London Fog** and others.

MANCHESTER SQUARE, *Routes 11 & 30, Manchester Center. Tel. 800/955-SHOP. Open daily. Major credit cards accepted at most stores.*

One of the largest collections of outlets and factory stores including **Brooks Brothers** *(Tel. 362-7044)*, **Giorgio Armani** *(Tel. 362-1166)*, **Emporio Armani**, **Maidenform**, **Tommy Hilfiger** *(Tel. 362-0888)*, **Levi's** *(Tel. 362-0995)*, among others.

NORTHSHIRE BOOKSTORE, *Corner of Route 7A and Route 30, Manchester Center. Tel. 802/362-2200, 800/437-3700. E-mail: usedbooks@northshire.com. Open Open Sunday-Thursday 10am-7pm, Friday-Saturday 10am-9pm. Credit cards: Mastercard, Visa.*

A more than decent used bookstore that also sells compact discs, tapes, and features a children's department.

THE ORVIS STORE, *Route 7A, Manchester Center. Tel. 802/362-3750. Open daily 9am-6pm. Major credit cards accepted.*

The oldest mail order company in the country (1856), Orvis specializes in upscale outdoor wear as well as hunting and fishing equipment and apparel.

Stratton

The **Village Square Shops**, *Tel. 802/297-2200*, in Stratton Village consist of more than two dozens stores and restaurants selling all types of Vermont specialty goods, sporting goods, clothing and apparel, and all types of souvenirs.

Weston

VERMONT COUNTRY STORE, *Route 100 (P.O. Box 128), Weston VT 05161. Open 9m-5pm Monday-Saturday (closed Sundays). Extended hours 9am-6pm July-October. Major credit cards accepted.*

Run by the Orton family since its founding in 1945, the highly venerated Vermont Country Store has achieved the status of standard bearer for Vermont's country stores – once pillars of most Vermont communities that many fear are endangered. It has flourished through expansion by way of its famous mail order catalog and opening a new store in Rockingham and several outlets, including one in Weston. But while the company has survived by adapting to the modern economy, the "Home Store" remains an old-fashioned affair, not only in its style and atmospherics (made complete an old-fashioned candystore counter), but in its products as well.

Selling everything seemingly everything under the sun, the store's inventory includes not only oodles of food, hardware, and clothing products typical of most country stores in Vermont, but all sorts of crazy items, from old-fashioned women's undergarments like girdles and bloomers to Goo Goo Supreme candies that you'll be hardpressed to find anywhere, period. For a preview, call or write for a catalog.

WESTON FUDGE SHOP, *Old Mill yard Road, Route 100, Weston. Tel. 800/824-3014. Web site: www.westonfudge.com. Open daily. Major credit cards accepted.*

WESTON VILLAGE STORE, *Route 100, Weston VT 05161. Tel. 802/ 824-5477.*

"Weston's original Country Store" (it was established in 1891), the Village Store features a wide selection of specialty foods, wines, cheeses, and a barn dedicated to Christmas items.

EXCURSIONS & DAY TRIPS

KILLINGTON & RUTLAND

An option for skiers, hikers, and out door buffs is the region around **Rutland** (25 miles north of Manchester on Route 7) and **Killington** (just north of Ludlow on Route 100). **Killington** and its sister ski resort of **Pico** offer the most extensive and diverse skiing in the east, as well as opportunities to enjoy hiking, biking, and other outdoors activites. Just about 10 miles north of Ludlow on Route 100 South is **Plymouth**, where on Route 100A you can visit the birthplace (and final resting place) of President Calvin Coolidge. His home village of Plymouth Notch has been restored and is now open to the public in the summer; it makes for a very enjoyable and educational experience. Just up the road, also on Route 100A, is the **Calvin Coolidge State Park**, where you can camp, hike, and enjoy the wilderness.

The city of **Rutland** is not generally thought of as a tourist destination, but having undergone a revival of sorts in recent years, it is a pleasant place to visit, and features a variety of good restaurants and shops. Just north of Rutland (and less than 20 miles from Brandon) is the **Chittenden Reservoir** with camping fishing, boating, hiking, and biking. Nearby attractions also include the **Marble Museum** in Proctor, the **Hubbarton Battle Monument and Museum**, and **Lake Bomoseen**, including Lake Bomoseen State Park, where you can hike, fish, or paddle and sail around in a boat. (See the "Rutland & Killington" chapter for more information.)

WOODSTOCK & QUECHEE

About 25 miles northeast of Ludlow by way of Routes 100, 100A, and 4 East, the **Ottauquechee River Valley** is one of the most popular destinations in Vermont. The town of **Woodstock**, often described the "quintessential New England village," is known for its village green, charming Victorian inns, restaurants and shops. It is also home to attractions such as the **Billings Farm and Museum**, a working dairy farm that was established according to the conservationist principles of Woodstock native Graham Perkins Marsh, who pioneered environmentalism in the 19th century. Across Route 12 from the Billings Farm and Museum, the **Billings-Marsh National Historic Park** was for many years a Rockefeller summer residence and is now open to the public as a museum.

Further east on Route 4, Quechee is the site of the famous **Quechee Gorge** and the **Simon Pearce Glass and Pottery Works**, located in a renovated mill. Quechee and Woodstock can be easily combined with a visit to Calvin Coolidge's homestead in Plymouth.

For more details, see the "The Ottauquechee River Valley" chapter.

THE PRECISION VALLEY

As an excursion, see Chapter 10, *Brattleboro & Windham County*. For much greater detail, see the Precision Valley chapter.

POINTS SOUTH - ARLINGTON, BENNINGTON & BRATTLEBORO

Fifteen and 25 miles south of Manchester respectively, by way of Route 7A and Route 7, are the towns of **Arlington** and **Bennington**. Arlington is handsome and picturesque and is home to several attractions, including a number of covered bridges and a museum about Norman Rockwell who lived there in the 1930's, 40's, and 50's. Bennington is one of the oldest towns in Vermont and is home to a beautiful old district which is the site of the Bennington Monument, built to commemorate the Battle of Bennington (1777), a cemetery where Robert Frost is buried, and an impressive museum housing the country's largest collection of Grandma Moses paintings, as well as a diverse assortment of American art and historic artifacts. See the "Bennington" chapter for more details.

From Bondville and the Stratton area, it is 30 miles south on Route 100 to Wilmington and the major resort areas of **Mount Snow** and **Haystack**, ski areas which attract tens of thousands of tourists and skiers annually. The countryside is beautiful and the region is teeming with quality inns, restaurants, and recreational opportunties. See the "Mt. Snow Region" chapter for more details.

Twenty miles east of Wilmington by way of a beautiful drive on Route 9 is **Brattleboro**, a town similar to Bennington in size and even appearance. It is home to an impressive little museum as well as several restaurants and inns. The surrounding towns of Newfane, Putney, and Marlboro all feature scenic drives, good restaurants, and various minor attractions. See the "Brattleboro" chapter for more information.

Going west from Wilmington on Route 9 (20 miles) will take you to Bennington. About halfway in between is **Woodford State Park** and **Adams Reservoir**. You can easily spend a day or two here (there is camping) hiking, fishing, swimming, or engaging in just about any outdoor activity. During the winter the area is popular with snowmobilers and cross-country skiers. See the "Sports & Recreation" section above for details.

PRACTICAL INFORMATION

Chambers of Commerce

LONDONDERRY AREA CHAMBER OF COMMERCE, *Mountain Marketplace Box 58, Londonderry VT 05148. Tel. 802/824-8178, Fax 802/824-5473. E-mail: londcham@vermontel.com. Web site: www.londonderryvt.com.*

LUDLOW AREA CHAMBER OF COMMERCE, *P.O. Box 333, Ludlow VT 05149. Tel. 802/228-5830, Fax 802/228-7642. Web site: www.vacationinvermont.com*

MANCHESTER AND THE MOUNTAINS CHAMBER OF COM-MERCE, *RR2 Box 3451, Manchester Center, VT 05255. Tel. 802/362-2100, Fax 802/362-3451. E-mail: mmchamber@sover.net. Web site: www.manchesterandmtns.com.*

Fire
   Bondville – *Tel. 824-3166*
   Dorset – *Tel. 911*
   Jamaica – *Tel. 603/352-1100*
   Londonderry – *Tel. 824-3166*
   Manchester – *Tel. 911*
   Peru (Bromley) – *Tel. 824-3166*
   Stratton Mountain – *Tel. 824-3166*
   Weston – *Tel. 824-3166*

Medical Emergencies
   All ski areas features emergency medical services.
   Rutland Regional Medical Center – *Tel. 802/775-7111, 160 Allen Street*
   Sherburne Health Center – *Tel. 802/422-3990*

Local Rescue Squads
   Bondville – *Tel. 824-3166*
   Dorset – *Tel. 911*
   Jamaica – *Tel. 603/352-1100*
   Londonderry – *Tel. 824-3166*
   Manchester – *Tel. 911*
   Peru (Bromley) – *Tel. 824-3166*
   Stratton Mountain – *Tel. 824-3166*
   Weston – *Tel. 824-3166*
   Vermont Poison Center – *Tel. 802/658-3456*

Police
   Bondville – *Tel. 297-2121*
   Dorset – *Tel. 362-3639*
   Jamaica – *Tel. 365-4949*
   Londonderry – *Tel. 824-3915*
   Manchester – *Tel. 911*
   Peru (Bromley) – *Tel. 824-3915*
   Stratton Mountain – *Tel. 874-4025*
   Weston – *Tel. 824-3915*

14. THE PRECISION TRAIL

- WINDSOR, ASCUTNEY, & SPRINGFIELD -

See the map on page 179 for destinations in this chapter.

Chances are your dreams of Vermont are cluttered with images of rolling green hills, covered bridges, and quaint villages with pointed steepled churches – and if you are driving along the Connecticut River on Route 5 between White River Junction and Windham County or strolling by vintage Victorian houses in Chester, these likely expectations will be met. But you might be surprised as you pass through sleepy Windsor or bike up Mt. Ascutney, that about 150 years ago the **Precision Valley**, as the southern portion of Windsor County is known, was once a 19th century version of Silicon Valley – the center of a technological revolution that changed the American economy.

For it was it first in **Windsor** in the 1820's and later in Springfield that the manufacturing of "machine tools" – tools used used to shape metal and other tools – was refined for the making of rifles. It was also in Windsor that the independent **Republic of Vermont** was born in July 1777 in a tavern on State Street (the Republic lasted until 1791), and the city remained the capital and largest town in the state until Montpelier became the capital in the early 19th century.

Today, the Precision Valley is less travelled than many regions of Vermont despite its more than worthy offerings of historical sites, recreational opportunities, and the assortment of old Yankee charm and natural beauty expected in Vermont. The tavern where the Republic was founded has since been renamed **"Constitution House"** (far more dignified), and is just one on a list of attractions that also includes the **Catamount Brewery**, **Simon Pearce Glass Works**, the **American Precision Museum** in Windsor (which contains one of the country's most extensive collection of 19th century machines and tools), and the **Cornish-Windsor Bridge** – the longest covered bridge in the world.

Just south of Windsor off Route 5 on Route 44 is **Mt. Ascutney**, featuring the Ascutney Mountain Resort with skiing and other recreational offerings, and Mt. Ascutney State Park with several hiking and biking trails to its peak from which you can peer over the Green Mountains, the Berkshires, and the Connecticut River Valley. Inland on Route 11, the town of **Springfield** was also a center of machine-tool manufacturing whose heritage can be explored at the **Hartness House**, a Victorian mansion-turned-inn that contains among other attractions, an old observatory. And finally, further easton Route 11 is **Chester**, a quaint and charming village known for its vintage Victorian buildings and classic inns and B&B's.

ARRIVALS & DEPARTURES

By Air

The nearest commercial airport is the **Lebanon Municipal Airport** in West Lebanon, New Hampshire, just 20-30 minutes from the town of Windsor (an hour from Springfield) by way of I-91 north and I-89 south. It is serviced by **USAir Express**, *Tel. 800/428-4322 at the airport, Tel. 800/943-5436 for general info and reservations.*

Also within a reasonable driving distance (about 80 miles from Windsor) is the upstart airport in **Manchester, N.H.**, serviced by Continental, United, USAir, and Southwest. The **Vermont Transit Line** bus company, *Tel. 802/864-6811,* operates bus routes directly from the airport to White River Junction where you can make connections to Ascutney and Springfield. Boston's **Logan Airport** is another option, and is a 2.5-3 hour drive to Windsor. All major rental car agencies operate out of Logan, and while Vermont Transit no longer provides direct service from Logan to White River Junction, there are frequent shuttles to the main bus depot at South Station in downtown from Boston, and there are no fewer than a half dozen departures daily to White River Junction.

By Car

All of Precision Valley destinations are on or within minutes of Interstate 91 (I-91), which skirts the Connecticut River and links the Canadian border with eastern Vermont, Massachussetts, and Connecticut where it joins I-95 and continues to New York City.

From Boston and southern New Hampshire and other points east, one is best advised to take I-89 to White River Junction; from there it is 10-12 miles to Windsor on I-91 or Route 5. Mount Ascutney is just another 3-5 miles from Windsor on Route 44. Route 5 runs alongside I-91 throughout the Precision Valley and most of Vermont, and is generally more scenic and a bit slower than I-91.

If you're approaching from the northwest on I-89, it is most efficient to take 5 or I-91 from White River. A more scenic but slightly slower route is to get off I-89 at Exit 2 and take Route 4 west through Quechee to the junction with Route 12 south at Taftsville. It's then 12 miles to Windsor.

If you're looking to go to Springfield or Mount Ascutney, continue on Route 4 west past Taftsville and the junction with 12 to Woodstock. You will then be treated to a 25-mile scenic drive along underdeveloped Route 106 to Springfield. To reach Mount Ascutney, hang a left (east) on Route 44, 13 miles south of Woodstock.

Finally, from the west, you'll have to find the most appropriate link from Route 100 to reach your destination. From the Killington area on north, you can take Route 4 east to Woodstock, and then make a right to go south on 106, 12, or Route 5/I-91. From Plymouth and Ludlow, take 103 east to Proctorsville and Route 131 to I-91 Route 5 at Ascutney Village just south of Windsor. Continue on 103 for Springfield and Chester. Finally, from all points south beginning with Weston, Route 11 east goes directly to Chester and Springfield where it meets Route 5 and I-91.

By Bus

Vermont Transit, *Tel. 802/864-6811,* with connecting Greyhound to major destinations across the northeast and the country, stops in Spring-field, *Tel. 802/885-2750*; Ascutney, *Tel. 802/674-6902* (stops at the Country Village Store); and White River Junction (15 miles north of Windsor). There are direct buses to Ascutney and Springfield from Springfield, Northamption, and Greenfield Massachussetts, as well as Brattleboro VT, Keene NH, Bellows Falls VT, and White River Junction, VT. There are also direct buses to White River Junction from Boston, Concord NH, Manchester NH, New York City, Rutland VT, Montpelier VT, Montreal, Canada, and Burlington VT, as well as other destinations in Vermont and New England.

By Train

Amtrak's **Vermonter** stops at Windsor-Ascutney in Windsor *on* Depot Avenue off Route 5 in downtown Windsor at 10:53am on its way south to Brattleboro; Springfield, MA; Hartford, CT; New Haven, CT; New York, NT; Philadelphia, PA; Wilmington, DE; Baltimore, MD; Washington, DC; and many other stops in between. It stops in the evening at 6:10pm going north to White River Junction, Randolph, Montpelier-Barre, Waterbury-Stowe, Burlington-Essex, St. Albans and Montreal. Tickets cost about $85 to Washington and less to other destinations. Reservations are required and can be made over the phone. There is no ticket window or service at the station and tickets can be picked up on the train itself. *Call 800/USA-Rail for information and reservations.*

ORIENTATION

The Precision Valley comprises the southeastern quadrant of Windsor County beginning with the town of **Windsor** to the north (about 10 miles south of White River Junction) and stretching about 30 miles south to the border of Windham County near Rockingham. **Interstate 91** (I-91) and **Route 5** are the main north-south arteries of the region and follow each other north-south along the Connecticut River through Windsor and link the region with Brattleboro, and eventually Massachussetts and Connecticut to the south, and with White River Junction and Saint Johnsbury to the north.

Just south of Windsor – not more than five miles – by way of **Route 44** is Mount Ascutney, home to the Ascutney Mountain Resort ski and vacation area, and the Ascutney State Park featuring hiking and biking trails, as well as facilities for camping, picnicing, and for those with a glider, hang-gliding. Four miles south of Windsor, Route 44A links Route 5 with Mount Asctuney and Route 44. The village of Asctuney is actually another several miles south on Route 5 off I-91's Exit 8. Route 44 (and 44A) continue west around Mount Asctuney, and through the hamlet of Brownsville to its end at the junction with Route 106 a north-south highway linking Springfield and Woodstock.

Route 5 and I-91 continue about another 15 miles south past the small Wilgus State Park and the penninsula at Weathersfield Bow, to a junction with Route 11 west. Just a couple of miles to the west in the Black River Valley lies Springfield, and another 10 miles beyond that, Chester and Chester Depot.

GETTING AROUND

Most visitors should and do have their own vehicles. There is a local bus service, **Town & Village Bus**, *Tel. 888/869-6287*, that stops at Chester, Chester Depot, Stone Hearth Inn, Cavenidh, Okemo, and Springfield. It runs from 7am-6pm and passes by each stop aproximately once every hour or so. Fares range from 50 cents to $2 per ride depending on distance, with seniors getting a discount.

WHERE TO STAY

Mt. Ascutney

ASCUTNEY MOUNTAIN RESORT, *Route 44 (meets Route 5 just south of Windsor), Brownsville VT 05037. Tel. 802/484-7711, 800/243-0011, Fax 802/484-3117. E-mail: skiascut@aol.com Web site: www.ascutney.com. Rates: $80-$315. Major credit cards accepted.*

This 800-acre family-friendly resort on the northwest slopes of Mount Ascutney is best known for its skiing – which is modest compared to

Killington or Stowe, but is still excellent (and cheaper). But the resort also offers guests the opportunity to explore other recreational activities on and around scenic Mount Ascutney. Lodging facilities include 250 deluxe hotel-style rooms and a variety of other suites and condos, some of which feature fireplaces and other amenities. There are several casual and fine dining eateries.

Other facilities include tennis and Racquetball courts, volleyball, saunas and steam baths, full sized indoor and outdoor swimming pools, miniature golf, and a gym. If mom and dad need some time to themselves, the resort offer a variety of day and half-day care programs that give children opportunities to enjoy the facilities and natural environment under qualified adult supervision. Call about ski and summer packages offering rates much improved on the rack rates listed above. Ski facilities, restaurants, and other facilities are open to use by non-resident guests for standard fees.

MOUNT ASCUTNEY STATE PARK, *1826 Back Mountain Road off Route 44A, Windsor VT 05089. Tel. 802/674-2060 summer; 802/886-2434 (off-season). Base rates: $11-$15. Open mid to late May through Columbus Day. Credit cards: Visa, Mastercard.*

Located on the eastern slope of Mount Ascutney, just minutes from Windsor, this state park contains 40 wooded tent and camper sites and 10 lean-to sites, as well as showers and restrooms, dumping station, and picnic facilities. The park also features a number of biking and hiking trails, and the summit includes two hang-gliding launches and superb views of the Green Mountains, Connecticut River Valley, and the Berkshires.

RUNNING BEAR CAMPING AREA, *P.O. Box 378 (at junction of routes 5 and 44A; I-91 Exit 8), Ascuutney VT 05030. Tel. 802/674-6417. Base Rates: $16-22. Open year around. Credit cards: Visa, Mastercard.*

This camp features more than 100 sites and some tents, with hook-ups, showers, stores, dumping station, and other amenities. Recreational opprtunities include basketball, a pool, horseshoes and others.

Chester
FULLERTON INN, *Village Green (Main Street/Route 11), P.O. Box 188, Chester VT 05143. Tel. 802/875-2444, 888/CHESINN, Fax 802/875-6414. E-mail: getaway@fullertoninn.com. Web site: www.fullertoninn.com. Rates: $70-$200. Major Credit cards accepted.*

This famous inn is a remnant of Chester's heyday as a stagecoach and rail hub and is a descendant of the famous American, Ingram Central and The Inn at Long Last hotels (the first two were destroyed by fire). With its columns, porches, and spacious rooms, today's rendition maintains some of the grandness of yesteryear. Each of the 21 rooms and suites are individually appointed and equipped with the necessary modern amenities. Other features include the Tavern, the Lounge, and the Library. Finally, the house food is excellent, but if you're a bit restless, the various options of the Village Green are within walking distance.

HENRY FARM INN, *2206 Vermont Turnpike, Chester VT 05143. (Off Route 11 northeast of the Green.) Tel. 802/875-2674, 800/723-8213, Fax 802/ 875-1510. E-mail: hfinn@vermontel.net. Web site: henryfarm.vermontel.net. Rates: $65-$115 depending on season.*

Nestled in a classic rural New England setting complete with woods, a stream-fed pond and meadows, this one-time 18th century stagecoach inn offers some of the best lodgings in the region.

INN VICTORIA, *Main Street (Route 11), (P.O. Box 788) Chester VT 05143. Tel. 802/875-4288, 800/732-4288, Fax 802/875-3529. Rates: $70-295. Credit cards: Visa, Mastercard.*

Another old style New Englandy inn with 9 individually decorated rooms, some of which feature fireplaces and/or jacuzzis, giving the Victoria a leg up on other local inns. Other features and amenities include an outdoor hot tub and deck, as well as good food.

THE MADRIGAL INN, *6 Williams River Road (off Route 103 between Chester and Rockingham), Chester VT 05143. Tel. & Fax 802/463-8169, 800/ 854-2208. E-mail: madrigal@sover.net. Web site: www.sover.net/˜madrigal. Rates: $90-$110. Credit cards: Visa, Mastercard.*

The main attraction of this inn – which made a recent addition in the traditional post & beam style – is its stunning setting in the hills between Chester and Rockingham. With more than 60 acres laden with meadows, woods, and a pond, the Madrigal really allows you to immerse yourself in rurality, and to do so in comfort in one of their beautifully decorated eleven rooms. The kitchen serves a full breakfast and beverages, but not dinner or lunch.

CHESTER HOUSE INN, *266 Main Street, Chester VT 05143. Tel. 802/ 875-2205; Tel. 888/875-2205, Fax 802/875-6602. E-mail: Randy@ChesterHouseInn.com. Web site: www. ChesterHouseInn.com. Rates: $90-150. Visa, Mastercard.*

This seven room Nationally Registered Historic Inn is located on the Village Green in a house that dates to the late 18th century. All rooms feature phones, a private bath, and air conditioning, and some have a fireplace. Also, homecooked breakfasts and dinners are served in the Keeping Room.

NIGHT WITH A NATIVE B&B, *266 Depot Street (off S. Main St.), Chester VT 05143. Tel. 802/875-2612. Rates: $60-90. Credit cards: Visa, Mastercard.*

With country-style appointments, Night with a Native (6th generation Vermont natives to be exact) is a warm and friendly inn, whose location in town is convenient for those who would enjoy an evening stroll through the village. Tasty breakfast included.

THE HUGGING BEAR INN & SHOPPE, *244 Main Street (Route 11), Chester VT 05143. Tel. 802/875-2412, 800/325-0519, Fax 802/875-3823. E-mail: huggingbear@vbv-online.com. Web stie: www.huggingbear.com. Rates: $60-$155. Major credit cards accepted.*

A comfy little inn on the Village Green with six rooms and a Teddy Bear motif that touches the child in each of us. Should you decide to adopt one of the cuddly little (or sometime cases not so little) bears, the "Shoppe" portion of the Inn has thousands of bears for sale as well as other toys and souvenirs.

KIMBERLY'S CHERUB B&B, *Route 103 (From Route 11 Main St. take Maple or Depot Street. It's on the right), (P.O. Box 62) Chester VT 05143. Tel. 802/875-3773. Rates: $75-115. Credit cards: Visa, Mastercard.*

Located in a 1906 Victorian beauty on Route 103 just down the block from Main Street and the center of town, Kimberly's features a small assortment of individually appointed rooms, each of which features private baths (some with Victorian-era clawfoot tubs). Only one room has cable television, but for the rest there is a communal game/television room. The house and setting are impressive, but it's the breakfast that really impresses many guests.

"SECOND WIND" B&B, *Corner of Grafton Street (Route 35) and River Street off South Main Street, Chester VT 05143. Tel. 802/875-3438. Rates: $60-$70. Credit cards: Visa.*

With more dogs (3) than suites (2), this may just be the most homey inn in Chester. Rooms arc simple but comfortable and the breakfast is excellent.

Windsor

JUNIPER HILL INN, *Juniper Hill Road, (RR1 Box 79) Windsor VT 05089. Tel. Tel. 802/674-5273, 800/359-2541, Fax 802/674-2041. E-mail: innkeeper@juniperhillinn. Web site: www.juniperhillinn.com. Rates: $90-$150. Credit cards: Visa, Mastercard.*

This grand mansion (listed in the National Historic Register) boasts one of the most spectacular settings in Vermont, offering views of Mount Ascutney and the beautiful surrounding countryside. But that's only the half of it – the mansion features a handsome dining room, a library, and a parlor, all littered with antiques, and the grounds comprise well-kept gardens and an inground pool.

Springfield

HARTNESS HOUSE, *30 Orchard Street, Springfield VT 05156. Tel. 802/885-2115, 800/732-4789, Fax 802/885-2207. E-mail: avstore@sover.net.*

Web site: avermontstore.come/hartness.html. Rates: $90-150. Major credit cards accepted.

The former home of a Vermont governor from a local industrial family, this handsome 1903 mansion (some rooms are in a modern addition) on the edge of Springfield is a historic landmark complete with historical exhibits including an old observatory. It is an elegant inn known for its excellent value. The building includes a sitting room and a charming dining room as well as 29 guest rooms. The 32 acres of grounds feature a tennis court and a pool, in addition to access to wooded trails on the one hand and Springfield on the other.

BULL RUN FARM B&B, *903 French Meadow Road, Springfield VT 05156. Tel. 802/886-8470. E-mail: ctm@vermontel.com. Rates: $45-55; discounts for extended stays. Visa.*

A modest but comfy and homey inn housed in an old farm house, the Bull Run offers good value, full breakfasts, a convenient location, and an opportunity to engage in a Vermont pastime by having a conversation with Alice the cow.

BAKER ROAD INN, *29 Baker Road, Springfield VT 05156. Tel. 802/ 886-6826. Rates: $50-60 per double. Credit cards: Visa, Mastercard.*

Sort of similar to the Bull Run in terms of value, modest size, and satisfying comfort. Breakfast is included and baths are shared.

HOLIDAY INN EXPRESS, *818 Charleston Road (off I-91 Exit 7), Springfield VT 05156. Tel. 802/885-4516, 800/HOLIDAY, Fax 802/885-4595. E-mail: hiexpress@aol.com. Rates: $80-$100. Major credit cards accepted.*

Standard franchise hotel offering some suites with whirlpool, and also features a restaurant, gym, and indoor pool.

TREE FARM CAMPGROUND, *53 Skitchewang Trail (1 mie east of town on Route 143), Springfield VT 05156. Tel. 802/885-2889. Rates: $13-$20. Open year around. Credit cards: Visa, Mastercard.*

Forty acre campround with more than 100 sites, extensive amenities (including cable TV hookups!), and direct access to trails for hiking, biking, cross-country skiing, snowmobiling, and snowshoeing.

WHERE TO EAT

Windsor

JUNIPER HILL INN, *Juniper Hill Road, (RR1 Box79) Windsor VT 05089. Tel. Tel. 802/674-5273, 800/359-2541, Fax 802/674-2041. E-mail: innkeeper@juniperhillinn. Web site: www.juniperhillinn.com. Hours: one seating at 7pm Monday-Saturday. Major credit cards accepted.*

Windsor's finest inn offers a set four course meal for $32.50 with one seating at 7pm. The food – haute American-continental – is fine but hearty. Each meal typically includes a soup, a salad and a choice of one of three entrees (usually a meat, fish or seafood, or poultry; vegetarians can be acccommodated) as well as a dessert and coffee. The setting in this vintage Victorian hilltop inn is nothing short of elegant, however smart casual dress (slacks and a sports shirt for example) is acceptable. Because tables are reserved for inn guests, you must call at least a day or two (more during foliage season and holidays) for a table; if you are a vegetarian or have other dietary needs, this is the time to bring it up.

WINDSOR STATION RESTAURANT, *Depot Avenue, Windsor VT. Tel. 802/674-2052. Hours: lunch 10am-2pm, dinner 5:30pm-9pm. Credit cards: Visa, Mastercard, American Express.*

Situated in Windsor's restored railroad station, the Station Restaurant offers diners fine food in a classic Victorian enviroment complete with brass railings and accents, wood paneling and velvet padded chairs. The food itself is continental-American and the menu typically features steaks, an assortment of pastas, chicken, and seafood such as grilled fish and shrimp. Entree prices range from $10-$20 and there is also a bar that serves adult refreshments from 4pm until the restaurant closes.

DEPOT DELI, *Depot Avenue, Windsor VT. Tel. 802/674-2675. Hours: 10am-2pm. Credit cards: Visa, Mastercard, American Express.*

This deli and catering service offers excellent freshly baked breads as well as salads and excellent sandwiches – great for picnic lunches at Mount Ascutney or stocking up for long Amtrak ride (sure beats those $4 microwaved ham croissants).

Weathersfield (Perkinsville)

INN AT WEATHERSFIELD, *Weathersfield Center Road (Route 106/ P.O. Box 106), Perkinsville VT 05151. (Located about 5 miles north of Springfield). Tel. 802/263-9217, Fax 802/263-9219. Hours: Two seatings nightly at 6pm and 8:30pm Monday – Saturday; sometimes closed Monday. Major credit cards accepted.*

Along with the Juniper Hill Inn at Windsor, the Inn at Weathersfield defintely takes honors for top dining in the Precision Valley. Located in a historic 19th century building, the dining room's intimate and elegant enviroment is enhanced by candlelight, a stone fireplace, and live piano music. The meal (there are two seatings at 6pm and 8:30 pm) is a set five course affair that includes drinks, soup, salad, appetizers, a main course, and coffee and dessert. The food is high-end, stylish American with – roasted and grilled meats, poultry, and seafood – perhaps an extra ethnic (usually Italian) touch. Meals cost $35.50 and you must call at least two days in advance for reservations, particularly during foliage and holiday seasons.

Springfield

HARTNESS HOUSE, *30 Orchard Street, Springfield VT 05156. Tel. 802/885-2115, 800/732-4789. E-mail: innkeeper@hartnesshouse.com. Hours: 5pm-9pm dail except Sunday. Credit cards: major credit cards accepted.*

In its vintage Victorian dining room (it was built in 1900), the Hartness serves a wide variety of hearty dishes from vegetarian pastas to ripe New York strip steaks. Though the menu rotates to a large degree, you can pretty much figure on steak, a fish dish or two (often grilled), several pastas, chicken, and vegetarian dishes; salads, soups, appetizers, and desserts are also plentiful. The food is not what some critics consider "fine dining" but is hearty and tasty – appropriate given Vermont's rurality and Springfield's industrial past. Entrees begin at $14 and wine, beer, and cocktails are also available.

B.J. BRICKER'S, *River Street, Springfield VT 05156. Tel. 802/885-6050. Credit cards: major credit cards accepted. Hours: Monday-Friday 11am-late.*

B.J. Bricker's might not be on the verge of earning a third star from Michelin, but its reasonable prices, friendly atmosphere, and decent food make it a good choice for families. Appetizers include the usual suspects (wings, potato skins et al), soups, and a variety of salads (incuding a salad bar), while entrees should also be recognizeable – steaks and seafood are the "Specialities" while pasta and chicken are also available. Most entrees are under $15 and some are under $12. On Friday's, Bricker's offers an all-you-can-eat buffet for $10.95 from 5pm-9pm.

Chester

YE OLDE BRADFORD TAVERN, *on the Village Green (Route 11), Chester VT -5143. Tel. 802/875-6094. Hours: daily except Wednesday 5pm until closing (somewhere between 9pm-11pm). Credit cards: Visa, Mastercard.*

This charming establishment features a handsome bar and an elegant but casual restaurant serving pasta, steak, poultry, and seafood by candlelight.

RASBERRIES AND THYME, *on the Village Green (Route 11), Chester VT 05143. Tel. 802/875-4486. Hours: 8am (lunch begins at 11am) to 5pm; dinner served 5pm-9pm Wednesday – Monday. Credit cards: Visa, Mastercard.*

A charming and casual Victorian establishment, Rasberries and Thyme serves excellent soups, salads, and sandwiches, baked goods for breakfast, and basic American-style fare for dinner.

SEEING THE SIGHTS

Windsor

The first major town south of White River Junction on Route 5 and I-91 is **Windsor**, cradle of industrial development in Vermont, and sometimes claimant to the title "Birthplace of Vermont" – a reference to adoption of the short-lived Republic of Vermont's constitution in a local tavern in 1777.

If you're not already on it, you should get on Route 5 at White Rvier Junction and head south through the villages of North Hartland and Hartland and on to Windsor. Taking Route 5 not only allows you to pass up the rush of the interstate in favor of the more leisurely and scenic state highway, but it will enable you to access two sights which are just north of downtown Windsor. (Get off at Exit 9 and head south if you're on I-91). Beer lovers will enjoy a visit to the **Catamount Brewery Co.**, where you can take a guided tour of brewery operations and sample what is considered by many to be the finest beer brewed in Vermont. There is of course, also a gift shop selling the usual assortment of t-shirts and other doo-dads. *The brewery and gift shop are open 9am-5pm Monday-Saturday; 1pm-5pm Sunday.*

Just south of the brewery is a second branch of **Simon Pearce Glass**, the world-renowned glass works based in Quechee. Visitors can observe master craftsmen and women blow glass, and peruse one or both of the two retail outlets located here. *Open 9am-5pm daily. Admission free.*

Apart from several sturdy brick buildings dating to its industrial heyday, Windsor itself hardly feels historic, let alone as if it was once one of the most techologically advanced places in the world. Like most Vermont towns and villages it consists of one major artery (Route 5 in this case) lined with 19th century churches and Victorian houses whose luster is lost to gas stations, convenience stores, and other modern and semi-modern buildings with little attraction.

The first site worth a visit on the northern side of town is the museum in **Old Constitution House**. This euphemistically named building was historically a tavern whose significance stems from its bygone status as a favorite watering hole for Vermont leaders keen on achieving independence from New York and New Hampshire, both which had claims on portions on the state. It was in Elijah West's tavern that the Republic of Vermont was founded on July 8, 1777, after the Continental Congress refused to nullify New York's claims to eastern portions of the state. According to Vermont legend, the convention which had been in session for a week was on the verge of breaking up in the face of the rapidly advancing armies of British General John Burgoyne, when in a stroke of "divine intervention," a wicked thunderstorm descended on the town, forcing the politicians and militiamen to stay put in the tavern, whereupon they finished the business of adopting the consitution and declaring Vermont's independence.

The Republic remained independent of the United States for almost 15 years until 1791, when New York finally acceded to Vermont's becoming the 14th state after agreeing to waive its own claims to the state in exchange for monetary compensation. Windsor continued to serve as Vermont's capital until 1805, when Montpelier assumed that status.

Just south of Old Constitution House (also on the west side of the street) are two of Windsor's more handsome buildings, **Windsor House** and the **Inn at Windsor**. Across from the Post Office at *54 Main Street (Route 5)*, Windsor House is home to the **Vermont State Craft Center**, an especially worthy destination for shoppers and those interested in Vermont arts and crafts. It features a museum exhibiting both antique and contemporary works as well as demonstrations by local artists. There is also a small library, and various crafts including textiles, ceramics, wood carvings, and sculptures are for sale as are books, food products, and other souvenirs. Those interested in learning craftsmanship may consider taking one of the many classes offered by the Center in conjunction with Lebanon College. *The Center is open Monday-Thursday 10am-5pm, Friday & Saturday 9am-6pm, and Sunday 11am-5pm.*

South of Windsor House stands the historic **Inn at Windsor**, once the home of the local indstrialist Roswell H. Lamson, and is now a small (three units), but functioning inn with a small exhibit of photos and historic relics relating to Windsor and Vermont history. *It is generally open to the public during regular business hours.*

Just about due east of the Inn at Windsor across Main St. (Route 5), the restored **Windsor-Ascutney Train Station** features a plushy and excellent restaurant (see *Where to Eat* above) and a modest exhibit about railroad history in Vermont. North of the rail station is the **Cone Blanchard Corporation**, a machine company whose status as the manufaturer of the largest grinders in the world is redolent of the 19th century Windsor industrialists who manufactured the most advanced firearms and machine-tools in the world.

Across from Windsor House stands **the oldest continuously used post office in America** and to the south, the **Cornish-Windsor Bridge** – the longest covered bridge in the world and the longest wooden span in the United States. This bridge – the fourth to be built here since 1796 – was completed in 1866 and stretches 460 feet. As the Vermont-New Hampshire border is drawn at the river's edge on the Vermont side, the bridge is technically the property of New Hampshire, which does pay the lion's share of dollars needed to maintain the bridge.

Many consider Windsor's crown jewel to be the **American Precision Museum** located on the west side of the street at the southern edge of the village. The building, built in 1848, was formerly the Robbins and Lawrence Armory where Windsor's most prominent industrialist, Richard Smith Lawrence and Nicanor Kendal, mastered the manufacture of rifles by machine rather than hand. This more efficient and cheaper way of maufacturing rifles was developed just in time for such major conflicts as the Mexican-American, Crimean and Civil wars. Later, in the 1860's Lawrence joined a partnership with Governor Oliver Winchester of Connecticut, to form the Winchester Repeating Arms Company, which pioneered the manufacture of rapid-fire rifles. During the second half of the 19th century and first decades of the 20th, Windsor also enjoyed the rise of its wool industry as well as the manufacture and use of machine-tools for non-military related products. The current museum contains a significant and fascinating collection of machines and tools from these eras. *Open from Memorial Day- November 1; Monday-Friday 9am-5pm; Saturday, Sunday & holidays 10am-4pm. Admission: Adults $3.50, seniors $3; students and children (6-12) $2; children under six enter free.*

Mount Ascutney

On Route 44 West, only four miles from Windsor, is **Mt. Asctuney** (and two miles beyond the junction with 44A) – a singular mountain with an inner core made of granite, and independent of nearby ranges such as the Green Mountains. (If coming from the south on Route 5, take Route 44A north of Ascutney village). Its northwestern slopes are dominated by the **Ascutney Mountain Resort**. Modest by the standards of Sugarbush or Killington, Asctuney is a family-friendly skiing resort complete with lift facilities, a variety of lodgings and restaurants, as well as summer recreation facilities for swimming and other activities. For more information see *Where To Stay* above or contact the Ascutney Mountain Resort at: *PO Box 494, Brownssville Vt 05037, Tel. 800/243-0011.*

The northeastern face of the mountain is now the **Ascutney State Park**, featuring four trails of two to four miles, 30 campsites, rest rooms, picnic areas, and a hang-glider launch site. The hiking is moderately difficult, but should you successfully make it to the top, you will be rewarded with an impressive 360 degree view (slightly marred by several nearby communications towers) that encompasses the Green Mountains, the Connecticut River Valley, and when visibility is decent, four states. For those not up to the task and walking 2-3 miles uphill, there is a toll road to the summit. The park is open from roughly mid-May thought mid-October, depending on when the trails recover from the last snow melt and the resulting mud. For more details about Ascutney State, including information and regulations for camping, *call 802/674-2060 in the summer,* or *802/885-8855 during the off-season.* Or write to the Ascutney State Park, *Box 186, HCR 71, Windsor VT 05089* in the summer and to *Vermont Department of Forests, Parks, and Recreation, RR 1 Box 33, North Springfield VT 05150-9726* during the off-season.

West of the Ascutney State Park and the Ascutney Mountain Resort, Route 44 joins Route 106, a scenic north-south strip linking Woodstock to the north with Springfield to the south. Just east of the junction on

Route 44 lies the hamlet of **Brownsville**, where the local **West Windsor Historical Society** features a very modest museum that . Each year a different theme of history is chosen and an exhibit is put together by members of the Society, along with schoolchildren and other folks of the community. To view the Society's collection during other times of the year call to make an appointment. *Open on Saturdays from July-August (3pm-8pm), Tel. 802/484-7474.*

Both 106 and Route 5 intersect less than five miles from Route 44 with Route 131, which strectches east-west from Ascutney village (east) to Cavendish (west). Just west of Ascutney on 131, take the Weathersfield Center Road going south to Weathersfield Center and Springfield. **Weathersfield Center** is a small village in the midst of some very beautiful rural country. Aside from the classic countryside scenery, Weathersfield's main attraction is the **Weathersfield Historical Society Museum** in the **Reverend Dan Foster House** on the main street. The museum features a variety of historical exhibits spanning a wide range of themes from the Civil War to local geneaologies. Portions of the complex date to the late 18th and early 19th centuries. If you'd like to arrange a visit during the off-season, call the museum's office. *Open from late June through early October, Tel. 802/674-6729.*

Springfield

To reach Springfield from Windsor or Mt. Asctuney, continue south on Route 5 along the Connecticut River and through Ascutney village and Weathersfield Bow (where a penninsula juts into the Connecticut River) to the junction with Route 11, which you follow two miles west. If you're coming on I-91, Route 11 begins at Exit 7. An alternative for those looking for a change from the Connecticut Valley scenery is to turn inland on Route 131 (at Exit 8 from I-91) and after about two miles turn south on the Weathersfield Center Road.

Known as the center of Vermont industry since the late 19th century when it assumed the status previously enjoyed by Windsor, Springfield was founded in the Black River Valley by laborers working on the **Crown Point Military Road**, which linked the British Fort No. 4 in Charlestown, New Hampshire with the Fort at Crown Point on Lake Champlain. While the earliest settlers built on the hills overlooking the valley, they were soon attracted to the river where a local entrepeneur, William Lockwood, constructed a dam on the second branch of the Black River to provide power for his sawmill. The operation was expanded in the early 19th century when a New Hampshire businessman, Isaac Fisher, purchased the operation and expanded it, building several mills and a foundry, and putting Springfield on the industrial map.

However, it was not until the later decades of the 19th century when the likes of Amasa Woolson, Fredson Lovejoy, and W. LeRoy Bryant pioneered the mechanization of manufacturing machine-tools (tools used to make other tools and machines) that Springfield found itself on the cutting edge of the Industrial Revolution. Facilitated by the Springfield Terminal Railway Company, at the time the only electric railroad in northern New England, Springfield's industrial development attracted many immigrants from Russia and Poland, many descendents of whom still live in the region.

Before encountering the town itself, Springfield's reputation as an industrial center manifests itself along Route 11 lined with machine and other factories. As you approach town, the **Eureka Schoolhouse** and the **Baltimore Covered Bridge** will appear on your right. Originally constructed in 1785 off the Crown Point Military Road, and completed in 1790 by some of Springfield's earliest settlers, the schoolhouse is Vermont's oldest. It was moved up the road and remodeled in 1837, and it closed in 1900. It remained idle until the 1950's when it was saved from demolition by concerned local citizens who raised the money to relocate it to its present location in 1968. The schoolhouse has been carefully renovated and redecorated to recreate its appearance from its heydey in the 19th century. It is usually closed to visitors, but is small enough that you can easily get a good look through the windows. *Open daily 9am-4pm mid-May through mid-October.*

Next to the Eureka Schoolhouse stands the **Baltimore Covered Bridge**. Like the Eureka Schoohouse, the bridge – the last covered bridge in Springfield – is a transplant from its original location on the Great Brook in North Springfield, where it was constructed in 1870 (it was moved in 1970).

Though Springfield has not made as much of its role in the Industrial Revolution in the way of tourist attractions to the same extent as Windsor, its roots in manufacturing are evident in the reconverted brick mills and other factories that dominate its downtown. The only true "tourist attraction" as such is the impressive **Hartness House**, a 1903 mansion built by a son of the Industrial Revolution and governor of Vermont, James Hartness. Located on Orchard Street *(turn onto Summer St. from Main St./Route 11 and follow the signs)*, this Victorian gem has been converted into an inn but is open to the public and features several small exhibits related to Springfield and James Hartness, including his observatory and early 20th century telescope (Hartness was a dedicated amateur astronomer). Guided tours are sometimes given in the evening; call *802/885-2779* for information and schedules.

Should you have the time, consider paying a short visit to the **Springfield Arts & Historical Society** *on Elm Street (north off Main Street),* home to a modest but fascinating photographic history of the machine-tool industry and Springfield.

From Springfield, the most efficient way to get back north to Windsor, White River, and other places north, or to Brattleboro and points south, is to take Route 11 to Route 5 and I-91 which runs north-south. A more quaint way north is Route 106 linking Springfield with Woodstock. To get back to Windsor, cut back east on 131 or 44 (also to Mt. Ascutney) to Route 5 and I-91. However, if you have the time, we'd recommend carrying on to the scenic village of **Chester** and **Chester Depot** by way of Route 11 (9miles) west which carries on to Londonderry and Manchester, as well as the ski resorts of Magic Mountain and Bromley.

Chester

Chester is one of those Vermont villages (and there are many) which you might miss if you blink for more than a moment as you pass through, which would be a shame because it boasts some of the most beautiful restored Victorian buildings in the state as well as several interesting gift shops, a handsome **Civil War Memorial and cemetery**, the renowned **Baba a Louis Bakery**, and the **National Survey Charthouse**.

Chester's main street is Route 11, which as it passes through town is flanked to the north by the long and thin **Village Green**, which itself is lined with an impressive assortment of Victorian homes, inns and other buildings. At the information booth across from Route 11, next to the cemetery and civil war monument across the street from the Green, you can pick up the pamphlet, *A Walking Tour of Chester*, which explains in detail the architectural history of Chester. Located at the junction of the Boston-Montreal and Hanover-Albany stagecoach highways, Chester prospered during the 19th century when most of the more than 150 buildings listed in the National Register of Historic Places were constructed. Some of the inns, such as the The Henry Farm Bed and Breakfast, date to the 18th century and are still among the nicest in all of Vermont.

Chester actually features two historic districts, one being the aforementioned Village Green; the second is the **Stone Village** along Route 103 which is a continuation of Route 11 after its turnoff towards Springfield. Consisting of about a dozen buildings, the Stone Village is so named for the sneckled ashlar type of masonry used in their construction during the 1830's. Among the buildings still intact are the First Universalist Church, an old schoolhouse, and the Stone Cottage Collectables Bed & Breakfast.

You can catch the Green Mountain Flyer Scenic Railroad here en route to Bellows Falls; see sidebar on page 67 for details.

NIGHTLIFE & ENTERTAINMENT

Though each features good restaurants and functional pubs and taverns, Windsor and Springfield are not known as hubs for high culture. Howeve,r the vibrant university town of Hanover, New Hampshire – home of Dartmouth College – is only about 20 minutes away up Route 5 (and I-91) and across the river. To find out what concerts, movies, and art shows are on the docket, pick up a copy of the readily available *Valley News.*

At the Ascutney Mountain Resort, you may enjoy an adult refreshment at **Brown's Tavern**, which also serves dinner. North of Windsor on Route 5, the **Skunk Hollow Tavern** in Hartland serves food and drink, and presents live music Wendnesdays and Fridays. *Tel. 802/436-2139.*

SHOPPING

You will not find the extensive shopping opportunities found in other, more tourist-traveled regions of Vermont, but there are an assortment of antique and handicraft shops in the area, particularly in and around Chester. Below is a listing of some of those shops. For a more complete list, contact the chambers of commerce listed in the "Practical Information" section at the end of this chapter.

Windsor

SIMON PEARCE GLASS, *Route 5 north of Windsor. (From I-91, get off at Exit 9). Tel. 802/674-6280. Hours: 9am-5pm daily. Major credit cards accepted.*

At this branch of the famous glass works based in Quechee, you can watch the craftsmen as they blow and shape glass jars, vases, and other containers. There are two retail outlets where you purchase all sorts of beautiful (and kitsch) glass items as well as other souvenirs. Keep in mind, should you purchase anything made of glass that it is very fragile and needs to be packed or shipped accordingly.

CATAMOUNT BREWING CO.,*Route 5 north of Windsor. Tel. 802/ 674-6700. (From I-91, get off at Exit 9). Open 9am-5pm Monday – Saturday, 1pm-5pm Sunday. Major credit cards accepted.*

In addition to taking tours and listening to making explanations of the brewing process, you may purchase all types of beers and other souvenirs at the gift shop.

VERMONT STATE CRAFT CENTER AT WINDSOR HOUSE, *54 Main Street (Route 5), Windsor VT. Tel. 802/674-6729. Hours: 10am-5pm Monday-Thursday, 9am-6pm Friday & Saturday, 11am-5pm Sunday. Major credit cards accepted.*

Located in a historic building in downtown Windsor, the Windsor House is now an all-around art center that includes galleries, a museum, a library and art classes. Avilable for sale are all types of Vermont-made crafts from textiles and ceramics to paintings and sculptures.

Chester

CARPENTERS'S EMPORIUM, *Main Street (on the Village Green), Chester VT 05143. Hours: 9am-5pm daily.*

A sort of all-purpose gift shop selling crafts, maple products, shirts and other apparel and just all types of souvenirs in a country store setting.

THE HUGGING BEAR INN & SHOPPE, *244 Main Street (Route 11), Chester VT 05143. Tel. 802/875-2412, 800/325-0519, Fax 802/875-3823. E-mail: huggingbear@vbv-online.com. Web stie: www.huggingbear.com. Open daily 10am-5pm. Major credit cards accepted.*

This inn and shop is just teeming with thousands of Teddy Bears – perfect if you're shopping for a child, a baby shower, or anybody whose heart melts at the sight of a loveable teddy. A great place for browsing.

MISTY VALLEY BOOKS, *Main Street (on the Village Green), Chester VT 05143. Tel. 802/875-3400. Hours: 10am-6pm Monday-Friday, 10am-5pm Saturday, 11am-5pm Sunday. Credit cards: Visa, Mastercard.*

A somewhat clogged shop with all sorts of interested used books – great browsing.

STONE COTTAGE COLLECTIBLES, *North Street, Chester VT 05143. Tel. 802/875-6211. Hours: 10am-5pm daily (usually). Credit cards: Visa, Mastercard.*

Situated in a B&B in the Stone Village, this shop sells a variety of antiques and stamps.

STONE HOUSE, *Route 103, Chester VT 05143. Tel. 802/875-4477. Hours: 9:30am-5pm daily.*

Sells a myriad of antiques, handicrafts, and other cool stuff.

THE VICTORIA TEAPOT SHOPPE, *at Inn Victoria on the Village Green on Main Street (Route 11), Chester VT 05143. Tel. 802/875-4288, 800/732-4288. Hours: 10am-6pm daily. Major credit cards accepted.*

Sells all types of tea brewing accessories from antiques to high tech gizmos.

SPORTS & RECREATION

Biking

Ascutney State Park, *Route 44/I-91 Exits 8 & 9,* is open from May until October and features several scenic but challenging trails for bikers. Maps and other information are available at the entrance.

It is also possible to cycle along main roads in the areas such as Routes 5, 44, and 131, as well local roads.

Cross-Country Skiing

There are no designated cross-country ski areas in the Precision Valley, but both **Woodstock** *(call 457-6674 or Tel. 800/448-7900 for info)* and **Quechee** *(call Wilderness Trails, Tel. 802/295-7620)* feature excellent cross-country opportunities and are 20-30 miles from Windsor and Springfield. There is also excellent cross-country skiing in the Green Moutains along Route 100 at the **Viking XC Ski Center** in Londonderry (see the "Manchester and the Heart of the Green Mountains" chapter for details).

Fishing

Talk to locals about what's biting where and pick up a copy of the *Vermont Guide to Fishing*, but unfortunately fishing is not one of the Precision Valley's better offerings. You can make your casts at **Wilus State Park** on Route 5, and in Springfield in the Black River, or at the **Springfield Nature Area** and the **Stoughton Pond Recreation Area**. However, there is no salmon or trout.

Golf

WINDSOR COUNTRY CLUB, *North Main Street (P.O. Box 263), Windsor VT 05143. Tel. 802/674-6491. Rates: $18 weekdays, $23. Major credit cards accepted. Nine holes*

TATER HILL RESORT, *Popple Dungeon Road, Windham VT. (Off Route 11 east of Chester). Tel. 802/875-2517. 18 holes. Rates: $65 weekends, $55 weekdays (carts included). Major credit cards accepted.*

CROWN POINT COUNTRY CLUB, *Weathersfield Center Road (P.O. Box 413), Springfield VT. Tel. 802/885-1010. 18 holes. Rates: $34 weekends, $27 weekdays, $14 after 5pm. Carts available. Major credit cards accepted.*

Hiking

Again, **Ascutney State Park**, *Route 44/ I-91 Exits 8 & 9*, features about a half dozen trails ranging from about 2-4 miles, most of which are challenging, and reward those who make it to the top with stunning views of the Connecticut Valley, the Green Mountains, and the Berkshires in Massachussetts.

In Springfield, the **Springfield Nature Area** on the **North Springfield Lake** *(entrance on Reservoir Road of 106 north of town)* features a modest 70 acres with trails, ponds, and wooded areas, as well as picnic facilities, restrooms, swimming areas, boating (no rentals). Just a few miles further north and accessible from Route 106 as well as the Reservoir Road is the **Stoughton Pond Recreation Area** with comparable facilities.

Skiing

ASCUTNEY MOUNTAIN RESORT, *Route 44, Brownsville. Tel. 802/ 484-7711. Web site: ww. ascutney.com. Credit cards: major credit cards accepted. Hours: 9am-5pm.*

Though it's not in the same league as Killington or Sugarbush in terms of extensive runs and variety of terrain, Acustney offers 47 runs and a good balance among difficult, easy, and in-between runs, and tends to be less crowded as it is not as accessible to major towns such as Rutland or Burlington – a factor that makes Stowe and Killington even more crowded. The resort offers lessons for adults and children, as well as childcare for children who may be too young or uninterested in skiing.

Finally, skiers who find Ascutney inadequate will be keen to head east to the "skiers' row" of **Route 100** where ski areas like Okemo, Bromley, Magic Mountain, Stratton and Killington offer some of the east's best and most varied skiing. From Springfield, **Magic Mountain** (20 miles) and **Bromley** (32 miles) are the closest ski areas and be reached directly on Route 11 west. From Windsor, the nearest ski areas are the modest **Suicide Six** at Woodstock and **Okemo**, which can reached by turning west from Route 5 onto 131 at Ascutney villlage. **Killington**, Vermont's most extensive ski area, is approximately 50 miles from Windsor and is best reached by taking Route 12 from Hartland (just north of Windsor) to Route 4 west which leads directly to Killington.

EXCURSIONS & DAY TRIPS

For most visitors, the Precision Valley itself is a day trip as few tourists actually stay in these towns, but should you decide to set yourself apart, there is plenty within reach of this region in addition to its own attractions.

Just about 20 minutes north and east of Windsor are the popular tourist destinations of **Quechee** and **Woodstock**. Teeming with restaurants and shops, these two towns have plenty to offer tourists of all ages, including Quechee Gorge ("Vermont's Grand Canyon"), the Billings Farm Museum, the Simon Pearce Glass works and restaurant, as well as many handsome buildings and several golf courses. Take I-91 or Route 5 to White River Junction and then one exit over on I-89 to Route 4. Or, from Windsor take I-91 or Route 5 north to Hartland and then get on Route 12 to Woodstock; from Springfield, the scenic Route 106 also goes straight to Woodstock (about 25 miles). For more details, see the "The Ottauquechee River Valley" chapter.

In the Connecticut Valley itself, not more than 15 miles north of Windsor is the hub town of **White River Junction**, and to its north the village of **Norwich**, home to nature-oriented Montshire Museum. White River doesn't offer much apart from some ordinary shops and restaurants, but **Hanover, New Hampshire** across the river from Norwich is a bustling and "happening" university town with many bars, restaurants, and shops. See the "Upper Connecticut Valley" chapter for more details.

To the south, **Windham County** features a very pleasant drive down Route 5 through towns like Bellows Fall, Dummerston (home of the longest covered bridge in Vermont), and Putney on your way to Brattleboro (about 50 miles south of Windsor) and Marlboro. Though **Brattleboro** is not considered the most attractive town in Vermont, its streets are lined with charming brick buildings that once were factories and mills but now bustle with lively shops, cafes and restaurants. Brattleboro's impressive but little known artistic heritage can be explored at the **Brattleboro Museum and Art Center**, which houses a number of fascinating exhibits including scultures by the renowned William Mead, an assortment of American paintings, and the famous Estey Organs, once manufactured in Brattleboro. See "Brattleboro & Windham County" chapter for more details.

From Brattleboro you can get on the scenic Routes 9 and 30. Route 9 leads east to **Marlboro** and the **Southern Vermont Natural History Museum**, featuring lots of animal and bird exhibits and dioramas. One good idea is to make your way to Springfield and Chester by way of Route 11 and then cutting south to Rockingham and Bellows Falls on the scenic Highway 103, which features three covered bridges. This is the same route you will enjoy should you indulge in the Green Mountain Flyer scenic train ride between Chester and Bellows Falls.

On Route 100, **Plymouth Notch** in Plymouth (10 miles north of Ludlow and 20 miles west of Woodstock) is noteworthy as the birthplace of President Calvin Coolidge and features a very well maintained and endowed museum and a beautiful state forest, as well as several quality inns and restaurants. To the south, the gentrified towns of **Ludlow** and **Londonderry** feature shops and restaurants; **Weston** (15 miles south of Ludlow) is home to the famous Vermont Country Store. Thirty miles east of Chester on Route 11 is **Manchester**, one of the most popular tourist destinations in Vermont known for its stately architecture, picturesque village center, and extensive high end outlet shopping. See "Manchester & The Heart of the Green Mountains" chapter for more details.

PRACTICAL INFORMATION

Banks & ATM's

VERMONT NATIONAL BANK (VNB), *50 Main Street, Windsor VT 05089. Tel. 802/674-2131.*

MERCHANTS BANKS, *160 Main Street, Windsor VT 05089. Tel. 802/ 674-6313.*

Medical Emergencies & Hospitals
> **Ambulance** – *Tel. 911*
>> **Ascutney** – *Tel. 603/542-2244 or 457-2323*
>> **Windsor** – *Tel. 802/674-2112*

WINDSOR HOSPITAL, *County Road, Windsor VT 05089. Tel. 802/674-6711.*

MOUNT ASCUTNEY HOSPITAL & HEALTH CENTER, *289 Windsor Road (off State Street which is off Main Street/Route 5), Windsor VT 05089. Tel. 802/674-6711. Includes 24 Emergency Service.*

SPRINGFIELD HOSPITAL, *25 Ridgewood Road, Springfield VT. Tel. 802/885-2151.*

DARTMOUTH-HITCHCOCK MEDICAL CENTER, *Medical Center Drive/Route 120 (Exit 18 I-91), Lebanon NH. Tel. 603/650-5848 (general information).*
> **Emergency Service** – *Tel. 603/650-5000*

Police & Fire Department
> **Ascutney** – *Tel. 802/674-2185 (Police); Tel. 802/674-2112 (fire)*
> **Windsor** – *Tel. 802/674-2112 (police and fire)*

15. THE OTTAUQUECHEE RIVER VALLEY

- QUECHEE, WOODSTOCK & PLYMOUTH -

Just west of White River Junction, along the modest **Ottauquechee River**, the 25-mile stretch of Route 4 from Route 100 to Interstate 89's Exit 1 draws perhaps more visitors and tourists than any in the state, with the possible exception of Route 100 between Warren and Stowe. The major attraction is the handsome, gentrified village of **Woodstock**. Known for its green, romantic Victorian inns, and the beautiful surrounding countryside with its rolling hills and classic farm houses, Woodstock is often described as the "quintessential New England village" and the "most photographed town in Vermont." But accolades aside, Woodstock is home to some fascinating attractions, including the **Billings Farm & Museum** where you can visit a working dairy farm that pioneered environment-friendly farming, and the **Marsh-Billings National Historic Park** on Mount Tom, featuring Laurence Rockefeller's former summer home-turned museum.

Almost as famous is the neighboring village of **Quechee**, site of "Vermont's Grand Canyon," the 165-foot deep **Quechee Gorge**, a famous balloon festival in June, and the renowned **Simon Pearce Glass and Pottery** works where you can watch master artists at work and eat in a fine restaurant in a renovated mill while gazing over waterfalls. Both Quechee and Woodstock boast among the best recreational facilities in Vermont, including fine golf courses and excellent cross-country skiing, hiking, and biking. The area is particularly popular during the foliage season in October, so be sure to make your reservations well in advance.

Situated about 12 miles west of Woodstock is the township of **Plymouth**. Not nearly as popular, gentrified, or developed as Woodstock and Quechee, Plymouth is the hometown of the 30th President of the

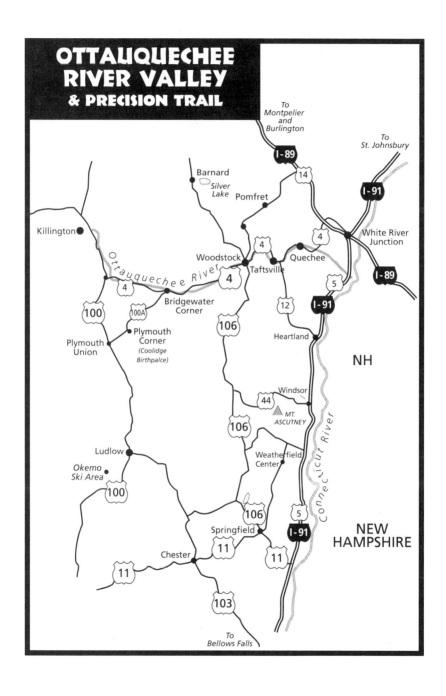

United States, **Calvin Coolidge**. On Route 100A, Silent Cal's home village of **Plymouth Notch** – from the room where he was born to the parlor in which he took the oath of office and the cemetery in which he is buried – has been entirely maintained and is open to the public from May until October.

Without subjecting you to a deluge of tacky souvenirs and meaningless exhibits, it not only teaches about Calvin Coolidge but provides a fascinating glimpse of life in rural New England around the turn of the century. Just up the road from Plymouth Notch is the **Calvin Coolidge State Park**. Part of the Coolidge State Forest (everything in these parts is named "Coolidge"), the park includes camping sites and trails for hiking and biking.

ARRIVALS & DEPARTURES

By Air

The nearest commercial airport is **Lebanon Municipal Airport** in West Lebanon, about 15 minutes away on Route 89 from Exit 1 and Route 4. However, Lebanon is only served by **USAir Express**, *Tel. 800/428-4322*, and flights are limited and expensive.

More convenient in terms of available flights and cost is **Manchester Airport** in Manchester, New Hampshire. Serviced by Southwest, *Tel. 800/435-9792*, Continental, *Tel. 800/525-0289*, USAir, *Tel. 800/428-4322*, and Delta Connection, *Tel. 800/345-3400*, Manchester is approximately two hours from Woodstock by car – most major rental companies operate out of Manchester. Otherwise, **Vermont Transit Lines**, *Tel. 800/552-8738, 800/451-3292*, offers direct service from the Manchester Airport to White River Junction four times daily (10:25am, 2:55pm, 5:55pm, & 10:40pm). From White River Junction you can take a 15-30 minute taxi ride to the Woodstock-Quechee region depending on where in the area you are going. If the departure times from the airport are inconvenient, take a taxi to the downtown depot where another half-dozen buses depart daily for White River Junction.

Another alternative is to fly into Boston's **Logan Airport** approximately 2.5 hours from the Woodstock-Quechee region by car. All major car rental companies operate out of Logan, or you can take one of the hourly shuttles to South Station in downtown Boston and catch one of a half-dozen daily buses to White River Junction. The advantages of flying to Boston, particularly if you are traveling some distance, include the availability of flights and lower costs than flying into one of the smaller regional airports.

By Car

Quechee, Woodstock, and Plymouth are all situated along **Route 4**, which is easily accessible from Interstate 89 (I-89) Exit 1, and from Interstate 91 (I-91) by getting off at Exit 10 at White River Junction and getting on I-89; it's then only a 5-10 minute drive to Exit 1. From Boston, it is approximately a 2.5 hour drive to Woodstock, and 1.5-2 hours from the Concord-Manchester area in New Hampshire.

From points northwest like Montpelier (one hour), Burlington (2 hours), and Montreal (3.5 hours), you can take **I-89** south to Exit 1, or you can get off at any one of several points from Montpelier on south and take a more intimate local road for the last stretch. For example, from Montpelier, you can take Route 12 south straight to Woodstock; or you can take Route 14 from Barre, Route 107 and Route 12 from Exit 3 and Bethel, or the Pomfret Road from Sharon (Exit 2).

From Killington and Rutland, it is an easy half hour-hour drive on Route 4. From other points west, find your way to West Bridgewater or Plymouth Union on Route 100 and take Route 4 east – it's 15 miles to Woodstock and another six or seven to Quechee.

By Bus

Vermont Transit Lines, *Tel. 800/552-8738, 800/451-3292,* offers direct service between White River Junction (*Tel. 802/295-3011*) – which is a 10-20 minute drive from Woodstock-Quechee – and major destinations throughout the Northeast, including New York City, Montreal, Boston, and Manchester NH, in addition to all areas of Vermont including Rutland, Burlington, Montpelier, the Northeast Kingdom, Bennington, the Precision Valley, all major ski areas, and Brattleboro. There are also two buses daily from Woodstock and Quechee to Rutland and White River Junction, but apart from saving a couple (and it really is just a couple) of dollars on a cab, it is almost always more convenient to take a taxi to White River Junction and catch buses from there.

By Train

Amtrak's **Vermonter**, *Tel. 800/USA-RAIL,* departs Washington, DC at 7:40am and stops at Baltimore, Wilmington DE, Philadelphia, New York City, Newark NJ, Metro Park NJ, Trenton, NJ, Bridgport CT, Hartford CT, Meriden CT, New Haven CT, Springfield MA, Amherst MA, Northampton MA, Brattleboro VT, Keene NH, Windsor VT, and arrives at White River Junction VT at 6:30pm. This is when you can also catch it to destinations north: Randolph VT, Montpelier VT, Waterbury-Stowe, Burlington VT, St. Albans, and Montreal Canada. For Woodstock and Quechee, White River Junction is most convenient for departures and arrivals as it is only 10-20 minutes by taxi or car. To destinations south, the Vermonter departs White River Junction at 10:35am. A one-way ticket to Washington DC costs about $85, New York City $65, and less to destinations in Connecticut, Massachusetts, New Hampshire, and Vermont.

For the Ottauquechee Valley, Amtrak's **Ethan Allen Express** is also a viable alternative. Departing Washington, DC at 3am daily (#299), and at 10:40am Monday-Thursday (#291), and 1:05pm Friday-Saturday (#293), it stops at Baltimore, Wilmington DE, Philadelphia, and New York City (arriving at 6:38am, 2:15pm, and 4:19pm respectively) where you must catch a connecting train with the same number. Train #299 departs Penn Station at 7:10am, Train #291 at 3:55pm, and Train #293 at 5:40pm en route to Yonkers, Croton-Harmon, Poughkeepsie, Rhinecliff-Kinston, Hudson, and Albany. Again, at Albany you must transfer or board trains with the same number departing at 9:55am, 6:40pm, and 8:20pm respectively and arriving in Rutland at 12:30pm, 9:05pm, and 10:45pm. Trains depart Rutland in the other direction at 1:25pm and 5:25pm.

A one-way fare from Rutland to New York City is approximately $55, and despite the connections the Ethan Allen is nearly 2 hours faster than the Vermonter. Rutland is approximately 15 miles from the Plymouth region by way of Route 4, 27 miles from Woodstock, and 35 miles from Quechee.

ORIENTATION

Entirely encompassed in Windsor County, Woodstock, Quechee, Plymouth and their environs and villages are all along **Route 4**, an east-west highway that follows the **Ottauquechee River** and links **I-89** at Exit 1 near White River Junction with **Route 100** just south of Killington. Quechee, which is a village in the town of Hartford is the furthest east and just off Exit 1. While many shops, inns, and attractions such as Quechee Gorge are on Route 4 itself, the actual village of Quechee is on the other side of the Ottauquechee River and can be reached taking Clubhouse Road (nearest Exit 1), Dewey Mills Road, and River Street from Route 4. All are well-marked by signs and all merge with Main Street in the heart of the village.

After passing by Quechee, Route 4 bends south with the Ottauquechee as it passes through the hamlet of Taftsville and intersects with Route 12 South which leads to Hartland, Windsor and I-91. Woodstock, the main destination for most visitors to the region, is about 4 miles beyond Taftsville. You'll know you're entering town when Route 4 makes a sharp right angle turn and you enter a stretch of filling stations that includes the rather unseemly looking State Corrections facility recognizeable by the razor wire surrounding its yards. It won't be long, however, before Route

4/Route 12 assumes its Pleasant Street identity, with B&B's and shops lining the road. Within a mile, you'll be in the village itself.

Pleasant Street continues right at the fork and leads to **Route 12** while Route 4 stays left on Central Street.The heart of the town is the junction of Central Street and Elm Street next to the thin, oblong Woodstock Village Green. Woodstock's signature landmark, the Green is lined with the Woodstock Inn, the Middle [Covered] Bridge, the old Courthouse, and numerous shops. Elm Street turns north and becomes Route 12 which continues on to the Billings Museum, Suicide Six, and eventually Montpelier and I-89 (about 50 miles). Just north of the Billings Museum, River Road leads east to Quechee, and beyond that, the scenic road through Pomfret (included in this chapter) leads to Sharon (about 10 miles) and I-89, Exit 2. South of the Green, **Route 106** leads to South Woodstock, the Kedron Valley Inn and eventually Springfield (25 miles). The country club, cross-country skiing, and hiking trails are also south of the Green off Cross Street and Golf Ave.

From Woodstock, Route 4 continues west eight miles through Bridgewater to Bridgewater Corners and the junction with Route 100A. Though only seven miles long, **Route 100A** is the address of major landmarks like Plymouth Notch, the Calvin Coolidge Birthplace historic site, and Calvin Coolidge State Park, on its way to the junction with Route 100 at Plymouth Union. Route 4 continues west to West Bridgewater and Route 100. The Killington ski area is just another seven miles north.

GETTING AROUND

The area is very easy to navigate by car – it doesn't take more than half an hour to drive from Quechee to the Plymouth area – and Woodstock and Quechee villages are best explored on foot. Indeed most inns and hotels in the region are located within walking distance of village centers.

If you are without a car and would like to rent one, **Avis**, *Tel. 603/298-7753, 800/331-1212*, **Hertz Rent-A-Car**, *Tel. 603/298-8927, 800/645-3131*, and **Enterprise Rent-A-Car**, *Tel. 603/448-3337, 800/325-8007*, all operate out of the Lebanon Municipal Airport, about 20 minutes from Woodstock-Quechee by taxi.

For a taxi, call **New Face Taxi** in White River Junction, *Tel. 802/295-1500*, or talk to an employee at your hotel. Give the taxi advance notice as it may take time for them to reach you before they can take you to your destination.

OTTAUQUECHEE VALLEY AREA SPECIAL EVENTS

Memorial Day Parade – *fourth weekend in May in Quechee.*

Annual Quechee Balloon Festival & Craft Fair – *third weekend in June. Call 802/295-7900 for information.*

July 4 – Woodstock Festival and Craft Fair – *Art displays, music, food, and fireworks held to celebrate Woodstock and the Fourth of July.*

Quechee Scottish Festival – *Fourth weekend in August. Features Scottish music, dancing, and arts and crafts, including clothing. Call 802/ 295-7900.*

Annual Apples and Craft Fair – *Second week in October, Bailey's Meadow Route 4 East.*

WHERE TO STAY

Woodstock & Plymouth

WOODSTOCK INN & RESORT, *14 Village Green, Woodstock VT 05091. Tel. 802/457-1100, 800/448-7900, Fax 802/457-6699. Web site: www.woodstockinn.com. Rates: rooms begin at about $100, and there are numerous 2 day, 3 day and longer packages that bundle meals, skiing, golf and other activities. Call for info. Major credit cards accepted.*

Perhaps the most famous – and certainly one of the finest – of all inns in Vermont, the Woodstock Inn combines the comfort and personal service of a country inn with the facilities of a resort in a classic Vermont setting on Woodstock's legendary green. There are 144 rooms, all tastefully furnished with country furniture and decor, featuring modern amenities such as air-conditioning, cable television, and telephones; 44 rooms also include a fireplace.

The main inn building includes a gift shop, tavern, and two eateries, including a very fine dining room serving gourmet continental and American country fare like grilled jumbo prawns and roast rack of lamb. There is also a fitness center with squash, indoor tennis, massage, and aerobics, and guests also enjoy access and special rates at the Suicide Ski Area and the Woodstock Country Club golf course designed by Robert Trent Jones. Be sure to call about special packages offered throughout the year that may enable you to enjoy all of these facilities and opportunities for less than if you paid for them separately.

Selected as one of my *Best Places to Stay* – see Chapter 9 for more details.

HAWK INN & MOUNTAIN RESORT, *Route 100, Plymouth VT 05056. Tel. 802/672-3811, 800/685-HAWK, Fax 802/672-5585. E-mail: hawkinn@vermontel.com. Web site: www.hawkresort..com. Rates: $170-$360 inn, $250-$825. Major credit cards accepted.*

Located somewhat off the beaten track in a beautiful mountain setting with easy access to skiing at Okemo and Killington, in addition to the shops, restaurants, and other attractions of Woodstock and Quechee. Hawk Inn and Mountain Resort is a full fledged resort offering seemingly limitless recreational opportunities. Lodging includes 50 rooms equipped with modern amenities like air-conditioning and cable television, and dozens of villas and townshouses with 1-4 bedrooms, also with full amenities. For warm weather recreation, you can engage in fly fishing (with guides and/or instruction), canoeing, sailing, lake or pool (indoor and out) swimming, horseback riding, and hiking and biking directly from the inn itself. Winter activities include cross-country skiing, snowshoeing, sledding, ice skating, and taking a sleigh ride; the fitness center includes a full weight room and gym as well as saunas. There is also fine dining and a pub at the River Tavern Restaurant.

JACKSON HOUSE INN & RESTAURANT, *37 Route 4 West, Woodstock VT 05091. (Located just beyond Woodstock High School west of the Woodstock Green on Route 4 on the right.) Tel. 802/457-2065, 800/448-1890, Fax 802/ 457-9290. E-mail: innkeepers@jacksonhouse.com, or posadajh@aol.com. Web site: www.jacksonhouse.com. Rates: $175-$200 for rooms, $250-$300 suites. Credit cards: Visa, Mastercard, American Express.*

One of the finest inns in Vermont, Jackson House features about a dozen rooms and suites, all elegant, comfortable, and laden with enough quality antiques to be museum exhibits in their own right. Each room includes air-conditioning and private bath and is individually appointed with first-rate furniture and ornamentation. The Josephine Tasher Bonaparte room (all rooms and suites have names) for example, features an antique mahogany bed with brass mounts, a gem of an old ceiling fan, and is decorated with bronze stauettes. Suites are even more fantastic – the Wales Johnson has a queen sleighbed made of cherry wood, a marble top bureau, a gas fireplace, and a jacuzzi in the bathroom. It also has a private entrance to the patio and gardens.

Jackson House Inn is also home to one of the finest restaurants in Woodstock, and while the prices are steep (they include breakfast, evening champagne refreshments and hors d'oeuvres), the experience is well worth the splurge.

Selected as one of my *Best Places to Stay* – see Chapter 9 for more details.

KEDRON VALLEY INN, *Route 106 (south of Woodstock), South Woodstock VT 05071. Tel. 802/457-1473, Tel. 800/836-1193. E-mail: kedroninn@aol.com. Web site: www.innformation.com/vt/kedron. Rates: $120-$240. Major credit cards accepted.*

Six miles south of Woodstock on Route 106, Kedron Valley Inn is a wonderful old inn that includes luxurious Victorian-style guestrooms (some of which feature canopied beds, hot tubs and fireplaces), a topnotch dining room, and a private lake for swimming. The building itself is something of a historic site; in the early 19th century it was a stagecoach inn, and later became a stop on the Underground Railroad where runaway slaves were given shelter on their way to Canada. The Woodstock Country Club, Kedron stables, and Woodstock Village are all within minutes by car.

CHARLESTON HOUSE, *21 Pleasant Street, Woodstock VT 05091. Tel. 802/457-3843, 888/475-3800. E-mail: nohl@together.net. Rates: $100-$200. Credit cards: Visa, Mastercard, American Express.*

Another gem of a small inn, the Charleston House is an 1835 Greek Revival brick house that includes nine individually appointed guest rooms, elegant and charming dining and sitting rooms, and a porch where you can relax and enjoy Vermont's fresh air during the fall and summer. Rooms range in price and amenities from the modest but elegant Hillary Underwood room with a queen bed and private bath for $110, to the B and B room featuring a queen bed, fireplace, jacuzzi and cable television. All rooms include a private bath, four have a jacuzzi and five have television. A final treat (for kitty lovers anyway) is meeting Ali Babs the cat.

CANTERBURY HOUSE B&B, *43 Pleasant Street, Woodstock, VT 05091. Tel. 802/457-3077. E-mail: innkeeper@thecanterburyhouse.com Web site: theconterburyhouse.com. Rates: $90-$175. Major credit cards accepted.*

Located in a Victorian townhouse within walking distance of the Woodstock Green and the surrounding shops and restaurants, the Canterbury House includes eight different rooms, each with a Canterbury Tales related name. They range from the "Friar's Tale" with twin canopy beds and blue and green floral walls ($120-$130 a night) to "Chaucer's Garrett," a third floor one-room suite with two double beds, a sofa and a full bath. The house includes a salon and a dining room, and is decorated throughout in the Victorian style.

ARDMORE INN, *23 Pleasant Street, Woodstock VT 05091. Tel. 802/457-3887, 800/497-9652, Fax 802/457-9006. E-mail: ardmoreinn@aol.com. Web site: ardmoreinn.com. Rates: $85-$150. Major credit cards accepted.*

Featuring five uniquely decorated rooms in a vintage white Greek Revival house dating to 1850, the Ardmore offers a combination of excellent location and comfort with ambiance to match. The rooms – all with Scottish and Irish names like McGovern and Tully – feature a variety of combinations of four post beds, marble bathrooms, and beautiful wooden furniture. The house also includes a screened veranda with wicker chairs where you take tea or another refreshment, an elegant dining room with beautiful wooden furniture, and a salon with a fireplace, handsome old-fashioned armchairs, and oriental carpeting.

LINCOLN INN AT THE COVERED BRIDGE, *530 Woodstock Road/ Route 4 West/, Woodstock VT 05091. (One mile and then some from the Woodstock Green and beyond the high school). Tel. 802/457-3312, Fax 802/ 457-5808. E-mail: lincon2@aoo.com. Web site: lincolninn.com. Rates: $100- $175. Major credit cards accepted.*

Set on a six acre estate by the Ottauquechee River and the Lincoln Covered Bridge, the Lincoln Inn includes six comfy rooms with private baths, a library kept warm by a fireplace, a tavern, and a dining room serving first-rate continental cuisine by candlelight.

THE 1830 SHIRE TOWN INN, *31 South Street, Woodstock. Tel. 802/ 457-1830. Website: www.scenesofvermont.com/shiretowninn. Rates: $70-$110. Major credit cards accepted.*

Situated a block from the Woodstock Green in a handsome building from the 1830's that is listed on the National Register of Historic Places, this small inn features three comfy guestrooms with private baths and antique furnishings, as well as a cozy salon warmed in the winter by a fireplace.

THE VILLAGE INN OF WOODSTOCK, *41 Pleasant Street (Route 4), Woodstock, VT 05091. Tel. 802/457-1255, 800/722-4571. Rates: $80-$160. Credit cards: Visa, Mastercard, American Express.*

Decked out in a fresh coat of lavender, the Village Inn (not to be confused with the more famous but less intimate Woodstock Inn) is a modest but elegant Victorian house-turned-inn featuring eight restored guestrooms with air-conditioning and private baths, a casual but elegant dining room, and salons in which to sit and relax. The restaurant, which opens four nights a week, serves elegant but hearty country fare, like roast turkey and roast duckling a l'orange.

THE SHIRE MOTEL, *46 Pleasant Street, Woodstock VT 05091. Tel. 802/457-2211. E-mail: dotcall@aol.com. Rates: $50-$170. Major credit cards accepeted.*

This motel offers a great combination of reasonably priced comfortable rooms (some with four postered beds) and a convenient location within a few minutes walk from the Woodstock green. All rooms include private bath, telephone, cable television, and air-conditioning.

FARMBROOK MOTEL, *P.O. Box 320, Plymouth VT 05056. (Located on Route 100A in Plymouth.) Tel. 802/672-3631. Web site: ww.vtliving.com. Rates: $40-$70.*

Situated on Broad Brook just minutes away from attractions such as the Calvin Coolidge State Park, Coolidge's historic birthplace, Woodstock Village, and the skiing areas at Killington and Okemo, this attractive little motel offers 12 simple but comfortable rooms with television and air-conditioning for reasonable prices. On-site amenities include a grill and picnic tables, and guests can relax strolling along the stream with a quaint water wheel.

Quechee & Taftsville

QUECHEE INN AT MARSHLAND FARM, *Clubhouse Road, Quechee VT 05059. Tel. 802/295-3133, 800/235-3133, Fax 802/295-6587. E-mail: quecheeinn@pinnacle-inns.com Web site: www.pinnacle-inns.com. Rates: $100-$260 (depending on meal plan). Major credit cards accepted.*

Featuring 24 handsome rooms decorated with an elegant country flavor, the "Quechee Inn," as it's known for short, is located in a 1793 building with access to wilderness trails for hiking, biking, and cross-country skiing. Guests also enjoy privileges at the exclusive Quechee Club with its golf courses and tennis courts, and can take advantage of the Inn's own recreational offerings such as the in-house fly fishing school. Finally, there is a fine restaurant on the premises serving gourmet country and American fare nightly in addition to breakfast for guests.

PARKER HOUSE INN & RESTAURANT, *1792 Quechee Main Street, Quechee VT 05059. Tel. 802/295-6077. E-mail: parker_house_inn@valley.net. Rates: $100-$140. Major credit cards accepted.*

This charming Victorian townhouse in "downtown" Quechee includes seven individually decorated rooms, each of which features its own combination of amenities and charms. The "Victoria" is a spacious third floor affair with a brass queen sized bed and a tub in its bathroom as well as air-conditioning, while the "Joseph" includes a brass queen sized bed and a large bath with a tub, in addition to a view of the river. The Parker House also includes a fine restaurant serving gourmet country fare four nights a week and breakfast daily.

COUNTRY GARDEN INN, *P.O. Box 404, Quechee VT 05059. (Located at 37 Main Street in Quechee.) Tel. 802/295-3023, 800/859-4191, Fax 802/295-3121. Web site: www.country-garden-inn.com. Rates: $100-$200. Credit cards: Visa, Mastercard.*

This fine B&B situated in an 1819 building offers a combination of intimacy, 19th century atmospherics, and excellent service with a location in Quechee Village that is close to the shops and restaurants of the Village as well as the outdoor recreational opportunties. Guests enjoy privileges at the Quechee Club golf course and tennis courts.

QUECHEE LAKES, *61 River Street (off Route 4) Quechee VT 05059. Tel. 802/295-1970, 800/745-0042, Fax 802/296-6852. E-mail: quechee.lakes.rentals@valley.net. Web site: www.pbpub.com/quecheelakes. Rates: $285-$680 for 2 nights; $575-$1310 weekly. Major credit cards accepted.*

Quechee Lakes Rentals offers an assortment of quality one-to-four bedroom condos and houses for rent, usually for at least a week. Guests enjoy privileges at Quechee Club, home to a very fine golf course in addition to featuring pools, tennis, exercise gym, and squash. A great way to spend time and money if you have both.

APPLEBUTTER INN, *Happy Valley Road, Taftsville, VT 05073. Tel. 802/457-4158, Fax 802/457-4158. E-mail: APLBTRN@aol.com. Rates: $75-$145. Credit cards: Visa, Mastercard.*

Located in an 1850 country home built in the Federal style, the Applebutter Inn is known for its combination of homey comfort, hospitality, and vintage Vermont atmospherics. There are six guestrooms, each with private bath as well as several sitting rooms with fireplaces in which to relax. The breakfasts also have an excellent reputation.

FOUR PILLARS B&B, *Happy Valley Road, Taftsville, VT 05073. Tel. 802/457-2797. E-mail: Fpillaras@vermontel.com. Web site: vermontel.com. Rates: $80-$130. Credit cards: Visa, Mastercard.*

This modest but elegant inn located in a restored 1836 Greek Revival mansion offers guests the combination of the intimacy people look for in Vermont inns, with the privileges and access to the Quechee Club (tennis and first-rate golf) that one generally enjoys only at a large resort. There are only three rooms, all with private bath and furnished with classy antiques and oriental rugs. A full and tasty breakfast is included.

QUALITY INN AT QUECHEE GORGE, *P.O. Box Q, Quechee VT 05059. (Located on Route 4 between the Exit 1 and the Gorge.) Tel. 802/295-7600, 800/732-4376. E-mail: joan@qualityinnquechee.com. Web site: www.qualityinnquechee.com. Rates: $50-$120. Major credit cards accepted.*

Offers clean comfortable rooms with air-conditioning and cable television within minutes of Quechee Gorge, Quechee Village, and I-89. On-site facilities include a modest outdoor pool, laundry machines, shuffleboard courts, picnic areas, and walking trails. The Wildflowers restaurant in the hotel serves decent food for reasonable prices. An all-around good choice for families interested in value.

Camping

COOLIDGE STATE PARK, *HCR 70 Box 105, Plymouth VT 05056. (The park is located off Route 110A near the Calvin Coolidge Homestead.) Tel. 802/672-3612 (summer), 802/886-2434 (off-season). Base rates: $11-$15. Credit cards: Visa, Mastercard. Open mid-May through Columbus Day (mid-October).*

Part of the Coolidge State Forest, Coolidge State Park features 25 tent and trailer sites as well as two shelters for groups and 35 rustic lean-to's constructed by the Civilian Conservation Corps during the Great Depression. Facilities include hot showers, sanitation dumps, and flush toilets. There is extensive and rewarding hiking and mountain biking throughout the area (pick up maps from the ranger station), as well as a playground and picnic areas.

QUECHEE GORGE STATE PARK, *190 Dewey Mills Road, White River Junction VT 05001. (Off Route 4 in Quechee) Tel. 802/295-2990 (summer), 802/886-2434 (off-season). Base rates: $12-$16. Credit cards: Visa, Mastercard. Open mid-May through Columbus Day (mid-October).*

This 600-acre park on the edge of Quechee Gorge includes more than 45 tent and trailer sites (seven lean-to's) as well as showers, picnic areas, a play area, and a dumping station. Hiking around Quechee sets it apart.

PINE VALLEY RV RESORT, *400 Woodstock Road, White River Junction VT 05001. (Off Route 4 beyond I-89 Exit 1 and Quechee Village). Tel. 802/296-6711. Base rates: $22-$26. Creditcards: Visa, Mastercard. Open late April through late October.*

PV is conveniently located off I-89 near its junction with I-91 and includes nearly 50 trailer sites, 40 of which feature water and electricity hookups; some also have cable television connections. On-site there is a shop selling camping supplies such as ice, firewood, and propane; there is also a laundry service.

SUGAR HOUSE CAMPGROUND, *HCR 70 Box 44, Plymouth VT 05056. (Located on Route 100 just north of the junction between Route 100 & Route 100A.) Tel. 802/672-5043. Base Rates: $12-$15. Credit cards: Visa, Mastercard. Open year around.*

Sugar House Campground has 45 winterized sites and rentals availables, and offers access to several nearby lakes and rivers as well as Killington and Coolidge State Park.

WHERE TO EAT

THE PRINCE & THE PAUPER, *24 Elm Street, Woodstock VT 05091. Tel. 802/457-1818 or 457-1648. Hours: 6pm-9pm. Major credit cards accepted.*

As some say, "you'll enter a prince and leave a pauper," but you'll be hard pressed to find anybody who has dined here to say it wasn't worth it – and to be fair, the $35 price tag for the prix fixe menu (includes an appetizer, salad, entree, dessert and coffee), is not at all unreasonable given the very high quality of food and service.

Owned and operated by Chef Chris Balcer, there is a rotating menu featuring primarily French and American dishes, such as lamb tenderloin in puff pastry with mushrooms and spinach, and Long Isand duckling with maple mustard glaze, but it usually includes an Asian flavored dish (very often fish) as well, such as seared tuna with wasabi flavoring. The same formula applies to the appetizer choices, which can range from grilled quail to Vietnamese spring rolls. For dessert, you may choose from an assortment of sinfully delicious pastries and/or ice cream. The Prince & the Pauper is located in a cozy dining room with wooden beams (some of the modern paintings seem a bit out of place though). Dress is smart casual (no tie necessary).

THE WOODSTOCK INN, *14 the Green on Route 4, Woodstock VT 05091. Tel. 802/457-1100. Hours: 6pm-10pm nightly. Major credit cards accepted.*

Though the Inn is more famous, it still gets second billing to the P&P (listed above); still it deserves high marks for its fine food and service. The cuisine is mainly fine American and continental and the menu typically features more seafood than you usually find in Vermont restaurants, in addition to the usual assortment of superb steak, lamb, and poultry dishes. Appetizers are typically $7-$8 while entrees range from $20 for the maple roasted chicken to $24 for double lamb chops au jus. The house specialty, char-grilled tiger shrimp and scallops, for example, costs $22. For dessert, there are pastries and baked goods, many of which are rich, but if you're watching calories, there is also sorbet and sometimes fruit. Reservations are advised, particularly during holiday and foliage seasons, and dress is just this side of formal – men are encouraged to wear jackets; jeans and t-shirts are prohibited.

JACKSON HOUSE INN & RESTAURANT, *37 Route 4 West, Woodstock VT 05091. (Located just beyond Woodstock High School west of the Woodstock Green on Route 4 on the right.) Tel. 802/457-2065., 800/448-1890, Fax 802/457-9290. E-mail: innkeepers@jacksonhouse.com, or posadajh@aol.com. Web site: www.jacksonhouse.com. Hours: Thursday-Monday 6pm-9pm. Credit cards: Visa, Mastercard, American Express.*

At the Jackson House, you can feast on variations of fine continental cuisine in a beautiful dining room distinguished by its cathedral style ceiling, beautiful wooden furniture, and an open hearth granite fireplace. But the food is the real star. While most dishes are from the continental old school, the chef has given them a little extra thrust without changing their essence or turning them into some fruity nouveau experiment.

Most recently, the menu included such items as the classic French seafood soup boullabaisse, grilled veal chop with merlot butter and jumbo asparagus, and Atlantic grilled grouper with fiddleheads and cabbage. He is a bit more experimental with appetizers like yellowfin tartar with pickled ginger and wasabi tobikko and eggplant canneloni. For dessert you may choose from the tray of fine pastries and baked goods. Expect to pay at least $40 per person including wine, but I don't think you'll regret it.

MEADOWS RESTAURANT, *Quechee Inn at Marshland Farm, Clubhouse Road (off Route 4), Quechee VT 05059. Tel. 802/295-3133, 800/235-3133. E-mail: quecheeinn@pinnacle-inns.com.*

Situated in Quechee's signature inn, Meadows offers gourmet fare in an elegant setting year around. Consisting primarily of continental and American dishes, the menu offers a variety of appetizers, soups, salads, and entrees ranging from grilled salmon to lamb loins.

THE VILLAGE INN OF WOODSTOCK, *41 Pleasant Street (Route 4), Woodstock, VT. Tel. 802/457-1255, 800/722-4571. Credit cards: Visa, Mastercard, American Express.*

This cushy Victorian inn includes an intimate and romantic restaurant, which receives praise for both its atmosphere and fine food. Using locally produced fresh ingredients whenever possible, the chef-owner, Mr. Clark, prepares an array of gourmet country fare, including the signature dishes Roast Vermont Turkey, Roast Duckling a L'orange, and Roast Rack of Lamb. Fine wines and high end-beers are also available and dress is smart casual. Call for reservations and expect to pay $25-$40 for a full including wine. A great place for a date.

PARKER HOUSE INN & RESTAURANT, *1792 QuecheeMain Street, Quechee VT 05059. Tel. 802/295-6077. E-mail: parker_house_inn@valley.net Major credit cards accepted.*

Yet another excellent eatery in the Woodstock-Quechee region, the Parker House Inn specializes in gourmet country cuisine and offers a more extensive menu than some of the other fine restaurants in the region. For appetizers ($6-$9) you typically have a choice of 6-8 items ranging from mushroom ravioli with fresh sage or jumbo shrimp cocktail to homecured salmon with horseradish-dill potato pancake with sour cream, and that does not include the soup of the day or the two or three salads also available. For main dishes, the meat dishes like loin of venison with reduction of balsamic vinegar and port wine, or the rack of lamb with white beans and wine-rosemary sauce, are probably the best, though seafood dishes like grilled yellowfin tuna and pan-seared flounder fillet are also excellent. And though it may not be on the menu, pasta can be ordered for vegetarians and children. Entrees typically cost from between $16 and $25.

KEDRON VALLEY INN, *Route 106 (south of Woodstock), South Woodstock VT 05071. Tel. 802/457-1473, 800/836-1193. E-mail: kedroninn@aol.com. Web site: www.innformation.com/vt/kedron.*

With a menu featuring gourmet yankee dishes, seafood, and cutting edge vegetarian fare, the Kedron Valley Inn has something for everybody and with its casual atmosphere, it's also perfect for families. The dishes themselves range from salmon stuffed with scallops and shrimp and wrapped in puff pastry to vegetarian wellington, a nouveau take on the traditional savory pastry that is stuffed with portabello mushrooms, vegetables and brie cheese. Often game meats like venison or quail are served as well. Desserts usually consist of tarts, pies, and other pastries and baked goods. Expect to pay at least $25 per person including wine.

SIMON PEARCE RESTAURANT, *located at the Mill off Route 4 (turnoff between Quechee and I-89), Quechee VT . Tel. 802/295-1470. Hours: 11:30am-2:45pm for lunch, 6pm-9pm for dinner. Major credit cards accepted.*

Situated at the renovated mill where Simon Pearce established his famous glass blowing and pottery center, the Simon Pearce Restaurant serves quality American and continental food in a casual but elegant setting overlooking the Quechee Falls. The menu features a variety of pasta, seafood, and meat and poultry dishes costing between $10-$20.

THE CORNERS INN & RESTAURANT, *Route 4, Bridgewater Corners VT. (8 miles west of Woodstock.) Tel. 802/672-9968. Hours: 5:30pm-9:30pm Wednesday through Saturday and seven days a week in summer and autumn. Major credit cards accepted.*

Situated in a farmhouse-type building, the Corners Inn restaurant offers both a tavern with appetizers and bar food like crab cakes and soups, as well as a more formal restaurant setting in a cozy dining room with a fireplace. The cuisine is mainly American and Italian, with interesting dishes such as salmon with rasberry glaze and veal with artichoke hearts. There are also more conventional dishes such as handcut, grilled New York steak and lobster ravioli. Ranging from $12-$18, entrees come with cheese and crackers and fresh bread with garlic flavored olive oil. The dessert menu rotates and typically features an assortment of pastries and baked goods.

PANE E SALUTE ITALIAN BAKERY, *61 Central Street, Woodstock VT 05091. Tel. 802/457-4882. Hours: 7am-5pm, 6pm-9pm for dinner in summer. Sunday Brunch 11am-2pm. Credit cards: Visa, Mastercard.*

An Italian espresso bar and bakery, Pane e Salute serves excellent coffee, pastries (biscotti and the like), breads, sandwiches and Italian deli items to go. You can also eat in the restaurant itself. The menu consists of the items just mentioned plus pastas and other Italian fare; in summer the menu is expanded for dinner (up to $15).

BENTLEY'S, *3 Elm Street (at the corner of Elm and Pleasant), Woodstoock VT 05091. Tel. 802/457-3232. Hours: 7-11am (breakfast), 11:30-9:30pm (lunch & dinner), bar stays open until 1am-2pm. Sunday brunch11am-3pm. Major credit cards accepted.*

This popular family eatery/tavern serves upscale bar and American food in a colorful setting that combines Victorian and Americana decor. Prices range from $3.50-$8 for breakfast and $8-$20 for full dinner meals; the menu includes, steak, pasta, and good bar food like nachos and burgers. On the weekend there is dancing and sometimes live entertainment beginning around 8pm-9pm. Next door on Elm Street, **Bentley's Cafe** is more of a take-out joint serving sandwiches, coffee and desserts *(Tel. 802/457-3400) .*

SPOONER'S STEAKHOUSE, *located at Sunset Farm on Route 4 in Woodstock. Tel. 802/457-4022. Hours: 5pm-10pm; lounge opens at 3:30pm. Credit cards: Visa, Mastercard.*

A decent eatery serving a variety of steaks (incuding prime rib), pasta and seafood, Spooner's is a bit cheaper than most of the fancier inns that dominate the region's dining scene; most dishes are under $15.

MOUNTAIN CREAMERY, *33 Central Street, Woodstock VT 05091. Tel. 802/457-1715. Hours: 7am-5pm restaurant, 7am-6pm bake shop.*

The casual low key old-fashioned bake shop and restaurant feels a bit out of place in the middle of ritzy Woodstock, but the upscale surroundings only enhance its charm and good value. The restaurant serves hearty no-frills breakfasts similar to what you expect in a diner, while for lunch you can take a salad and/or your choice of sandwiches ranging from toasted cheese or a BLT to roast beef and turkey. For dessert, try whatever homemade ice cream or pie suits your fancy. Speaking of pies, the bake shop on the lower floor sells excellent homemade cakes and pies, custom-made if you like. Neither breakfast nor lunch will set you back much more than $5.

THE CHOCALATE COW, *24 Elm Street (1 block from the Green,) Woodstock. Tel. 802/457-9151, 888/TRUFFLE. Open 9am-5pm (later in summer and during the Christmas season). Credit cards: Visa, Mastercard.*

Features superb gourmet chocalates in addition to ice cream, baked goods, and coffee.

THE FARINA FAMILY DINER & RESTAURANT, *Quechee Gorge Village, Route 4 between I-89 and Waterman Hill Road, Quechee. Tel. 802/295-8955, Fax 802/295-8997. Hours: 7am-8pm Monday-Saturday & Sunday 7am-3pm.*

A casual diner with a hint of kitsch, the Farina serves decent diner food including sandwiches and salads. It makes a good change from all that high-end, rich gourmet food served at the inns, and its great choice for lunch with the kids. You can eat a filling meal for $8-$10 or less!

SEEING THE SIGHTS
Route 4 from I-89 to Quechee

Route 4 from I-89 to Quechee is – apart from Quechee Gorge – not especially impressive. Lined with all sorts of souvenir and antique shop complexes, RV camps, and hotels, it offers little in the way of historic sites or scenic views.

One landmark that is definitely worth stopping for is the aforementioned **Quechee Gorge**, *approximately four miles from I-89 Exit 1 off Route 4 (one mile east of Quechee Village)*. Created through erosion by water produced by melting glaciers at the end of the ice age about 13,000 years ago, the Gorge – sometimes called "Vermont's Grand Canyon" – is now part of the 600-acre **Quechee Gorge State Park**, which includes camping sites, picnic areas, and hiking trails. Visitors can admire the gorge – which is beautiful in summer, autumn, and winter – from a picnic and parking area just west of the bridge off Route 4.

If you have time, though, you should hike down to the **Ottauquechee River** itself. This will enable you to immerse yourself in the natural beauty of the gorge and the river without the distractions of traffic. If you like, you can also follow the trail north up to **Mill Pond** and check out the **dam**; up and back, it's not much more than a mile. For more information about the natural history of Quechee Gorge, pick up a copy of the pamphlet *Quechee Gorge*, published by the Vermont Agency of Natural Resources at the Department of Forests, Parks and Recreation. *For information about camping in the State Park, call 802/295-2990 (summer), 802/886-2434 (off-season).*

Quechee

Named for the Ottauquechee – an Abenaki Indian word meaning "swift mountain stream" – **Quechee** was founded in the 1760's and, though it never became a major economic center, it was renowned for its wool industry which produced enough wealth to build many attractive buildings, a good number of which remain today. The mill industry is gone, but tourism has been a more than adequate economic replacement and Quechee remains one of the weathiest villages in Vermont. Though most of the area's attractions are natural, like Quechee Gorge, or recreational like Quechee Club with its fine golf courses, the village itself does include several attractions worth taking in, namely the Simon Pearce Glass Works, and the village center that contains numerous historic buildings.

Route 4 actually skirts Quechee Village, so you must take Clubhouse Road, Dewey Mills Road, or if coming from Woodstock, River Road, to reach Main Street and the heart of Quechee Village.

SIMON PEARCE THE MILL, *The Mill on Main Street, Quechee VT 05056. (From Route 4, turn north on Waterman Road and pass through the covered bridge.) Tel. 802/295-2711. Hours: Daily 9am-9pm. Major credit cards accepted.*

Established in 1981 by Irish glassblowing and pottery maestro Simon Pearce, this factory is located in a beautifully restored mill. Visitors can watch as the masters craft first-class glass and pottery, and then shop in the a retail store selling glass and pottery of all quality levels – indeed many of the best bargains are seconds (items with minor defects). The complex also contains the **Simon Pearce Restaurant** serving quality American cuisine in a gorgeous setting overlooking the waterfalls and the mill's hydroelectric dam *(restaurant is open 11:30am-2:45pm, 6pm-9pm, Tel. 802/295-1470; see above for review under Where to Eat).*

In addition to the Simon Pearce complex, Main Street and the surrounding environs are dotted with historical buildings. They range from the **Village Green** and **Meeting House**, first built in 1833 for "those Congregationalists known as Orthodox" and restored in 1873 by T.W. Silloway (who also renovated the State House in Montpelier) after becoming a school; to the **Marshland Farm**, built in 1793 by Vermont's first Lt. Governor and grandfather of George Perkins Marsh, famous diplomat and a founder of the American conservation movement. If you're interested in exploring such buildings – many of which are on or within minutes' walk of Quechee's Main Street – pick up a copy of the pamphlet *By the Old Mill Stream: An Architectural and Historical Walking Tour of Quechee, Vermont,* published by the Quechee Chamber of Commerce, *Tel. 802/296-8280.*

COVERED BRIDGES IN WOODSTOCK & QUECHEE

The Middle Bridge, off the Green & Route 4 in Woodstock, is the 1969 replacement for a bridge originally built in the 1870's.

Lincoln Bridge spans the Ottauquechee, just west of the center of Woodstock off Route 4. It was constructed in 1865 and named for the slain President.

Taftsville Bridge also crosses the Ottauquechee next to Route 4 in Taftsville between Quechee and Woodstock. Built in 1836, it is the oldest covered bridge in the region.

Quechee Bridge, on Waterman Road off Route 4 (down the road from Simon Pearce Glassworks) is the newest Ottauquechee bridge, having been built in 1970.

Quechee to Woodstock

From Quechee, you have two major ways to head west. One is to return to Route 4 and pass through the hamlet of **Taftsville**, home of one of the more famous **country stores** in Vermont and site of the **Taftsville Bridge**, the oldest and one of the most impressive covered bridges in the region.

The alternative is to take **River Road**, a less developed route to Woodstock and Route 12. Should you take this route, consider a detour on Hillside Road or High Pastures Road to the **Sugarbush Farm**, where you can take a tour of a sugaring house and purchase a variety of locally made products. Also in the summer, children can pet baby calves – a real thriller for city kids especially.

Woodstock

With its classic green flanked by a covered bridge, a handsome courthouse, and the most famous inn in northern New England, Woodstock boasts a reputation as *the* quintessential New England village. Whether it tops your own list will depend on your own personal tastes – many find it overly gentrified and overrun with tourists – but it's hard to deny the charm of its buildings and the quality of its inns and restaurants. In any case, Woodstock features many attractions which, if you can spare some time from the golf course and ski slopes, are well worth a visit.

There is of course, the Village Green, but Woodstock is also home to the Woodstock Institute of Natural Science & Vermont Raptor Center, featuring fine natural history exhibits; one of the country's premier agricultural museums, the Billings Farm & Museum; and the Marsh Billings National Historic Park, the former home of Laurence and Mary Rockefeller, which only recently opened to the public. These and other attractions are described below.

Situated at the junction of Route 4 (Central Street) and Route 12 (Elm Street), the **Village Green** is Woodstock's signature landmark and a logical place to begin any tour. It has retained its oblong shape since it was formed very soon after the town's founding in 1761 by a Harvard graduate

---

PAUL REVERE'S CHURCH BELL LEGACY

Did you know that Woodstock is home to more church bells (four) crafted by Paul Revere than any other town in America? Though he is best known for his "Midnight Ride" alerting the Minute Men to the arrival of British troops in Boston, he was best known in his own time as one of Boston's premier silversmiths.

named **Timothy Knox**. Apart from its publishing industry that flourished from the early 19th century on, Woodstock did not build itself on a specific industry the way many other Vermont towns did.

However, because of its central location in Windsor County, the site of a major techonological revolution in the development of machine tools during the 19th century, Woodstock was a logical choice to be the seat of the county court and was also the site of the **Windsor County Fair** – a major event until its discontinuance during the Great Depression. There is nothing left of the fair, but the **courthouse** still stands on the Green just east of the Woodstock Inn. The wealth and importance of the region also manifested itself in the fact that Woodstock was the first town in Vermont to have a medical school, and it was a terminal for one of the country's first railroad express lines. Built in the 1820's by **Alvin Adams**, founder of the Adams Express Company, the rail line connected Woodstock to Windsor, the region's economic hub at the time.

In any case, the Green has been a hub since the town's founding and remains so today. On its southern side is the **Woodstock Inn & Resort**, one of the finest in Vermont, and the old courthouse. On the northern side, the **Middle Bridge** is one of the most visited covered bridges in Vermont. However, it is also one of the newest bridges, officially built in 1969 as a replacement for the original Union Street Bridge (built in 1877), though the present version dates to 1974 when local youngsters got out of control at the firemen's ball and set the new bridge ablaze. The bridge you see today is 140 feet long and consists of more than 80,000 feet of lumber board. Crossing it will lead you to River Street and a mostly residential section of Woodstock.

At the eastern end of the Green, there is fork in the road where Elm Street and Route 12 go north. Continuing east, Route 4 and Route 12 merge on **Central Street**, Woodstock's "Main Street" and home to many of its best known shops. A block or so from the Green by the brook is a small park named for one of Woodstock's favorite sons, George Perkins Marsh, a distinguished diplomat who is best known as one of America's earliest environmentalists (see sidebar on the next page). After another block or so, Central Street merges with Pleasant Street, address for many of the elegant and charming Victorian B&B's in Woodstock.

Off the eastern side of the Green, Elm Street (Route 12) branches north. It is lined with such landmarks as **Gillingham's Country Store** – one of the oldest and most endearing in Vermont; a gourmet chocolate shop called the **Chocolate Cow**; **The Prince & The Pauper** gourmet restaurant; and just beyond the **Woodstock Historical Society**.

GEORGE PERKINS MARSH

*A distinguished politician, diplomat, and a founder of the Smithsonian Institute, **George Perkins Marsh** is best known as one of America's earliest and most important conservationists. Born in 1801, he served in the U.S. House of Representatives from 1844-1849, when be became the American minister (ambassador) to Turkey and the Ottoman Empire where he served for six years. After a five year stint at Columbia University, where he was recognized as one of America's leading scholars in linguistics and literature, President Lincoln sent him once again overseas, this time as U.S. Minister to Italy where he served an astounding 21 years.*

*An author of more than 20 books about subjects ranging from zoology to philosophy, Marsh's most important literary contribution was **Man and Nature**, a seminal work for the conservation movement in America, and the earliest articulations of the need for restoration of balance between human industries and their natural surroundings. Marsh passed away in 1882, shortly after returning from Italy.*

THE WOODSTOCK HISTORICAL SOCIETY (THE DANA HOUSE MUSEUM), *26 Elm Street, Woodstock VT 05091. Tel. 802/457-1822. Museum & Shop hours: 10am-5pm Monday – Saturday, noon-4pm Sunday mid-May through October; by appointment in winter. Research Library open 10am-3pm Tuesday through Friday. Museum Office open 9am-5pm Monday – Friday. Admission: $1.*

Situated in a Federal-style building built in 1807 by a local merchant named Charles Dana, the Historical Society contains a wonderful little museum and a shop. The Dana House Museum features a colorful array of furnitiure, tools, paintings, dolls and toys, textiles and clothing, and other artifacts that bring Woodstock's past back to life. The complex also contains a small library used by historians for research.

Route 12

Beyond the Historical Society, Elm Street assumes its Route 12 identity as it makes its way out of the village center and towards such attractions as the Billings Farm & Museum, the Marsh-Billings National Historic Park, and Suicide Six.

BILLINGS FARM & MUSEUM, *Route 12 (Elm Street) about a mile north of the Woodstock Green. Tel. 802/457-2355. Open daily 10am-5pm May 1-October 31; Thanksgiving weekend, December weekends & December 2-31 10am-4pm.*

This working dairy farm-turned-museum has been in operation since the prominent lawyer, railroad mogul, and Woodstock resident **Frederick**

Billings bought it in the 1860's. Run in partnership with the Marsh-Billings-Rockefeller National Historical Park, this still functioning farm offers visitors a genuine opportunity to experience the ins and outs of a Vermont dairy farm. Visitors may take a self-guided tour through the dairy barn, calf nursery, and other functioning sections. You'll learn about regional history and past farming practices from the many historical exhibits, including a renovated farm house from the 1890's complete with residential quarters and a creamery; also very insightful are the recreated farm workshop and the general store where the products remind us not only of how far consumerism has come in the past century, but also the extent to which people's basic needs and habits remain the same.

When you visit Woodstock, call the Billings Farm to determine if you will be around for one of the special events or days held each month. These range from the 1890's celebration of July 4, complete with old time political speeches, traditional music, and plenty of bunting; to Apple Day in late September and Pumpkin Day in early October, when the many culinary uses of these two autumn products can be explored and enjoyed.

MARSH-BILLINGS HISTORICAL PARK, *Route 12 opposite the Billings Farm & Museum (P.O. Box 178), Woodstock VT 05091. Tel. 802/457-3368. Hours: 9am-5pm daily May-October. A small fee is charged for guided tours.*

Given to the federal government by Laurence Rockefeller after his wife Mary passed away in 1998, the Marsh-Billings National Historical Park offers visitors a wonderful opportunity to enjoy a unique blend of American history and the outdoors. It includes the mansion where Mr. and Mrs. Rockefeller lived, which has been converted into a museum, and dozens of forest stands on Mt. Tom where you can hike in the summer and cross-country ski in the winter.

The **mansion** is pretty much as it was when Mr. Rockefeller moved, and is full of all sorts of wonderful stuff from railroad memorabilia handed down from Mr. Billings to furniture collected throughout the 20th century and much of the past residents' personal affects. The Rockefellers used the estate primarily as a summer residence for more than 40 years. Those with a bit of time should consider hiking to the top of Mt. Tom for the fine views of the neighboring countryside – the climb is not especially difficult.

Just beyond the Billings Farm & Museum and the Marsh-Billings Historical Park are two roads to the east (right). The first, known as River Road, is largely undeveloped and leads to Quechee – great for biking and quite scenic. The second road, also very scenic, passes through the picturesque township of **Pomfret**, characterized by rolling hills and beautiful farms, and eventually eventually leads to Sharon. You can return

MARSH, BILLINGS & EARLY ENVIRONMENTALISM IN WOODSTOCK

*At first it seems odd that the park is named "Marsh-Billings" when the benefactor and most recent resident was Rockefeller, but there is a good reason that actually ties into the significance of the estate and Woodstock's place in the early environmentalist movement. As mentioned in the sidebar above, **George Perkins Marsh**, a native son of Woodstock, was among the earliest, if the not first, to articulate the need for human civilization, specifically American society, to reestablish the balance in nature lost to man's overuse of natural resources.*

*Marsh owned the land now in the park until it was purchased by **Frederick Billings**, owner of the Pacific Northwest Railroad for whom the town of Billings, Montana, is named, who upon reading Marsh's watershed book, **Man and Nature**, was converted to environmentalism. He sought to continue Marsh's work by establishing an efficient environment-friendly farm (now the Billings Farm & Museum across Route 12), and by reclaiming treeless land on Mount Tom. Indeed, many of the forest stands on Mt. Tom today date to Billing's time in the late 19th century, and are considered to be the oldest in America. The recently deceased Mary Rockefeller was Frederick Billings' granddaughter.*

to the Woodstock-Quechee region by taking Route 14 east to Route 4 or you can continue north on Route 14, get Route 107 to Bethel and then take Route 12 south. In either case, the entire loop shouldn't take much more than an hour.

Beyond the Pomfret Road (still less than five miles from Woodstock Village) is the **Suicide Six** alpine ski area and Route 12's intersection with the **Appalachian Trail**. Ten miles north of Woodstock is the rural town of **Barnard** and the **Silver Lake State Park** offering camping, fishing, swimming, and boating opportunities.

Route 106 South of the Green

Taking South Street from the Green takes you past the Woodstock Inn and on to Route 106 South, from which you can access the Woodstock Country Club and the Mt. Peg hiking and cross-country skiing trails by way of Cross Street. About 4-5 miles south of the Green, you will come upon the very fine **Kedron Valley Inn** and the **Kedron Valley Stables** *(Tel. 802/457-1480)* where you can take horseback riding lessons, sleigh and carriage rides, and buy maple syrup. Also five miles south of Woodstock in South Woodstock is the Green Mountain Perkins Academy:

GREEN MOUNTAIN PERKINS ACADEMY, *Route 106 five miles south of Woodstock across from the South Chapel, South Woodstock VT. Tel. 802/457-1710. Hours: Saturdays, 2pm-5pm in July and August. Also open 2pm-5pm Saturday-Monday on Labor Day Weekend. Admission: free but donations are appreciated.*

This prestigious academy was open from 1848 until 1898, when many of Woodstock's most prominent families sent their children here. Today, visitors can visit the academy in its 19th century condition, including a science room, study hall, and classrooms featuring a number of physical and photographic exhibits.

From there, Route 106 passes through the hamlet of Hammondsville on its way to Springfield 25 miles south of Woodstock. About halfway down, Route 44 turns east leading to the Ascutney Mountain Resort (with skiing), the Mt. Ascutney State Park (excellent hiking and biking, wonderful views), and Route 5 and I-91 at Windsor in the Connecticut River Valley.

Church Street & the Raptor Center

Back at the Woodstock Green, take Prospect Street (a.k.a. Church Hill Road, *not* Church Street) from the west end of the Green to reach the Raptor Center:

VERMONT INSTITUTE OF NATURAL SCIENCE & RAPTOR CENTER, *Church Hill Road, 1.5 miles from Woodstock Green, Woodstock. Tel. 802/457-2779. Open 10am-4pm daily May-October; 10am-4pm Monday-Saturday, Novermber-April. Admission: $6 adults, $3 students, $2 children (5-11).*

Dedicated to the preservation of and education about birds, the "Raptor Center," as it's known, features exhibits with more than 25 types of birds of prey in outdoor cages, a 78-acre nature preserve with walking trips, and a rehabilitation center for injured and sick birds. There are also displays concerning other animals including turtles, bees, and spiders. Guided tours are offered, as are classes and demonstrations for schools and other groups. Call for information. A thrilling and educational experience for children.

Route 4 West onto Plymouth

Beyond the Woodstock Green to the west, Route 4 leads you through the area known as West Woodstock where you pass numerous landmarks, such as the **Woodstock High School**, the opulent extravagant **Jackson House Inn & Restaurant**, and the **Lincoln Inn** and the **Lincoln Covered Bridge**. Built in 1877, the Lincoln Bridge is significant as the covered bridge in the U.S. in which the wood and iron truss method was used. The bridge underwent a major renovation in 1988. Beyond the bridge you will pass the **Old Mill Marketplace** and the **Charles Shackleton Furniture and**

Miranda Thomas Pottery complex as you enter Bridgewater (see "Shopping" below).

Plymouth

Five miles west of the Lincoln Bridge (six miles beyond Woodstock), Route 4 intersects with Route 100A which branches south. Here you ener the municipality of Plymouth, known as the hometown of President Calvin Coolidge. Along this rural seven-mile road are two major attractions: the **Calvin Coolidge Historic Site** and the **Calvin Coolidge State Park** in Coolidge State Forest, where you can enjoy hiking, camping, and biking (see "Sports & Recreation" below). If you continue on Route 4, it will shortly intersect and merge with Route 100 at Bridgewater Corners as it turns north towards the Killington-Pico ski areas (6 miles).

CALVIN COOLIDGE STATE HISTORIC SITE, at plymouth Notch six miles north of Route 4 on Route 100A. Tel. 802/672-3773. Open 9:30am-5:30pm from late May to mid-October. Admission: $5.

Few sites in Vermont or anywhere in the region retain the essence of old New England like this exhibit, which contains virtually the entire village where President Calvin Colidge was born and raised. Visitors begin their tour at the **Calvin Cololidge Visitors Center**, where you can buy a ticket and look at a small photographic exhibit tracing Coolidge's life from his birth here in 1872, through his tenure as Governor of Massachusetts, and the US Presidency, which he assumed after the unexpected passing of President Warren G. Harding. At the Visitors center, you should pick up a copy of the guide that will explain the exhibits and the order in which you should visit them. Hold on to your ticket, because at each exhibit you will need it for entrance to each of the 12 exhibits.

The tour begins at two buildings, named for Coolidge's mother's brother-in-law, John Wilder, who inherited them. The **Wilder Barn** is a three story barn featuring dozens of 19th century tools and equipment, including carriages used in farming and in Calvin Coolidge's cheese factory. The **Wilder House** was the childhood home of Coolidge's mother, Victoria Josephine Moor, who married his father there in 1868. Originally a tavern when it was built in the early 19th century, the Wilder House is now a restaurant serving lunch when the Historic Site is open.

One of the most interesting and moving sites is the **Coolidge Homestead** itself. A restored typical turn of the century Yankee house, the homestead was Coolidge's boyhood home, and it was here where he received the news of Harding's death and took the oath of office which was administered by his father at 2:47am. The house, which includes parlors, bedrooms, bathrooms, and a kitchen and breakfast nook, has been restored to its 1923 condition.

From the Homestead, move on to the **Plymouth Cheese Factory**, opened by Calvin's father John in 1890, and the **One Room Schoolhouse**, a replacement of the one in which Calvin Coolidge went to grade school. Unfortunately, the Schoolhouse is usually closed to the public, nor is the Azro Johnson Farmhouse up the road. Instead, cross the street from the homestead to visit the **Carrie Brown Coolidge Garden**, originally planted by Calvin's stepmother. Next to the Garden stands the very handsome Greek Revival **Union Christian Church**, built in 1842.

There are several exhibits in and attached to the **Florence Cilley General Store**, including the **Calvin Coolidge Birthplace**, where Silent Cal was born on July 4, 1872. The store itself was built in the 1850's and was managed by Calvin's father John, who also served as the town post master, and manufactured cheese; the modest **post office** is located in a carraige barn attached to the store. Above the store is **Coolidge Hall** where the town held dances and other gatherings, and which Coolidge turned into his "Summer White House" during the summer of 1924. Today it contains numerous historic photos and some of the original furnishings.

The rest of Plymouth Notch consists of the **Aldrich House** where the Site's administration is located, the **Top of the Notch** (prefabricated) **Cabins** built for the President's Secret Service detail in the 1920's and later used by tourists, and the **Brown Family Farmhouse**, part of a prominent local farmer's estate that is not open to the public.

If you walk or drive to the Site's entrance and cross Route 100A, and take the local road on the other side, you will shortly come to the **Plymouth Cemetery**. Here Calvin Coolidge is buried alongside many of his family members in a grave marked by a surprisingly modest granite gravestone and the roadside of the cemetery.

The Calvin Coolidge Historic Site is just a couple of miles from the Juntion of Route 100A and Route 100 at the modest village of Plymouth Union. If you continue south, you will shortly find yourself in the town of Ludlow (see the "Manchester & the Heart of the Green Mountains" chapter), but not before passing the **Hawk Mountain Inn & Resort** (see *Where to Stay* above), an upscale resort with numerous outdoorsy recreation facilities, and Echo and Amherst Lake.

SHOPPING

With the high volume of tourist traffic that passes through the area, the Woodstock-Quechee region is particularly well endowed with shops and boutiques, selling everything from handcrafted pottery to Christmas ornaments. Listed below is just fraction of the shops in the area; for a more complete directory of shops and stores, contact the **Quechee**

THE OTTAUQUECHEE RIVER VALLEY 205

Chamber of Commerce, *P.O. Box 15, Quechee VT 05059. (Located at #15 on Main Street.) Tel. 802/296-8280. E-mail: quechee@quechee.com. Web site: www.quechee.com.*; or the **Woodstock Area Chamber of Commerce**, *P.O. Box 486, Woodstock VT 05091. (Located at #18 on Central Street.) Tel. 802/457-3555, Tel. 888/496-6378, Fax 802/457-1601. Web site: www.woodstockvt.com*

Quechee

ANTIQUE COLLABORATIVE, *Waterman House, Route 4, Quechee. Tel. 802/296-5858. Email: collab@sover.net. Hours: daily 10am-5pm. Credit cards: major credit cards accepted.*

A wide selection of antiques available from various dealers.

FAT HAT FACTORY etc*..., *Route 4 & Clubhouse Road, Quechee. Tel. 802/296-6646, Fax 802/296-3080. Website: www.pbpub.com/fathat.htm. Hours: 9am-5pm daily. major credit cards accepted.*

A colorful and slightly offbeat shop selling all types of hats and other apparel.

LARO'S NEW ENGLAND SPECIALTIES SHOPPE, *Route 4 East of the Quechee Gorge, Quechee. Tel. 802/295-6163. Hours: daily 9am-5pm. Major credit cards accepted.*

MESA FACTORY STORES, *next to Quechee Gorge on Route 4, Queechee. Tel. 802/295-0604. Hours: 9am-5pm daily. Major credit cards accepted.*

An outlet store selling a variety of ceramics, glassworks, and other crafts for wholesale prices.

QUECHEE GORGE VILLAGE, *Route 4, Quechee between Exit 1, I-89 and Waterman Hill Road turnoff to Quechee Village. Tel. 800/438-5565, Fax 802/295-6759. Email: Gary@QuecheeGorge.com. Hours: open daily; hours may vary according to store. Major credit cards accepted at most stores.*

This huge complex is a stretch mall gone kitsch, but with a definite Vermont flavor. It contains a half dozen shops, including the huge **Antique Center**, *Tel. 802/438-5565*, with thousands of pieces, crafts, and a country store section selling Vermont specialty foods; the colorful **Christmas Loft**, *Tel. 802/295-5404*, featuring all sorts of wonderful Christmas ornaments, gifts, and decorations; **New England Candles**, *Tel. 802/295-5775*, where you can enjoy candle dipping demonstrations; **Stellare Stained Glass**, *Tel. 802/296-3788*, selling home windows and repair supplies; and the **Farina Family Diner & Restaurant**, *Tel. 802/295-8997*, located in a vintage 1946 Wocerseter Semi-Streamliner. In the summer there is even a small amusement park for children that includes a wee choo-choo train.

SCOTLAND BY THE YARD, *Route 4, Quechee, 05059. Tel. 802/295-5351; 800/295-5351. Hours: 10am-5pm daily. Major credit cards accepted.*

Kilts, tweeds, and ties in every variety of plaid known to man are just some of the Scottish products available at Scotland by the Yard. Apart from clothing, merchandise includes, jewelry, pottery, books about everything Scottish from clan histories to cookbooks, and other souvenirs and knickknacks.

VERMONT'S HISTORIC TAFTSVILLE COUNTRY STORE, *Route 4 Taftaville. Tel. 802/457-1135; toll free 800/854-1120. Hours: daily 8am-8pm.Major credit cards accepted.*

One of the most famous country stores in Vermont, the Taftsville branch sells a variety of specialty foods and Vermont products and souvenirs.

Woodstock

F.H. GILLINGHAM & SONS, *16 Elm Street, Woodstock. Tel. 802/457-2100. Major credit cards accepted.*

Allegedly the oldest country store in Vermont, Gillingham's is certainly one of the most charming, though it hasn't been the same since Henry the cat (pictured threee times in *The New York Times*) passed away. Merchandise includes an extensive selection of wines and specialty foods as well as Vermont goods and souvenirs.

MIRANDA THOMAS PATTERY & CHARLES SHACKLETON FURNITURE, *Route 4 West (5 miles beyond Woodstock), Bridgewater VT. Tel. 802/672-5175. Open 10am-6pm. Major credit cards accepted.*

Miranda Thomas's handcrafted pottery and Charles Shackleton's furniture are both considered amongst the finest in their trade. Their shops are located in the **Old Mill Marketplace**, a complex that also includes a country store, a bookstore, and the **Bridgewater Mill Antique Centre**, *Tel. 802 672-3049.*

CHRISTMAS TREASURES, *73 Central Street, Woodstock. Tel. 802/457-4054. Open Monday-Saturrday 10am-5pm & Sunday 11am-4pm. Major credit cards accepted.*

A Christmas speciality store.

THE CHOCALATE COW, *24 Elm Street (1 block from the Green), Woodstock. Tel. 802/457-9151; Tel. 888/TRUFFLE. Open 9am-5pm (later in summer and during the Christmas season). Credit cards: Visa, Mastercard.*

Features superb gourmet chocalates in addition to ice cream, baked goods, and coffee.

MORGAN-BALLOU, *23 Elm Street, Woodstock. Tel. 802/457-1321.*

Specializes in rustic but elegant women's apparel.

NORDISKA, *5 The Green, Woodstock. Tel. 802/457-4005. Open daily 9am-5pm. Major credit cards accepted.*

Situated on the Woodstock Green, this gallery features an interesting collection of American, Scandanavian, and Inuit (Eskimo) arts and crafts.

WOODSTOCK CLAYWORKS, *Route 4 West, Woodstock. Tel. 802/ 672-5005. Open daily except Tuesdays, May-November. Credit cards: Visa, Mastercard.*

First rate hand-made pottery.

SUGARBUSH FARM, *Hillside Road off Route 4 in Taftsville, Woodstock. Tel. 802/457-1757; 800/281-1757, Fax 802/457-3269. Email: Sugarbsh@sover.net. Open daily 7:30am-5pm weekdays, 9am-5pm weekends and holidays. Credit cards: Visa, Mastercard.*

Sugarbush Farm is a working dairy and mapling farm selling dairy and maple products. You can also take tours of the farm – a worthwhile experience. Call in advance to inquire about tours.

SPORTS & RECREATION

Biking

The Woodstock-Quechee region offers some of the most scenic cycling in Vermont along roads like Route 106, Route 12, and many of the various local town roads, particularly River Road which links Woodstock from The Billings Museum on Route 12 with Quechee. For ideas about tours, talk to the local cycle shops listed below and pick up copies of Vermont Life's *Bicycle Vermont Map and Guide*, and *25 Bicycle Tours in Vermont* (Backcountry Press) by John Friedin. There are other publications about cycling in Vermont that are widely available in bookstores acrosss the state.

BIKE VERMONT, *P.O. Box 207, Woodstock VT 05091. Tel.Tel. 800/ 257-2226. Major credit cards accepted.*

Bike Vermont is an outfit that organizes and operates bike tours throughout the state and the Connecticut River Valley. Their tours can last from one to six days and are often inn-to-inn. They can also help you with equipment, instruction, and maps and directions.

CYCLERY PLUS, *36 Route 4, West Woodstock VT 05091. Tel. 802/457- 3377. Major credit cards accepted.*

CP rents and sell bikes as well as cycling apparel and accessories.

WILDERNESS TRAILS AT THE QUECHEE INN AT MARSH- LAND FARMS, *one mile from Quechee Gorge on Clubhouse Road, Quechee VT 05059 . Tel. 802/295-7620.*

Rents mountain and hybrid bikes for $17 a day ($30 for couples, $11 for additional days) and provides maps of biking trails, many of which are just a mile or so north of the Quechee Inn.

WOODSTOCK SPORTS, *30 Central Street, Woodstock VT 05091. Tel. 802/457-1568. Major credit cards accepted.*

This sporting goods shop specializes in bike and ski equipment service.

Canoeing

WILDERNESS TRAILS AT THE QUECHEE INN AT MARSH-LAND FARMS, *Clubhouse Road (one mile from Quechee Gorge), Quechee VT 05059. Tel. 802/295-7620. Email: quecheeinn@pinnable-inns.com. Major credit cards accepted.*

Rents canoes for $18 a day, $12 for a half-day. Most folks just paddle around Dewey Lake and the Dewey Mills Waterfowl Sanctuary for views of blue heron, kingfisher, and some of the beautiful fowl that inhabit the lake. Wilderness Trails also arranges day and half-day self-guided excursions on the Connecticut River. Essentially they drop you off and pick you at a designated spot downriver, and handle transporting the canoes.

Cross-Country Skiing

WILDERNESS TRAILS AT THE QUECHEE INN AT MARSH-LAND FARMS, *Clubhouse Road (one mile from Quechee Gorge), Quechee VT 05059. Tel. 802/295-7620. Email: quecheeinn@pinnable-inns.com. Major credit cards accepted.*

Wilderness Trails in Quechee operates about 20 kilometers of beautiful trails north of Quechee Village, and provides rentals, instruction, and equipment tune-ups and sales. The Weekend trail fee is $6. Avid skiers should consider asking about weekend and weekday packages combining lodging, dining and skiing and Quechee Inn (see *Where to Stay* above).

WOODSTOCK SKI TOURING CENTER, *Route 106 just off Woodstock Green, Woodstock VT 05091. Tel. 802/457-6674, 800/448-7900. Trail fees $8-$12. Major credit cards accepeted.*

The Woodstock Ski Touring Center operates approximately 60 kilometers of cross-country ski trails most ly in the Mount Peg area south of the Green off Route 106. There are also trails on Mt. Tom off Routes 12 and Route 4 West. The Center rents, sells, and repairs equipment, and can provide instruction. Call the Touring Center for information.

You can also cross-country ski in **Hawk Mountain Inn and Resort** off Route 100 in Plymouth, and there are many opportunities along Route 100 in the **Killington-Pico** area just to the north (see the "Rutland & Killington" chapter for more information); south in the **Ludlow -Okemo** region (see the "Manchester & the Heart of the Mountains" chapter for more information); and off Route 5, Route 44 and I-91 in **Mt. Ascutney State Park** (see the "Precision Valley" chapter for more information).

Fishing

Near Quechee and Woodstock, there are fish in the **Ottauquechee**, **White** and **Connecticut** rivers, and in **Dewey Pond**, **Barnard Brook**, and the **Gulf Stream**. In the Plymouth region, there is also fishing in **Broad**

Brook, and the **Black River**. You can also go **Amherst Lake** and **Echo Lake**, roughly five miles south of Plymouth Union on Route 100. About ten miles north of Woodstock in Barnard is the **Silver Lake State Park**, *Tel. 802/23409451,* where you can rent boats or fish from the shore.
WILDERNESS TRAILS AT THE QUECHEE INN AT MARSH-LAND FARMS, *one mile from Quechee Gorge on Clubhouse Road, Quechee (05059). Tel. 802/295-7620. Email: quecheeinn@pinnable-inns.com. Major credit cards accepted.*

The **Vermont Fly Fishing School** can provide equipment, fishing licenses (one day license, $7), and ideas for good fishing spots. Clinics for all levels of fishermen are also given by the School's director, Marty Banak. A private lesson (including a one hour precourse, three hours of on-stream instruction, and any necessary euipment) costs $85 for one, and $35 for each additional participant.

Golf
In addition to the two clubs below, you may also consider **Green Mountain National**, *Tel. 802/ 422-3241,* and the **Killington Golf Course**, *Tel. 802/422-4100,* in Killington; the **Montague Golf Course** in Randolph, *Tel. 802/728-3806*; the **Windsor Country Club** in Windsor, *Tel. 802/674-6491*; and the Hanover Country Club in Hanover, New Hampshire, *Tel. 603/646-2000.*
WOODSTOCK COUNTRY CLUB, *14 The Green, Woodstock VT 05091. Tel. 802/457-2114. Rates: $59 weekends, $49 weekdays, $25 after 4pm. Carts avialable for rent. Major credit cards accepted.*

Designed by Robert Trent Jones, this beautiful course is one of the finest and most popular in Vermont, so be sure to call for reservations.
QUECHEE LAKELAND & HIGHAND (Quechee Club), *1 River Road, Quechee VT 05059. Tel. 802/295-6245. Rates: $73 weekends, $69 weekdays, $42 after 4pm. Major credit cards accepted.*

This fine and exclusive club is private, so it's very difficult to access unless you are a member or staying at one of the select hotels in the Quechee area (see *Where to Stay* above).

Hiking
There are plenty of hiking opportunties – mostly very easy – in and around Quechee and Woodstock villages, as well as at the Calvin Coolidge State Park in Plymouth. For information, maps, and specific directions, contact the **Touring Center at the Woodstock Inn and Resort**, *Tel. 802/457-2114,* in Woodstock, and/or **Wilderness Trails**, *Tel. 802/295-7620,* at the Quechee Inn at Marshland Farms in Quechee. For comprehensive information about hiking in the rest of Vermont, contact the **Green Mountain Club**, *Tel. 802/244-7037,* or pick up one of their many guides

and other publications readily available at bookstores throughout Vermont.

Hiking in Plymouth

Calvin Coolidge State Park *off Route 100A, Plymouth, Tel. 802/672-3612/summer, Tel. 802/886-2434/winter,* is part of the Calvin Coolidge State Park and features miles of hiking as well as camping sites, picnic areas, and a playground. One of the easiest and most rewarding hikes is to the summit of **Slack Hill** where a vista offers impressive views. Maps detailing this trail and othes can be picked up at the ranger station at the park's entrance, where you will pay a nominal fee for entering the park.

Hiking in Quechee

Quechee Gorge State Park, *off Route 4 in Quechee, Tel. 802/295-2990/summer, Tel. 802/886-2434/off-season,* is a 600-acre park with miles of hiking trails around the beautiful Gorge as well as camping facilities (see *Where to Stay* above).

There is also extensive hiking north of Quechee Village, which you can access by taking the Quechee West Hartford Road north from Main Strreet and the Safford Road past the Equistrian Center. Contact **Wilderness Trails**, *Tel. 802/295-7620.* at the Quechee Inn at Marshland Farms in Quechee for information.

Hiking in Woodstock

Mt. Tom in west Woodstock is popular with hikers and rewards those who make it to the top (the climb is not very difficult) with great views of the Ottauquechee Valley. Trails begin at Mountain Avenue, River Street (west of Route 12), and in the Marsh-Billings National Historic Park. Covered by more than 50 forest stands (some of which date to the 1800's and are considered the oldest in the United State) that include groves of Norway spruce, a variety of pines (red and white among others), and hemlocks.

If you drive down 106 (a.k.a. South Street) from the Woodstock Green onto Cross Street and then Golf Avenue, you will be able to access the **Mt. Peg** hiking trails. Also very easy, they make for a relaxing stroll and afford some good views of neighboring Mt. Tom. Like Mt. Tom, its topography is largely covered with trees planted and managed by humans over the past century. Contact **Touring Center at the Woodstock Inn and Resort**, *Tel. 802/457-2114,* in Woodstock for more information.

Horseback Riding & Sleigh Rides

KEDRON VALLEY STABLES, *Route 106, South Woodstock VT 05091. Tel. 802/457-1480. Open 10am-4pm daily. Credit cards: Visa, Mastercard.*

Offers trail and carriage rides, horseback riding lessons, inn-to-inn tours and sleigh rides in the winter.

Mini Golf

QUECHEE GORGE MINI GOLF, *Route 4 between Quechee Village and I-89 (Exit 1) next to Quality Inn. Tel. 802/296-6669. Open 10am-11pm late spring through autumn.*

With its waterfalls, surrounding trees, and grass lawns, the setting is first-rate for mini golf. Operated by Quechee Pizza Chef restaurant which operates next door – a nice place to fill up before or after a cut-throat round of putt-putt.

Skiing

Dedicated skiers should consider heading over to **Killington-Pico**. Only a half-hour drive from the Woodstock-Quechee region on Route 4 West, it's the largest and most extensive skiing area in the east. Another option is to head south on Route 100 to **Okemo**, another major ski area with much more to offer than Suicide Six or Quechee Lakes. Finally, a third option is **Mt. Ascutney** – about 20 miles away and accessible by taking Route 106 or I-91/Route 5 south to Route 44.

Otherwise, try:

SUICIDE SIX, *Route 12, Woodstock VT 05091. Tel. 802/457-6661. Hours: 9am-4pm daily. Daily ski pass rate $25-$45. Major credit cards accepted.*

This modest ski area features 50 acres, 22 trails, and three lifts. Snowboarding is allowed, equipment for snowboarding and apline can be rented, and clinics are offered.

QUECHEE LAKES, *off River Road & Route 4, Quechee VT 05059. Tel. 802/295-9356. Open 9am-4pm on weekends & holidays. Daily ski passes: $20-40. Major credit cards accepted.*

So modest as to make Suicide Six look like Val D'Isere (actually its acreage is greater), Quechee Lakes only operates during holidays and the weekends, but is convenient for those staying in Quechee. Rentals and clinics are available and snowboarding is allowed.

WOODSTOCK SPORTS, *30 Central Street, Woodstock VT 05091. Tel. 802/457-1568. Major credit cards accepted.*

This sporting goods shop specializes in bike and ski equipment service.

Tennis

Both the **Quechee Club**, *Tel. 802/295-9356,* and the **Woodstock Health & Fitness Center** at the **Woodstock Inn**, *Tel. 802/ 457-1100,* feature tennis courts and give priorities to members and guests at selected hotels. Others should call regarding court times.

EXCURSIONS & DAY TRIPS

With access to major highways like Interstates 89 and 91, and Routes 4 and 100, the Ottauquechee River Valley is a convenient location from which to explore central Vermont and the Connecticut River Valley.

WEST OF WOODSTOCK

Route 4 West leads straight to Route 100 at Plymouth. Just north of Plymouth on Route 4 is the **Killington-Pico** area, featuring the most extensive alpine skiing east of the Rocky Mountains as well as opportunities for hiking, biking, golfing, cross-country skiing and other outdoorsy activities. There are also many fine inns and restaurants. However, the area lacks the charm of Woodstock, Quechee and other older towns and villages across Vermont.

Just about 10 miles beyond Killington on Route 4 is **Rutland**, Vermont's second biggest city, but not much in the way of an attraction for most tourists. From Rutland you can take Route 7 north to explore the beautiful region around **Middlebury**, including the **Lake Champlain Valley** and the **Green Mountain National Forest** with its extensive hiking, biking, and snow-related outdoors activities. (See the "Rutland & Killington" and the "Middlebury & the Lower Champlain Valley" chapters for more information.)

Eleven miles south of Plymouth Union on Route 100 is the **Ludlow-Okemo** region, also a major skiing area teeming with inns, restaurants, shops, and recreational opportunities. (See the "Manchester & the Heart of the Green Mountains" chapter for more info.)

THE CONNECTICUT RIVER VALLEY

Taking Route 4 and/or I-89 east will lead straight to the Connecticut River Valley. In the immediate vicintiy of White River Junction, where all of the region's major highways (I-89, I-91, Route 4, Route 5, and Route 14) intersect, is the picturesque town of **Norwich**, home to the famous Norwich Inn and the Montshire Museum devoted to natural history and science. Across the river in New Hampshire, the town of **Hanover** is the quintessential college town (some might also say a preppies' paradise) and home to **Dartmouth College**. It features many shops and eateries and, at only 20 minutes away from the Woodstock-Quechee area, makes for an easy half-day trip.

From White River Junction, you can also take Route 5 (or I-91) north along the scenic Conncecticut River. Depending on how much of an excursion you want to make of it, you can do a number of loops back west and come back to the Ottauquechee region inland by way of local roads, many of which are quite pretty. From Norwich, for example, you can take

Route 132 west through Union Village, Thetford, and Strafford, where a short detour on the Justin Smith Morrill Road will take you to the handsome village of **Strafford** and the **Justin Smith Morrill Homestead**, the restored Victorian home of one of Vermont's most famous legislators. Route 132 continues south to Sharon from where you can take the scenic **Pomfret Road** back to Woodstock (half an hour). this scenic drive only takes a couple of hours or more, depending on how much you stop.

Or you can continue further along Route 5 and take **Route 113** to **Lake Fairlee** where you can fish, hike, or boat. Route 113 continues to Chelsea on **Route 110**, a road lined with classic Vermont farms and rolling hills which, if you take south, will lead you to South Royalton. From Royalton, take Route 14 and Route 107 to Bethel where it joins Route 12 back to Woodstock. An alternative is to go south on Route 14 six miles to Sharon and take the Pomfret Road back to Woodstock. Both Route 12 and the Pomfret Road are largely undeveloped and scenic, though the Pomfret Road is perhaps a bit prettier. (See the "Upper Connecticut Valley" chapter for more information.)

Finally, you can even take Route 5 or I-91 from White River all the way to **St. Johnsbury** in the Northeast Kingdom, about 1.5-2 hours one way by car. A colorful little town of just under 10,000, St. Johnsbury is home to the **Fairbanks Museum and Observatory**, as well as many handsome buildings and churchs. The countryside around St. Johnsbury is quite picturesque. See the "Northeast Kingdom" chapter for information.

THE PRECISION VALLEY

There are also excellent opportunities for exploration to the south. Southern Windsor County and the area around the towns of Windsor and Springfield is known as the Precision Valley because it was here that the machine-tool industry was developed. From Woodstock, you can take the quiet Route 106 about 25 miles south to **Springfield**, where you can visit the **Hartness House** mansion, a former home of a Vermont Governor and industrialist James Hartness. The mansion is now an inn with a fine restaurant and several small historical exhibits, including a fascinating antique observatory. From Springfield, you can take Route 11 ten miles west to the picturesque village of **Chester**, known for its many beautiful Victorian buildings and quaint green. To get back to the Woodstock-Quechee region, take 103 west from Chester to Route 100 North to Plymouth Union and then Route 4 east.

The alternative is to take Route 11 east from Springfield to Route 5 and come back north along Route 5 and the Connecitcut River. Should you do this during the summer, you can stop at the **American Precision Museum** in Windsor which contains a wonderful collection of tools, machines and firearms from the 19th century. Also just north of Windsor on Route 5 are the **Simon Pearce Glass** (a second branch of the operation in Quechee) and the **Catamount Brewery**. From Windsor, it's less than 15 miles to Woodstock-Quechee by way of Route 12 from Hartland (just north of Windsor) to Taftsville. Of course, you can skip Springfield and Chester and go straight to Windsor, or you can cut from Route 106 13 miles south of Woodstock on Route 44 to Windsor. This takes you past **Mount Ascutney**, where there is a resort with a skiing area and Mt. Ascutney State Park, where you can hike or bike to the summit and enjoy magical views of the Connecticut River Valley, the Berkshires, and the Green Mountains. (See the "Precision Valley" Chapter for more information.)

THE WHITE RIVER VALLEY & MONTPELIER

Finally, there is plenty to explore along the White River that flows from the Montpelier region (there are actually four branches) to the Connecticut River at White River Junction. From Woodstock and Quechee, you can take Route 4 to White River Junction and then take Route 14 along the White River as far as you like; it's quite a pretty drive.

At **Sharon**, 13 miles from White River Junction, you can take a scenic detour on **Route 132** to the beautiful village of **Strafford**, known for its Meeting House and the **Justin Smith Morrill Homestead**, a historic Victorian mansion that was once the home of the man who drafted the Morrill Homestead Acts that provided land grants for colleges across the United States. You can also reach Sharon by taking the scenic Pomfret Road (off Route 12 just beyond the Billing Museum) from Woodstock. Five miles beyond Sharon, just before South Royalton, with its classic village green and church steeple, is Dairy Hill Road and **Joseph Smith Monument**, built to commemorate the Mormon prophet's birthplace. Yet another scenic rural road, Dairy Hill Road will eventually (after 5 or 6 miles) lead you to Turnbridge and Route 110. You can also get on Route 110 at South Royalton itself. It is a scneic 27-mile drive lined with farms; you'll pass the villages of Tunbridge and Chelsea from South Royalton to the eastern edge of **Barre** which borders Montpelier.

You can also continue along Route 14 for about 30 miles from South Royalton to Montpelier. This will take you through Bethel, East Randolph, North Randolph, and the town of **Brookfield**, home of the famous **Floating Bridge** (take a detour on Route 65 west) before the final 11 miles to Barre. **Barre** itself is home to the **Rock of Ages Granite Quarries** (the largest in the world), which you can visit along with the manufacturing division. You can watch as dozens of craftsmen carve and engrave headstone, statues, and other granite products.

Just northwest of Barre is **Montpelier**, the charming and handsome state capital distinguished by the elegant capital building and several fine restaurants, including two operated by the **New Engand Culinary Institute**. You can also reach Montpelier and Barre directly from the Woodstock-Quechee region by taking Route 12 straight north, getting on I-89 at Exit 1, and from there it's a straight shot – or by taking Route 12 to Bethel and getting on I-89 at Exit 3 (take Route 107 east). For this whole area, see the "Montpelier and Central Vermont" chapter.

PRACTICAL INFORMATION

Chambers of Commerce

QUECHEE CHAMBER OF COMMERCE, *P.O. Box 15, Quechee VT 05059. (Located at #15 on Main Street.) Tel. 802/296-8280. E-mail: quechee@quechee.com. Web site: www.quechee.com.*

WOODSTOCK AREA CHAMBER OF COMMERCE, *P.O. Box 486, Woodstock VT 05091. (Located at #18 on Central Street.) Tel. 802/457-3555, 888/496-6378, Fax 802/457-1601. Web site: www.woodstockvt.com*

Gas Stations

Route 4 on the eastern edge of Woodstock is lined with several filling stations. The **Quechee Mobil Mart**, *on Route 4 off Exit 1, I-89*, is open 24 hours and has an ATM, restrooms, coffee, snacks, and beer available in addition to gas.

Medical Emergencies & Services

Ambulance – *Tel. 911*
Fire – *Tel. 911*
DARTMOUTH-HITCHCOCK MEDICAL CENTER, *Medical Center Drive/Route 120 (Exit 18 I-91), Lebanon NH. Tel. 603/650-5848 (general information).*

The best medical facility in the region with walk-in clinic, emergency services, and specialized care in all medical areas.

Police

Tel. 911, Tel. 802/457-1416 or 457-1420

Post Office

WOODSTOCK POST OFFICE, *22 Central Street, Woodstock VT 05091. Tel. 802/457-1323. Open 8:30am-4:45pm Monday – Friday, 9am-noon Saturday.*

QUECHEE POST OFFICE, *Main Street (by the Green), Quechee VT 05059. Tel. 802/295-3535. Open 8:30am-4:45pm Monday – Friday, 9am-noon Saturday.*

16. KILLINGTON & RUTLAND

According to Vermont legend, a certain 18th century traveler, Rev. Samuel Peters, was traveling the Green Mountains. After ascending what we now know as Mt. Killington (then called Mt. Pisgah after the mountain in Jordan from which Moses first saw the Promised Land), and beholding the beautiful green expanse of mountains and valleys, he christened the area "Verd Mont." Later the area's English-speaking settlers shortened the name out of linguistic convenience to "Vermont" and the name – meaning "Green Mountains" – has remained ever since.

Should Rev. Peters ascend Killington today (probably in a gondola) he would hardly recognize the area, for now **Killington** and its sister peak and resort **Pico** is the largest ski area east of the Mississippi, with more than 200 trails. The surrounding area is covered with condos, lodges, shops, and other facilities to accommodate the tens of thousands of visitors who come to ski, bike, and hike the mountain slopes. Unfortunately, the developments are almost exclusively modern and the area lacks the old New England charm that characterizes most of Vermont, though many find it a worthy tradeoff for Killington's excellent recreational opportunities and facilities.

Just 15 miles east of Killington on Route 4, Vermont's traditional second city, **Rutland**, was the capital of the country's marble industry in the 19th century. While it has not been a major tourist destination, the city's recent renaissance makes it worthy of a visit. Its downtown has been revitalized and the town makes an excellent base not only for accessing Killington, but for visiting nearby attractions such as the **Marble Museum** in Proctor and **Lake Bomoseen** near Vermont's border with New York.

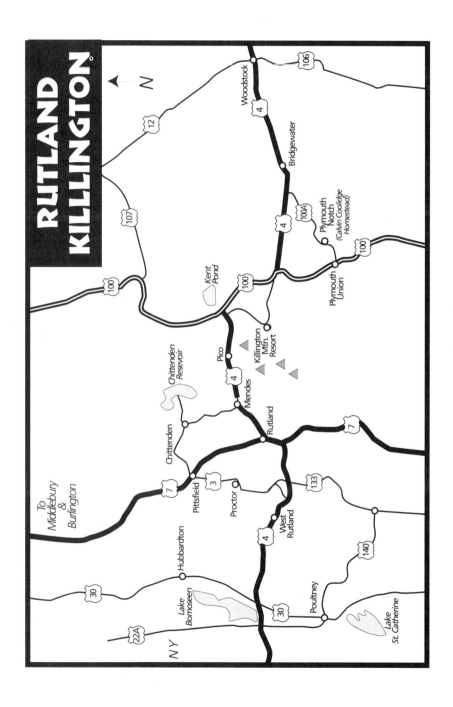

ARRIVALS & DEPARTURES

By Air

Continental's **Colgan Air**, *Tel. 800/253-FARE,* flies two-to-four times daily between Rutland and Boston. Otherwise **Lebanon Municipal Airport** in West Lebanon, New Hampshire, is about 55 miles from Rutland by way of Interstate 89 and Route 4 (from I-89 Exit 1 at Quechee). It is serviced by **USAir Express** but flights are relatively expensive and infrequent *(Tel. 800/428-4322 at the airport, Tel. 800/943-5436 for general info and reservations).*

Also within a reasonable driving distance (about 110 miles from Rutland by way of I-89 and Route 4) is the upstart airport in **Manchester, N.H.**, serviced by Continental, United, USAir, and Southwest. The Vermont Transit Line, *Tel. 802/864-6811,* operates bus routes directly from the airport to White River Junction where you can make connections to Rutland. Boston's **Logan Airport** is another option, and is a 3-4 hour drive to Windsor. All major rental car agencies operate out of Logan, and while Vermont Transit no longer provides direct service from Logan to White River Junction, there are frequent shuttles to the main bus depot at South Station in downtown Boston; there are no fewer than a half-dozen departures daily to White River Junction, where connections can be made for Rutland and Killington.

Rutland is situated at the junction of **Route 7** (north-south) and **Route 4** (East-West). From points north such as the Canadian border, Burlington (70 miles), and Middebury (35 miles), take Route 7 South. From Manchester (30 miles) and Bennington, take Route 7 North.

Killington is 17 miles east of Rutland on Route 4 near the intersection of Route 4 and Route 100.

From points south of Montpelier on **I-89**, or if you're coming up or down **I-91** in the Connecticut Valley, find your way to I-89 Exit 1 just west of White River Junction, and get on Route 4. It is then a straight 30 mile shot to Killington and 40 miles to Rutland. Slower but more direct alternatives include taking Route 12 south from Montpelier and then Route 4 west from Woodstock, or getting off I-89 at Bethel (Exit 3), and then taking Route 107 to Route 12, and on to Route 4.

By Bus

Rutland and Sherburne Village (Killington Village as opposed to the Killington Resort on Killington Road) are both serviced by **Vermont Transit Lines** bus company. Three buses depart Rutand daily for **Burlington** (stopping at Brandon, Middlebury, and Vergennes); **Albany** (via Wallingford, Manchester, and Bennington); four daily for **Boston** (stopping at Brattleboro and Keene, or Sherburne, White River Junction,

Woodstock) and again for Burlington. At Burlington, connections can be made for points in northwestern Vermont, Montreal, Waterbury-Stowe, and Montpelier; while from White River Junction connections can be made for Montpelier, Manchester N.H., Boston, New York, and the Northeast Kingdom.

By Train

Amtrak's **Ethan Allen Express** departs **Washington, DC**, at 3am daily (#299), and at 10:40am Monday-Thursday (#291), and 1:05pm Friday-Saturday (#293), it stops at Baltimore, Wilimington DE, Philadelphia, and **New York City** (arriving at 6:38am. 2:15pm & 4:19pm respectively), where you must catch a connecting train with the same number. Train #299 departs Penn Station at 7:10am, Train #291 at 3:55pm, and Train # 293 at 5:40pm en route to Yonkers, Croton-Harmon, Poughkeepsie, Rhinecliff-Kinston, Hudson, and **Albany**. Again you must transfer or board trains with the same number departing at 9:55am, 6:40pm, and 8:20pm respectively and arriving in Rutland at 12:30pm, 9:05pm, and 10:45pm. Trains depart Rutland in the other direction at 1:25pm and 5:25pm. A one-way fare from Rutland to New York City is approximately $55.

The **James Jeffords Railroad Station** is located next to the transportation center behind the Walmart in downtown Rutand. There are virtually no facilities. Call *800/USA-RAIL* to make reservations and inquire about Amtrak schedules and fares.

ORIENTATION

Situated at the junction of **Route 4** (east-west) and **Route 7** (north-south), **Rutland** is the commercial, transportation, and economic center of the region, while **Killington-Pico**, at the junction of Route 4 and Route 100 (north-south), is the state's premier ski area. The two are about 17 miles apart on **Route 100** and are separated by the hotel-filled town of Mendon. About 10 miles north and west of Rutland on the short Route 3 is the famous marble town of Proctor, while west of Rutland Route 4 continues approximately 20 miles to the state border with New York and passes through the towns of West Rutland, Castleton, and Fair Haven.

Just east of the border, **Route 30** (north-south) intersects with Route 4. North on Route 30 immediately is Lake Bomoseen, the third largest lake in the state and a popular venue for fishing and boating. Meanwhile, about eight miles south of the intersection on Route 30 is the town of Poultney, of little significance, and Lake St. Catherine, another popular destination for fishermen and boaters. There are state parks with campsites at both Lake Bomoseen and Lake St. Catherine.

GETTING AROUND

If you do not have a car, most resorts and major lodges offer shuttle service to and from the ski slopes, while the **Diamond Express** shuttles between Killington and Rutland stopping at most resorts and other landmarks, such as the Diamond Run Mall. Ask at your hotel for schedule information or call *802/772-3244 (Ext. 62)*. A daily fare is $2.

For renting a car, **Avis** has an office in Rutland, *Tel. 802/773-1317*. **Enterprise Rent-A-Car** has outlets in Rutland, *Tel. 802/773-0855*; Barre, *Tel. 802/479-5400*; and South Burlington, *Tel. 802/863-2111*. Cars can also be rented at major airports in the region including Albany, Burlington, Montreal, Boston, Manchester, and West Lebanon.

WHERE TO STAY

Killington-Pico & Mendon

KILLINGTON RESORT VILLAGES, *Killington Village/ Killington Road, Killington VT 05751Tel. 802/422-3101, 877/4KTIMES, 800/621-MTNS. Web site: www.killing.tom*. Rates begin at about $50 a night. Major credit cards accepted.

Killington (the resort company owned by the American Skiing Company, not to be confused with the town or the region generally), operates numerous condo complexes at the Snowshed base of the Killington Ski Area and on Killington Road (a.k.a. "Mountain Road") that links the ski area with Routes 4 and 100. Within walking distance of the lifts,

Trail Creek, **Highridge**, and the spanking new **Killington Grand Resort Hotel** (a hotel with condo-like studios and suites) offer condos and studios with 1-4 bedrooms and full amenities, including baths, kitchens, premium cable television, saunas and/or hot tubs, and access to recreation facilities like tennis courts, fitness centers etc. **Whiffletree**, **Sunrise**, **Fall Line**, and **Pinnacle** are all approximately a half-mile from the lifts and offer similar condos with slightly fewer amenities and conveniences. Finally, at the base of the Pico Ski Area, the **Pico Resort Hotel & Condominiums** offers similar accommodations, amenities and access to facilities. To sort out which combination of accommodation best fits your needs, call the number above and request comprehensive information. Don't forget to ask about multi-day packages featuring discounted condo rates, ski tickets, and meals. In the summer ask about golf, tennis, and biking packages.

CORTINA INN, *Route 4, 6 miles east of Rutland between Killington and Rutland. Tel. 802/773-4735, 422-2121, 800/579-4735. E-mail: cortina1@aol.com, Web site: www.cortinainn.com. Rates $100-4170. Major credit cards accepted.*

Located halfway between Killington and Rutland and just two miles from Pico Mountain, Cortina features the most extensive recreational facilities of any establishment in the area, in addition to modern rooms with full amenities. On-premise facilities include numerous tennis courts (instruction available), a pool, a biking center, a nature trail for hiking, and a full-fledged fitness center with saunas, exercise machines, and spa.

MOUNTAIN GREEN RESORT, *Killington Road, Killington VT 05751. Tel. 802/422-3000, 800/336-7754, Fax 802/422-2328. E-mail: stay@mtgreen.com. Web site: www.mtgreen.com. Rates begin at about $50 per person. Major credit cards accepted.*

Located within feet of the lifts at Snowshed, Mountain Green Resort includes more than 200 apartments ranging from 1-4 bedrooms and furnished with kitchens, cable television, private baths, and some fireplaces. On-premise facilties include a spa, a shopping arcade, a video store, a ski shop, and a restaurant.

GLAZEBROOK TOWNHOUSES, *.75 miles from Snowshed lifts on Killington Road (P.O. Box 505), Killington VT 05751. Tel. 802/422-4425, 800/544-8742, Fax 802/422-2221. E-mail: VT4ME@sover.net. Web site: www.skigkg.com. Rates begin at around $20 per person per night. Major credit cards accepted.*

An assortment of townhouses, some of which can sleep up to ten. Many include full kitchens, saunas, hot tubs, several baths, dishwasher, laundry machines, and other amenities. There is also a ski shop, two eateries, and a lounge on the premises.

RED CLOVER INN, *7 Woodword Road (off Route 4), Mendon VT 05701. (Between Killington and Rutland.) Tel. 802/775-2290, 800/752-0571, Fax 802/773-0594. E-mail: redclovr@vermontel.net. Web site: redcloverinn.com. Rates: $150-$300. Major credit cards accepted.*

A restored 1840 home, Red Clover offers some of the finest and most romantic lodging in the area with 14 rooms featuring fireplaces and private baths, some with whirlpools. The dining room in which guests take a first class breakfast in the morning serves excellent American cuisine by candlelight in the evening.

INN AT LONG TRAIL, *Route 4 at Sherburne Pass, Killington VT 05751. Tel. 802/775-7181, 800/325-2540, Fax 802/747-7034. E-mail: ilt@vermontel.com. Web site: www.innatlongtrail.com. Rates: $60-$210. Credit cards: Visa, Mastercard, American Express.*

Situated at the intersection of Route 4 and the Long Trail, the ILT features 22 rooms, including six suites with fireplaces. Some rooms have no phone or television. Common areas include an Irish Pub presenting live Irish music on the weekends, a sitting room with a fireplace, and a restaurant with a boulder, of all things, in it. In business since the 1930's, it is one of the oldest lodges in the Killington area.

SUMMIT LODGE, *Killington Road (Mountain Road) (P.O. Box 119), Killington VT 05751. Tel. 802/422-3535, 800/635-6343, Fax 802/422-3536. E-mail: summit@vermontel.com. Web site: www.summitlodgevermont.com. Rates: $75-$175. Major credit cards accepted.*

The Summit offers guests clean, comfortable rooms with modern amenities, but its real attractions are the fine views, the convenient location just a mile or so from the slopes, and most of the recreational facilities: five tennis courts, saunas, a giant jacuzzi, a heated outdoor pool, and a spa. There are also two restaurants and a pub on the premises. The resident St. Bernard adds a homey touch.

BIRCH RIDGE INN, *Butler Road off Killington Road, Kiinglinto VT 05751. Tel. 802/422-4293, 800/435-8566, Fax 802/422-3406. E-mail: innkeepers@birchridge.com. Web site: www.birchridge.com. Rates: $130-$250 per room. Major credit cards accepted.*

A first-rate inn offering luxury, intimacy, and convenience. There are 10 rooms including six with fireplaces, of which four have whirlpools; also a cozy lounge with a slate fireplace and a top-notch restaurant.

FOX & PHEASANT INN, *Bear Mountain Road, Sunrise Village, Killington VT 05751. Tel. 802/422-8770, Fax 802/422-4242. E-mail: unwind@foxpheasantinn.com. Rates: $90-$160. Credit cards: Visa, Mastercard, American Express.*

Fox and Pheasant offers six comfortable rooms furnished with queen beds, private baths, and cable television, as well as access to the resort facilities including the pool, sauna, and fitness center.

CASCADES LODGE, *Off Bear Mountain Lodge in Killington Village, Killington VT 05673-0766. Tel. 802/422-3731, 800/345-0113, Fax 802/422-3351. E-mail: info@cascaseslodge.com. Web site: www.cascadeslodge.com. Rtes: $50-$250. Major credit cards accepted.*

Located within walking distance of the slopes at Snowshed, the Cascades offers one of the top combinations of convenience, value, and amenities. Accommodations include a variety of rooms and suites, all with private bath and cable television. Other amenities include a lounge with a fireplace, a more-than-adequate restaurant, and a fitness center with saunas, exercise machines, whirlpools, and an indoor pool.

GREY BONNET INN & RESTAURANT, *Route 100 North, Killington VT 05751. (North of the intersection with Route 4 and four miles north of Snowshed lifts.) Tel. 802/775-2537, 800/342-2086, Fax 802/775-3371. Rates: $70-$110. Major credit cards accepted. Closed in May and November.*

The Grey Bonnet features 21 rooms with private baths, cable television, air-conditioning and antique furnishings, which lend it some of the old-time inn atmosphere that most establishments around Killington lack. On-site facilities include tennis, a fitness center with a sauna, jacuzzi, exercise machines, swimming pools (one indoor, one out) and cross-country skiing. There is also a restaurant and a pub that sometimes has live entertainment.

KILLINGTON-PICO MOTOR INN, *HC 34 on Route 4, Killington VT 05751. Tel. 802/773-4088, toll fre Tel. 800/548-4713, Fax 802/775-9705. E-mail: KPMI@webTv. Web site: www.killingtonpico.com. Rates: $65-$120. Major credit cards accepted.*

Decent rooms with private baths, cable television, convenient parking, and in-room telephones. Other on-site facilities include a large hot tub and a nice pub with a fireplace. Call about multi-packages which offer great value.

Rutland

THE INN AT RUTLAND, *70 North Main Street, Rutland VT 05701. Tel. 802/773-0575, 800/808-0575, Fax 802/775-3506. E-mail: inrutlnd@vermontel.com. Web site: innatrutland.com. Rates: $60-$180. Major credit cards accepted.*

The Inn at Rutland is a restored victorian home, originally dating from the 1890's. There are two common rooms, a nice fireplace, and a wraparound porch. The Inn has a carriage house for bicycle and ski storage, and mountain bikes are available for guests. Each room has a private bath, color television, and telephone. Breakfasts are a gourmet affair.

HOLIDAY INN, CENTRE OF VERMONT, *411 South Main (Route 7), Rutland VT 05701. Tel. 802/77501911, 800/462-4810, Fax 802/775-0113. E-mail: info@holidayinn-vermont.com. Web site: www.holidayinn-vermont.com. Rates: $60-$200. Major credit cards accepted.*

Modern and charmless, but features modern comfortable rooms with full amenities as well as a restaurant, fitness center, and pub that packs 'em in for karaoke on Friday nights (ouch!).

HOWARD JOHNSON, *South Main Street (just north of the Holiday Inn), Rutland VT 05701. Tel. 802/775-4303, Fax 802/775-6840. Rates: $45-$110. Major credit cards accepted.*

Not quite as well endowed with amenities as the Holiday Inn, but better value.

Fair Haven (Lake Bomoseen)

MAPLEWOOD, *Route 22A South, Fair Haven VT. Tel. 802/265-8039, 800/253-7729, Fax 802/265-8210. Web site: www.sover.net/~maplewd/ index.html. E-mail: maplewd@sover.net. Rates: $75-$140. Major credit cards accepted.*

Situated on an old dairy farm in a farmhouse dating to the 1840's, Maplewood is listed on the National Historic Register. The inn is off by itself and, as such, offers a very nice escape. All rooms have air-conditioning, cable TV, telephone, private bath, and four of the five rooms have fireplaces. The suites are larger and feature a living room. Breakfasts are hearty but not gourmet.

Camping

BOMOSEEN STATE PARK, *West Shore Road (RR#1 Box 2620), Fair Haven VT 05743. (Take Route 5A to West Shore Road in Hydesville.) Tel. 802/ 265-4242 (summer), 802/483-2001 (off-season). Base rates: $13-$15. Credit cards: Visa, Mastercard. Open mid-May through Labor Day (first weekend in September).*

The lakefront location is great for fishermen, swimmers, and boaters (boats can be rented). There are also numerous hiking trails, including several routes to Half Moon State Park. Camping facilities include 66 sites and 10 lean-to's, as well as restrooms, showers, and dumping stations.

HALF MOON POND STATE PARK, *Moscow Road (RR#1 Box 2730), Fair Haven VT 06743. (Take Town Road from Roue 30 north of Hubbardton west to Moscow Road.) Tel. 802/273-2848 (summer), 802/483-2001 (off-season). Base rates: $13-$17. Credit cards: Visa, Mastercard. Open mid-May through Labor Day (first weekend in September).*

Half Moon offers 60 sites for tents and trailers (10 lean-to's) with facilities including showers, restrooms, and dumping stations. Recreationally, there is fishing, boating and swimming in the pond; you can also hike to the much larger Lake Bomoseen.

GIFFORD WOODS STATE PARK, *Route 100, Sherburn (Killington) VT 05751. Tel. 802/775-5354 (summer), 802/886-2434 (off-season). Base rate:$11-$15. Credit cards: Visa, Mastercard. Open mid-May through Columbus Day (mid-October).*

Developed by the Civilian Conservation Corps in the 1930's, Gifford Woods is bisected by the Appalachian Trail (which meets the Long Trail 1.5 miles to the south) and is within walking distance from Kent Pond, a popular fishing spot. Ther are 27 wooded sites for tents and trailers and 21 lean-to's. Facilities include showers, restrooms, and sanitary dumping stations.

LAKE ST. CATHERINE STATE PARK, *Route 30 3 miles south of Poultney, (RD 2 Box 1775), Poultney VT 05764. Tel. 802/287-9158. Base rates: $13-$17. Credit cards: Visa, Mastercard. Open mid-May through Columbus Day (mid-October).*

Located on Lake St. Catherine, the park is ideal for those interested in swimming, boating (there is an access ramp at the park), and fishing. It contains 50 sites, and facilities include showers, restrooms, and dumping stations.

KILLINGTON CAMPGROUND, *Killington Road (Alpenhof Lodge Box 2880), Killington VT 05751. Tel. 802/422-9787. Base rates: $14-$20. Credit cards: Visa, Mastercard. Open from May 1 through mid-October.*

Located within a mile of the Killington Resort, this modest campground features 10 sites for tents and four for campers. Facilities include showers, laundry machines, a hot tub, and a bike repair shop.

LAKE BOMOSEEN CAMPGROUND, *Route 30 (HCR 62, Box 173), Bomoseen VT 05732. Tel. 802/273-2061. Base rates: $18-$25. Major credit cards accepted. Open May 1 through October 15.*

Features 99 sites, cabins, and trailors with full hookups. Other facilities include a pool with slides, rental boats, arcades and rec rooms, a general store, and a playground for kids.

WHERE TO EAT
Killington

HEMINGWAY'S, *Route 4, Killington VT. Tel. 802/422-3886. E-mail: hemwy@sover.net. Web site: www.hemingwayrestaurant.com. Open daily except Monday from 6pm. Major credit cards accepted.*

Widely regarded as the finest restaurant in the region, if not the state, Hemingway's serves superb American and continental cuisine in three elegant dining rooms in a restored 1860's house. Prix Fixe menus cost $50-$70 and typically feature a selection of game meats and fowl, seafood, and freshly made pasta, as well as soups, salads, appetizers, and fantastically rich and delicious pastries for dessert (or lighter sorbets and fruit). Reservations recommended; dress well.

RED CLOVER INN AT WOODWARD FARM, *Woodward Road, Mendon (between Killington and Rutland). Tel. 802/775-2290, 800/752-0571. Open nightly except Sunday 6pm-9pm. Credit cards: Visa, Mastercard, Discover.*

Located in an 1840's farmhouse, the Red Clover features a rotating menu that typically includes gourmet lamb, fresh game, vegetarian, and seafood dishes, in addition to salads, appetizers, soups, and desserts. The wine list is extensive. Expect to pay $40-$50 per person for a full meal including wine.

CATAMOUNT GRILL & TAVERN, *74 Route 4, Mendon (between Rutland and Killington). Tel. 802/773-5411. Open nightly at 5pm and for lunch in the summer and fall. Major credit cards accepted.*

The Catamount is a casual but fine place to dine outdoors or by fireside depending on the season. There are two dining rooms – one non-smoking – and a gem of a 170-year old bar. The menu includes an array of simple but fine American dishes like rainbow trout, grilled free range fowl, BBQ ribs, steaks, lobsters and vegetables (organic) all cooked fresh with fresh ingredients. The bar menu includes eight microbrews. During the summer live folk music is presented on the weekends.

THE GARLIC, *Killington Road, Killington VT. Tel. 802/422-5055. Open from 3pm daily. Major credit cards accepted.*

Cozy, casual and classy, The Garlic serves an array of hearty old style cuisine that includes pastas, meats, and seafood. Those who do not like garlic need not fear, but those who do can certainly indulge.

CASEY'S CABOOSE, *Killington Road, Killington VT 05751. Tel. 802/422-3795. Open daily 3pm-11pm and for lunch on Saturdays, Sundays and holidays. Mjor credit cards accepted.*

One of the most popular and highly acclaimed family restaurants in the area, Casey's is a friendly and colorful establishment distinguished by its railroad-motifed decorations and reasonably priced, quality food. The cuisine is mostly no-fooling-around American fare like hand-cut prime rib, burgers, pastas, seafood, and for the truly hungry a variety of surf and turf combinations. There are also a half-dozen salads and appetizers like wings, nachos, and chicken fingers. Entrees (except for the surf and turf combos) range form $11-$18, while a salad or appetizer will set you back $4-$8.

PPEPPERS BAR & GRILLE, *end of Killington Road, Killington VT. Tel. 802/422-3177. Open daily 7am-11pm. Major credit cards accepted.*

Casual, friendly establishment serving breakfast, lunch and dinner. Except for breakfast (which consists of the usual eggs, omelets, and pancake variations), the cuisine is basically American-Italian with lots of pastas, chicken parmesan, and calamari marinara for starters. For lighter fare there are a half-dozen salads on the menu, and for lunch there are numerous sandwiches, burgers, and other typical dishes. In the summer outdoor seating is usually available. Appetizers, lunch dishes, and salads typically cost $5-$8, while pastas and dinner entrees range from $10-$15.

OUTBACK PIZZA, *located at the Nightspot at the top of Killington Road, Killington. Tel. 802/422-9885. Hours: 3pm (winter & spring) & 5pm (summer & fall) until late. Credit cards: Visa, Masercard, American Express.*

Specializes in woodfired pizza, beer, and acoustic music presented nightly. Often a stop on the way to the adjunct Nightspot, one of Killington's most popular nightclubs.

Rutland

ROYAL'S 121 HEARTHSIDE, *Junction of Route 4 and Route 7, Rutland VT. Tel. 802/775-0856. Open for dinner nightly. Credit cards: Visa, Mastercard, American Express.*

In business for more than 30 years and located in a 19th century Colonial style home – the atmospherics of which are enhanced by the roaring fire (at least during cooler weather), Royal's specializes in haute American cuisine. The menu typically features such such favorites as prime rib, roast duck, and a variety of seafood dishes, all cooked with fresh ingredients.

BISTRO CAFE, *3 Center Street, Rutland VT. Tel. 802/747-7199. Open for breakfast lunch and dinner. Major credit cards accepted.*

Located right in the center of town, the establishment is part cafe, part bistro. The cafe is in the tradition of Starbucks, serving gourmet coffees, pastries, sandwiches and soups in a hustle and bustle environment where you can sit at European-style cafe chairs and tables, or simply take your goods to go. The sit-down restaurant is an ornate affair redolent of an Art Deco restaurant or cafe from the '20's, only with pale versions of '90's dishes ranging from chicken sandwiches, glorified burgers and calamari salad to grilled "Spanish cedar roasted salmon." Live jazz is featured on weekend evenings.

SIRLOIN SALOON, *200 South Main Street (Route 7), Rutland VT. Tel. 802/773-7900. Major credit cards accepted. Open for lunch and dinner.*

Popular with tour groups and locals, the Sirloin Saloon is a roomy steakhouse serving decent but not overwhelming steak and grilled fare, salads, and pastas. The dining areas are distinguished by Native American décor, lending the atmosphere a toush of the American West.

Bomoseen

LAKEHOUSE PUB & GRILLE, *Route 30, Bomoseen VT. Tel. 802/273-3000.*

Offers standard pub fare, grilled meat dishes and sandwiches, etc.

SEEING THE SIGHTS

Killington to Rutland

Despite its 200 year old charter, **Killington** is essentially a late 20th century creation and does not even feature the charming old churches and meeting houses that grace even the most ordinary Vermont hamlet. In fact, the 20-odd mile stretch of Route 4 between the junctions with Routes 107 and 100 and Rutland has something of a strip mall quaility to it that is less than appealing. In any case, there are several attractions you may or may not find worth paying a visit, some of which, like the Billings Farm in Woodstock and the Calvin Coolidge Historic Site in Plymouth, are covered in the "Ottauquechee River Valley" chapter.

If you're interested in seeing a brewery in action, stop by the **Long Trail Brewery Company**, *Route 4, Bridgewater VT, Tel. 802/672-5011. Open daily. Call for tour information.* You can take a tour and buy souvenirs.

Behind the Sugar Spice Restaurant in **Mendon** (the municipality between Killington and Rutland) is the interesting, if less than overwhelming, **grave of Old John**, the beloved horse of Civil War General Edwar Ripley. A boulder marks the site.

NORMAN ROCKWELL MUSEUM, *Route 4 East, Rutland VT 05701. (Just east of downtown Rutland.) Tel. 802/773-6095. Open daily 9am-6pm. Admission: $3 adults, $2.50 seniors, $.75 children.*

Norman Rockwell spent more than 20 years in the 1930's through the 1950's living in Arlington, Vermont, where there already is a museum – which begs the question: why is there one here? In any case, this one does features a video about Rockwell, hundreds of exhibits of his work from his famous *Saturday Evening Post* covers, and dozens of advertisements and portraits of presidents and other world leaders. The exhibits are accompanied by insightful audio and written explanations. The gift shop sells postcards, posters and other Rockwell and Vermont memorabilia.

Rutland

Chartered in 1761, and situated on the site of the old Fort Rutland (built in 1784), the city and town of **Rutland** (the two were separated in the 1880's) rose to prominence in the mid-19th century, when its location near Lake Champlain Valley and New York State in the valley between the Green and Taconic mountain ranges made it a natural junction for the region's rapidly growing network of railroad lines.

A bit later, in the post-Civil War period, Rutland developed another engine of economic growth in the marble industry, largely the child of Redfield Proctor who founded the town of Proctor and established a dynasty in the Republican Party that dominated Vermont politics for more than a quarter of a century. Known as the "Marble City," Rutland underwent an ugly political period in the 1880's and '90's when, largely under the direction of Governor Proctor, the township was divided into new towns, Proctor, West Rutland, and the City of Rutland, leaving the Town of Rutland as something of a rump – relations between the city and town have been strained ever since.

With the decline of the railroads and the marble industry, Rutland spent much of the 20th century struggling to establish a new identity, and until recently was considered a bottom feeder on the list of destinations for tourists in Vermont. However, in recent years Rutland has undergone something of a revival and Merchants Row and the rest of downtown are again vibrant and bustling with restaurants, shops, and businesses. Part of Rutland's rebirth has been its development as a retail center, with Route 7 South assuming a strip mall identity reminiscent of say Route 1 in Saugus Massachusetts, and the erection of a Walmart smack dab in the middle of town. However, the **old downtown** around Merchants Row and Center Street is still lined with restored 19th century buildings many of which, naturally, are well endowed with beautiful marble fixtures, and visitors can keep themselves busy visiting a number of attractions ranging from the **Trinity Church** to the **Chaffee Center for the Arts**.

WALKING TOURS IN RUTLAND

From the beginning of July to mid-October, the Visitor's Center in Rutland offers free guided walking tours in the city's historic district. If guided tours are not offered during your visit or if you would prefer to go it alone, pick up a copy of the guidebook Views Through Time ($2), available at local book and newspaper shops. Call 802/747-3590 for information.

CHAFFEE CENTER FOR THE VISUAL ARTS, *16 South Main Street, Rutland VT 05701. Tel. 802/775-0356. Open daily 10am-5pm June-December, 11am-4pm Friday-Monday December-June. Admission free.*

Located in a Victorian style building listed in the National Register of Historic Places, the Chafee Center features photographic, painting, and sculpture exhibits representing more than 200 artists past and present. It also sponsors special exhibits, classes, and the **Art in the Park** arts and music festival held once in August and again in October.

RUTLAND HISTORICAL SOCIETY, *96 Center Street, Rutland VT 05701. Tel. 802/775-2006. Open 6pm-9pm Monday, 1pm-4pm Saturday. Free admission.*

Located in the Nickwackett Firehouse built in 1849, the Historical Society includes a modest collection of artifacts, photographs, and documents relating to Rutland area history.

Proctor & Pittsford

From Rutland, Route 7 North leads to Middlebury (34 miles) and Burlington (69 miles), but not before passing through the scenic towns of **Proctor** and **Pittsford**, both of which warrant a visit on account of their marble related museums and exhibits (Proctor), and covered bridges and maple museum (Pittsford).

Proctor is easily combined with a visit to Pittsford. You can either take Route 7 north from Rutland to Pittsford, visit the Maple Museum and the covered bridges and then take Route 3 south through Proctor en route back to Rutland; or ride Route 4 west of downtown and then Route 3 north through Proctor to Pittsford.

A relatively new creation by the standards of Vermont townships, **Proctor** was founded in 1886 when then-Governor and marble mogul Redfield Proctor threw around his political weight to force its partition from Rutland against that town's wishes. They resisted in futililty but argued with good sense that the Governor was cutting off part of their tax base while creating his own fiefdom; indeed he did own 97% of the land that became the town of Proctor. The marble industry has fallen off significantly, but the town still features marble factories and its main attraction, the Vermont Marble Exhibit, does a fine job of articulating the industry's story as well as the processes of marble production.

VERMONT MARBLE EXHIBIT, *Route 3, Proctor VT. Tel. 802/459-3311, 800/451-4468 (ext. 436). Open daily 9am-5:30pm mid-May through mid-October. A nominal admission fee is charged.*

This exhibit, dating to 1933, is one of the most fascinating attractions in Vermont. Using video, displays and live demonstrations, it provides insight into the production of beautiful marble products. Many interesting and unique – as well as not so interesting or unique – souvenirs are available in the gift shop.

PROCTOR & THE MARBLE INDUSTRY

*In the late 19th century, Proctor assumed from Middlebury the status as capital of Vermont's marble industry in the post-Civil War period, after a wily and entrepreneurial Civil War veteran, **Colonel Redfield Proctor** founded the Vermont Marble Company. So successful and popular was Proctor that he built enough of a political base to establish a family dynasty that dominated Vermont politics for more than a quarter of a century. In 1878 he won his first of six terms as Vermont Governor, a position of power which he used against the powerful interests of Rutland, to break off the town of Proctor which bears his name and 97% of the land of which he owned. He was then elected to the U.S. Senate in 1890, leaving the statehouse in the hands of his descendants, three of whom also became governor.*

While in the Senate, Proctor used his political acumen to acquire the chairmanship of the committee responsible for awarding federal building contracts, a position of influence which he used to promote the commissioning of such prominent Washington landmarks as the Jefferson Monument and the United States Supreme Court, among others – all of which, naturally, are made of Vermont marble and stand as reminders not only of America's commitment to democracy and justice, but also that politicians, even in the good old days, were beholden to special interests and and unapologetic masters of pork barrel politics.

WILSON CASTLE, *West Proctor Road off Route 4, Proctor VT. Tel. 802/ 773-3284. Open daily 9am-6pm mid-May through late October. Admission: $6.50 adults, $5.75 seniors, $2.10 children 6-12, children under 6 admitted free of charge.*

Easily combined with a visit to the Marble Exhibit, the Wilson Castle is an ornate 19th century gem of a mansion featuring a real hodge-podge of architectural and interior design styles. Situated on a 115 acre estate, it is loaded with European and oriental antiques and furnishings, as well as 13 (imported) tiled fireplaces, numerous stained glass windows, immaculately hand-painted ceilings, and other fascinating touches that you simply don't find in many American homes, even those that remain from the 19th century.

More than a hundred years older than Proctor, **Pittsford** was once known as the site of two sanitoriums and for its **covered bridges** (see sidebar on next page); indeed, Pittsford favorite son Nicholas Powers was Vermont's premier builder of such bridges in the 1840's and '50's. A handsome town, its main claim to fame today – at least according to regional chamber of commerce materials – is the **New England Maple Museum**, though many find its covered bridges and such landmarks as the **Old Cemetery** (dating to 1774) to be of more interest.

To reach Pittsford, take Route 7 North from Rutland; the drive is scenic and dotted with covered bridges (see sidebar below). An alternative is to take Route 4 west from downtown Rutland, then take Route 3 north through Proctor where – if it's summer – you can visit Wilson Castle and the Vermont Marble Exhibit (see above).

NEW ENGLAND MAPLE MUSEUM, *Route 7, Pittsford VT. Tel. 802/ 483-9414. Open from March 15- May 20: daily 10am-4pm daily. May 20- October 31: 8:30am-5:50pm. November 1-December 23 10am-4pm daily. Closed from Christmas until March 15. Admission: $1.50 adults, $.50 children.*

Dedicated to the history and process of "sugaring," the New England Maple Museum features a variety of exhibits that includes antique and modern equipment. Demonstrations are also given, however it is best to visit in March and April when the real sugaring season is in process. Also during this period, sugar-on-snow parties (a Vermont rite of spring) and other special events are held.

PITTSFORD HISTORICAL SOCIETY, *Eaton Hall on Route 7, Pittsford VT. Tel. 802/483-6623. Open Tuesdays from 9am-4pm March through November and on Saturdays from 9am-4pm in July and August. Admission by donation.*

In addition to the usual photographs, documents and modest artifact exhibits found in most local historical societies, the Pittsford Society features videos about local history, a sports exhibit, and information for those interested in taking a local walking tour.

COVERED BRIDGES IN THE PITTSFORD AREA

Otter Creek, which flows alongside Route 7 through Pittsford, is lined with a series of covered bridges which can be combined with a visit to the Marble Exhibit, the Wilson Castle and the Maple Museum. They are covered (excuse the pun) below from south to north.

__Twin Bridge__ – Off Route 7 on the East Pittsford Road halfway betwen Pittsford Village and Rutland. No longer a bridge, but rather a shed, the Twin Bridge was the second of two built in 1940-50 when the East Creek changed course after a high flood. It was relocated to its present location after the Chittenden Reservoir overflowed in 1947 and washed it out. It is now used for storage by the Rutland highway department.

__Gorham Bridge__ – Route 3 on the Proctor-Pittsford line. Also known as the "Goodnough Bridge," the Gorham Bridge was constructed in 1841-42 and washed out in the famous Flood of 1927. Restored in 1929, it is named for two prominent local families.

__Cooley Bridge__ – On Elm Street on mile north of the junction of Routes 7 & 3. Built 1849 by Nicholas Powers – who also built the Twin and Gorham bridges – the Cooley Bridge is named for a local resident and Revolutionary War veteran Benjamin Cooley.

__Depot Bridge__ – On Depot Road off Route 7 just north of Pittsford Village. Named for a nearby railroad station, the Depot Bridge has undergone numerous renovations since its construction in 1840.

__Hammond Bridge__ – On Kendall Hill Road off Route 7, 1.1 miles north of Pittsford Village. At 139 feet long and constructed in 1842, the Hammond Bridge is handsome, worn and well traveled – literally. In the Flood of 1927 it was washed more than mile from its original site. But thanks to the ingenuity of local resident James Tennien, it was saved by filling metal drums with air, placing them under the bridge to float it and then employing a team of horses to pull it back up stream.

The Chittenden Reservoir Area

East of Pittsford and northeast of Rutland, the 675-acre **Chittenden Reservoir** is a terrific venue for water and outdoor recreation in a beautiful mountain setting. The Reservoir contains largemouth bass, trout and walleye, and is accessible to boats (15 horsepower is the maximum allowed) from a ramp off Chittenden Dam Road. Nearby **Lefferts Pond** features extensive wetlands where otters, beavers and other wildlife and fowl flourish. Hikers can also take advantage of the Canty Trail up the Blue Ridge Mountain and the Long Trail which passes through the area.

To reach the area, take the East Pittsford Road from Route 4 in Mendon (east of Rutland) or the Holden Road through Holden from Pittsford.

West of Rutland on Route 4

From downtown Rutland, Route 4 and Route 4A continue west through **West Rutland** en route to Fair Haven and the New York border 18 miles away. Like Proctor and the city of Rutland, West Rutland was partitioned from the town of Rutland in the late 1800's. **Castleton**, the next town west, is a quiet hamlet where Ethan Allen and Seth Warner planned their attack on Fort Ticonderoga; today it is home of Castleton State College. The town's historic district includes a number of handsome houses and businesses built in the Federal and Greek Revival styles.

CASTLETON HISTORICAL SOCIETY MUSEUM, *Main Street, Castleton VT 05735. Tel. 802/468-5523. Open on Sundays from 1pm-4pm in summer and fall. Admission by donation.*

The Historical Society contains a varied collection of furnishing, painting, artifacts and photographs related to local history, including the Battle of Hubbardton.

West of Castleton, Routes 4 and 4A intersect the north-south highway Route 30. Just north of this intersection is **Lake Bomoseen**, 17 miles long and the third largest lake in the state. Surrounded by a town of the same name and **Lake Bomoseen State Park** on the western banks, Lake Bomoseen is a popular venue for fishing and boating though it is quite built up.

Hubbardton

At the northern end of Lake Bomoseen is the town of **Hubbardton**, known for the Revolutionary Battle of the Same Name.

HUBBARDTON BATTLEFIELD & MUSEUM, *Route 4 Exit 5, Hubbardton VT. Tel. 802/759-2412. Open 10am-5pm Wednesday-Sunday from Memorial Day (late May) through Columbus Day (mid-October). Admission: $1.*

Apart from minor skirmishes and Indian raids, the only battle of the Revolutionary War fought in Vermont, occurred here in Hubbardton when colonists temporarily stopped the forces of **General John Burgoyne** moving south on July 7. Despite suffering heavy casualties, Burgoyne continued his march south through the Champlain Valley until he was stopped for good at the Battle of Bennington (fought in New York state) in August, and forced to retreat back north until he surrendered in October after the fall of Fort Ticonderoga.

Today visitors can take a guided tour of the battlefield site and stop by the visitors' center, featuring artifacts, dioramas, and explanations.

During the summer there are occasional reenactments and other com-memorative events; call for details.

Poultney & Lake St. Catherine

From Lake Bomoseen and the junction with Route 4, Route 30 South leads six miles to **Poultney** and **Lake St. Catherine**, site of **Lake St. Catherine State Park** *(Tel. 802/287-9158/summer, Tel. 802/484-2001/off-season)* and a popular venue for fishing, boating and camping. East of Poultney on Route 140, is – no surprises here – **East Poultney**, a handsome village characterized by Federal and Greek Revival styles buildings, including the East Poultney Baptist Church designed by **Elisha Scott**.

POULTNEY HISTORICAL SOCIETY, *Route 30, Poultney VT 05764. Tel. 802/287-5268. Open on Sundays 1pm-5pm from June to August.*

The Historical Society features several restored buildings including a schoolhouse, an academy, and Melodean Factory, all dating to the 19th century.

NIGHTLIFE & ENTERTAINMENT

Rutland

There are several bars on Main Street (Route 7) near downtown and on around Center Street. The **Holiday Inn** has a typically dull hotel bar, that comes alive on Friday when locals invade for a night of karoake.

Killington

NIGHTSPOT, *top of Killington Road. Tel. 802/422-9885. jor credit cards accepted.*

One of Killington's most popular night spots with DJ's, dancing, and live music; joined at the hip with the Outback Pizza joint which often features live acoustic music.

THE KILLINGTON MUSIC FESTIVAL

*Held annually in the glory of the Green Mountains at the Ram's Head Base Lodge (at the end of Killington Access Road) in July and August (every Sunday evening), the **Killington Music Festival** is a celebration of chamber music that brings together music students, teachers, and professionals of the highest level. Each year, dozens of students audition for an opportunity to study in residency and perform at this festival. For details call 802/773-4003. E-mail: kmfest@sover.net. Web site: www.killingtonmusicfest.com.*

MCGRATH'S IRISH PUB AT THE INN AT LONG TRAIL, *Route 4 Sherburne Pass, Killington VT 05751. Tel. 802/775-7181, 800/325-2540. open nightly. Credit cards: Visa, Mastercard, American Express.*

A popular pub serving Guinness and British and American bar food, whose atmospherics improve when live Irish music is presented on weekends and holidays.

MOTHER SHAPIRO'S RESTAURANT, *Killington Road, Killington VT 05751. Tel. 802/422-9933. Web site: www.mothershapiros.com. Open from breakfast until late. Major credit cards accepted.*

A colorful and popular restaurant and *apres ski* locale that includes a bar, a game room, and even Victorian cigar room. In the winter, folks can eat and drink by fire, and in the summer, there is the outdoor garden "oasis."

SUMMER RUTLAND/KILLINGTON AREA EVENTS

CHAFFEE CENTER ANNUAL GARDEN IN THE PARK – *A garden fest featuring vendors, artists, music, food, and other attractions; held in early June. Call 802/775-0356 for information.*

INDEPENDENCE DAY PARADE, BRANDON – *The annual Fourth of July festivities include colorful floats, marching bands, and oodles of beautiful fire trucks and antique motorcars.*

JULY 4 FIREMEN'S BBQ & FIREWORKS – *A benefit for the local fire squad, and a great place to mingle with local types; held in Sherburne Town Park, Killington.*

ANNUAL RAVE CAR SHOW – *Held annually in mid-July at Rutland Fairgrounds off Route 7. Call 802/747-9076 for information.*

KILLINGTON MUSIC FESTIVAL – *Features Saturday evening chamber music concerts by faculty from prestigious music schools like Julliard, from early July through the last week in August. Tel. 802/773-4003. Website: www.killingtonmusicfest.com. E-mail: kmfest@sover.net.*

MICROBREW FESTIVAL – *Held in Killington in early August, and featuring food, live, music, and great beer! Call 802/422-3333 for information.*

CHAFFEE CENTER'S ANNUAL ART IN THE PARK SUMMER FESTIVAL – *Held in the Main Street Park in Rutland, this summer art fest features the work of more than 100 local artists and crafters, as well as food, live music, and demonstrations. Call 802/775-0356 for information.*

VERMONT STATE FAIR – *Ten-day agrictultural fair beginning on the first Saturday of September, off Route 7 just south of Rutland. Call 802/775-0356 for information.*

Others – *There are dozens of other regional events open to the public each summer, including all types of musical concerts, plays, art exhibitions, and others. Check local publications, or the Rutland (Tel. 802/773-2772; e-mail: www.rrccvt@aol.com) or Killington (Tel. 802/773-4181; e-mail: kpaacofc@vermontel.com) chambers of commerce for more information.*

SPORTS & RECREATION

Biking

From the last weekend in May through the second weekend in October, **Killington Resort** opens its trails on Killington Mountain to bikers and provides access by way of ski lifts. The trails and rental shops are open from 9am-6pm (last ride up 5pm). Trail access costs $8, a full day of lifts is $30. Rates per day go down with multi-day passes (a season pass is $200), and there are 40% discounts for children and youth under 18. Call the **Mountain Bike Center**, *Tel. 802/422-6232* for general information; call *800/372-2007* for information about multi-day bike packages the include rentals and passes.

On the other side of Rutland mountain, bikers should also consider the **Delaware and Hudson Rail Trail** – a 10 mile long abandoned rail trail from Casteton to Poultney. The riding is quite easy and the scenery includes farm, hills, and two slate quarries. There is also mountain biking in **Coolidge State Park** in Plymouth less than ten miles down Route 100 from Killington on Route 100A. **Road bikers** can pretty much bike where they like, though getting off Routes 7 and 4 is advised for better safety and scenery.

THE GREAT OUTDOOR TRADING COMPANY OF VERMONT AND ADVENTURE BIKE TOURS, *219 Woodstock Avenue, Rutland VT 05701. Tel. 802/775-9989, 800/345-5182, Fax 802/775-981. Web site: www.greatoutdoorsvt.com Open daily. Open daily. Major credit cards accepted.*

Adventure Bike Tours offers a full range of biking opportunities throughout Vermont, including a variety of multi-day tours and packages, while the store itself is fully stocked with all types of bikes and equipment for rent and sale.

FIRST STOP SKI & BIKE SHOPS, *8474 Route 4 Killington VT 05751. Tel. 802/422-9050. Open Daily. Major credit cards accepted.*

Provides bike rentals, maps and directions for self-guided tours in the area, including the Coolidge State Forest.

GREEN MOUNTAIN CYCLERY, *133 Strong Avenue, Rutland VT. Tel. 802/775-0869.*

Sells and rents all types of bikes as well as biking accessories, including maps and guides.

NORTHERN SKI WORKS, *Killington VT. Tel. 802/422-4800. Major credit cards accepted.*

Rentals, sales of equipment and accessories.

Boating, Canoeing & Kayaking

Lake Bomoseen, 15 miles west of Rutland by way of Routes 4 and 30 (north), or the first road north after Route 30, is the area's main body of water and is a venue for sailing, canoeing, rowboating, and kayaking. Most access points are on the western side of the lake in or near **Lake Bomoseen State Park**, *Tel. 802/273-2061.*

Covering more than 900 acres, **Lake St. Catherine** in Poultney (20 miles west and south of Rutland on Route 30) can be enjoyed in all types of boats. **Lake St. Catherine State Park**, *Tel. 802/287-9159,* features an access ramp and provides boats for rent. The lake is also popular with fishermen and swimmers, and the State Park includes about 50 campsites.

THE GREAT OUTDOOR TRADING COMPANY OF VERMONT, *219 Woodstock Avenue, Rutland VT 05701. Tel. 802/775-9989, 800/345-5182, Fax 802/775-981. Web site: www.greatoutdoorsvt.com Open daily. Major credit cards accepted.*

Rents and sells kayaks, canoes and boating accessories; also can arrange tours.

MOUNTAIN TRAVELER, *Woodstock Avenue, Rutland VT 05701. Tel. (Tel. 802/775-0184).*

Sells kayaking equipment and accessories for all types of outdoors activities.

Cross-Country Skiing
MOUNTAIN MEADOWS CROSS-COUNTRY SKI RESORT, *Route 4 one quarter mile east of the Killington Road turnoff, Killington 05751. Tel. 802/775-7077, 800/221-0598. Trail fee: $13. Major credit cards accepted.*

Conveniently located within minutes of the Killington Ski Area, Mountain Meadows features 60 kilometers of trails and offers instruction and rentals.

MOUNTAIN TOP CROSS-COUNTRY SKI RESORT, *Route 7 (10 miles north of Rutland), Chittenden 05751. Tel. 802/483-2311, 800/445-2100. Trail fee: $13. Mjor credit cards accepted.*

Mountain Top is one of the premier cross-country skiing areas in Vermont with 85 kilometers of trails and a full range of services and facilities including rentals, guided tours, instruction, and retail sales. There is also snowshoeing, sleigh rides and ice skating.

Fishing
Kent Pond in Gifford Woods State Park (south of Killington) **Lake Bomoseen** (15 miles west of Rutand by Route 4), **Lake Hortonie** and the **Chittenden Reservoir** contain a variety of fish including pike and bass.

Golf
GREEN MOUNTAIN NATIONAL, *Barrows Towne Road, Sherburne (Killington). Tel. 802/422-3241. Green fees: $30-$40..Major credit cards accepted. Carts available.*

KILLINGTON GOLF COURSE, *705 Killington Road, Killington. Tel. 802/422-6700; Tel. 800/343-0762 for packages and golf getaways. 18 holes. Green fees: $23-$44. Carts available. Major credit cards accepted.*

Designed by Geoffrey Cornish, the Killington Golf course is an 18-hole, 6300 yard par 72 course, which is tough on duffers – but even if your score doesn't qualify you for the PGA, the beautiful surroundings are well worth the humiliation and the 40 bucks. The course also features a well-stocked pro shop and offers club and cart rentals as well as lessons. Call *800/343-0762* for information about special golf holiday packages beginning at around $100 per day per person, including greens fees and lodging at the Killington Grand Resort Hotel.

LAKE ST. CATHERINE COUNTRY CLUB, *Route 30, Poultney. Tel. 802/287-9341. 18 holes. Green fees: $18-$22. Carts available. Major credit cards accepted.*

PROCTOR-PITTSFORD COUNTRY CLUB, *Corn Hill Road, Pittsford VT. Tel. 802/483-9379. 18 holes. Semi-private. Green fees: $17-$25. Carts available. Major credit cards accepted.*

PROSPECT BAY COUNTRY CLUB, *Route 30, Bomoseen VT. Tel. 802/468-5581. 9 holes. Green fees: $8-$20. Carts available. Credit cards: Visa, Mastercard, American Express.*

RUTLAND COUNTRY CLUB, *Grove Street, Rutland. Tel. 802/773-9153. 18 holes. Semi-private. Green fees: $50. Major credit cards accepted.*

WHITE RIVER GOLF CLUB, *Route 100 Rochester (about 15 minutes north of Killington. Tel. 802/767-4653. 9 holes. Green fees: $18. Carts available.*

Hiking

Both **Killington** and **Pico Peak** feature a variety of trails of various distances and difficulties. From the Inn at the Long Trail on Route 4, you can take the Long Trail 2.5 miles to the trails at the Pico ski area.

On Route 4 opposite Pico (on the northern side) is the **Deer Leap Rock**, a series of cliffs with fine views of the area. It's a 1.6 miles hike each way beginning on the Long Trail at the Long Trail Inn, which will lead you to the Deer Leap Trial after a bit more than half a mile.

There is also good hiking in the **Calvin Coolide State Park** in Plymouth (about 10 miles south of Killington on Route 100 on Route 100A), and at **Moosalamoo** and the **Bread Loaf Wildderness** to the north in the Brandon-Middlebury area 25-35 miles north of Rutland by way of Route 7.

MOUNTAIN TRAVELER, *Woodstock Avenue, Rutland VT 05701. Tel. (Tel. 802/775-0184). Major credit cards accepted.*

Sells hiking and camping equipment.

Horseback Riding & Sleigh Rides
MOUNTAIN TOP CROSS-COUNTRY SKI RESORT, *Route 7 (10 miles north of Rutland), Chittenden 05751. Tel. 802/483-2311, 800/445-2100.*
Horse-drawn sleigh rides over the Resorts many miles of trails and roads.
HORSE AMOUR, *Eaton Hill Road, Castleton VT. Tel. 802/468-2200.*
RIVERSIDE FARM STABLES, *Route 100 (7 miles north of Killington), Pittsfield. Tel. 802/746-8544.*
VERMONT HORSE RIDING VACATIONS, *Mountian Top Inn, Mountain Top Road, Chittenden VT. Tel. 802/483-2311.*
Offers trail rides of varying distances and time periods as well as instruction.

Ice Skating
CORTINA INN, *Route 4, 6 miles east of Rutland between Killington and Rutland. Tel. 802/773-4735, 422-2121, 800/579-4735. Hours: 9am-9pm. Major credit cards accepted.*
The rather roomy three acre pond is open to the public and skates are available for rental.
GIORGETTI ICE SKATING RINK, *Preville Avenue, Rutland. Tel. 802/775-7976.*
The rink is open to the public, but skates are not available for rental.
HAWK INN & MOUNTAIN RESORT, *Route 100, Plymouth. Tel. 802/672-3811. Major credit cards accepted.*
ROYCE MANDIGO ARENA, *Rutland. Tel. 802/773-9416.*
Indoor rink is open to the public; lessons and skates available.
PROCTOR SKATING RINK, *Proctor. Tel. 802/459-2819.*

Miniature Golf
SUNRISE MINI-GOLF, *Junction of Routes 100 and 4 at the Cedarbrook Motor Inn, Killington. Tel. 802/422-9666. Rates: . Credit cards accepted .*
PICO MINI-GOLF & DRIVING RANGE, *Route 4, Pico, Killington (10 miles east of Rutland). Tel. 802/775-4346.*

Skiing
KILLINGTON AND PICO MOUNTAIN AT KILLINGTON, *Killington Resort, Killington VT 05751. Tel. 802/422-6200. Tel. 800/621-MTNS. Web site: www.killington.com. Lift rates begin $54 per adult for a full day. Discoutns for chldren, youths and senior. Lower rates for multi-day packages.*
Killington's main **Snowshed Base Lodge**, the **Rams Head Base Lodge**, and the **Killington Lifts and Alpine Training Center** are located at the end of **Killington Road** (a.k.a. "Mountain Road"), which turns off

Route4/Route100 roughly 15 miles east of downtown Rutland. Two other base stations, **Sunrise** and **Skyeship** are located several miles south on Route 4 and Route 100. **Pico Mountain's** base lodges and lifts are located off Route 4, three miles west of the Killington Road turnoff.

Skiing is Killington's raison d'etre, and no ski area east of the Mississipi offers more miles of runs and lifts with more variety and better maintained conditions than this jewel in the American Skiing Company's crown. Indeed, what Killington resort lacks in charm and character, it makes up with what is probably the best skiing this side of the Rockies.

And if Killington's 1,200 acres, 205 trails, and 33 lifts worth of skiing doesn't satisfy your appetite, or if on the other side of the coin, seems a bit daunting, the next door resort of **Pico** (also recently acquired by the American Skiing Company) is more modest but still features more than forty additional trails serviced by nine lifts and superb views of the Green Mountains from Pico Peak. Pico's own baselifts are several miles west of the Killington Road turnoff on Route 4. The "Ultimate Connection" gondola will soon link the slopes of Pico and Killington.

Snowmobiling

CORTINA INN, *Route 4 6 miles east of Rutland between Killington and Rutland. Tel. 802/773-4735, 800/579-4735. Open 9am-9pm. Major credit cards accepted.*

It may seem odd that the home of the Killington School for Tennis – the Cortina Inn – also offers snowmobiling, an activity usually identified with working class locals, but they do offer a variety of tours as well as necessary equipment rentals.

KILLINGTON SNOWMOBILE TOURS AT SUNRISE, *Sunrise Base Lodge, Killington Ski Area. Tel. 802/422-3339. Open daily during ski season. Credit cards: Visa, Mastercard.*

Rents snowmobiles and offers tours (including dinner tours) during ski season.

KILLINGTON SNOWMOBILE TOURS, *Route 4 at the base of Killington Road net to Bill's Country Store, Killington. Second branch: next to Chinese Gourmet on Killington Road, Killington. Tel. 802/422-2121. Mastercard, Visa, Discover accepted.*

Killington Snowmobile Tours offers tours on local trails and rents all necessary equipment.

VERMONT SNOWMOBILE TOURS, *Happy Bear Motel on Killington Road, Killington. Second branch: Junction of Routes 100S and 4 in West Bridgewater. Tel. 800/286-6360. Major credit cards accepted.*

This respected snowmobile company offers tours in the Coolidge State Forest and rents all equipment.

Snowshoeing

CORTINA INN, *Route 4 6 miles east of Rutland between Killington and Rutland. Tel. 802/773-4735, 800/579-4735. Open 9am-9pm. Major credit cards accepted.*

HIGH COUNTRY TOURING CENTER AT KILLINGTON, *Killington VT. Tel. 802/422-6200. Major credit cards accepted.*

High Country Touring Center offers guided tours around Killington and Skye Peak (tours begin with a gondola ride to the top).

MOUNTAIN MEADOWS CROSS-COUNTRY SKI RESORT, *Route 4 one quarter mile east of the Killington Road turnoff, Killington 05751. Tel. 802/775-7077, 800/221-0598. Trail fee: $13. Major credit cards accepted.*

Swimming

Many of the resorts and hotels in the Killington-Pico area have pools open to their guests. **Lake Bomoseen** 15 miles west of Rutland on Route 4, and **Glen Lake** just west of Lake Bomoseen also feature good swimming; and finally, there's a great old-fashioned river swimming pool at McLaughlin Falls on Wheelerville Road of Route 4 east of Mendon.

Tennis

Many hotels and resorts in the Rutland-Killington region include tennis courts of varying quality and accessibility. Serious tennis players might consider looking into the Killington School for Tennis listed below.

KILLINGTON SCHOOL FOR TENNIS/CORTINA INN TENNIS CENTER, *Cortina Inn, Route 4, Killington (6 miles east of Rutland). Tel. 802/773-3333, 800/451-6108. Credit cards: major credit cards accepted.*

The Cortina Inn Tennis Court features eight courts and offers clinics, memberships, and private lessons. It is also home to the renowned Killington School for Tennis, offering clinics and lessons for adults, and the Junior Tennis Academy offering instruction for youth ages 9-16. Two, three, and five day vacations are available for those looking to commit their hard-earned vacation to tennis.

SHOPPING

Killington & Mendon

BILL'S COUNTRY STORE, *Routes 4 & 100, Killington VT 05752. Tel. 802/773-9313. Web site: www.billscountrystore.com. Open 9am-6pm daily. Major credit cards.*

Offers a full assortment of Vermont specialty products and foods.

BURNHAN HOLLOW, *Route 4, Mendon VT. Tel. 802/773-8830, 800/582-0044. E-mail: bestofvt@aol.com Web site: ww.bestofvt.com. Major credit cards accepted.*

Specializes in Vermont specialty foods and features mail order.

Rutland
   DIAMOND RUN MALL, *Route 7 South, Rutland VT 05701. Tel. 802/773-1145.*
   Shopping mall featuring brand name goods and a food court.
   ESSENTIAL ALTERNATIVES, *22 Center Street, Rutland VT 05701. Tel. 802/773-8834. Open daily. Major credit cards accepted.*
   Vermont handcrafts and souvenirs.
   NUSANTRA, *43 Strongs Street, Rutland VT 05701. Tel. 802/775-3027. Open Monday-Friday 9am-5pm. Major credit cards accepted.*
   Specializes in textiles, jewelry and other high end souvenirs.

EXCURSIONS & DAY TRIPS
   With its central location at the junction of major highways such as Routes 4, 7, and 100, the Rutland-Killington region is a convenient location from which to explore other areas of Vermont.

WOODSTOCK & QUECHEE
   Just about 20 minutes north and east of Windsor are the popular tourist destinations of **Quechee** and **Woodstock**. Teeming with restaurants and shops, these two towns have plenty to offer tourists of all ages including Quechee Gorge ("Vermont's Grand Canyon"), the Billings Farm Museum, the Simon Pearce Glass works and restaurant, as well as many handsome buildings and several golf courses.
   On the way to Woodstock, you can take Route 100 beyond the intersection with Route 4 another five miles to the junction with Route 100A and the **Calvin Coolidge Birthplace** at Plymouth Notch. Silent Cal's entire hometown has been restored to its condition when he lived there a century ago and has been converted into a very fine museum.
   For more details, see the "The Ottauquechee River Valley" chapter.

MANCHESTER
   Roughly 30 miles south of Rutland you'll come to **Manchester**. Known for its picturesque village and outlet shopping, it is a mecca of sorts for high-end tourists and is loaded with shops, restaurants, and inns including the venerable Equinox, widely recognized as the first to cater to tourists visiting Vermont for pleasure. Other attractions include the beautiful **Hildene** mansion and estate; the longtime residence of Abraham's Lincoln's children and descendants. The mansion is open to visitors during the summer and the grounds are used for cross-country skiing in the winter.
   Less than ten miles east of Manchester, **Bromley Mountain** is a major ski area. North of Manchester, **Dorset** and its various villages on the

Memorial Highway and Route 7 are quite scenic and the surrounding wilderness is prime territory for snowmobilers, hikers, bikers, and cross-country skiers.

See the "Manchester & the Heart of the Green Mountains" chapter for more information.

BENNINGTON

Twenty-five miles beyond Manchester, **Bennington** is one of the oldest towns in Vermont and is home to a beautiful old district which is the site of the impressive **Bennington Monument**, built to commemorate the Battle of Bennington (1777), a cemetery where **Robert Frost** is buried, and an impressive museum housing the country's largest collection of Grandma Moses paintings, and a diverse variety of American art and historic artifacts.

Fifteen miles north of Bennington on scenic Route 7A, **Arlington** is attractive and picturesque. It is home to several attractions, including several covered bridges and a museum about Norman Rockwell who lived there in the 1930's, '40's, and '50's.

See the "Bennington" chapter for more details.

PRACTICAL INFORMATION

Chambers of Commerce

KILLINGTON CHAMBER OF COMMERCE, *P.O. Box 114, Route 4, Killington VT 05751. Tel. 802/773-4181, Fax 802/775-7070. E-mail: info@killingtonchamber.com. Web site: www.killingtonchamber.com.*

RUTLAND REGION CHAMBER OF COMMERCE, *256 North Main Street, Rutland VT 05701. Tel. 802/773-2747, toll free 1-800756-8880, Fax 802/773-2772. E-mail: rrccvt@aol.com. Web site: www.rutlandvermont.com.*

Medical Emergencies & Services

For ambulance service:

Rutland – *Tel. 911*

Killington & Chittenden – *Tel. 802/773-1700*

Rutland Regional Medical Center – *160 Allen Street, Tel. 802/775-7111*

Sherburne Health Center – *Tel. 802/422-3990*

Police

Rutland – *Tel. 911*

Killington & Chittenden – *Tel. 802/773-9101*

17. MIDDLEBURY & THE LOWER CHAMPLAIN VALLEY

Though virtually all of Vermont is visually attractive, no region features the beautiful combination of the Green Mountains and Lake Champlain as does the **Lower Champlain Valley**. On the eastern side of Addison County is the heart of Green Mountain National Forest, where the **Bread Loaf Wilderness** and **Moosalamoo Wilderness** areas offer limitless opportunities for hikers, bikers, skiers, fishermen, and campers. Not nearly as crowded with tourists as those wilderness areas near popular resorts, the likes of **Lake Dunmore**, **Silver Lake**, the **Middlebury College Ski Bowl**, and dozens of trails, brooks, and streams offer visitors the chance to experience Vermont's natural beauty without having to compete or wait in line for a ski lift, a tent site, or a parking lot.

Meanwhile, the western section of the region consists of what many consider quintessential Vermont scenery – low rolling hills dotted with picturesque farmhouses and barns that gradually cascade down to **Lake Champlain**, with an environment much different from the Green Mountains less than 30 miles to the east.

In addition to it natural beauty, the Lower Champlain Valley features a number of interesting towns and sites of historical significance. **Middlebury**, home to a college of the same name that is regarded as the finest in Vermont, is the cultural and social hub of the region. Once a center of the marble industry, its village center – bisected by the quaint Otter Creek – consists of hundreds of historic buildings, many of which have been converted to shops, restaurants, and other businesses. Attractions include the **Sheldon Museum** dedicated to preserving the memory of life in 19th century Vermont; the **UVM Morgan Horse Farm**, and the **Vermont Folklife Center**. Other attractions in the region include the **Lake Champlain Maritime Museum** near America's smallest incorporated

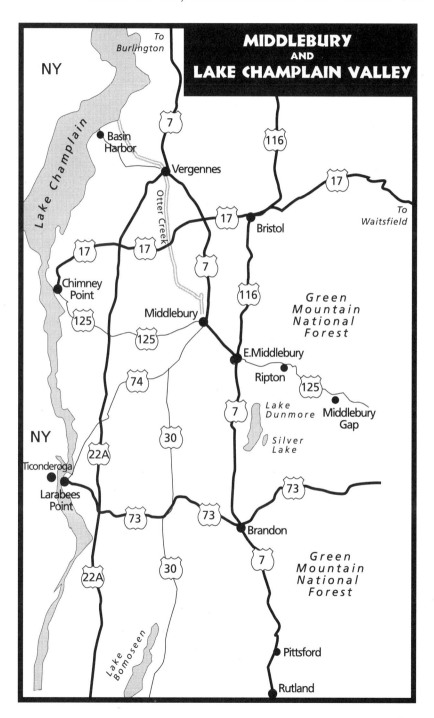

city, Vergennes; the Revolutionary War-era encampment and museum at **Mt. Independence State Historic Site** in Orwell; and the **Rokeby Museum** in Ferrisburgh which was once of the home of a prominent abolitionist family.

ARRIVALS & DEPARTURES

By Air

Burlington International, *Airport Drive (off Williston Road), Burlington VT 05401,* is the closest major commercial airport to the Middlebury area (35 miles), and is served by Continental, United, USAir, and the commuter airlines, Business Express, *Tel. 800/345-3400,* and Comair, *Tel. 800/927-0927.*

If you're arriving from overseas, you'll probably find it cheaper and more convenient to fly into **Montreal** where you can make a connection by bus or rent-a-car. Montreal is roughly two hours from Middlebury, but can be longer depending on traffic and delays at the border. Other options include Albany NY, Manchester NH, and Boston's Logan Airport. Major rental car comapanies operate out of these cities, which are also serviced by the **Vermont Transit Lines** bus company, *Tel. 800/552-8738, 800/451-3292.*

By Car

Middlebury is 35 miles south of Burlington and 32 miles north of Rutland on Route 7. If you're coming from southeast on **Interstate 89**, you can take **Route 4** from Exit 1 just west of White River Junction, to Rutland (35 miles) and then head north on Route 7. A more scenic alternative is to continue on I-89 to Exit 3 at Bethel, and then take Route 107 West to Route 100 at Stockbridge (13 miles), Route 100 north 13 miles to Hancock, and then Route 125 east 20 miles west to Middlebury.

From the Montpelier region, get off I-89 at Exit 9 or 10 and then head south on Route 100A and Route 100 to Waitsfield, where you need to take Route 17 west to Route 7 at New Haven, which you take south. This drive should take about an hour.

From New York State and points west, you can get off I-87 at Albany and Troy, and then take Route 4 north to Route 30 north just over the Vermont border. An alternative, particularly if you're coming from the north, is to get off I-87 at Exit 25, and then take Route 8 to Ticonderoga and Route 74 to Middlebury.

By Bus

Middlebury, Brandon, and Vergennes are all on **Vermont Transit Line's**, *Tel. 800/552-8738 or 800/451-3292,* Burlington-Rutland-Albany route, which also stops in Bennington and Manchester. Buses depart Middlebury three times daily (12:01pm, 5pm & 9:15pm) for Burlington, where you can make connections for Montreal and Montpelier; and three times daily (5:45pm, 12:10pm, & 7:25pm) for Rutland, Bennington, and Albany. At Rutland you can make connections for Boston, Brattleboro, White River Junction, and smaller destinations like Ludlow, Killington, Springfield, and Keene, NH. At White River Junction you can catch buses for the Northeast Kingom, New Hampshire, and New York City.

Buses depart from Middlebury at the Middlebury Exxon *(Tel. 802/388-4373)* ; from Brandon at Rosen's National *(Tel. 802/247-5520)* ; and from Vergennes at the Masi Radio Shack *(Tel. 802/877-6805)* .

By Train

Amtrak's **Ethan Allen Express** departs Washington DC at 3am daily (#299), and at 10:40am Monday-Thursday (#291), and 1:05pm Friday-Saturday (#293), it stops at Baltimore, Wilimington, DE, Philadelphia, and New York City (arriving at 6:38am. 2:15pm & 4:19pm respectively), where you must catch a connecting train with the same number. Train #299 departs Penn Station at 7:10am, Train #291 at 3:55pm, and Train # 293 at 5:40pm en route to Yonkers, Croton-Harmon, Poughkeepsie, Rhinecliff-Kinston, Hudson, and Albany. Again you must transfer or board trains with the same number departing at 9:55am, 6:40pm, and 8:20pm respectively and arriving in Rutland at 12:30pm, 9:05pm, and 10:45pm. Trains depart Rutland in the other direction at 1:25pm and 5:25pm (on Sundays only). A one-way fare from Rutland to New York City is approximately $55.

The **James Jeffords Railroad Station** is located next to the transportation center behind the Walmart in downtown Rutland. There are virtually no facilities. Call *800/USA-RAIL* to make reservations and inquire about schedules and fares.

ORIENTATION

Route 7 is the main artery for the Southern Lake Champlain Valley and the Middlebury region. It enters the region at **Brandon** in northern Rutland County before entering Addison County in Leicester and passing through Salisbury and East Middlebury on its way to **Middlebury**, the region's hub, 20 miles to the north. It then continues to skirt Weybridge as it passes through New Haven, Waltham, **Vergennes**, and Ferrrisburgh before continuing on to Burlington 35 miles north of Middlebury.

East of Route 7 is the Green Mountain National Forest – a major area for hiking, biking, and other outdoors activities – accessible from Brandon by way of **Route 73** and from Middlebury by Route 125. **Route 116** is a north-south highway that skirts the Forest north of East Middlebury. It joins Route 17 at Bristol which continues north and east to Route 100 at Waitsfield in the Mad River Valley. Running parallel to Route 7 to the west is **Route 22A**, which passes through Orwell, Shoreham, Bridport, Addison, and Panton before joining Route 7 at Ferrisburgh.

Lake Champlain is reached by Route 7 via Route 125 from Middlebury, and Route 17 at New Haven Junction. These roads meet at **Chimney Point** where the **Lake Champlain Bridge** crosses into New York State and Route 22. A second place to cross the lake (by way of a car ferry) is at **Larabees Point** in Shoreham. From Middlebury, you must take Route 30 south to Route 73 West.

GETTING AROUND

Apart from a local shuttle between the Middlebury campus and the village center, it is virtually impossible to get around without a car unless you are one heck of a serious biker. Cars can be rented at all major airports in Canada and the northeast. **Avis**, *Tel. 800/331-1212*, **Budget**, *Tel. 800/244-9429*, and **Hertz**, *Tel. 800/654-3131,* all operate out of Burlington International Airport. **Avis** also has an office in Rutand, *Tel. 802/773-1317).* **Enterprise Rent-A-Car** has outlets in Rutland, *Tel. 802/773-0855*, Barre, *Tel. 802/479-5400*, and South Burlington, *Tel. 802/863-2111.*

WHERE TO STAY

For an updated information about lodging in Middlebury and Addison County, contact the **Heart of Vermont Lodging Association**, *Tel. 802/388-0800; e-mail: stay@vermont-lodging.com.*

BASIN HARBOR CLUB, *Basin Harbor Road, Vergennes VT 05491. Tel. 802/475-2311, 800/622-4000, Fax 802/475-6545. E-mail: info@basinharbor.com. Web site: www.basinharbor.com. Rates: $150-$375. Credit cards; Visa, Mastercard. Open mid-May through October. Closed for winter.*

This 700-acre self-contained resort is somewhat un-Vermontlike in its size and grandeur, but its extensive facilities, colonial architecture and its location on the shores of Lake Champlain make it an excellent choice for those interested in sports and recreation, or just plain getting away from it all. Guests have a choice between staying in one of the elegantly appointed lodge rooms or suites, or in one of the 77 cottages, which feature 1-3 bedrooms, a fridge, and other basic amenities.

Recreational facilities include an 18-hole golf course, tennis courts, a fitness center, miles of hiking and biking trails on the estate grounds, and all sorts of watercraft from sailing boats and canoes to cruisers and motorboats for water skiing. If that isn't enough, there is even a 3,200-foot airstrip. In July and August, free supervised activities for children are offered, and bringing pets can also be accommodated. Call Basin Harbor or your travel agent to inquire about package deals, especially if you're interested in staying for a week or longer. Finally, there are various casual and fine dining options available on the estate, and when booking your reservation you may customize your eating plan.

Brandon, Orwell & Goshen

HISTORIC BROOKSIDE FARMS COUNTRY INN & ANTIQUE SHOP, *Route 22A, Orwell VT 05760. (Due west of Brandon via Route 73 west). Tel. 802/948-2727, Fax 802/948-2800. E-mail: hbfinnvt@aol.com. Web site: www.brooksideinnvt@aol.com. Rates: $85-$165. No credit cards.*

Situated on a historic 300-acre property, this inn and antique shop consists of a country farm house with seven guest rooms, and a downright stately Greek Revival-style main house where the dining room and an assortment of sitting and library rooms are located. Hiking, biking, and cross-country skiing are all possible in the immediate vicinity, and the dining room (open to the public by reservation) serves first-rate gourmet food.

LILAC INN, *53 Park Street, Brandon VT 05733. Tel. 802/247-5463, 800/221-0720, Fax 802/247-5499. E-mail: lilacinn@sover.net. Web site: www.lilacinn.com. Rates: $120-$275. Credit cards: major credit cards accepted.*

Award-winning cuisine, immaculate landscaping and turn of the 19th century Victorian decor make this upper-scale inn popular for marriages and honeymoons. The building, constructed in 1909, contains nine elegant guestrooms, a bevelled glass ballroom, and other meticulously decorated salons and parlors, all maintaining the inn's Victorian character.

BLUEBERRY HILL, *Goshen-Ripton Road, Goshen VT 05733. (Take 73 east from Brandon 6 miles to Goshen-Ripton Road and go north 4 miles). Tel. 802/247-6735, 800/448-0707, Fax 802/247-3983. Web site: www.blueberryhillinn.com. Rates: $85-$120. Credit cards: Visa, Mastercard.*

Situated a bit out of the way in woods of the Green Mountain Forest in the ever-rural town of Goshen, Blueberry Hill engenders a special esprit de corps among its guests who take breakfast and dinner communally at one table in the inn's post & beam dining hall. The main attraction of Blueberry Hill is its setting in the Green Mountain National Forest, where guests can hike and cross-country ski on the 30 miles of trails maintained by the inn itself (the inn rents equipment and offers lessons). Vermont's most famous trail, the Long Trail, is also very nearby. Rooms are minimalist with no air-conditioning, or in-room phones, but communal facilities include a sauna and a library.

BRANDON INN, *20 Park Street, Brandon VT 05733. Tel. 802/247-5766, toll free Tel. 800/639-8685. E-mail: splattis@sover.net. Web site: www.brandoninn.com. Rates: $70-$190. Credit cards: major credit cards accepted.*

Situated in a historic 18th century building on the village green, the Brandon Inn offers a variety of unique rooms and suites (35 rooms total), as well as various meal plans (the food is quite good). Call about package rates for extended stays and low season stays.

CHURCHILL HOUSE INN, *RR 3 Box 3265, Brandon VT 05733. Tel. 802/247-3300, 800/838-3301. Web site: www.churchillhouseinn.com. Rates: $70-$100. Credit cards: Visa, Mastercard.*

With its wilderness setting in the Green Mountains, Churchill caters to hikers, bikers, and cross-country skiers, all of whom have direct access to trails from the inn itself. The eight guestrooms feature basic amenities, including private bath and a dining room serving breakfast and dinner. Bicycles can be rented at the inn.

ADAMS MOTOR INN & RESTAURANT, *RR 1 Box 1142, Brandon VT 05733. Tel. 802/247-6644, 800/759-6537. Rates: $50-$65. Credit cards: Visa, Mastercard. Open mid-May through October only. Closed for winter.*

Very good value, considering that in addition to clean comfortable rooms (some of which have fireplaces), the Adams also offers trout fishing in the nearby pond, miniature golf, and a pool.

Middlebury, East Middlebury & Ripton

THE MIDDLEBURY INN, *14 Courthouse Square, Middlebury VT 05753-0798. Tel. 802/388-4961, 800/842-4666. E-mail: midinnvt@sover.net. Rates: $90-$260. Credit cards: major credit cards accepted.*

This historic 75 room inn (50 in the historic building, the remainder in a modern annex) is situated in an 1827 building in the center of town on the village green and features beautifully appointed rooms, all with private baths, cable television, and air-conditioning. The elegant mansion also contains old fashion parlors (where afternoon teas are served) and balconies for lounging, and from Sunday brunch to the fine dinners, the food is superb. Call as far in advance as you can for reservations if you'd like to stay during the foliage season (essentially all of October) or Middlebury's commencement weekend, which is usually held in the last week of May.

THE INN ON THE GREEN, *19 South Pleasant Street, Middlebury VT 05753. Tel. 802/388-7512, 888/244-7512, Fax 802/388-4075. E-mail: innongreen@aol.com. Rates: $100-$200. Major credit cards accepted.*

With only 11 rooms, this historic inn (the building dates to 1803) engenders a sense of intimacy and personal service not found at the

Middebury Inn. Having been perfectly renovated, the rooms are comfortable and feature private baths and air-conditioning.

SWIFT HOUSE INN, *Route 7 and Stewart Lane, Middlebury VT 05753. (North of the village center off Route 7). Tel. 802/388-9925, Fax 802/388-9927. E-mail: shi@toether.net. Rates: $90-$185. Major credit cards accepted.*

Built by Vermont Governor Samuel Swift in 1814, this historic inn features 21 rooms, some of which have been equipped with in-room whirlpools, fireplaces, and/or cable television; and all of which are individually appointed with antiques, four poster beds, and homey quilts and comforters. Breakfast is complimentary, and the restaurant serves excellent dinners.

CHIPMAN INN, *Route 125, Ripton VT 05766. (East of Middlebury via Route 125 East). Tel. 802/388-2390, 800/890-2390, Fax 802/388-2390. E-mail: smudge@together.net. Rates: $85-$120. Credit cards: Visa, Mastercard.*

Located east in "Robert Frost Country" in the Green Mountains, the cozy Chipman Inn features eight meticulously decorated rooms, all with private bath and a dining room where breakfast and dinner are served. Outdoor activities such as hiking and cross-country skiing are easily accessible.

WAYBURY INN, *Route 125, East Middlebury VT 05740. (About 5 miles south of Middlebury) Tel. 802/388-4015, 800/348-1810, Fax 802/388-1248. E-mail: thefolks@woyburyinn.com. Web site: www.wayburyinn.com. Rates: $50-$115. Credit cards: Visa, Mastercard, Discover.*

This former stagecoach station dates back nearly two centuries and features 14 rooms furnished and decorated with antiques. There's a bar and restaurant, nice porches for sitting and eating, and several meeting rooms. Very comfortable.

LINENS & LACE B&B, *29 Seminary Street, Middlebury VT 05753. Tel. 802/388-0832, 800/808-3897. Rates: $89-$109. Credit cards: Visa, Mastercard.*

A Victorian-style B&B, Linens & Lace offers a combination of comfortable and cozy accommodations, and easy access to Middlebury and the college, which is within walking distance.

BLUE SPRUCE MOTEL, *2428 Route 7 South, Middlebury VT 05753. (Approximately 3 miles south of Middlebury village center. Tel. 802/388-3233, 800/640-7671, Fax 802/388-3003. E-mail: stpadd@aol.com. Rates: $50-$125. Credit cards: major credit cards accepted.*

Blue Spruce offers a variety of options including basic hotel rooms, cottages, suites, and suites with kitchenettes. Cable television is available.

GREYSTONE MOTEL, *RR 4 Box 1284, Route 7 South, Middlebury VT 05753. Tel. 802/388-4935. Rates: $40-$70. Credit cards: Visa, Mastercard, American Express.*

Quiet and well-kept, the Greystone contains only 10 rooms furnished with air-conditioning, cable television, and telephones.

SUGARHOUSE MOTEL, *Route 7 North, Middlebury VT 05753. (3 miles north of Middlebury village center). Tel. 802/388-2770, 800/ SUGARHOUSE.*

Another small family-run motel with basic amenities including phones, fridges, and cable television. Location only miles away from the college is great for visiting parents.

Vergennes

STRONG HOUSE INN, *82 West Main Street, Vergennes VT 05491. Tel. 802/877-3337, Fax 802/877-2599. E-mail: shi@flinet.com. Rates: $75-$165.Credit cards: American Exprees, Visa, Mastercard.*

Built in the Federal style in the 1830's, Strong House features eight superbly appointed rooms, some of which have televisions and/or fireplaces. Attractions include views of the Green Mountains and the Adirondacks across the lake in New York, and an old-fashioned library and a classic Victorian parlor where tea is served. Breakfast is complimentary and the dining room is generally open to guests only.

EMERSON'S B&B, *82 Main Street, Vergennes VT 05491. Tel. 802/877-3293. Rates: $60-$100. Credit cards: Visa, Mastercards.*

Situated in downtown Vergennes, Emerson's offers six guestrooms (two with private bath, four with shared) in a Victorian home, laden with antiques. Homemade breakfast included.

SKYVIEW MOTEL, *Route 7, Ferrisberg VT 05456-9769. Tel. 802/877-3410. E-mail: jdegraaf@sover.net. Rates: $45-$85. Credit cards: Visa, American Express, Mastercard.*

Rooms feature cable television and other basic amenities. The location is pleasant and the grounds feature grills and picnc tables as well as lawn games. Good value.

Addison

WHITFORD HOUSE INN, *RR 1 Box 1490, Vergennes VT 05491. (Whitford is actually located on Grandey Road in Addison between Middlebury and Vergennes). Tel. 802/758-2704, 800/746-2704, Fax 802/758-2089. E-mail: whitford@together.net. Rates: $110-$175. Credit cards: Visa, Mastercard.*

Situated in relative obscurity between Middlebury and Vergennes and overlooking the Adirondacks, the Whitford is a gem of an inn housed in a classic 1790's country house. With only four rooms and a small guesthouse/cottage (bathrooms are private), it is intimate and cozy, a feeling which is enhanced by the personal service and wood burning fires. Guests can hike and bike around the region, including by Lake Champlain, and the hub of Middlebury is only minutes away by automobile.

Camping

BRANBURY STATE PARK, *RR 2 Box 2421 (10 miles north & east of Brandon on Route 53 via Route 73 east from Brandon), Brandon VT 05733. Tel. 802/247-5925 (summer), 802/483-2001 (off-season). Base rates: $13 $17. Credit cards: Visa, Mastercard. Open mid-May through Columbus Day.*

This beautiful state park, nestled between Lake Dunmore and Mount Mooslamoo, has 40 tent sites (some near the beach, some across the road) and six lean-to's. Facilities include beaches, picnic areas, and boat rentals. Recreational opportunities range from picnicing on the beaches of Lake Dunmore to hiking on one or more of the park's beautiful trails.

BUTTON BAY STATE PARK, *5 Button Bay State Park Road (on Panton Road, 6.5 miles east from Route 22A south of Vergennes), Vergennes VT 05491. Tel. 802/475-2377 (summer), 802/483-2001 (off-season). Base rates: $13-$17. Open mid-late May to Columbus Day. Credit cards: Visa, Mastercard.*

Situated on Lake Champlain, this park contains more than 70 grassy tent sites and 13 lean-to's as well as picnic areas, boat launch sites, a swimming pool, and hiking trails. The Lake Champlain Maritime Museum is just north of the park.

MT. PHILO STATE PARK, *5425 Mt. Philo Road, Charlotte VT 05445. Tel. 802/425-2390 (summer), 802/483-2001 (off-season). Base rates: $11-$15. Open mid May to mid October. Credit cards: Visa, Mastercard.*

Known for its stunning views and rich horticultural diversity, Mt. Philo State Park features a modest seven tent camp site with three lean-to's, as well as hot showers, toilets, and a dumping station, but no hookups.

LAKE DUNMORE KAMPERSVILLE, *Box 56 Salisbury VT 05769. Tel. 877/250-2568, Fax 802/352-6017. Base rates: $17-$26. Major credit cards accepted. Open year around.*

Situated on the edge of the Green Mountain National Forest on Lake Dunmore, Kampersville offers an extensive array of facilities beginning with 210 tent and trailer sites. For practical matters, there are showers, LP gas, a dumping station, a camp store and snack bar, and firewood. Visitors can take advantage – weather permitting of course – of the Lake Dunmore location, to swim (there are also two pools), or take advantage of the softball, basketball, and volleyball facilities. Hiking, fishing, sightseeing and other activities can also be arranged.

GRIFFIN'S (MILLS) TEN ACRE CAMPGROUND, *9 Ten Acres Drive, Addison VT 05491. (15 miles due west of Middlbury on Route 125). Tel. 802/759-2662, Fax 802/759-2662. Base rates: $16-$22. Credit cards: Visa, Mastercard.*

Griffin's (now run by the Mills) is located mere meters away from Lake Champlain and and offers sites for tents, lean-to's, and on-site camper rentals with electricity, water, and sanitation facilities. Other features include a dock, a heated pool, a game room and horseshoe pit, laundry facilities, LP gas, and the sale of items related to camping.

ELEPHANT MOUNTAIN CAMPGROUND, *RD 3 Box 850, Bristol VT 05443. (Located on Route 116 between Bristol and East Middlebury). Tel. 802/453-3123. Base rates: $10-$15. Open first of May through October. Credit cards: Visa, Mastercard.*

Features 50 trailer and tent sites with water and sanitation facilities, and electricity.

WHERE TO EAT

Brandon, Orwell & Goshen

LILAC INN, *53 Park Street, BrandonVT 05733. Tel. 802/247-5463, 800/221-0720, Fax 802/247-5499. E-mail: lilacinn@sover.net. Web site: www.lilacinn.com. Open 5:30-9pm Wednesday-Saturday.Credit cards: major credit cards accepted.*

One of the most charming establishments in all of Vermont, the Lilac Inn with its beautiful oak paneled dining room is a great place to take a meal, and by the standards of inn restaurants it's actually quite a good bargain as well. The menu typically (it changes weekly) features an assortment of American country fare (herb roasted free range chicken, pecan encrusted roast pork loin), pasta (shrimp mushroom diablo, linguine with mixed seafood), and slightly offbeat creations such as sauteed jerk shrimp or Moroccan vegetable stew with cous cous and toasted Syrian bread with goat cheese. You can also go old school American with a roast turkey dinner or meatloaf. Meals begin with your choice of salad and or a soup as well.

For desserts, there are fancy tarts and pastries and their signature dessert dish, the double chocolate brulee which you must order with dinner so that it will be ready by dessert time. As the Lilac is a favorite venue for special functions ranging from Mozart Society concerts to private weddings, it is imperative to call in advance for a table. Entree prices range from $10-$25, with most betwteen $15 and $20.

BRANDON INN, *20 Park Street, Brandon VT 05733. Tel. 802/247-5766, toll free Tel. 800/639-8685. E-mail: splattis@sover.net. Web site: www.brandoninn.com. Credit cards: major credit cards accepted. Open Thursday-Sunday 6pm-9pm.*

At the oldest continuously operating inn in Vermont, diners feast on assortment of conventional American country and continental cuisine, as well as nouveau dishes in an elegant but casual dining room characterized by white columns. A meal typically includes a green salad and appetizers, before moving on to entrees that range from rack of lamb to a lightly seared tuna with red pepper known as "Almost Sushi." Expect to pay $20-$30 for a full meal with wine.

Bristol

MAIN STREET DINER, *34 Main Street, Bristol. Tel. 802/453-4394. Open 5:30am-9pm Monday-Friday, 6:30am-10pm Sturday, 8am-10pm Sunday.*

Good diner food ranging from vegetarian specials to turkey dinners, and of course breakfast which is served all day.

CUBBERS, *Main Street, Bristol. Tel. 802) 453-2400. Open 10:30am-10om daily. Credit cards: Visa, Mastercard, American Express.*

A modest take-out joint with onsite seating in the warmer months, Cubbers serves a variety of pizzas, calzones, and subs. Good for getting a meal to go.

Middlebury, East Middlebury & New Haven

MIDDLEBURY INN, *Court House Square, Middlebury VT 05753. Tel. 802/388-4961, 800/842-4666. Web site: www.middlebury.com. Hours: 7:30-10am for breakfast daily, 10:30am-2pm Sunday brunch, 11:30am-2pm Monday-Saturday for lunch, 5:30-9pm for dinner nightly. Major credit cards accepted.*

Middlebury's signature dining and lodging establishment, the Middlebury Inn serves breakfast, a terrific Sunday brunch, lunch (mostly good soups, salads, and sandwiches) and dinner, for which they feature one of the most extensive menus of any inn in the region. Appetizers range from a sampler of Vermont cheeses, and mushroom saute of grilled polenta to Maine crab cakes and several soups and salads. Entrees include New York sirloin, grilled chicken breast with goat cheese and spinach, and farm raised trout with sweet potato cakes and thyme beurre meuniere. The setting is elegant, but not particularly formal.

ROLAND'S PLACE, *Route 7, New Haven VT. (Five minutes north of Middlebury.)Tel 802/453-6309. Open for dinner & brunch year around, and lunch in the summer and autumn. Credit cards: Visa, Mastercard, American Express.*

Situated in an inn and tavern that dates to 1796, Roland's is the perfect place to enjoy good hearty country and New England fare. The menu is extensive, and beginning with the appetizerss, it's impossible to choose between the shrimp quesadilla with roasted peppers, the Maine crab cakes, steamed mussels, or the escargot broiled with red potatoes and garlic butter – and how about trying smoked Vermont emu with sour cherry sauce and mesclun salad!? Luckily you can solve this question by ordering a sample platter for two ($10), four ($18), or six ($24), but this solution won't work for entrees (if there's any room left) for which you have a choice of various meats (Vermont lamb chops, Beef Wellington, or venison medallions for example), poultry (roast turkey, chicken or duck), and seafood (lobser, almond crusted trout, or red snapper in a potato paupiette). For the food and atmosphere, Roland's is quite a bargain; appetizers typically cost $4-$8, and entrees ranges from $12-$19.

CAFE SWIFT HOUSE, *25 Stewar Lane, Middlebury. Tel. 802/388-9925. Open 5:30pm-9pm THursday-Wednesday. Major credit cards accepted.*
Located in an 1814 house built by then-Vermont Governor Samuel Smith, the Cafe Swift House features a beautiful cherry-paneled dining room where you can enjoy continental and American cuisine. Appetizers ($4-$8) include oven roasted little neck clams, grilled andouille sausage, and duck confit salad, while entrees ($10-$22) range from roast chicken and roast lamb to game meats such as venison cooked any number of ways. Dishes are well-prepared and feature local produce and meats.

DOG TEAM TAVERN, *Dog Team Road (off Route 7), New Haven VT. Tel. 802/388-7651. Tavern open 8am-9pm, dinner served from 5pm-9pm Monday-Friday, noon-9pm Saturday and Sunday. Major credit cards accepted.*
Popular with locals and flatlanders alike, the Dog Team includes a dining area and bar, and is known for its sticky buns, local color, and the New England specialties like prime rib, chicken and a variety of seafood dishes. A good choice.

FIRE & ICE RESTAURANT, *26 Seymour St., Middlebury. Tel. 802/388-77166, 800/367-7166.*
Known for its huge salad bars and colorful decor (witness the 21-foot mohogany motor boat at the salad bar), this casual family restaurant serves primarily American and Yankee favorites such as prime rib, steak, and the like.

WAYBURY INN, *Route 125, East Middlebury VT. Tel. 802/388-4015, 800/348-1810. Dinner serverd 4pm-9pm. Credit cards: Visa, Mastercard.*
The Waybury Inn features a happening little pub, which is a great place to wind down after a good ski or hike, and a dining room serving a wide variety of American and continental cuisine in a casual atmosphere. The pub menu is extensive with more than 100 types of beer and two pages worth of light fare and pub food, ranging from three types of green salads and three types of soups to tempura fried mushrooms, a Vermont cheddar burger, and pecan-friend calamari; no dish costs most than $6. The pub menu is also available in the dining room where you can also sample a variety of entrees including scallops & ravioli, three cuts of steak, rock cornish game hen, and several types of pasta. Entrees cost between $12 and $22.

WOODY'S, *5 Bakery Lane, Middlebury. Tel. 802/388-4182, 800/346-3603. Open 11:30am-3pm for lunch, dinner served 5pm-10pm. Same hours durin winter, except closed on Tuesdays, and closes for dinner at 9pm. Major credit cards accepted.*
Featuring a three storied Art Deco style dining room and a deck overlooking Otter Creek, Woody's serves a wide variety of American and international dishes but specializes in seafood offerings like mixed

seafood grill, lobster and stuffed filet of sole. Expect to pay $15-$30 for a full meal including wine or beer.

STORM CAFE, *3 Mill Street, Middlebury VT 05753. Tel. 802/388-1063. open 11am-3pm (lunch), 5pm-9pm Dinner) Monday-Saturday. Credit cards: Visa, Mastercard.*

Located on the waterfront, this cutting edge cafe (at least by Vermont standards) serves a wonderful array of coffees, beers, baked goods (made fresh on the premises), and sandwiches, in addition to an assortment of entrees.

MISTER UP'S, *25 Bakery Lane, Middlebury VT. Tel. 802/388-6724. Open 11:30am-midnight. Major credit cards accepted.*

Located on Otter Creek, which its deck overlooks, Mister Up's is a popular and pleasant place in which to enjoy a relaxing drink or meal. The menu features pasta, steak, and seafood, and the salad bar is renowned. Expect to pay $10-$20 for a meal with a drink or two.

NEIL & OTTO'S PIZZA EXPERIENCE, *11 Merchants Row (int he basement of the Baptist Church), Middlebury. Tel. 802/388-6774/6776. Hours: 11am-2am. Credit cards: Visa, Mastercard.*

This popular pizzeria located in the basement of a Baptist Church serves a variety of pizza dishes that begin around $5.

Vergennes

CHRISTOPHE'S ON THE GREEN, *5 Green Street (on the Green), Vergennes VT. Tel. 802/877-3413. Open 5:30pm-9:30pm mid-May through mid-October. Credit cards: Visa, Mastercard.*

Located in the historic Stevens building on the Vergennes Green, Christophe's serves first-rate French country cuisine made with fresh local ingredients and produce. Expect to pay $25-$35 for a full meal plus wine.

BASIN HARBOR CLUB, *Basin Harbor Road, Vergennes VT 05491. Tel. 802/475-2311, 800/622-4000, Fax 802/475-6545. E-mail: info@basinharbor.com. Web site: www.basinharbor.com. Dining room open 12:30pm-2:30pm (lunch), 6:30pm-8:30pm (dinner). The Red Mill is open 11:30am-10pm. Open mid-May through mid-October only. Major credit cards accepted.*

The Basin Harbor offers two dining options. The dining room proper overlooking Lake Champlain is a formal and expensive affair, where men are expected to wear jackets and ties and the menu consists of haute American and continental cuisine. Lunch is served buffet style and on Sunday morning a "Jazz" brunch is served accompanied by live music. The Red Mill is a cheaper and more casual dining option, probably more appropriate for families with children. Its menu consists primarily of steaks, burgers, and other American favorites. The dining in both establishments is considered quite good.

SEEING THE SIGHTS

Brandon

The southernmost town in the Lower Champlain Valley on Route 7, **Brandon** apparently derived its current name (it was originally called "Neshobe") from the phrase "Burnt Town" – a reference to the torching it suffered in a 1777 Indian raid. Today, this town, birthplace of Abraham Lincoln's most famous political opponent, Stephen Douglas, is a typically handsome Vermont town whose streets are lined with 19th and early 20th century buildings.

There is little to see in the town, but with lodging establishments such as the Lilac Inn and the Brandon Inn, it the perfect place to set up a base for a day or two during which you take in the historical sites of **Mt. Independence** and **Fort Ticonderoga**, both less than 20 miles to the east; and/or hike, bike or ski in the wilderness areas of **Moosalamoo** and **Bread Loaf** to the east. If nothing else, these destinations will give you an excuse to explore the many scenic roads in the area, including Route 73, Route 30, Route 22A, and countless local roads. **Route 73 East** over the Brandon Gap is especially beautiful in the summer and autumn, and when combined via Route 100 north with Route 125 over the Middlebury Gap.

Orwell

MT. INDEPENDENCE HISTORIC SITE, *Mt. Independence Road, Orwell VT. (Located 16 miles west of Brandon by way of Route 73 & Route 73A to Mt. Independence Road.) Tel. (8020 948-2000. Open from mid-May through Columbus Day (mid-October) from 9:30am-5:30pm Wedbesday through Sunday. Admission is free.*

Situated across Lake Champlain and a bit to the south, Mt. Independence was the site of a major army encampment used by the Continental Army during the Revolutionary War. After Benedict Arnold and the **Green Mountain Boys** led by Ethan Allen managed a successful surprise attack on Fort Ticonderoga in 1775, Mt. Independence was constructed as a base for soldiers deployed to protect Ticonderoga. However, its evacuation was forced on July 6, 1777, after British forces led by **General John Burgoyne** took Ticonderoga on their way to Bennington, where they were defeated. The camp was retaken for good following the **Battle of Bennington** in August 1777. As is so often the case in war, most American casualties at Ticonderoga and Mt. Independence did not succumb in battle, but rather to a variety of illnesses and epidemics; many of them are buried in the area.

The site today features an archaeological center that includes items relating to the Revolutionary War era (including a 3,000 pound cannon) and the French era when the area was first developed by Europeans. You can hike around the area on the various trails and, if you're lucky, enjoy one of the various reenactments held during the summer. A great trip combines visiting Mt. Independence with a ferry ride from Larabees Point (north in Shorcham, scc below) to **Ticondcroga** where you can visit the more significant and famous fort.

Shoreham

From Orwell, you can take Route 22A north up to **Shoreham** and then cut back east to Route 30 and Middlebury by way of Route 74 east; or you can continue north to Bridport and on to Chimney Point by way of Route 125 west. Whatever you do, exploring all these towns and routes won't take you much more than a couple of hours, or less if you don't stop. To reach the car ferry in Shoreham, take Route 73 East from Orwell Village to **Larrabee's Point**. Once a center of commercial transport before trains replaced ferries, Larrabee's Point is a shell of its former self, but some docks, a warehouse, and an assortment of other older buildings remain from the old days. The **car ferry**, *Tel. 802 897-7999,* operates continuously from 7am-8pm and costs $6 one way per vehicle, and $10 round-trip.

THE CHAMPLAIN WEEKEND SCENIC RAILROAD

*On weekends from July 3 through September 6, the **Champlain Valley Weekender** offers railroad tours between Burlington, Shelburne, Vergennes, and Middlebury that enable you to enjoy the Lake Champlain Valley and surrounding landmarks such as the Camel's Hump and Mount Mansifled from the comfort of a 1930's passenger coach. A round-trip fare for an adult is $12, $8 for children under the age of 12 (children under 3 travel free). Trains depart twice from Burlington (10am & 2:30pm, arriving at Middlebury at 11:15am & 3:45pm) and twice from Middlebury (11:50am and 3:45pm); you can make the round-trip journey from either end and you can board and get off at Vergennes and Shelburne as well. Call the Green Mountain Railroad Corp. for more information, Tel. 800/707-3530 or 802/463-3069.*

Middlebury

One of Vermont's largest towns before the Civil War, **Middlebury's** charter was granted in 1761 at the same time as Salisbury and New Haven. It received its name because it was in between the other two towns. The first resident, a farmer named Benjamin Salley, moved in around 1773, and despite being temporarily uprooted by a raid by Indians and Tories

(British sympathizers) in 1778, the town flourished as a center for the marble industry and wood production, and was among the biggest in the state by the time **Middlebury College** was founded in 1800. Eight years after the college's founding, Middlebury's legacy of dedication to education was furthered with the founding by Emma Hart (later Emma Willard) of one of the earliest and most prestigious girls' schools in the region, the **Middlebury Female Academy**.

With the transformation of the region's economy in the 19th century as a consequence largely of the introduction of the railroad, and the machine tool industry in Windsor on the other side of the state, Middlebury lost its status as one of Vermont's premier towns. However, the college has retained an excellent reputation, despite some troubled periods financially in the 19th century, providing the town an economic base and a reputation as a cultural center.

Visiting Middlebury today, you will find that it is a vibrant and colorful village that has retained much of its 18th and 19th century charm and flavor. The hub is the village center between Otter Creek and the intersection of Route 125 and Route 7 to the east. Despite suffering a major fire in 1891, the area, known as the "historic district," includes more than 200 buildings dating the 18th and 19th centuries. Mostly renovated old marble factories and mills, they have been converted to shops, eateries, and other businesses.

The most famous building is the **Congregational Church**, designed by Lavius Fillmore (who also designed the Old Congregational Church in Bennington) and built during the first decade of the 19th century. In addition to the buildings, a major attraction is **Otter Creek** and the waterfalls in the middle of the village. You can cross the creek by way of a foot or auto bridge to the west side, which is dominated by Middlebury College, but includes other attractions as well, such as the Vermont Folklife Center:

VERMONT FOLKLIFE CENTER, *2 Court Street (P.O. Box 442), Middlebury VT 05753. Tel. 802/388-4964. Open Memorial Day (lat weekend in May) through December 9am-5pm Monday-Friday, noon-4pm Saturday. Admission free but donations are appreciated.*

Dedicated to the preservation of Vermont's folkloric and artistic traditions, this center features exhibits relating to folklore from pieces of actual art to videos and recordings. A special exhibit is held during the first two weeks in December.

Beer afficianados should consider paying a visit to the **Otter Creek Brewery**, *85 Exchange Street, north of the village center.* A serious challenger to Catamount for the title of Vermont's premier brewery, Otter Creek produces a wide variety of ales and lagers which you can sample after joining one of the guided tours of the brewery. *The brewery and **gift shop** are open daily from 10am-6pm with free tours beginning at 1pm, 3pm, and 5pm. Tel. 800/473-0727 . Website: www.otterbreekbrewing.com.*

> ## MIDDLEBURY COLLEGE
>
> *The western side of Otter Creek in Middlebury is dominated by **Middlebury College**, Vermont's oldest and most prestigious institution of higher learning. Founded in 1800, it developed an excellent reputation for its English studies, in no small part because of the generosity of Joseph Battell, a Middlebury dropout (for health reasons) who purchased the land southeast of town in the Green Mountains that became the Bread Loaf Wilderness. In the region near Ripton, Middlebury developed a second campus, now famous for the annual Bread Loaf Writers' Conference held there annually (Robert Frost was often a headliner) as well as ski facilities: the **Middlebury College Snowbowl** and **the Rikerts' Ski Touring Center** which operates more than 40 kilometers of trails. Middlebury has also earned a reputation for foreign language studies that is rooted in its intense summer programs. Prominent graduates include several governors and other politicians in Vermont.*
>
> *The campus itself is now mostly a pretty hodge-podge of buildings built over the past two centuries as the college has made every effort to upgrade its facilities. Most visitors find the older buildings known as "Old Stone Row" to be the most attractive. These range from the **Old Chapel** built in in 1836, **Mead Memorial Chapel** (1917), and **Painter Hall**, the oldest building on campus (1816). For examples of some of the newer buildings, check out the relatively new **Middlebury College Center for the Arts**, on Route 30.*

Attractions West of Otter Creek

One of the great pleasures of visiting Middlebury is strolling over the bridge, admiring Otter Creek and the waterfalls, and making your way to the attractions on the western side of the Creek like the Sheldon Museum, the Frog Hollow Craft Center, and the beautiful campus of Middlebury College.

SHELDON MUSEUM, *1 Park Street, Middlebury VT 05753. (Located of Route 30 just over Otter Creek from the village center.) Tel. 802/388-2117. Open 9am-5pm Monday-Friday June-October, Wednesdays and Fridays in the off-season.*

Situated in a house built in 1829 by a local merchant, the Sheldon Museum contains a wonderful assortment of relics relating to life in 19th century Vermont. Echibits range from black marble fireplaces and furniture to clocks, kitchen utensils and children's dolls. It also includes an assortment of art from the period. Guided tours are given in the summer and fall.

FROG HOLLOW CRAFT CENTER, *1 Mill Street, Middlebury VT 05753. Tel. 802/388-3177. Web site: www.froghollow.org. Admission free. Open daily 9-5pm. Check for times of classes, demonstrations and other special events.*

Located across the Middlebury River from the village center in a restored mill, this gallery overlooks the Otter Creek Falls and features a variety of arts and crafts made by local and visiting artists. Check for special exhibits, demonstrations, classes and other events.

MIDDLEBURY COLLEGE MUSEUM OF ART, *Route 30 Middlebury, Middlebury VT 05753. Tel. 802/443-5007. Web site: middlebury.edu. Open 10am-5pm Tuesday – Friday, noon-5pm Saturday and Sunnday. Closed Mondays. Admission free.*

This small museum includes a variety of paintings, sculptures, and other exhibits of Vermont, American, and international art, primarily from the 20th century. The Museum is part of the **Middlebury College Center for the Arts**, a spanking new multimedia center that includes theaters, a music library, studios, and a cafe, in addition to the Museum of Art.

North of Middlebury – Weybridge

UVM MORGAN HORSE FARM, *74 Battell Drive (Morgan Horse Farm Road), Weybridge. (Take Route 23 from Route 125 almost immediately across Otter Creek from the Middlebury Village center and take the first major right, which is Morgan Horse Farm Road through the covered bridge about two miles.) Tel. 802/388-2011. Open 9am-4pm daily May through the first week in October. Admission: .*

In operation since the 1870's, this working horse farm operated by the University of Vermont now contains about 70 horses used for breeding, training, and research. Visitors can take a tour, learn about the farm and horse breeding from a video, and watch the horses work out and train (but probably not breed).

East of Middlebury – Robert Frost, Bread Loaf, & The Middlebury Gap

From Middlebury, it only takes five miles on Route 125 East before you pass through East Middlebury and into the Green Mountain National Forest near Ripton. Purchased by Middlebury's chief benefactor **Joseph Battell** mountain by mountain in the latter half of the 19th century, this portion of the Green Mountain National Forest was donated to Middlebury College, which established a second campus, known as **Bread Loaf**, and turned most of the land over to the Green Mountain National Forest.

Known for the famous writers' conference of the same name, the Bread Loaf region (much of which is encompassed in the Bread Loaf Wilderness) features some of the best hiking, biking, and skiing in the state. It was also in this region that the quintessential New England poet **Robert Frost** maintained a summer cottage for nearly the last quarter century of his life.

Just beyond the hamlet of Ripton is the **Robert Frost Wayside** with some exhibits about his life. The cabin itself is a little more than half a mile from the Wayside on the gravel road. The road is not marked, and may even be closed off, but you can still walk up to the cabin (past the Homer Noble Farm) and peek inside. For information about the Robert Frost Interpretive Trail and other hiking and recreational opportunities in the Bread Loaf area, check out "Sports & Recreation" below.

Route 125 West of Middlebury

From Middlebury to Chimney Point on Lake Champlain, it is 15 pastoral miles on Route 125, which is bisected by Route 22 about halfway in between at Bridport. A minor hub for sheep farmers in the 19th century, this is a quaint and charming little village.

BRIDPORT HISTORICAL SOCIETY MUSEUM, *Route 22A (RR1, Box656), Bridport VT 05734. Tel. 802/758-2654. Father's Day and by appointment. Call Margaret Sunderland at number above.*

This 19th century house features several small exhibits concerning local history over the past 200 years.

Chimney Point

Situated on Lake Champlain 15 miles west of Middlebury at the junctions of Route 17 and 125, Chimney Point has always been important as a point for crossing the lake.

CHIMNEY POINT STATE HISTORIC SITE, *Junction of Route 17 & 125, Addison VT 05641. Tel. 802/759-2412. Hours: 9:30m-5pm Wednesday-Sunday mid-May through Columbus Day (mid-October). Admission: $3 adults, children under 12 enter free.*

Located in an 18th century tavern, the Chimney Point Historic Site is interesting because of its emphasis on Vermont's and Lake Champlain's Native American and French heritage. It includes a variety of artifacts and documents relating to the history of the region dating to the pre-European era.

Route 17

If you came to Chimney Point by Route 125, you might consider returning to the Middlebury region on Route 17. In addition to the beautiful surrounding countryside, there are two attractions I'd recommend on this route between Chimney Point and the junction with Route 7 in New Haven:

D.A.R. JOHN STRONG MANSION, *Route 17 just north of Chimney Point, Addison VT 05641. Tel. 802/759-2309. Open 9am-5pm Friday-Monday from mid-May through October. Admission is free but donations are appropriate (indeed, expected).*

More than 200 years old, this building was once the home of a famous Revolutionary War hero, John Strong. Maintained by the Daughters of the American Revolution, it includes five rooms furnished as they were in the 18th and 19th centuries. Guided tours are given regularly.

DEAD CREEK WILDLIFE MANAGEMENT AREA, *Route 17, Addison VT 05641. From Vergennes take Route 22A to the junction with 17 in Addison; from Middlebury, take Route 7 North to the junction with Route 17 in New Haven, then go 11 miles west. The Area is accessible from points on Route 17 and Route 22A. Vermont Fish & Wildlife Department, Tel. 802/878-1564. Open year around.*

Created to provide a sanctuary (perhaps not the right term since hunting is allowed) for migratory birds and other wildlife, the Dead Creek Wildlife and Management Area covers nearly 3,000 acres and is home to hundreds of varieties of plants and wildlife. Most people come to watch migratory birds, such as ducks and Canadian geese, in the spring and autumn. Since the area is dominated by wetlands, it is possible to canoe here, but whether you're birdwatching from boat or on land, be aware that during the autumn people do come here to hunt.

Route 116 from East Middlebury to Bristol

Skirting the western edge of the Green Mountain Forest and linking East Middlebury with Bristol and Route 17 (which continues east to the Mad River Valley), **Route 116** is a beautiful drive lined with classic Vermont scenery that includes farms, meadows, and the Green Mountains. About eight miles south of Bristol, there is a gravel road east to **Abbey Pond**, around which you can hike for four miles.

On Baldwin Creek on the edge of the Green Mountains, **Bristol** is a handsome little town with a classic village green that made its name as a center for the manufacture of wood products; indeed, the Bristol Manufacturing Company was renowned for its burial caskets. Bristol is also the address for an inn, **Mary's at Baldwin**, *Tel. 802/453-2432*, renowned for its fine dining. Just a bit more than a mile from the village green are the **Bristol Ledges** to which you can hike and enjoy great views of the village, Lake Champlain, and on to the Adirondacks in New York.

BRISTOL HISTORICAL SOCIETY MUSEUM, *Howden Hall Community Center, Main Street Bristol VT 05443. Tel. 802/453-6029. Hours: 10am-4pm daily June through August, Thursday nights 7:30-9:30pm March, April, September & October, and by appointment.*

Situated in Bristol's historic community center, the Historical Society Museum features a modest collection of artifacts, documents, and photographs relating to local history.

Less than two miles east of Bristol are **Bartlett Falls**, where the New Haven River cuts through a quartzite gorge where there is a small waterfall, before cascading towards Bristol – a great place to picnic and swim in the summer. Nearby, **Bristol Memorial Forest Park Gorge**, built as a memorial to World War II and Korean War veterans, consists of a small waterfall and a modest stone monument. Take Route 116 north to Route 17 and then it's a bit less than two miles to the parking area.

ROBERT COMPTON POTTERY, *Route 116 (5 miles north of Bristol Village), Bristol VT. Tel. 802/453-3778. Web site: www.RobertComptonPottery.com. open 10am-6pm dialy except Wednesday mid-May through mid-October. Major credit cards accepted.*

About five miles north of Bristol, Robert Compton Pottery offers visitors an opportunity to watch a master potter at work as he uses a variety of methods, techniques, and kilns. All sorts of ceramic goods are for sale as well as textiles woven by Mrs. Christine Compton.

The Lincoln Gap

From Bristol it's a short drive on Route 17 to **Waitsfield** and the **Mad River Valley**, one of Vermont's top ski resort areas. Between the last snow melt in the spring and the first snowfall in late autumn-early winter, it is possible to reach the Mad River Valley and Route 100 by taking the Lincoln Gap Road that leads to Warren. This road also accesses the Bread Loaf Wilderness area and its many hiking and outdoors recreational opportunities (see the "hiking" portion of the "Sports & Recreation" section below).

Vergennes & Ferrisburgh

"The smallest city in America," **Vergennes** was incorporated in 1788 as the third oldest city in New England after its original settler, Colonal Reid from New York, was driven out by the Green Mountain Boys led by Ethan Allen and Seth Warner (of Battle of Bennington fame) who were committed to keeping Vermont free of New York's rule. Built along Otter Creek, Vergennes was primarily a mill town in the 19th century when the mills off Main Street were used to power furnaces which produced cannonballs used in the War of 1812. In 1814, Colonel Macdonough manufactured an entire fleet of ships, including the *Saratoga*, that were used in the famous defeat of the British at the Battle of Plattsburg. Today, dozens of old brick buildings remain as a reminder to Vergennes' industrial roots.

BIXBY MEMORIAL LIBRARY, *258 Main Street VT 05491. Tel. 802/ 877-2211. Open Monday & Friday 12:30ppm-8pm, Tuesday & Thursday 12:30pm-5pm, and on Wednesday from 10am-5pm.*

This handsome Greek Revival style library features several modest exhibits of local art, historic documents including stamps, and Native American artifacts.

West of Vergennes on Lake Champlain

During the summer you can take Route 22A south of Vergennes for just half a mile, and then get on the Panton Road west to the **Button Bay State Park** and the **Lake Champlain Maritime Museum**.

Button Bay State Park is open from mid-May through Columbus Day in October and features camp sites, beaches, hiking, a picnic area, and a boat launch. Fishing, boating, and swimming are favorite activities. For information about camping, call *802/475-2377 (summer)* or *802/483-2001 (off-season)* and see the "Camping" portion of the "Where to Stay" section of this chapter.

LAKE CHAMPLAIN MARITIME MUSEUM, *4472 Basin Harbor Road, Vergennes VT 05491. (Located next to the Basin Harbor Resort. Take Route 22A south from Vergennes to the Basin Harbor Road West.) Tel. 802/475-2953/475-2022. Opend 10am-5pm daily from the first week of May through mid-October. Admission: $7audlts, $6 seniors, $3 for children under 12.*

This fascinating museum traces the natural and human-related history of Lake Champlain through exhibits ranging from dioramas, virtual underwater explorations to reenactments and a replica of the gunboat, *Philadelphia II*. There is also a working metal forge, picnic area, a gift shop, and even boat rentals for taking a quick jaunt into the lake. Kids love it and it's educational for youngsters and adults alike.

North of Vergennes – Ferrisburgh

ROKEBY MUSEUM, *Robinson Road off Route 7 (to the east), Ferrisburgh VT. Tel. 802/877-3406. Open May through October Thursday through Sunday. Admission: $4 adults, $3 students, $1 for children under 12 .*

Home of the prominent abolitionist Rowland Robinson's family dating to the 1790's, and once a stop on the Underground Railroad that harbored escaped slaves on their way to Canada, this museum offers interesting insights into life in rural 19th century Vermont. A restored farm, it includes a smokehouse, a creamery, an ice house and a variety of exhibits concerning everyday life on a Vermont farm. Guided tours can be taken.

DAKIN FARM, *Route 7, Ferrisburgh VT. Tel. 802/425-3971, toll free 993-2546, Fax 9802) 425-2765. E-mail: dakin@vbimail.champlain.edu. Web site: www.dakinfarm.com.*

This family-run farm/business specializes in producing and swelling Vermont specialty foods, from smoked ham to maple syrup. Visitors can take a tour of the operations and watch the various processes in addition, of course, to shopping. Dakin, which also has an operation in Winooski near Burlington, also runs a mail order business, so put yourself on the mailing list if you'd like to enjoy their products long after making your last exit off Route 7.

SHOPPING

Bristol

ROBERT COMPTON POTTERY, *Route 116 (5 miles north of Bristol Village), Bristol VT. Tel. 802/453-3778. Web site: www.RobertComptonPottery.com. Open 10am-6pm daily except Wednesday mid-May through mid-October. Major credit cards accepted.*

Features a variety of ceramic products made on-site, as well as textiles woven by Mrs. Compton.Lincoln

LINCOLN COUNTRY STORE, *Lincoln Center at 17 East River Road, Lincoln VT 05443. Tel. 802/453-2981. Open 7am-7pm daily. Major credit cards accepted.*

This country store sells a variety of Vermont specialty foods and product, as well as more mundane every day products like basic foods and toiletries.

Middlebury

THE COUNTRY PEDDLER GIFT SHOP, *in the Middlebury Inn on Route 7, Middlebury. Tel. 802/388-4961, 800/842-4666, Fax 802/388-4563. Email: midinnvt@sover.net. Hours: 7am-10pm daily. Credit cards: major credit cards accepted.*

MAPLE LANDMARK, INC., *1297 Exchange Street, Middlebury. Tel. 802/388-0627, 800/421-4223. Web site: www.maplelandmark.com. Hours: Monday-Friday 9am-5pm, Saturday 9am-4pm. Major credit cards accepted.*

Maple Landmark offers visitors an opportunity to watch the manufacture of quality wooden toys and other products – a great place to buy gifts for grandchildren and others.

MARSDEN'S COUNTRY STORE, *Route 7 South, Middlebury VT 05753. Tel. 802/388-227. Major credit cards accepted.*

Features a variety of Vermont specialty foods and souvenirs.

SKIHAUS, *Main Street, Middlebury VT 05753. Tel. 802/388-6762, toll free 499-6762. Major credit cards accepted.*

Skihaus specializes in casual and outdoor clothing as well as selling skis, bikes, and other outdoor equipment and accessories.

MIDDLEBURY ANTIQUE CENTER, *Route 7, East Middlebury VT. Tel. 802/388-6229. Major credit cards accepted.*

Features a wide selection of antiques, representing more than 50 dealers.

ANNUAL MIDDLEBURY CRAFT FEST

*Held in the third week in August, this relatively new event (started in 1998) is organized by the **Vermont Hand Crafters** and features work of more than 50 Vermont crafters. For exact dates and other details, contact the Vermont Hand Crafters, Tel. 802/223-2636; vhc@together.net; P.O. Box 967, Montpelier VT 05601-0967; and see local publications.*

New Haven

CRAFT COUNTRY FARM, *Dog Team Road, New Haven VT. Tel. 802/388-8212, 888/388-8212. Open daily 5pm-9pm and on Sunday from 1pm-9pm May through October, or by appointment. Major credit cards accepted.*

While you're waiting for a table at the Dog Team Tavern, you can browse in this colorful little shop featuring a variety of Vermont products and souvenirs.

WEST MEADOWS FARM, *Pearson Road, New Haven VT. Tel. 802/545-2338. Open 10am-6pm from second weekend in September until Halloween.*

If you're in the area during the autumn, you can enjoy picking your own apples as well as stocking up on cider and other apple products.

Vergennes

KENNEDY BROTHERS FACTORY MARKETPLACE, *11 Main Street, Vergennes VT 05491. (Located on Route 22A off Route 7.) Tel. 802/877-2975.*

SPORTS & RECREATION
Biking

There is excellent biking throughout the Lower Champlain Valley, both on paved roads, and mountain biking.

THE BIKE & SKI TOURING CENTER, *74 Main Street, Middlebury VT 05753. Tel. 802/388-6666. Open daily. Major credit cards accepted.*

Come here for all your mountain biking needs.

Cross-Country Skiing

RIKERT'S SKI TOURING CENTER, *Route 125, Ripton VT 05766. Tel. 802/388-2759.*

Like the Snowbowl for alpine skiing, this cross-country ski center is operated by Middlebury College, which has a campus here known as Bread Loaf. Set in the Green Mountain National Forest, their network of more than 40 kilometers of trails is among the most scenic in Vermont (meaning among the most scenic anywhere!), and the trails lead right into town where they are often lighted until 10pm. The trail fee is $9 and instruction, rentals, and guided tours are available.

THE BIKE & SKI TOURING CENTER, *74 Main Street, Middlebury VT 05753. Tel. 802/388-6666. Open daily. Major credit cards accepted.*

In addition to biking equipment, you can get cross-country skis here too.

Golf

NESHOBE GOLF CLUB, *Route 73 (east of downtown Brandon). Tel. 802/247-3611. Web site: www.neshobe.com. Major credit cards accepted.*

A beautiful 18 hole, 6,400-yard course open to the public.

RALPH MYHRE GOLF COURSE AT MIDDLEBURY, *Route 30, Middlebury VT 05753. Tel. 802/443-5125.*

18 holes.

Hiking

Situated between Route 7 and Route 125 southeast of Middlebury, the **Moosalamoo wilderness area** is a mix of private, national forest, and state lands managed through a partnership of all involved, and is a goldmine for hikers, bikers, and snowmobilers. The most famous and accessible trail is the **Robert Frost Interpretive Trail** (on Route 125 seven miles south of the junction with Route 116 in East Middlebury), a well-groomed mile-long loop with signs linking and interpreting Frost's relationship with nature and the manifestation of that relationship in his poetry.

Other easily accessible trails include **Mount Horrid** on the **Long Trail** (0.7 miles one way; take Route 73 east from Route 53 and look for signs); **Branbury State Park** *(Tel. 802/247-5925 in summer)* on **Lake Dunmore** with a 0.7 mile trail to the Falls of Lana, and a 2.3 mile trail to Rattlesnake Point (take Route 53 3.5 miles south from the Junction of Routes 7 and 53 between Brandon & Middlebury); the **Mt. Moosalamoo Camground** *(Tel. 802/388-4362)* with trails to Lake Dunmore and Mt. Moosalamoo itself (take Forest Road 32 of Route 125 6 miles east of the junction of Route 116 and 125 in East Middlebury); and the **Falls of Lana**, a series of waterfalls accessible from Branbury State Park, Silver Lake, and a parking site on Route 53. More difficult hiking can be explored in the **Silver Lake Recreation Area** around Silver Lake, which is only accessibly by trail from Forest Road 27 off Forest Road 32 and Route 73.

There are oodles more hiking opportunities in the area around the Chittenden Reservoir on the south side of Route 73. See the "Rutland & Killington" chapter for more information.

Consisting of more than 21,000 acres of federally protected mountains and woods that are teeming with plant and wildlife, the **Bread Loaf Wilderness Area** features some of the most beautiful and extensive hiking in Vermont. There are three main ways to access the area: you must take Route 125 10 miles east to the Middlbury Gap, or take the Lincoln Road from Route 116 east of Bristol south past Lincoln; when the Gap Road splits with the River Road, continue south of River Road (a.k.a. the Natural Turnpike, Big Basin Road) along the river south. The third way is to continue on Route 125 to Route 100 and then turn north to Granville, or continue east on Lincoln Gap Road to Route 100 and turn south.

From the Basin Road, you can access the **Cooley Glen** and **Emily Proctor Trails** with more than 12 miles over the area's "Presidential Range" (not to be confused with New Hampshire's mountains of the same name) where they criss-cross the Long Trail. South of the access for Cooley Glen and Emily Proctor is the trailhead for the **Skylight Pond Trail**, which leads to a pond of the same name (2.5 miles), the site of the famous **Skyline Lodge** originally built in 1955 by the Green Mountain Club. From the Lodge and Pond, it is another 1.2 miles to **Bread Loaf Mountain**. Off the summit of Bread Loaf is a short detour trail that offers superb views of the Champlain Valley.

On Route 125, roughly halfway between Hancock and the Middlebury Colleeg Snow Bowl, is the turnoff for the **Texas Falls Recreation Area** with picnic areas and trails to the **Texas Falls**, among the most beautiful and accessible in the state – a great destination for a family expedition.

From Route 100, it is ten miles south of Warren and the junction with the Lincoln Gap Road to the **Moss Glen Falls**, a scenic waterfall accessible directly from the roadside parking site.

There are several hikes around the scenic village of **Bristol**, located at the junction of Routes 116 and 17. From the village green in the center of Bristol, you can make the scenic and easy 1.5 mile (3 miles roundtrip) trek to **Bristol Ledges** where you can enjoy great views of the village, Lake Champlain, and the Adirondacks in New York. A more difficult off-trail hike is on South Mountain in the **Bristol Cliffs Wilderness**, which you can reach by taking Route 116 1.5 miles west from Bristol, then turning right of Lincoln Hill Road and after two miles another right on York Hill Road. The hiking is difficult and off-trail, so find yourself a map and give yourself plenty of daylight.

West of Brandon, the **Mt. Independence Historic Site**, *located 16 miles west of Brandon by way of Route 73 & Route 73A to Mt. Independence Road*, was where a large army encampment was built to house Continental Army soldiers. It was connected to Fort Ticonderoga across the lake in New York by a floating bridge. There are several trails in and around the site that make for relaxing and scenic hikes. *Tel. 802.948-2000. Open: mid-May to Columbus Day (mid-October) 9:30am-5:30pm, Wednesday – Sunday.*

Skiing

MIDDLEBURY COLLEGE SNOWBOWL, *12 miles east of Middlbury Village on Route 125. Middlebury VT 05753. Tel. 802/388-4356. Lift tickets: $30weekends, $25 weekdays. Credit cards: Visa, Mastercard. American Express.*

Owned and operated by Middlebury College, the Snowbowl offers great skiing at all levels without the crowds you expect at the Stowe's and Killington's of the world. Rentals, instruction, and snowboarding are available.

Skiers may also consider trekking the 20 miles on Route 17 East over to the Mad River Valley, famous for the **Sugarbush** and **Mad River Glen** ski areas. Twenty miles north of the Mad River Valley on Route 100 is **Stowe** at Mt. Mansfield, another major ski area.

Snowmobiling

There are many snowmobiling opportunities throughout the western half of Vermont, particularly in the Green Mountain National Forest. To snowmobile in Vermont, you must join a local club and pay annual dues to them (usually under $20 a year) as well as a fee known as the Trail Maintenance Assessment, or TMA. This money goes towards the maintenance of trails and, once paid, enables you to snowmobile anywhere in Vermont. For more information about snowmobiling in the region – including tours, rentals, and lessons – and throughout Vermont generally, contact the **Vermont Association of Snow Travelers** (V.A.S.T.) at *P.O. Box 839, Montpelier VT 05601. Tel. 802/229-0005, Fax 802/223-4316, Website: www.vtvast.org.*

Listed below are snowmobile clubs in the Middlebury and Vergennes region:
- **Bridport Snobirds** – *Tel. 802/758-2225*
- **Foote of the Mtn. Sno-Travelers** – *Tel. 802/247-4708*
- **Green Mountain Sno Owls** – *Tel. 802/623-6197*
- **Little Otter Scramblers** – *Tel. 802/877-2813*
- **Mount Abe Sno Sports** – *Tel. 802/453-4264*
- **Shellhouse Nostalgic Mountain Jumpers** – *Tel. 802/877-2273*
- **Vergennes Otter Creek Sliders** – *Tel. 802/877-2726*
- **Weybridge Trail Blazers** – *Tel. 802/545-2280*

EXCURSIONS & DAY TRIPS

Perhaps the easiest and most fun excursion from the Vermont side of the Lower Champlain Valley is **Fort Ticonderoga** in New York. The most strategic military fort in the Champlain Valley, it was founded by the French and changed hands several times in the early years of the Revolutionary War. It is easily combined with a visit to its sister base on the Vermont side, **Mt. Independence**; just take Route 73 a couple miles north to the ferry of Larrabbee's Point in Shoreham. The ferry costs $6 per vehicle one way, $10 round-trips, and runs constantly from 7am-8pm.

Burlington, Vermont's largest city, is 35 miles north of Middlebury on Route 7, and is a happening little city offering a variety of culinary, cultural, and shopping opportunites. There are a variety of interesting attractions, including the **Ethan Allen Homestead** where the leader of the Green Mountain Boys spent his last years; in **Shelburne** you can visit **Shelburne Farms** with its famous Vistorian Inn and cheese factory on Lake Champlain, and the **Shelburne Museum** featuring various exhibits about life in 19th century Vermont ranging from exhibits of tools, furniture, and other artifacts, to a restored general store. On and around **Lake Champlain** near Burlington, and particularly on the Lake Champlain islands to the north, there are numerous opportunities for swimming, fishing, and boating.

Skiers looking to ski somewhere other than the Middlebury College Snow Bowl might consider a visit to the **Mad River Valley**, which is 32 miles from Middlebury by taking Route 7 north to New Haven and then Route 17 east to Waitsfield. The Mad River Valley is home to the Sugarbush and Mad River Glen ski areas, and features a variety of other recreational opportunities ranging from kayaking to taking a tour of the valley in a glider. There are also numerous shops, charming inns, and fine restaurants; besides, the drive itself is quite beautiful. See the "Mad River Valley" chapter for more information.

Just another 15-20 miles north of Warren and the Mad River Valley on Route 100 is the area around **Mt. Mansfield**, including **Waterbury**, **Smugglers' Notch** and the famous resort town of **Stowe**. Like the Mad River Valley, it offers great skiing and other recreation, dozens of inns and restaurants, and an assortment of other attractions like the **Ben & Jerry's Ice Cream Factory** in Waterbury. Just down the road at the junction of Route 100B (which you get on just north of Waitsfield in the Mad River Valley) and I-89 at Exit 9 is **Middlesex**, home of **Camp Meade**, a restored military camp and museum dedicated to the heroism of the World War II generation where you can even stay in cabins and wake to the sound of bugles at the crack of dawn (8am).

Another option for skiers, hikers, and outdoor buffs is the region around **Rutland** (35 miles south of Middlebury on Route 7) and **Killington** (45 miles from Middlebury). **Killington** and its sister ski area of **Pico** offer the most extensive and diverse skiing in the east as well as opportunities to enjoy hiking, biking, and other outdoors activites. Just about 10 miles beyond Killington on Route 100 South is **Plymouth**, where on Route 100A you can visit the birthplace (and final resting place) of President Calvin Coolidge. His home village of Plymouth Notch has been restored and is now open to the public in the summer; it makes for a very enjoyable and educational experience. Just up the road, also on Route 100A, is the **Calvin Coolidge State Park**, where you can camp, hike, and enjoy the wilderness.

The city of Rutland is not generally thought of as a tourist destination, but having undergone something of a revival in recent years, it is a pleasant place to visit, and features a variety of good restaurants and shops. Just north of Rutland (and less than 20 miles from Brandon) is the **Chittenden Reservoir** with camping fishing, boating, hiking, and biking. Nearby attractions also include the **Marble Museum** in Proctor, the **Hubbardton Battle Monument and Museum**, and **Lake Bomoseen**, including Lake Bomoseen State Park, where you can hike, fish, or paddle and sail around in a boat. See the "Rutland & Killington" chapter for more information.

Finally, the state capital, **Montpelier**, at 52 miles (most of which must be driven on non-interstates) from Middlebury might be a bit of a hike for a day trip, but it can be done, and makes a particularly nice visit if you can spend the night. The smallest state capital in the Untied States, Montpelier is a charming little town whose signature landmark is the modest but elegant gold domed state capital building. Other attractions include the exhibits at the **Vermont Historical Society** and many shops and restaurants, several of which are operated by the **New England Culinary Institute** which is based in Montpelier. Nearby in **Barre** is one of the most fascinating sites in all of Vermont, the **Rock of Ages granite quarries**, which are the largest in the world, and the **Cabot Creamery** about 20 miles north of Montpelier.

PRACTICAL INFORMATION

Chambers of Commerce
ADDISON COUNTY CHAMBER OF COMMERCE (including Middlebury), *2 Court Street, Middlebury VT 05753. Tel. 802/388-7951, 800/ SEE-VERMONT, Fax 802/388-8066. E-mail: accoc@sover.net. Web site: www.midvermont.com.*

BRANDON CHAMBER OF COMMERCE, *P.O. Box 267 (Route 7), Brandond VT 05733. Tel. 802/247-6401. E-mail: brandon@sover.net. Web site: www.brandon.org.*
VERGENNES CHAMBER OF COMMERCE, *P.O. Box 335, Vergennes VT 05491. Tel. 802/877-0080.*

Medical Emergencies & Services
Ambulance – *Tel. 911*
Porter Medical Center, *South Street, Middlebury VT. Tel. 802/388-7901*
Medical Health Care Info Center (incuding 24 hour emergency and walk-in clinic), *Colchester Avenue, Burlington VT. Tel. 802/864-0454*

Pharmacies
MARBLE WORKS PHARMACY, *Marble Works (southern end of Maple Street), Middlebury VT 05753. Tel. 802/388-3783. 8am-6pm Monday-Friday, 8am-5pm Saturday, 9am-2pm Sunday. Major credit cards accepted.*
MARBLE WORKS PHARMACY (Vergennes), *187 Main Street, Vergennes VT. Tel. 802/877-1190, 800/684-8300. 8am-6pm Monday-Friday, 8am-5pm Saturday, 9am-2pm Sunday. Major credit cards accepted.*

18. THE MAD RIVER VALLEY

The **Mad River Valley** south of I-89 and Stowe, between Montpelier and Burlington, is also one of the oldest ski regions in the state. In addition to featuring two of Vermont's most established and esteemed ski areas, and the only one managed by a cooperative in Mad River Glen, the area offers visitors more opportunities to sample vintage old school accommodations and eateries than other ski areas in the state.

Waitsfield and **Warren** serve as the commercial and social anchors for the region, and have weathered the development that big time tourism entails better than most and have. by and large, maintained their historic character. Besides skiing, the two resorts, **Mad River Glen** and **Sugarbush**, offer unlimited opportunities for skiers, hikers, cyclists, as well as shoppers, and if the local offerings are not enough, the Mad River Valley is within easy driving distance of attractions ranging from the art galleries and cultural happenings of Burlington to the most famous hike in Vermont – the Camel's Hump near Huntington and Bolton.

ARRIVALS & DEPARTURES
By Air
Burlington International Airport, *Airport Drive (off Williston Road), Burlington VT 05401,* is the closest major commercial airport and is an hour from the Mad River Valley. The airport is served by Continental, United, USAir, and the commuter airlines, Business Express, *Tel. 800/ 345-3400*, and Comair, *Tel. 800/927-0927.*

Other airports within 2-4 hours by car include Lebanon NH, Manchester NH, Boston, and Montreal. All are serviced by major airlines and major car rental companies operate out of all of them.

By Car

The towns of the Mad River Valley are basically located where Routes 100, 100B, and Route 17 meet. The area is usually accessed by taking Exits 9 & 10 from **I-89** between Burlington and Montpelier. **Route 100** south takes you straight to Waitsfield and Warren. If you're coming from Massachussets or beyond to the south, you'll probably come north on I-91 or I-89. If you're coming from I-91, get on I-89 north at White River Junction. For a more scenic drive, get on Route 14 at White River, switch to 107 West in Royalton and then take Route 100 north (35 miles). From points in southern Vermont, find your way to Route 100 (probably by Route 9, Route 11, or Route 4) and simply go straight north.

If coming from west from New York State on Interstates 90, 81 on 87 (coming from New York City), take I-87, get off at Exit 20, and go east on Route 149 which turns into Route 4 in Vermont. Continue through Rutland and on to Route 100 North (50 miles).

By Bus

Vermont Transit Lines, *Tel. 800/552-8738, 800/451-3292,* go in and out of Waterbury at the Gateway Hotel and links the region to all parts of Vermont. Through Vermont Transit's connection with Greyhound, you can link up with the rest of the U.S. and Canada as well.

By Train

Amtrak's **Vermonter** links Vermont with major cities on the northeastern seaboard, including New York, Philadelphia, Baltimore, Washington and numerous towns in Connecticut, central Massachusetts, and New Jersey, as well as Montreal. The closest station to the Mad River Valley is **Waterbury-Stowe**, about 15 miles north on Route 100. From points in New York (New York City, Albany, Groton and others), the **Ethan Allen Express** stops in Rutland (about 40 miles south of the Mad River Valley), from which you can take a bus, rent a car, or hire a taxi to the Mad River Valley. Call Amtrak, *Tel. 800/USA-RAIL,* for reservations and information regarding schedules and fares. Generally tickets to the major cities above range from $50-$100 depending on how far you go.

ORIENTATION

Most visitors approach the region from the north on either **Route 100B** or **Route 100**. The main artery for the Mad River Valley, Route 100 skirts the Mad River itself, and links the villages of Warren and Waitsfield (the villages are about six miles apart) to each other as well as to I-89 and the outside world. Several miles north of Waitsfield Village in the sleepy municipality of **Moretown,** Route 100 splits into two: Route 100 continues on to Waterbury where it meets Route 2 and I-89 at Exit 10; it then

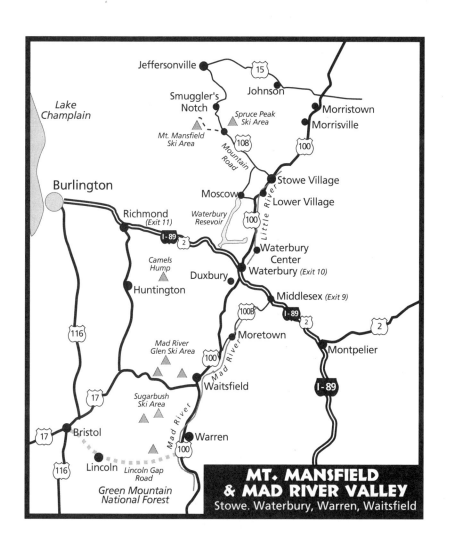

MT. MANSFIELD
& MAD RIVER VALLEY
Stowe. Waterbury, Warren, Waitsfield

moves on north to Stowe and the Mt. Mansfield area, also a major destination for skiers.

Both Warren and Waitsfield are small historic villages containing shops, restaurants, and quaint old buildings, but Waitsfield is slightly more commercially developed and many of the area's businesses, including restaurants and lodgings, are situated along Route 100 on a 3-4 mile strip beginning just north of the junction with Route 17. Route 17 links Waitsfield with the **Mad River Glen** skiing area and the Appalachian Gap where you can access Vermont's famous **Long Trail**. The Long Trail is also reachable by way of the Lincoln Gap Road, which has a junction with Route 100 just south of Warren Village. The **Sugarbush Village and Ski Area** is connected to Route 100 a mile north of Warren by the **Sugarbush Access Road**, which is also the address of many resorts and lodges. Linking the Sugarbush Access Road with Route 17 is the **German Flats Road**, which also accesses the **Mount Ellen Sugarbush Ski Area**. Also off Route 100 are numerous local roads offering scenic Vermont landscapes, and good opportunities for biking and also hiking.

GETTING AROUND

If you don't have a car and can't get where you need to go on skis, a snowboard, or perhaps a single chair lift, there are several taxi services that can also drive you up to Burlington or Waterbury to catch a plane, bus, or train:
• **C&L Taxi**, *Tel. 802/496-4056.*
• **Morf Transit**, *Tel. 802/864-5588, Tel. 800/696-7433.*

Also, **Hap's Auto Store** on Route 100 in Waitsfield rents cars as well as providing 24-hour car service. *Tel. 802/496-3948. Hours: 8am-6pm Monday-Saturday. Credit cards: major credit cards accepted.*

WHERE TO STAY

SUGARBUSH RESORT LODGING, *RR 1 Box 350, Warren VT 05674. (Located at the Sugarbush Ski Area; take the Sugarbush Access Road from Route 100 between Warren and Waitsfield villages). Tel. 802/583-6160, 800/53-SUGAR, groups and functions 802/583-6114, Fax 802/583-3209. E-mail: sugarbush.com. Web site: www.sugarbush.com. Rates: $40-$200 per person per night and up. Credit cards: major credit cards accepted.*

Owned by the same folks who own the ski area itself (the ubiquitous but unprofitable American Skiing Company), Sugarbush features an assortment (more than 180) of modern 1-4 bedroom condos located in and around the Sugarbush Village. They provide easy access to the ski lifts and health club facilities, but lack the charm of Warren and Waitsfield or the many inns in the area. Most units contain an in-house phone, private or semi-private baths (shared with one other unit), cable television, and a living room that may or may not have a fireplace. Lodgers also enjoy free access to the gym facilities at the Sugarbush Health and Racquet Club. Look into package deals and weekly rates that include skiing passes, meal plans, and other bundled goodies like discount golf and bike rentals. The Sugarbush Inn (see below) is also part of the village complex and offers similar access to skiing and the health club with lodging in more charming quarters.

THE BRIDGE FAMILY RESORT AND TENNIS CLUB, *Sugarbush Access Road, Warren VT 05674. Tel. 802/583-2922, 800/453-2922, Fax 802/ 583-1018. E-mail: bridges@madriver.com. Web site: www.bridgesresort.com. Rates: $100-$400 per condo per night. Credit cards: major credit cards accepted.*

Situated on 45 acres less than half a mile from the Sugarbush Ski Area, this resort features modern condos with 1-3 rooms equipped with amenities such as full baths, telephones, televisions and VCR's, and microwaves. Other facilities on the resort grounds include three swimming pools, more than 10 indoor and outdoor tennis courts, hot tubs and saunas, a full gym, and a child care center where youngsters participate in fully supervised indoor and outdoor activities; free shuttle service to the ski slopes is also provided. Call for package deals including lodging, ski passes, and access to all resort facilities. Tennis players should inquire about special tennis packages during the summer. There is a restaurant on the resort grounds, but meals are generally not included in rates – a good excuse to sample the region's extensive fine dining opportunities.

EAGLES RESORT, *Route 100/P.O. Box 208, Waitsfield VT 05673. Tel. 802/496-5700. Rates: $100 and up. Major credit cards accepted.*

With 16 condos and fewer recreation facilities than Sugarbush or the Bridge Family Resort, Eagles Resort may not seem like a "resort" as such, but semantics aside it features more than a dozen individual standing units, each equipped with bedrooms, full kitchens, a fireplace, a Swedish sauna (steambath), a fireplace, and a parking garage. The resort also includes a recreation clubhouse with racquetball courts, a rec room, and a social lounge, while outdoors there is one tennis court and a swimming pool. There is no restaurant. Call about weekend, weekly, and off-season discount rates and packages.

INN AT THE ROUND BARN FARM, *East Warren Road, Waitsfield VT 05673. Tel. 802/496-2276, Fax 802/496-8832. E-mail: roundbarn@madriver.com. Web site: innatroundbarn.com. Rates: $135-$240. Credit cards: Visa, Mastercard, American Express.*

Situated in a beautifully restored white 1810 farmhouse, this inn – named for its rare 12 sided barn – is a gem that will pamper you with delicious breakfasts (included in the price), jacuzzis, beautiful pastoral scenery, on site cross-country skiing, and luxurious and cozy rooms featuring canopied beds, fireplaces, and other old-fashioned furnishings. With cows, five ponds, and dozens of acres littered with beautiful perennials, it is as gorgeous in the summer and fall as it is in the winter when it's a real winter wonderland.

HAMILTON HOUSE, *Hamilton House Drive, Warren VT 05674-9712. Tel. 802/583-1066, 800/760-1066, Fax 802/583-1776. E-mail: james@hamiltonvt.com. Web site: www.hmiltonvt.com Rates: $150 per room. Credit cards: Visa, Mastercard.*

With four beautiful rooms in a country house on a 25 acre estate, this small establishment offers a combination of intimacy and privacy in a beautiful setting. The house and appointments are elegant, and this makes for an excellent choice for a romantic getaway. Breakfast included.

1824 HOUSE INN, *P.O. Box 159, Waitsfield 05673. (Route 100). Tel. 802/496-7555, 800/426-3986, Fax 802/496-7559. E-mail: 1824@madriver.com. Web site: 1824@madriver.com. Rates: $100-$150. Credit cards: major credit cards acepted.*

This cozy but elegant restored farmhouse-turned-B&B is listed in the National Historic Register and features eight beautifully furnished rooms with antique furnishings, comfy featherbeds, and private baths but no phones. The inn is set on an estate with 23 acres on which you can stroll about or snowshoe depending on the weather, and which also features an outdoor hot tub and a "private" swimming hole in the Mad River. The 1824 house is well known for its multicourse gourmet breakfasts; in the evening hors d'oeuvres and snacks are often served, giving guests a chance to socialize with one another.

BEAVER POND FARM INN, *Golf Course Road, Warren VT 05674. (Golf Course Road is off the Sugarbush Access Road). Tel. 802/583-2861, Fax 802/583-2860. E-mail: beaverpond@madriver.com. Web site: www.beaverpondfarminn.com. Rates: $85-$120. Credit cards: Visa, Mastercard.*

With its location next to the golf course, it makes sense that the Beaver Pond Farm Inn caters to golfers who can literally walk to the course, and the inn often offers special packages for golfers. The inn itself is a comfortable but modest old farmhouse with views of nearby ponds and meadows and five guestrooms, each of which is uniquely decorated with Victorian and Vermonty decor and contains a private bathroom.

THE SUGARTREE, *2440 Sugarbush Access Road, Warren VT 05674. Tel. 802/583-3211, 800/666-8907, Fax 802/583-3209. E-mail: sugartree@madriver.com. Web site: www.sugartree.com. Rates: $85-$160. Credit cards: major credit cards accepted.*

The Sugartree features about 10 rooms with canopied beds and private baths (but no phones or television) and one larger suite with a fireplace. Breakfast, which is excellent, is included.

FINDING DISCOUNT PACKAGES

At virtually any time of year, and particularly during weekdays and the off-season, you can find package deals at resort destinations such as Sugarbush in the Mad River Valley. There are a number of ways to find out about such packages, which often include lodging, ski tickets, a meal plan, and discounts for other recreational activities like golf and tennis. For starters you can look up the various resorts and hotels on the web or call them for information.

*However, this can be time-consuming and you will probably miss some good deals. We'd recommend beaming up the Vermont Department of Tourism Marketing at **www.travel-vermont**, or calling **Central Reservations of Vermont** at 802/583-3007 or 800/451-4574; E-mail: oto@vtvacation.com; web site: www.vtvacation.com. They offer free quotes and information about packages through Vermont for all budgets. **Sugarbush Reservations** is a similar service, but only provides for the Mad River Valley, Tel. 800/53-SUGAR, web site: www.sugarbush.com.*

SUGARBUSH INN, *RR1 Box 350, Warren VT 05674. (Located in Sugarbush Village at the end of the Sugarbush Access Road). Tel. 802/583-2301, 800/53-SUGAR, Fax 802/583-3209. E-mail: sugarbush.com. Web site: www. sugarbush.com. Rates: $70-$150. Major credit cards accepted.*

Located in the heart of Sugarbush Village at the base of the Sugarbush ski area, the Inn has more charm than the condos and offers the same access to the Sugarbush Health and Racquet Club, as well as discounted ski tickets. However, its atmosphere is really no match for the fine inns in the region located in vintage Vermont farmhouses. In any case, the rooms feature television, in-room phones, and clean modern baths. In the summer, consider looking into the special golf and tennis packages offering discounts on tennis clinics and court time, as well as discounted greens fees at the Robert Trent Jones Sr. designed Sugarbush golf course just down the road.

THE SUGAR LODGE AT SUGARBUSH, *Sugarbush Access Road, Warren VT 05673. Tel. 802/583-3300, 800/982-3465, Fax 802/583-1148. Web site: www.sugarlodge.com. Rates: $50-$150. Major credit cards accepted.*

Situated about half a mile down the road from the Sugarbush Village, the Sugar Lodge offers smartly decorated, modern hotel rooms with in-room phone, cable television, and clean, private baths. Though it doesn't have quite the same flavor that some of the older inns do, it's a warm and friendly sort of place where cider and other refreshments are served during the early evenings. Free shuttle to the slopes is provided.

LAREAU FARM COUNTRY INN, *P.O. Box 563, Waitsfield VT 05674. (Located on Route 100). Tel. 802/496-4949, 800/833-0766, Fax 802/496-7979. E-mail: lareau@madriver.com. Web site: www.lareaufarminn.com. Rates: $75-$140. Credit cards: Visa, Mastercard.*

Once the home of the area's first physician, this restored farmhouse with a touch of Greek Revival is situated on a 67 acre estate on the Mad River, and features 13 guestrooms (11 with private bath) and the American Flatbread Kitchen, recently recognized by *Vermont* magazine as serving the best pizza in the state. Rooms are artfully decorated and comfortable but do not contain phones, air-conditioning, or television. The location on the river is ideal for those interested in hiking, biking, and swimming in the river, and sleigh rides are offered on-site. Breakfast is included and is excellent.

MAD RIVER INN, *P.O. Box 75, Waitsfield VT 05673. (Located on Tremblay Road off Route 100). Tel. 802/497-7900, 800/TEA-TART. Fax. 802/496-5390. E-mail: madinn@madriver.com. Web site: www. madriver.com/ lodging. Rates: $70-$130. Credit cards: Visa, Mastercard.*

The handsome grounds of this vintage Victorian inn include beautiful gardens, a jacuzzi, a gazebo, and a swimming hole in the Mad River, while the building itself features 11 guestrooms (each with private bath), a cozy library, billiards and a lounge to which you can bring your own refreshments. To top it off, the views of the neighboring mountains are beautiful and hiking, biking, and other outdoor activities are readily accessible.

TUCKER HILL LODGE & RESTAURANT, *Route 17 Box 147, Waitsfield VT 05674. Tel. 802/496-3983, 800/543-7841. E-mail: tuckhill@madriver.com. Rates: $75-$135. Credit cards: Visa, Mastercard, American Express.*

Tucked away on Route 17, this restored 1820's farmhouse is secluded but still close to skiing and other regional attractions. It features about 20 comfy guestrooms with private bathrooms and various common rooms, the atmosphere of which is enhanced in the winter by cozy fires. However, the food, both breakfast and the Italian-flavored fare served at Georgio's, is the biggest star here.

MILLBROOK INN & RESTAURANT, *533 McCullough, Waitsfield VT 05673. Tel. 802/496-2405, 800/477-2809, Fax 802/496-9735. E-mail: milbrkinn@aol.com. Web site: www.millbrookinn.com. Rates $80-$150. Credit cards: Visa, Mastercard.*

With its handmade quilts, hand stencilled bed rooms, and antique furnishings, this 19th century inn is a real winner in the atmospherics department, and the food cooked and served at the in-house restaurant isn't too shabby either.

CHRISTMAS TREE INN, *Sugarbush Access Road, Warren VT 05674. Tel. 802/583-2800, 800/535-5622, Fax 802/583-2826. Rates: $80-$250. Major credit cards accepted.*

This Christmas-motifed establishment offers reasonably priced rooms ($80-$140) with private baths and television,s in addition to an assortment of 1-3 room condos, all of which include kitchens, laundry facilities, and comfy living rooms with fireplaces, televisions and VCR's. Breakfast is included in the inn rates.

GOLDEN LION RIVERSIDE INN, *Box Route 100, Warren VT 05674. (Located at the junction of Route 100 and the Sugarbush Access Road about one mile north of the village). Tel. 802/496-3084, Fax 802/496-7438. E-mail: gldnlion@madrivervalley.com. Rates: $50-$90. Credit cards: major credit cards accepted.*

With a river beach, grills, a lobby with a fireplace, and a hot tub, the Golden Lion offers more than the usual motel accoutrements. In addition, the management and staff are friendly and rooms are equipped with a range of amenities, from cable television and in-room telephones to private baths and extra space. Pets are welcome, but arrangements should be made in advance.

WAIT FARM MOTOR INN, *4805 Main Street (Route 100), Waitsfield VT 05673. Tel. 802/496-2033, 800/887-2828. Rates: $45-$70. Credit cards: Visa, Mastercard.*

This small family-run motor inn consists of ten rooms with private showers and cable television, but no in-room phones; some also feature kitchenettes. It's not particularly charming or special in any way, but the management is friendly and helpful, the rates are reasonable, and the location halfway between the Route 17 turnoff and Waitsfield village is convenient in terms of proximity to shopping and dining.

WHERE TO EAT
Expensive

THE COMMON MAN, *German Flats Road (between Lincoln Peak and Mount Ellen Peak), Warren VT 05673. Tel. 802/583-2800, Fax 802/583-2826. E-mail: comman@madriver.com. Opens: December-April 5:30pm Saturday &holidays, 6pm weekdays; rest of the year 6pm Saturdays & holidays, 6:30pm weekdays. Closed on Mondays. Major credit cards accepted.*

Serving superb continental and American cuisine in the interior of a huge barn with a large fireplace, the Common Man offers diners a romantic, elegant, yet rustic dining experience. Parisienne Chef Jean-Patrick Matecate rotates the menu, but it typically includes game meat, lamb, seafood, steak, and pasta prepared in sensuous and rich wine and cream sauces, or in lighter herb-favored olive oil sauces. A meal might begin with a typical French appetizer such as soupe a l'oignon or escargots before moving on to a light salad and the main course. Prices range from $2-$6 for appetizers and salads, to $20 and more for main courses such as roast rack of lamb. It's wise to call for reservations, particularly on weekends and holidays, and during the foliage season.

CHEZ HENRI'S, *Sugarbush Village, just left of the entrance. Tel. 802/ 583-22600. Hours: 11:30am – midnight daily, Sunday brunch, 10am. Major credit cards accepted.*

This famous French eatery includes a casual and intimate bistro with a bar, as well as a more upscale dining room. Both are a bit pricey, and both are well worth it, particularly if you're looking to fill an empty stomach after a day out on the slopes or perhaps the golf course. The handsome dining room in the back is a romantic sort of place complete with white table clothes and a stone fireplace, which sometimes features after-dinner dancing. A bit more casual, the bistro contains a bar ideal for a taking an apres-ski aperatif, or if the weather permits, you may sit outside beside a small brook. Both the bistro and the dining room serve lunch and dinner.

Supper is a fine dining experience which you might begin with a classic French hors d'oeuvres ($4-$10.50) such as moules mariniere (mussels in white wine and cream sauce) or perhaps something lighter such as green salad with Vermont goat cheese (yum!). Entree choices include a wonderful carre d'agneau aux herbes (rack of lamb with rosemary and garlic), bouillabaisse (a mixed seafod soup), and pasta with mixed shellfish, among others. The lunch menu has more "bistro" in it and features an assortment of appetizers and lighter food such as onion soup and salads, in addition to simpler, heartier fare such as cheese fondue, beef bouguignon, and a sinfully rich coq au vin.. Prices range from $3.50 for soup to more than $10 for meat dishes.

THE PITCHER INN, *275 Main Street, Warren VT 05673. Tel. 802/ 496-6350, Tel. 888/TO-PITCH. Web site: www.pitcherinn.com. Open 6:30pm until closing. Credit cards: major credit cards accepted.*

With its classic Vermont inn setting, Pitcher Inn features a more cutting edge menu than the Common Man or Chez Henri. Using fresh, locally produced ingredients when possible, the chefs prepare a limited but imaginative variety of dishes, such as grilled cherry wood smoked duck and vegetarian cassoulet with tomato confit. Appetizers tend to be vegetable based, but are no less interesting. When I was last here, offerings included tomatoes with Vermont goat cheese and roasted garlic; grilled bruschetta (toasted bread spread with olive oil) with garlic marmalade; and warm spinach salad with squash and lentils. Prices range from $6-$10 for appetizers, and $18-$30 for entrees.

THE SPOTTED COW, *Bridge Street Marketplace, Waitsfield VT 05673. Tel. 802/496-5151. Hours: 11:30am-2:30pm for lunch, 5:30pm-9pm for dinner. Credit cards: Visa, Mastercard.*

Trust me, the restaurant is far more elegant and interesting than the name suggests. Indeed, with such nouveau dishes as steamed grouper en papillote (whatever that is), seared black sesame salmon medallion, and Bermuda fish chowder, your dining experience is bound to be delicious and distinctly un-Vermont like.

THE WARREN HOUSE RESTAURANT & BAR, *Sugarbush Access Road, Warren, 05674. Tel. 802/583-2421. Hours: open nightly for dinner at 5:30pm. Credit cards: Visa, Mastercard.*

This cozy restaurant serves a well rounded assortment of conventional seafood, pasta, meats and fowl – grilled Angus tenderloin with vegetables and mashed potatoes – as well as more cutting edge dishes, such as grilled yellowfin tuna with kiwi lime chutney and sweet mango coulis. For drinks, there is a healthy choice of beers and wines.

Moderate

FLATBREAD KITCHEN, *Route 100, Waitsfield VT 05673. Tel. 802/496-8856. Hours: 5;30pm-9:30pm Friday and Saturdays only! Closed November and May. Credit cards: Visa, Mastercard.*

Situated in the Lareau Farm Country Inn, this fantastic little restaurant serves the tastiest and most interesting pizza in the Mad River Valley, perhaps even all of Vermont and New England. Prepared in an old-fashioned wood-fire earthen oven, pies come with all combinations of toppings, ranging from free range chicken and home-made sausage to sun-dried tomatoes and shrimp. Furthermore, the atmosphere is casual, the staff friendly, and the prices extremely reasonable – you'll be splurging if it comes to $15 a person for food, salad, and beverages. They are only open on Fridays and Saturdays and close during May and November.

GIORGIO'S CAFE, *Route 17 Waitsfield (in the Tucker Hill Lodge), Waitsfield VT 056743. Tel. 802/496-3983. E-mail: millbrkinn.com. Open for dinner 6pm. Credit cards: Visa, Mastercard.*

This family-operated eatery serves very good Italian food in a pleasant dining room setting, and on Thursdays features live entertainment. The menu includes a variety of antipasti (appetizers) ranging from a light but crispy calamari (fried squid) for $5.95 and a number of salads dressed in vinaigrettes ($4-$5) to the antipasto misto, featuring an assortment of cheeses, cold cuts, and salads for $6.95. For entrees you can choose from among eight different pasta dishes ($8-$12) ranging from vegetable lasagna to linguine ai frutti di mare (linguine pasta with mixed seafood steam in white wine). If you're interested in an alternative to pasta, the menu typically features tasty meat, chicken, seafood, and vegetarian dishes such as cappesante alla Veneziana (scallops with raisin, cream and pine nuts) and spiedino vegetariano – vegetable kebabs with portabello, eggplant, onion, pepper, and tomato. Entrees typically range in price from $12-$17.

MILLBROOK....A COUNTRY INN, *Route 17 (less than one mile from Route 100), Waitsfield VT 05673. Tel. 802/496-2405. Hours: open daily 6pm-9pm. Major credit cards accepted.*

With only a handful of candlelit tables (capacity is less than 20), and a dining setting distinguished by a roaring fire and antique Yankee furnishings, Millbrook offers a vintage Vermont dining experience. Together with a menu featuring American dishes (roast meats, home-made pies and cakes for dessert) as well as Italian and Indian cuisine, it adds up to an odd combination, but it works, especially given the warm hospitality and the reasonable prices (appetizers $3-$7, entrees $9-$17).

THE DEN, *Junction of Routes 100 and 17 in Waitsfield. Tel. 802/496-8880). Hours: 11:30am-11:30pm. Credit cards: Visa, Mastercard.*

This family-friendly pub (no smoking) features very good food for reasonable prices: sandwiches and burgers during the day, and pasta, seafood, and a wide selection of other entrees during the evening. Soups, particularly seafood chowder and crab bisque, are especially good. Sandwiches and appetizers range from $3-7, while dinner entrees generally top $10.

ARVADS, *Route 100 about a mile north of the Junction with Route 17 and just south of Waitsfield Village. Tel. 802/496-9800. Hours: 11:30am-11:30pm. Credit cards: major credit cards accepted.*

The food is decent, but not as good or as varied as the Den's. Appetizers and "Lite Bites" feature the usual suspects like wings and nachos. Lunch concentrates on sandwiches (which are quite good), dinner on steaks and pastas ($9-15). There is also a full bar with televisions if you want a bit of spectator sports with your refreshments.

JAY'S (JW's of Vermont), *located in the Mad River Shopping Center on Route 100 (about a quarter of a mile from the junction with Route 17), Waitsfield VT 05673. Tel. 802/496-8282. Hours: 8am-11am for breakfast in winter an durin foliage, (opens 9am in off-season); 11am-5pm for lunch, 5pm-10pm for dinner. Credit cards: major credit cards accepted.*

Though the Mad River Green Shopping center location is less than idyllic, Jay's offers an assortment of decent Italian-style food (pizzas, calzones, pastas) and typical American appetizers (wings, potato skins et al.) and entrees (steak and roast chicken) for reasonable prices. Prices range from $2-$5 for appetizers and from $5-$13 for entree's. The breakfast menu features the usual assortment of egg and omelet combos, and sweet dishes such as waffles, pancakes, and French toast.

Baked Goods, Cafe's & Sandwich Shops

K.C.'s BAGEL CAFE, *Route 100 (next to Arvad's between the junction with Route 17 and Waitsfield Village), Waitsfield VT 05673. Tel. 802/496-9955. Hours: Monday – Friday 6am-3pm, Saturday & Sunday 7am-2pm. No credit cards accepted.*

This small shop serves freshly baked bagels with the typical assortment of toppings and is an excellent choice for a quick bite or perhaps a packed lunch for the slopes or the road. Coffee and other beverages are also served.

THREE MOUNTAIN CAFE, *Mad River Green Shopping Center on Route 100 (just north of the Junction with Route 17), Waitsfield VT 05673. Tel. 802/496-5470. Hours: 7am-5pm. Credit cards: Visa, Mastercard.*

In the tradition of Starbucks, the often bustling Three Mountain Cafe serves a wide variety of coffees, teas, baked goods and sandwiches as well as coffee-related equipment and apparel and newspapers to go with a morning cup of joe. The cafe also serves as something of an art gallery where paintings by Vermont artists (many of them locals) are displayed in rotating exhibits.

THE VERY SMALL DONUT COMPANY, *located in the Village Square Shopping Center on Route 100 (just beyond the junction with Route 17), Waitsfield VT 05673. Tel. 802/496-4534. Hours:: 7am-7pm daily.*

This small shop serves an assortment of tasty bagels, donuts and other baked goods, as well as custom-made sandwiches and salads.

BRIDGE STREET BAKERY, *Bridge Street in historic Waitsfield Village off Route 100, Waitsfield VT 05673. Tel. 802/496-0077. Open daily except Tuesday 7am-7pm. Credit cards: Visa, Mastercard.*

Located in the charming historic Waitsfield village next to the covered bridge, the Bridge Street Bakery is operated by a graduate of the prestigious Ecole Lenotre in Paris, and offers an assortment of gourmet breads, cakes, and pastries baked on the premises. Also available are sandwiches, soups, and coffees.

COUNTRY CREEMEES, *Village Square Shopping Center off Route 100 just north of the junction with Route 17), Waitsfield VT 05673. Open from early May to September and possibly October from about 10am-mid-evenin. No credit cards.*

Sort of an old-fashioned ice cream and hot dog stand serving all sorts of summer refreshments from cones, shakes, and sundaes to hot dogs and soft drinks – a great place to take the kids on a hot summer day.

SEEING THE SIGHTS

Chances are the most satisfying sights you'll experience in the Mad River Valley will be the area's beautiful natural and pastoral landscapes – or perhaps something like a golf ball flying 250 yards up the middle of the fairway, or trees gone blurry as you fly down the slopes at 60 miles an hour. Indeed, the Mad River Valley offers little in the way of historical sights, but with its natural beauty, handsome villages, and classic Vermont pastoral scenery, the Valley is certainly worth exploring.

The area is small enough that you can tour it in a car in a mere hour or so, or if biking it may take the better part of a day. Basically, seeing the area entails following **Route 100** from Warren to Waitsfield (or vice versa) and then making a loop on the **East Warren Road** (a.k.a. "Common Road" and "North Road") while taking as many detours on local roads as you like.

Let's begin in **Warren**, the southernmost of the two towns. Named for Dr. Joseph Warren, President Pro Tempore of the Provincial Congress and the first American killed at the Battle of Bunker Hill in Charleston, Massachussetts, the town was founded by John Thorp in 1789. Until the tourism industry began to flourish with the establishment of the Mad River Glen Ski Area in 1946 (Sugarbush was founded in the 1950's), Warren was not a town of particular significance. Initially its economy was entirely tied to agriculture, and though the lumber industry developed in the 19th century when mills were built on the Mad River, the town remained small – a consequence of its distance from major railroad lines and highways.

Warren's darkest hours were in the 1930's, when the Great Depression hit an economy that was already on its knees after the Flood of 1927 wiped out virtually all the lumber mills as well as many homes, farms, and other businesses. Today, despite the town's economic ups and downs, and the extensive development of the region that came with tourism, Warren Village has retained its 19th century Yankee charm and is littered with handsome structures, including the **Warren Bridge**, a covered bridge that dates to 1880.

From Warren Village you can head north on Route 100 through Irasville, a small hamlet between Warren and Waitsfield, and on to Waitsfield; you cross Route 100 and take **Lincoln Gap Road** (closed in the winter) that leads to the Long Trail and excellent hiking country (see Hiking in the "Sports & Recreation" section below); or you can take Fullerhill Road or Brook Road from Main Street to the East Warren Road.

Taking the **East Warren Road** north (left) to Waitsfield and Route 100 will enable you to enjoy classic Vermont scenery dotted with old-fashioned country houses and barns. This road is also great for biking, and you shouldn't hesitate to explore some of the local roads that branch off it. As you approach Waitsfield, which is only six miles or so from Warren, I'd recommend bearing left on the East Warren Road or continuing on the Common Road and turning left on the Joslyn Hill Road. Both of these lead to Bridge Street, where you will pass through a 100-foot covered bridge and find yourself in the heart of Waitsfield's historic village. The covered bridge, formally the **Village Bridge**, was originally built in the 1830's.

During the summer and autumn when the **Roxbury Mountain Road** is open, you can continue your detour off the East Warren Road onto the Roxbury Road and make a longer loop by continuing north and then west to Moretown, which is about five miles north of Waitsfield. While longer than the simple East Warren Road route to Waitsfield, it should still take you less than an hour assuming you don't stop. Should you take Route 100 you make a slightly longer trip by taking the Sugarbush Access Road, which leads to the ski area, and then the German Flats Road, leading to Route 17 and the **Mad River Glen Ski Area**. Beyond Mad River Glen, Route 17 leads to the **Appalachian Gap** and the **Long Trail**, where in the summer and autumn you can enjoy some excellent hiking (see Hiking in "Sports & Recreation" below).

Given their proximity to each other, it makes sense that Warren's and Waitsfield's histories are virtual parallel. Founded by and named for **General Benjamin Wait**, a Revolutionary War hero, Waitsfield too was a modest settlement whose economy was dominated by dairy farming and lumber until the Flood of 1927. Since the founding of the Mad River Glen Ski area in the 1940's and that of Sugarbush in the 1950's, tourism has dominated the local economy and changed the area's landscape literally and figuratively. Historic Waitsfield Village is now a flourishing little hamlet bustling with small shops, restaurants, and handsome buildings, such as the **Joslin Memorial Library** and the **Federated Church** with its classic steeple.

Opposite Waitsfield on Route 100 lies the sparsely popular municipality of **Fayston**, distinguished by its lovely back roads and its claim to be the town in Vermont with the highest average elevation. Also, just a handful of miles north of Waitsfield, Route 100 splits into Route 100 and Route 100B. On Route 100B is **Moretown**, another village whose history is steeped in logging and agriculture, but which lacks the tourism industry of Warren and Waitsfield. Beyond Moretown, Route 100B leads to **Middlesex**, site of historic **Camp Meade** (see the Mt. Mansfield chapter) and meets I-89 & Route 2, major east-west highways leading to Burlington (west) and Montpelier (east). Meanwhile Route 100 leads to Duxbury, from whence you can make your way to the famous **Camel's Hump Mountain** (see Hiking in the "Sports & Recreation" section below), as well as Waterbury, Stowe, and other points north.

South of Warren, Route 100 is largely undeveloped as it skirts the **Green Mountain National Forest** and heads to the small towns of Granville, Rochester, and on to Killington and Rutland. About 10 miles south of Warren on the west side of the road is the scenic **Moss Glen Falls**.

MAD RIVER VALLEY ANNUAL EVENTS

There are literally hundreds of public events, performances, and festivals held in the Mad River Valley annually. We have listed some of the major ones below. For more information about these events and others, contact the **Sugarbush Area Chamber of Commerce**, *Tel. 802/496-3409, 800/82-VISIT, chamber@madriver.com, or check out their web page at www.sugarbushchamber.org.*

NEW YEAR'S CELEBRATIONS – *Sugarbush sponsors a series of celebratory events to welcome the New Year including parades, fireworks, and numerous parties, performances and other events for adults and children. Other hotels, restaurants and nightclubs also hold special celebrations.*

WINTER CARNIVAL – *First week of February. Warren and Waitsfield go bonkers and put on dozens of winter-related events including ski and snowboarding races, snowshoe races, ice sculpturing, late night skiing and skating, music, dancing, and a whole host of other activities.*

EASTER AT MAD RIVER GLEN – *Festivities include a huge Easter egg hunt, barbeques and other food feasts, music, and other activities.*

BEN & JERRY'S ONE WORLD, ONE HEART FESTIVAL - *Sponsored by Vermont's best loved ice cream makers, this annual late-June festival held at Mount Ellen features dozens of vendors selling food, clothing, and other goodies, as well as music by popular rock and folk acts.*

FOURTH OF JULY – *A colorful and terrific parade is held on Main Street in Warren, and on Brook Street you can visit a myriad of booths and tents where puppet shows and other entertainment are presented. Food, beer, and other goodies can also be enjoyed.*

MAD RIVER MUSIC FESTIVAL – *A feature of the Vermont Festival of the Arts held in late August, this special event includes a variety of local and national acts performing all different types of music.*

VALLEY CRAFT FAIR – *Held on Labor Day Weekend at Kenyon's Variety Store on Route 100 in Waitsfield, this celebration of the arts features exhibits and sales of crafts produced by dozens of Vermont artisans as well as music and food.*

SUGARBUSH BREWERS' FESTIVAL – *The foliage season kicks off in late September with this event held on Lincoln Peak. Brewers from across Vermont and New England all have booths and tents where you can taste all varieties of beer and food, watch demonstrations about the brewing process, and ride chairlifts from which you can enjoy spectacular views of the Mad River Valley.*

NIGHTLIFE & ENTERTAINMENT

Nightlife in the way of drinking and dancing is concentrated at the junction of Route 17 and Route 100, where **Gallagher's** and the **Mad Mountain Tavern** compete for the business of those keen to enjoy some apres-ski social activity. Both are large beer-hall sort of places with jukeboxes, pool tables, and plenty of televisions for sports viewing. Live rock, country, and folk acts are also regularly featured.

The Blue Tooth on the Sugarbush Access Road is another happening night spot. It also features live music, billiards, darts, and serves good food.

Performing Arts

You can begin by calling the **Chamber of Commerce Events Line**, *Tel. 802/496-7907,* which lists major area events and performances and often include performances by major state and national acts, such as the Vermont Symphony Orchestra. Live rock and pop music is most likely to be enjoyed in the bars and taverns mentioned above.

The **Green Mountain Cultural Center** is a local non-profit organization that brings performing artists to the region as well as various visual arts shows. For information, check local flyers and publications; otherwise, call the Chamber of Commerce listed above or Joslyn at the Inn at Round Barn Farm on the East Warren Road in Waitsfield, *Tel. 802/496-7722.*

VERMONT FESTIVAL OF THE ARTS IN THE MAD RIVER VALLEY

In August 1999, the Mad River Valley hosted the first annual **Vermont Festival of the Arts**. *This 10-day celebration of Vermont's and the Valley's creative talent features a deluge of musical performances, exhibits of all types of visual arts, and other activities ranging from food tasting to art classes and demonstrations. To find out more about this festival in coming years, call 802/496-7907 or look up the festival's web site at* **www.vermontartfest.com.**

The **Valley Players** are a local theater goup who perform full productions of major musicals and plays three or four times a year, in addition to several smaller programs including a Christmas Special. For a schedule, check local publications and bulletins or call *802/583-1674.*

Finally for something a bit less traditional, the **Phantom Theater** is a local theater group often joined by professionals from New York. They perform original and less known works for children and adults. Call for performance dates and for information about acting classes and workshops, *Tel. 802/496-5997 (summer); Tracy Martin, Tel. 802/496-6361 (winter).*

SHOPPING

There are more than one hundred stores and shops in the Mad River Valley, virtually all of which are on Route 100, the Sugarbush Access Road, and in the Warren and Waitsfield villages. There are two main shpping centers, the **Village Square Shopping Center** and the **Mad River Green Shopping Center**, which are located opposite each other on Route 100 in Waitsfied just north of the junction with Route 17. We have listed below just a fraction of the antique and handicraft stores that dominate the shopping scene, as well as some that cater to practical needs.

For a more complete listing, contact the **Sugarbush Chamber of Commerce**, *Tel. 802/496-6273 or 800/82-VISIT,* or pick up a copy of the *Mad River Valley Four Season Guide* that is widely available throughout the Mad River Valley.

Antiques, Art Galleries, Crafts & Souvenirs

BARN-IT-ALL ANTIQUES, *Main Street, Warren Village, Warren VT 05674. Tel. 802/496-7007.*

STEP BACK IN THYME ANTIQUES, *Route 100 & Bridge Street, Waitsfield Village, Waitsfield VT 05674. Tel. 802/496-9744. Hours vary according to season, but basically follow 9am-5pm. Credit cards: Visa, Mastercard.*

WARREN VILLAGE POTTERY,*Main Street (across from the covered bridge), Warren Village, Warren VT 05674. Tel. 802/496-4162. Hours: 10am-5pm daily. Credit cards: Visa, Mastercard.*

Specializes in ceramic pots, bowls, vases, and all types of containers and cookware; some functional, some decorative.

WARREN AND MORE STORE, *Main Street (across from the Pitcher Inn), Warren Village, Warren VT 05674. Tel. 802/496-3864. Hours: Monday-Saturday 8am-7pm, Sunday 8am-6pm. Credit cards: Visa, Mastercard.*

An old-fashioned country store, the Warren and More Store sells deli and Vermont specialty products, wine, baked goods and other foods on the bottom floor, and clothing and knick-knacks on the second floor of an old stage-coach inn. Well worth a visit if only just to look.

PARADE GALLERY, *Main Street (opposite the Pitcher Inn), Warren Village, Warren VT 05674. Tel. 802/496-5445. Open usually from 9am-5pm on business days. Credit cards: Visa, Mastercard, American Express.*

Features a wide variety of paintings, photos, sculptures, and other arts produced by local artisans, including Sabra Field.

THE STORE, *Route 100, Waitsfield VT 05673. Tel. 802/496-4465. Web site: www.vermontstore.com. Hours 10am-6pm daily. Credit cards: major credit cards accepted.*

Situated in a former Methodist meeting house dating to the 1830's, this voluminous store sells a variety of goods from Vermont specialty foods to antiques and souvenirs.

Food & Provisions

MEHURON'S SUPERMARKET, *Village Square Shopping Center on Route 100 (north of the Junction with Route 17), Waitsfield VT 05673. Tel. 802/496-3700. Hours: Monday-Saturday 8am-8pm, Sunday 8am-6pm. Credit cards: Visa, Mastercard.*

A fairly comprehensive supermarket selling basic food provisions such as meats, baked goods, vegetables, and beverages, as well as Vermont specialties like maple syrup and cheeses.

WARREN AND MORE STORE – see above.

GRAND UNION, *Mad River Green Shopping Center on Route 100 (just north of the Junction with Route 17), Waitsfield VT 05673. Open 8am-9pm daily. Major credit cards accepted.*

The region's dominant supermarket chain, Grand Union is your typical supermarket selling fresh produce, meats, deli and baked items, frozen foods, and beer and wine.

During the summer and fall a **farmer's market** where local farmers sell fresh produce is also held in the Green Mountain Shopping Center. Check local publications for the schedule.

SWEET PEA NATURAL FOODS, *Village Square Shopping Center on Route 100 (north of the junction with Route 17), Waitsfield VT 05673. Tel. 802/496-7763. Open Monday-Saturday 8:30am-6pm, Sunday 11:30am-5pm. Credit cards: Visa, Mastercard.*

Specializes in organic produce and health foods and body-care products.

Sporting Goods

Look under specific sporting activities in the "Sports & Recreation" section below for more specific listings.

KENYON'S VARIETY STORE, *Route 100 (north of the Village), Waitsfield VT 05673.*

A sort of country store with an outdoorsy bent; the place to come for snowmobile passes, and hunting and fishing licenses. Also a variety of equipment and apparel for winter (snowshoeing, sledding, ice skating, etc.) and summer (some fishing equipment, shoes) sports.

CLEARWATER SPORTS, *Route 100, Waitsfield VT 05673. (Located in Waitsfield Village). Tel. 802/496-3343. Major credit cards accepted.*

Probably the best sports store in the Mad River Valley, Clearwater Sports can outfit you with everything from a kayak or a canoe to sleds and ice skates.

MAD RIVER SNOWBOARDS, *Junction of Route 100 and Route 17, Waitsfield VT 05673. Tel. 802/496-9996. Major credit cards accepted.*

Specializes in Snowboard sales and rentals, as well as winter sporting apparel.

SPORTS & RECREATION

Biking

There are numerous opportunities for cyclists of all levels in the Mad River Valley. The various local roads off Route 100 are one place (or rather many places) to start from. For example, from Waitsfield Village you can pass through the covered bridge and continue on the East Warren Road as far as you like before turning back to Route 100 on the Airport Road or the Brook Road. Or you can bear left on the Joslyn Hill Road after the bridge and then turn north (left) on the North Road, which will lead you right back to Route 100. For those interested in a more difficult route, you can make the loop beginning on the center Fayston Road and continue on the Vasseur and Bragg Hill roads. Also, the Sugarbush Access Road and the German Flats Road are quite challenging.

For guided tours or simply advice about biking in the area, contact the **Sugarbush Mountain Biking & Technica Hiking Center** *by Lincoln Peak at the end of the Sugarbush Access Road, Tel. 802/583-6572.* This center also rents equipment, gives lessons, and operates hiking tours. Listed below are other outfits that rent bikes and will be happy to provide information about local cycling opportunities:

MAD RIVER CYCLERY, *Junction of Routes 17 and Route 100, Waitsfield VT 05673. Tel. 802/496-9996. Major credit cards accepted.*

CLEARWATER SPORTS, *Route 100, Waitsfield VT 05673. (Located in Waitsfield Village). Tel. 802/496-3343. Major credit cards accepted.*

Canoeing & Kayaking

The Mad River and the Winooski River are canoeable (and kayakable) in April and May, and if there's been a big, late snowmelt or lots of rain, in June as well. Contact the outfits listed below for rentals, tours, and information about how and where to go about riding the white water.

MAD RIVER CANOE, *Mad River Green, Route 100, Waitsfield VT 05673. (Located just west of the junction of Route 100 and Route 17) Tel. 802/496-3127. Hours: Monday-Friday 10am-4pm. Major credit cards accepted.*

Mad River Canoe is one of the premier manufacturers of high quality canoes in the world and concentrates primarily on manufacturing, wholesale and retail sales.

CLEARWATER SPORTS, *Route 100, Waitsfield VT 05673. (Located in Waitsfield Village). Tel. 802/496-3343. Major credit cards accepted.*

Clearwater Sports offers a variety of boating services, including canoe and kayak rentals, guided day trips, and a kayaking camp for children ages 7-16.

Fishing

Fishermen can try their luck both in the **Mad River** which flows right through both Warren and Waitsfield, or you can make a bit of a journey up Route 2 or I-89 to **Lake Champlain**, where there are unlimited fishing opportunities from Ferrisburg in the south all the way to the Canadian border.

Licenses can be purchased at **Kenyons' Variety Store** *on Route 100 in Waitsfield*, Tel. *802/496-3922*; **Kingbury's Store** *on Route 100, Warren*; and the **Moretown General Store** *on Route 100B, Moretown.*

Fly Fish Vermont *on Route 100 in Waitsfield* features a wide selection of equipment and offers lessons and tours.

Gliding

SUGARBUSH SOARING, *Warren-Sugarbush Airport on Airport Road (P.O. Box 123), Warren VT 05674. (Take the Airport Road from Route 100 between Warren and Waitsfield, or take Brook Road from Main Street in Warren Village). Tel. 802/496-2290, 800/881-7627. Major credit cards accepted.*

It may set you back a few smackers ($75-$125 approximately) but the experience and memory of soaring through the Mad River Valley, particularly during the foliage season, is special. Glider planes seat two passengers (300 pound weight maximum for two people) and a pilot. Twenty and thirty minute rides are available as are instruction for singles that will allow you to actually fly the glider.

Golf

SUGARBUSH GOLF COURSE, *Golf Course Road, Warren. Tel. 802/ 583-6725, Tel. 800/53-SUGAR.*

This beautiful 18-hole course designed by famed golf course architect, Robert Trent Jones, Senior, is one of the finest in Vermont, not in the least because of its spectacular setting. Facilities in addition to the course include a practice range, putting greens, and a cafe on the clubhouse deck. The **Mountain Golf School** offers an assortment of clinics including 2 day, 3 day, and weekend programs.

Gyms, Spas, and Fitness Centers
   BRIDGE FAMILY RESORT AND TENNIS CLUB, *Sugarbush Access Road, Warren. Tel. 802/583-2922, Tel. 800/453-2922. E-mail: bridges@madriver.com. Web site: bridgesresort.com.*
   SUGARBUSH HEALTH & RACQUET CLUB, *Sugarbush Village, Warren. Tel. 802/583-6700.*
   Facilities include a climbing "rock gym," a well-endowed fitness center, 24 tennis and squash courts, indoor and outdoor pools, and of course a few hot tubs and saunas. Tennis and swimming lessons for children and adults are offered.

Hiking
   Those interested in exploring the beautiful terrain in and around the Mad River Valley have numerous options ranging from mountain hikes on the famed Long Trail and the Camel's Hump, Vermont's third tallest peak, to easy strolls along trails in the woods of Route 100 near Warren and Waitsfield. Whatever your interest in hiking, we'd recommend studying your options before setting out. The **Green Mountain Club**, based in Waterbury, publishes dozens of books concerning hiking in Vermont, including *A Hiker's Guide to Vermont* and *Guide Book of the Long Trail*, both of which contain information relating to hiking in the Mad River Valley and surrounding areas.
   For guided hikes, contact the **Sugarbush Mountain Biking & Technical Hiking Center** by Lincoln Peak at the end of the Sugarbush Access Road, *Tel. 802/583-6572*. Finally, information about trail conditions is often posted at the **Temptest Book Store** on Route 100 in Waitsfield, and the **Mad River Recreation Path Association**, a local organization dedicated to preserving and maintaining trails in the Mad River Valley. Call them for information about local trails in the woods and wilderness around Warren and Waitsfield.
   The **Long Trail**, which stretches the length of the state and is Vermont's most famous trail, skirts the Mad River Valley to which it is linked by the Lincoln Gap Road (connected to Route 100 opposite Warren). From the junction of the Long Trail and the Lincoln Gap Road, you can either take the trail north 2.5 miles up to **Mount Abraham** (elevation 4,050 feet), or you can hike the Long Trail South to the **Sunset Rock** (elevation 2,420 feet) – an easy half hour walk ideal for family outings and picnics. You can also reach the Long Trail by taking Route 17 past the Mad River Glen Ski Area to the Appalachian Gap. From there it is a bit more than a three mile hike to **General Stark Mountain** (elevation 3,660 feet). There are several shelters for camping along this trail.
   Another famous mountain hike is up Vermont's third highest peak (elevation 4,803 feet), the **Camel's Hump**, famous for the fantastic views

of the Green Mountains from its summit. To reach the trail, take Route 100 north ten miles to Duxbury, turn left on River Road, and follow the signs.

An alternative to hiking in the mountains is simply to stroll along the country roads off Route 100, many of which offer great views of the area's farms and pastoral countryside; or to hike trails and paths off of those roads. For example, the River Road along the Mad River between Waitsfield Village and Moretown to the north is an easy, relaxing, and scenic hike. Pick up a copy of the *Mad River Valley Four Seasons Guide* for specific directions and more ideas about local hikes.

Horseback Riding

DANA HILL STABLE, *Route 17, Fayston VT 05675. Tel. 802/496-6251. Credit cards: Visa, Mastercard.*

VERMONT ICELANDIC HORSE FARM, *Waitsfield Common, Waitsfield VT 05674. Tel. 802/496-7141.*

MAD RIVER STABLES, *Route 100B between Moretown and Middleseax. Tel. 802/223-2359.*

NAVAJO FARM, *Moretown VT. (North of Waitsfield on Route 100B). Tel. 802/496-3656.*

Ice Skating

You can ice skate at the **Skatium** next to the Grand Union in Waitsfield and rent ice skates at the **Inverness Ski Shop**, *Tel. 802/496-3343*, and at **Clearwater Sports**, *Tel. 802/496-2708*, both of which are on Route 100 in Waitsfield.

Skiing & Snowboarding

SUGARBUSH, *RR1 Box 350, Waitsfield VT 05673. (Located at the end of the Sugarbush Access Road off Route 100 between Warren and Waitsfield). Tel. 802/583-2381. Web site: www.sugarbush.com. Rates: $45-$55 (less for multi-day passes, children, and seniors). Major credit cards accepted.*

One of the giants of Vermont skiing, Sugarbush features more than 100 trails on 430 acres serviced by 18 lifts, including four gondolas. Most trails are on Lincoln Peak, recently connected by gondola to Mount Ellen, which you can also reach by driving several miles north. Skis, boots, poles, and snowboards can be rented at the base lodges at Sugarbush at **Crisports** *(open 8:30am-5pm weekdays, 8am-5pm weekends; Tel. 802/583-6516)* which has outlets both at Lincoln Peak and Mount Ellen. You can also join group lessons at all levels or arrange private lessons. There are also organized activities and a ski school for children of all ages. Call the number above for more information.

MAD RIVER GLEN, *P.O. Box 1089, Route 17, Waitsfield VT 05674. Tel. 802/496-3551. E-mail: ski@madriver.com. Web site: www.madriverglen.com. Rates: $35-$45 (less for multi-day passes, children and youth, and seniors). Major credit cards accepted.*

The only ski area owned and managed by a cooperative (and the only ski area in Vermont to turn a profit in 1997-98), Mad River Glen is renowned for its challenging slopes. Of course there are also easy and only modestly difficult slopes and lessons are available for skiers of all levels. However, snowboarding is prohibited here. Mad River Glen is also considerably smaller than Sugarbush, with 44 runs accessed by four chair lifts.

Ski & Snowboard Rentals

CRISPORTS SERVICE CENTER, *Sugarbush base lodge, Sugarbush Ski Area at the end of the Sugarbush Access Road, Waitsfield VT 05673. Tel. 802/583-6516. Major credit cards accepted. Open 8:30am-5pm weekdays, 8am-5pm weekends & holidays.*

CLEARWATER SPORTS, *Route 100, Waitsfield VT 05673. (Located in Waitsfield Village). Tel. 802/496-3343. Major credit cards accepted.*

INVERNESS SKI SHOP, *Route 100, Waitsfield VT 05674. Tel. 802/496-3343. Major credit cards accepted.*

MAD RIVER SNOWBOARDS, *Junction of Route 100 and Route 17, Waitsfield VT 05673. Tel. 802/496-9996. Major credit cards accepted.*

NORTH VERMONT SKI SHOPS, *Sugarbush Access Road, Warren VT 05673. Tel. 802/583-2511. Major credit cards accepted.*

ALPINE OPTIONS, *Sugarbush Access Road, Warren VT 05673. Tel. 802/583-1763, Tel. 888/888-9131. Major credit cards accepted.*

Sled Rentals

CLEARWATER SPORTS, *Route 100, Waitsfield VT 05673. (Located in Waitsfield Village). Tel. 802/496-3343. Major credit cards accepted.*

MAD RIVER SNOWBOARDS, *Junction of Route 100 and Route 17, Waitsfield VT 05673. Tel. 802/496-9996. Major credit cards accepted.*

CRISPORTS SERVICE CENTER,*Sugarbush base lodge, Sugarbush Ski Area at the end of the Sugarbush Access Road, Waitsfield VT 05673. Tel. 802/583-6516. Major credit cards accepted. Open 8:30am-5pm weekdays, 8am-5pm weekends & holidays.*

Sleigh and Horse Cart Rides

MOUNTAIN VALLEY FARM, *Common Road, Waitsfield VT 05673. Tel. 802/496-9255. Credit cards: Visa, Mastercard.*

The Mountain Valley Farm offers you the opportunity to ride about in a sleigh during the winter or in a covered wagon, formal carriage, or hay cart during the summer and autumn – a great photo op and lots of fun for kids.

Snowmobiling
Before hitting the trails you should contact Kenyon's Store on Route 100 in Waitsfield (see above under "Shopping"), for information regarding rentals and tours, and to purchase a club membership in the Mad River Ridge Runners, *Tel. 802/496-3922,* and pay your Trail Maintenance Assessment fee; both are prerequisites for anybody interested in snowmobiling in Vermont. For comprehensive information about tours, lessons, rentals, and all information regarding snowmobiling, contact **V.A.S.T.**, *P.O. Box 839, Montpelier VT 05601, Tel. 802/229-0005.*

Snowshoe Rentals & Tours
CLEARWATER SPORTS, *Route 100, Waitsfield VT 05673. (Located in Waitsfield Village). Tel. 802/496-3343. Major credit cards accepted.*

In addition to renting snowshoes, Clearwater also offers guided day tours – a good way to experience the Mad River Valley's beautiful terrain.

NORTH VERMONT SKI SHOPS, *Sugarbush Access Road, Warren VT 05673. Tel. 802/583-2511. Major credit cards accepted.*

INVERNESS SKI SHOP, *Route 100, Waitsfield VT 05674. Tel. 802/496-3343. Major credit cards accepted.*

Tennis
THE BRIDGE FAMILY RESORT AND TENNIS CLUB, *Sugarbush Access Road, Warren. Tel. 802/583-2922, Tel. 800/453-2922. E-mail: bridges@madriver.com. Web site: www.bridgeresort.com.*

Resort facilities include ten Har-Tru courts (two indoors) and several all-weather courts, in addition to pools, spas, weights, etc. But getting back to the tennis: private and group clinics are offered all year, and professional tournaments and exhibitions, including some USTA events, are held throughout the year here. Call for details.

SUGARBUSH HEALTH AND RACQUET CLUB, *Sugarbush Resort, Sugarbush Village. Tel. 802/583-6700.*

The resort features more than 20 courts, most of which are Har-Tru and clay, and offers lessons and clinics for youth and adults.

EXCURSIONS & DAY TRIPS
With its location in the middle of the state, the Mad River Valley is within reach of many of Vermont's other natural, historic, and cultural attractions. Vermont's largest city, **Burlington**, and **Lake Champlain** are about an hour away via Route 100 north and I-89 (north). With its recently

restored downtown and the pedestrian mall known as the **Church Street Marketplace**, Burlington boasts Vermont's most active cultural scene, extensive shopping, and an urban flavor not found in the rest of the state. It is also on Lake Champlain, offering innumerable opportunities for boating and fishing during the summer. The islands (**Isle La Motte**, **North Hero**, and **South Hero**) can all be reached by taking Route 2, and feature some of Vermont's most beautiful wilderness. Along the shores of the lake, both on the mainland and the islands, are a number of state parks that during the summer are accessible for hiking, biking, fishing, and camping.

Just south of Burlington on Route 7 is **Shelburne**, home to some of Vermont's most popular tourist destinations, including the **Shelburne Museum**, featuring extensive exhibits about life in 19th century America; **Shelburne Farms**, a huge Victorian-era estate turned inn where you can take horse cart tours and watch cheese being made; and the **Vermont Teddy Bear Company**, manufacturer of customized teddy bears that make great gifts for children and adults alike. See the "Burlington & Champlain Valley" chapter for details.

Vermont's capital, **Montpelier**, is about a half an hour away by taking Route 100 and Route 100B north, and then Route 2 or I-89 southeast. Not as large or busy as Burlington, Montpelier is an attractive little town featuring dozens of historic buildings, the most important of which is the **Vermont Capital Building**, a modest but elegant granite structure topped with a gold dome. The capital is open to the public and contains a number of interesting paintings and historical exhibits. Just beyond Montpelier on Route 2 and/or I-89 is **Barre**, home of the **Rock of Ages Quarry**, the largest granite quarry in the world. An amazing site, it is open for public viewing, while nearby at the Rock of Ages Manufacturing Division you can watch as craftsmen chisel and saw granite products from headstones to statues. See the "Montpelier & Central Vermont" chapter for more info.

Finally, and closest to home, **Waterbury** is roughly 15 miles and **Stowe** about 20 twenty miles north and offer more skiing, tons of restaurants and lodging establishments, as well as unique attractions such as the **Ben & Jerry's Ice Cream Factory** where you can watch the ice cream-making process and sample the product. Of course, tacky souvenirs are also for sale. Up Route 100B in Middlesex is **Camp Meade**, a former military camp turned museum dedicated to the 1930's and '40's, the Great Depression and World War II. The camp also includes cabins where visitors can stay for about $45 a night. See the "Stowe & Mt. Mansfield Region" chapter for more information.

PRACTICAL INFORMATION

Auto Services

FISHER AUTO PARTS, *Fiddlers' Green, Waitsfield. Tel. 802/496-3188. Hours: 7:30am-5:30 pm Monday-Friday; 8am-2pm Sunday. Credit cards: major credit cards accepted.*

HAP'S SERVICE STATION, *Route 100, Waitsfield. Tel. 802/496-3948. Hours: 8am-6pm Monday-Saturday. Credit cards: major credit cards accepted.*

Hap's is AAA-affiliated, offers 24 hour road service, and rents cars.

SUGARBUSH, *Route 100 200 yards south of Sugarbush Access Road. Tel. 802/496-3977. Hours: 7:30am-5:30pm. Credit cards: major credit cards accepted.*

Banks & ATM's

There are ATM's in the villages of Warren and Waitsfield, as well as at the base lodge of the ski areas and in the Grand Union supermarket in the Mad River Green Shopping Center on Route 100 in Waitsfield (north of the junction with Route 17).

NORTHFIELD SAVINGS BANK, *Mad River Green Shopping Center on Route 100 (north of the junction with Route 17), Waitsfield VT 05673. Tel. 802/496-9700. Hours: 9am-5pm Monday through Friday & 9am-2pm Saturdays.*

NSB offers banking services and features an ATM.

CHITTENDEN BANK, *Mad River Green Shopping Center on Route 100 (north of the junction with Route 17), Waitsfield VT 05673. Tel. 802/496-2585. Hours: 9am-5pm Monday through Friday & 9am-2pm Saturdays.*

Full service bank with public ATM's.

Business Services

EASTERN SYSTEMS GROUP, *7 Irasville Common on Route 100, Waitsfield. Tel. 802/496-1000, Fax 802/496-6222. E-mail: hello@easternsys.com. Credit cards: major credit cards accepted.*

Offers copying, fax, and printing, as well as computer rentals, secretarial, accounting, and other office services.

Chamber of Commerce

SUGARBUSH AREA CHAMBER OF COMMERCE, *Tel. 802/496-3409, Tel. 800/82-VISIT. E-mail: chamber@madriver.com. Web site: www.sugarbushchamber.org.*

Medical Emergencies

Ambulance – *Tel. 802/496-3600*

Pharmacies

THE DRUG STORE, *located in the Village Square Shopping Center on Route 100 (north of the junction with Route 17), Waitsfield VT 05673. Tel. 802/ 496-23345. Hours: 8:30am-6pm. Major credit cards accepted.*

Post Office

WAITSFIELD POST OFFICE, *located in the Mad River Green Shopping Center on Route 100 Waitsfield (just north of the junction with Route 17), Waitsfield VT 05673. Tel. 802/496-2391. Hours: 8:30-5pm Monday through Friday, 9am-noon Saturday. Closed on federal and state holidays.*

19. STOWE & MT. MANSFIELD

> *See the map on page 277 for destinations in this chapter.*

To many, **Stowe** is synonymous with Vermont. For skiers, between **Stowe Mountain Resort** and **Smugglers' Notch**, the area offers more than 100 runs and 500 acres of world class skiing on Vermont's highest peak, **Mt. Mansfield**, as well as unlimited opportunities for cyclists, hikers, showshoers, cross-country skiers, or virtually anybody else who enjoys sports and recreation in a beautiful natural setting. Combine that with a picturesque village, complete with steepled churches and a classic village green; classic inns and resorts like the Trapp Family Lodge; and the Ben & Jerry's headquarters in nearby Waterbury, and you could argue – though certainly against the objections of a few locals – that few destinations in Vermont offer a more complete version of the "Vermont Experience."

But one of the beauties of Vermont, and Stowe is certainly no exception, is that even when you're in a major tourist hub, you only have to jump in your car or even your bike, and within minutes you can sample the true Vermont of working dairy farms and country stores.

ARRIVALS & DEPARTURES

By Air

The closest major commercial airport to the Mt. Mansfield area is **Burlington International Airport** *on Airport Drive (off Route 2) in Burlington.* Usually not more than a half-hour by automobile, it is serviced by Continental, *Tel. 800/525-0289*, United, *Tel. 800/241-6522*, USAir, *Tel. 800/428-4322*, and the commuter airlines, Business Express, *Tel. 800/345-3400*, and Comair, *Tel. 800/927-0927*.

Sometimes it is cheaper to fly into large hub airports such as Montreal (a bit more than two hours away by car), Manchester, NH (three hours by car), or Boston's Logan Airport (3.5 hours by car).

Rental cars are available at all of these airports, and the Manchester airport is also directly serviced by the Vermont Transit Lines bus company which stops in Waterbury. You'll have to switch buses in White River Junction, or you can take one of the more frequent buses to Montpelier or Burlington and from there you can take a taxi to the Mt. Mansfield region.

By Car
Automobile is defintely the easiest way to reach the Mt. Mansfield area. To reach the area, you simply need to take **Route 100** to Exit 10 at Waterbury, or Exit 9 to reach Middlesex. From Waterbury it's a straight shot north on **Route 100** to Waterbury Center (4 miles), Stowe (10 miles) and up to Morristown. Many of the resorts are on Route 100, also known as the **Mountain Road**, which leads to the Mt. Mansfield Ski Area and Smugglers' Notch.

During the winter, the road at Smugglers' Notch is closed, in which case you should take Route 15 to Route 108 south at Jeffersonsville if you are coming from Burlington. If you are traveling from the south or west, take Route 100 from I-89, Exit 10 at Waterbury, north through Stowe to Morrisville where it connects with Route 15 east, which you need to take to Jeffersonville; from there it's just about ten miles on Route 108 south to Smugglers' Notch.

In Waterbury, cars can be rented at **Thrifty** by the Amtrak depot at *1 Demeritt Place off Route 100, Tel. 802/244-8800.* **Avis**, *Tel. 800/331-1212,* **Budget**, *Tel. 800/244-9429,* and **Hertz**, *Tel. 800/654-3131,* all operate out of Burlington International Airport. Avis also has an office in Rutland, *Tel. 802/773-1317.* **Enterprise Rent-A-Car** has outlets in Rutland, *Tel. 802/773-0855,* Barre, *Tel. 802/479-5400,* and South Burlington, *Tel. 802/863-2111.*

By Bus
Vermont Transit Lines, *Tel. 802/864-6811,* provides direct service to **Waterbury**, stopping at Depot Beverage, *Tel. 800/552-8737.* There is one bus daily departing at 2:25pm to Burlington, St. Albans, Swanton, the US-Canadian border, St. Jean (Quebec), and Montreal.

The southbound bus (coming from Montreal and Burlington) departs at 8:50am for Montpelier, Randolph Center, White River Junction (with connections to Rutland, the Northeast Kingdom, Portland ME, and Brattleboro), Hanover NH, New London NH, Concord NH, Manchester NH, Nashua NH, Lowell MA, and Boston MA. The 4:15 bus from Boston (which passes through the just mentioned towns) drops off passengers but does not pick up riders. The same goes for the 6pm coach from Boston, which only stops at Nashua, Hanover, White River Junction, and Montpelier en route.

A one-way adult fare to Boston is approximately $32, with tickets to destinations in between costing less depending on how close they are to Waterbury. For destinations beyond Boston, such as New York and Philadelphia, connections can be made in White River Junction and Boston. Call for details. Finally, taxis can take you from the bus depot to your hotel or inn – see "Getting Around" below for details.

By Train

Amtrak's **Vermonter** stops in **Waterbury** *(depot at Demeritt Place by Foster's Chevrolet of Route 100)* at 7:52pm on its way to Burlington-Essex (8:35pm), St. Alban's (9:20pm), and Montreal, Quebec (10:55pm). The Vermonter departs Waterbury at 8:28am on its way to Montpelier-Barre, Randolph, White River Junction, Windsor-Ascutney, Claremont NH, Bellows Falls, Brattleboro, Amherst MA, Springfield MA, Hartford CT, Berlin CT, New Haven CT, Bridgeport CT, Stamford CT, New York Penn Station (6pm), Newark NJ, Metropark NJ, Trenton NJ, Philadelphia PA (7:47pm), Wilmington DE (9pm), BWI Airport MD (9:13pm), New Carrollton MD, & Washington, DC (9:45).

Trains depart for Waterbury from Washington, DC (7:40am), Baltimore (8:06am), Philadelphia (9:48am), New York City (11:30am) and other cities mentioned above. There is no ticket office at the Waterbury Depot, so you must call in advance to get a reservation and confirmation number, and the conductor will issue a ticket. A one-way fare to New York is approximately $65, $90 to Washington DC.

A second option is Amtrak's **Ethan Allen Express**, departing Washington, DC at 3am daily (#299), and at 10:40am Monday-Thursday (#291), and 1:05pm Friday-Saturday (#293), it stops at Baltimore, Wilimington DE, Philadelphia, and New York City (arriving at 6:38am. 2:15pm & 4:19pm respectively) where you must catch a connecting train with the same number. Train #299 departs Penn Station at 7:10am, Train #291 at 3:55pm, and Train # 293 at 5:40pm en route to Yonkers, Croton-Harmon, Poughkeepsie, Rhinecliff-Kinston, Hudson, and Albany. Again you must transfer or board trains with the same number departing at 9:55am, 6:40pm, and 8:20pm respectively and **arriving in Rutland** at 12:30pm, 9:05pm, and 10:45pm. Trains depart Rutland in the other direction at 1:25pm and 5:25pm (on Sundays only). A one-way fare from Rutland to New York City is approximately $55.

The **James Jeffords Railroad Station** is located next to the transportation center behind the Walmart in downtown Rutand. There are virtually no facilities.

Call 800/USA-RAIL for schedules, fare information, and reservations.

ORIENTATION

The main artery for the Mt. Mansfield area is **Route 100** that leads north through Waterbury, Waterbury Center, Stowe Village (ten miles from Exit 10), and on to Morrisville and other points north. At Stowe Village, **Route 108** – also known as **Mountain Road** – branches northwest to the Mt. Mansfield Ski Area and Smugglers' Notch. This road is lined with most of Stowe's major resorts, hotels, restaurants and shops; hugging it for much of the way is the **Recreation Path**, a popular route for hikers and cyclists in the summer and cross-country skiers and snowshoers in the winter.

As mentioned above, Route 108 between the Mount Mansfield ski area and Smugglers' Notch closes for the winter (usually in mid-to-late November), forcing those looking for Smugglers' Notch to continue on Route 100 to Morrisville, where Route 15 west leads to Route 108 south at Jeffersonville. This detour may add an extra 20 or 30 minutes of driving time, but the scenery is very pleasant. If you are traveling from the Burlington area, take Route 15 east from Burlington to Jeffersonville and then 108 south.

GETTING AROUND

Stowe Village itself is small enough to get around by walking. Throughout the day the **Inter-Mountain Bus Service** runs a route from the base lodges and ski areas to Stowe by way of the Mountain Road (Route 108). It departs from the mountain every 20 minutes from 8am to about 10pm, except between the hours of 10:30am to 2:30 pm, and from 5:30pm to 10 pm, when it departs every hour.

If you are without a car, consider renting one or calling a taxi. Listed below are car rentals and taxi and limousine companies:

In Waterbury, cars can be rented at **Thrifty** by the Amtrak depot at *1 Demeritt Place off Route 100, Tel. 802/244-8800.* In nearby transportation hubs, **Avis**, *Tel. 800/331-1212*, **Budget**, *Tel. 800/244-9429*, and **Hertz**, *Tel. 800/654-3131,* all operate out of Burlington International Airport. Avis also has an office in Rutland, *Tel. 802/773-1317.* **Enterprise Rent-A-Car** has outlets in Rutland, *Tel. 802/773-0855*, Barre, *Tel. 802/479-5400*, and South Burlington, *Tel. 802/863-2111.*

THRIFTY CAR RENTAL, *Route 100, Waterbury. Tel. 802/244-8800. Website and E-mail: www.thrifty.com/vermont. Major credit cards accepted.*

Thrifty offers a wide variety of cars and rental packages. With locations throughout Vermont and the United States, as well as Amtrak and corporate rates, it's quite convenient.

PEG'S PICK UP, *Tel. 802/253-9490, 800/370-9490, Tel. 800/293-PEGS. Major credit cards accepted.*

Peg's offers limousine and taxi service within the Stowe area and to Burlington, as well as further destinations such as Boston, Montreal and other points in Vermont.

RICHARD'S LIMOUSINE SERVICE LTD, *Morrissvile. Tel. 802/888-3176, 800/698-3176. Major credit cards accepted.*

Richard's provides bus/limo/van service to Burlington International Airport and other regional destinations; also rents limos and luxury sedans for weddings or other occasions.

WHERE TO STAY
Stowe & Waterbury

TOPNOTCH AT STOWE RESORT & SPA, *4000 Mountain Road (Route 108), Stowe VT 05672. Tel. 802/253-8585, 800/451-8686, Fax 802/253-9263. E-mail: topnotch@sover.net. Web site: www.topnotch-resort.com. Rates: $75 per person per night & up. Major credit cards accepted.*

Situated on a 120-acre property overlooking Mt. Mansfield, this highly acclaimed modernist (many ceiling-to-floor glass walls) resort lives up to its name as it features the most impressive facilities and amenities in Stowe, if not all of Vermont. Guests have a choice between staying in one of the 92 individually and lavishly appointed rooms and suites, or one of the 15 fully equipped townhouse condos with fireplaces, kitchens, balconies, and other amenities.

The most impressive aspects of Topnotch, however, are the recreational facilities: indoor and outdoor tennis courts, on-site cross-country skiing, an acclaimed spa and fitness center, two swimming pools, mountain bike rentals, and horseback riding. There's a beauty shop, a gift shop, a bar, fine dining at the highly regarded restaurant Maxwell's, and movies on the big screen four times a week. Finally, if nothing else, the lobby with its freestanding stone fireplace and gothic-like ceiling is worth a visit. Call for package deals with discounts for rooms, the spa, skiing, golf, and tennis.

Selected as one of my *Best Places to Stay* – see Chapter 9 for more details.

TRAPP FAMILY LODGE, *700 Trapp Hill Road, Stowe, VT 05672. Tel. 802/253-8511, 800/826-7000. Fax. 802/253-5740. E-mail: info@trappfamily.com. Web site: www.trappfamily.com. Rates: $100-$250. Major credit cards.com.*

"A mountain resort in the European tradition" founded and owned by the Trapp family, whose story inspired the smash musical and movie

The Sound of Music. The Trapp Family Lodge is a 2,500 acre resort with a myriad of facilities and a hillside setting overlooking the Little River Valley that is nothing less than breathtaking. Lodging options include a variety of rooms and suites, ranging in price (not including holiday rates or special packages) from $98 to $650 in one of two main lodge buildings. Though the original lodge burned down in the early 1980's, the new lodges have recaptured much of the Austrian mystique. Rooms combine modern amenities with old world standards of decor and comfort. There are also condos available on a time-share basis.

Facilities include a full service cross-country ski center with more than 100 kilometers of groomed trails, three pools indoor and out, a fitness center, sleigh riding, miles and miles of hiking and biking trails, and lots of planned activities, ranging from Vermont Mozart Society outdoor concerts to volleyball and tennis tournaments. There are also three restaurants: an Austrian tea house serving breakfast and lunch; the main semi-formal dining room serving fine continental cuisine with a German twist; and a handsome lounge serving refreshments and upscale bar food. Various meal plans are available; call or talk to your travel agent about special packages with cheaper rates than the rack rates listed above. Even if you do not stay at the Trapp Family Lodge, it is well worth a visit.

Selected as one of my *Best Places to Stay* – see Chapter 9 for more details.

STOWE MOUNTAIN RESORT, *5781 Mountain Road (Route 108), Stowe VT 05672. Tel. 802/253-3000, 800/253-4754, Fax 802/253-3659. Rates: $100 & up. Major credit cards accepted.*

The Stowe Mountain Resort is a massive complex at the base of Mt. Mansfield (it is the closest lodging to the ski area) that includes the **Inn at the Mountain**, the **Townhouse and Lodge Condominiums** (with one, two, or three bedrooms), and an assortment of recreational facilities like the cross-country ski center, a full fledged fitness center, and a handful of eateries.

The Inn and Condominiums lack the vintage Yankee atmosphere that characterizes many of the region's inns and hotels, but they are more than comfortable and well equipped with modern amenities; plus, staying at Stowe Mountain Resort offers proximity to the Spruce and Mt. Mansfield ski areas, as well as access and discounts at the fitness center and golf course not available at other establishments. The Inn, which is more cozy and intimate, features 34 rooms with in-room phones, cable television, balconies, refrigerators, and air-conditioning. Condominiums all feature fireplaces, cable television, balconies, and kitchens. Call about special packages with discounts for rooms, and ski passes in the winter or tennis and golf rates in the summer and autumn.

SMUGGLERS' NOTCH RESORT, *Route 108 South, Smuggler's Notch VT 05672. Tel. 802/664-8851, 800/451-8752, Fax 802/644-1230. E-mail: smuggs@smuggs.com. Web site: www.smuggs.com. Rates: $50 per person per night & up. Major credit cards accepted.*

Smugglers' Notch Resort is a self-contained slope-side resort village that offers a variety of accommodation options from hotel rooms to three-room condos. An array of recreational opportunities is available, including skiing, snowboarding, and cross-country skiing in the winter and golf, tennis, and swimming in one of 11 ponds and pools (with four water slides). Spas, saunas, tennis, shopping, live entertainment, guided canoe and fishing tours, and supervised activities for children are all available. Great for family recreation, but lacks the charm and atmosphere of the old villages and inns.

STOWEFLAKE MOUNTAIN RESORT & SPA, *1746 Mountain Road (Route 108), Stowe VT 05672. Tel. 802/253-7355, 800/253-2234, Fax 802/253-6858. E-mail: stoweflk@sover.net. Web site: www.stoweflake.com. Rates: $60 per person per night & up. Major credit cards accepted.*

A modern resort on a slightly smaller scale than the Topnotch's of the world, Stoweflake does a good job of combining recreated Yankee charm with modern comforts and amenities. Guests have a choice between a large variety of rooms, suites and condos. Most units are one of four types (distinguished by room size, views, and other factors). "Resort" hotel rooms featuring fireplaces, mountain views of varying quality, satellite television, mini-bars, and tasteful though not opulent decorations and furnishings. Ideal for honeymooners and others willing to splurge are the "Deluxe Suites," all of which include jacuzzis, large bedrooms, sitting rooms, fireplaces, balconies, and good views. On the condo front, "Townhouses" are available in one, two, or three bedroom units, all with kitchens, living rooms, fireplaces, bathrooms, and decks. Finally, for larger groups, there is the "Baraw Family Ski House," a full-scale mountain mansion with four bedrooms, four bathrooms, a kitchen, and several comfortable sitting areas.

On-site recreational facilities include a deluxe fitness center with a weight room, squash and racquetball courts, saunas and steamrooms, indoor pool, and a spa where you can indulge in all sorts of facials, massages, and other body pampering. Dining options include the formal and elegant Winfield's, where you can enjoy continental and American cuisine by candlelight; and Charlie's, a more casual eatery favored by many for breakfast and lunch. There is also a bar serving refreshments and munchies until 1am.

THE MOUNTAIN ROAD RESORT AT STOWE, *Mountain Road (Route 108) Stowe VT 05672. Tel. 802/253-4566, 800/367-6873, Fax 802/253-7397. E-mail: stowevt@aol.com. Web site: www.stowevtusa.com. Rates: $89-$195 per unit per night. Credit cards: major credit cards accepted.*

With only about 40 units, the Mountain Road Resort is more intimate than the other large resorts, but still offers comfortable lodging in style, as well as a variety of facilities. Lodging units include deluxe rooms and suites furnished with phones, cable television, and refrigerators, as well as "condo-suites" with more space and the same amenities; many of the condos also feature in-room jacuzzis and fireplaces. Sporting facilities include a small gym with a weight room, a spa, tennis, saunas and whirlpools, and two swimming pools, one of which is indoors. There is also a restaurant and a bar. Call for package deals.

GOLDEN EAGLE RESORT, *Mountain Road (Route 108), Stowe VT 05672. Tel. 802/253-4811, 800/626-1010, Fax 802/253-2561. E-mail: info@stoweagle.com. Web site: www.stoweagle.com. Rates: $80-$200 per room. Major credit cards accepted.*

The Golden Eagle is set on an 80-acre property that contains several nature trails with bird watching, in addition to an assortment of lodgings and fine dining. There's a fitness center (including whirlpools and massage), two swimming pools (one indoor, one out), a tennis court, a childrens' playground, and fishing ponds. Accommodations include standard guestrooms, suites with jacuzzis and fireplace, and family efficiencies with extra space and some kitchen equipment. For dining there is the Colonial Cafe serving breakfast and lunch, and the more upscale Partridge Inn serving fine versions of New England style seafood dishes. Call for special multiday packages.

COMMODORES INN, *Route 100 South (between Stowe Village & Waterbury), Stowe VT 05672. Tel. 802/253-7131, 800/44-STOWE, Fax 802/253-2360. E-mail: commodores@mtmansfield.com. Rates: $85-$140 per room. Major credit cards accepted.*

A rather modern affair on thirty acres, Commodores Inn features modern rooms equipped with standard amenities, such as full baths, telephones, air-conditioning and cable television. The grounds also include an outdoor and indoor pool, a spa with jacuzzis and saunas, and conference facilities. There is also a casual quality restaurant, a sports lounge, a cozy living room with a large fieldstone fireplace, cushy sofas, board games, and a widescreen television with a VCR for movies. Call about multiday packages in summer and winter. During warm weather months, the resident Stowe Yacht Club stages model sailboat races.

GREEN MOUNTAIN INN, *Main Street (P.O. Box 60), Stowe VT 05672. Tel. 802/253-7301, 800/253-7302, Fax 802/253-5069. E-mail: info@gminn. Web site: www.greenmountaininn.com. Rates: $90-$340. Major credit cards accepted.*

Situated in an expanded and renovated 1833 house in the heart of Stowe Village, the Green Mountain Inn offers visitors the charm and intimacy of a genuine 18th century inn with the comfort and amenities one typically expects in a mid- or large-sized luxury hotel. The inn's 76 guestrooms and suites are individually appointed with country furnishings and décor, includingg many canopy beds, fireplaces, and jacuzzis. It also features fine dining in the Main Street Dining Room and casual dining in the Whip & Grill, a health club, an outdoor pool, and cozy sitting rooms.

THE GABLES INN, *1457 Mountain Road, Stowe VT 05672. Tel. 802/ 253-7730, 800/GABLES-1. Fax. 802/253-8989. E-mail: inngables@aol.com Web site: www.gablesinn.com. Rates: $60-$200 per double. Major credit cards accepted.*

Known for its superb dining, beautiful surrounding gardens, and warm hospitality, the Gables Inn is romantic and charming. It is endowed with all sorts of pampering amenities, from suites with four poster beds, fireplaces and hot tubs, to first-rate dining, a health club, and an outdoor pool.

INNSBRUCK INN AT STOWE, *4361 Mountain Road (Route 108), Stowe VT 05672. Tel. 802/253-8582, 800/225-8582, Fax 802/253-2260. E-mail: seestowe@together.net. Web site: ww.stoweinfo.com. Rates: $130-$300. Major credit cards accepted.*

Located in an Austrian-style lodge, the Innsbruck Inn features guestrooms (some with jacuzzis), efficiency suites with extra space and cooking facilities, and a 5-bedroom rental chalet. The inn boasts six acres of landscaped lawns and gardens, a pool, a fitness room, a fireside sitting area where you can sip coffee or a cocktail.

FIDDLERS GREEN INN, *4859 Mountain Road, Stowe VT 05672. Tel. 802/253-8124, 800/882-5346. E-mail: fiddlersgreen@pwshift.com Web site: fiddlersgreeninn.com Rates: $75-$200. Major credit cards accepted.*

Situated in a renovated and expanded early 19th century house in beautiful grounds by a small brook, the Fiddlers Green Inn features seven elegant guestrooms with private baths.

YE OLDE ENGLAND INNE, *433 Mountain Road (Route 108), Stowe VT 05672. Tel. 802/253-7558, Fax 802/253-8944. E-mail: englandinn@aol.com. Web site: www.oldenglaeinne.com. Rates: $100-$400. Major credit cards accepted.*

Built successfully – apart from the large swimming pool out back – in the tradition of an English country inn right down to the kippers and eggs for breakfast, Ye Olde English Inne offers fine lodging in rooms with Laura Ashley decor, and suites with four-poster beds, fireplaces, and jacuzzis. On-site facilities include a fitness center, an outdoor pool, and two eateries serving quality and interesting game meats (roast leg of antelope, for example), English cuisine, and American and international food as well; the pub serves more than 100 different domestic and imported beers. This is the place to come if you need a European football (soccer) fix.

STOWE MOTEL & SNOWDRIFT, *2043 Mountain Road, (Route 108), Stowe VT 05672. Tel. 802/253-7629, 800/829-7629. Rates: $58-$116 (motel rooms), $66-$150 (efficiency units), $100-$300 for apartments and houses. Major credit cards accepted.*

Though it sounds like a motel and features comfortable and well-equipped motel rooms, the Stowe Motel & Snowdrift actually offers a lot more. In addition to the motel rooms, which include private baths, television, and an in-room phone, they also offer efficiency units with extra sitting rooms and kitchens; and an assortment of 2-5 bedroom houses and apartments, most of which include a hot tub, a kitchen, VCR, and sometimes maid service. On-site facilities include a pool, hot tubs, badminton, croquet, and a tennis court; mountain bikes are also provided for free. Be sure to call about their special five-day and weekly rates.

HOLIDAY INN, *Route 100 (just off I-89 Ext 10), Waterbury VT 05676. Tel. 802/244-7822, 800/621-7822. Rates: $60-$150. Major credit cards accepted.*

Offers all the conveniences of a brand name hotel, including comfortable rooms with all expected amenities, a fitness center, indoor pools, saunas, and hot tubs (all located in a glass adjunct), a tennis court, dining, a lounge, and even a covered bridge.

TOWN & COUNTRY RESORT & MOTOR LODGE, *Mountain Road (Route 108) one mile north of Stowe Village, Stowe VT 05672. Tel. 802/ 253-7595, 800/323-0311, Fax 802/253-4764. E-mail: tnc@together.net. Web site: www.townandcountrystowe.com. Rates: $60-$140. Major credit cards accepted.*

Town and Country offers spacious, comfortable rooms with private baths and cable television, in addition to a convenient location on the Rec Path. On-site facilities include a hgue outdoor pool, an indoor pool, saunas, a tennis court, a lounge, and a restaurant. Good value.

CRIMSON KING MOTEL, *Route 100 four miles north of Stowe (HC Box 260), Morrisville, VT -5661. Tel. 802/888-4210. Rates: $40-$70. Credit cards: Visa, Mastercard.*

Very simple but adequate rooms with private baths.

Smugglers' Notch

SMUGGLERS' NOTCH INN, *55 Church Street Jeffersonville, VT 05464. Tel. 802/644-2412, 800/845-3101, Fax 802/644-2881. E-mail: info@smugglers-notch-inn.com. Web site: www.smugglers-notch-inn.com. Rates: $60-$150. Credit cards: Visa, Mastercard.*

The Smugglers' Notch Inn is a handsome little establishment in a 1791 building with eleven guestrooms. All rooms feature a private bath, and one has a jacuzzi.. The inn also features a pool, a hot tub, and a salon with a fireplace where guests can get to know each other over a refreshment.

MANNSVIEW INN, *Route 108 S., Smugglers' Notch VT 05464. Tel. 802/644-8321, 888/937-6266, Fax 802/644-2006. E-mail: rsvp@mannsview.com. Web site: www.mannsview.com. Rates: $50-$140. Credit cards: Visa, Mastercard.*

Situated at the base of Mt. Mansfield in a restored colonial-style house dating to the 1870's, the Mannsview features six guestrooms decorated and furnished with country and antique decor, as well as private jacuzzi baths. The house also includes a cozy library and sitting room with a fireplace, a billiards room, and a hot tub. There is also an antique center on the premises and you can organize canoe tours out of the inn.

STERLING RIDGE INN & CABINS, *Junction of Hill Road and Route 100 (RR Box 5780), Jeffersonville VT 05464. Tel. 802/644-8265, 800/347-8266. E-mail: vtcabins@sover.net. Web site: www.vermont-cabins.com. Rates: $50-$85 for rooms, $75-$175 for cabins. Credit cards: Visa, Mastercard, American Express.*

Located on its own quiet 80 acres, Sterling Ride features eight guestrooms in the inn with Laura Ashley decor and private baths, and several new log cabins. The cabins include two bedrooms, a full kitchen, and a fireplace. On the premises is a heated swimming pool, a hot tub, and hiking trails.

Camping & Cabins

1836 CABINS, *Route 100 (5 miles south of Stowe), Waterbury Center VT 05677. Tel. 802/244-8533. Rates: $60-$120. Credit cards: Visa, Mastercard.*

Well, it's not as rustic as you might imagine. There are three standards of cabins, the most modest of which (standard) includes a queen sized bed, a bunk, a fully equipped kitchen (pots, pans, utensils included), a full bath, television, and a deck with a barbeque. The Semi-Deluxe and Deluxe cabins are even bigger and more equipped with fireplaces and other amenities. Also, all cabins are clean and carpeted, and many enjoy pleasant views of the surrounding countryside and woods. Great for families.

LITTLE RIVER STATE PARK, *RD 1 Box 1150, Waterbury VT 05676. (on the west shore of the Waterbury Reservoir – take Route 2 west from Waterbury .5 miles and then north of Little River Road.) Tel. 802/244-7103 (summer), 802/479-4280 (off-season). Base rates: $13-$17. Credit cards: Visa, Mastercard. Open mid-May through Columbus Day (mid-October).*

Little River State Park offers campers and visitors a wide array of recreational opportunities, including swimming, boating, and fishing in the Reservoir and the Little River, plus hiking, guided nature tours, and of course access to the Stowe-Mt. Mansfled region. For campers, there are 81 tent and trailer sites (20 lean-to's), sanitary facilities, showers, and toilets. Call for a reservation if you plan to stay during holidays or in high season (October and the height of summer).

SMUGGLERS' NOTCH STATE PARK, *7248 Mountain Road (Route 108), Stowe VT 05672. Tel. 802/253-4014 (summer), 802/479-4280 (off-season). Base rates: $12-$16. Credit cards: Visa, Mastercard. Open mid-May through Columbus Day (mid-October).*

Situated at the notch itself at the base of Mt. Mansfield, this state park features designated Natural Areas that include 1,000 foot cliffs off Route 108 and just great views and hiking generally. Camping facilities include 21 tent and trailer sites (14 lean-to's), showers, restrooms, and sanitary facilities.

GOLDBROOK CAMPGROUND, *Route 100 7.5 miles north of Exit 10 (Box 1028), Sowe VT 05672. Tel. 802/253-7683. Base rates: $16. Credit cards: Visa, Mastercards. Open year around.*

A private campground, Goldbrook includes 100 sites with amp hook-ups, cable television, and free telephone connections. There are also hot showers, a playground, swimming pool, and shuffleboard.

WHERE TO EAT

There are literally dozens, if not hundreds, of eateries in the Stowe and Mt. Mansfield area; virtually every resort and major inn has as at least a restaurant serving quality country and continental cuisine. To learn more about the restaurants listed below and to obtain a more complite listing of all restaraunts, pick up a copy of the *Stowe Guide to Dining* which is widely available in the area at inns, restaurants, rest stops and anywhere else visitors might be likely to pass; or contact the **Stowe Area Association**, *P.O. Box 1350/Main Street, Stowe VT 05672, Tel. 802/453-7371, 800/24-STOWE, Fax 802/253-2159. E-mail: stowe@sover.net, Web site: www.Stoweinfo.com.*

THE GABLES INN AND RESTAURANT, *1457 Mountain Road, Stowe VT 05672. Tel. 802/253-7730. Fax. 802/253-8989. E-mail: inngables@aol.com Web site: www.gablesinn.com. Open nightly from 5:30pm-*

9pm, 8am-10:30am for breakfast on weekdays & 8am-12:30am on weekends and holidays. Major credit cards accepted.

The Gables Inn is renowned for its restaurant, which offer diners some of the best food in the region. Meals are served in a charming dining room with views of Mt. Mansfield for very reasonable prices. Appetizers ($2.50-$7) typically include soups, salads, and continental and American favorites ranging from escargot to shrimp cocktail. The entree menu offers a well balanced selection of seafood, poultry, meat, and there is always a vegetarian dish as well as special selections for children. For seafood, you might have a choice between poached salmon with roasted red pepper hollandaise sauce, broiled scallops in white wine and herbs, or shrimp scampi. Meats and poultry usually include a selection of steaks with a delicious herbed butter or some other sauce, a classic roast chicken with herbs and garlic, and a rotating selection of other entrees. Prices range from $8.50 (for the vegetarian selection) to $18. Reservations are recommended, and the alcoholic beverage policy is BYOB ("bring your own").

The Gables Inn is also open for breakfast, served on the porch or in the dining room. Selections range from the usual American favorites like omeletes, eggs & sausage, bacon, corned beef hash, and ham; pancakes; and fresh coffee. There is also a selection of gourmet selections like portabello mushroom eggs benedict, sauteed chicken livers with onions, eggs, and toast; or if you're not planning on eating lunch, the "Lumber Jack," which includes a Black Angus top sirloin with eggs, potatoes, baked beans and toast. No item on the breakfast menu costs more than $8.

ISLE DE FRANCE, *Mountain Road (Route 108), Stowe VT 05672. Tel. 802/253-7751. Open for dinner 6pm-10pm, apres ski from 4pm, Sunday Brunch 11:30am-2:30am. Major credit cards accepted.*

If it's first-rate old school French cuisine you're interested in, the Isle de France offers you the choice of enjoying an excellent meal either in a casual bistro atmosphere in Claudine's or in the formal setting of the Pierre Bonnard Dining Room, modeled after the Rtiz Carlton in Paris. The bistro, which is ideal for an apres-ski drink and gourmet snacks such as pate, clams casino, and onion soup gratinee. Or if you're hungrier, you might indulge in one of the hearty entrees like the "bistro" filet mignon with bearnaise sauce, or breast of chicken forestiere in mushroom garlic sauce. Appetizers range from $2.75 for the soup de jour to $5.50 for clams casino; entrees hover between $12 and $15.

While that's high class stuff for some of us, it's minor league compared to the cuisine served in the Pierre Bonnard Dining Room. Here the menu features such French classics as the appetizer Escargot Borguignonne (snails in herbed butter and white wine), Cuisses de Grenouilles a la Provencale (frog legs sauteed with garlic butter and white wine sauce), and the magnificent Le Chateaubriand (lightly roasted tenderloin carved at the table and served with bearnaise sauce, for two). The menu also includes more than a dozen other gourmet dishes ranging from Ris de Veau (sweet breads sauteed with mushrooms in brown sauce) and roast duck with apple flavored sauce, to veal cutets and a handful of high-end steaks. Appetizers typically cost $7-$9 with entrees costing $17-$50and up for some dishes for two. Dress well.

THE SEASONS AT STOWEHOF INN, *434 Edson Hill Road (off the Mountain Road/Route 108), Stowe VT 05672. Tel. 802/253-9722. Open 8am-10am for breakfast, 6pm-9:30pm for dinner, Tap Room (lounge/bistro) opens at 4pm. Major credit cards accepted.*

Situated in the Austrian-style Stowehof Inn, the Seasons serves fine continental cuisine in an elegant dining room with gorgeous views, as well as glorified bar food (barbequed duck quesadilla, smoked pork chops with apple cider and braised sauerkraut) in the Tap Room. In the main dining room, many choose one of the two house specialties, Wiener Schnitzel with spatzle ($18.95), or Beef Wellington (filet mignon in a puff pastry with mushrooms and bordelais sauces for $21.95). Other entrees might include (menus rotate) grilled pork medallions with rosemary papardelle, button mushrooms, scallions and sun-dried tomatoes; winter cassoulet with duck, andouille sausage, shimp and vegetables with cilantro cream sauce; or roast leg of antelope with garlic flavored potatotes. Appetizers, such as stuffed quail and mixed bruschetta, range from $6-$9, while entrees typically hang around $18-$21. Salads are also available and for dessert you may choose from an ever changing selection of freshed pastries and baked goods.

THE TRAPP FAMILY LODGE, *700 Trapp Hill Road, Stowe, VT 05672. Tel. 802/253-8511. dinner served 5:30pm-9pm, bar open from 3:30pm until closing, Austrian Team Room open daily from 10:30am-5:30pm (Bake Shop open 8am-4pm). Major credit cards accepted.*

One way to experience the Trapp Family Lodge and its beautiful hillside setting is to make a culinary excursion to one or more of its three dining venues: the Dining Room, the Lounge, and the Austrian Tea Room. The **Dining Room** is a formal affair and serves elegant European 3 and 5 course meals. Entrees include roast duckling in port wine sauce, weinerschnitzel, and medallions of Vermont venison with potato pancakes among others. The more casual **Lounge** features a bar and a heartier bistro-like menu that includes bratwurst, tournedos of beef bordelaise, and a broiled hamburger as well as soups, salads, and appetizers.

Finally, below the main lodge in its own little Austrian=style cottage is the **Austrian Tea House**, a great family venue serving three kinds of wursts (knackwurst, bratwurst, and bauernwurst), as well as half a dozen other sandwiches, entrees like sauteed veal with noodles and Westphalian Ham with melon, and an assortment of pastries and cakes like Bavarian chocolate torte and Vermont maple cream pie. Also located in the Tea House is a bake shop that bakes and sells breads and pastries, and a souvenir shop selling every imaginable Trapp Family souvenir (their story *inspired The Sound of Music*) and memorabilia, from CD's to coloring books.

THE PARTRIDGE INN SEAFOOD RESTAURANT, *504 Mountain Road (Route 108), Stowe VT 05672. Tel. 802/253-8000. Dinner served nightly 5:30pm-9:30pm. Major credit cards accepted.*

The Partridge Inn specializes in fine New England seafood, though it also serves a variety of meat and poultry dishes, such as steak, lamb chops, and baked stuffed chicken. For starters there are a dozen appetizers ($5.50-$8), ten of which are a variety of seafood favorites such as oysters on the half shell, Maryland crab cakes, and crab stuffed artichoke bottoms. There is also New England clam chowder and lobster bisque in a bowl or a cup. Main dishes include an assortment of grilled, broiled, and baked fish (sole, salmon, swordfish, scallops; fried shrimp, scrod, and scallops; and seafood specialties such as broiled lobster, Alaskan King crab legs, and Thai shrimp. For those who want it all, there are also "By Land & By Sea" combinations like lobster tail and filet mignon, and baked stuffed shrimp and filet mignon. Price for entrees range from $15-$22, and all dishes come with popovers and a choice of rice, potato, or vegetable.

EDSON HILL MANOR, *1500 Edson Hill Road (off the Mountain Road/ Route 108), Stowe VT 05672. Tel. 802/253-7371. Open 5:30pm-10pm. Major credit cards accepted.*

Edson Hill Manor offers a fine assortment of country, continental, and international fare in an elegant dining room (and on the terrace in warm weather months). Appetizers range from Korean pork and cabbage soup ($4.75) and Thai steamed mussels (with coconut milk, lemongrass and chili sauce for $7.50) to smoked duck French toast ($8) and cajun paella ($8.50). Entrees ($15-$24) are no less enticing or interesting. In the winter of '98-'99, they included, among others, grilled Atlantic salmon with port lobster sauce, roasted peppers, and wasabi-potato gratin; seared tuna loin with nishaki rice, Panang mussel sauce and peanut leek salad; and roasted rack of New Zealand lamb. For dessert there is an assortment of puddings, pies, and other gourmet pastries.

VILLAGE TRAGARA, *Route 100 (6 miles south of Stowe Village), Waterbury VT. Tel. 802/244-5288, Fax 802/244-4130. Open for dinner 5:30pm-9:30pm. Major credit cards accepeted.*

The Village Tragara specializes in northern Italian cuisine and Italian "tapas," appetizer-sized dishes that are ordered by the handful and shared amongst a group. Also, the Tragara sometimes features live entertainment ranging from cabaret-style variety shows, music, and dinner theater. Expect to pay $20-$30 for a full meal with wine, and a bit more if there is an entertainment charge.

MR. PICKWICK'S, *In Ye Olde England Inne at 433 Mountain Road (Route 108), Stowe VT 05672. Tel. 802/253-7558. Open 8am-midnight daily. Major credit cards accepted.*

A classy British-themed restaurant and tavern, this self-proclaimed "Dickens of a Place" serves breakfast, lunch, and dinner, for all of which there is an extensive menu featuring British, American, and international cuisine. For example, for breakfast you can choose from typical American dishes like eggs, pancakes, and Belgian waffles, or you can opt for the British style kippers (smoked mackerel) and eggs. For lunch there is a wide selection of sandwiches and other moderately sized dishes like chicken pie, curried chicken salad, and Thai stirfry with tofu. Things really get interesting at dinner when the menu extends to – in addition to the usual steaks, wings, and seafood – British dishes like Beef Wellington, fish & chips, and steak and kidney pie, as well as far-out game meats such as skewered kangaroo, cajun alligator medallions, boar ribs, and more conventional game like rabbit, pheasant, and venison. Also, the beer and wine lists are extensive, and the atmosphere is casual, and at times lively – a nice change from the conventional inn setting. Most entrees cost $10-$20 with most at the lower end of that spectrum.

SWISSPOT, *Main Street, Stowe Village VT 05672. Tel. 802/253-4622. Open 11:30am on weekends and holidays for lunch, 5pm for dinner nightly. Major credit cards accepeted.*

Located in charming Stowe Village, the Swisspot serves fondue, quiche, and other Swiss and continental specialties for very reasonable prices. House specialties include Swiss Air Dried Beef (an appetizer for $7.95), Swiss Cheese Fondue ($24.95 for two), and the Swiss Reuben sandwiche ($7.95). Other items include escargot (snails in white wine and garlic-parsley butter) bruschetta, and raclette (melted cheese over steamed potatoes) for appetizers, and for dinner you'll be treated to quiches, fondues (beef, shrimp, vegetable), sandwiches, steaks and pastas, and more than ten burgers.

THE SHED RESTAURANT & BREWERY, *Mountain Road (Route 108), Stowe VT 05672. Tel. 802/253-4364. Major credit cards accepted. Open from 11am-midnight (dinner 5m-10pm). Major credit cards accepted.*

Open since 1965, the Shed is a nice family restaurant for lunch, dinner and Sunday brunch, that also caters to those over 21 keen to enjoy locally produced adult refreshments. In a fireside setting in the winter or a greenhouse-garden setting in warm weather, diners can choose from an extensive menu that includes more than ten sandwiches, a half dozen vegetarian dishes (quesadillas, flatbread sandwiches), steaks, a half dozen salads, a full list of traditional American appetizers (potato skins, nachos et al), poultry soups, seafood (shrimp scampi, grilled tuna and others), and a kids' menu. On Sunday for brunch, there is an all you can eat buffet that includes waffles, omeletes, pastries, and other hot and cold items, and in the evening you can sample one or more of the various beers brewed at the Shed's brewery and take in a game on the satellite-fed television.

MIGUEL'S STOWE AWAY, *3148 Mountain Road (Route 108), Stowe VT 05672. Tel. 802/253-7574. Open noon-3pm for lunch (Saturdays & Sundays); Cantina (lounge) 4pm-midnight Monday-Friday, 3pm-midnight Saturday and Sunday; dinner 5:30pm-10pm Monday-Friday, 5pm-10pm Saturdays and Sundays. Major credit cards accepted.*

Miguel's offers reasonably priced Mexican fare served in a cozy fireside setting, and is also known and for its weekend late nights which often include dancing and live entertainment.

PIE IN THE SKY, *492 Mountain Road (Route 108), Stowe VT 05672. Tel. 802/253-5100. Open for lunch and dinner . Major credit cards accepted.*

Specializes in pizza, for which there are literally dozens of choices ranging from create-your-own to "Not-so-Traditional Specialty Pizzas" like bianchi all vongole (pizza topped with white clans, garlic, olive oil, oregano and asiago) and Mexicana (spicy salsa, peppers, onions, olives and roast chicken). Also available are numerous appetizers (garlic bread, focaccia, and salads), pastas (garlic, meatballs, pesto to name a few), and baked specialties like lasagna and ravioli. Pizzas cost between $7.50 for 12 inch create-your-own, to $15.95 for 16 inch specialty pizzas. All other entrees are less than $10. The Pie in the Sky stays open until midnight.

GRACIE'S, *in the Carlson Building on Main Street in Stowe Village, Stowe VT 05672. Tel. 802/253-8741. Open 11:30am-4:30pm, dinner 4-:30pm-11pm, late night bar open until midnight.*

Located in Stowe Village among dozens of gentrified inns and restaurants, Gracie's is refreshingly middle class, or even blue collar. It's atmosphere is casual, its prices downright cheap compared to other area establishments, and the menu is a mile long – there are a dozen burgers alone. Also available are appetizers, salads, steaks and chops, Mexican specialties, fish and seafood, and desserts, speaking of which consider the house specialty "Doggie-Bag," a white chocolate bag with peppermint schnapps flavored chocolate mousse on top of hot fudge. There are also vegetarian and children's menus. Apart from the Mexican items, the menu is all-out American. Ninety percent of the menu is available for less than $8.

Bakeries, Sandwich Shops, & Take-out

CAFE VERMONT, *33 Coffee Lane behind the Stowe Emporium, Waterbury. Tel. 802/244-5621. Hours: 6:30am-5pm Monday-Friday. Credit cards: Visa, Mastercard, American Express.*

Dealing in Vermont's own acclaimed Green Mountain Coffee, this cafe specializes in coffee and coffee-making accessories, and also serves pastries, bagels and other baked goods.

THE BAGEL, *Baggy Knees Shopping Center on Mountain Road (108), Stowe VT 05672. Tel. 802/253-9943. Open daily from 7am-5pm. Credit cards: Visa, Mastercard.*

Bakes bagels, muffins, and other goods daily. Fresh coffee, deli-style sandwiches, and soup are also available for take-out.

HARVEST MARKET, *1031 Mountain Road (Route 108), Stowe VT 05672. Tel. 802/253-3800. Open 7am-7pm daily. Major credit cards accepted.*

The Harvest market is an upscale bakery and prepared foods store that sells fresh baked goods of all types, gourmet coffees, wines, cheeses, and deli items like sandwiches and salads.

SEEING THE SIGHTS

There is admittedly little in the way of interesting historic sites in the Stowe region, but there are a few attractions, such as the Ben & Jerry's Ice Cream Factory, the Red Hollow Cider Mill, and Camp Meade in Middlesex. Of course, there the beautiful natural scenery that can be enjoyed just by hopping in the car and exploring the area.

Waterbury

BEN & JERRY'S ICE CREAM FACTORY, *Route 100 (one mile north of Exit 10), Waterbury VT. Tel. 802/244-TOUR. Web site: www.benjerry.com.*

America's favorite ice cream makers have opened their headquarters here in Waterbury to the public, and it has recently become one of the most popular attractions in the state. Visitors can take a tour of the ice cream factory, sample the product, and of course shop the well-endowed gift store. A must for kids.

COLD HOLLOW CIDER MILL, *Route 100 (Box 430), Waterbury Center VT 05677. Tel. 802/327-7537, (mail order) Tel. 800/3-APPLES. Open 8am-6pm daily year around. Major credit cards accepted.*

In terms of expanding your cultural knowledge and experience, the over-hyped Cold Hollow Cider Mill falls short; indeed, it's one of those attractions that is 20% attraction, 80% gift shop. But having pointed that out, it must be said that the expansive, never-ending gift shop is one of the best endowed in the state, and in itself warrants a visit. There are oodles of souvenirs and handicrafts from stuffed animals and toy trains, to

Vermont key chains and handcrafted wooden toys. There are also thousands of specialty food items like maple flavored mustard, cheeses, baked goods, and of course cider and other apple products. A great place to buy souvenirs and gifts.

Stowe

One of the most pleasant ways to pass a little time in the Stowe area is simply to hop in the car and drive around a bit. Route 100 north of the village, for example, is far less developed than the Mountain Road and very shortly beyond the village the surrounding countryside gives way to picturesque rolling hills dotted with farms. You can also turn off Route 100 onto one or more of the local roads such as **West Hill Road**, where you can stop off at the **Sage Sheep Farm** *(open afternoons form June through October; Tel. 802/253-8532)*, where Elizabeth Squire tends sheep and grows herbs and other plants. Ms. Squire also sells interesting and charming wool products and often serves tea and a homecooked lunch for about $5.

Other roads include Stagecoach Road and Sterling Ridge Road, where you can visit the **Sterling Falls Gorge**, a series of picturesque waterfalls and pools with walking trails. Continuing north on Route 100 will lead you to **Morrisville**, home of the **Noyes House Museum** featuring exhibits about local and state history. *Main Street Morrisville. Tel. 802/888-7617/888-5605. Open July & August Wednesday-Saturday 1pm-4pm.*

From Morrisville take Route 15 west up through Johnson, famous for its textiles, and Jeffersonville (11 miles from Morrisville), where Route 108 South leads to the ultra-scenic **Smugglers' Notch** (the road is open only when there's not snow) and on back to Stowe via the Mountain Road. South of Smuglers' Notch it is possible to drive up the **Mt. Mansfield Auto Toll Road** *($12 per automobile, $7 per motorcycle)* for 4.5 miles, where you can take a picnic or just suck up some fresh air and enjoy the great views.

HELEN DAY ART CENTER, *School Street (off the village center), Stowe VT 05672. Tel. 802/253-8358. Open noon-5pm daily except Monday from July 4-mid-October, and from Tuesday-Saturday in the off-season. Admission: $2, $1 for seniors, fifty cents for children.*

Located in a restored schoolhouse built in the Greek Revival style during the 1860's, the Helen Day Art Center is a visual arts center that features all types of art exhibits and offers art classes and demonstrations. Next door is the restored Bloody Brook schoolhouse, which is maintained by the Stowe Historical Society and contained school materials from the past.

STOWE HISTORICAL SOCIETY MUSEUM, *in the Akeley Building on Main Street (in the village), Stowe VT 05672. Tel. 802/253-6133. Open by appointment .*

The historical society maintains a modest museum with local art, and historic artifacts such as furniture, photographs, and tools.

Middlesex
CAMP MEADE VICTORY MUSEUM, *Route 2 (off I-89 Exit 9), Middlesex VT. Tel. 802/223-5537. E-mail: cmpmeade@together.net. Web site: www.campmeade.com. Open*

Dedicating to preserving the glory of the World War II generation and their struggles and sacrifices during the Great Depression and World War II, Camp Meade features more than two dozen displays and exhibits from dioramas and videos to artifact and photographic exhibits. On Saturdays between June and October, there are also rides for kids on antique military vehicles, and very often lectures are given by veterans and other members of that generation about their experiences.

NIGHTLIFE & ENTERTAINMENT
Dancing & Entertainment

During the summer, there are numerous public concerts given in all sorts of venues from the **Russ Parker Memorial Park** in Waterbury in Waterbury by the train depot to the magical hillside setting of the **Trapp Family Lodge**. Check local publications and bulletin boards for schedules. For rock'n'roll and other popular music and dancing, check with the establishments listed below:

THE ROADHOUSE MOUNTAIN R&B GRILL, *Mountain Road (Route 108), Stowe VT 05672. Tel. 802/253-2800. Open 4pm until late. Major credit cards accepted.*

The Roadhouse features live (mostly rhythm & blues) entertainment, dancing and general late night fun, as well as quality barfood like seafood corn chowder, grilled chicken and steaks, seafood pot pie, pasta, and a variety of burgers. Most eats will set you back $5-$10.

THE MATTERHORN, *End of the Mountain Road (Route 108), Stowe VT 05672. Tel. 802/253-8198. Open daily 4pm until late (past midnight). Major credit cards accepted.*

The Matterhorn is one of the most popular apre-ski spots in Stowe, and features live music on the weekends as well as all sorts of munchies from brick oven pizza and chicken wings to sushi. Other attractions include pool tables, video games, and televisions for watching the big games.

VILLAGE TRAGARA, *Route 100 (6 miles south of Stowe Village), Waterbury VT. Tel. 802/244-5288, Fax 802/244-4130. Open for dinner 5:30pm-9:30pm. Major credit cards accepeted.*

The Tragara specializes in northern Italian cuisine and often features live entertainment ranging from cabaret-style variety shows, music, and dinner theater. Expect to pay $20-$30 for a full meal with wine, and a bit more if there is an entertainment charge.

MIGUEL'S STOWE AWAY, *3148 Mountain Road (Route 108), Stowe VT 05672. Tel. 802/253-7574. Open noon-3pm for lunch (Saturdays & Sundays); Cantina (lounge) 4pm-midnight Monday-Friday, 3pm-midnight Saturday and Sunday; dinner 5:30pm-10pm Monday-Friday, 5pm-10pm Saturdays and Sundays. Major credit cards accepted.*

Miguel's offers reasonably priced Mexican fare served in a cozy fireside setting, and is also known and for its weekend late nights which often include dancing and live entertainment.

Movies

STOWE CINEMA 3-PLEX, *Mountain Road, Stowe. Tel. 802/253-4678.*

SHOPPING

Routes 100 & 108 as well as the villages themselves are teeming with ski shops, antique dealers, and souvenir shops. We've listed only a fraction of those shopping opportunities here. For complete listings, contact the **Stowe Area Association**, *Tel. 802/453-7371, 800/24-STOWE, E-mail: stowe@sover.net, Web site: www. Stoweinfo.com*; or the **Stowe Reporter** for a copy of *The Stowe Guide* featuring complete listings of businesses in the Stowe area, *Tel. 802/253-2102, Tel. 800/734-2102, E-mail: stwerep@sover.net, Web site: www.stowereporter.com.* A yearly subscription costs $10.

General Souvenirs & Gifts

THE CHRISTMAS PLACE, *1800 Mountain Road, Stowe. Tel./Fax 802/253-8767. Email: NoelStowe@aol.com. Hours: Credit cards: major credit cards accepted.*

Mostly Vermont Christmasy stuff.

PUZZLE PUZZLE!, *1056-13 Mountain Road, Stowe. Tel. 802/253-8121. Credit cards: major credit cards accepted.*

Sells mostly puzzles and games.

SAMARA'S CARDS & GIFTS, *Red Barne Shops, Route 108, Stowe. Tel. 802/253-8318. Credit cards: major credit cards accepted.*

Art Galleries & Antiques
CLARKE GALLERIES, AMERICAN PAINTINGS, *123 Mountain Road, Stowe. Tel. 802/253-7116. Credit cards: major credit cards accepted.*
Situated in a 150-year-old farmhouse, Clarke Galleries specializes in 19th and 20th century painting in New England.
ROBERT PAUL GALLERIES, *394 Mountain Road, Stowe. Tel. 802/ 253-7282; Tel. 800/873-3791.Credir cards: major credit cards accepted.*
One of the biggest galleries in the region, Robert Paul features a wide selection of art from across America, including paintings and sculptures. Shipping and framing services offered.
STOWE CRAFT GALLERY & SHIMMERING GLASS, *Simmering Glass Stoudio is on Route 100 in Waterbury. Tel. 802/244-8134. Stowe Craft Gallery is on Route 108 in Stowe. Tel. 802/253-4693. Hours:. Credit cards: major credit cards accepted.*
These sister shops feature all types of lamps and glass, and offer glass blowing classes.
VERMONT CLAY STUDIO, *2802 Waterbury-Stowe Road. Route 100 Waterbury Center. Tel. 802/244-1126. E-mail: Vtclay@aol.com. Hours: Daily from 10am-6pm. Major credit cards accepted.*
Complete with a gallery, a gift shop, and ceramic classes, the Vermont Clay Studio features some beautiful examples of ceramics and pottery from jars and vases to coffee cups and mugs.
VERMONT HERITAGE GIFTS & CRAFTS, *48 South Main Street, Stowe. Tel. 802/253-7507. Hours: 10am-6pm daily. Major credit cards accepted.*
VERMONT GIFT BARN, *32 South Main Street., Stowe. Tel. 802/253-6798. Hours: daily 10am-6pm. Credit cards: major credit cards accepted.*
Situated in a 150 year old barn, this shop features wide variety of Vermont gifts and souvenirs from ceramics and other crafts to maple syrup and gourmet foods.

Film Development & Photography
THE CAMERA STORE & LAB, *Stowe Center Shops on Mountain Road, Stowe. Tel. 802/253-4842. Hours: 9:30am-5:30pm Monday-Saturday; 10am-5pm Sunday. Credit cards: major credit cards accepted.*
OPRAH MOORE, *175 Depot Street, Hyde Park. Tel. 802/888-2309. Hours: . Credit cards: major credit cards accepted.*
Specializes in photography for weddings and other important events.

Food & Provisions
While eating out is the norm for most visitors, it can be costly and those in condos and apartments especially may wish to take advantage of in-house kitchen facilities to eat in. Listed below are some options for grocery and food shopping:

EDELWEISS COUNTRY STORE, *Mountain Road (Route 108), Stowe VT 05672. Tel. 802/253-4034. Major credit cards accepted. Open 8am-9pm daily.*

FOOD FOR THOUGHT NATURAL MARKET, *Route 100, Lower Village, Stowe. Tel. 802/253-4733. Credit cards: Visa, Mastercard.*

Specializing in high quality produce, Food for Thought sells primarily organic local foods including organic veggies, cheeses, wines, and free range poultry as well as homeopathic medicine, herbs, and other such products.

CABOT ANNEX STORE, *Route 100 Waterbury between Ben &Jerry's ad Cold Cider Mill. Tel. 802/244-6334. Hours: 9am-6pm daily. Credit cards: major credit cards accepted.*

COLD HOLLOW CIDER MILL, *Route 100, Waterbury Center. Tel. 802/244-8771; toll free 800/327-7537, Fax 802/244-7212. Website: www.coldhollow.com. Hours: Credit cards: major credit cards accepted.*

Though the pamphlets tend to push your opportunity to watch the cider making process (nothing special really), the gift shop is the true star. One of the largest in Vermont, it sells everything from stuffed animals and t-shirts to maple flavored cheese and Christmas ornaments.

GREEN MOUNTAIN COFFEE ROASTERS, *2 branches at Route 33 Coffee Lane and on Route 100, both in Waterbury. Tel. Coffee Lane 802/244-5621; Route 100 802/244-8430. Hours: 6:30am-5pm Monday-Friday, 8am-1pm Saturday. Credit cards: major credit cards accepted.*

A factory outlet for Vermont's best known gourmet coffee producers, selling all sorts of coffee and coffee accessories.

Sporting Goods

If you're just in Stowe for the day, renting equipment is most convenient at the Spruce and Mansfield base lodges. The standard boot, poles, and skis package cost $25 per adult for one day ($18 for each additional day); $15 for children (12 and younger); and $25 for a snowboard package ($15 for 12 and under). They can also tune, sharpen, and wax your skis. *Tel. 802/253-3000. Hours: 7:30am-5pm Monday-Friday; 7am-5pm weekends and holidays.*

SKI MAGAZINE DEMO CENTER, *Upper Mountain Road (Route 108), Stowe. Tel. 802/253-7222; Tel. 800/458-9996.*

AJ'S SKI & SPORTS/WOODIE'S SNOWBOARDS, *Mountain Road, Stowe. Tel. 802/253-4593, 800/226-6257. E-mail: ajssports@pwshift.com. Hours: Credit cards: major credit cards accepted.*

The tag team of Al and Woodie boast one of the largest ski and snowboard inventories in Stowe. Clothing and other accessories are also in good supply.

SNOWBOARD ADDIC, *Mountain Road, Stowe. Tel. 802/253-2996. Hours: 8am-6pm daily; open until 8pm on holidays.*

INNER BOOTWORKS, *Mountain Road Stowe. Tel. 802/253-6929. Hours: 8am-6pm (8pm on weekends and holidays). Credit cards: major credit cards accepted.*

BOOTS 'N BOARDS, *430 Mountain Road, Stowe. Tel. 802/253-4225, Fax 802/253-5039. Rental reservations: Tel. 800/298-5574. E-mail: Bootsnbrds@aol.com. Hours: Credit cards: major credit cards accepted.*

Boots 'n Boards specializes in snowboard rentals and equipment and is also a major dealer for The North Face sporting wear company.

SPORTS & RECREATION

Biking

One place to start is the **Stowe Recreation Path**, which runs parallel to the Mountain Road from the Village center to the Topnotch Resort. Otherwise, major roads such as Route 100 and Route 108 and local roads are excellent for road cycling. For mountain biking, the **Cotton Brook Road** off the Moscow Road two miles west of the hamlet of Moscow, and the **Haul Road** linking the Trapp resort with Mt. Mansfield, are both challenging and rewarding. Pick up maps for specific directions at one of the establishments listed below. You can also pay a flat fee of $25 a day at Stowe Mountain Resort for riding the lifts up Mt. Mansfield and cycling down the dry ski runs and trails. Rentals are also available; call *800/253-4754* for more information.

AJ'S SKI & SPORTS, *Mountain Road, Stowe. Tel. 802/253-4593, Tel. 800/226-6257. E-mail: ajssports@pwshift.com. Credit cards: major credit cards accepted.*

Deals in all types of bikes (including rentals) and biking accessories.

MOUNTAIN BIKE SHOP, *Mountain Road (Across from the Golden Eagle), Stowe VT 05672. Tel. 802/253-7919. Open daily. Major credit cards accepted.*

Deals in bikes and other outdoor accessories and equipment.

STOWE HARDWARE, *Main Street (in the village), Stowe VT 05672. Tel. 802/253-7205. Major credit cards accepted.*

Rents and repairs all types of bikes.

Boating, Canoeing & Kayaking

The Waterbury Reservoir and the Lamoille River are the primary venues for boating. You can access the **Waterbury Reservoir** by taking the Old River Road west off Route 100 just south of the Cold Hollow Cider Mill and from the Little River State Park. Lake canoeing, kayaking, and motor boats are all available. The **Lamoille River** features easy river canoeing or kayaking between Cady's Falls Dam (in Hyde Park west of Morrisville) and the Dog's Head by the Johnson Bridge, and between Johnson and Cambridge.

UMIAK VERMONT ADVENTURE CENTER, *Lower Stowe Village Route 100, Stowe VT 05672. Tel. 802/253-2317.*

Organizes and operates hiking, canoeing, rafting, and kayaking tours and lessons as well as rentals.

SMUGGLERS' NOTCH CANOE TOURING, *Mannsview Inn on Route 108, Jeffersonville VT. Tel. (Tel. 802/644-8321, 888/937-MANN.*

Offers canoe and kayak rentals as well as tours and trips, including shuttles and pick-ups.

Cross-Country Skiing

Stowe's cross-country skiing opportunities may be even better than its downhill.

STOWE MOUNTAIN RESORT, *5781 Mountain Road (Route 108), Stowe VT 05672. Tel. 802/253-3000, 800/253-4754, Fax 802/253-3659.*

The resort maintains 35 kilometers of trails and also features 40 kilometers of backcountry trails. Tickets, equipment, and lessons can be arranged and purchased at the **Stowe Mountain Cross-Country Center** *located on the Mountain Road (Route 108) about a quarter of a mile from the Inn at the Mountain and the Spruce and Mansfield base lodges.* The daily trail access fee is $10 for adults ($6 for children 6-12), and season passes are $120 per individual and $239 for a family of up to two parents and two kids. To join a one and a half hour group lesson costs $20. Private lessons are $45 an hour for the first skier and $15 for each additional student. *Hours of operation: 8:30am-4pm. Tel. 802/253-3000 (ext. 3688).*

The Stowe Mountain Resort also rents **telemarking** equipment and runs a telemarking clinic that you can join for $40, which includes equipment and a trail pass.

TRAPP FAMILY LODGE SKI CENTER, *42 Trapp Hill Road, Stowe VT 05672. Tel. 802/253-5716., 800/826-7000. Web site: www.trappfamily.com. Trail rates: $12 daily. Major credit cards accepted.*

The Trapp Family Lodge maintains a whopping 100 kilometers of trails, considered by many to be some of the best cross-country skiing in Vermont. In addition to trails, the Lodge's Ski Center offers rentals, retail sales, instruction, guided tours, and equipment repairs and tune-ups. Multiday packages are available for equipment rentals and trail passes.

TOPNOTCH, *Route 108 (Mountain Road), Stowe VT 05672. Tel. 802/ 253-8585. Web site: www. topnotch-resort.com. Trail fees: $10 daily. Major credit cards accepted.*

Topnotch operates 25 kilometers of trails and offers rentals, guided tours, instruction, and retail sales.

EDSON HILL MANOR, *Edson Hill Road off Route 108, Stowe VT 05672. Tel. 802/253-8954. Trail fees: $10 daily. Major credit cards accepted.*

Edson Hill Manor offers skiers 55 kilometers of trails and a full range of services, from equipment rentals and ski instruction to guided tours and retail sales.

SMUGGLERS' NOTCH RESORT, *Route 108 , Smugglers' Notch VT 05464. Tel. 802/644-8851 (Extension 1208). Trail fees: $12. Major credit cards accepted.*

Smugglers' Notch features 25 kilometers of trails and the ski center offers instruction, rentals, and guided tours.

SUMMER RECREATION AT STOWE MOUNTAIN RESORT

After the last (usually manmade) snow melts sometime in April or May, Mt. Mansfield and Spruce Peak are converted into a series of sightseeing and sporting venues that include an alpine slide, an in-line skate park, biking trails, and a scenic Gondola Skyride.

Gondola Skyride *– Take a ride up to the summit of Mt. Mansfield where you can take in the views, eat lunch at the Cliff House Restaurant, and/or hike the various trails. Fees: Adult round-trip $10, children under 12 $6, one-way $7. Family of four $25. Open 10am-5pm mid-June through mid-October.*

Alpine Slide *– A sort of 2,300 foot dry toboggan or sled run. Fees: single ride $7.50, five rides $25. Open 10am-5pm mid-June through mid-October.*

Mountain Biking *– Take a ski lift up Mt. Mansfield and then cycle down one of the many trails. Lift tickets: $25 full day, $16 half-day, two hour instruction and guided tour $25. Rentals available.*

In-Line Skating *– One of those Xtreme activities that involves jumping, swooping, and sommersaulting on roller blades or a skateboard through slalom courses, half-pipes, and ramps. Admission: $15 full day, $8 half-day. Rentals and instruction available at extra cost.*

*For more information contact the Stowe Mountain Resort, Tel. 800/253-5754, or look up their web site at **www.stowe.com**.*

Fishing

In and around Stowe and Waterbury, the **Little River** features decent fishing, but the **Lamoille River** which flows east-west through Jeffersonville and Morrisville north of Stowe and Smugglers' Notch is considered the best in the region. Teeming with trout (brook, rainbow and brown), perch, smallmouth bass, and other types of fish, the river can be accessed near Jeffersonville – which can be reached from Smugglers' Notch by way of Route 108, or from Stowe by taking Route 108 or Route 100 and Route 15 West. Near Smugglers' Notch, you can also try **Brewster River** and **Sterling Pond**, which is stocked with brook trout. Also, in Morrisville, the **Green River Reservoir** on Garifield Road (off Route 15 at Morrisville) is known for excellent perch and bass fishing (motor boats not allowed).

FLY ROD SHOP, *954 South Main Street/P.O. Box 960, Stowe VT 05672. (On Route 100 about 2 miles south of Stowe Village). Tel. 802/253-3964, 800/ 535-9763. E-mail: angler@flyrodshop.com. Web site: www.flyrodshop.com. Hours: 9am-6pm Monday – Friday, 9am-5pm Saturday, 10am-4pm Sunday. Hours may be shortened during winter, call to check. Major credit cards accepted.*

This wonderful shop, offering with hundreds of beautifully made rods, thousands of flies and lures, and hundreds of reels, is worth a visit even for those not interested in the sport of angling. For those who are, it's like a candy shop for children. In addition to selling excellent equipment, the Fly Rod Shop can give good advice about how and where to fish in the Mt. Mansfield area, and it offers a variety of guided tours and clinics. It also sells equipment for salt water fly fishing and arranges saltwater fishing tours in the Caribbean and other places.

THE FISHING HOLE, *Bridge Street, Morrisville VT 05661. Tel. 802/ 888-6210. Open daily. Major credit cards accepted.*

The Fishing Hole features a wide selection of fresh water fishing equipment, including rods, reels, flies, and apparel, as well as offering fishing tours. It also sells hunting gear and equipment for ice fishing in the winter.

BEAVER LAKE TROUT CLUB, *P.O. Box 5270, RFD#1, Morrisville VT 05661. (Take 15 or 15A east of Morrisville to Garfield Road which will be to the north shortly after the junction of Route 15 and 15A; at the intersection bear right). Tel. 802/888-3746. Credit cards: Visa, Mastercard. Open May through September.*

The Beaver Lake Trout Club operates a private lake stocked with trout. Licenses are not needed, and equipment and boats are available for rental. Call in advance to make a reservation as daily spaces are limited.

Golf

THE STOWE COUNTRY CLUB & GOLF SCHOOL, *5781 Mountain Road, Stowe. Tel. 802/253-3000, 800/253-4754. Pro Shop 802/253-4893, Fax 802/253-3618. Web site & e-mail: www.stowe.com. Hours: . Credit cards: major credit cards accepted. Soft spikes required.*

In addition to the 18-hole 6,213 yard (blue tees) Championship Golf Course, among the finest in the state, the Country Club features more than forty acres of practice facilities, a fully equipped pro shop, and a golf school offering instruction for players of all levels from certified PGA and LPGA pros.

COPLEY GOLF COURSE, *Golf Course Road, Morrisville. Tel. 802/888-3013. Major credit cards accepted. Nine holes.*

FARM RESORT, *Route 100, Morrisville VT. Tel. 802/888-3525. Major credit cards accepted. Nine holes.*

SMUGGLERS' NOTCH DRIVING RANGE, *Smugglers' Notch Resort, VT. Tel. 800/451-8752. Major credit cards accepted.*

Hiking

Apart from that muddy month that begins sometime in early or mid-April, Stowe features superb hiking year 'round. For an evening stroll and great views of Mount Mansfield, the **Recreation Path** stretches more than five miles between Stowe Village and the covered bridge behind the Topnotch Tennis Center on Route 108 (a.k.a. the Mountain Road), and is a favorite with snowshoers and cross-country skiers in the winter, and hikers and bikers in the summer and autumn. Running virtually parallel to Route 108, the Path is also accessible from Weeks Hill Road (across from the Golden Eagle just outside Stowe Village), at the Stonybrook condos, and from many of the hotels and other establishments on Route 108 between the Village of Topnotch and Brook Road.

More ambitious climbers should consider **Mount Mansfield**, which at 4,393 feet is the tallest peak in Vermont; **Stowe Pinnacle** (2,740 feet); and **Mount Hunger** (3,538 feet). To reach Mt. Mansfield, get on the Long Trail 8.5 miles from Stowe Village on Route 108; the hike is 2.3 miles each way, and typically takes 5-6 hours round-trip. Stowe Pinnacle, which is easier and more popular, is accessible from Upper Hollow Road in Stowe Hollow, which you can reach from the village by taking School Street south to Stowe Hollow Road and following it as it bends east. For Mount Hunger, which is known for offering perhaps the best views of all, take Maple Street from Waterbury Center to Loomis Hill Road where the trail head is located 4 miles from Route 100. The hike is almost 4 miles round-trip (approximately 4 hours).

Near Smugglers' Notch, there is a moderately difficult mile-plus hike on the Long Trail to **Sterling Pond**, where you can look over the ski runs. Also reachable from the Mt. Mansfield region is the famous **Camel's Hump**. Take Route 100 south through Waterbury and onto River Road for 4.5 miles and follow the signs another 3-4 miles on a road up the left. It is 3.5 easy miles to the summit. Further south of Route 100 in the Mad River Valley, **Mt. Abraham** at 4,006 feet is one of the highest peaks in the state and is accessible from the Lincoln Gap Road off Route 100 in Warren. The climb is 4 miles and takes 2-4 hours.

There are numerous other less sensational hikes in the area, at places like the Little River State Park; contact the organizations below or pick one of the many pamphlets available throughout the region for more details.

GREEN MOUNTAIN CLUB, *4711 Waterbury-Stowe Road (Route 100), Waterbury Center VT -5677. Tel. 802/244-7037, Fax 802/244-5867. E-mail: gmc@sover.net. Web site: www.greenmountainclub.org.*

Vermont's premier hiking club, the GMC publishes numerous guides, books, and pamphlets concerning hiking in the Stowe-Waterbury region as well as the whole state; they also organize hikes in the region and throughout the state.

UMIAK VERMONT ADVENTURE CENTER, *Lower Stowe Village Route 100, Stowe VT 05672. Tel. 802/253-2317.*

Organizes and operates hiking, canoeing, rafting, and kayaking tours and lessons as well as rentals.

Horseback Riding
EDSON HILL MANOR RIDING STABLES, *Tel. 802/253-7371.*

STOWE MOUNTAIN RESORT ACTIVITIES FOR KIDS

After a lesson or two most teenagers and old preteens can easily stay with mom and dad on the slopes if they're not already zooming ahead. For toddlers and younger children, Stowe operates a child care center called **CUB's** *located next to the Sruce Base Lodge. The staff is trained by Early Childhood Development and a staff member trained in first aid and CPR is always on duty. Facilities include toy and play rooms, cribs and nap rooms, a small library, climbing equipment and slides, as well as all sorts of toys, puzzles, and other devices designed to stimulate and occupy children. Kids 3 and older may take part in ski lessons. Call 802/253-3000 or 802/253-3686 for more details, or if you have questions or concerns about security, food, or other issues. A full day (8am-4:30pm) costs $55, half-days (8am-noon, or 12:30pm-4:30pm) cost $40, and beepers are issued for a $5 deposit.*

For older kids, the **Kid's Adventure Center** *located next to the Spruce Base Lodge offers half and full day programs that include ski lessons and passes (half-day $35, full day $75). Children ages 3-12 are eligible to join alpine clinics, while snowboarding is available to 6-12 year olds.*

Skiing & Snowboarding

STOWE, *Route 108 (Mountain Road), Stowe VT 05672. Tel. 802/253-7311, 800/24-STOWE. Web site: www.stowe.com. Lifts open 8pm-4pm (7:30am on weendends). Major credit cards accepted.*

During the 1998-99 season lift ticket prices for adults ranged from $38 from a half-day pass (beginning at noon) to $270 for a seven day pass. During major holidays (Christmas-New Years week, the Martin Luther King Jr. weekend, and Presidents' Day weekend) rates are 15%-20% higher. For children (ages 6-12) and seniors (65 and older) prices range from $22 for a half-day pass to $158 for a seven day pass. Again, these rates go up 15% during peak weekends. Night skiing (5pm-9pm Thursday-Saturday) passes are $20 for adults ($22 during peak weekends), and $16 ($18 during peak weekends) for children and seniors. Ski lesson prices usually include a ski pass.

Lessons for skiers of all levels can be arranged by phone, at any one of the base lodges, and at the Burton Riding Center or the K2/Olin Demo Center. For $30 ('98-'99 prices) both novices, intermediate and advanced adult skiers can join 90 minute ski or snowboard group lessons. For those just beginning there is the Stowe for Starters adult package, which offers two 90 minute lessons (one am and one pm) for $65, or one session in the afternoon for $45. Rates include lift tickets.

Private lessons can also be arranged at the Mansfield and Spruce Base lodges with rates beginning at $65 for one hour and going up to $365 for a full day for 2-5 skiers.

For kids, the Ski and Snowboard Schools at the Children's Adventure Center by the Spruce Base Lodge runs half and full day clinics. Programs begin at 9:30 am and last until 1pm for a half-day ($35), and 3:30pm for the full day ($75). Alpine clinics are open to children ages 3-12, while prospective snowboarders must be at least six.

If you're just in Stowe for the day, renting equipment is most convenient at the **Spruce** and **Mansfield base lodges**. The standard boot, poles, and skis package cost $25 per adult for one day ($18 for each additional day); $15 for children (12 and younger); and $25 for a snowboard package ($15 for 12 and under). They can also tune, sharpen, and wax your skis. *Tel. 802/253-3000. Hours: 7:30am-5pm Monday-Friday; 7am-5pm weekends and holidays.*

SMUGGLER'S NOTCH, *Route 108, Smugglers' Notch, VT. Tel. 802/644-8851, 800/523-2754. Lifts open 8am-4pm. Lift tickets begin at $42 for a single week day adult pass ($32 for a half-day). Tickets for seniors and children from seven to seventeen (under seven ski free) are about 30% cheaper and tickets during major holidays (Christmas-New Years, and Presidents' Weekend) are about 10% more, while passes for dates prior to mid-December or after the end of*

March are 30% less. Vermonters may be eligible for further discounts. Major credit cards accepted.

Smuggler's Notch enjoys a 250-foot higher verticle rise than Stowe, and offers comparble skiing for about 15% less. Eight lifts take skiers to three peaks from which they can enjoy more than sixty trails. The lowest peak, **Morse Mountain**, is serviced by lifts based in the village itself, and provide the easiest runs, most appropriate for novice and beginner skiers. Those who take the lift to Morse Mountain can also ski to the base lodges for **Madonna Mountain** (2640 feet) and **Sterling Mountain** (3010 feet). Madonna Mountain features the most difficult trails (a couple of double and triple diamonds).

For skiing lessons, Peter Ingvoldstad's **Snow Sport University** offers a variety of clinics and lessons for children and adults of all levels. Children from three years and up can participate in day and weeklong ski camps ($60 for one day, $159 for five days). Also, snowboarding is offered to children six years and up. For adult (13 and up) beginners, lessons begin at $49 for a three hour session. Joining a five day package is quite a deal $150, including equipment and lift tickets.

Equipment can be rented at base lodges. Skis, poles, and boots cost $26 per adult per day ($20 for youth and children. A snowboard and boots cost $28, while cross-country equipment is $16.

Sleigh Rides

Favored by lovebirds and children in particular, sleigh rides offer you a great opportunity to capture all the mystique of the Vermont winter. With its pictureqsue landscapes and classic New England village scenes, Stowe is an ideal locale for sleigh rides, so while you're here try one of the following places:

• **Charlie Horse Sleigh Rides at Topnotch**, *Tel. 802/253-2215.*
• **Edson Hill Manor Riding Stables**, *Tel. 802/253-7371.*
• **Pristine Meadows**, *Tel. 802/253-9901.*
• **Stoweflake Resort**, *Tel. 802/253-7355.*

Snowmobiling

For comprehensive information about snowmobiling in Vermont, including the Stowe-Smugglers' Notch-Mt. Mansfield reagion, contact the **Vermont Association of Snow Travelers** (V.A.S.T.), *Tel. 802/229-0005.*

STOWAWAY SNOMOBILE TOURS, *located in Umiak Outfitters on Route 100 in Stowe (just south of the Route 108). Tel. 802/253-6221. Open daily. Credit cards: Mastercard and Visa.*

Rents snowmobiles (including boots and helmets), and offers tours.

Snowshoe Rentals and Tours
   TRAPP FAMILY LODGE SKI CENTER, *42 Trapp Hill Road, Stowe VT 05672. Tel. 802/253-5716., 800/826-7000. Web site: www.trappfamily.com. Trail rates: $12 daily. Major credit cards accepted.*
   TOPNOTCH, *Route 108 (Mountain Road), Stowe VT 05672. Tel. 802/ 253-8585. Web site: www. topnotch-resort.com. Trail fees: $10 daily. Major credit cards accepted.*
   EDSON HILL MANOR, *Edson Hill Road off Route 108, Stowe VT 05672. Tel. 802/253-8954. Trail fees: $10 daily. Major credit cards accepted.*
   SMUGGLERS' NOTCH RESORT, *Route 108 , Smugglers' Notch VT 05464. Tel. 802/644-8851 (Extension 1208). Trail fees: $12. Major credit cards accepted.*
   MOUNTAIN BIKE SHOP, *Mountain Road (Across from the Golden Eagle), Stowe VT 05672. Tel. 802/253-7919. Open daily. Major credit cards accepted.*

Tennis & Racquet Sports
   TENNIS ACADEMY & INDOOR COURTS @ TOPNOTCH, *Mountain Road, Stowe. Tel. 802/253-9649. Credit cards: major credit cards accepted.*
   The Tennis Academy offers lessons and clinics and contains four indoor courts. Call for court reservations and information.

EXCURSIONS & DAY TRIPS

   Burlington, Vermont's largest city, is about a half-hour northeast of Stowe and is a happening little city, offering a variety of culinary, cultural, and shopping opportunites. In terms of sightseeing, there are a variety of interesting attractions, including the **Ethan Allen Homestead** where the leader of the Green Mountain Boys spent his last years; and in **Shelburne** you can visit **Shelburne Farms** with its famous Vistorian Inn and cheese factory on Lake Champlain, and the **Shelburne Museum** featuring various exhibits about life in 19th century Vermont, ranging from exhibits of tools, furniture, and other artifacts, to a restored general store. On and around **Lake Champlain** near Burlington, and particularly on the Lake Champlain islands to the north, there are numerous opportunities for swimming, fishing, and boating.
   The state capital, **Montpelier**, is only 22 miles from Stowe by way of I-89 and Route 2. The smallest state capital in the Untied States, Montpelier is a charming little town whose signature landmark is the modest but elegant gold domed state capital building. Other attractions include the exhibits at the **Vermont Historical Society** and many shops and restaurants, several of which are operated by the **New England Culinary Institute** which is based in Montpelier. Nearby in **Barre** is one of the most

fascinating sights in all of Vermont, the **Rock of Ages granite quarries**, which are the largest in the world; and the **Cabot Creamery** about 20 miles north of Montpelier.

Skiers looking to ski somewhere other than Stowe and Smugglers' Notch might consider a visit to the **Mad River Valley**, approximately 20 miles south on Route 100. The Mad River Valley is home to the **Sugarbush** and **Mad River Glen** ski areas – known for its challenging runs – and features a variety of other recreational opportunities ranging from kayaking to taking a tour of the valley in a glider. There are also numerous shops, charming inns, and fine restaurants; besides, the drive itself is quite beautiful. See the "Mad River Valley" chapter for more information.

South and East of the Mad River Valley is the **Green Mountain National Forest** where areas such as the **Bread Loaf Wilderness** and **Moosalamoo** features some of the best hiking and camping in Vermont. The area is accessible by taking Route 100 south to the Mad River Valley, where you can take Route 17 over the Appalachian Gap to Route 116 and Bristol (20 miles west of Waitsfield); or when there is no snow, you can take the scenic Lincoln Road from Warren over the Lincoln Gap. Finally you can also take Route 100 south to Hancock or Rochester and then cut west into the Forest on Route 125 or Route 73. Route 125 leads to **Middlebury**, a picturesque and culturally vibrant town that is home to Vermont's oldest and most prestigious college. Route 73 leads to another charming village, Brandon. See "Middlebury & the Lower Champlain Valley" chapter for more information.

Another option for skiers, hikers, and outdoor buffs is the region around **Rutland** (80 miles from Stowe) and **Killington** (75 miles from Stowe), both reachable by heading straight south on Route 100 and going west on Route 4 for Rutland. Killington and its sister ski area of Pico offer the most extensive and diverse skiing in the east, as well as opportunities to enjoy hiking, biking, and other outdoors activites. Just about 10 miles beyond Killington on Route 100 South is **Plymouth**, where on Route 100A you can visit the birthplace (and final resting place) of President Calvin Coolidge. His home village Plymouth Notch has been restored and is now open to the public in the summer; it makes for a very enjoyable and educational experience. Just up the road, also on Route 100A, is the **Calvin Coolidge State Park**, where you can camp, hike, and enjoy the wilderness.

Rutland is not generally thought of as tourist destination, but having undergone something of a revival in recent years, it is a pleasant place to visit and features a variety of good restaurants and shops. Just north of Rutland (and less than 20 miles from Brandon) is the **Chittenden Reservoir** with camping, fishing, boating, hiking, and biking. Nearby attractions also include the **Marble Museum** in Proctor, the **Hubbarton**

Battle Monument and Museum, and **Lake Bomoseen**, including Lake Bomoseen State Park, where you can hike, fish, or paddle and sail around in a boat. See the "Rutland & Killington" chapter for more information.

PRACTICAL INFORMATION

Automobile Service & Rentals

STOWE AUTO SERVICE & CAR RENTAL, *Mountain Road, South. Tel. 802/253-7608, 253-8194. Open daily. Major credit cards accepted.*

Stowe Auto Service features a Texaco station with diesel fuel and offers repair services for foreign and domestic makes (they specialize in Saab, Mercedes, BMW, Volkswagen, Audi and Porsche). Rentals offered include economy, midsize, and minivans for daily, weekly, and monthly rates. An AAA Emergency Service.

THRIFTY CAR RENTAL, *Route 100, Waterbury. Tel. 802/244-8800. Website and E-mail: www.thrifty.com/vermont. Hours: Credit cards: .*

Thrifty offers a wide variety of cars and rental packages. With locations throughout Vermont and the United States, as well as Amtrak and corporate rates, it's quite convenient.

Banks & ATM's

UNION BANK, *ATM's in Stowe Village, Stowe Mountain Resort, & Trapp Family Lodge.*

Business Services

THE X PRESS, *Stowe Village. Tel. 802/253-9788, Fax 802/253-7883. Hours: 8am-4:30pm Monday- Friday. Credit cards: major credit cards accepted.*

The X Press prints business cards, letterheads, and provides other basic services including making copies.

Chambers of Commerce

STOWE AREA ASSOCIATION, *P.O. Box 1350/Main Street, Stowe VT 05672. Tel. 802/453-7371, 800/24-STOWE, Fax 802/253-2159. E-mail: stowe@sover.net. Web site: www.Stoweinfo.com.*

SMUGGLERS' NOTCH AREA CHAMBER OF COMMERCE, *info@smugnotch.com. Web site: www.smugnotch.com.*

LAMOILLE VALLEY CHAMBER OF COMMERCE, *Tel. 802/888-7607, 800/849-9985. E-mail: lvcc@together.net. Web site: www.together.net/ ˜lvcc/homepage.htm.*

WATERBURY TOURISM COUNCIL, *P.O. Box 468, Waterbury VT 05676. Tel. Tel. 800/800-2224.*

Gas Stations

MAPLEFIELDS/MOBIL, *Stowe Village. Tel. 802/253-8932. Major credit cards accepted.*

A substantial convenience store and gas station.

Medical Emergencies & Services

Ambulance & Medical Emergencies– *Tel. 911*

Police – *Tel. 911, 802/253-7126*

Fire – *Tel. 911, 253-4315*

Stowe Rescue Squad – *Tel. 802/253-9060*

Poison Center – *Tel. 802/658-3456*

COPLEY HOSPITAL, *Located on Washington Highway, Morrisville. 802/888-4231.*

Offers comprehensive services including 24 hour emergency care and walk-in clinic.

Pharmacies

HERITAGE PHARMACY, *1878 Mountain Road, Stowe VT 05672. Tel. 802/253-2544. Major credit cars accepted.*

Travel Agencies

STOWE TRAVEL SERVICE, *51 Main Street, Stowe. Tel. 802/253-7752.*

20. BURLINGTON & THE CHAMPLAIN VALLEY

Charted in 1763 by the Province of New Hampshire, and named for a prominent local family (the Burlins), **Burlington** got its true start in the early 1770's when **Ira Allen** (brother of the Revolutionary War hero Ethan) built the first shipyard on the Winooski River. After a respite in growth during the Revolutionary War, Burlington's potential as a maritime center was realized by the likes of Allen and an entrepreneurial shipping manufacturer named Gideon King, who came to dominate shipping in Lake Champlain.

In 1791, when Vermont became a state, the **University of Vermont** was chartered and it was decided that Burlington was to be its home; ever since the identities of Burlington and the university have been intertwined. The city's growth was further enhanced by the opening of the Champlain Canal connecting the Lake with Hudson River. Throughout the early 19th century, shipping helped Burlington develop into the largest and most cosmopolitan city in Vermont, a status it retains today.

With the introduction of the railroads in the mid-19th century and the consequential reduction of the shipping industry, Burlington's growth slowed, but its status and the presence of the university ensured that it remained an economic and cultural hub. The city essentially treaded water for much of the twentieth century until recent decades, when an influx of immigrants ranging from urban professionals looking to escape America's megalopolises to immigrants of non-European origins (there is a particularly large Vietnamese community) gave Burlington a boost. An urban renaissance, like many throughout the country, has made Burlington a tourist and cultural center whose economy is now thriving.

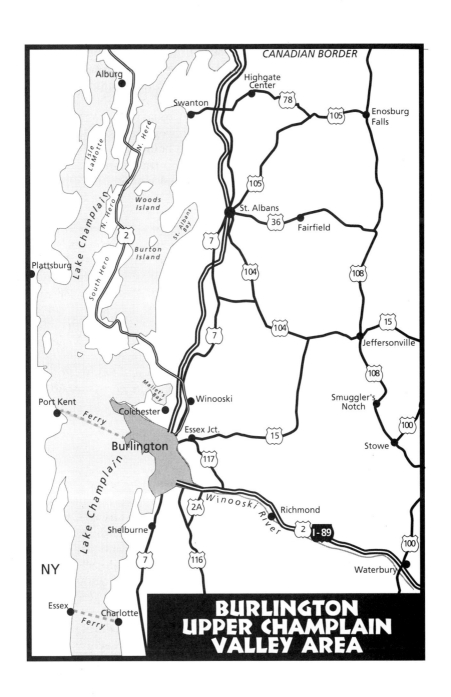

CANADIAN BORDER

Alburg

Highgate
Center

Swanton

78

105

Enosburg
Falls

Isle
LaMotte

N. Hero

Woods
Island

105

St. Albans

36

Fairfield

2

St. Albans
Bay

7

Lake Champlain

N. Hero

Burton
Island

104

108

South Hero

Plattsburg

7

104

15

Jeffersonville

Mallet's
Bay

108

Port Kent

Winooski

Smuggler's
Notch

100

Colchester

Ferry

Essex Jct.

15

Stowe

Burlington

117

Lake Champlain

2A

Winooski River

Richmond

NY

Shelburne

2

I-89

7

116

100

Waterbury

Essex

Charlotte

Ferry

BURLINGTON
UPPER CHAMPLAIN
VALLEY AREA

ARRIVALS & DEPARTURES

By Air

Burlington International Airport, *on Airport Drive (off Route 2) in Burlington,* is serviced by Continental, *Tel. 800/525-0289,* United, *Tel. 800/241-6522* , USAir, *Tel. 800/428-4322,* and the commuter airlines, Business Express, *Tel. 800/345-3400,* and Comair, *Tel. 800/927-0927.*

If you're arriving from overseas, you'll probably find it cheaper and more convenient to fly into **Montreal**, where you can make a connection by bus or rental car. Montreal is roughly an hour and a half drive from Burlington, but can be longer depending on traffic and delays at the border. Boston's **Logan Airport** is another viable option and is approximately four hours from Burlington.

By Car

From points east and south including Boston (240 miles from Burlington) and New Hampshire, **Interstate 89** via White River Junction (91 miles from Burlington) is the most direct and efficient route to the Burlington area and northwest Vermont. From Montpelier (38 miles from Burlington) and the Northeast Kingdom (St. Johnsbury, 77miles), it is also a straight shot on Route 2 which intersects with I-89 in Montpelier. From points due south in the Lower Champlain Valley and the Green Mountains, Route 7 is a direct route from Middlebury (35 miles), Rutland (69 miles), Manchester (99 miles), and Bennington (123 miles). From points along Route 100, take Route 100 north or south to I-89 at Exit 10.

From New York, take I-87 to Exit 34 and take the ferry from Port Kent to Burlington; see below for more details on catching the ferry.

By Boat

Ferries link **Port Kent, New York** and **Burlington** at the King Street Dock off College Street. Ferries leave every 70 minutes from 9am-8:30pm) for $12.75 per vehicle and driver one-way ($23 round-trip), $3.25 every additional adult passenger. To reach points north of Burlington including the islands, take Route 87 to Exit 39 at Plattsburg and take the ferry to Grand Isle, Vermont. Ferries depart every 20 minutes in each direction; fees for car and driver is $7, extra additional passengers $2.50 (children under 12 cost 50¢). South of Shelburne, there is another ferry off New York's I-87 (Exits 31 or 33) in Essex, New York to Charlotte, Vermont (hourly and half hourly departures from 6:30am-11pm during summer, less frequently during other seasons; car and driver $7, additional adult passengers $2.25).

For further information about ferries between northern Vermont and New York, contact the **Lake Champlain Transportation Company**, *King Street Dock, Burlington VT 05401, Tel. 802/864-9804, Web site: www.ferries.com*; or pick up one of their schedule pamphlets available at hotels, highway rest-stops and other sources of tourist information.

By Bus
Vermont Transit Lines, *345 Pine Street, Burlington, Tel. 802/864-6811,* offers direct service between Burlington and major destinations in Vermont, including White River Junction, Rutland, Middlebury, St. Albans, Swanton, Montpelier, and Waterbury-Stowe, as well as major regional destinations including Montreal, Albany, Boston, Manchester NH, and Toronto. At Rutland you can make connections to Ludlow, Brattleboro, Mancheser, and Bennington, while at White River Junction you can make connections for St. Johnsbury and the Northeast Kingdom, Maine, and New York City. Call above for schedule and fare information.

By Train
Amtrak, *Tel. 800/USA-RAIL,* links the Burlington area with St. Albans and Montreal to the north (buses are generally more convenient for northbound travelers), and most of central and southeastern Vermont, as well as the Northeastern seaboard to the south. The southbound train departs the Burlington-Essex Junction station at 8:30am and continues on through Vermont to Waterbury-Stowe, Montpelier-Barre, Randolph, White River Junction, Windsor-Mount Ascutney, Claremont NH, Bellows Falls, and Brattleboro. It then passes through Massachusetts (Amherst, Springfield); Connecticut (Hartford, Berlin, Meriden, New Haven, Bridge-port, Stamford), New York City's Penn Station; New Jersey (Newark), Metropark, Trenton); Philadelphia; Wilmington, Delaware; Maryland (Baltimore, BWI Airport, and New Carrollton); and Washington DC.

Amtrak's **Ethan Allen Express**, which currently links New York and points south with Rutland via Albany and the Hudson River Valley, is planned to extend to Burlington in 2000. Call *Tel. 800/USA-RAIL* for information.

ORIENTATION/GETTING AROUND
By Car
As in most of Vermont, having your own car is by far the easiest way to get around the northwestern portion of the state. The only exception to this is getting around downtown Burlington, where during rush hours and major events (we'll include road work), traffic can back up both downtown and on Routes 7 (especially south into Shelburne) and 2.

Compared to the rest of Vermont, it is relatively easy to rent a car in the Burlington area.

Avis, *Tel. 800/331-1212*, **Budget**, *Tel. 800/244-9429*, and **Hertz**, *Tel. 800/654-3131*, **Thrifty**, *Tel. 802/863-5500, 800/FOR-CARS.* all operate out of **Burlington International Airport**. **Enterprise Rent-A-Car** has an outlet in South Burlington, *Tel. 802/863-2111.* All rental car agencies accept major credit cards.

By Bus

The **Vermont Transit Lines** Burlington-Montreal route departs Burlington for St. Albans (40 minutes) at 6:15am, 3:20pm, 8:15pm and 11:05pm. The 3:20pm bus also stops in Swanton. In the other direction, buses depart St. Albans for Burlington at 7:15am and 9:50am. *Call 802/864-6811 for more information.*

Within Burlington, the **CCTA** operates more than a half-dozen routes connecting all communities with the greater Burlington area, including Winooski, North Avenue, South Burlington, Shelburne, and Essex Junction. Fares are typically $1 one way, though multi-ride tickets are cheaper. You can pay on the bus, but only with exact change. Pamphlets with detailed maps and ticket information are available through the city and at the airport.

WHERE TO STAY

Burlington Area
Includes South Burlington, Shelburne, Colchester, Essex, Richmond, Jericho, & Underhill

RADISSON HOTEL BURLINGTON, *60 Battery Street, Burlington VT 05401. Tel. 802/658-6500, 800/333-3333, Fax 802/658-4659. Web site: www.radisson.com. Rates: $80-$180. Major credit cards accepted.*

It has all the charm of a chain hotel that you might find anywhere in the U.S. (or nowadays the world), but the location just a few minutes' walk from the Church Street Marketplace, and the views overlooking Lake Champlain, are first-rate and make the Radisson worth choosing over other brand name hotels in the area. Facilities are comparable to those you might expect in such an establishment and include two restaurants (one casual, one upscale), an assortment of meeting rooms, business services, a gift shop, and a comedy club. Rooms overlooking the lake are the more expensive, but it's worth it.

SHERATON BURLINGTON HOTEL & CONFERENCE CENTER, *870 Williston Road, Burlington VT 05403. (Off intersection of Route 2 & Exit 14E, I-89). Tel. 802/865-6600, 800/677-6576. E-mail: conthlsvt@aol.com. Web site: www.sheraton.com. Rates: $90-$175. Major credit cards accepted.*

It's very much like the Radisson, only the view is of the strip malls on Williston Road and downtown Burlington is just out of reach for most people who might consider walking. The Sheraton is very comfortable, however, and offers the service and amenities you would expect from one of the world's largest and most successful hotel chains. In addition to standard "deluxe" rooms and suites with cable television, in-room coffee makers and all the rest, the hotel complex features a gym, an indoor pool, jacuzzis, a restaurant, a pub, and business services. There is also an airport shuttle.

HOLIDAY INN BURLINGTON, *1068 Williston Road, South Burlington VT 05403. (Off intersection of Route 2 and Exit 14E, I-89). Tel. 802/863-6363, 800/799-6363, Fax 802/863-3061. Rates: $69-$150. Major credit cards accepted.*

More of the same: decent rooms with amenities, and an assortment of fitness and pool facilities, eateries, and business services, all in a complex with the charm of an airport.

RAMADA INN, *1117 Williston Road, Burlington VT 05403. (Off intersection of Route 2 & Exit 14E, I-89). Tel. 802/658-0250, 800/RAMADA, Fax 802/863-0376. Web site: www.ramada.com. Rates: $69-$150. Major credit cards accepted.*

Another big name cookie cutter hotel offering the usual comfortable rooms with cable television, coffee markers and all the rest. The hotel also features a restaurant, Trader Dukes, with a little more pizzazz than your typical hotel eatery, as well as a bar, pool, and fitness center. Free shuttle service to the airport is also offered.

HAMPTON INN & CONFERENCE CENTER, *6 Mountain View Drive, Colchester VT 05446. (Off Exit 16, I-89). Tel. 802/655-6177, 800/ HAMPTON. Rates:$75-$100. Major credit cards ccepted.*

This second tier brand name hotel and conference center has more than charm and better views than the Sheratons and Holiday Inns of Burlington, and practically the same facilities and services, including standard rooms with cable television, coffee makers, and so on, as well as the obligatory indoor pool, fitness center, and jacuzzis.

HAWTHORNE SUITES HOTEL, *401 Dorset Street, Burlington VT 05401. Tel. 802/860-1212, 800/527-1133. Web site: www.harthotels.com. Rates: $75-$125. Major credit cards accepted.*

Basically a standard brand hotel with amenities like the fitness room and pool, Hawthorne Suites sets itself apart in that it offers rooms and two bedroom suites with actual kitchens. Some rooms also have fireplaces.

INN AT SHELBURNE FARMS, *1611 Harbor Road, Shelburne VT 05482. (Turn west from Route 7 At Shelburne, or west of Bay Road 4 miles south of the junction of Route 7 and I89 which connects Route 7 with I-89). Tel. 802/ 985-8498, Fax 802/985-8123. Web site: www.shelburnefarms.org. Rates: $85-*

$285. Major credit cards accepted. Guestrooms available from mid-May through mid-October.

There is no place in Vermont, or possibly the United States, quite like Shelburne Farms, a 1,400 acre working farm estate on Lake Champlain with a classic Victorian inn containing 26 guestrooms and suites. The rooms vary in furnishings and decor, with some featuring private baths and others shared. But while the rooms are more than decent, it is the grounds themselves that are the attraction. Formerly the estate of Dr. Seward Webb and Lila Vanderbilt, its grounds were landscaped by Frederick Olmstead and contain the 110 room "cottage," a barn with a two-acre courtyard, a mansion where Dr. Webb and Mrs. Vanderbilt lived, as well as several trails for walking or hiking, and a cheese shop (open all year) featuring cheese made on the premises. Tours are available to guests and other visitors from mid-May through mid-October. Not to be confused with the nearby Shelburne Museum, also well worth a visit.

THE INN AT ESSEX, *70 Essex Way, Essex VT 05452. Tel. 802/878-1100, 800/727-4295, Fax 802/878-0063. E-mail: innessex@together.net. Web site: www.innatessex.com. Rates: $130-$200. Major credit cards accepted.*

Featuring nearly 100 rooms (a quarter of which have fireplaces) complete with amenities, this modern hotel was built to capture the atmosphere of the colonial era, and it does quite a convincing job. It also contains a pool, a library, an art gallery, a lounge, and best of all, a first-rate restaurant operated by the New England Culinary Institute. The setting and views are classic Vermont, and hiking trails are accessible directly from the hotel – indeed within its own grounds. An excellent choice overall.

HEART OF THE VILLAGE INN, *P.O. Box 953/2130 Shelburne Road, VT 05482. Tel. 802/985-2800, Fax 802/985-2870. E-mail: bmaynes315@aol.com. Rates: $95-$225. Credit cards: Visa, Mastercard, American Express.*

This recently restored Queen Anne Victorian first opened as a stage coach inn in 1886. Today it features nine lushly decorated rooms and offers a location conveniently near Shelburne attractions, such as the Shelburne Farms and the Shelburne Museum.

POOR FARM INN, *30 Poor Farm Road, Colchester VT 05446. Tel. 802/872-8712, 800/872-8712, Fax 802/872-8711. E-mail: jrogersvt@aol,com Web site: www.poorfarminnvt.com. Rates: $90-$120. Credit cards: Visa, Mastercard.*

This special inn has only four guestrooms, each with its own private entrance and sitting salon, and is surrounded by more than 100 acres on which you can hike, cross-country ski, and snowmobile. There is also a horse farm.

WILLIARD STREET INN, *349 South Williard Street, Burlington VT 05401. Tel. 802/651-8710, 800/577-8712, Fax 802/651-8714. Web site: www.williardstreetinn.com. Rates: $80-$150. Major credit cards accepted.*

For those looking to combine a downtown location, a view of Lake Champlain, and the experience of lodging in a classic Vermont inn, the Williard Street Inn is the choice. There are 15 handsomely appointed rooms (10 with private bath), most of which offer lake views. Breakfast is served in the solarium, and downtown Burlington is within easy walking distance.

WOODBURY GUESTHOUSE, *91 Brookes Venue, Burlington VT 05401. Tel. 802/863-9748. Rates: $75-$90. Credit cards: Visa.*

Located only four blocks from Church Street, this turn of the century Colonial Revival Victorian inn offers four antique decorated rooms (sharing two baths), a convenient location, and a more than adequate breakfast.

CATAMOUNT BED & BREAKFAST, *592 Governor Chittenden Road, Williston VT 05495. (Off Route 2A between 2A's junctions with Route 2 and Route 15 and 117 near the Burlington Airport). Tel. 802/878-2180. Rates: $60. Rates: Visa, Mastercard.*

This quaint B&B features only three rooms with a shared bath, but its significance looms large as it was constructed in 1796 by Thomas Chittenden, Vermont's first Governor. It also offers easy access to Burlington and the factory outlet shopping at Essex.

HARTWELL HOUSE BED & BREAKFAST, *170 Ferguson Avenue, Burlington VT 05401. Tel. 802/658-9242, 800/871-0630. Web site: www.members.aol.com/hartwellbb. Rates: $45-$65. Credit cards: Visa, Mastercard.*

Located in a Burlington residential neighborhood, the Hartwell House features three guestrooms, a common room with a fireplace, and a pool.

HOWDEN COTTAGE BED & BREAKFAST, *32 North Champlain Street, Burlington VT 05401. Tel. 802/864-7198, Fax 802/658-1556. Rates: $39-$79.*

This intimate establishment housed in an 1825 artist's home contains three rooms. Two share a bath (they do have private sinks) while the larger room has its own. Downtown Burlington is within walking distance.

MAMA BOWER'S BED & BREAKFAST, *PO Box 22, Richmond VT 05477. Tel. 802/434-2632. Rates: $35-$60. Credit cards: Visa, Mastercard.*

Situated in Richmond village, this restored 18th century home offers three guestrooms equipped for five people and sharing one bath. The best parts are the delicious breakfast, the friendly hosts, and the convenient location between Stowe and Burlington.

Area Camping

LONE PINE CAMPSITES, *104 Bay Road, Colchester VT 05446. Tel. 802/878-5447. E-mail and web site: www.lonepine.together.com. Base rates: $23. Major credit cards accepted.*

One of the largest campgrounds in Vermont, Lone Pine features more than 250 sites for tents and trailers, as well as trailer rentals. The grounds include two swimming pools, tennis courts, an assortment of recreation rooms and arcades, miniature golf, horseshoe pits, and shuffleboard. As far as practical matters are concerned, there are toilets, wood, ice, showers, and a store. It is not located on Lake Champlain itself, but it is just miles away.

MALLETS BAY CAMPGROUND, *209 Lakeshore Drive, Colchester VT 05446. (Located off Blake Road three miles from Route 7, Exit 16 I-89). Tel. 802/ 863-6980. Base rates: $20-$27. Credit cards: Visa, Mastercard. Open May 1 – October 15.*

Located on Mallets Bay just miles north of Burlington, this campground features nearly 120 sites for tents and campers with flush toilets, showers, laundry facilities, and a pool. Visitors have access to the Bay via a public beach as well as to nearby tennis courts, miniature golf, and (the ads make a point of it) a bingo parlor.

BURLINGTON'S NORTH BEACH CAMPGROUND, *60 Institute Road, Burlington VT 05401. (North of Downtown). Tel. 802/862-0942, 800/ 571-1198. Fax. 802/865-7087. Base rates: $16-$25. Credit cards: Visa, Mastercard. Open May 15 – October 15.*

Operated by the Burlington Parks and Recreation Department, this campground is on a 45-acre plot of beach and woods, and features more than 120 sites for trailers (with hookups), and tents. It's not exactly wilderness, but can be a nice refuge from the nearby city.

SHELBURNE CAMPING AREA AND DUTCH MILL MOTEL & FAMILY RESTAURANT, *4385 Shelburne Road (1 mile north of the Shelburne Museum on Route 7), Shelburne VT 05482. Tel. 802/985-2540 (camping), 802/985-3568 (motel), Fax 802/985-4130. Base rates: $16 (camping) – $28 and up for motel rooms. Major credit cards accepted.*

This complex features 76 camping sites, a simple hotel, and a kind of hokey restaurant built to resemble a Dutch windmill. Its major attraction is the proximity to nearby attractions such as the Shelburne Museum, the Vermont Teddy Bear Company, and boating and fishing opportunities at Lake Champlain.

Franklin County
St. Albans, Swanton, Highgate, Fairfax, Enosburg Falls

TYLER PLACE FAMILY RESORT ON LAKE CHAMPLAIN, *Box 804, Highgate Springs, VT 05460. (Located on Old Dock Road off I-89, Exits 21*

& 22). Tel. 802/868-4000, Fax 802/868-7602. E-mail: tyler@together.net. Web site: www.tylerplace.com. Rates: $42-$75 per child, $80-$175 per adult. Credit cards: Visa, Mastercard, Discover. Open mid-May through Labor Day.

Situated on 160 acres, this family-friendly resort features an assortment of inn rooms and cottages, many of which contain fireplaces. Open only in the summer, its primary attractions are its recreational opportunities. A mile of private beach offers access to swimmers and boaters who can indulge in kayaking, canoeing, windsurfing, waterskiing, and fishing, while on shore the grounds include six tennis courts, a softball field, a petting farm, an indoor pool, hiking and biking trails, and riding about on hay wagons. Golf and horseback riding are possible nearby. For adults keen to enjoy their own playtime without kids, there are supervised activities for children.

COMFORT INN & SUITES, *167 Fairfax Road, St. Albans VT 05478. (Off I-89, Exit 19). Tel. 802/524-3300, 800/228-5150, Fax 802/524-3300. E-mail: comfort2@together.net. Web site: www.selectvermont.com/comfortinn. Rates: $60-$130. Major credit cards accepted.*

This modern hotel offers rooms and suites equipped standard amenities such as cable television, in-room phones and coffee-makers, and air-conditioning, as well as a fitness room and indoor pool. A bit lacking in the charm department.

INN AT BUCK HOLLOW FARM, *RR 1 Box 680, Fairfax VT 05454. Tel. 802/849-2400, Fax 802/849-9744. E-mail: buckholl@together.net. Rates: $60-$90. Credit cards: Visa, Mastercard.*

Set on a 400-acre estate, the Inn at Buck Hollow Farm spoils guests with classic Vermont scenery, jacuzzis, and rooms with canopied beds and decorated with antiques. During the winter, cross-country skiing is accessible from the inn itself.

CADILLAC MOTEL & RESORT, *213 Main Street, St. Albans VT 05478. (On Route 7 off Exit I-89, Exit 19). Tel. 802/524-2191, Fax 802/527-1483. E-mail: cadmotel@together.net. Web site: www.motel-cadillac.com. Rates: $50-$80. Credit cards: Visa, Mastercard, Discover.*

A bit chintzy in decor (witness the Vegas-like heart shaped jacuzzi in the "Honeymoon Suite"), the Cadillac Motel & Resort (a bit of a stretch there) features more than 50 comfortable rooms with cable television, and 3.5 acres of grounds with a swimming pool, picnic tables and grills, and gardens overflowing with more than 10,000 plants and flowers.

Area Camping

LAKEWOOD CAMPGROUND, INC., *RFD 2 Box 482, Swanton VT 05488. (Located on Tabor Road off Route 78 10 miles west of Swanton &). Base Rates: $12-20. Credit cards: Visa, Mastercard. Open May 1 through October 1.*

Lakewood features more than 250 sites for trailers and tents as wells as a provisions store, a pool, tennis courts, a recreation room, and a baseball field. Practical facilities include a dumping station, toilets, showers, and washing machines. Fishermen, swimmers, and boaters can enjoy easy access to Lake Champlain.

LAKESIDE CAMPING, *1348 Route 105, East Brighton Road, Island Pond VT 05846. (1 moe from island Pond on Route 105). Tel. 802/723-6649, 723-6331. Base rates: $16-$22. Credit cards: Visa, Mastercard. Open mid-May through Labor Day.*

In addition to 200 sites for trailers and tents, Lakeside offer visitors 1,500 feet of beach and nice views of Lake Champlain. Facilities include showers, toilets, a game room, a camp store sellling basic food and other supplies, picnic tables, sanitation stations, full hookups for trailers, and LP metered gas. Recreational opportunities include fishing, boating, hiking, and swimming.

The Islands

THE NORTH HERO HOUSE, *Box 155, North Hero VT 05474. (Off Route 2). Tel. 802/372-4732, toll free, 1-8880525-3644, Fax 802/372-3218. E-mail: NHHLAKE@aol.com. Rates: $89-$285. Major credit cards accepted.*

The most distinguished establishment on the islands, the North Hero House offers magnificent views of Lake Champlain and the Green Mountains, a 19th century building with 26 handsomely decorated rooms, a cozy lobby with a fireplace, and access for boats and people to the lake. The rooms vary in terms of amenities and decor with some featuring hot tubs, fireplaces, and private balconies or patios.

SHORE ACRES INN AND RESTAURANT, *Route 2, North Hero VT 05474. Tel. 802/372-8722. E-mail: info@shoreacres.com. Rates: $78-$140. Mastercard, Visa, Discover.*

Shore Acres features nearly 25 rooms overlooking Lake Champlain, in addition to a good restaurant, two tennis courts, and a private beach.

THOMAS MOTT HOMESTEAD, *Blue Rock Road (off Route 78), Alburg 05440-9620. Tel. 802/796-3736, 800/348-0843. Rates: $69-$79. Credit cards: American Express,Discover, Visa, Mastercard.*

This is a restored 19th century guesthouse overlooking Lake Champlain with five rooms, and cross-country skiing on and directly off the premises. Breakfast is included, and guests are often spoiled with complimentary ice cream as well.

CHARLIE'S NORTHLAND LODGE, *RR 1 Box 88, North Hero 05474. Tel. 802/372-8822, Fax 802/372-5215. Rates: $55-$65. Credit cards: Visa, Mastercard.*

This modest establishment contains only two rooms (shared bed) in a 19th century building decorated with antiques. Boats are rented and hiking, fishing, canoeing, and sailing are all accessible.

Area Camping

NORTH HERO STATE PARK, *3803 Lakeview Drive (after crossing the bridge on the North Hero, continue for two mile and take a left on Lakeview Road for two miles), North Hero VT 05474. Tel. 802/372-8727 (summer), 802/879-5674 (off-season). Base rates: $12-$16. Open late May through Labor Day. Credit cards: Visa, Mastercard.*

Facilities include about 100 tent and trailer sites and 18 lean-to's. Sites features toilets, picnic tables, and showers, but no hookups for trailers.

KNIGHT ISLAND STATE PARK, *c/o Burton Island State Park, P.O. Box 123, St. Alban's Bay VT 05481. (Knight Island is a separate island east of North hero and is only accessible by boat from Burton Island off St. Albans'). Tel. 802/524-6353 (summer), 802/879-5674 (off-season). Base rate: $12. Open late May through Labor Day. Credit cards: Visa, Mastercard.*

Situated on its own island between North Hero and the Vermont mainland, this state park is special because of its remoteness. There are no vehicles permitted. Nor for that matter are there any flushing toilets or running water. Though the island and park cover nearly 200 acres, there are only seven campsites and two lean-to's, so you should definitely call for reservations in advance. Apart from the remoteness, Knight Island offers good hiking and excellent views of the Lake Champlain region.

BURTON ISLAND STATE PARK, *P.O. Box 123, St. Alban's Bay VT 05481. (Burton Island is accessible only by boat from Kill Kare State Park on Hathaway Point Roadabout three miles from St. Alban's). Tel. 802/524-6353 (summer), 802/879-5674 (off-season). Base rates: $12-$17. Credit cards: Visa, Mastercard.*

Like Knight Island, Burton Island (as the name obviously suggests) is an island in Lake Champlain, only accessible by boat. However, compared to Knight, Burton is laden with developed amenities, including a 100-slip marina with gasoline and power, a store, and even carts to lug your stuff around. The campground itself features nearly 50 sites, about half with lean-to's, equipped with showers (not free) and toilets.

KINGS BAY CAMPGROUND, *1088 Lakeview Drive, North Hero VT 05474-9689. (Across from Alburg off Route 2 on Lakeview Drive. Tel. 802/372-3735. Base rates: $13-$16. Credit cards: Visa, Mastercard. Open First week of May through Labor Day.*

With only 40 sites for trailers and tents, Kings Bay offers 1,300 feet of lakefront with docks and opportunities for swimming, boating, and fishing. Facilities include free hot showers, toilets, 20 amp electric hookups, and fresh water. Gas and other supplies are available within three miles.

ALBURG RV RESORT, *P.O. Box 50, Alburg VT 05440-0050. (Located on Blue Rock Road off Route 78 two miles east of the junction of Route 2 and Route 78). Tel. 802/796-3733. Base rates: $20-$24. Credit cards: Visa, Mastercard. Open May 1 through October 1.*

More than 175 sites (150 with electric hookups) are on offer along with hot showers, toilets, laundry machines, a convenience store, and air conditioning (for an extre fee). Visitors can take advantage of the 1,500 foot beach to enjoy swimming, boating, waterskiing, canoeing, fishing, and windsurfing; or you can work up a sweat playing basketball, volleyball, and/or softball. And oh yeah, there's a pool as well.

CAMP SKYLAND ON LAKE CHAMPLAIN, *398 South Street, South Hero VT 05486. (Take Route 2 ten miles from Exit 17, I-89; 3.5 miles on South Street). Tel. 802/372-4200. Base rates: $16 (camping sites) – $250 (most expensive cabins). Credit cards: Visa, Mastercard. Open Memorial Day (end of May) through September.*

Camp Skyland offers a choice between one (or more) of the 33 campsites and staying in one of the cabins designed to house 2-6 people. Cabins feature fully equipped bathrooms, a fridge and cooking facilities, and bedding. Facilities for campers include showers, toilets, laundry machines, picnic tables, and campfire rings. Visitors can spend their time, fishing, swimming, boating (rowboats and canoes available for rental), and generally enjoying the Lake.

WHERE TO EAT
BURLINGTON
Church Street Marketplace & Downtown

LEUNIG'S, *on the corner of College and Church Streets in the Church Street Marketplace, Burlington. Tel. 802/863-3759. Open for breakfast 7am-11am Monday-Friday, 9am-3:30pm for brunchon Saturday & Sunday, Lunch served 11am-5pm Monday-Friday, lite fare 3.30pm-5pm Saturday and Sunday, dinner served nightly 5pm-10pm, Late Night: fare served from 10pm-midnight. Major credit cards accepted.*

"An old world Cafe" and longtime Burlington landmark under new management, Leunig's Bistro combines old world atmospherics and recipes with nouveau American cuisine and a vibrancy stemming from a constant flow of customers and the live jazz featured several nights a week. For breakfast and brunch there is an extensive choice of high-end omelets, pancakes, waffles, and other egg dishes, costing between $4 and $10. Before dinner is served at 5pm, diners may choose from the bistro menu that includes nouveau American and continental dishes, such as Tuscan-style mussels ($6.95), spinach salad with Vermont goat cheese, red peppers and a maple flavored vinaigrette ($5.50), and farfalle bow tie pasta with exotic mushrooms, artichoke hearts, and sundried tomatoes (7.75). After 5pm, you may also choose from the dinner menu with larger more gourmet dishes like shrimp and scallops provencal ($15.50), New York Steak au Poivre ($16.95), and roasted rack of lamb with medallions of Vermont goat cheese for $24.95 (full), or $16.50 (half rack). After 10pm some of the liter items from the bistro menu are available as the bar remains open until midnight

SWEETWATERS, *on the corner of Church and College Streets in the Church Street Marketplace, Burlington. Tel. 802/864-9800. Open daily from 11:30am until midnight and beyond. Sunday Bruch served from 10:30am. Major credit cards accepted.*

Sweetwaters features one of the most extensive and interesting menus in Burlington. For those with less than an entirely empty stomach, there is a wide variety of soups (onion soup, bison chili, soup de jour), salads, and appetizers ranging from quality bar food like wings and nachos to salmon cakes and portabello caponata (grilled portabello with vegetables, balsamic vinegar sauce, and topped with goat cheese). Also good are sandwiches and bistro items like flatbreads, risotto with smoked chicken ($10.95), fajitas ($8-$10), and garlic herbed mussel with linguine ($10.95). There is also a special assortment of moderately sized bison features, such as bison chili ($6.95), bison loaf, and three types of bison burgers.

Finally, entrees ($10-$20) run the gamut in terms of ingredients and types of cuisine. There are American dishes such as grilled pork tenderloin, T-bone steak, and crab stuffed trout, as well as international flavors in teriyaki steak, and several types of pastas. Sweetwaters is also open for Sunday brunch, where you can choose from gourmet egg dishes, waffles, and other breakfast items served from 10:30am. Sweetwaters is a smartly decorated but casual establishment with bar, dining room, and outdoor seating.

FIVE SPICE CAFE, *175 Church Street, Burlington. Tel. 802/864-4045. Hours: 11am-10pm daily, Sunday brunch at 11:30am. Major credit cards accepted.*

The Five Spice Cafe is a distinctly Burlingtonian Asian restaurant. It features a menu long enough to make any Chinese restaurant owner proud, with dishes reflecting a variety of Asian culinary traditions from Chinese and Vietnamese to Burmese and Indonesian. Entrees such as Thai Red Snapper in Spicy Sweet Sauce, Vegetarian Vindaloo, and Sichuan beef with broccoli range from $10-$16 ($6-$9 for lunch portions), while there is also a selection of bistro items like Thai noodles in green curry and Five Spice Rice, all of which are under $10. Most items can be made in vegetarian form, while shrimp, chicken, beef, and tofu can be added to vegetarian dishes. The food is delicious and impressively

352 VERMONT GUIDE

authentic, even though the staff is 90% Caucasian and the dining room decor is pure Americana with pictures of pop and movie stars, and old posters and newspaper clippings. Dim Sum brunch on Sundays is excellent and very popular.

NECI COMMONS, *25 Church Street, Burlington VT. Tel. 802/862-6324. Open 11:30am-9:30pm Monday-Saturday, 10:30am-9pm Sunday. Major credit cards accepted.*

The New England Culinary Institute's Burlington branch features a slightly eclectic, ever-changing selection of contemporary American dishes ranging from sandwiches, breads, and baked goods, to full-fledged pasta and meat entrees. Take-out and on-site dining are both available, and classes and demonstrations are sometimes open to the public.

BOURBON STREET GRILL, *213 College Street (just off the Church Street Marketplace), Burlington. Tel. 802/2800. Open daily from 11am until late.*

Colorful, fun, and happening, the Bourbon Street Grill really does capture the fun-loving spirit of New Orleans as well as its culinary essence. Jambalaya, crab cakes, jerked chicken, grilled catfish, and dozens of other southern and American favorites not available anywhere else in Vermont can be had "as hot as you like." Makes for a great change from the mild and subtle flavors of most New England cuisine, no matter how good it is. Also a great place to throw a few back with some friends over a game of pool.

On the Waterfront

ISABEL'S ON THE WATERFRONT, *112 Lake Street, Burlington VT. Tel. 802/865-2522. Open for lunch Monday-Friday 11am-2pm, brunch 10:30am-2pm Saturday & Sunday, dinner nightly 5:30pm-9pm. Major credit cards accepted.*

Located in a renovated 19th century industrial complex, Isabel's serves excellent nouveau American cuisine in a beautiful setting overlooking the Waterfront Park and Lake Champlain. "Accessible by car, bike, and boat," it features outdoor seating during the summer, while the interior features paintings by local artists. For appetizers, there is a choice of more than a dozen items ranging from baked goat cheese flavored with pesto and Maine crab cakes, to chicken quesadilla, and a seafood sampler. Entrees are no less diverse or eclectic, as you can choose between cashew-vegetable stirfry, maple ginger chicken, or salmon and artichoke heart pasta. Lunch features a rotating menu of similar fare, while the highly acclaimed Sunday brunch features more traditional items such as pancakes, french toast, and Eggs Benedict.

MONA'S, *3 Main Street, Burlington. Tel. 802/658-6662. Open from 11:30am-11pm Monday-Wednesday, 11:30am-midnight Thursday-Saturday, 10:30am-10pm Sunday. Major credit cards accepted.*

Specializing in anything grilled from steak and prime rib to yellowfin tuna steak or portabello mushrooms, Mona's is a classy but casual eatery with views of Lake Champlain and outdoor deck seating in the summer. The menu is extensive, prices are reasonable (most items are under $15), and the Sunday brunch buffets are well known throughout the region.

DOCKSIDE CAFE, *209 Battery Street on Perkin's Pier, Burlington VT. Tel. 802/864-5266. Open for lunch and dinner.*

The Dockside serves a variety of quality dishes for lunch and dinner at a very scenic waterfront setting. For lunch, there is a choice of salads such as ceasar, tossed cucumber (really a full Greek salad), and Greek salad; and sandwiches ranging from fresh salmon and crab cake sandwich, to grilled steak and chicken ceasar roll-ups. Lunch items cost between $5 and $8. The dinner menu features a wider variety of choice. Appetizers ($6-$9) include calamari, buffalo shrimp, and perhaps a quesadilla; while entrees feature "VT Chicken" with Macintosh apples, cheddar cheese and cured ham with potato, grilled tuna, vegetarian lasagna and lamb chops marinated in garlic and balsamic vinegar. Entrees price between $9 and $20.

SHANTY ON THE SHORE, *181 Battery Street (off the Church Street Marketplace), Burlington VT. Tel. 802/864-0238. Major credit cards accepted. Open daily 11am-10pm.*

Located on the waterfront in a renovated commercial building with indoor and outdoor seating, the Shanty specializes in seafood and features a variety of raw bar favorites like oysters on the half-shell, steamers, and oysters Rockefeller. Entrees include blackened swordfish, yellowfin tuna, and salmon as well as non-seafood items like vegetarian pasta and chicken teriyaki. For lunch, there are a number of sandwiches like grilled chicken and lobster roll, as well as fish and chips and several salads. Apart from the lobster, most entrees are under $18.

Bakeries, Ice Cream & Coffee

BEN & JERRY'S, *36 Church Street, Burlington. Tel. 802/862-9620. Hours: . Credit cards:*

This is the flagship scoop shop for America's most famous ice cream manufacturers. A great place to sample and stock up on Vermont's newest signature export.

DOUGHBOY'S BAKERY & PASTRY SHOP, *85-87 Pearl Street, Burlington. Tel. 802/658-1425. Hours: daily.*

Specializes in baked goods, including breads, cakes, pastries, and other baked desserts.

KLINGER'S BREAD, *at the corner of Church and College Streets in the Church Street Marketplace, Burlington. Hours: 7:30am-6pm Monday-Wednesday & Saturday; 7:30am-9pm Thursday & Friday; 9am-5pm Sunday. Credit cards:*

Northern Vermont's favorite bakers (their bread is found on the tables of many of Burlington's finer eateries), the self-annointed "Best Bread Under the Sun" can be sampled at this small kiosk. Offerings include scones, muffins, patries, and sandwiches as well as loaves of whole wheat, sourdough, and other types of bread. No seating.

Diners

THE OASIS DINER, *189 Bank Street (off the Church Street Marketplace), Burlington VT. Tel. 802/864-5308. Open 6am-11pm.*

Founded in the 1950's, this chrome diner is popular with folks from all walks of life, including politcians like Senator Patrick Leahy and Governor Dean, who brought President Clinton here as you can see from the various photographs and news clips dotting the place.

HENRY'S DINER, *155 Bank Street (off the Church Street Marketplace), Burlington VT. Tel. 802/862-9010. Open 6:30am-3:45pm Monday-Saturday, 6:30am-3:45pm Sunday.*

In business since 1925.....a classic.

SOUTH BURLINGTON & SHELBURNE

PERRY'S FISH FOUSE, *1080 Shelburne Road (Route 7), South Burlington. Tel. 802/862-1300. Major credit cards accepted.*

Widely regarded as serving the best seafood in Burlington, if not Vermont, Perry's offers reasonably priced New England-style fish and shellfish dishes as well as some meat, poultry, and vegetarian fare. Appetizers include calamari, almond fried shrimp and of course a delicious clam chowder; for non-seafood lovers, there are french fries, a salad bar, and roasted garlic whipped potatoes among others. For entrees there is a wide selection of seafood, including all sorts of fried, roasted, grilled, and poached fish, clams, shrimp, fish, crab, scallops, and lobster. There are also several seafood pasta selections, as well as steaks, grilled chicken, and upon request, vegetarian pasta. Entrees (apart from lobster) are typically between $10 and $16, while starters hover around $5-$6. The atmosphere is casual and family-friendly.

LA VILLA MEDITERRANEAN BISTRO & PIZZERIA, *Tennybrook Square on Route 7, Shelburne VT. Tel. 802/985-2596. Open 11am-9:30 Monday-Saturday, 4pm-9pm Sunday. Major credit cards accepted.*

La Villa serves a balanced assortment of Italian dishes including pizza, antipasti (appetizers), pasta, upscale entrees, and casual bistro fare. Appetizers include spicy crabcakes, artichoke and spinach dip and grilled focaccio, and there are a half-dozen salads from simple green salads for $3.25 to Miskell's Tomato Plate with a variety of cheeses and greens for $6.95. Pizzas come in three sizes ($9.95, $13.55, $17.55) and include a Greek spinach special with garlic, black olives, mushrooms, and a variety of cheeses, provencal with Vermont goat cheese, artichoke hearts and other vegetables and herbs. For other main dishes, you can choose between entrees such as grilled salmon with pesto potatoes ($12.95), shrimp farfalle (bow tie pasta with shrimp, roasted red peppers, and artichokes in a pesto chardonnay sauce) for $12.95, and baked trout with risotto ($11.95); or casual bistro fare like lasagna ($7.95) and lemon chicken salad ($5.95).

SIRLOIN SALOON, *2545 Shelburne Road (Route 7), Shelburne VT. Tel. 802/985-2200. Open 4:30pm Monday-Friday, 4pm Saturday & Sunday. Major credit cards accepted.*

Owned by the same folks who operate Perry's and Sweetwaters, the Sirloin Saloon serves a variety of steaks and other grilled fare in a casual setting distinguished by the Native American decor which gives it a bit of a western flavor. Steaks and other grilled fare such as chicken and seafood typically costs $10-$20 per platter (salad bar, potato included). For those not so keen on eating grilled meat, the salad bar is extensive and can easily be made into an entire meal. There are also veggie appetizers and vegetarian pasta.

Diners

COSMOS DINER, *1110 Shelburne Road (Route 7), South Burlington. Tel. 802/651-8774. Open 6:30am-11pm.*

Feast on classic diner food in a vintage 1954 Worcester diner car.

ESSEX

BUTLER'S, *Located in the Inn at Essex at 70 Essex Way, Essex VT. (Off Exit 10, I-289). Tel. 802/878-1100. Open for breakfast, lunch (11:30am-2pm), tavern opens at 2pm, and dinner from 6pm-10:30pm. Major credit cards accepted.*

Located in the neo-Colonial Inn at Essex and operated by the New England Culinary School (based in Montpelier), Butler's is one of the most popular restaurants in the area. The prix-fixe menus (usually around $25) rotate nightly and features cutting edge gourmet American and continental cuisine. Dress is smart casual (no need for a tie, but no jeans either).

WINOOSKI
WATERWORKS, *Champlain Mill, Winooski VT. Tel. 802/655-2044. Open daily 11:30am-closing (around 11pm-midnight). Major credit cards accepted.*

Waterworks serves moderately priced (entrees $8-$20) American cuisine in a beautifuly restored mill over looking the Winooski River. Seating options include a solarium, outdoor deck, balcony, and platform, while the menu includes great salads, pastas, meats, and fowls, and vegetarian fare as well as appetizers and desserts.

COLCHESTER
SKILLETS RESTAURANT, *Creek Farm Shopping Center on Route 7, Colchester VT. Tel. 802/878-3435. Open for lunch and dinner daily except Monday. Credit cards: Visa, Mastercard.*

Skillets serves a variety of American and international dishes ranging from New York Strip Steak and Cajun Jambalaya to Asian Barbequed Shrimp, wok stirfrys and pizzas.

FRANKIE JUNIORS RESTAURANT & JUNIORS PIZZA, *6 Roosevelt Highway, Colchester VT. Tel. 802/655-5555. Open for lunch and dinner until late.*

Casual and cheap Italian food and pizzas; take-out and delivery available.

LIBBY'S BLUE LINE DINER, *Across from the Marriot Fairfield Inn on Route 2/7 (off Exit 16), Colchester VT. Tel. 802/863-3759. Open from 7am-10pm.*

Classic diner food and a great place to sample local color.

ST. ALBANS
JEFF'S MAINE SEAFOOD, *65 North Main Street (Route 7), St. Albans VT. Tel. 802/524-6135. Open 10am-9pm/10pm, retail stores closes at 7pm daily except Sunday when it closes at 2pm. Credit cards: Visa, Mastercard.*

A lively and casual seafood restaurant and retail store, Jeff's is located at the northern end of Taylor Park. The specialties are seafood – live lobster, clam chowder – though there are plenty of chicken, meat, and vegetarian dishes. The wine list is extensive and on the weekends live music is provided. The retail store sells both prepared and fresh fish as well as numerous salads, sandwiches, terrific desserts, and ethnic foods from Chinese noodle salad to savory Greek pastries to go. Expect to pay $15-$25 for a full seafood dinner plus wine, less if you choose other fare.

OLD FOUNDRY RESTAURANT, *Corner of Federal Street & Lake Street (one block west from Main Street), St. Albans VT. Tel. 802/524-9665. Open for lunch 10:45am-2pm, and 5pm until closing for dinner. Major credit cards accepted.*

Situated in an old foundry where railroad wheels were produced, this testament to St. Albans' railroad heritage serves quality American cuisine including steaks, seafood and pasta for moderate prices (full dinner $20-$30 including wine or beer).

CHOW! BELLA, *28 Main Street, St. Albans VT. Tel. 802/524-1405. Open 11am for lunch and dinner. Major credit cards accepted.*

Casual but classy bar serving upscale munchies, like salads and flatbreads as well as quality beers and wines. Entrees include seafood, steak, and pastas.

HIGHGATE SPRINGS

TYLER PLACE FAMILY RESORT ON LAKE CHAMPLAIN, *Box 804, Highgate Springs, VT 05460. (Located on Old Dock Road off I-89, Exits 21 & 22). Tel. 802/868-4000, Fax 802/868-7602. E-mail: tyler@together.net. Web site: www.tylerplace.com. Credit cards: Visa, Mastercard, Discover. Dining room open 12:30pm-1:30pm (lunch), 6:30pm-8pm (dinner) mid-May through Labor Day.*

Standard family fare.

FAIRFAX

THE COUNTRY PANTRY, *Junction of Route 104 and Route 128, Fairfax VT. Tel. 802/849-6364. Open for breakfast, lunch and dinner.*

Cheap, hearty American country food – even dinner entrees are under $10.

SWANTON

MARBLE MILL CAFE, *Merchant's Row, Swanton VT. Tel. 802/868-5019. Open for lunch and dinner. Credit cards: Visa, Mastercard.*

Very pleasant dining, especially when the weather cooperates and you can sit out on the deck overlooking the Missisquoi River. Cuisine is standard American and prices are moderate – you can eat a full diner for $10-$20 and lunch for under $10.

ENOSBURG FALLS

ABBEY RESTAURANT, *Route 105, Enosburg Falls VT. Tel. 802/933-4747.*

Nice place, moderate prices.

MONTGOMERY & MONTGOMERY CENTER
BLACK LANTERN INN, *Route 118, Montgomery Village VT 05470. Tel. 802/326-4507, 800/255-8662. E-mail: blantern@together.net. Web site: www.blacklantern.com. Open 6pm-9pm Wednesday through Sunday. Major credit cards accepted.*

Serves fine American and gourmet country cuisine in an elegant candlelit setting.

JR's, *Main Street, Montgomery Center VT. Tel. 802/326-4682. Open 6:30am-10pm.*

Serves cheap, no-frills, but more than adequate American food.

THE ISLANDS
THE NORTH HERO HOUSE INN & RESTAURANT, *Route 2, North Hero. Tel. 802/372-4732, Tel. 888/525-3622. Web site: www.northherohouse.com. Open daily for dinner 5:30pm-8:30pm. Major credit cards accepted.*

The Island's most popular and probably finest dining can be enjoyed at the charming North Hero House Inn, where dinner is served nightly and the menu includes steaks, pastas, seafood, among others. On Friday night, the menu is null and void as they spread out the lobster buffet with salads, lobster and other seafood dishes, and a variety of side plates ($25.95). There is seating in the dining room and on the porch, which is recommended if you can make a reservation which you should do in any case, particularly on weekends. Entrees price between $13 and $23.

MARGO'S CAFE & BAKERY, *Route 2 (across from the Post Office), Grand Isle Village VT. Tel. 802/372-6112. Credit cards: Visa, Mastercard.*

Serves coffees, fresh pastries and baked goods, in addition to soups, sandwiches, salads, and other light fare such as quiche.

SEEING THE SIGHTS
Burlington
Commercial, cultural, and culinary activity in Burlington is centered around the **Church Street Marketplace** on Church Street between Main and Pearl Streets. Recently restored, the Marketplace has breathed much needed life not only into downtown Burlington, but the city and the state as a whole. Some complain about features like the enormous Border's bookstore and the Burlington Square Mall, which they feel give the Marketplace an over-commercialized "Anywhere USA" feel, but by and large most of the hundreds of shops and restauranta are owned and operated by local merchants and chefs. For a complete directory of all of the Marketplace's restaurants and businesses, asa well as other information, call *802/863-1648* or write *Church Street Marketplace, 135 Church Street, Suite 4, Burlington VT 05401.*

Important downtown landmarks on **Church Street** include the colonial revival style City Hall, the City Hall Park, the Federal Unitarian Church and the Richardson Romanesque Masonic Temple. Along the **waterfront,** the docks on Battery Street were the shipping hub of Lake Champlain and Burlington's primary engine of economic growth. Today there are several restaurants serving quality food and offering even better sunset views, as well as the **Burlington Bike Path**, **Battery Park**, and the **Community Boathouse**, the hub of recreational boating in the area. During the summer, the waterfront buzzes with activity as it hosts activities from brewfests to Fourth of July firework displays. East of Church Street the commercial district gives way to the **"Hill Section"** with its Victorian and Queen Anne houses and villas and eventually the **University of Vermont campus**, itself home to an assortment of 19th and early 20the century buildings.

VERMONT STATE CRAFT CENTER-FROG HOLLOW ON THE MARKETPLACE, *85 Church Street, Burlington VT 05401. Tel. 802/863-6458. Open 10am-6pm Monday-Saturday, noon-5pm Sunday. Admission free.*

Dedicated to the promotion of Vermont-produced arts and crafts, this 1991 branch of the Center (the orginal is in Middlebury) features displays of art from more than 250 Vermont artists, and also presents special classes, lectures, and demostrations.

ROBERT HULL FLEMING MUSEUM, *61 Colchester Street, Burlington VT. (about 6 miles east from Church Street on Pearl Street). Tel. 802/656-0750. Open 9am-4pm Tuesday-Friday & 1pm-5pm Saturday and Sunday Labor Day through May 1; noon-4pm Tuesday-Friday & 1pm-5pm Saturday & Sunday May through Labor Day (early September). Admission: $2 donation.*

Operated by the University of Vermont, the "Fleming," as it's known, features a modest (but still Vermont's top) collection of art from the United States, Europe, Ancient Egypt, Asia and Africa. Call about special lectures, classes, and guided tours.

PERKINS MUSEUM OF GEOLOGY, *Colchester Avenue, Burlington VT 05401. Tel. 802/656-8694. Open daily 9am-5pm. Admission free.*

Popular with children and natural history buffs, the Perkins features a colorful assortment of displays featuring numerous fossils, skeletons, dioramas, and other multimedia exhibits.

BAILEY/HOWE SPECIAL COLLECTIONS, *Main Street, Burlington VT 05401. Tel. 802/656-2138. Open during the academic year (September-May) 10am-9pm Monday -Thursday, 10am-5pm Saturday and Sunday, 9am-5pm Monday-Friday during the summer. Admission free.*

The University of Vermont's Bailey/Howe Library contains the Wilbur Collection of historic Vermont documents including maps, manuscripts, and books about early Vermont and Canadian history. Probably of interest only to history buffs.

FLETCHER FREE LIBRARY, *235 College Street, Burlington VT 05401. Tel. 802/863-3403. Hours: 8:30am-6pm Monday-Friday (except Wednesday), 8:30am-9pm Wednesday, 9am-5:30pm Saturday, noon-6pm Sunday from September through May. Free admission.*

The city library, Fletcher includes a room dedicated to local history that features historic documents, photographs, and artifacts relating to local and state history.

Route 127 North of downtown

Off Route 127 just north of downtown, the **Ethan Allen Homestead** features the revolutionary hero's restored 1787 farm and final residence as well as historical exhibits (including a recreated tavern), a multi-media show, and a gift shop. *Hours: 1-5pm daily mid-May -mid-June; 10am-5pm Monday-Sutrday, 1-5pm Sunday; and by appointment in the off-season. Tel. 802/865-4556. E-mail: ethan@vbimail.champlain.edu.*

Winooski

As Burlington grew into a major shipping center, the town of the **Winooski** across the Winooski River developed as an industrial center, and throughout the 19th century it remained an important producer of textiles. Today, the town is essentially a suburb of Burlington, though its industrial past is evident in several remaining mills. Major attractions are the **Champlain Mill**, now renovated and home to a great restaurant overlooking the Winooski River, and a shopping center that includes an outlet of **Dakin Farm**, a producer of Vermont specialty foods.

WINOOSKI HISTORIC SOCIETY, *73 East Allen Street, Winooski VT 05404. Tel. 802/655-3561. Open on the last Sunday of every month except December. Tours given .*

This historical society houses a small collection of historic artifacts, photographs, and documents relating to local history.

Essex

East of Burlington at the junctions of Routes 15, 2A, 128 and 117, the town of **Essex** (including Essex Center and Essex Junction) became a prominent transportation and industrial hub in the mid-19th century, when the railroad revolutionized transportation and three Vermont Central R.R. lines intersected at Essex Junction. The railroad industry has largely faded, though Amtrak still stops in Essex, and today the town is known for its outlet shopping and an IBM plant with 8,000 employees (making it the largest employer in Vermont, and Essex the second largest city in the state).

ESSEX COMMUNITY HISTORICAL SOCIETY, *Junction of Routes 15 and 128, Essex Center VT. Tel 802/878-6486. Open noon-4pm Saturday and Sunday from Memorial Day (late May) through Columbus Day (mid-October). Admission free.*

Located in an old schoolhouse, this modest museum features a number of school items and other exhibits relating to local history.

Shelburne

Just south of Burlington on Route 7, **Shelburne** is best known for the Frederick Law Olmstead-designed Shelburne Farms and the nearby Shelburne Museum, both of which are very worth a visit. Unfortunately, Shelburne itself has assumed something of a strip mall identity.

SHELBURNE FARMS, *1611 Harbor Road, Shelburne VT 05482. (Turn west from Route 7 at Shelburne, or west of Bay Road four miles south of the junction of Route 7 and I89 which connects Route 7 with I-89). Tel. 802/985-8498, Fax 802/985-8123. Web site: www.shelburnefarms.org. Admission: $4 adults, $3 children. Tours: $6.50 adults, $5.50 seniors, $3.50 children. Open Mid-May through mid-October.*

There is no place in Vermont, or possibly the United States, quite like Shelburne Farms, a 1,400-acre working farm estate on Lake Champlain. The farm also includes a classic Victorian inn containing a variety of 26 guestrooms and suites. Formerly the estate of Dr. Seward Webb and Lila Vanderbilt, its grounds were landscaped by Frederick Law Olmstead and feature the 110 room "cottage," a barn with a two-acre courtyard, a mansion where Dr. Webb and Mrs. Vanderbilt lived, several trails for walking or hiking, and a cheese shop (open all year) selling cheese made on the premises. Tours are available from mid-May through mid-October. Not to be confused with the nearby Shelburne Museum (see below) – also well worth a visit.

SHELBURNE MUSEUM, *Off Route 7 in Shelburne. Tel. 802/985-3346. Open 10am-5pm daily from late May through October. Admission (for two days): $17.50 adults, $10 students, $7 children. Family rates are also available.*

This fantastic museum features a wide array of exhibits in nearly 40 rooms, ranging from a restored 19th century village complete with a general store, jail, and sawmill, to natural history exhibits and an extensive collection of American art.

VERMONT TEDDY BEAR COMPANY FACTORY AND MUSEUM, *2236 Shelburne Road (Route 7), Shelburne. Tel. 802/985-3001. Open 9am-6pm Monday through Saturday, 10am-5pm Sunday. Admission is free, tours cost $1. Major credit cards accepted.*

Visitors can take a tour of a small museum dedicated to the history of teddy bears, but the main attraction is the shop where you can pick from among hundreds of teddy bears dressed in every costume imaginable.

St. Albans

Roughly 30 miles north of Burlington on Route 7 or I-89, **St. Albans** was once a major railroad stop for cargoes coming and going between New York and Vermont, and from Montreal. Though not a major tourist destination, its museum is quite impressive.

ST. ALBANS MUSEUM, *Off Main Street (Route 7), St. Albans. Tel. 802/527-7933. Open 1pm-4pm Tuesday-Saturday from June through September. Admission free.*

Located in an 1860's schoolhouse, the St. Albans Museum features a wide variety of exhibits dedicated to local history. In addition to the usual assortment of clothing, tool, and photographic exhibits, the museum includes an interesting display dedicated to the railroad that played such an important role in the town's history, as well as a recreated doctor's clinic from a century ago.

East of St. Albans

CHESTER A. ARTHUR BIRTHPLACE AND HISTORIC SITE, *North Fairfield, Vermont. Take Route 36 east from St. Albans seven miles to Fairfield and then take the local road north. Take the road east at the fork just north of Fairfield, 5 miles east. Open 9:30am-5:30am Wednesday-Sunday from June through October.*

Poor Chester A. Arthur, who succeeded the assassinated President James Garfield in 1881 – he always plays second fiddle to Calvin Coolidge as Vermont's favorite presidential son, and this exhibit, when compared to the fine museum dedicated to Coolidge at Plymouth Notch, is a perfect example. It is essentially a replicated version of the home in which Arthur was supposedly born, though the exact location of his birth is in dispute. It features a modest exhibit about Arthur's presidency and his early life in Vermont.

NIGHTLIFE & ENTERTAINMENT

Theater & Performing Arts

THE FLYNN THEATRE, *153 Min Street, Burlington. Tel. 802/863-5966 (86-Flynn). Box office hours: Monday-Friday 10am-5pm; 11am-4pm Saturday . On performance days, the box office remains open until half an hour before showtime. Tickets also available at the UVM Campus Bookstore (Monday-Friday 10am-3pm), and at Copy Ship Fax Plus in Essex Junction at 159 Pearl Street. 8am-6pm Monday-Friday & 9am-1pm. Credit cards: major credit cards accepted.*

This venerable little theater may just be Vermont's premier arena for the performing arts. All year round its docket is packed with a variety of acts, from Shakespeare and the VSO (Vermont Symphony Orchestra) to the Neville Brothers and David Grisman. For info and tickets, call the box office; to check out coming attractions, browse local Burlington publications such as the *Free Press* and the *Vermont Times*. The Flynn Box Office is also the main Burlington ticket outlet for major events in Canada, and all ticket prices for Flynn events include a $1 Preservation Fee which goes to maintaining the Flynn.

THE COMEDY ZONE, *Radisson Hotel Burlington, 60 Battery Street, Burlington. Tel. 802/658-6500. Shows at 8pm & 10pm on Fridays and Saturdays. Credit cards: all major credit cards.*

Nationally acclaimed and lesser known local comedians alike perform here twice a night on Friday and Saturday nights. Ticket prices range from $5 on up depending on the status of the performer. Alcohol is served and to combine dinner, call in advance.

RHOMBUS GALLERY/ARTS SPACE, *186 College Street, Burlington. Tel. 802/865-9603, 865-3144. Hours and tickets: varies according to event schedule.*

This non-profit volunteer-run center features an ever-rotating schedule of visual and performing arts. including film screenings, literary lectures, music, and plays. Check local publications or call for a schedule.

Bars & Taverns

There are numerous bars on and around **Church Street** – you'll never have trouble finding a cold one, but on Fridays and Saturdays, particularly in the summer and autumn (when UVM kicks into gear), you might have a hard time finding a seat. Major hotels like the Radisson, the Holiday Inn, the Sheraton, and others have bars as well.

THE VERMONT PUB & BREWERY, *144 College Street, Burlington. Tel. 802/865-0500. Hours: 11:30am-2am daily. Major credit cards accepted.*

A popular late-night spot with young folks, the Vermont Pub and Brewery serves an extensive assortment of their lagers and ales as well as numerous domestics and imports. The menu features more than adequate American bar food and British fare, like shepherd's pie and fish 'n' chips. Brewery tours are given at 8pm on Wednesdays and on Saturday mornings, and live entertainment is usually featured Thursdays through Saturdays from 9pm or 10pm until closing.

BOURBON STREET GRILL, *213 College Street (just off the Church Street Marketplace), Burlington. Tel. 802/2800. Open daily from 11am until late.*

Colorful and usually active, the Bourbon Street Grill features a full-fledged menu from N'Awluns that, in addition to jambalaya and gumbo, includes that staple of any cajun bar: Hurricanes.

RATHSKELLER, *Route 7 off I-89 Exit 16, Colchester VT. Tel. 802/655-9792. Open from morning until late. Major credit cards accepted.*

In addition to a restaurant and cafe, the Rathskeller includes a lounge serving adult refreshments and bar food until midnight. Located in Colchester outside of Burlington.

SHOPPING

CHURCH STREET MARKETPLACE, *135 Church Street, Burlington. Tel. 802/863-1648, Fax 802/865-7024. Website: www.together.net/~market-place.*

Vermont's premier example of urban renewal – to the extent such a thing is possible in Vermont – the Church Street Marketplace is a pedestrian mall in Burlington's renovated downtown district, located on Church Street between Main Street on the south and Pearl Street on the north. Boasting more than 150 shops and restaurants from Borders to the Bone Appetit ("gourmet treat boutique for dogs and cats"), the Market-place offers more shopping choices and culinary variety than anywhere in Vermont. For a complete directory of shops contact the Marketplace at the listings above, or pick up the *Blue Map* or the *Burlington Magazine* at your hotel or at virtually any commercial establishment in Burlington.

Many of the shops below are part of the Church Street Marketplace:

BURLINGTON SQUARE MALL, *5 Burlington Square. Tel. 802/658-2545.*

Featuring such mall stalwarts as the Body Shop, Victoria's Secret, and the Gap, the Mall may be the least interesting chunk of the Church Street Marketplace in that it resembles the typical suburban shopping center we've all learned to love and hate. But with more than 60 shops it's a good place to begin if you need something in particular, whether it be glasses (Champlain Valley Eyecare), a manicure (the Nail Emporium) or anything else. If you're planning to shop often consider applying for the Burlington Square Mall Gold Membership Club, which entitles members to discounts and other special offers.

Apparel & Clothing

BURLINGTON ARMY AND NAVY STORE, *9 Center Street, Burlington. Tel. 802/862-0223. All major credit cards accepted.*

Specializing in outdoor and military style clothing and accessories, the Army-Navy Store also sells a wide variety of goods, from biker-style bandanas to Swiss Army knives.

GET FLEECED, *136 1/2 Church Street (across from City Hall), Burlington. Tel. 802/864-7907.*

Specializing in fleece and wool, Get Fleeced is a good place to prepare for confronting the elements.

Gifts & Souvenirs

APPLE MOUNTAIN, VERMONT GIFTS AND SPECIALTY FOODS, *30 Church Street, Burlington; second branch in Champlain Mill, Winooski. Tel. 802/658-6452; 802/654-7450 in Winooski. Hours: 9am-9pm Monday-Wednesday; 9am-9:30pm Thursday-Saturday; 10am-6pm Sunday. Credit cards accepted.*

If you're looking for Vermonty souvenirs to bring to the folks back home, this is your place. From maple syrup (and maple everything else) to Vermont sweatshirts and Cabot cheese, Apple Mountain is a quintessential Vermont gift shop. And while that includes by necessity more kitsch than I'd care to mention, it also means that whatever it is you want, you'll probably find it here. If the loot is more than your suitcase can handle, they can ship it home for you for a handling charge.

BENNINGTON POTTERS NORTH, *127 College Street, Burlington. Tel. 802/863-2221. Hours: 9:30m-9pm Monday-Friday; 9:30am-6pm Saturday; noon-5pm Sunday.*

Specializing in the Bennington pottery for which it is named, this multi-leveled store is housed in a 19th century building and features a large variety of home furnishings, decorations, kitchen products and glassware.

PEACE & JUSTICE STORE, *21 Upper Church Street, Burlington. Tel. 802/863-8326. Hours: daily. .*

This "socialy responsible marketplace," with its recycled paper goods and crafts made by independent artists, is right at home here in Burlington and makes for interesting browsing even if you don't buy.

Books & Music

In addition to Borders, you can shop at:

BYGONE BOOKS, *31 Main Street, Burlington. Tel. 802/862-4397. Hours: Monday-Saturday 10am-5:30pm.*

Specializes in rare, out of print, and used books.

CROW BOOKSHOP, *14 Church Street. Tel. 802/0848.*

Selling a wide variety of mostly second-hand books, the Crow makes for excellent browsing even if you don't buy, and if you find something, it's invariably cheaper than Borders.

DISC GO AROUND, *198 College Street, Burlington. Tel. 802/660-8150. Hours: 9:30am -8pm Monday-Saturday; noon-5pm Sunday. Credit cards: Visa, Mastercard.*

Disc Go Around features an excellent selection of used CD's (and some tapes) and buys as well as sells CD's. Most sell from $6-12 unless it's one of those Bob Marley imports, in which case the sky's the limit. As always, you should listen to a disk before buying.

PYRAMID BOOKS, *96 Church Street, Burlington. Tel. 802/660-8060.*
Another worthy used/discount bookstore, which at least deserves a good browse before you give in to Borders.

Photography & Film Development
VERMONT COLOR PHOTO LABS, *192 College Street, Burlington. Tel. 802/864-7318. Other branches in South Burlington (1140 Williston Road), Essex Junction (94 Pearl Street), and Shelburne (1950 Shelburne Road). Major credit cards accepted.*
Offers one hour development, black and white development, and digital imaging.
PHOTOGARDEN, *206 College Street, Burlington. Tel. 802/863-1256. Second branch at Taft Corners Shopping Center, Williston. Major credit cards accepted.*
In addition to developing film, Photogarden sells a wide assortment of photo accessories including different films, frames and albums, lenses, instant passport photos, and of course cameras.

Specialty Stores
GARCIA TABACCO SHOP, *in the Burlington Mall, 135 Church Street. Tel. 802/658-5737, 800/587-5737. Major credit cards accepted.*
Pipe tobacco, cigars, fancy lighters, and imported cigarettes – this is the place.
PURPLE SHUTTER HERBS, *100 Main Street, Burlington. Tel. 802/ 865-HERB.*
Medicine, teas, culinary flavors – anything herbal, they have it along with an assortment of books explaining how why herbs may be useful for everythin from shampooing your rug to curing cancer.

Sporting Goods
BURTON SNOWBOARDS, *80 Industrial Parkway, Burlington. Tel. 802/862-4500. Hours: 8am-6pm Monday-Friday; noon-5pm Saturdays. Major credit cards accepted.*
In business since the ark came down (1977 for snowboarders), Burton specializes in all things related to snowboarding from the boards themselves to clothing and lip balm. Boards are manufactured at their own factory. A good place to seek advice about how to get involved in this cutting edge sport.
THE BSIDE, *145 Cherry Street just off the Church Street. Marketplace. Tel. 802/863-0539. Major credit cards accpted.*
A snowboard specialty store, the BSIDE also features a wide variety of winter sports apparel and accessories.

DAKIN FARM, *135 Church St., (Church St. Marketplace), Burlington. Tel. 802/658-9560.*

SOUTH BURLINGTON
UNIVERSITY MALL, *Dorset St. at Williston Road (off exit 14E, I-89), South Burlington. Tel. 802/863-1066. Fax: 802/863-5836. Hours: Monday-Saturday 9:30am-9:30pm; Sunday 11am-6pm.*
With more than 70 shops and restuarant, the University Mall is the largest in Vermont.
CHEESE TRADERS, *1186 Williston Road (just off Exit 14E, I-89), South Burlington. Tel. 802/863-0143, Tel. 800/540-4261. Major credit cards accepted.*
Cheese Traders features a huge variety of local, domestic, and international cheeses and wines. Breads, and other products are also sold.

NORTH HERO ISLAND
CHARLIE'S NORTHLAND, *Route 2, North Hero. Tel. 802/372-8822.*
HERO'S WELCOME, *Route 2, North Hero Village. Tel. 802/372-4161, Fax 802/372-3205. Website: www.heroswelcome.com.*

SOUTH HERO ISLAND
THE GREEN FROG GIFT SHOP, *Route 314 Ferry Road, South Hero. Tel. 802/372-5031. Hours: 9am-6pm daily, July & August; 10am-5pm May-December.*

JOHNSON
THE FORET-ME-NOT SHOP, *Route 15, Johnson. Hours: 9am-9pm daily.*
With two full floors of clothing, jewelry and other accessories to be worn, the Forget-Me-Not Shop is worth a good browse for any committed bargain hunter.
JOHNSON WOOLEN MILLS, INC., *Main Street, Johnson. Tel. 877/635-WOOL. E-mail: woolen4u@pshift.com. Website: www.johnsonwoolenmills.com.*

SHELBURNE
BURLINGTON CENTRE FOR ANTIQUES, *3039 Shelburne Road, Route 7, Shelburne. Tel. 802/985-4911. Hours: 10am- daily.*
SHELBURNE COUNTRY STORE, *The Village Green, Shelburne. Tel. 802/985-3657. Hours: 9am-6pm daily, 10am-5pm Sunday.*
VERMONT TEDDY BEAR COMPANY, *6655 Shelburne Road, Shelburne. Tel. 800/829-BEAR. Website & e-mail: www.vtbear.com. Major credit cards accepted.*

VERMONT WILDFLOWER FARM, *Route 7, Charlotte. Tel. 802/985-9455, Fax 802/985-9268. Hours: 10am-5pm daily May-October.*

ESSEX
ESSEX OUTLET FAIR, *21 Esses Way in Essext off Toues 15 at Exit 10 -I89. Tel. 802/657-2777.*

A brand name outlet festival featuring shops bearing the names of Adidas, Levi's, Polo Ralph Lauren, Jockey, Samsonite, and Dockers, among others.

VERGENNES
KENNEDY BROTHERS FACTORY MARKETPLACE, *Route 22A, Vergennes. Tel. 802/877-2975, 800/451-4387. Website: www.kennedy-brothers.com. Hours: open daily year around.*

SPORTS & RECREATION
BIKING
Burlington Area

In Burlington itself, there are the beautiful **Burlington** and **South Burlington Bike Paths**, which wind along the waterfront south to Shelburne when they cut in to Spear and Dorset streets. In Williston, the **Catamount Family Center**, *Tel. 802/879-6001,* features 30 kilometers of trails through woods, meadows, and other countryside and wilderness. You can reach the center by taking Route 2 east to North Williston Road, on which you turn left and continue to Governor Chitteden Road and take a right on it. The Center also rents bikes and gives lessons.

Also, for road cycling, many of the regional roads outside of Metropolitan Burlington both to the north and south – particularly inland – are quite good and there are limitless possibilities interms of loops and routes you can take. Just pick up a biking guide like *25 Bicycle Tours in Vermont* by John Freidin (Backcountry Publications), talk to somebody in the know like a local cylce enthusiast, and always carry good maps when you hit the road.

EARL'S CYCLERY & FITNESS ("Downtown"), *135 Main Street, Burlington, VT 05401. Tel. 800/287-9197. Open daily. Major credit cards accepted.*

EARL'S CYCLERY & FITNESS ("Suburbs"), *2500 South Burlington, VT 05403. Tel. 800/287-9197. Open daily. Major credit cards accepted.*

Rentals, accessories, retail sales.

SKIRACK, *85 Main Street, Burlington VT 05401. Tel. 802/658-3313. Open daily. Major credit cards accepted.*

ESSEX JUNCTION BICYCLES, *50 Pear Street, Route 15, Essex Junction VT. Tel. 802/878-1275, 800/64-WHEEL. Open daily. Major credit cards accepted.*

CLIMB HIGH, *1861 Shelburne Road, Shelburne VT. Tel. 802/985-5055. Open daily. Major credit cards accepted.*

St. Albans & The Islands

Very fit cyclists can tour the entire Islands' region in one day (60-70 miles round-trip); take Route 2 through South Hero, North Hero, past South Alburg, then take Route 128 onto the Grande Isle, see what you want and turn back. You can also take numerous detours anywhere in between.

There are also numerous road cycling opportunities around St. Alban's and to the west. For example, you take Route 7 up to Swanton and then take Route 36 south along the coast back to St. Alban's. There is also the scenic **Missisquoi Valley Rail Trail** linking St. Alban's (near the intersection of Routes 105 and 7) with Richford (27 miles one way). Routes 108, 118, 104, and 36 are also viable for cyclists as are numerous local and town roads.

HERO'S WELCOME, *Route 2, North Hero VT. Tel. 802/372-4161. Open daily. Credit cards: Visa, Mastercard.*

A general store with a marina that rents bikes as well as kayaks and canoes.

BOATING

There are oodles of boating opportunities throughout the region, and you shouldn't have much of a problem finding access to the Lake or renting a boat of any type. Many of the state and private campgrounds (see the "Camping" subsections in *Where to Stay* above) offer both access to the lake as well as boat rentals. Generally the boating season runs from mid-

---

REMINDERS FOR LAKE CHAMPLAIN BOATERS

*1. All boats must be equipped with a **personal flotation device** ("pfd" – also known as life jackets) for each passenger.*

2. Continuous weather forecasts can be found at 162 MHZ.

3. The U.S. Coast Guard radio frequencies: 156.8 MHZ FM & VHF channels 9 & 16.

4. Always stay within your own limits, and if you're sailing, canoeing, kayaking, or boating in a small or medium size motor boat, by all means get off the Lake when lightning is occurring or is near.

May through mid-September. For complete information about rental locations as well as rules and regulations, contact the **Lake Champlain Regional Chamber of Commerce**, *P.O. Box 453, 60 Main Street, Suite 100, Burlington VT 05402-0453. Tel. 802/863-3489.*

Burlington

Virtually all boating, including rentals and cruises, operates out of the **Burlington Community Boathouse** where you can rent jet-ski's, sailboats, and various inflatable crafts. *The Boathouse is located off the end of College Street downtown. Tel. 802/863-5090.*

Listed below are some outfits offering boating lessons, cruises, and tours.

WINDS OF IRELAND *at the Burlington Community Boathouse on the Waterfront in Burlington. Tel. 802/863-5090. Hours: 10am-6pm. Credit cards: major credit cards accepted.*

Offers captained sailing tours, boat rentals, and private charters from May 15–October 15. Captained sails during the day and at sunset (departures at 11:30am, 2pm, & 6pm) last two hours and cost $20. Rental rates depend on the type of boat and range from $35 for half an hour in a Sea Doo to $460 for eight hours in a Hunter 40.5. Rentals include instruction, and anybody looking to operate a boat born after 1975 must have proof of boating education. Reservations are advised.

LAKE CHAMPLAIN CRUISE & CHARTER, *King Street ferry dock, Burlington Community Boathouse (end of College Street, downtown). Tel. 802/ 864-9804. Major credit cards accepted.*

This outfit offers cruise excursions with a historical bent. The routes follow the corridor taken by Samuel De Champlain himself.

SEAHORSE CHARTERS, *Burlington Community Boathouse, Burlington.*

CRUISES ON LAKE CHAMPLAIN

Supposing you don't fancy yourself as skipper or even first mate material – one way to enjoy the beauty of Lake Champlain is to take one of the various cruises offered by the **Lake Champlain Scenic Shoreling Cruises***. They offer an assortment of choices, including scenic day cruises, sunset cruises, Sunday Brunch cruises, evening dinner cruises, and variety show & dinner cruises. Prices range from $8 an adult for the 1.5 hour "Scenic Narrated Cruise" to $35 an adult for the "Murder Mystery Dinner Cruise." Cruises depart from the Burlington Community Boathouse on the lake front at the end of College Street in downtown. Call 802/862-8300 for info. E-mail: spiritsoea.com. Web site: soea.com. Major credit cards accepted.*

Tel. 802/863-6142.
Primarily fishing excursions aboard a 24-foot boat.

CANOEING & KAYAKING
Burlington Area
For canoeing and kayaking, there is obviously Lake Champlain itself, accessible from many points including North Beach just north of downtown, as well as the Winooski River for river kayaking and canoeing.

CANOE IMPORTS, INC., *370 Dorset Street, South Burlington VT. Tel. 800/985-2992. Open daily. Major credit cards accepted.*

Rents and sells canoes, kayaks, and sailboats as well as all accessories and related equipment.

St. Albans & The Islands
There is boating virtually everywhere you look on and around Lake Champlain from May through September. Throughout the islands, virtually hotel, sporting goods store, and state park rents boats of some sort. The **state parks**, such as Sand Bar, Knight Island, Burton, and Grand Isle, all feature boating including rentals. Also, about 20 miles north of St. Albans, Lake Carmi State Park covers 600 acres and boats are available for rent.

HERO'S WELCOME, *Route 2, North Hero VT. Tel. 802/372-4161. Open daily. Credit cards: Visa, Mastercard.*

A general store with a marina that rents bikes as well as kayaks and canoes.

Further east around Jeffersonville off Route 15 near Smugglers' Notch and the Stowe region, the **Lamoille River** features passive and scenic paddling between Hyde Park and Cambridge.

SMUGGLERS' NOTCH CANOE TOURING, *Mannsview Inn on Route 108, Jeffersonville VT. Tel. 802/644-8321, 888/937-MANN.*

Offers canoe and kayak rentals as well as tours and trips including shuttles and pick-ups.

CROSS-COUNTRY SKIING
CATAMOUNT FAMILY CENTER, *Governor Chittenden Road, Williston VT 05495. Tel. 802/879-6001). Trail fees: $12.*

The Center maintains 40 kilometers of trails and provides rentals and cross-country ski instruction.

HAZEN'S NOTCH CROSS-COUNTRY SKI CENTER, *Montgomery Center VT. 05471. Tel. 802/326-4708. Trail fees: $8.*

Off Routes 118 and 242 in Franklin County, there are 45 kilometers of trails and provides rentals, nordic instruction, and guided tours.
FISHING

Lake Champlain offers more fishing opportunities than any other place in the state by far, with more than 435 miles of lake surface and 80 different types of fish from channel catfish, smelt, and a variety of bass to the prized landlocked Atlantic salmon and the largest assortment of trout in New England.

Other good fishing can be enjoyed at **Lake Iroquois** and the **Lamoille River** to the east, **Arrowhead Lake**, and the **Winooski River**.

GOLF

ALBURG COUNTRY CLUB,_Route 129, South Alburg VT -5440. Tel. 802/796-3586. E-mail: alburgcc@together.net. Web site: www.homepages.together.net/~alburgcc. 18 holes. Green fees : $15-$10. Carts $15-$20. Credit cards: Visa, Mastercard, American Express. Driving range, club rentals, pro shop._

CHAMPLAIN COUNTRY CLUB, _Route 7, St. Albans VT. Tel. 802/527-1187. 18 holes. Green fees: $21-$24, $12 after 5pm. Major credit cards accepted._

KWINIASKA GOLF CLUB, _Spear Street, Shelburne VT. Tel. 802/985-3672. 18 holes.Green fees: $15-$20. Rental clubs and carts available. Major credit cards accepted._

MARBLE ISLAND RESORT, _Colchester Vt. Tel. 802/864-6800. 9 holes. Green fees $12-$18. Carts available. Credit cards: Visa, Mastercard, American Express._

ROCKY RIDGE C.C., _68 Ledge Road at the Intersection of Routes 2A and 116, St. George VT. (10 miles south of Burlington.) Tel. 802/482-2191. 18 holes. Green fees: $21. Club rentals and carts available. Credit cards: Visa, Mastercard, American Express._

VERMONT NATIONAL COUNTRY CLUB, _1227 Dorset Street, South Burlington VT. Tel. 802/864-7770. 18 holes. Major credit cards accepted._ The first Jack Nicklaus/Jack Nicklaus II designed golf course in Vermont.

WILCOX COVE GOLF COURSE, _3 Camp Vermont Ct., Grand Isle VT. Tel. 802/372-8343. 9 holes. Green fees: $5-$9.50. Credit cards: Visa, Mastercard._

WILLISTON GOLF COURSE, _88 Gof Course Road (P.O. Box 541), Williston VT. Tel. 802/878-3747. 18 holes. Carts available. Credit cards: Vis, American Expres, Mastercard._

HIKING

There are plenty of areas in which to hike throughout the region, from the waterfront in Burlington to the beaches of the Islands. For real wilderness or mountain hiking, the **Camel's Hump** in Huntington is one of the most famous and popular hikes in Vermont, and rewards those who make it (usually) with amazing veiws of the Green Mountains. To reach the trail take Route 2 or I-89 east from Burlington to Richmond (Exit 11), and continue south about ten miles to Hungtinton center. Then get on Camel Hump Road and follow the signs 3.5 miles to the trail head. Count on 5-6 hours to make the 4.8 mile round-trip.

Otherwise head to the Green Mountain areas in **Addison County** (roughly 30-40 miles south of Burlington on Route 7), the **Mad River Valley** (40 miles on I-89, Route 100 South), and the **Stowe** and **Smugglers' Notch** region where you can climb the tallest peak in Vermont, **Mt. Mansfield** (it's about 40 miles on I-89, Route 100 north and Route 108).

SKIING

BOLTON VALLEY, *Bolton VT 05477. (25 miles from Burlington on Route 2 East. Tel. 802/434-213. Lifts open 9am-4pm. Lift fees $15-$30 daily. Rentals available.*

Bolton Valley is a modest ski area with 48 trails/runs over 100 acres with 6 lifts. For more extensive skiing, head to the **Stowe** and **Smugglers' Notch** ski areas (40 minutes from Burlington on Route 89,Exit 10 and Route 100 North); or the **Sugarbush** and **Mad River Glen** ski areas in the Mad River Valley, also off Exit 10 – only take Route 100 South 15 miles.

SNOWMOBILING

There are many snowmobiling opportunities throughout the Champlain Valley and northwestern Vermont. To snowmobile in Vermont, you must join a local club and pay annual dues to them (usually under $20 a year), as well as a fee known as the Trail Maintenance Assessment, or TMA. This money goes towards the upkeep of trails and, once paid, enables you to snowmobile anywhere in Vermont.

Listed below are snowmobile clubs in the northern Champlain Valley and northwestern Vermont that can license you and provide information about rentals, maps and lessons. For more information about snowmobiling in the region – including tours, rentals, and lessons – and throughout Vermont generally, contact the **Vermont Association of Snow Travelers (V.A.S.T.)**, *P.O. Box 839, Montpelier VT 05601. Tel. 802/229-0005, Fax 802/223-4316. Website: www.vtvast.org.*

Chittenden County
- **Arrowhead Mountain Snowmobile Club** – *Tel. 802/655-0725*
- **Cobblehill Snowmobile Club** – *Tel. 802/893-7792*
- **Crouching Lions Snow Sledders** – *Tel. 802/434-4359*
- **Green Mountain Snow Cats** – *Tel. 802/863-2160*
- **Iroquois Sno-Beavers** – *Tel. 802/482-3321*
- **Jericho Sno-Drifters** – *Tel. 802/899-1928*
- **Mallets Bay Lakers** – *Tel. 802/658-1887*

- **Richmond Ruff Riders** – *Tel. 802/434-3512*
- **Saxon Hill Riders** – *Tel. 802/879-4089*
- **S.C.A.T.** – *Tel. 802/879-4089*
- **Williston Hill Hawks** – *Tel. 802/862-6333*

Franklin County
- **Bakersfield Valley Drifters** – *Tel. 802/827-3288*
- **Cold Hollow Barons** – *Tel. 802/933-2437*
- **Covered Bridge Snowmobile** – *Tel. 802/326- 4687*
- **Fletcher Rough Riders** – *Tel. 802/849-6174*
- **Franklin County Snow Raiders** – *Tel. 802/849-6619*
- **Missisquoi Bearcats** – *Tel. 802/848-7659*
- **North West Riders** – *Tel. 802/868-2038*

PRACTICAL INFORMATION

Chambers of Commerce
   LAKE CHAMPLAIN REGIONAL CHAMBER OF COMMERCE, *60 Main Street, Suite 100, Burlington VT05401-8418. Tel. 802/863-3489, Fax 802/863-1538. E-mail: vermont@vermont.org Web site: www.vermont.org/ chamber.*

Medical Emergencies & Services
   Emergencies – *Tel. 911*
   MEDICAL CENTER CAMPUS, *111 Colchester Avenue, Burlington VT 05401. Tel. 802/656-2434, 656-2345 (Emergency Department), 802/658-3456 (Vermont Poison Center).*
   FANNY ALLEN CAMPUS, *101 College Parkway, Burlington VT 05401. Tel. 802/654-1170 (Walk-In Clinic).*
   Walk-In Clinic – Essex: *Junction of Routes 15 & 2A. Tel. 802/879-4242;* Burlington: *Dorset Street off Williston Road. Tel. 802/658-5756*

21. THE NORTHEAST KINGDOM

Often described by its inhabitants as the "Vermonters' Vermont," the **Northeast Kingdom** (a term coined in the 1940's by U.S. Senator George Aiken) is the most remote and, many claim, the most beautiful, part of the state. In large part because of its isolation, the Kingdom has not seen the massive development linked to tourism like some other parts of the state, and while this certainly means that those who make the extra effort to reach it are rewarded with the most pristine wilderness in Vermont, it also translates into fewer economic opportunities for its residents.

In any case, its offerings for travelers are many and diverse. The region's main town, **St. Johnsbury**, is home to the famous **Fairbanks Museum and Planetarium**, as well as numerous beautiful buildings like the **St. Johnsbury Athenaeum**, one of the oldest unadulterated art galleries in America and a gem of Victorian building. For skiers, **Jay Peak** and **Burke Mountain** are smaller than the Killingtons and Stowes of the world, but their nothern locations mean the best snow in the state and smaller crowds. For cyclists, hikers, and cross-country skiers, the same rule applies and the scenery is consistently beautiful. Finally, the Kingdom's many small villages, the best known of which is **Craftsbury Common**, are among the most charming in the state, and again, without being overrun by tourists, they have retained their original character.

ARRIVALS & DEPARTURES
By Air
The nearest commercial airports are in **Burlington**, **Montreal**, and **Lebanon Municipal Airport** in West Lebanon. Montreal is served by virtually every major airline on the planet, but is roughly 200 miles from St. Johnsbury and unless you have your own car, that trip will be significantly lengthened with bus connections, (and that's not even

factoring in whatever delays you may face at the Canadian border). Just over the Connecticut River from White River Junction, which is an easy one hour drive and an easy bus ride from St. Johnsbury, **Lebanon** is the closest airport to the Kingdom, but it is only served by USAir Express, *Tel. 800/428-4322* and flights are limited and expensive.

More convenient in terms of available flights and cost is **Manchester Airport** in Manchester, New Hampshire. Serviced by Southwest, *Tel. 800/435-9792*, Continental, *Tel. 800/525-0289*, USAir, *Tel. 800/428-4322*, and Delta Connection, *Tel. 800/345-3400*. Manchester is a straight 1.5-2 hours drive from St. Johnsbury on I-93; most major rental companies operate out of Manchester.

Burlington is serviced by Continental, *Tel. 800/525-0289*, United, *Tel. 800/241-6522*, USAir, *Tel. 800/428-4322*, and the commuter airlines, Business Express, *Tel. 800/345-3400*, and Comair, *Tel. 800/927-0927*. Burlington is a relatively short 77 miles from St. Johnsbury but, as with Lebanon, flights are expensive and somewhat infrequent.

Another alternative is to fly into Boston's **Logan Airport**, which is approximately four hours from St. Johnsbury by car, all on I-93. All major car rental companies operate out of Logan, or you can take one of the hourly shuttles to South Station in downtown Boston, catch one of a half-dozen daily buses to White River Junction, and make a connection for St. Johnsbury or Newport. The advantages of flying to Boston, particularly if you are traveling some distance, include the availability of flights and lower costs than flying into one of the smaller regional airports.

By Car

Interstate 91 (I-91) begins in Hartford, Connecticut, where it intersects with I-95 coming from New York and continues through central Massachusetts and along the Connecticut River in eastern Vermont – all the way through St. Johnsbury and on to Lyndon, Barton, Orleans, past Newport and up to Derby Line at the Canadian border. **Route 5** also runs up the Connecticut River Valley, and is slower but more scenic than I-91. The Kingdom is also fed directly by **I-93**, which begins in Boston and continues through Manchester and central New Hampshire en route to St. Johnsbury; it is roughly four hours plus from Boston to St. Johnsbury assuming no major delays.

From points west like Burlington (75 miles to St. Johnsbury) and the Lake Champlain area, the most efficient way of reaching the Kingdom, unless you're headed for Montgomery, Jay Peak, or some other point in the far northwest portion of the Kingdom, is to get on **I-89** to Montpelier and then take **Route 2 East** to St. Johnsbury.

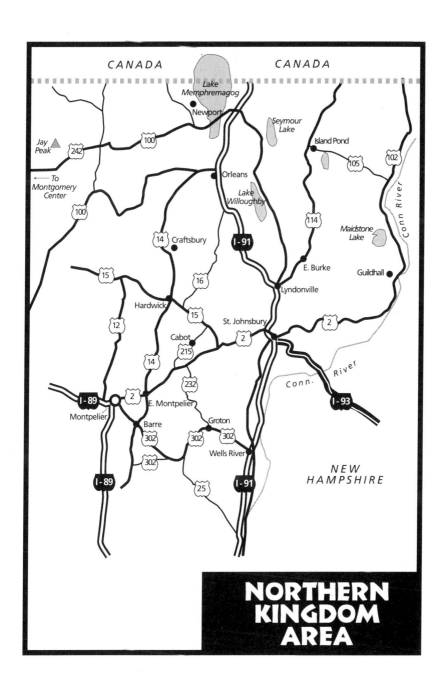

NORTHERN KINGDOM AREA

By Bus

Vermont Transit Lines, *Tel. 800/552-8738, Tel. 800/451-3292,* offers direct service between Barnet, St. Johnsbury, Lyndonville, Barton, Newport and White River Junction. Buses depart Newport at 7:30am, Lyndonville 8:20am, and St. Johnsbury at 8:40am, arriving at White River Junction at 10:20am. From White River Junction, you can make connections for points all over Vermont, including Montpelier, Burlington, Rutland, Brattleboro, and all major ski areas except Mount Snow. You can also make connections for major destinations in the Northeast including Boston, Manchester NH, New York, Hartford, and Montreal.

Buses depart White River Junction for the Northeast Kingdom once a day at 5:20pm, arriving at St. Johnsbury at 6:30pm, Lyndonville 6:45pm, Barton, 7:10pm, and Newport at 7:30pm. A one-way ticket between any destination in the Kingdom and White River Junction is $10-$15.

By Train

Amtrak's **Vermonter** route departs Washington DC at 7:40am and stops at Baltimore, Wilimington DE, Philadelphia, New York City, Newark NJ, Metro Park NJ, Trenton, NJ, Bridgport CT, Hartford CT, Meriden CT, New Haven CT, Springfield MA, Amherst MA, Northampton MA, Brattleboro VT, Keene NH, Windsor VT, and arrives at White River Junction VT at 6:30pm, and Montpelier at 7:52pm. This is when you can also catch it north to destinations: Randolph VT, Montpelier VT, Waterbury-Stowe, Burlington VT, St. Albans, and Montreal, Canada.

Going south to destinations above (except Randolph, Montpelier, Waterbury-Stowe, Burlington, St. Albans, and Montreal), the Vermonter departs Montpelier at 9:12am, and White River Junction at 10:35am. A one way ticket to Washington DC from White River costs about $85, New York City $65, and less to destinations in Connecticut, Massachusetts, New Hampshire, and Vermont.

Inquire at your hotel about pick-up options, because unless somebody is meeting you or you plan to rent a car in White River Junction, getting from either town to the Kingdom may be a problem.

For more information about fares, call Amtrak, *Tel. 800/USA-RAIL.*

ORIENTATION

Comprising Orleans, Essex, and Caledonia counties, the Northeast Kingdom vaguely resembles an upside down triangle, with the upper side running along the Canadian border and bisected by **Lake Memphremagog**, at the southern end of which is **Newport**. The major highway through the Kingdom, **I-91**, leads from just west of Newport south through the relatively major towns of **Orleans**, **Barton**, **Lyndon**, and **St. Johnsbury**, where it meets I-93 coming from Boston. St. Johnsbury is the biggest town in the Northeast Kingdom and with I-91, I-93, and Routes 2 & 5 intersecting there, it is also the regions's main transportation hub. Running roughly alongside I-91 is **Route 5**, and both continue south of St. Johnsbury en route to the southernmost point of the Kingdom at Wells River and on to White River Junction.

Other main roads include **Route 2**, which cuts west-east through northern Vermont from Burlington through Montpelier and into the Kingdom at **Danville**, ten miles west of St. Johnsbury. It continues through St. Johnsbury and into New Hamshire at Guildhall, where it meets **Route 102** which continues along the Connecticut River north to Canadian border. Running roughly parallel to and between Route 102 and Route 5 is **Route 114**, linking Lyndon and the Canadian border. En route it passes through the ski resort of **East Burke**, seven miles from Lyndon. On the western side of the Kingdom, **Route 14**, which begins at White River Junction and passes through Barre in the Montpelier area, passes through **Craftsbury Common** on its way to the Newport area. Finally, Vermont's most remote ski area, **Jay's Peak**, is on **Route 242** at the far northwestern edge of the Kingdom.

GETTING AROUND

Apart from shuttles between hotels and ski slopes, and Vermont Transit's once-daily bus route linking Newport, Barton, Orleans, Lyndon, and St. Johnsbury with White River Junction, you're pretty much left to your own devices, meaning basically that you need a car. If you do not have one, rent one in Burlington, White River Junction, or wherever else possible. See those destination chapters for car rental options.

WHERE TO STAY

Averill

QUIMBY COUNTRY LODGE, *Forest Lake Road Route 114 (PO Box 20), Averill, VT 05901. Tel. 802/822-5533, Fax 802/822-5537. Email: quimbyc@together.net. Rates: $100-$200. Credit cards: Visa, Mastercard, American Express. Closed in winter.*

Situated on Forest Lake in the northeast of the Kingdom, this rustic lodge may be the most remote in the state. Comprising 20 cottages and a main lodge on nearly 700 acres with a restaurant, this "resort" offers access to three lakes and offers great opportunities for fishing, hiking, boating, and generally getting away from it all. And while it's defintely not The Four Seasons, it certainly is comfortable and amenities such as showers are more than adequate.

Barnet

THE OLD HOMESTEAD, *1573 Route 5 (PO Box 150), Barnet, VT 05821. (Located about eight miles south of St. Johnsbury.) Tel. 802/633-4016, Fax 802/633-4924. Email: oldhomestead@connriver.net. Web site: www.connriver.net/odhomestead.Rates: $45-$100. Call about credit cards.*

An 1850 colonial home with a screened porch, nice views, and charming antique decor and furnishings, the Old Homestead is a modest and intimate B&B with five comfortable rooms, all of which include private baths. Breakfast is prepared fresh on the premises. If you wake early enough, the sunrise views of the White Mountains can be quite a treat.

Barton & Lake Willoughby/Westmore
Includes Glover & West Glover

WILLOUGHVALE INN & RESTAURANT ON LAKE WILLOUGHBY, *Route 5A (RR 2 Box 403), Westmore VT 05860. Tel. 802/525-4123, 800/594-9102, Fax 802/525-4514. E-mail: info@willoughvale.com. Web site: www.willoughvale.com. Rates: $70-$130. Major credit cards accepted.*

Part rustic but mostly elegant, the Willoughvale on Lake Willoughby features several cottages with two bedrooms, kitchens, fireplaces, living rooms, and porches. There are also seven individually decorated rooms, all of which have private baths (some with jacuzzi or whirlpool), hand-crafted furnishings, and televisions. The restaurant is a casual affair serving hearty country cuisine, while the tap room is a relaxing place to enjoy a refreshment. Boats and bikes can be rented on the premises.

ANGLIN B&B, *Lakeside Lane (PO Box 403), Barton VT 05822-0403. Tel. 802/525-4548, Fax 802/525-8840. Email: fay@anglinbb.com. Web site: www.anglinbb.com. Rates: $45-$65.*

This small cottage run by Ms. Fay Valley includes only four rooms With its waterfront location on Crystal Lake, it caters primarily to those interested in fishing, boating and other water recreation, though Ms. Valley also welcomes others of course, including hunters in the fall and snowmobilers in the winter.

RODGERS COUNTRY INN, *RFD# 3 (Box 57), West Glover, VT 05875-9124. Tel. 802/525-6677, Fax 802/525-6677. Weekly rates: $250 adult, $140 children under 12. Daily rates: $45 adult, $25 children under 12. Credit cards: Visa.*

Situated in a building dating to 1840 on a 350-acre estate, Rodger's (James and Nancy Rodgers are the hosts) Country Inn includes five guestrooms (shared bath). Breakfast and dinner are included in the rates.

Burke Mountain Area

Includes East Burke, Lyndon & Lyndonville

BURKE MOUNTAIN, *Mountain Road (PO Box 247), East Burke, VT 05832-0247. Tel. 802/626-3305, 800/541-5480, Fax 802/626-1323. Email: reserve@burkemountain.com. Rates begin around $100 per night. Major credit cards accepted.*

The Burke Mountain resort operates about 80 modern condos, an assortment of 1-3 bedroom units with private baths, cable television, telephones, kitchens, and other amenities. There is a restaurant and some spa facilities at the resort, and in the summer there is hiking, biking, and other outdoor activities. Inquire about special "ski & stay" and summer package deals.

BURKE VACATION RENTALS, *East Burke VT 05832. Tel. 802/626-1161, 888-327-2850, Fax 802/626-3706. E-mail: BVR@together.net. Rates begin at around $100 per night. Major credit cards accepted.*

Rents an assortment of fully equiped condos, most of which are very close to the lifts.

WILDFLOWER INN, *Darling Hill Road, Lyndonville, VT 05851. Tel. 802/626-8310, 800/627-8310, Fax 802/626-3039. Rates: $85-$250. Major credit cards accepted.*

Situated on a 500-acre estate, the Wildflower Inn includes a beautifully restored and maintained farmhouse with a fine restaurant, and an array of recreational facilities for children. The main inn features about a dozen elegant suites, all beautifully decorated and equipped with private baths, and there are also nine rooms in an old carriage house and one extra suite in an old school house that also has an in-room whilrpool. Facilities include tennis and basketball courts, a beautiful pool, playing fields, and a play area and petting barn for children (special supervised activities are provided for kids so that parents may enjoy skiing and other activities on their own). The food, both breakfast and dinner, is superb.

INN MOUNTAIN VIEW CREAMERY, *PO Box 355, East Burke, VT 05832. Tel. 802/626-9924, 800/572-4509. Email: innmtnvu@plainfield.bypass.com. Rates: $95-$175. Credit cards: Major credit cards accepted.*

Featuring 12 rooms in a restored dairy farm that includes a handsome neo-Georgian main building and several marvelous restored barns, the Inn at the Mountain View Creamery is ideal for those interested in hiking, snowshoeing, and cross-country skiiing. The inn's more than 400-acre estate is suited perfectly for such activities. Rooms are appointed with elegant country decor, and there is a charming sitting room and a bistro restaurant serving continental and American cuisine.

GARRISON INN, *Burke Hollow Road (PO Box 177), East Burke, VT 05832-0177. Tel. 802/626-8329, 800/773-1914. Rates: $55-$75. Credit cards: Visa, Mastercard.*

This quiet six room B&B includes six simple but charming and comfortable rooms, all of which feature private baths. Breakfast is prepared fresh daily and the Inn is located three miles from the slopes at Burke Mountain.

THE OLD CUTTER INN, *Next to the Burke Mountain Ski Resort (RR1, Box 62), East Burke VT 05832. Tel. 802/626-5152, 800/295-1943. Web site: www.pbpub.com/cutter.htm. Rates: $50-$65. Credit cards accepted.*

Located in a renovated farmhouse from the 1840's, the chef-owned Old Cutter Inn includes nine rooms and a suite (all with private bathrooms), as well as a fine restaurant serving Swiss-style continental cuisine.

THE VILLAGE INN OF EAST BURKE, *Route 114 (PO Box 186), East Burke, VT 05832-0186. Tel. 802/626-3161. E-mail: villginn@pllainfield.bypass.com Rates: $60-$70. Credit cards: Visa, Mastercard.*

Located within walking distance of the slopes at Burke Mountain, the Village Inn is a homey affair featuring five guestrooms, all of which include a private bath. There is also a common room with a fireplace, a kitchen available for use by the guests, and a stream flowing through the meadows where guests can cool off in the summer.

The Craftsbury Common Area

INN ON THE COMMON, *Main Street, Craftsbury VT 05826. Tel. 802/586-9619, 800/521-2233, Fax 802/586-2249. E-mail: info@innonthecommon.com. Web site: www.innonthecommon.com. Rates: $200-$300 (meals included). Major credit cards accepted.*

Perhaps the most luxurious inn in the Northeast Kingdom, the Inn on the Common is located in the heart of Craftsbury and offers a complete package of elegant accommodations, gourmet dining, and on-site recreational opportunities including tennis, croquet, and swimming. Spread over three historic buildings, lodging includes 15 rooms and one suite, all of which are immaculately appointed with handcrafted furnishings and antique decor. The restaurant, serving fine country and continental cuisine, is renowned as the finest in the area and boasts a world class wine selection.

CRAFTSBURY INN, *Main St. (PO Box 36), Craftsbury, VT 05826-0036. Tel. 802/586-2848, 800/336-2848, Fax 802/586-6952. Rates: $60-$100. Credit cards: Visa, Mastercard.*

Situated in an 1850 building in the heart of Craftsbury, this classic Vermont inn includes ten comfortable, antique-decorated rooms and a fine restaurant serving hearty country cuisine four nights a week (the dining room is open to the public during the summer).

CRAFTSBURY OUTDOOR CENTER, *Lost National Road (PO Box 31), Craftsbury, VT 05827. Tel. 802/586-7767, 800/729-7751, Fax 802/586-7768. Email: crafts@sover.net. Web site: www.craftsbury.com. Rates: $55-$100. Major credit cards accepted.*

A sort of summer camp for adults and families (even though it's very active in the winter), the Outdoor Center offers its guests a great combination of lodging, dining, and access to their extensive recreational facilities. Situated on 140 acres on Lake Hosmer, the Center includes a 100-kilometer network of trails for snowshoeing, cross-country skiing, hiking, and biking, while the lake is used for kayaking, canoeing, sculling (Olympic-style rowing), and swimming. Guests can participate in these activities with groups in an instructive environment, or you can go at it alone. There is an assortment of cottages, multiroom apartments, and rooms that are something in between a simple hotel and dormitory where baths are shared. Meals are served buffet in a communal setting, and the food tends to resemble the type of nourishment one might expect in a home rather than a restaurant; nutrition is emphasized and vegetarian dishes are readily available.

CRAFTSBURY BED & BREAKFAST ON WYLIE HILL, *Craftsbury Common VT 05827. Tel. 802/586-2206. Rates: $55-$75. Credit cards: Visa, Mastercard.*

This small hilltop 1860's B&B features just five rooms, three with shared baths.

Derby & Derby Line

DERBY VILLAGE INN, *46 Main St. (PO Box 1085), Derby Line, VT 05830. Tel. 802/873-3604, Fax 802/873-3047. Email: dvibandb@together.net. Rates: $75-$110 Major credit cards accepted.*

A true period piece, the Derby Village Inn is an intimate five room B&B that was originally built by a retired Civil War colonel at the turn of the century. Though comfortable and well endowed with modern amenities including private baths, its original character, right down to the fixtures and woodwork, has been remarkably well maintained.

THE BIRCHWOOD BED & BREAKFAST, *48 Main St. (PO Box 550), Derby Line, VT 05830. Tel. 802/873-9104, Fax 802/873-9121. Email: birchwd@together.net. Rates: $75. Checks accepted.*

Greensboro

HIGHLAND LODGE, *Caspian Lake Road, Greensboro, VT 05841. Tel. 802/533-2647, Fax 802/533-7494. Email: Hlodge@connriver.net. Rates: $90-$130. Major credit cards accepted.*

Overlooking Caspian Lake, the Highland Lodge offers elegant accommodation either in the main building or in one of several lakeside cottages. The main inn is a restored Civil War-era mansion with a fine restaurant and a screened porch with terrrific lake views. Other on-site facilities include a tennis court, lawn bowling, boating (rentals available), a private beach and, in the winter, more than 50 kilometers of cross-country ski and snowshoe trails.

Guildhall

MAIDSTONE STATE PARK, *RR1, Box 338, Guildhall VT 05905. (Take Route 102 11 miles north of Guildhall village to the State Forest Highway.) Tel. 802/676-3930 (summer), 802/479-4280 (off-season). Base rates: $13-$17. Open from late May through Labor Day. Credit cards: Visa, Mastercard.*

This remote state park and campground on Lake Maidstone is especially attractive to fishermen, as the lake is home to salmon and several types of trout, of which the lake variety purportedly can weigh in at more than 20 pounds. The camground itself features about 50 trailer and tent sites, with more than 35 lean-ton's and basic amenities like showers, toilets, and sanitation dumping facilities.

Hardwick

SOMERSET HOUSE BED & BREAKFAST, *24 Highland Avenue (PO Box 1098), Hardwick VT 05843-1098. Tel. 802/472-5484, 800/838-8074. Email: gaillard@plainfield-bypass.com. Rates: $70-$90.*

Personable and comfortable, this Victorian mansion-turned-B&B includes four individually decorated rooms, all of which come with a private bath. Breakfast, which is prepared fresh every morning, is of course included.

Island Pond

LAKEFRONT INN & RESORT (LAKEFRONT MOTEL), *Cross Street (PO Box 448), Island Pond, VT 05846-0448. Tel. 802/723-6507. Rates: $65-$300. Major credit cards accepted.*

Overlooking Island Pond, the Lakefront features a variety of accommodations (hence the range in price), including 20 well-maintained motel rooms (some with kitchenettes), and two 2-bedroom suites, also with kitchens. It has a private boat dock and is with walking distance from town, with its various restaurants, and a recreation area with tennis courts and other facilities.

BRIGHTON STATE PARK, *Island Pond VT 05846. (Two miles east of Island Pond on Route 105). Tel. 802/723-4360 (summer), 802/479-4280 (off-season). Base rates: $13-$17. Credit cards: Visa, Mastercard. Open late Mate through mid-October.*

The campsite features more than 60 tent and trailer sites with 21 lean-to's, and is situated on Spectacle Pond around which is scenic hiking.

Jay Peak Area

Includes Montgomery & Troy

JAY PEAK RESORT, *Route 242, Jay, VT 05859. Tel. 802/988-2611; toll free 151 4449, Fax 802/988-4049. Email: jaypeak@together.net. Rates: begin at about $90 per night during the winter. Credit cards: major credit cards accepted.*

Offers an assortment of slopeside and near slopeside 1-4 bedroom studios, condos, and townhouses, all of which feature modern amenities like cable television and at least a kitchenette.

NORTHERN LIGHTS RESORTS, *Route 242, Jay VT 05859. Tel. 802/ 988-2880, 800/331-4346, Fax 802/988-2260. E-mail: skilodge@together.net. Web site: www.skilodge.com.*

In addition to the Inglenook Lodge and the Jay Village Inn, Northern Lights operates Trillium Woods featuring eight-room townhouses. Each includes kitchens, sitting areas with televisions and VCR's, laundry facilities, and access to a modest gym, saunas and whirlpools.

ALPINE HAVEN CHALETS AND FOUR SEASON RESORT, *Route 242 (Box 359), Montgomery Center. Tel. 802/326-4567, Fax 802/326-4009. Rates: begin at around $110 a day (more in winter). Major credit cards accepted.*

Alpine Haven is a resort three miles from the Jay Peak ski area and includes nearly 100 2-6 bedroom chalets and a 25-room lodge. Other facilities include tennis courts, a pool, andon-site cross-country skiing.

BLACK LATERN INN, *Route 118, Montgomery Village, VT 05470. Tel. 802/326-4507, 800/255-8661, Fax 802/326-4077. Email: blantern@together.net. Rates: $85-$165. Major credit cards accepted.*

A stagecoach inn dating to 1803 and listed in the National Register of Historic Places, the Black Lantern is located in the heart of Montgomery Village and features 16 rooms and suites. Rooms are not especially spacious but are charming and nicely furnished with private baths, while the more luxurious suites are larger and include fireplaces and whirlpools. The inn also includes a stove-warmed salon, a porch, and an intimate and elegant dining room where breakfast and dinner is served.

JAY HOTEL, *Route 242, Jay VT 05859. Tel. 802/988-2611, 800/451-4449. E-mail: jaypeak@together.net. Web site: www.jaypeak.com. Rates: begin at around $80 per day (more during ski season and holidays). Major credit cards accepted.*

Situated slopeside at the heart of the resort within meters of the lifts, the Jay Hotel is a modern ski lodge with about 50 rooms, all of which are equipped with amenities including in-room phones and cable television. Other facilities include a restaurant, a lounge area, and a modest spa with sauna and jacuzzi.

INN ON TROUT RIVER, *Main St. (PO Box 76), Montgomery Center, VT 05471. Tel. 800/338-7049, Fax 802/326-3194. Email: troutinn@sover.net. Rates: $85-$120. Credit cards accepted.*

More homey and casual than the Black Lantern, the Inn on Trout River is a turn of the century Victorian Mansion with ten comfy rooms and a suite, as well as restaurant and tavern. Rooms are furnished with quilt-covered queen size beds and include private baths.

INGLENOOK LODGE, *Route 242, Jay, VT 05859. Tel. 802/988-2880, 800/331-4346, Fax 802/988-2686. Email: skilodge@together.net. Rates: $50-$120. Major credit cards accepted.*

Perched on the slopes of Jay Peak, this modernist alpine style lodge includes about 20 rooms, an indoor pool, a restaurant, a lounge with a fireplace, and a spa with a jacuzzi and sauna.

HAZEN'S NOTCH B&B AND CROSS-COUNTRY SKI CENTER, *Hazen's Notch Road (PO Box 730 Route #58), Montgomery Center, VT 05471. Tel. 802/326-4708. Email: hazens@together.net. Rates: $40-$50. Credit cards: Vis, Mastercard*

Best known for its cross-country skiing facilities, including 45 beautiful kilometers of trails, Hazen's Notch features three recently restored rooms with private baths, as well as a sitting room and dining room.

Morgan & Seymour Lake

SEYMOUR LAKE LODGE & INN, *Route 111 (PO Box 61), Morgan, VT 05853-0061. Tel. 802/895-2752. Rates: $50-$110 (cheaper rates for the winter). Credit cards: Visa, Mastercard.*

An ideal choice for fishermen given its location on Seymour Lake. Host Dave Benware is a fishing expert who rents equipment and gives lessons. There are only a half-dozen bedrooms, of which only one has a private bath. There is a dining room serving breakfast and dinner as well a lounge where you can take refreshments.

Newport

NEWPORT CITY MOTEL, *974 East Main St., Newport, VT 05855. Tel. 802/334-6558, 800/338-6558, Fax 802/334-6557. Rates: $60-$85. Major credit cards accepted.*

A full-fledged motel featuring rooms with balconies, coffee makers, cable television and in-room modem links and phones. There is also a modest gym, an indoor pool, and basic business services.

BAY VIEW LODGE & MOTEL, *Route 5, Newport, VT 05855. Tel. 802/334-6543, Fax 802/334-6781. Email: bayview@together.net. Rates: $40-$50. Credit cards: Visa, Mastercard.*

Bay View features basic motel rooms with air conditioning, cable television, and in-room phones; some also have viewsof Lake

CAMPING IN THE GROTON STATE FOREST

The 25,000-plus acres of Groton State Forest in the southeast portion of the Kingdom offers the best and most extensive camping opportunities in northeastern Vermont, particularly for those interested in tent and wilderness camping. Situated on a huge mass of granite (which gives it elevation), the Forest contains four state parks with campgrounds (and three with no campgrounds); several great fishing ponds, lakes and streams; hiking, biking, and ski trails; and a rich variety of plant and animal life. Officials are on duty in all of the state parks and can assist you with directions, information about the park's natural features and history, and maps and other information about trails, water areas, and campgrounds. The Forest surrounds Route 232, which links Route 2 between Montpelier and St. Johnsbury, and – via Route 302 – Interstate 91 and Route 5, making it easily accessible (less than a half hour) from both Montpelier and St. Johnsbury. If you're comming on Route I-91, get off at Exit 17 and take Route 302 west.

__KETTLE POND STATE PARK,__ RD Box 600, Marshfield VT 05658. (5.5 miles south of the junction of Routes 2 and 232; get directions from ranger at New Discovery State Park Entrance). Tel. 802/584-3820 (summer), 802/479-4280 (off-season). Rates: $4 per person per night. Credit cards: Visa, Mastercard. Open from late May through mid-October.

The Kettle Pond State Park features about 30 lean-to's divided into small groups, and a handful of sites on the pond itself. Facilities are minimal, and the pond is an excellent place for hiking and watching wildlife.

__RICKER POND STATE PARK,__ RD, Groton VT 05046. (Ricker is the souterhnmost of the state parks in the forest). Tel. 802/584-3821 (summer), 802/479-4280 (off-season). Base rates: $13-17. Open third week in May through Labor Day. Visa and Mastercard accepted.

Developed by the Civilian Conservation Corps during the Great Depression, the campgrounds feature 32 tent and trailer sites with 23 lean-to's, some fire pits, a sanitary dump, and a boat launch ramp. Ricker also offers good access to the Forest's main trail – the former rail line for the Montpelier-Wells River Railroad.

__STILLWATER STATE PARK,__ RD 2 Box 332, Groton VT 05046. Tel. 802/584-3822 (summer), 802/479-4280 (off-season). (Located off Route232 south of Little Deer Mountain on Lake Groton.) Base rates: $13-$17. Credit cards: Visa, Mastercard. Open May 21-October 11.

With more than 60 campsites for trailers and tents with 17 lean-to's, Stillwater contains the largest campground in Groton State Forest. Situated on the beach of Lake Groton, it is convenient for boaters, swimmers, and fishermen, and with nearby access to most of the Forests trails, hikers and bikers as well.

__NEW DISCOVERY STATE PARK,__ RD 600, Marshfield VT 05658. (New Discovery is the first camground coming from the north on Route 232). Tel. 802/584-3820 (summer), 802/479-4280 (off-season). Base rates: $11-$15; $25 per group of four at remote sites on Osmore Pond. Credit cards: Visa, Mastercard. Open May 21 through Labor Day.

New Discovery is unique in that it is the only park where you can bring your horse (but you should call for reservations first). It also offers, in addition to three dozen trailer and tent sites, remote camping on Osmore pond, not accessible by automobile.

Memphremagog. There is also a game room, jacuzzi, and a decent restaurant.

TOP-OF-THE HILLS COUNTRY INN & MOTEL, *Route 5 & Route 105 of Exit 28 1 mile west of I-91, Newport, VT 05855. Tel. 802/334-6748, 800/258-6748, Fax 802/334-1463.*

The St. Johnsbury Area

RABBIT HILL INN, *Route 18 (PO Box 55), Waterford VT 05848. Tel. 802/748-5168, 800/76-BUNNY, Fax 802/748-8342.*

Recently restored and refurnished, the Rabbit Hill Inn is a quintessential country inn with an accent on romantic atmospherics. A colonial building dating to the 1790's, most of its 20 individually decorated rooms have fireplaces and most suites also include whirlpool-style jacuzzis. For recreation, there is on-site snowshoeing, cross-country skiing and sledding in the winter, canoeing, fishing, and golf privileges in the summer. The handsome grounds include a pond and a gazebo, and the restaurant is no slouch either, serving slightly eccentric but good cuisine and fine wines in an intimate and romantic environment – the charm of which is enhanced by the candlelit tables and live flute music.

BROADVIEW FARM, *McDowell Road (RFD 2, Box 153, St. Johnsbury VT 05819), North Danville. Tel. 802/748-9902. Rates: $50-$75. Closed in April and May.*

Situated on a beautiful 300-acre estate, this attractive antique-filled 19th century farmhouse was recently renovated and includes five unique guestrooms (shared baths). The farm is also known for its maple syrup and the views are magnificent.

FAIRBANKS INN, *32 Western Avenue (off Exit 21, I-91), St. Johnsbury VT 05819. Tel. 802/748-5666. Rates: $60-$90. Major credit cards accepted.*

A newish luxury motel, if you will, with rooms that include balconies, cable television, and telephones. Other faciliities include a swimming pool and a gym.

ECHO LEDGE FARM, *Route 2 (PO Box 46), East St. Johnsbury, VT 05838-0046. Tel. 802/748-4750. Rates: $50-$75. Credit cards: Visa, Mastercard.*

This simple but comfortable family-run bed and breakfast features six bedrooms (most with private baths) on a vintage 1790's farm.

SLEEPY HOLLOW B&B, *546 Roy Road, Danville, VT 05828. Tel. 802/748-8066, 800/213-8180, Fax 802/748-5185. Rates: $65-$80. Credit cards: Visa, Mastercard*

Situated on a secluded estate with grounds that include a small brook and a pond, the Sleepy Hollow B&B is a restored 19th century home with a handful of comfy rooms; private and shared baths available.

AIME'S MOTEL, *Intersection routes 2 and 18 a quarter mile pas Exit 1 of I-93, St. Johnsbury, VT 05819. Tel. 802/748-3194. Rates: $40-$75. Credit cards: Visa, Mastercard.*

Aime's offers simple motel style rooms with air conditioning, cable television, and telephones.

WHERE TO EAT

Barton & Lake Willoughby

WILLOUGHVALE INN & RESTAURANT ON LAKE WILLOUGHBY, *Route 5A (RR 2 Box 403), Westmore VT 05860. Tel. 802/525-4123, 800/594-9102. Web site: www.willoughvale.com. Open nightly for dinner at 5:30pm. Major credit cards accepted.*

Casual and rustic with great views of Lake Willoughby, the Willoughvale serves a wide assortment of dishes, including New England fare and seafood, vegetarian specials, and unique specialties – like shepard pie spud. The Tap Room tavern serves pub fare and is a pleasant place in which to unwind in the evening.

CANDLEPIN RESTAURANT, *Route 5 (a half mile north of the village center), Barton. Tel. 802/525-6513. Open daily 7am-9:30pm, closes at 3pm on Sundays.*

A sort of no-frills blue collar family restaurant adjacent to a bowling alley, you can get steak, seafood, sandwiches and other typical middle American fare. Prices are moderate; you can eat a full meal for less than $15.

Burke Mountain Area
Includes East Burke, Lyndon & Lyndonville

THE OLD CUTTER INN, *Burke Hollw Road, East Burke VT 05832. Tel. 802/626-5152, 800/295-1943. Web site: www.pbpub.com/cutter.htm. Open nightly except Wednesdays from 6pm. Credit cards accepted.*

Owned and operated by a Swiss chef, the elegant intimate dining room at the Old Cutter Inn features excellent French and Swiss-style continental cuisine. Specialties include beef wellington, bratwurst and seafood, meat, and poultry dishes prepared in wine and cream sauces. Main entrees typically range from $13-$25.

WILDFLOWERS INN, *Darling Hill Road, Lyndonville, VT 05851. Tel. 802/626-8310, 800/627-8310, Fax 802/626-3039. Major credit cards accepted.*

The dining room at this wonderfully restored farmhouse serves a rotating menu that features multicourse meals, with a variety of interestingly prepared seafood, steak, and vegetables reflecting New England, Mediterranean and American cuisine. A full meal costs between $20-$30.

RIVER GARDEN CAFE, *Route 114 in East Burke. Tel. 802/626-3514. Open for lunch and dinner. Credit cards accepted.*

A casual but classy cafe serving a wide selection of excellent salads, sandwiches and desserts for lunch, as well as pastas and main entrees the include fish, chicken, and meat dishes for dinner. Popular for Sunday brunch. Prices are low to moderate.

MISS LYNDONVILLE DINER, *Route 5, Lyndonville. Tel. 802/626-9890. Open from 6am until 8pm, sometimes later.*

This venerable old-fashioned diner is among the most popular eateries in the Kingdom with locals and tourists alike. The food has the homecooked hearty diner quality and the menu features a wide selection of breakfast, lunch and dinner fare. Of course, it's also cheap.

The Craftsbury Common Area

INN ON THE COMMON, *Main Street, Craftsbury VT 05826. Tel. 802/586-9619, 800/521-2233, Fax 802/586-2249. E-mail: info@innonthecommon.com. Web site: www.innonthecommon.com. Major credit cards accepted. Call for reservations and seating times.*

The renowned Inn on the Common features perhaps the finest restaurant in the area, a formal candlelit affair serving multicourse, prix fixe ($35 not including wine) dinners that usually offer a choice of several items for each course. Entrees typically include a seafood, meat (often game meats such as venison), and poultry. Finally, the wine list is considered world class.

CRAFTSBURY INN, *Main St. (PO Box 36), Craftsbury, VT 05826-0036. Tel. 802/586-2848, 800/336-2848, Fax 802/586-6952. open to the public in the summer. Reservations required. Credit cards: Visa, Mastercard.*

Situated in an 1850 building in the heart of Craftsbury, this classic Vermont inn features a small dining room that seat about 20, where the $25 prix fixe menu features a modest assortment of superbly prepared lamb, chicken, and game meats (pheasant, venison), fish, soups, salads, and bread baked fresh on the premises.

Derby

BORDER RESTAURANT, *135 North Main Street (at Routes 5 & 105), Derby. Tel. 802/766-2088, 800/280-1898. Open daily.*

A popular establishment serving average American fare (chicken, steaks, veal, pasta) for moderate prices.

Greensboro

HIGHLAND LODGE, *Caspian Lake Road, Greensboro, VT 05841. Tel. 802/533-2647, Fax 802/533-7494. Email: Hlodge@connriver.net. Major credit cards accepted. Open for breakfast 8am-9:30am, lunch 11:30am-2pm, dinner 6pm-9pm. Major credit cards accepted.*

The Highland Lodge serves quality country cuisine in a classy but casual dining room. Meals often begin with soups and salads made fresh with local produce, while the selection of entrees includes seafood, chicken and meats, including such Vermont mainstays as roast rack of lamb. Most dinner entrees are under $20. For breakfast there is an assortment of quality pastries, egg dishes, and fruit while the lunch menu typically includes soups, salads, and sandwiches as well as light entrees.

Jay Peak Area
Includes Montomery & North Troy

ZACK'S ON THE ROCKS, *Route 58, Montomery Center. Tel. 802/326-4500. Open nightly from 6pm-9pm. Reservations required. Major credit cards accepted.*

Zany but luxurious, this one-of-a-kind restaurant is the brainchild of Zack, the quirky owner-chief-maitre'd-jester-in-chief, whose favorite color permeates the place which features great views of Jay Peak. If that scares you off, keep in mind that the nouveau cuisine served is considered among the best and most innovative in Vermont. Just be prepared to fork out $30-$40 per person for a full meal.

BLACK LANTERN INN, *Route 118, Montgomery Village, VT 05470. Tel. 802/326-4507, 800/255-8661, Fax 802/326-4077. Email: blantern@together.net. Major credit cards accepted.*

This highly regarded inn serves continental and country cuisine, in an intimate candlelit dining room. Entrees range from $15-$25.

LEMOINE'S AT INN ON TROUT RIVER, *Main St. (PO Box 76), Montgomery Center, VT 05471. Tel. 800/338-7049, Fax 802/326-3194. Email: troutinn@sover.net. Credit cards accepted.*

The Inn at Trout River operates a popular tavern serving bar food and light fare, in addition to its dining room Lemoine's, which serves continental and American country cuisine in casual country inn atmosphere.

JAY HOTEL, *Route 242, Jay VT 05859. Tel. 802/988-2611, 800/451-4449. E-mail: jaypeak@together.net. Web site: www.jaypeak.com. Rates: begin at around $80 per day (more during ski season and holidays). Major credit cards accepted.*

The restaurant at the Jay Hotel specializes in continental cuisine, with an accent on the French dishes such as escargots, as well as meats and seafood prepared with rich suces, often wine-based. Expect to pay at least $25 per person for a full meal.

THE BELFRY, *Route 242, Montgomery Center. Tel. 802/326-4400. Open daily from 4pm. Major credit cards accepted.*

This popular pub and restaurant serves good old school American cuisine and tavern food: burgers, steaks, soups, salads and an array of appetizers. Most dishes are under $12.

The St. Johnsbury Area

RABBIT HILL INN, *Route 18 (PO Box 55), Waterford VT 05848. Tel. 802/748-5168, 800/76-BUNNY, Fax 802/748-8342.*

In a romantic environment shaped by candlelight and live harp or flute music, the $35 prix fixe dinner are multicourse affairs featuring gourmet continental and country cuisine, but often with international twists (spicey Asian or Carribean sauces for example) that set them apart from your typical gourmet inn dinner.

THE CREAMERY RESTAURANT, *Off Route 2 in Danville. Tel. 802/684-3613. Open 11am-2pm & 5pm-9pm Tuesday through Friday and for dinner on Saturday. Credit cards: Visa, Mastercard.*

Famous for its pies and old time atmosphere (shaped by its last life as a dairy creamery), this eatery serves quality American cuisine including steaks, seafood, and usually a pasta or two, as well as fresh salads and home-style soups. A full meal can be had from $15-$25.

MISS VERMONT DINER, *Route 5 in St. Johnsbury. Tel. 802/748-9751. Open 6am-9pm Monday-Friday, 9am-9pm Saturday, and 7am-1pm Sunday.*

This popular sister of the more famous Lyndonville Diner serves good hearty no-frills diner food, from ultra-calorific burgers to fried clams.

SEEING THE SIGHTS

Route 5 South of St. Johnsbury

If you're not racing up I-91 or coming from the west on Route 2, you will probably enter the Kingdom by coming up Route 5, through Barnet and Rygate from the south.

Settled primarily by Scots, **Barnet** is a small Connecticut Valley village whose main landmarks include a Presbyterian Church, a Buddhist meditation center, a general store, and the **Barnet Historical Society** in the Goodwillie House. Reportedly a station on the Underground Railroad which smuggled freed slaves to Canada, today the Historical Society includes a small collection of the usual photographs and artifacts relating to local history. *Open daily 10am-4pm from July through September. Tel. 802/633-2611 for appointments and guided tours.*

St. Johnsbury

Though it was founded by a group of settlers from Rhode Island led by Jonathan Arnold in 1786, **St. Johnsbury** was actually named for a French consul in New York, Saint-Jean de Crevecoeur, who happened to be a good friend of Ethan Allen. But it was not until the mid-19th century when the inventor of the lever scale, **Thaddeus Fairbanks**, established the Fairbanks Scale Works here and St. Johnsbury became the economic, social and political center of the Kingdom – a status that became official in 1856 when the Caledonia County seat was moved there from Danville, and which it retains today.

Thanks not only to the economic contributions of the Fairbanks, but also to their dedicated leadership and philanthropy, St. Johnsbury thrived thrived culturally and socially. The Fairbanks endowed such institutions as the Museum of Natural Science (now the Fairbanks Museum & Planetarium) and the St. Johnsbury Athenaeum, one of the oldest and beautiful unadulterated art galleries in the United States. During the late 19th and early 20th century, beautiful churches were built, the town enjoyed excellent schools, and the arts thrived.

The Fairbanks were finally bought out in the 1960's and, while it has not recently been blessed with the prosperity that it enjoyed in its heyday a hundred years ago, St. Johnsbury is still a handsome town whose landmarks and cultural vibrancy make it worthy of at least a cursory visit.

ST. JOHNSBURY ATHENAEUM, *30 Main Street (one block left from Route 5 if you're coming from the south). Tel. 802/748-8291. Open 10am-8pm Monday & Wednesday, 10am-5:30pm Tuesdy, Thursday, Friday, and Saturday. Admission free.*

Designed by J.D. Hatch and dedicated by Horace Fairbanks in 1871 (Fairbanks became governor five years later), this must be among the most beautiful town libraries anywhere in the United States – but it is the art gallery for which most visitors come. One of the oldest "pure" galleries in the US, its most famous piece is the huge Domes of Yosemite by Albert Beirstadt, one of the largest landscape paintings of its type.

The real artistic gem, however, is the building itself. While visiting the Athenacum, take time to stroll up Main Street and examine such interesting architectural works as the Gothic North Congregations Church, and the South Congregational Church with its conical spire and open bell tower. Another church worth a visit, on Western Avenue, is the old Methodist Episcopal Church featuring stained glass windows by Tiffany.

THE FAIRBANKS MUSEUM & PLANETARIUM, *Corner of Main Street & Prospect Street (south of the Atheneum). Tel. 802/748-2372. Open 10m-4pm (6pm in summer) Monday through Saturday and from 1pm-5pm on Sunday. Admission: $4 adults, $2.50 children.*

Dedicated by Colonel Franklin Fairbanks in 1890 as the Museum of

Natural Science, the **Fairbanks Museum and Planetarium** is itself a historic relic as well as an architectural gem. Its collections include thousands of specimens of birds, mammals, insects and plants, as well as ethnographic and anthropological exhibits about peoples and cultures from all over the world, including Egypt, Africa, and Asia. The intimate planetarium section upstairs makes daily astronomy presentaitons; call for schedules, information, and other details.

Route 2 West of St. Johnsbury

You can begin a variety of driving tours from St. Johnsbury by taking Route 2 ten miles west of St. Johnsbury to West Danville, and then turn north on 15 which leads to Hardwick (17 miles) and Route 14 north, up to the famously scenic village of Craftsbury Common (ten miles north of Hardwick). From Craftsbury, you can take the local road east to Greensboro and back on Route 16 to the Hardwick area. You can also simply retrace your steps, or continue north on Route 14 to Orleans, from where you can return to St. Johnsbury directly on I-91 or by Route 5 or 122 – both of which pass through Lyndon. Route 16 which leads back to Hardwick is another alternative.

Danville

A rural town with a classic Vermont village complete with a green and bandstand, **Danville** (seven miles west of St. Johnsbury) is definitely worth passing through, though there isn't much to visit unless you're interested in dowsing. What's dowsing, you say? That's the now all but defunct practice of using a divining rod to locate water or minerals underground. Find out all about it at the **American Society of Dowsers'** headquarters, *in Dowsers Hall, Danville, open Monday-Friday from 9am-5pm, Tel. 802/684-3417.*

If you have time to spare, consider taking a 10-mile detour south to **Peacham**, a handsome gentrified village with many historic buildings and nice views of the White Mountains in New Hampshire. Three miles beyond Danville, West Danville is situated on Joe's Pond at the intersection with Route 15. As mentioned, you can turn north up to Hardwick, which presents an excelllent opportunity to visit the Cabot **Creamery**, Vermont's most famous and highly decorated producer of cheeses, simply by turning south from Route 15 on Route 215 at Walden Station; the creamery will be four miles south.

CABOT CREAMERY VISITORS' CENTER, *Route 215 in Cabot. Tel. 802/563-2231. Open mid-June through mid-October from 8am-4pm Monday through Saturday and from 11am-3pm on Sundays. Admission free.*

Highly promoted by the folks at the state's marketing and tourism department, the Creamery offers visitors the opportunity to view the cheese making process and to sample some of Vermont's best known cheeses. There is also a gift shop selling all sorts of cheeses and other Vermont specialty foods and souvenirs.

Hardwick

Back on Route 15, it's about seven miles north through the town of Walden to **Hardwick**, a former granite town whose major claim to fame nowadays is the annual **Vermont Reggae Festival**. A free one-day concert held recently on a local farm, it has attracted such stars as Burning Spear and Buju Banton in recent years. *For details about dates and camping, call 802/-862-3092 and/or check out the festival's web site: www.vtreggaefest.org.*

Route 14 & Craftsbury

Seven miles north of Hardwick, on Route 14, a local road (there are plenty of signs) will lead to the town of Craftsbury and its most famous village, **Craftsbury Common**. Founded by a Yale-educated tavern owner and merchant, **Ebenezer Crafts**, Craftsbury Common with its classic colonial and federal-style buildings and village green is among the most picturesque in Vermont. Though Craftsbury gets more than enough tourist traffic as it is (which of course is important for business), it seems blessed in that its more isolated Kingdom location has kept it from being gentrified and overrun with tourists to the extent of Woodstock.

From Craftsbury, you can take the local road a dozen miles through Greensboro to Route 16, or you can continue north on Route 14 along the Black River and enjoy some classic pastoral Vermont scenery. It is roughly 15 miles to Irasburg and Orleans.

Route 16

You can reach the quiet resort town of **Greensboro** and pristine **Lake Caspian** either by taking Route 16 for the Hardwick area (the junction with Route 15 is actually two miles east of Hardwick village), or directly from Craftsbury Common. There is little to see apart from the lake itself, which is quite beautiful.

Sixteen miles north of Hardwick in the township of Glover, Route 16 intersects with Route 122 which leads south directly 25 miles to St. Johnsbury. Glover is best known as the home of the **Bread & Puppet Theater Museum**, where you can view an amazing array of fantastic larger-than-life puppets built and played by the Bread and Puppet Theater Troupe. *Open daily from June through October from 10am-5pm. Admission free.*

THE BREAD & PUPPET THEATER

Founded by the Polish-born German-American Peter Schumann, the Bread and Puppet Theater based in Glover has been presenting its overtly leftist morality plays to audiences across the Northeast and America, as well as abroad, for more than 25 years. The plays, which invariably take aim at corporatism, greed, and other evils of capitalist society, are witty and entertaining, but the greatest attraction are the puppets themselves and the amazing effort put into creating them and performing with them. Mostly fantastic caricatures of the good (the honest working folks and the poor), and the evil (any corporate, right-wing type often represented by a sinister witch or devil) the colorful papier-mache puppets – some of which are more than 20 feet tall – require hours and hours of tedious work to create, and often as many as four puppeteers to operate.

For 23 years, the pinnacle of each Bread and Puppet Theater season was the annual Domestic Resurrection Circus. Held in Glover and of course free of charge, the two day orgy of taunting the establishment grew to the extent that by the early '90's it attracted tens of thousands, some of whom unfortunately made the event an excuse to get overly rowdy and it has been indefinitely canceled. However, the Theater still performs across the region and the country.

Lyndonville & the Burke Mountain Area

Eight miles north of St. Johnsbury by way of I-91 and Route 5, the town of Lyndon and especially its primary village of **Lyndonville** is a commercial hub, but offers little for visitors apart from a handful of covered bridges, the famous Lyndonville Diner, and annual country fair held at the end of the summer.

Far more inviting is the Burke Mountain resort area in **East Burke** five miles to the northeast on Route 114. Though it's known primarily for its skiing, East Burke itself is a pretty village featuring many shops and restaurants. The **White School Museum** is a restored one-room schoolhouse originally built in 1818. *Open on Wednesday and Saturday afternoons from June through October; Tel. 802/626-9823.*

From East Burke, it's a pleasant but uneventful drive up Route 114 to Island Pond. There is also a little traveled local road to Guildhall in the Connecticut River Valley. From Guildhall, it's a twenty mile drive on Routes 102 and 2 to St. Johnsbury.

Essex County

East of Route 114 (which runs south-north from Lyndonville to the Canadian border), **Essex County** is the least developed, most sparsely populated area in Vermont, and is primarily the domain of loggers. From St. Johnsbury, it is – apart from the odd abandoned trailer – a pleasant drive, with many views of the White Mountains on Route 2 through the towns of Concord and Lunenburg to the Connecticut River and the junction with Route 102. At this point, just south of the town of Guildhall, Route 2 crosses into New Hampshire. Meanwhile, **Route 102** is a scenic if lonely drive up the Connecticut River. Roughly 20 miles north of the junction is a turnoff west to Lake Maidstone and **Maidstone State Park**. The lake itself is beautiful and, because it is more secluded than many in Vermont, it is less crowded and features more wildlife in the way of waterfowl, moose, and even bear.

North of Lake Maidstone, Route 105 turns west 16 miles to the town and body of water known as **Island Pond**, while Route 102 continues north to the junction with **Route 114** at the village of **Canaan** in the very northeastern coerner of Vermont. Just off Route 114 ten miles west of Canaan, you can stay at the Quimby Country Lodge on Forest Lake (see above under *Where to Stay*, and fish and swim at the Great and Little Averill Ponds as well.

Barton & Crystal Lake

Roughly 30 miles north of St. Johnsbury by way of Route 5 and I-91, **Barton** was once a modest rail hub and popular resort. Though the railroad is gone, it remains a great destination for those who enjoy lakes, fishing, and boating. In terms of sights, the Pierce House on Water Street includes a modest collection of photographs and artifacts relating to local history. *Open Tuesday and Thursday 2pm-4pm from mid-June through mid-September. Admission free. Tel. 802/525-6251.*

Lake Willoughby

This stunningly beautiful lake, resembling a Norwegian fjord or Scottish loch, can be reached by way of Route 5A from the north and south (15 miles north of Lyndonville), and by Route 16 from Barton (seven miles). There is little in the way of historic sites or picturesque villages here; **Willoughby State Park** at the southern end of the lake is a beautiful venue for hiking, fishing, and boating.

Echo Lake & Seymour Lake

Situated between Island Pond and Newport along Routes 111 (Seymour Lake) and Route 105 (Echo Lake), these two lakes are both excellent venues for fishing and boating.

Newport & Lake Memphremagog

It might seem as though this lake – the second largest in Vermont (even though two-thirds of it are in Canada) – has vast potential as a resort that has yet to be realized; indeed, **Newport** (45 miles north of St. Johnsbury on I-91) offers little in the way of facilities and amenities for tourists. Having said that, the lake still offers great fishing and boating opportunities and the surounding countryside is beautiful, sparsely populated, and hardly visited by tourists.

Jay Peak & the western Kingdom

West of the Lakes Region, there is little in the way of sights apart from the beautiful scenery you can enjoy on Routes 100, 242, 105 and 101, and various local roads. The **Jay Peak** area, known primarily for its skiing, is also a popular venue for biking and hiking in the summer. You can also take the scenic **Jay Peak Tram**, which ferries skiers in winter and affords beautiful views in the summer and in foliage season. West of Jay Peak (less than five miles) at the junction of Routes 242 and 118, **Montgomery Center** is a pleasant village with an assortment of country inns, restaurants, and shops.

NIGHTLIFE & ENTERTAINMENT

The **Catamount Arts Center** in St. Johnsbury supports local artists and presents a variety of performances in the Northeast Kingdom, and has done so for more than 20 years now. There's a film series, theater series, family fun series, and a classical series. Movies, dance, plays – it's a cultural mecca here, and both local artists and nationally known (and international) performers appear.

The theater seats 85 people, and there's also an art gallery on-site. For schedule and price information, contact them at *60 Eastern Avenue, St. Johnsbury, VT 05819, Tel. 802/748-2600. Web site: www.ourkingdom.com/ nonprofit/catamount/index.html.*

If you're just looking to take in a movie, see what's playing at the **Star Theatre**, *18 Eastern Avenue, St. Johnsbury, Tel. 802/748-9511.*

Traveling with kids? Over in Lyndonville, check out the **Vermont Children's Theater**, *Darling Hill Road, Lyndonville, VT 05851, Tel. 802/ 626-5358.*

And if you're looking for some live music and good fun, we'd recommend the following:

• **Jasper's**, *Main St., Newport, Tel. 802/334-2224.* Live rock music on Friday nights.
• **Phat Kats**, *Depot Street, Lyndonville, Tel. 802/626-3064.* Local rock acts.
• **The Pub Outback**, *Route 114, East Burke, Tel. 802/626-1188.* The place for jazz and blues in the Northeast Kingdom.

There's also usually live music at the resorts (**Jay Peak**, **Burke Mountain**) during ski season, so call ahead and find out.

SPORTS & RECREATION

Biking

With a natural beauty and a sparse popularion even by Vermont standards, the Northeast Kingdom is a fantastic place for biking. Most of the state parks and forests – notably **Groton State Forest** between Montpelier and St. Johnsbury, and **Willoughby State Forest** 25 miles due north of St. J's – feature a rich diversity of terrain for mountain bikers. Biking on the road is also very good assuming that you are careful. Though Vermont's and the Kingdom's roads are well maintained and low in traffic volume, they are often curvy with blind corners and do not have special biking lanes.

For specific information about where to rent bikes, and ideas for bike tours, pick up a copy of *25 Bicycle Tours in Vermont* published by Backcountry Publications or the Vermont Life magazine's pamphlet and map, *Bicycle Vermont*. Both publications are widely available at bookstores and gift shops throughout the state. The Vermont Department of Tourism and Marketing also publishes a pamphlet, *Biking Tours in the Northeast Kingdom*, available at rest stops on major highways and by calling *800/VERMONT*.

NORTHEAST KINGDOM GUIDE SERVICES, *P.O. Box 269, Albany VT 05820. Tel. 800/723-4117.*

Organizes bike tours.

EAST BURKE SPORTS, *Route 114, East Burke VT 05832. Tel. 802/ 626-3215. Open daily. Major credit cards accepted.*

In addition to selling and renting canoes, skis, and bikes (including mountain bikes), these folks can also give advice and tips about how and where to ski, bike, boat, and fish. They also deal in camping equipment, outdoor apparel, and clothing generally.

CRAFTSBURY OUTDOOR CENTER, *Lost National Road (PO Box 31), Craftsbury, VT 05827. Tel. 802/586-7767, 800/729-7751, Fax 802/586-7768. Email: crafts@sover.net. Web site: www.craftsbury.com. Major credit cards accepted.*

Primarily a cross-country ski facility, you can rent bikes here and get information about area biking options.

Boating

With its many lakes, the Northeast Kingdom offers many opportunities for boating. With its secluded location, the lakes are much less crowded than Lake Champlain. Bigger lakes, such as **Willoughby**, **Memphremagog**, **Crystal Lake**, and **Island Pond**, are popular venues for all types of boating, including motorboats, canoes, sailing, and even jetskiing, while smaller lakes, particularly those in state parks like **Lake Maidstone** and **Lake Groton**, are better suited to those interested in enjoying the wilderness and wildlife.

For more information about boating and the lakes, contact the Northeast **Kingdom Travel & Tourism Association**, *P.O. Box 355, Island Pond VT 05907-0355. Tel. 802/723-9800, Tel. 888/884-8001, Fax 802/723-5300, E-mail: info@travelthekingdom.com, Web site: www.travelthekingdom.com*; and/or **Vermont Department of Forests, Parks, and Recreation.** *324 North Main Street, Barre VT 05461-4109, Tel. 802/476-0170, 802/479-4280.*

CRAFTSBURY OUTDOOR CENTER, *Lost National Road (PO Box 31), Craftsbury, VT 05827. Tel. 802/586-7767, 800/729-7751, Fax 802/586-7768. Email: crafts@sover.net. Web site: www.craftsbury.com. Major credit cards accepted.*

Rents and provides instruction for canoeing, kayaking, sailing, and sculling (Olympic rowing). Also features lodging and other outdoor recreation facilities.

EAST BURKE SPORTS, *Route 114, East Burke VT 05832. Tel. 802/ 626-3215. Open daily. Major credit cards accepted.*

In addition to selling and renting canoes, skis, and bikes (including mountain bikes), these folks can also give advice and tips about how and where to ski, bike, boat, and fish. They also deal in camping equipment and outdoor apparel and clothing generally.

ANGLIN' CANOE & BOAT RENTAL, *Crystal Lake, Barton. Tel. 802/ 525-3750.*

Cross-Country Skiing & Snowshoeing

BURKE MOUNTAIN CROSS-COUNTRY SKI CENTER, *Burke Mountain (Route 114), East Burke VT 05832. Tel. 800/786-8338. Trail fees: $12.*

Burke Mountain has 80 kilometers of trails and provides rentals, instruction and tours. Call about special lodging packages.

CRAFTSBURY OUTDOOR CENTER, *Lost National Road (PO Box 31), Craftsbury, VT 05827. Tel. 802/586-7767, 800/729-7751, Fax 802/586-7768. Email: crafts@sover.net. Web site: www.craftsbury.com. Major credit cards accepted.*

The Center maintains nearly 100 kilometers of trails for cross-country skiing and snowshoeing. Lodging, rentals, and instruction are also available.

HAZEN'S NOTCH CROSS-COUNTRY SKI CENTER, *Montogomery Center. Tel. 802/326-4708. Trail fees: $8.*

Nearly 50 kilometers of trails as well as rentals, instruction, and tours.

HIGHLAND LODGE, *Greensboro. Tel. 802/533-2647. Trail fees: $10.*
65 kilometers of trails, rentals and instruction.
SUGARMILL FARM, INC., *Barton. Tel. 802/Tel. 800/688-7978. Trail fees: $5. 25 kilometers of trails.*
A pretty place with nice trails.

Fishing

All of the major lakes in the kingdom contain fish, as do many of the rivers and streams. For comprehensive information about fishing, including regulations, contact the **Vermont Department of Forests, Parks, and Recreation,** *324 North Main Street, Barre VT 05461-4109, Tel. 802/476-0170, 802/479-4280.* Or contact the state parks listed in the *Where to Stay* section above.

Lake Willoughby in Orleans County in the heart of the Northeast Kingdom is not only one of the most beautiful sites this side of the Canadian border, but is home to some of the biggest trout and landlocked salmon (20-plus pounds) in Vermont. Lake Willoughby is roughly 25 miles north of St. Johnsbury and is accessbile from I-91, by getting off at Exit 25 and taking Route 16 east; or by way of Route 5 and continuing on Route 5A. You can also continue on Route 5 itself to **Willoughby State Forest**. There are several boat ramps into the lake, including a few from the State Forest – just look for signs.

Groton State Forest, nestled in the southeast corner of the Northeast Kingdom, features seven state parks with several lakes and ponds where you can try your luck for lake trout among others. Two of these bodies of water, **Peacham Pond** and **Lake Groton**, are equipped with boat ramps for those with boats. Four of the state parks (New Discovery, Kettle Pond, Stillwater, and Ricker) features camgrounds (see above in the *Where to Stay* section). Camping fees are typically $11-$17 and there is also a small entrance fee for day use.

Lake Maidstone in **Maidstone State Park** off Route 102 about ten miles north of the village of Guldhall on the eastern edge of the Kingdom, *Tel. 802/ 676-3930 in season; Tel. 802/479-4280 in off-season,* is home to landlocked salmon and several varieties of trout (brook, rainbow, and lake trout), with the lake variety sometimes weighing in at more than 20 pounds. The park is open from about the third week in May through Labor Day, and has campsites (see *Where to Stay* above) for accommodation. Loons and moose are also major attractions.

Golf

ST. JOHNSBURY COUNTRY CLUB, *St. Johnsbury VT. Tel. 800/748-8899, 802/748-9894. Rates: $30 weekdays, $34 weekends, $15 twilight, $13 per person for carts. Major credit cards accepted.*

ORLEANS COUNTRY CLUB, *Route 58 one mile east of Orleans town/ P.O. Box 8, Orleans VT 05860. Tel. 802/754-2333. 18 holes. Green fees: $10-$20. Major credit cards accepted.*

NEWPORT COUNTRY CLUB,*Newport VT. Tel. 802/334-2391. 18 holes. Green fees: $11-$21. Credit cards accepted. Carts available.*

Hiking

There is an abundance of excellent hiking in the Northeast Kingdom, particularly in state parks and forests. For comprehensive information about hiking in the Kingdom and Vermont generally, contact the **Vermont Department of Forests, Parks, and Recreation**, *324 North Main Street, Barre VT 05461-4109, Tel. 802/476-0170, 802/479-4280.* Also the Green Mountain Club's book *Day Hiker's Guide to Vermont* and many of their other publications have good ideas and tips about hiking in the region.

Hunting

Hunting is very popular in the Northeast Kingdom as in the rest of Vermont, and in addition to deer, the Kingdom features a greater abundance of moose than other regions in the state. For detailed information about seasons, licenses, and other regulations, as well as the pamphlet, *Vermont Lodging Directory – Hunter's Edition,* contact the **Vermont Department of Fish and Wildlife**, *103 South Main Street, Waterbury VT 05671, Tel. 802/241-3700.*

Skiing & Snowboarding

BURKE MOUNTAIN, *Burke Mountain on Route 114 8 miles north of Lyndon (P.O. Box 242), East Burke VT 05832. Tel. 802/626-3305, 800/922-BURK, Tel. 800/541-5480. Web site: www.burkemountain.com. Lift Rates: $25-$40 per adult for one day (lower rates for Vermonters, youth, seniors, and multiday passes). Lift hours: 8:30-4pm.*

With four lifts and 30 trails covering only 60 acres, Burke Mountain is much smaller than the Mount Snows and Killingtons of the world, but its remote location – which is more convenient than Jay Peak's remote location – ensures that crowds are smaller and lines shorter. Also, it is considerably cheaper than the bigger resorts.

Equipment can be rented at the base lodge (skis, poles, and boots for an adult begin at about $25), and group and individual lessons can be joined and arranged for adults and children. Call for further information about lessons, discounts, and special packages and promotions that include lodging and skiing.

JAY PEAK, Route 242, Jay VT 05859. Tel. 802/988-2611, Tel. 800/451-4449. E-mail: jaypeak@together.net Web site: www.jaypeakresort.com. Rates begin at $45 a day for adults ($32 for children) and get cheaper for each day (for a example a five day ticket costs $185 for an adult ($130 for children under 14). Rentals (including boots, bindings,ski's, and poles) begin at $25 a day for adults ($19 for children under 14). Snowboard rentals (boots and boards) begin at $30 a day. Lift hours: 9am-4:30pm.

With its remote northern location, Jay Peak can boast lower lines in addition to an annual snowfall of more than 330 inches – highest in Vermont – as well as 65 trails and seven lifts. Jay Peak is particularly popular for its chutes and glades skiing.

For those interested in lessons, group ski lessons for all levels (two hours a day) range from $25 a day to $105 for five days of lessons. Lessons for skiers and snowboarders begin at $40 a day (lifts, equipment, and two hours of lessons) and go up to $160 for five days.

There are also special programs for children. The Kinderschool Nursery offers supervised activities for children ages 2-7 ($15 half-day, $30 full day). For young children interested in skiing (or with parents interested in their skiing), the Kinderschool Ski Program offers lessons for $30 a pop. Finally, the SKIwee program offers day long lessons for children 5-12 at $50 a day (rentals $10, lift tickets not included).

Contact Jay Peak at the numbers/addresses above for information about discounts and package deals that bundle lodging, skiing, and meals for a price well below what you would pay for each separately.

Snowmobiling

Vermont is a dedicated snowmobiling state, and the Northeast Kingdom is no exception. In fact, **Island Pond** bills itself the "Snowmobile Capital of Vermont" and there is excellent snowmobiling throughout the region. Areas considered particularly good include **Groton State Forest**, **Canaan**, **Lyndonville**, **Burke**, **Derby**, and the aforementioned Island Pond.

To snowmobile in Vermont, you must join a local club (contacts listed below) for an annual membership fee (usually about $15), and pay a Trail Maintenance Assessment (usually $50 – $100). For detailed information, contact the **Vermont Association of Snow Travelers (V.A.S.T.)**, *P.O. Box 839, Montpelier VT 05601, Tel. 802/229-0005, Tel. 888/884-8001, Fax 802/223-4316, Web site: www.vtvast.org.* Listed below are snowmobile clubs in the Northeast Kingdom:

- **Brighton Snowmobile Club** – *Tel. 802/334-2208*
- **Canaan Border Riders** – *Tel. 802/266-8864*
- **Connecticut Valley Sno-Riders** – *Tel. 802/328-4106*
- **Lunenburg Polar Bears** – *Tel. 802/695-2919*

- **Moose River Rock Dodgers** – *Tel. 802/328-2191*
- **Snow Rollers** – *Tel. 802/433-5519*
- **Barton Snow Hawks** – *Tel. 802/525-3574*
- **Clyde River Riders** – *Tel. 802/895-4422*
- **Country Riders** – *Tel. 802/334-8056*
- **Creek Runners** – *Tel. 802/754-2218*
- **Drift Dusters** – *Tel. 802/895-4689*
- **Glover Trailwinders** – *Tel. 802/525-6985*
- **Hazen's Notch Snowmobile** – *Tel. 802/744-6217*
- **North Country Mountaineers** – *Tel. 802/755-6218*
- **Orleans Snow Stormers** – *Tel. 802/754-2085*
- **Westfield Trail Cats** – *Tel. 802/744-6542*
- **Bayley Hazen Snowmobile Club** – *Tel. 802/592-3382*
- **Buckaroos of 302** – *Tel. 802/584-3101*
- **Caledonia County Snowmobile Trails Club** – *Tel. 802/684-2584*
- **Coles Pond Sledders** – *Tel. 802/563-9985*
- **Danville S-Ski-Mos** – *Tel. 802/684-3372*
- **Drift Skippers** – *Tel. Tel. 802/626-5274*
- **Lyndon Sno Cruisers** – *Tel. 802/626-3174*
- **Newark E-Z Riders** – *Tel. 802/467-3436*
- **Ryegate Rovers** – *Tel. 802/757-3034*
- **St. Johnsbury Sno-Blazers** – *Tel. 802/748-3833*
- **Snowflake Ridge Runners** – *Tel. 802/472-6850*
- **Waterford Ridge Runners** – *Tel. 802/748-4367*
- **Winter Wanderers** – *Tel. 802/626-5582*

SHOPPING

Albany

   McCLEARY BROOK ANTIQUES & GIFTS, *HC 65 one mile north of Albany and 11 miles from I-91. Tel. 802/755-6344. Email: Inteslen@together.net. Open daily. Credit cards: Visa, Mastercard.*

   Situated in a restored carriage barn, McCleary's features a variety of Vermont specialty foods and goods as well as antiques.

Barton & West Glover

   JAN'S ORIGINALS, *RFD 1, Barton. Tel. 802/525-6608.*
   Baskets and other handmade arts and crafts.

   COMSTOCK'S SMOKEHOUSE, *Crystal Lake Plaza, Barton. Tel. 800/89-BACON. Open daily 10am-5pm. Credit cards: Visa, Mastercard.*

   Specializing in cob-smoked ham, bacon, and other meats, Comstock's also sells maple syrup and other Vermont specialty foods. Mail order catalog available.

SOUTHWIND NORTH, *Route 16, Glover. Tel. 802/525-8891. Open Monday-Saturday 10am-5pm & from 10am-4pm on Sunday. Credit cards: Visa, Mastercard.*

Features a wide variety of antiques, old jewelry, art, quilts and other textiles, and all sorts of other interesting stuff.

Danville

FARR'S ANTIQUES, *on Peacham Road off the Danville Green (4/10 mile from Route 2). Tel. 802/684-3333. Hours: 10am-4pm daily except Sunday. Open year around. Credit cards: Visa, Mastercard.*

LAUGHING FIRE POTTERY, *Off Route 2, West Danville, VT 05873.*

CASEY BROOKS CRAFTS, *3/4 mile off Route 2 at 848 Jamieson Road, Danville. Tel. 802/748-4494.*

HARRINGTON'S RED LOFT, *Junction of Routes 2 & 15, West Danville. Hours: "Open by appointment or by chance."*

East Burke

BAILEY'S COUNTRY STORE, *Route 114, East Burke. Tel. 802/626-3666. Open daily. Credit cards: Visa, Mastercard.*

An old-fashioned Vermont country store featuring souvenirs and t-shirts, fine wines, maple syrup and freshly prepared baked goods.

EAST BURKE SPORTS, *Route 114, East Burke VT 05832. Tel. 802/626-3215. Open daily. Major credit cards accepted.*

In addition to selling and renting canoes, skis, and bikes (including mountain bikes), these folks can also give advice and tips about how and where to ski, bike, boat, and fish. They also deal in camping equipment and outdoor apparel, and clothing generally.

Greensboro

VERMONT DAYLILIES, *Barr Hill Road (PO Box 216), Greensboro. Tel. 802/533-7155.*

THE OLD FORGE, SCOTTISH WOOLENS LTD., *Across from Willey's Store, Greensboro (PO Box 105). Tel. 802/533-2241. Open from May to December – call ahead for. Credit cards: major credit cards accepted.*

The Old Forge features a beautiful assortment of textiles from the British Isles (Scotland, Ireland, Englad, and Wales), including tweeds, leathers, and knits.

Jay

JAY COUNTRY STORE & CHRISTMAS WORLD, *Route 242, Jay. Tel. 802/988-4040. Email: jcountry@together.net. Open daily. Major credit cards accepted.*

One of the Kingdom's most famous country stores selling everything from deli sandwiches and groceries to pottery and limited edition lithographs and paintings.

THE TRICKLE TRUNK, *Jay Village, Jay. Tel./Fax 802/988-4731. Hours: 10am-5pm Thursday-Monday.*

WHITNEY MC DERMUT, BOOKSELLER, *P.O. Box 789, Jay, VT 05859. Tel. 802/988-4349.*

Montgomery Center

TERRY'S FINE WOOLENS & ANTIQUES, *Route 118, Main St. (PO Box 412), Montgomery Center. Tel. 802/326-4118.*

Newport

COUNTRY THYME VERMONT, *Derby Road, Newport. Tel. 802/334-7906; toll free 888-334-7906. Open daily. Major credit cards accepted.*

A classic Vermont gift shop featuring crafts, jewelry, candles, stuffed animals and much more.

WOODKNOT BOOKSHOP, *49 Main St., Newport. Tel. 802/334-6720, Fax 802/334-1322.*

St. Johnsbury

MAPLE GROVE MUSEUM & GIFT SHOP, *off Exit 1 (I-93) and Exit 20 (I-91); Route 2 East from downtown at 167 Portland St., St. Johnsbury. Tel. 802/748-5141. Open daily May-October. Major credit cards accepted.*

REDBERRY SPECIALTY FOODS & GIFTS, *109 Railroad St., St. Johnsbury. Tel. 802/748-8093, 800/641-4928, Fax 802/748-9783. Email: redberry@together.net. Hours: 10am-5:30pm Monday-Thursday, Saturday. 10am-8pm Fridays and daily during X-mas holiday. Credit cards: Visa, Mastercard, Discover.*

A small shop big enough to operate its own mailing order business, Redberry's specializes in gourmet Vermonty souvenirs that are both tasty and easy to carry home.

NORTHERN LIGHTS BOOKSHOP & CAFE, *79 Railroad St., St. Johnsbury. Tel. 802/748-4463. Open daily. Credit cards: Visa, Mastercard.*

The book selection is more than decent for a small town bookstore, and the cafe gives it a nice buzz of activity as well as a place to sit down, sip coffee, and read the paper. The menu is extensive and features breakfast dishes, about 20 hot and cold sandwiches, other entrees and a wide variety of beverages from coffee to beer and wine.

PETER GLENN SKI & SPORTS, *115 Railroad St., St. Johnsbury. Tel. 802/748-3433, Fax 802/748-1611. Summer hours: 10am-6pm Monday-Thursday, Sat.urday; 10am-8pm Friday; closed Sunday. Winter hours: daily 10am-8pm; 10am-4pm on Sundays. Credit cards: Visa, Mastercard, Discover.*

"Snow ski specialists since 1958," the folks at Peter Glenn can hook you up with all types of ski equipment from long underwear to sun goggles, as well as other general winter sports gear.

EXCURSIONS & DAY TRIPS

The Northeast Kingdom is so large that unless you're based in St. Johnsbury or some other locale on the edge of the Kingdom, it's difficult to make a day trip out of the region. Having said that, there are numerous attractions within 100 miles of any location in the Kingdom.

Montpelier, Vermont's charming state capital, is 35 miles west of St. Johnsbury on Route 2. Its main landmark is the handsome state capitol building, with other attractions including the **Vermont Historical Society**, featuring an extensive library and collection of documents, photos, and other artifacts related to the state history. Montpelier is also home to the **New England Culinary Institute** and three of its eateries where you can sample cutting-edge cuisine prepared by the chefs of tomorrow. Just east of Montpelier, **Barre** is the granite capital of the world and the **Rock of Ages Quarry** is among the most interesting attractions in Vermont.

For a nice drive, simply head south from St. Johnsbury on Route 5 to sample the beauty of the **Connecticut River Valley**. There is little in the way of major attractions but the villages like Newbury and Bradbury are quite charming, and if you have time, **Norwich** (about an hour south of St. J), is home to the **Montshire Museum of Science**.

PRACTICAL INFORMATION

Chambers of Commerce & Information

NORTHEAST KINGDOM TRAVEL & TOURISM ASSOCIATION, *Located in the Historic Railroad Station on Main Street (P.O. Box 355), Island Pond VT 05907-0355. Tel. 802/723-9800, Tel. 888/884-8001, Fax 802/723-5300. E-mail: info@travelthekingdom.com. Web site: www.travelthekingdom.com.*

Medical Emergencies

Ambulance & Rescue– *Tel. 911 or 334-7331;* **Albany** – *Tel. 525-3505*

North Country Hospital, *Prouty Drive, Newport. Tel. 802/750-7331, 800/750-7331.*

Northeastern Vermont Regular Hospital, *Hospital Drive, St. Johnsbury. Tel. 802/748-8141.*

Police –*Tel. 911*

State Police in Derby – *Tel. 802/766-2211*

Albany – *Tel. 525-3505*

Newport – *Tel. 766-2211*

408

22. THE UPPER CONNECTICUT RIVER VALLEY

The **Upper Connecticut River Valley** between **White River Junction** to the south and **Newbury** to the north is one of those regions that most visitors to Vermont pass through on their way to either the Northeast Kingdom or the Green Mountain ski resorts. Those of you with a bit of time, however, might consider stopping and taking in the beauty of the river valley itself, if not the scenic villages of **Norwich**, **Bradford**, and **Newbury**. Most of these towns serve as bedroom communities for the economically booming region of Hanover, New Hampshire (home to Dartmouth College) and the neighboring commercial center of West Lebanon, New Hampshire.

Indeed, many residents of the Upper Connecticut River Valley interact and associate themselves with the neighboring communities in New Hampshire more than they do with the rest of Vermont. However, they will also tell you that despite higher taxes and a longer commute, they would not give up the better maintained natural preserved character of their Vermont communities for anything.

ARRIVALS & DEPARTURES

By Air

The nearest commercial airport is **Lebanon Municipal Airport** in West Lebanonm only about 10 minutes on I-89 from White River Junction. However, Lebanon is only served by USAir Express, *Tel. 800/428-4322* and flights are limited and expensive.

More convenient in terms of available flights and cost is **Manchester Airport** in Manchester, New Hampshire. Serviced by Southwest, *Tel. 800/435-9792*, Continental, *Tel. 800/525-0289*, USAir, *Tel. 800/428-4322*, and Delta Connection, *Tel. 800/345-3400*, Manchester is approximately 1.5 hours from White River Junction by car – most major rental companies operate out of Manchester. Otherwise, **Vermont Transit Lines**, *Tel. 800/552-8738, Tel. 800/451-3292*, offers direct service from the Manchester

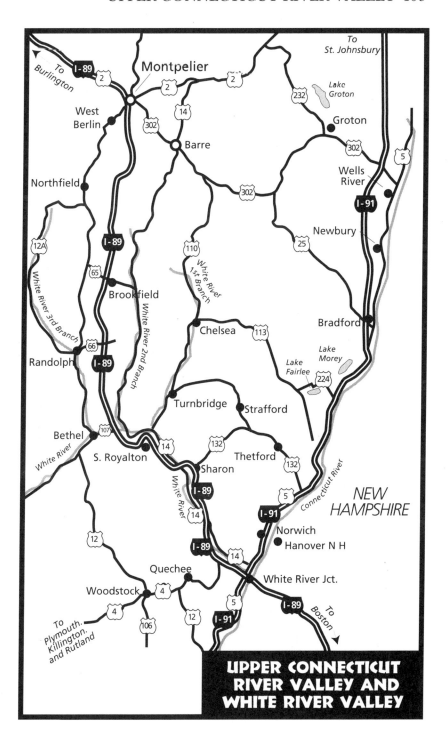

UPPER CONNECTICUT
RIVER VALLEY AND
WHITE RIVER VALLEY

Airport to White River Junction four times daily (10:25am, 2:55pm, 5:55pm, & 10:40pm). If the departure times from the airport are inconvenient, take a taxi to the downtown depot where another half-dozen buses depart daily for White River Junction.

Another alternative is to fly into Boston's **Logan Airport**, approximately 2.5 hours from the Woodstock-Quechee region by car. All major car rental companies operate out of Logan, or you can take one of the hourly shuttles to South Station in downtown Boston and then catch one of a half-dozen daily buses to White River Junction. The advantages of flying into Boston, particularly if you are traveling some distance, include the availability of flights and lower costs than flying into one of the smaller regional airports.

By Bus

Vermont Transit Lines, *Tel. 800/552-8738, Tel. 800/451-3292*, offers direct service between **White River Junction**, *Tel. 802/295-3011*, which is a 10-20 minute drive from Woodstock-Quechee, and major destinations throughout the Northeast, including New York City, Montreal, Boston, and Manchester NH, in addition to all areas of Vermont including Rutland, Burlington, Montpelier, the Northeast Kingdom, Bennington, the Precision Valley, all major ski areas, and Brattleboro. There are also two buses daily from Woodstock and Quechee to Rutland and White River Junction, but apart from saving a couple (and it really is just a couple) of dollars on a cab, it is almost always more convenient to take a taxi to White River Junction and catch buses from there. A one-way fare to Boston is approximately $30.

By Train

Amtrak's **Vermonter**, *Tel. 800/USA-RAIL*, departs Washington, DC at 7:40am and stops at Baltimore, Willmington DE, Philadelphia, New York City, Newark NJ, Metro Park NJ, Trenton, NJ, Bridgport CT, Hartford CT, Meriden CT, New Haven CT, Springfield MA, Amherts MA, Northampton MA, Brattleboro VT, Keene NH, Windsor VT, and arrives at **White River Junction** at 6:30pm. This is when you can also catch it north to Randolph, Montpelier, Waterbury-Stowe, Burlington, St. Albans, and Montreal, Canada. Going south to destinations above (except Randolph, Montpelier, Waterubur-Stowe, Burlington, St. Albans, and Montreal), the Vermonter departs White River Junction at 10:35am. A one-way ticket to Washington DC costs about $85, New York City $65, and less to destinations in Connecticut, Massachusetts, New Hampshire, and Vermont.

GETTING AROUND

If you are without a car and would like to rent one, **Avis**, *Tel. 603/298-7753, 800/331-1212*, **Hertz Rent-A-Car**, *Tel. 603/298-8927, 800/645-3131*, and **Enterprise Rent-A-Car**, *Tel. 603/448-3337, 800/325-8007*, all operate out of the **Lebanon Municipal Airport**, which is about 20 minutes from White River Junction by taxi.

For a taxi in or around White River Junction, call *Tel. 802/295-1500*.

ORIENTATION

White River Junction is the hub of the region, if not the entire state. Major interstates, I-91 and and I-89, meet here, as do routes 4, 5, and 14. **Routes 5** and **I-91** are the major arteries for the region as they lead north along the Connecticut River to Wilder, Norwich, Thetford, and Fairlee, before continuing north to St. Johnsbury and the Northeast Kingdom.

Other important roads include **Route 132** (a very scenic drive) which links Route 5 and I-91 with Sharon on Route 14 and I-89 to the west via South Strafford; and **Routes 113** and **244** that lead to the popular recreation area of Lake Fairlee north of Thetford.

WHERE TO STAY

Norwich

NORWICH INN, *225 Main Street (P.O. Box 908), Nowich VT 05055. Tel. 802/649-1143. Rates: $55-$100. Major credit cards accepted.*

This famous and popular inn has been renovated in recent years since being taken over by new management. Built in the late 18th century as a stage coach inn, it features 14 inn-style rooms in the main building as well as four suites and seven motel rooms in an adjunct. All rooms have private baths and television, and the restaurant and tavern, Jasper Murdock's Alehouse (named for the original builder of the inn), is a popular eatery serving English-style ales and lagers brewed on the premises.

Thetford

THE STONE HOUSE INN, *Off Route 5 on the Connecticut River in North Thetford VT 05054. Tel. 802/333-9124). Rates: $35-$55.*

This reasonably-priced B&B was originally built in 1835 and includes three rooms, some of which overlook the river, with three baths.

Fairlee

LAKE MOREY INN RESORT COUNTRY CLUB, *Lake Morey Road Road, Fairlee VT 05045. Tel. 802/333-4311, 800/423-1211, Fax 802/333-4553. E-mail: lakemoreyinn@msn.com. Web site: www.lakemoreyinn.com. Rates: $65-$150 (depending on meal plan). Major credit cards accepted.*

Located on Lake Morey, this resort caters to golfers and lakers in the summer and snowmobilers, cross-country skiers, and sledders in the winter. Accommodations include cottages and rooms with full amenities. There's a dining room serving country cuisine, a golf course, indoors and outdoor swimming pools, exercise facilities and on-site cross-country skiing and smowmobile trails.

SILVER MAPLE LODGE AND COTTAGES, *Route 5 (RR 1 Box 8), Fairlee VT 05045. Tel. 802/333-4326, 800/666-1946. E-mail: silvermaple@connriver.net. Web site: www.silvermaplelodge.com. Rates: $55-$80. Credit cards: Visa, Mastercard.*

This beautifully restored 19th century farmhouse inn features eight guestrooms in the main building and seven cottages that include kitchenettes and private baths. The hosts are known for their hospitality and knowledge of the region. On-site activities include horseshoes and shuffleboard, biking and hiking.

White River Junction

Not much in the way of charm here: most lodgings, other than the Coolidge, are of the chain motel variety.

COOLIDGE HOTEL, *Main Street, White River Junction VT 05001. Tel. 802/295-3118, 800/622-1124, Fax 802/291-5100. E-mail: hotel.colidhe@valley.net. Web site: www.coolidgehotel.com. Rates: $40-$100. Major credit cards accepted.*

A relic from White River's railroad glory days in the 1990's, the Coolidge has been touched up and retains some of its old charm, but is still a victim of the town's decline. Nonetheless, the rooms are clean, comfortable, and include private baths, telephones, air-conditioning, and television. Recently added are hostel-style dorm rooms costing $15-$20. There is a coffee shop on the premises.

BEST WESTERN AT THE JUNCTION, *Off I-91 Exit 11 on Route 5, White River Junction 05001. Tel. 802/295-3015, 800/370-4656, Fax 802/296-2581. Rates: $50-$130. Major credit cards accepted.*

A decent motel featuring modern rooms with queen or king-sized beds, television and pay-per-view movies, and in-room coffee makers. Other facilities include a heated pool, sauna and hot tub, and a modest gym. Breakfast is complimentary.

HAMPTON INN, *Route 5, White River Junction VT 05001. Tel. 802/ 296-2800, 800/HAMPTON, Fax 802/296-2884. Rates: $65-$135. Major credit cards accepted.*

The newest of the chain motels in White River, the Hampton Inn offers spacious new rooms with air-conditioning, television with HBO, and in-room coffee makers. There is also a gym and an indoor pool, and breakfast is complimentary.

COMFORT INN, *8 Sykes Avenue (just off Exit 11, I-91), White River, 05001. Tel. 802/295-3051, Tel. 800/628-7727. Website: www.hotelchoice.com. Rates: $65-$120. Major credit cards accepted.*

A modern chain motel, Comfort Inn features 71 standard rooms and several suites. Facilities include a heated outdoor pool, meeting facilities for up to 25, and use of a nearby health center. The rooms could be in any city or town in America, but are clean, decently spacious, and have television. A simple continental breakfast is free of charge, but there are no other dining facilities (there are plenty in town and Hanover anyway).

WHERE TO EAT

Bradford

BANK STREET CAFE, *Main Street, Bradford. Tel. 802/222-4646. Open April through October for dinner 5pm-9pm Wednesday through Sunday, 11am-2:30pm Wednesday through Saturday. Credit cards: Visa, Mastercard.*

This interesting little cafe serves an assortment of international dishes from curries and Asian fare to Carribean and American food.

Fairlee

POTLATCH TAVERN, *Main Street, Fairlee. Open for lunch and dinner. Credit cards: Visa, Mastercard.*

This comfortable and casual restaurant serves a variety of sandwiches, salads, pastas, meat and seafood dishes for lunch and dinner. A full lunch should cost under $10 while dinner entrees rarely top $12.

FAIRLEE DINER, *Route 5 in Fairlee. Open daily from 5:30am-2pm (8pm on Thursdays and Fridays).*

Another one of those classic diners that might have difficulty surviving elsewhere, but does just fine in Vermont. The menu features typical diner fare including sandwiches, breakfast fare, and pies. It's a challenge to eat for more than $10.

Norwich

LA POULE A DENTS, *Main Street, Norwich. Tel. 802/649-2922. Open for dinner from 6:30pm Monday through Saturday and from noon-2:30pm for lunch Monday through Friday. Major credit cards accepted.*

This elegant and expensive (expect to pay at least $30 for dinner) specializes in traditional French cuisine and offers an assortment of seafood, game meats, and fowl in wine and cream sauces. There is also an extensive list of excellent wines.

NORWICH INN, *Main Street, Norwich. Tel. 802/649-1143. Open for breakfast, lunch, dinner, and Sunday Brunch (call for exact hours). Major credit cards accepted.*

The famous Norwich Inn features an elegant dining establishment as well as a pub known for the Jasper Murdock beers brewed on the premises. The dining room(s) serves upscale New England and country cuisine. Appetizers range from warm goat cheese salad ($6.50) and New England oyster cobbler ($7.25) to rosemary-flavored grilled quail ($7.25), while entrees ($15-$22) include such items as venison in wine sauce, roast chicken and pan-seared seafood. The pub is a more casual affair serving a rotating variety of the famous Jasper Murdock brews, as well as tavern classics like Maine crab cakes, steak sandwich, and fried oysters.

ALICE'S BAKERY & CAFE, *Corner of Main and Elm streets, Norwich. Tel. 802/649-2846. Open Tuesday through Friday 9:30am-5:30pm (3:30pm Saturday. Credit cards: Visa, Mastercard.*

Famous for its breads baked fresh on the premises, Alice's also serves a changing assortment of gourmet sandwiches and salads.

DINING OPTIONS IN HANOVER, NEW HAMPSHIRE

*While dining options in White River Junction and Norwich are limited, fear not, for there are dozens of quality eateries of all types just over the Connecticut River in **Hanover, New Hampshire**, a dynamic town and home to Dartmouth College. On Main Street, **Molly's** (Tel. 603/643-2570) serves a wide variety of appetizers, pastas, wood-fired pizzas, sandwiches and Mexican fare in a festive and colorful atmosphere. More formal dining can be enjoyed at the famous **Hanover Inn** (Tel. 603/643-4300) featuring a wine bar and a formal dining room. For soups and sandwiches served in a cozy environment, try **Patrick Henry's** also on Main Street, (Tel. 603/643-2345), or **Murphy's Tavern** on Main Street (Tel. 603/643-4075), which also serves a wide variety of pub fare and entrees in a tavern environment.*

White River Junction

GILLIAM'S, *Sykes Avenue off I-91 Exit 11 and I-89 exit 1 next to the Vermont Transit bus station. Tel. 802/296-3071. Open 11am-10pm daily (closes at 8pm on Sunday). Major credit cards accepted.*

This family restaurant serves decent American dishes like pasta primavera, steak, and grilled seafood, as well as soups, salads, sandwiches, and appetizers for reasonable prices. Most dinner entrees cost around $12 while appetizers and entrees hover around $5.

THE POLKA DOT, *Main Street, White River Junction. Open 5am-8am.* An old-time diner serving an assortment of cheap soups, sandwiches, and other typical diner food.

SEEING THE SIGHTS

White River Junction

A major rail hub in the 19th and early 20th centuries, White River has retained its role as a major transportation hub as the junction of interstates 89 and 91, as well as routes 4, 5 and 14. Yet most travelers see little more than the interstate interchange or the Vermont Transit bus depot. The village is still a shell of its former self.

Norwich

This handsome and wealthy village is primary a bedroom community for doctors, professors and other professionals working at Dartmouth College in Hanover, NH, just over the river. Norwich's centerpiece is a green, surrounded by many 18th century federal-style buildings, including the famous **Norwich Inn** where you can sample good country cuisine and an assortment of lagers and ales brewed on the premises.

MONTSHIRE MUSEUM OF SCIENCE, *Montshire Road off I-91 Exit 13, Norwich Museum. Tel. 802/649-2200, Fax 802/649-3637. E-mail: montshire@valley.net. Open 10am-5pm daily. Admission: $5 adults, $3 children 3-17 years.*

Dedicated to the natural physical sciences, this impressive museum on a 100-acre estate offers a number of interactive exhibits, an aquarium, walking tours, and a playground. It also sponsors special events such as lectures and theme days.

Thetford

Consisting of several villages, all of which have "Thetford" in their names (North Thetford, Thetford Hill, Thetford Center, and East Thetford), **Thetford** is also a residential town populated by folks who primarily work at Dartmouth in Hanover. The natural beauty both along the river and inland is impressive. Thetford Hill, with its many Civil War and pre-Civil War, buildings is quite handsome, but there is little in the way of "attractions" as such.

THETFORD HISTORICAL SOCIETY MUSEUM, *Thetford Hill, Thetford. Tel. 802/785-2430, 333-4613. Museum open 2pm-4pm on Sundays in August. Call for library hours.*

The museum features a number of exhibits dedicated to local history that include photos, manuscripts, vehicles, tools, and furniture. The library, which is open year around, also includes a number of the town's historical documents as well as artwork.

Fairlee

Fairlee is modest town known primarily for its two lakes, **Lake Morey** (just west of Route 5) and the larger **Lake Fairlee** southeast of town on Route 244.

Bradford

Situated at the confluence of the Wells and Connecticut rivers, Bradford was developed as a modest industrial center, where industrialist Asa Low built a number of mills and kilns. The wealth created by this industry funded the construction of a number of handsome federal and Greek Revival style buildings, many of which can still be seen in the village center.

Newbury

The northernmost town in the Connecticut River Valley before the beginning of the Northeast Kingdom at Wells River, **Newbury** features a modest but classic village center that includes a green dotted with memorials to its founder, Jacob Bayley, a renowned Revolutionary War hero.

Strafford

JUSTIN SMITH MORRILL HOMESTEAD, *Located on Justin Morrill Highway just off the green of the Upper Village in Strafford. Tel. 802/765-4484. Hours: 11am-5pm Wednesday-Sunday from April 15 to October 15. Admission: $2 donation per adult; children under 12 are free.*

The restored home of one of Vermont's – and the nation's most important legislators of the 19th century, the Justin Smith Morrill Homestead is an excellent example of a rural upper class residence, and provides fascinating insights into the domestic life of the time. A tour of the complex should begin with the 17-room mansion, a masterpiece in Gothic Revival if ever one existed. Pay your $2 and you are entitled to a guided tour of the home, or pick up a written pamphlet and take yourself on a walking tour.

NIGHTLIFE & ENTERTAINMENT

To say there's not much going on here after hours is quite an understatement. Head on down the road to Killington or Woodstock if you're in the mood to party.

SPORTS & RECREATION

Biking

Route 5 and many of the local roads that branch off of it make for good, scenic road cycling, but there isn't much in the way of mountain biking unless you head 15 miles south of White River Junction to **Mount Ascutney State Park** on Route 44 from Windsor.

The **Silver Maple Lodge** off Route 5 in Fairlee, *Tel. 802/333-4326*, rents bikes and organizes tours as do **Bike Vermont**, *Tel. 802/457-3553, 800/257-2226*, and the **Cyclery**, *Tel. 802/457-3377*, in Woodstock.

Boating

Lake Morey in Fairlee and the **Connecticut River** are the main venues for boating in the area. At Lake Morey, motorboats and canoes can be rented at in town at **Fairlee Marine**, *Tel. 802/333-9745*, while for canoeing on the Connecticut, **Wilderness Trails at the Quechee Club** in Quechee, *Tel. 802/295-7620*, organizes tours and rents boats.

Cross-Country Skiing

LAKE MOREY INN RESORT COUNTRY CLUB, *Lake Morey Road Road, Fairlee VT 05045. Tel. 802/333-4311, 800/423-1211, Fax 802/333-4553. E-mail: lakemoreyinn@msn.com. Web site: www.lakemoreyinn.com. Trail fees: $8 per day. Major credit cards accepted.*

There are about 15 kilometers of trails at Lake Morey. Another option is the Mount Ascutney Resort just south of Windsor, 15 miles south of White River Junction, where there are about 35 kilometers of trails.

Fishing

There are fish in **Lake Morey** and the **Connecticut River**, the latter of which is primarily known for trout.

Golf

LAKE MOREY COUNTRY CLUB, *Lake Morey Road, Fairless. Tel. 802/333-4800. 18 hoes. Green fees: $16-$31. Major credit cards accepted. Carts available.*

Hiking

You can always find room to stroll just about anywhere in the area. There are a couple of miles of trails at the Montshire Museum in Norwich, but for more challenging hikes and great views of the Connecticut River Valley, head to **Ascutney State Park** 15 miles south of White River Junction. There are more than a dozen miles of trails and several paths to the summit.

SHOPPING

Norwich

THE KING ARTHUR FLOUR BAKER'S STORE, *133 US Route 5 South, Norwich. Tel. 802/649-3361, Fax 802/649-3365. Website: www.kingarthurflour.com. Hours: 9am-5pm Monday-Saturday, 11am-4pm Sunday. Major credit cards accepted.*

Something of the proverbial "candy store" for novice and experienced bakers alike, King Arthur features all sorts of baking-related products and accessories – from flours and cookbooks to bread machines and baking stones. Worth a visit if you enjoy baking or need a gift for somebody who does.

NORWICH BOOKSTORE, *Main Street, Norwich. Tel. 802/649-1114. Open daily. Credit cards: Visa, Mastercard.*

A very impressive independent bookstore, especially considering its location in a small Vermont town.

STAVE PUZZLES, *Off Route 5 south of the Norwich village center. Tel. 802/295-5200. Call for times.*

Stave manufactures high-end puzzles, many of which are customized. Visitors can watch the puzzles being made.

EXCURSIONS & DAY TRIPS

Just 10-20 minutes from White River Junction by way of Route 4 are the popular tourist destinations of **Quechee** and **Woodstock**. Teeming with restaurants and shops, these two towns have plenty to offer tourists of all ages, including **Quechee Gorge** ("Vermont's Grand Canyon"), the **Billings Farm Museum**, the **Simon Pearce** glass works and restaurant, as well as many handsome buildings and several golf courses. See the Ottauquechee River Valley Chapter for more details.

If you have more time, or are particularly interested in historical sites, **Plymouth Notch** in Plymouth is noteworthy as the birthplace of President Calvin Coolidge and features a very well maintained and endowed museum and a beautiful state forest, as well as several quality inns and restaurants. To the south, the gentrified towns of **Ludlow** and **Londonderry** feature shops and restaurants, and **Weston** (15 miles south of Ludlow) is home to the famous Vermont Country Store. Thirty miles east of Chester on Route 11 is **Manchester**, one of the most popular tourist destinations in Vermont, known for its stately architecture, picturesque village center, and extensive high-end outlet shopping.

There are also excellent opportunities for exploration to the south. Southern Windsor County and the area around the towns of Windsor and Springfield is known as the Precision Valley, because it was here that the machine-tool industry was developed. From Woodstock, you can take the quiet Route 106 for 25 miles south to **Springfield**, where you can visit the **Hartness House** mansion, a former home of a Vermont Governor and industrialist James Hartness. The mansion is now an inn with a fine restaurant and several small historical exhibits, including a fascinating antique observatory. From Springfield, you can take Route 11 ten miles west to the picturesque village of **Chester**, known for its many beautiful Victorian buildings and quaint green. To get back to the Woodstock-Quechee region, take 103 west from Chester to Route 100 North to Plymouth Union and then Route 4 east.

The alternative is to take Route 11 east from Springfield to Route 5 and come back north along Route 5 and the Connecitcut River. Should you do this during the summer, you can stop at the **American Precision Museum** in Windsor which contains a wonderful collection of tools, machines and firearms from the 19th century. Also just north of Windsor on Route 5 are the **Simon Pearce Glass** (a second branch of the operation in Quechee) and the **Catamount Brewery**. From Windsor, it's less than 15 miles to Woodstock-Quechee by way of Route 12 from Hartland (just north of Windsor) to Taftsville.

Of course, you can skip Springfield and Chester and go straight to Windsor, or you can cut from Route 106 13 miles south of Woodstock on Route 44 to Windsor. This takes you past **Mount Ascutney**, where there is a resort with a skiing area, and **Mt. Ascutney State Park** where you can hike or bike to the summit and enjoy magical views of the Connecticut River Valley, the Berkshires, and the Green Mountains. See the "Precision Valley" Chapter for more information.

The White River Valley & Montpelier

There is plenty to explore along the White River, which flows from the Montpelier region (there are actually four branches) to the Connecticut River at White River Junction. From White River Junction take Route 14 along the White River as far as you like; it's quite a pretty drive. At **Sharon**, 13 miles from White River Junction, you can take a scenic detour on Route 132 to the beautiful village of **Strafford**, known for its Meeting House and the **Justin Smith Morrill Homestead**, a historic Victorian mansion.

Five miles beyond Sharon, just before **South Royalton** with its classic village green and church steeple, is **Dairy Hill Road** and the **Joseph Smith Monument**, built to commemorate the Mormon prophet's birthplace. Yet another scenic rural road, Dairy Hill Road will eventually (after 5 or 6 miles) lead you to Turnbridge and Route 110. You can also get on Route 110 at South Royalton itself. It is a scenic 27-mile drive lined with farms and the villages of Tunbridge and Chelsea from South Royalton to the eastern edge of Barre, which borders Montpelier.

You can also continue along Route 14 for about 30 miles from South Royalton to Montpelier. This will take you through Bethel, East Randolph, North Randolph, and the town of Brookfield, home of the famous **Floating Bridge** (take a detour on Route 65 west) before the final 11 miles to **Barre**, itself is home to the **Rock of Ages Granite Quarries** (the largest in the world). Just northwest of Barre is **Montpelier**, the charming state capital distinguished by the elegant capital building and several fine restaurants, including two operated by the **New Engand Culinary Institute**. For this whole area, see the "Montpelier and Central Vermont Chapter."

PRACTICAL INFORMATION

Chamber of Commerce

  UPPER VALLEY CHAMBER OF COMMERCE, *P.O. Box 697, Old River Road, White River Junction VT 05001. Tel. 802/295-6200, Fax 802/295-3779.*

Medical Emergencies

  Ambulance & Fire:

• **White River Junction & Norwich**, *Tel. 911*
• **All other Valley towns**, *Tel. 603/353-4347*

23. MONTPELIER &
THE WHITE RIVER VALLEYS

From its headwaters in the Green Mountains west of Montpelier, the **White River** winds through the heart of Vermont, where it is joined by its three main branches before continuing to the state's eastern border where it meets the Connecticut River at White River Junction. Not especially well-worn by tourists, this region is characterized by quintessential Vermont trademarks: picturesque villages, covered bridges, and green rolling hills dotted with old farms that make it the perfect place for driving tours.

At the northern end of the region covered by this chapter is the graceful town of **Montpelier**, home to Vermont's State House and legislatures, and America's smallest state capital. **Barre**, which is just minutes away from Montpelier, is the granite capital of the world, and offers visitors an opportunity to visit the world's largest granite quarry to watch master craftsmen turn the stone into beautiful sculptures, headstones, and monuments of all types. Once a region that grew from heavy rail traffic, the area is now traversed by Interstate-89, making it easily accessible from much of the state, New Hampshire, and Boston.

ARRIVALS & DEPARTURES
By Air

The nearest commercial airport to most White River Valley is **Lebanon Municipal Airport** in West Lebanon, which is only about 10 minutes from White River Junction on I-89 from White River Junction. However, Lebanon is only served by USAir Express, *Tel. 800/428-4322,* and flights are limited and expensive.

More convenient in terms of available flights and cost is **Manchester Airport** in Manchester, New Hampshire. Serviced by Southwest, *Tel. 800/435-9792,* Continental, *Tel. 800/525-0289*, USAir, *Tel. 800/428-4322*, and

Delta Connection, *Tel. 800/345-3400.* Manchester is approximately 1.5 hours from White River Junction by car, and most major rental companies operate out of Manchester. Otherwise, **Vermont Transit Lines**, *Tel. 800/552-8738, Tel. 800/451-3292,* offers direct service from the Manchester Airport to White River Junction four times daily (10:25am, 2:55pm, 5:55pm, & 10:40pm). If the departure times from the airport are inconvenient, take a taxi to the downtown depot where another half dozen buses depart daily for White River Junction.

The closest major commercial airport to Montpelier itself is **Burlington International Airport**, on Airport Drive (off Route 2) in Burlington. Usually not more than an hour by automobile, it is serviced by Continental. *Tel. 800/525-0289,* United, *Tel. 800/241-6522,* USAir, *Tel. 800/428-4322,* Business Express, Tel. 800/345-3400, and Comair, Tel. 800/927-0927.

Another alternative is to fly into Boston's **Logan Airport**, which is approximately 2.5 hours from the Woodstock-Quechee region by car. All major car rental companies operate out of Logan, or you can take one of the hourly shuttles to South Station in downtown Boston and catch one of a half-dozen daily buses to White River Junction. The advantages of flying to Boston, particularly if you are traveling some distance, include the availability of flights and lower costs than flying into one of the smaller regional airports.

By Car

Interstate 89 (I-89) runs straight from White River Junction along the White River and on to Montpelier before carrying on to Burlington. It also provices a direct link to Manchester, NH, and Boston via I-93. From the south, **I-91** intersects I-89 at White River Junction.

By Bus

Vermont Transit Lines bus company, *Tel. 802/864-6811,* has its main hub in White River Junction, which is within an hour from virtually every destination in the White River Valleys. Within the region it offers direct service to Montpelier and Randolph Center and major destinations across Vermont. From White River, there is also direct service to Montreal, Boston, New York, as well as Manchester, Hanover, New London, and Concord in New Hamshire. Within Vermont, most fares are under $15, while a one-way fare to Boston from White River is approximately $30.

By Train

Amtrak's **Vermonter,** *Tel. 800/USA-RAIL,* stops in White River Junction, Randolph, and Montpelier, and offers direct service to and from Washington DC, Baltimore, Wilimington DE, Philadelphia, New York City, Newark NJ, Metro Park NJ, Trenton, NJ, Bridgport CT, Hartford CT, Meriden CT, New Haven CT, Springfield MA, Amherts MA, Northampton MA, Brattleboro VT, Keene NH, and Windsor VT to the south, as well as Waterbury-Stowe, Burlington, St. Albans, the Canadian border, and Montreal to the north. It departs and arrives once daily.

An alternative is Amtrak's **Ethan Allex Express** that offers service between Rutland, VT and Albany, NY, New York City, and points south. It is a bit quicker than the Vermonter, and Rutland is within an hour and a half from most points in the White River Valleys.

ORIENTATION

Montpelier is just north of the geographic center of the state off of **Interstate 89** (I-89), which links it directly to Burlington to the north and west and White River Junction to the southeast. It passes by major towns in the White River Valleys, such as **Randolph**, **Brookfield**, **Bethel**, **Royalton**, and **Sharon**, all of which are between Montpelier and White River Junction. Running alongside I-89 is **Route 14** which is more scenic; it actually cuts north a little to the east at Royalton and runs north directly to **Barre** (which is just southeast of Montpelier). The same point also marks the beginning of **Route 107**, which heads west and south to the villages of **Bethel** and **Stockton** where it intersects the main north-south artery, **Route 100**.

Another important road in the region is **Route 110**, which begins at South Royalton and goes north along the First Branch of the White River through **Tunbridge**, **Chelsea**, and **Washington** before ending in East Barre. Finally **Route 12** runs north-south from Woodstock through Barnard and to to Randolph, Northfield and Montpelier.

The **White River** itself features three main branches that split from the main branch around South Royalton. The First Branch is the furthest east and flows from South Royalton along Route 100 past Tunbridge and Chelsea. The Second Branch is to the west and flows along Route 14 through the eastern parts of the Randolph and Brookfield townships. The Third Branch joins the main branch at Bethal after flowing south from Northfield through Randolph. The river itself traces Route 100 to the west and Route 107 before joining the other branches. The main river then flows from the Royalton area to White River, where it joins the Connecticut at White River Junction.

See the map on page 377 for the main destinations in this chapter.

GETTING AROUND

Montpelier is a great town for walking, but otherwise a car is imperative if you want to enjoy the beautiful scenery along Routes 14, 110, and 12, as well picturesque villages like South Royalton, Tunbridge, Chelsea and Strafford.

WHERE TO STAY

Montpelier & East Montpelier

THE INN AT MONTPELIER, *147 Main Street, Montpelier VT 05602. Tel. 802/223-2727, Fax 802/223-0722. E-mail: mail2inn@aol.com. Web site: www.members.aol.com/innvt/index. Rates: $100-$200. Major credit cards accepted.*

Certainly the most elegant Montpelier inn, it features beautifully decorated and comfortable rooms with private baths, telephones, cable television, and air-conditioning; some also include fireplaces. The federal-style buildings are historic and charming; especially the wrap-around porch. Breakfasts are delicious and hearty.

CAPITOL PLAZA HOTEL & CONFERENCE CENTER, *100 State Street, Montpelier VT 05602. Tel. 802/223-5252, 800/274-5252, Fax 802/229-5427. Web site: www.capitolplaza.com. Rates: $69-$149. Major credit cards accepted.*

Located almost directly opposite Vermont's beautiful State Capitol, the Capital Plaza is an intimate and old fashioned hotel, popular with politicians as well as tourists. Rooms feature amenities such as phones, cable television, and air-conditioning, while downstairs the house restaurant, J. Morgan's, is favorite with schmoozing politicians and serves very good steak (and other dishes too).

COMFORT INN AT MAPLEWOOD, *Route 62 (just of I-89 Exit 7), Montpelier VT 05602. Tel. 802/229-2222, Fax 802/229-2222. E-mail: comfortin@aol.com. Rates: $ 59-$210. Major credit cards accepted.*

A typical modern motel, Comfort Inn features about 100 standard rooms (air-conditioning, cable television, phone, bath) and an assortment of luxury and efficiency suites with kitchenettes. Other amenities and facilities include free continental breakfast, laundry machines, in-room modem connections, and an on-site family-style American restaurant called Shoney's (it's a chain).

BETSY'S BED & BREAKFAST, *74 East State Street, Montpelier VT 05602. Tel. 802/229-0466, Fax 802/229-5412. E-mail: betsybb@together.net. Wen site: www.central-vt.com/business/betsybb. Rates: $55-$95. Credit cards: Visa, Mastercard.*

Situated in a real knock-out Victorian mansion, Betsy's offers spacious, antique-laden rooms and suites, in addition to a very convenient downtown location. All rooms and two-room suites include privates baths, in-room telephones, and cable television.

MONTPELIER GUEST HOUSE, *22 North Street, Montpelier VT 05602. Tel. 802/229-0878. Rates: $35-$55; 15% discount for stays longer than two nights and traveling cyclists! Credit cards: Visa, Mastercard.*

This very intimate and personable establishment is located in a Victorian home, and that's exactly what it feels and looks like – a home. Rooms are individually appointed with handmade quilts, hand-stenciled walls, and family antiques. In warm weather, there are also beautiful gardens. The only potential drawback might be the shared bath.

Barre & Environs

REYNOLD'S HOUSE B&B, *773 Graniteville Road, Graniteville VT 05641. Tel. 802/476-8313, Fax 802/476-9960. E-mail: rrey1892@aol.com. Rates: $110-$200. Visa, Mastercard.*

Containing only three bedrooms, the Reynold's House B&B is in a beautiful Victorian home dating to the 1890's and is decorated accordingly with gorgeous antiques and furniture. Even more than most Victorian inns in Vermont, this one truly captures the essence of it's 19th century origins.

DAYS INN, *173-175 South Main Street, Barre VT 05641. Tel. 802/476-6678, 800/329-7466. Rates: $50-$90 per double. Major credit cards accepted.*

Days Inn is a fully equipped modern motel that includes a dining room, lounge, and an indoor pool, in addition to nothing-special-but-more-than-adequate rooms featuring air-conditioning, phones, cable television, and clean private baths.

Bethel

GREENHURST INN, *Just east of Bethel Village on Route 107 West, Bethel VT 05032. Tel. 802/234-9474, 800/510-2553. Web site: www.innsandouts.com/propoerty/greenhurstinn.html. Rates: $50-$100. Credit cards: Visa, Mastercard.*

A classic Victorian affair listed in the National Register of Historic Places, the Grenhurst offers 13 guestrooms.

THE VILLAGE INN BED & BREAKFAST, *Church Street (P.O. Box 68, Bethel VT 05032. (Take 107 west from Exit 3 through Bethel, and cross the bridge on Route 12, the B&B will be on your right after the church.) Tel. 802/234-5440. Rates: $55-$65. Credit cards: Visa, Mastercard.*

Managed by a German mother and daughter pair, the Village Inn features comfortable four rooms, two with private bath. Breakfast (included in the price) is prepared on the premises and include German-style crepes

426 VERMONT GUIDE

Chelsea

SHIRE INN, *Main Street (Route 110), Chelsea VT 05038. Tel. 802/685-3031, 900/441-6908, Fax 802/685-3871. E-mail: hosts@shireinn.com Web ste: www.shireinn.com. Rates: $90-$215. Credit cards: Visa, Mastercard, American Express.*

A nice place; the more expensive rates include a meal plan other than just B&B.

Randolph & Brookfield

THREE STALLIONS INN, *Stock Farm Road off Route 66 just off I-89 Exit 4. Tel. 802/728-5575, 800/424-5575, Fax 802/728-4036. E-mail: tsinn@sover.net. Web site: 3stallioninn.com. Rates:$70-$120. Major credit cards accepted.*

Located on the outskirts of Randolph just off Interstate 89 (Exit 4), the Three Stallions Inn is a traditional New England inn on an old 1,300-acre stock farm with 15 comfortable singles, doubles and suites and extensive recreational facilities that include the Green Mountain Ski Touring Center with 50 kilometers of cross-country skiing, snowshoeing and hiking trails, tennis courts and a modest fitness center with excersise machines, saunas and a swimming pool.

Also, just next door is the 18-hole Montague Golf Club where Three Stallion guests enjoy discounts on greens fees. In the main building, Morgans Pub serves lite fare and and drinks, while the main dining room serves quality American and country cuisine seven nights a week. Three Stallions hosts a variety of public functions each year, including an outdoor Vermont Symphony Orchestra concert in mid-July. Call about special golf and ski packages.

GREEN TRAILS INN, *Route 65, Brookfield VT 05036. Tel. 802/276-3412, 800/243-3412. E-mail: greentrails@quest-net.com. Rates: $79-$130 per room. Credit cards: Visa, Mastercard, Discover.*

Consisting of two buildings on a 17-acre estate by the famous Floating Bridge, the Green Trails features 14 rooms and suites with various combinations of shared and private baths, in-room jacuzzis, and fireplaces. All room are uniquely appointed with country and Victorian decor and antiques. The main building, the Marcus Peck House, was built in the 1840's and was the home of Jessie Fisk, a pioneer in breaking down barriers to women in higher education who taught at Rutgers; the second is a teak guest house. Recreationally, there is plenty of hiking, cross-country skiing, biking, and swimming literally right out the front door. Among the unique characteristics of the Green Trails Inn is the antique clock collection and the clock repair shop on the premises.

BROOKFIELD GUEST HOUSE, *Pond Village (P.O. Box 500), Brookfield VT 05036. Tel. 802/276-3146. Rates: $85 per room. Cash and checks only.*
Situated in quaint Pond Village off Sunset Lake and the Floating Bridge in Brookfield, the Guest House offers guests a suite with private bath, warm hospitality, and personal attention.

Rochester

LIBERTY HILL FARM, *Liberty Hill Road (RR 1 Rox 158), Rochester VT 05767. Tel. 802/767-3926. E-mail: liberty.hill.farm@quest-net.com. Rates: $70 per adult, $30 per child. Credit cards: Visa, Mastercard.*
Those keen to really immerse themselves in the "real Vermont" should cancel their reservations they have at whatever fancy inn or B&B and call up the Liberty Hill Farm. A working dairy farm with seven guestrooms (4 baths), it is nothing short of the real deal, from the scent of manure and the morning cow milking to the fresh meals preapred daily by Mrs. Kennett.

HARVEY'S MOUNTAIN VIEW INN, *RR 1 Box 53, Rochester VT 05767. Web site: www.vtchamber.com. Rates: $35-$75 for inn rooms, $550 for chalet (weekly). Credit cards: Visa, Mastercard.*
Beautifully situated in Rochester's farm country, Harvey's Mountain View Inn offers comfy inn rooms or a chalet for weekly rentals. Nearby and on-premise attractions and facilities include a trout pond, a heated pool, walking trails, and pony riding. Rates include breakfast and dinner served in an intimate candlelit dining room (BYOB).

Royalton & South Royalton

FOX STAND INN & RESTAURANT, *Route 14, Royalton VT 05068. (Located just south of the Junction of Route 107 & 14 and I-89 Exit 3.) Tel. 802/ 763-8437. E-mail: foxstand@aol.com. Rates: $50-$75. Credit cards: Visa, Mastercard.*
A handsome 1818 brick stagecoach "stand" (inn) overlooking the White River, that according to local legend onced hosted Le Marquis de Lafayette during his 1824-25 American tour, the Fox Stand features five individually appointed, comfortable rooms with shared baths. Downstairs are two intimate dining rooms where breakfast and dinner (open to the public) are served, as well as a tavern serving refreshments and lite fare. During warm weather, there is also seating outside.

Sharon

THE INN AT IDLEWOOD, *Route 132, Sharon VT 05065. Tel. 802/ 763-5236. Rates: $85-$135. Credit cards: Visa, Mastercard.*
Set in a beautiful off-the-beaten-track setting, but less than 20 minues from Hanover, Quechee, and Woodstock, the Inn at Idlewood features

three guestrooms in an early 20th century mansion on a 75-acre estate with walking trails and a pond. However, while the setting and accommodations are first-rate, the real star is the restaurant, operated by the owners and well-traveled culinary masters Alex Bird and Marcy Marceau. The small dining room seats about a dozen and the prix fixe five course meals (featuring haute contiental and American cuisine) routeinly receive rave reviews.

THE COLUMNS MOTOR LODGE, *Route 14 (off Exit 2), Sharon VT 05065. Tel. 802/763-7040. Email: vtlodge@aol.com. Rates: $40-$50. Credit cards: Visa, Mastercard.*

A small motor lodge offering rooms with twin and double beds, telephones, television, and private baths.

CAMPING & RV'S
East Montpelier

GREEN VALLEY CAMPGROUND, *P.O. Box 21 (on Route 2 5 miles from Montpelier), East Montpelier VT 05651. Tel. 802/223-6217. E-mail: ggosselin@aol.com. Base rates: $20. Visa, Mastercard. Open May 15-November 1.*

Smaller than some other campgrounds with about three dozen sites. Facilities include store, bathhouse, swimming, ice, etc.; cable television, air-conditioning, and heating for extra cost.

Randolph

ALLIS STATE PARK, *RD 2 Bos 192 (Off Route 12 between Northfield & Randolph), Randolph VT 05060. Tel. 802/276-3175 (summer), Tel. 802/886-2434 (offseason). Base rates $11-$15. Credit cards: Visa, Mastercard. Open mid to late May through Labor Day.*

Situated at the top of Bear Mountain, this state park features 18 tent/trailer slots, and 10 lean-to's in addition to picnic facilities, flush toilets, showers, a dumping station, and a play area. Attractions include include a hiking trail and superb views from the fire tower at the summit.

MOBILE ACRES CAMPGROUND, *354 Mobile Acres Road (on Route 12a off Route 66 2.5 miles from I-89 Exit 4), Randolph VT 05060. Tel. 802/728-5548, 7655-6700. Base rate: $20. Open May 15-October 15. Credit cards: Visa, Mastercard.*

Offers access to the Third Branch of the White River for fishing and tubing. Facilities include a pool, bathhouse, laundry facilities, LP gas, and more than 93 sites.

Barnard

SILVER LAKE FAMILY CAMPGROUND, *Box 111 (7 miles south of Bethel on Route 12, on Stage Road), Barnard VT 05031. Tel. 802/234-9974. Base rates: $18. Open early May through October 15. Visa, Mastervard.*

This campground features more than 60 campsites and cabins, as well as a private beach on Silver Lake in which visitors may participate in swimming fishing, and canoeing. Other facilities include showers, toilets, and a recreation room.

WHERE TO EAT

Montpelier & Barre

CHEF'S TABLE, *118 Main Street, Montpelier. Tel. 802/229-9902. Open for dinner 6pm-10pm Monday through Saturdays. Seasonally open for lunch. Major credit cards accepted.*

The piece de resistance of the New England Culinary Institute, the Chef's Table features a constantly changing assortment of nouveau and traditional American and continental-style dishes, ranging from almond-crusted trout and citrus glazed pork loin to venison medallions sauteed in port. The environment is semi-formal and meals typically range from $25-$40 per person.

THE INN AT MONTPELIER, *147 Main Street, Montpelier. Tel. 802/ 223-2727. Open for dinner from 6:30pm Tuesday throuh Sunday. Major credit cards accepted.*

Fine American dining with a few twists served in a classic inn setting. Dishes range from roast lamb and steak to broiled salmon and other seafood specialties. A full dinner costs from $20 to $40 depending on whether you take wine and/or appetizers.

MAIN STREET BAR AND GRILL, *118 Main Street, Montpelier. Tel. 802/223-3188). Open daily from 11am-11pm. Major credit cards accepted.*

The less formal of the New England Culinary Insitute's two main Montpelier restaurants, the Main Street Bar and Grill serves innovative American and international cuisine in a bustling and casual atmosphere. The menu features a wide assortment of dishes from corn chowder and colorful flatbreads to wood-fired steak, bouillabaise, and grilled portabello mushrooms. For lunch, salads and sandwiches comprise the main offerings. Most lunch entrees are under $10 while dinner, few top $15.

J. MORGAN'S, *100 State Street (opposite the State Capitol in the Capitol Plaza), Montpelier. Tel. 802/223-5252. Web site: capitolplaza.com. Open daily from 7am until late. Major credit cards accepted.*

Situated in the Capitol Plaza Hotel across from the State Capitol, J. Morgan's is a railroad-motifed steakhouse with lots of wood paneling and a nice bar. It's specialty is steaks, though the menu also includes several pasta offerings, roast chicken, salads, and sandwiches for lunch. Most entrees are between $10 and $20. The place is especially active when the legislature is in session.

SARDUCCI'S, *3 Main Street, Montpelier. Tel. 802/223-0229. Open daily from 11:30am-midnight except Sunday when it opens at 4pm. Major credit cards accepted.*

Casual, colorful, inexpensive and very popular, Sarducci's serves a wide array of Italian dishes, from wood-fired pizza and salads to 20 types of pasta, most of which cost under $10. There are fancier meat, chicken and seafood entrees avaialble for dinner after 5:30pm. Most dishes are under $10.

LA BRIOCHE BAKERY & CAFE, *89 Main Street, Montpelier. Tel. 802/ 229-0443. Open from 8am-7pm. Major credit cards accepted.*

Also operated by the New England Culinary Institute, La Brioche is a casual soup-and-sandwich operation that also sells pastries and a host of breakfast items, like muffins and coffee cake.

Randolph & Brookfield

THREE STALLIONS INN, *Stock Farm Road off Route 66 just off I-89 Exit 4. Tel. 802/728-5575   800/424-5575, Fax 802/728-4036. E-mail: tsinn@sover.net. Web site: 3stallioninn.com. Open 5pm-9pm nightly. Major credit cards accepted.*

Located in a restored 19th century farmhouse, the Three Stallions Inn Dining Room serves New England and American cuisine in a relaxed and comfortable environment. Appetizers range from soups lake New England clam chowder and a variety of fresh salads to small quesadillas, while for entrees ($10-$20) there is typically a choice of steaks, pastas, and other favorites like roast chicken seasoned with fresh herbs. Adjoining the dining room is Morgans Pub, a pleasant setting in which to enjoy a post-ski, pre-meal refreshment and/or hors'd'oeuvres and tavern food.

AUGUST LION, *Main Street, Randolph. Tel. 802/728-5043. Open daily except Sunday for lunch and dinner. Credit cards accepted.*

Located in downtown Randolph, the August Lion serves decent steak, pasta and other American favorites for moderate prices (most dinner entrees cost between $10 and $20). For lunch, the menu includes pasta, soups, salads, and sandwiches.

FOUNDRY PARK RESTAURANT & BREW PUB, *Print Street, Randolph. Tel. 802/728-3788. Open daily from 11:30am until about midnight. Major credit cards accepted.*

Situated in a former Vermont Castings foundry, the Foundry Park offers an assortment of modertely priced tavern and American fare and beer.

Royalton

FOX STAND INN & RESTAURANT, *Route 14, Royalton VT 05068. (Located just south of the Junction of Route 107 & 14 and I-89 Exit 3.) Tel. 802/ 763-8437. E-mail: foxstand@aol.com. Open for dinner from 6pm-9pm Tuesday throuh Saturday. Credit cards: Visa, Mastercard.*

A cozy and casual inn eatery, the Fox Stand serves a three course meal for $19 in two intimate dining rooms with fireplaces. Dinner includes a soup, salad, fresh bread, and a choice of entree including broiled or blackened salmon or swordfish, steak, roast chicken, and pasta. There is also a small tavern featuring pub food like crab cakes, shrimp cocktail, and wings. Good value and very decent food.

SOUTH ROYALTON HOUSE, *On the Green, South Royalton. Tel. 802/763-8315. Open for lunch and dinner except Monday. Credit cards: Visa and Mastercard.*

Owned by the Vermont Law School, South Royalton House serves moderately priced standard fare such as roast chicken, steak and pasta for dinner as well as sandwiches and salads for lunch, in a pleasant, casual, and dignified dining room. When the weather is warm, lunch can be taken outside on the terrace/porch, and during summer barbequed dinners are served informally in the yard, sometimes with informal entertainment provided by a local state representative who sings folk and rock tunes and plays guitar.

VERMONT SUGAR HOUSE, *Junction of Route 14 and Route 107, Royalton. Tel. 802/763-8809. Open from 7am to 7pm (usually). Credit cards: Visa, Mastercard.*

This quirky restaurant and souvenir shop is especially popular with tourists and locals for breakfast, when you can enjoy a typical cholesterol-laden American breakfast. Lots of eggs and sausage dishes as well as pancakes, french toast, and waffles. all served with Vermont maple syrup.

Strafford

STONE SOUP, *Village center, Strafford. Tel. 802/765-4301. Open Wednesday 6pm-9pm. Checks accepted, no credit cards.*

Known for its rustic atmosphere, the Stone Soup is one of the more popular eateries in the region, though many feel the food is not what it once was. The menu typically features hearty soups, salads, and American and continental style dishes like roast chicken, roast lamb and scallops in white wine sauce. Most entrees are under $20.

SEEING THE SIGHTS

Montpelier

America's smallest and arguably most charming state capital, **Montpelier** was chosen to succeed Windsor as home of the statehouse in 1805, primarily for its central location. Apart from being the state capital, Montpelier is also the birthplace of Admiral George Dewey, who sunk the Spanish fleet in Manilla Bay in 1898 without firing a shot. Dewey's father founded the National Life Insurance company, which played a large role in Montpelier's economic success following the Civil War.

VERMONT STATE HOUSE, *115 State Street, Montpeleri. Tel. 802/ 828-2228. Open 8am-4pm Monday-Friday. Guided tours offered from 10am-3:30pm from July through mid-October. Admission free.*

Dignified but modest, Vermont's present Renaissance Rivival-style **State Capitol** building was constructed in 1859 after two earlier versions were demolished and destroyed by fire. Very well preserved, the building still features many of its original furnishings, including gas lamp fixtures and hundreds of beautiful paintings of prominent Vermonters and important events in Vermont history. The most impressive of these paintings is *The Battle of Cedar Creek, 1864,* portraying Vermonters fighting in of the most bloodiest battles in the Civil War (Vermont lost more men per capita than any state on the Union side). The statue on the capitol steps is Vermont's founding father, Ethan Allen, and the sculpture atop the gold-leafed dome is Ceres, the classical goddess of agriculture.

THE VERMONT HISTORICAL SOCIETY (including the Museum), *109 State Street, Montpelier. Tel. 802/828-2291. E-mail: vt_hist_soc@dol.state.vt.us. Open 9am-4:30pm Tuesday-Friday, 9am-4pm Saturday, noon-4pm Sunday. Admission: $2 adults, $1 children.*

Located in a replica of the Pavilion Hotel, the Vermont Historical Society includes a great museum featuring all sorts of paintings, furniture, photographs, weapons (including Ethan Allen's gun), and costumes reflecting the breadth of Vermont's history. The Society also includes the most comprehensive collection of books, documents, and maps relating to Vermont history.

On Country Road in Montpelier less than three miles from the Main Street traffic circle, the **Morse Farm Sugar Works** has been in operation in some form or other since 1787, and features a variety of exhibits and demonstrations about maple sugaring and the manufacture of maple syrup. A Country Store sells all types of maple products and other souvenirs; a catalog is available for ordering from home. *Tel. 802/223-2740, 800/242-2740, Fax 802/223-7450, E-mail: Maplespeak@aol.com.*

Barre

Synonymous with granite – it is home to the largest quarries in world – **Barre** was a ho-hum sort of place before the arrival of the railroad and the granite boom at the end of the 19th century attracted thousands of skilled stone cutters and sculptors from Italy and across Europe. Granite and the quarries, which are located southeast of town in the appropriately named Graniteville, still define the town and city (Barre city is a separate municipality within Barre town) and its main attraction, the Rock of Ages Quarry, is one of the most fascinating attractions in Vermont.

ROCK OF AGES VISITORS CENTER, *773 Main St., Graniteville. Tel. 802/476-3119. Website: rockofages.com. Open 8:30am-5 pm daily except Sunday (noon-5pm) from May 1- October 31. Entrance: free.*

One of the most fascinating and awesome sites in Vermont is that of the huge piles of granite stones and rubble next to the huge holes in the ground, from which they and so much of American's granite has been cut. The biggest granite quarries in the world, it is estimated that these stretch ten miles (!) beneath the earth's surface and contain enough granite to sustain the world for 4,500 years according to current estimates. In addition to viewing the site itself, take the time to watch the explanatory video which tells the fascinating history of the granite industry in Barre and Vermont, and does a good job explaining the processes of quarrying granite and manufacturing granite products. Also, between June and October, you can take one of the guided shuttle tours around the active quarries and during the entire season, you can meander down to the **Rock of Ages Manufacturing Division**, where in a huge factory building you can watch dozens of craftspeople manufacture statuettes, headstones, and other granite products with lasers, chisels, and a variety of other tools and technologies.

MOUNT HOPE CEMETERY, *Route 14 north of downtown Barre.*

This wonderful cemetery features amazing examples of granite sculpture, which makes sense given that many of the stonecutters themselves are buried here. Very worthy of a stroll.

Northfield

Now known as the home of the Norwich University (a military academy), Northfield is ten miles south of Montpelier on Route 12.

NORWICH UNIVERSITY MUSEUM, *Norwich University. Open during the academic year 2pm-4pm Monday-Friday. Admission free.*

This interesting little museum features a variety of exhibits concentrating on the achievements of the academy's alumnae, many of whom participated in the Civil War and other military conflicts.

Between Northfield & Randolph

Between Randolph and Northfield off Route 12 (or west of Brookfield and Route 14 by Route 65 west) is the **Allis State Park** at the summit of **Bear Mountain**. The park was created in the 1930's by the Civilian Conservation Corps, after the owner of the land, Walter Allis, gave it to the state in his will. The area around Bear Mountain had been in Allis family hands since the 1700's. Though not filled with recreation opportunities and facilities, the park does contain some campsites; a hiking trail, along which is an interesting cave known as the **Bear's Den**; and at the summit, the fire tower features superb views of the Green Mountains, including such famous Vermont landmarks as the Camel's Hump and Mount Mansfield to the northwest and the White Mountains to the east.

Practical facilities include a rather pretty picnic site, restrooms, and a dumping station. There is a small fee for entrance to the park, and if you plan to camp, call in advance (particularly on holiday weekends) to make reservations. See the "Allis State Park" entry above in *Where to Stay*.

Randolph

First settled in the 1780's, Randolph features a historic distrcit that in recent years has suffered from a major fire. The town was laid out with the anticipation that it might become the state capital; of course, Montpelier was selected instead. Some of the more impressive landmarks include the beautiful **Chandler Music Hall**, which dates to the early 20th century, and the Gothic Revival Baptist Church.

Route 14

Following the Second Branch of the White River from Barre to Royalton, Route 14 is a scenic alternative to I-89. The area around **Brookfield** is especially attractive, and if it's open, consider a visit to the famous **Floating Bridge** – the longest floating bridge east of the Mississippi!

Route 110

From Montpelier and Barre, you can take Route 302 east and then Route 110 south. Route 110 offers a wonderful drive along the First Branch of the White River through the villages of **Washington**, **Chelsea** and **Tunbridge**, all of which are very attractive Vermont villages, before meeting Route 14 at South Royalton. Of course, you can also enjoy the ride going the other way by turning onto Route 110 from Route 14 at South Royalton. You may be especially interested in checking out the various covered bridges around Tunbridge and Chelsea (see sidebar on next page).

Royalton

Located at the junction of Routes 14 and Route 110, where the First Branch of the White River meets the main river about 40 miles from Montpelier on I-89, **South Royalton** is the bigger of the two villages in the town of Royalton. The village of Royalton itself is just north on Route 14 and was the major village in the area, until the railroad led to South Royalton's superceding it in the middle of the 19th century. Royalton has

CHELSEA-TUNBRIDGE AREA COVERED BRIDGES

There are a half-dozen covered bridges in the Chelsea-Tunbridge area. They are here from north to south:

Moxley Bridge - *Located 2.5 miles south of the Route 110-Route 113 junction in Chelsea, the Moxley Bridge was built in the queen post style in 1883 and is about 55 feet long.*

Flint Bridge - *Located 3.2 miles south of the junction of Route 110 and Route 113, the Flint Bridge was built in 1845 and is almost 90 feet long.*

Larkin Bridge - *This 68-foot-long bridge is about 2 miles south of the Flint Bridge in Tunbridge and is one of only a few covered bridges built in the 20th century (it was built in 1902).*

Mill Bridge - *Located off Spring Road that branches west from Route 110 just north of Tunbridge village, the Mill Bridge is 72 feet long and was constructed in 1883.*

Howe Bridge - *Situated just south of the Tunbridge village center off Route 110, the Howe Bridge is named for the famliy that owned the adjacent farm and was built in 1879. It is 75 feet long.*

Cilley Bridge - *Take the Ward Hill Road from just south of the village by the cemetery. The Cilley Bridge is named for a local family and was built in 1883.*

never quite recovered. With its steepled churchs and village green, complete with a bandstand and a handsome Civil War monument, South Royalton is many ways a quintessential Vermont village whose authenticty has not been compromised by tourist-related commercialization. Once a modest railstop, its current population includes a mixture of farmers and other native Vermonters, as well as flatlander migrants, many of whom are retirees and professionals working in the Hanover region in the Connecticut Valley a half hour away. The town is also home to the **Vermont Law School**, the only law school in Vermont, which is becoming increasingly respected for its academic program, particularly in the field of environmental law.

The main attraction in the Royalton region is the **Joseph Smith Memorial** on Dairy Hill Road, which turns off Route 14 just south of South Royalton Village. Smith, who founded the Church of the Latter Day Saints (the Mormon faith), was born here (technically in Sharon), which is marked by a obelisk-style monument made of Barre granite. There is no admission fee and the site is always accessible. During the day, Mormon missionaries hand out literature.

NIGHTLIFE & ENTERTAINMENT

Montpelier & Barre

LOST NATION THEATRE COMPANY, *128 Elm Street, Monpelier. Tel. 802/229-0492.*

Sponsors a number of plays and musical productions each year.

BARRE OPERA HOUSE, *Downtown Barre. Tel. 802/476-8188.*

A beautiful turn-of-the century building, the Barre Opera House hosts musical, theater, and other events throughout the year.

SAVOY (MOVIE THEATER), *26 Main Street, Montpelier. Tel. 802/229-0509.*

Shows independent and art films.

CAPITOL (MOVIE THEATER), *93 Main Street, Montpelier. Tel. 802/229-0343.*

Shows feature films.

Randolph

CHANDLER MUSIC HALL, *Randolph. Tel. 802/728-9133.*

Attending a performance at the Chandler Music Hall is worth it just to enjoy the beautiful interior acoustics of this well-preserved, turn-of-the-century venue. Call for concert schedules, prices, etc.

THE TUNBRIDGE WORLD'S FAIR

*Held at the Tunbridge Fairgrounds from Thursday through Sunday on the third week in September, the **Tunbridge World's Fair** is one of Vermont's greatest events. While other fairs have become huge commercial affairs, the World's Fair has retained its local flair and old-timey feel. Attractions include vendors selling all sorts of handicrafts, foods, and souvenirs, live music, buggy racing, livestock competitions, and the ever-popular demolition derby held on the final evening. For years, the event was known for turning raucous in the evenings when the free-flowing beer and girly shows seemed to give folks of the male persuasion carte blanche to go wild. Recently, however, the burlesque has disappeared and beers have become more regulated, making the event family-friendly for the whole day. For information, call 802/889-5555.*

SHOPPING
Barre & Environs
 EAST BARRE ANTIQUE MALL, *133 Mill Street, East Barre. Tel. 802/479-5190.*
 RED WAGON ANTIQUES AND USED FURNITURE, *1079 South Barre Road, Barre. Tel. 802/479-3611. Email: RedWagonAntiques@connriver.net.*

Montpelier
 BERLIN MALL, *Exit 7 (I-89), second light, Montpelier. Tel. 802/229-4151, 800/660-4151, Fax 802/229-4918. Website: www.ddrc.com.*

Sharon
 COLUMNS WOODCRAFT & GIFT SHOP, *Route 14 off Exit 2 (I-89), Sharon Village. Tel. 802/375-6928. Email: vtlodge@aol.com. Hours: 9am-5pm Monday through Friday. Credit cards: Visa, Mastercard, American Express.*

SPORTS & RECREATION
Biking
 For mountain biking, there are numerous trails in **Groton State Forest**, 25 miles east of Montpelier by way of Route 302 and Route 232; and also in the Mad River Valley and around Stowe and Mt. Mansfield, both off I-89, Exit 10. See the respective chapters for more information.
 ONION RIVER SPORTS, *20 Langdon Street, Montpelier VT 05601. Tel. 802/229-9409; also 395 North Main Street, Barre VT. Tel. 802/476-9750.*
 Sells cycling and other outdoor recreational equipment and accessories; also a good source of information.
 Around Randolph, Routes 12A to Northfield and 65 to Brookfield are both quite scenic, as are Route 14 and Routes 110 and 132 near Royalton and Strafford. For mountain biking, the **Maple Ridge Sheep Farm** in Brookfield (take the path from the church in West Brookfield off Route 12) features about nine miles of steep and challenging trails.

Boating, Canoeing & Kayaking
 The **White River**, particularly between Stockbridge and Sharon, offers some of the most beautiful and challenging river canoeing and kayaking in Vermont. The **Winooski** between Middlesex(I-89, Exit 9) and Waterbury (I-89, Exit 10) is a more modest ride, and the **Connecticut** features rapids of varying derees of difficulty. For lakes and ponds, try **Lake Fairlee** and **Lake Morey** off I-91 north of White River Junction and **Silver Lake** in Barnard.

Cross-Country Skiing

GREEN TRAILS INN & CROSS COUNTRY CENTER, *Brookfield VT. Tel. 802/7276-3412. Trail fees: $9. Major credit cards accepted.*

Green Trails features more than 35 kilometers of trails, ski rentals, and instruction.

THREE STALLIONS INN CROSS COUNTRY CENTER, *Randolph VT. Tel. 802/728-5575. Major credit cards accepted.*

Three Stallion offers 50 kilometers of trails in addition to rentals, instruction, and guided tours.

Fishing

The **Second** and **Third Branches** of the White River are considered particularly good for trout (brown and rainbow), and the Winooski is also a possibility.

Golf

COUNTRY CLUB OF BARRE, *Plainfield Road, Barre VT. Tel. 802/476-7658. 18 holes. Green fees: $30. Major credit cards accepted. Carts available.*

GOLF MONTAGUE GOLF COURSE, *Randolph Ave (downtown), Randolph. Tel. 802/728-3806. 18 holes. Green fees: $18-$24. Major credit cards accepted. Carts available.*

MONTPELIER COUNTRY CLUB, *Montpelier VT. Tel. 802/223-7457. 9 holes. Green fees: $17-$20. Credit cards accepted.*

Hiking

ALLIS STATE PARK, *Routes 12 & 65 between Randolph & Northfield and west of Brookefield, Randloph. Tel. 802/276-3175 (summer), Tel. 802/886-2434 (offseason). Open mid to late May through Labor Day. Camping available.*

Situated at the top of Bear Mountain, the Allis State Park features one major hiking trail, along which is the famous **Bear's Den,** a cave so named because it was believed to have served such a function in the past. The main attraction, however, is the view in all directions from the fire tower at the peak. To the north and west are stunning views of the Green Mountains, and to the east you'll see the White Mountains in New Hampshire.

Snowmobiling

There are many snowmobiling opportunities in central Vermont, and even more if you scoot over to **Groton State Forest** on Route 232 about half an hour east of Montpelier via Route 2. To snowmobile in Vermont, you must join a local club and pay annual dues to them (usually under $20 a year) as well as a fee known as the Trail Maintenance Assessment, or TMA. This money goes towards the maintenance of trails and, once paid, enables you to snowmobile anywhere in Vermont. Listed below are snowmobile clubs in central Vermont as listed by the **Vermont Association of Snow Travelers (V.A.S.T.)**. For more information about snowmobiling in the region – including tours, rentals, and lessons – and throughout Vermont generally, contact V.A.S.T. at *P.O. Box 839, Montpelier VT 05601. Tel. 802/229-0005, Fax 802/223-4316, Website: www.vtvast.org.*

All these clubs are in Washington County:
- **Barre Town Thunder Chickens** - *Tel. 802/479-2448*
- **Cabot Skilighters** - *Tel. 802/563-3230*
- **Demons Snowmobile Club** - *Tel. 802/426-3383*
- **East Montpelier Gully Jumpers** - *Tel. 802/223-7416*
- **Green Mountain Roamers** - *Tel. 802/244-7826*
- **Montpelier Trackmakers** - *Tel. 802/223-3179*
- **Mountain Tamers** - *Tel. 802/456-8862*
- **Northfield Snowmobilers** - *Tel. 802/485-3001*
- **Riverton Sno-Dusters** - *Tel. 802/223-5619*
- **Sno-Bees of Barre** - *Tel. 802/476-3760*
- **Spruce Mountain Ridge Runners** - *Tel. 802/476-7680*
- **Tri-Town Snow Travelers** - *Tel. 802/767-3350*
- **Worcester Rangers** - *Tel. 802/223-7626*

EXCURSIONS & DAY TRIPS

With its central location, Montpelier is an easy base from which to enjoy many of Vermont's offerings. To the west by way of Route 2 or I-89, the **Stowe** and **Mad River Valley** ski areas offer some of the best downhill and cross-country skiing in the east and are just a half hour away. Farther west, and usually less than an hour from Montpelier, **Burlington** is Vermont's largest city and offers numours opportunities to enjoy restaurants, shopping, watersports on Lake Champlain, and cultural events.

East of Montpelier on Route 2, you will shortly enter the **Northeast Kingdom**, one of the most beautiful regions in Vermont. Within a half hour, you can learn about the process of making award-winning cheese at the **Cabot Creamery** in Cabot, while a bit further east, **St. Johnsbury** is home to a wonderful historic planetarium and the beautiful St. Johnsbury Athenaeum, one of the oldest art galleries in America.

From the southern areas around the White River, it's a straight shot on I-89 or Route 14 to White River Junction (one hour-plus from Montpelier) and the **Connecticut River Valley**, which includes the happening town of Hanover, NH, home of Dartmouth College. Also within minutes of White River Junction is the Ottauquechee River Valley and the popular tourist destinations of **Quechee** and **Woodstock**, known for their beautiful buildings, shopping, and eateries. Another twenty minutes south on I-91 is **Windsor** and the Precision Valley, where the machine tool industry was revolutionized in the 19th century. Windsor itself is home to the impressive Precision Museum and the Consitution House, where the shot-lived Republic of Vermont was founded in 1777.

PRACTICAL INFORMATION

Chambers of Commerce

RANDOLPH AREA CHAMBER OF COMMERCE, *66 Central Street, P.O. Box 9, Randolph VT 05060. Tel. 802/728-9027, Fax 802/728-4705. E-mail: mail@randolph-chamber.com. Web site: www.randolph-chamber.com.*

Medical Emergencies & Services

CENTRAL VERMONT HOSPITAL, *Off I-89, Exit 7, Berlin VT. Tel. 802/229-9191.*

Facilities include a 24-hour emergency room as well as general and specialized care. The most convenient hospital in the Montpelier area.

GIFFORD MEMORIAL HOSPITAL, *44 South Main Street, Randolph VT. Tel. 802/728-3366.*

Services include a 24-hour emergency room and general and specialized care.

DARTMOUTH HITCHCOCK MEDICAL CENTER, *Route 120 off I-89 Exit 18, Lebanon New Hampshire. Tel. 603/650-5000.*

Services include a 24-hour emergency room, walk-in clinic, and general and specialized care. The best hospital this side of Boston. Most convenient for all communities south of Bethel.

INDEX

THINGS CHANGE!

Phone numbers, prices, addresses, quality of food, etc, all change. If you come across any new information, we'd appreciate hearing from you. No item is too small! Drop us an e-mail note at: Jopenroad@aol.com, or write us at:

Vermont Guide
*Open Road Publishing, P.O. Box 284
Cold Spring Harbor, NY 11724*

TRAVEL NOTES

TRAVEL NOTES

448